Modern
Food Service
Purchasing

Robert Garlough, MS, FMP, AAC

Grand Rapids Community College

DELMAR
CENGAGE Learning™

Australia • Brazil • Japan • Korea • Mexico • Singapore • Spain • United Kingdom • United States

Modern Food Service Purchasing
Robert Garlough

Vice President, Career and Professional
   Editorial: Dave Garza

Director of Learning Solutions: Sandy Clark

Senior Acquisitions Editor: Jim Gish

Managing Editor: Larry Main

Product Manager: Nicole Calisi

Editorial Assistant: Sarah Timm

Vice President Marketing, Career
   and Professional: Jennifer Baker

Executive Marketing Manager:
   Wendy Mapstone

Senior Marketing Manager: Kristin McNary

Marketing Coordinator: Scott Chrysler

Production Director: Wendy Troeger

Senior Content Project Manager:
   Kathryn B. Kucharek

Senior Art Director: Casey Kirchmayer

Technology Project Manager: Chris Catalina

Production Technology Analyst: Tom Stover

Cover Images: Used under license from iStockphoto.com: Eggplant: Image copyright Paul Johnson, 2009; Swiss Chard: Image copyright Suzannah Skelton, 2009; Acorn Squash: Image copyright, 2009; Heirloom Tomatoes: Image copyright, Kelly Cline, 2009; Portabello Mushroom: Image copyright, 2009; Olives: Image copyright, 2009; Artichoke: Image copyright, Benjamin Brandt, 2009; Morel Mushroom: Image copyright, 2009; Blue Crab: Image copyright, Justine Gecewicz, 2009; Snow Peas: Image copyright, 2009; Pear: Image copyright, 2009; Salmon: Image copyright, Vyacheslav Anyakin, 2009; Grouper Fish: Image copyright, Serdar Yagci, 2009; Pistachios: Image copyright, 2009; Eggs: Image copyright, 2009. Used under license from Shutterstock.com: Sage: Image copyright Ultimathule, 2009; Green beans: Image copyright Thumb, 2009; Cantaloupe: Image copyright William Berry, 2009; Grapes: Image copyright Robyn Mackenzie, 2009; Clams: Image copyright Norman Chan, 2009; Pasta: Image copyright Ultimathule, 2009; Spices: Image copyright Elena Elisseeva, 2009; Lobster: Image copyright Mikael Damkier, 2009; Chili Peppers: Image copyright Irabel8, 2009; Lemons: Image copyright Angelo Gilardelli, 2009; Jalapeno Peppers: Image copyright Greenfire, 2009; Anise Seed: Image copyright Ewa Walicka, 2009; Strawberries: Image copyright Alphacell, 2009; Chanterelle Mushrooms: Image copyright Gala Kan, 2009.

Front Matter Graphics: Image copyright, 2010. Used under license from iStockphoto.com: Page viii - Avocados; Page ix - Vegetable market; Page xiii - Wine glass; Page xv - Mushroom; Page xviii - Apple.

Back Matter Graphics: Used under license from iStockphoto.com: Page 569 Peppers: Image copyright Jill Chen, 2010; Page 596 Bok Choy: Image copyright Jill Chen, 2010; Page 607 Sage: Image copyright Jill Chen, 2010.

People Places Thing icon: People: ©iStockphoto.com 4964459; Field: ©iStockphoto.com 8864284; Market: ©iStockphoto.com 4691841

Library of Congress Control Number: 2009933906

ISBN-13: 978-1-1111-2837-1
ISBN-10: 1-1111-2837-5

Delmar
5 Maxwell Drive
Clifton Park, NY 12065-2919
USA

Cengage Learning is a leading provider of customized learning solutions with office locations around the globe, including Singapore, the United Kingdom, Australia, Mexico, Brazil, and Japan. Locate your local office at:
international.cengage.com/region

Cengage Learning products are represented in Canada by Nelson Education, Ltd.

To learn more about Delmar, visit **www.cengage.com/delmar**

Purchase any of our products at your local college store or at our preferred online store **www.CengageBrain.com**

Notice to the Reader

Publisher does not warrant or guarantee any of the products described herein or perform any independent analysis in connection with any of the product information contained herein. Publisher does not assume, and expressly disclaims, any obligation to obtain and include information other than that provided to it by the manufacturer. The reader is expressly warned to consider and adopt all safety precautions that might be indicated by the activities described herein and to avoid all potential hazards. By following the instructions contained herein, the reader willingly assumes all risks in connection with such instructions. The publisher makes no representations or warranties of any kind, including but not limited to, the warranties of fitness for particular purpose or merchantability, nor are any such representations implied with respect to the material set forth herein, and the publisher takes no responsibility with respect to such material. The publisher shall not be liable for any special, consequential, or exemplary damages resulting, in whole or part, from the readers' use of, or reliance upon, this material.

PART I OPENER: Pyramid: © iStockphoto.com; Eggs: 8685545; Spices: 4970418; Pear: 4624110. PART II OPENER: Cookies: © iStockphoto.com; Salad: © iStockphoto.com/Vetta Collection; Items on shelf: © Randy Van Dam 2008; Tomatoes: © iStockphoto.com; Spoons with coins: Image copyright marekuliasz, 2009. Used under license from Shutterstock.com; Cameras: © iStockphoto.com. PART III OPENER: Spices: Image © Elena Elisseeva, 2009. Used under license from Shutterstock.com; Flour, Meat, Fruit, Dairy: iStockphoto.com; Chicken: Image © Janet Faye Smith, 2009. Used under license from Shutterstock.com; Shell and Radishes: © Randy Van Dam 2008; Noodles: Image © ultimathule, 2009. Used under license from Shutterstock.com; Tea: Image © Katarzyna Walecka, 2009. Used under license from Shutterstock.com. PART IV OPENER:

Printed in the United States of America
1 2 3 4 5 6 7 14 13 12 11 10

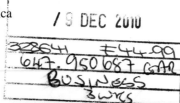

DEDICATION

I am forever grateful to the many friends around the world who have opened their hearts and homes to me, so that I may learn from them and share in the hospitality that is their own cuisine and culture. As a willing explorer of this planet, they have been my able guides. This book is respectfully dedicated to their treasured homelands and unique food ways.

ABOUT THE
Author

Robert Garlough
MS, FMP, AAC

Professor of Hospitality
Education and Chef-Emeritus
Secchia Institute for
Culinary Education
Grand Rapids Community College

With a passion for exploration of distant cultures, and a fascination with global cuisine, Chef Garlough has led international cuisine and culture study-tours to over 30 countries on 6 continents. Many hundreds of culinary students and food service professionals have traversed the planet with him, as he continues to study world gastronomy.

Chef Garlough has taken seminars in various culinary schools in Italy, France, Greece, Mexico, Australia, South Africa, Scotland, Brazil, and Malta. He has shopped the world's food markets, including those in Barcelona, Nassau, Zurich, Istanbul, Auckland, Sydney, New York, Paris, Puerto Vallarta, Lucerne, Glasgow, Athens, Rome, Valetta, Hong Kong, Oaxaca, Frankfurt, San Salvador, London, Cairo, Beijing, Johannesburg, Guadalajara, and Lisbon.

As founding director of the Secchia Institute for Culinary Education at Grand Rapids Community College (GRCC) in Grand Rapids, Michigan, Chef Garlough has over 40 years of experience in the food service industry with over 30 years in culinary education. He has held food service management positions in New York, Ohio, Florida, and Michigan. Chef Garlough is a founding partner in the catering corporation of My Chef, Inc. located in Naperville, Illinois, which received the 2007 U.S. Chamber of Commerce National Small Business of the Year award. Garlough is also principal to his consulting company, The Culinary Group, and his culinary adventure tour company, Mexican Travel Adventures. With his various supervisory positions, Chef Garlough has established or managed food service storeroom operations in family dining, fine dining, catering, and institutional food service.

The Educational Foundation of the National Restaurant Association certifies Chef Garlough as a Food Service Management Professional. He is a Fellow of both the American Academy of Chefs and the Honorable Order of the Golden Toque, and a member of the Craft Guild of Chefs. He holds an Associate in Occupational Studies degree in Culinary Arts from the Culinary Institute of America, a Bachelor of Business Administration degree in Restaurant and Lodging Management from Davenport University, and a Master of Science in Occupational Education degree from Ferris State University.

A recipient of numerous culinary salon competition awards, Chef Garlough was awarded the Chef Herman Breithaupt Memorial Award by CHRIE, naming him their national chef-instructor of the year in 1984. Garlough personally earned silver and bronze medals at the 1988 *Internationale Kochkunst Ausstellung* (considered the "Culinary Olympics") in Frankfurt, Germany while managing a six-member team of GRCC faculty and graduates. The American Culinary Federation Educational Institute honored him as their National Educator of the Year in 1992. He served as Manager for the 1993 Pastry Team USA that represented the United States at the 1993 *Coupe du Monde de la Patisserie* (World Pastry Cup) in Lyon, France. Chef Garlough also served as Manager for Team USA 1998, a culinary student team representing America at the Malta International Students Culinary Salon in St. Julian's Bay, Malta.

His professional affiliations included serving as President of the Michigan Council on Hotel, Restaurant and Institutional Education, President of the American Culinary Federation Greater Grand Rapids

Chapter, Chairman of the American Culinary Federation Educational Institute Accrediting Commission, and Executive Director of the International Consortium of Hospitality and Tourism Institutes.

Chef Garlough is co-author of *Ice Sculpting the Modern Way* (Thomson Delmar Learning, 2004) and *Modern Garde Manger* (Thomson Delmar Learning, 2006). *Modern Garde Manger* received the 2007 IACP Cookbook Award in the Food Reference/Technical category at the 2007 International Association of Cooking Professionals Conference.

Foreword

My God! What a body of work! *Modern Food Service Purchasing* could not have come at a better time. In a world where the economy is about as consistent as the weather, the bottom line of the hospitality business has never been more scrutinized. As chefs and managers, where does the bottom line start? At the back door! What comes in, or does not come in through receiving, can make or break a great chef and can dictate whether an operation will be successful or not.

Chef Garlough has compiled what seems to be a life's work between these two covers. It is certainly the most complete resource for food service purchasing on the market today; identifying the most commonly used food products while establishing and managing storeroom operations that work in any sized food service establishment. I don't care if you run a $30-million or $2-million operation; there is something in this book for everyone.

With over 30 years as a culinary educator and 40 years in the food industry, the author understands selection and procurement as only an experienced operator can. Chef Garlough has captured the essence of purchasing and cost controls, while also challenging the reader to consider the modern food chain—including the myriad of circumstances that affect how the food is raised, harvested, processed, shipped, stored, and sold. I am telling you now that if a person can identify and see firsthand what work goes into the growing, nurturing, and harvesting of any vegetable, that person would have a new found respect for that plant. That same person is certainly less apt to whack two inches off the top of the vegetable and toss it into the garbage. To me, procurement is like sanitation, you can never be too good at it. No one in the industry has a kitchen that is too clean. And you can never know too much about researching, sourcing, buying, storing, and delivering the best product possible.

This book *has* it all! Chef Garlough has done his due diligence, and researched this vital aspect of food service operations with a breadth and depth that is truly remarkable. From buyer-seller relationships, making important buying decisions, governmental regulations, grading processes, current food science practices, packaging, proper storage, staffing, and actual physical requirements needed to lay out a storeroom, financial management, security, commodities, developing product knowledge and so much more! Give me a break, where else are you going to get all of that in one book? This is such an incredible resource! There is no other text on the market that so thoroughly combines product identification with complete storeroom operations and cost controls. *Modern Food Service Purchasing* is truly an amazing resource that no food service purchasing agent or working chef should be without. It should find a permanent home in every office, directly next to their copy of Escoffier's cookbook; it is that important. In my mind, it will prove to be an ageless resource, and the new bible in purchasing.

In addition to Chef Garlough's insights, close to 30 seasoned food service professionals who represent the day-to-day food service industry and culinary education, in both buying and selling, offer their fascinating experiences to the reader. "It Happened to Me" are real-life experiences passionately told by the professionals, offering their advice in their own words, based on a lifetime in food service. Bona fide stuff that really happened to them and proved to be important life lessons.

With over 900 color photographs, diagrams, tables, and charts, this manual is also visually stunning. This tool alone sets this text apart from any other reference book! And coming from a chef who believes strongly in policies, procedures, and forms to run a tighter ship and make your life easier, I have found the instructor's CD-ROM to have countless forms that students, chefs, purchasing agents and managers can use to learn the important calculations that set the standard in today's hospitality environment.

Modern Food Service Purchasing should not be looked upon merely as a textbook for students or those just entering the food service industry; rather, it's the most thoroughly developed reference manual on food service purchasing and storeroom operations *EVER*

PRINTED! Therefore, anyone involved in the circle of buying food, cooking food, being responsible for the cost of goods sold, or simply responsible for the cooking of foods bought . . . needs this book. I don't care if you are working in white tablecloth or no tablecloth operations—if you are working with food, this is your book. In too many cases, chefs get caught up in the business at hand, and do not take time to get more involved in the proper procurement of great product. Now is your time, and this is your book.

As a successful culinary competitor on an international level, and a seven-time member of the United States Culinary Olympic Team, I can personally attest to the imperative for quality standards in purchasing. Even though customers don't award points for your work (like a food show judge), if you provide a consistent quality product, they will reward you with their continued patronage. It all starts with proper selection and procurement.

We currently do over 9.5 million in annual food and beverage sales, making us one of the busiest country clubs in the United States. Even though I have been in this business all of my life, I still feel that the practices in our purchasing office can be improved upon, perhaps even to light-years ahead of where they are now. We have been steadily working on the revamping of our policies and procedures, while doing our best to keep current with today's technology. *Modern Food Service Purchasing* will now be a big part of our own storeroom and cost control operations, and regularly referenced by all of my chefs and storeroom personnel.

Rich with hundreds of customized photographs and forms, *Modern Food Service Purchasing* is a must for anyone who is involved in the broad functions of food service purchasing and stockroom operations. *It is simply that good!* This is a mountain of work desperately needed by our industry, and I have the greatest respect for its creator. As an author myself, I recognize the yeoman's efforts involved in visualizing and assembling such an incredible resource. Hats off to Chef Garlough and Team! *Modern Food Service Purchasing* is this Culinary Olympian's dream work.

Charles M. Carroll CEC, AAC
Executive Chef
River Oaks Country Club
Houston, Texas

Preface

"To see what is in front of one's nose needs a constant struggle."
GEORGE ORWELL

Of crucial importance to the food service operator, and ultimately their customers, is the timely procurement of healthful products at reasonable costs. Chefs and managers involved in the purchase of food and beverages must carefully evaluate the innumerable variables that in due course influence their purchasing decisions. Countless forces, both controllable and unforeseen, can affect the flow of goods, availability, condition, price, and market form of the assorted products. A comprehensive understanding of these considerations, as well as the products themselves, is essential to the success of any food service operation.

Also inherent in procurement, are the established business practices the professional food service operator must undertake. To be viable, businesses must control their costs and manage their assets with certainty. Reliable financial information, readily available to the chef or manager, is indispensable when making purchasing decisions.

This text seeks to create awareness in its readers. Its goal is to present information in a politically neutral manner, and to refrain from serving as a platform for any personal beliefs held by the author, whether by the inclusion or exclusion of topics contained herein. That being said, the text strives to bring a sense of consciousness to the culinarian, so he or she may be informed on various issues relevant to food. It is the author's hope that critical thinking and passionate discussion will follow the reading of this text.

Modern Food Service Purchasing: Business Essentials to Procurement was written for the individual who is either currently involved in the selection, procurement, receiving, storing, and issuing of food service related products, or studying to become a chef or food service manager. Whether for institutional food service, retail, business, and industry, casual or fine dining, this primer will address the many aspects relative to the purchaser's responsibilities. Presented in a practical format for both the reader and instructor, the text is designed for immediate application in the workplace.

Modern Food Service Purchasing contains 21 chapters that are divided into 4 sections. The first part deals with market influences and purchasing considerations outside the actual food service operation, the second section covers the organization of the internal system and its management controls, while the third segment focuses on identifying the various commodities. The last section and chapter looks ahead to the near future in food service, and is offered as insight into forthcoming issues in the opinion of the author.

Organization of the Text

The book begins with **Part I Procurement: Dynamics of Food Service Purchasing**. This section provides a brief overview of the historical perspectives that brings the subject of food sourcing forward from antiquity to the modern food service establishment. It provides a detailed description of the buyer-seller relationship and the attributes necessary to be a successful buyer. It discusses, in general terms, the myriad of considerations that must be made when conducting the buying decision in today's global marketplace. Common market and distribution systems are discussed, as well as the multidimensional nature of the decision process. An up-to-date section on laws governing food production and distribution is included, as well as grading processes. The section concludes with an interesting, and possibly controversial, explanation of the many practices that currently exist in food science, relative to food production and preservation.

The text continues with **Part II Purchasing Management: Mastering the Storeroom Function**. This section begins with the common methods of measuring and packaging ingredients, basic to the understanding of proper storage. The ingredient process follows, beginning with the menu and concluding with the selection of needed ingredients. Requisite staffing and the storeroom's physical requirements, including space for receiving, buyer's office, and storage spaces are detailed along with specific equipment, including shelving, sinks, scales, and refrigeration. The receiving, storing, and issuing processes are discussed, together with the documents used to organize the flow of goods. Flow charts are included, with photographs and drawings, to illustrate the proper means of organizing the storeroom and buyer's workplace. A comprehensive and practical chapter on financial management of the storeroom is provided, along with a unique chapter on storeroom security.

The third section of text, titled **Part III The Commodities: Developing Product Knowledge** focuses directly on the products and their various market forms. A thorough understanding of the numerous available ingredients is essential to proper storeroom administration. Included in this section are several chapters dealing with the many products available. All commonly used ingredients from herbs to shellfish are discussed, and suggested considerations for buying and storing them are listed. Useful reference charts to aid in the identification and decision-making process, and color photographs of regularly purchased items for the purpose of teaching product identification, are featured.

The last section, **Part IV Postscript: Looking Ahead**, consists of only one chapter. The purpose for its inclusion in the text is to highlight relevant areas for probable growth in the present and near future. Chefs and managers should always maintain an eye on the horizon in order to be prepared for future realities.

Chapter and Text Features

Written with the classroom coach in mind, the text is organized in a logical sequence for instruction. Each chapter will include: *learning objectives* and a *chapter introduction*, plus a *Chapter in Review,* which includes *Review Questions, Individual and Group Activities* for students, and *Key Words and Concepts* to assist the learner with useful pedagogy. Succinct sections titled *People, Places, Things* are used to relate personal experiences by the author and to offer vignettes about specific subjects—all to enhance the chapter readings. Further insights into the purchasing and cost control process are provided by various food service personalities, in each chapter, when they are introduced in sections titled either *Ask the Expert* or *Professional Profiles*. Additionally, the use of numerous charts, color photographs, and drawings will augment both the visual impact and learning process for the reader. Part III contains a comprehensive collection of product and commodity photographs, to aid the learner in product identification. In addition, each chapter in Part III contains a useful list of value-added products in features titled *Convenience Corner*.

Additionally, the text contains a useful *Glossary,* common to the functions of purchasing and cost controls. An extensive collection of *Appendices* with handy tables, addresses, and costing formulas is also included to assist the working chef and food service manager in operating a successful business. A student accessible online companion is available with practical forms and checklists, all editable and reproducible.

Ancillary Materials

A valuable Instructor's Resource is available in CD or online format to those who teach a purchasing and cost control course using this text. It provides an Instructor's Manual and Test Bank with over 500 constructive questions and chapter outlines to aid in presenting the material in lecture. Also included, are editable and reproducible forms used in food service operations, such as make-or-buy analysis, butcher's yield tests, recipe costing, requisitions, and purchase orders. These are included as available masters for the instructor to reproduce as handouts to support classroom discussions and exercises. Also included is an image library that includes a variety of photos from the text to aid in instructor lectures and presentations. Additionally, an Electronic Classroom Manager CD-ROM is available with PowerPoint slides outlining each chapter, color photographs of all products specified in the text, and checklists and forms that are editable and reproducible.

Multimedia Resources

INSTRUCTOR'S MANUAL

The *Instructor's Manual* provides chapter outlines, answers to end-of-chapter review questions, and additional assessment questions and answers. The *Instructor's Manual* is available at no charge to adopters of the text on a CD and online.

Instructor Resources CD

The Instructor Resources CD is designed as a complete teaching tool for *Modern Food Service Purchasing*. It assists instructors in creating lectures, developing presentations, constructing quizzes and tests. This valuable resource simplifies the planning and implementation of the instructional program. This complimentary resource package is available upon adoption of the text and consists of the following components:

- PowerPoint® Lecture Slides, divided by chapter, offer a visually appealing way to extract key points of the textbook and enhance class lectures.
- Computerized Test Bank consists of a variety of test questions including multiple choice and true/false.
- Image library that includes a variety of photos from the text to aid in instructor lectures and presentations
- Editable standard forms used in food service operations are included as available assets for the instructor to support classroom discussions and exercises
- The Instructor's Manual contains a number of useful tools including the Chapter Introduction, Chapter Outline, Definitions for the Chapter Key Words and Concepts, and Answers to the Chapter Review Questions.

Key Features

OBJECTIVES

Answering the question "What am I about to learn?" will best describe this chapter-opening feature. These learning objectives are used to help students understand that by the end of the chapter they will have a working knowledge of the material presented.

KEY WORDS AND CONCEPTS

Key Words and Concepts are listed at the end of each chapter enforcing the importance of new terminology presented in each chapter. Key Words and Concepts are also bolded blue at first use within the chapters for easy identification.

PHOTOGRAPHS

This beautifully illustrated textbook contains nearly 1,000 full color photographs and illustrations.

BUYER'S NOTE

Buyer's notes elaborate on essential information valuable to the future buyer.

PEOPLE, PLACES, THINGS

People, Places, Things boxes are used to relate personal experiences by the author and to offer vignettes about specific subjects, all to enhance the chapter readings.

ASK THE EXPERT AND PROFESSIONAL PROFILE

Further insights into the purchasing and cost control process are provided by various food service personalities, in each chapter, when they are introduced in sections titled either "Ask the Expert" or "Professional Profile."

CONVENIENCE CORNER PRODUCT EXAMPLES

Convenience Corner sidebars provide future buyer's with information on where to buy quality pre-made or ready-mix convenience products.

CHAPTER IN REVIEW

Each chapter ends with a "Chapter in Review" section, which includes Review Questions, Individual and Group Activities for students, and Key Words and Concepts to assist the learner with useful pedagogy.

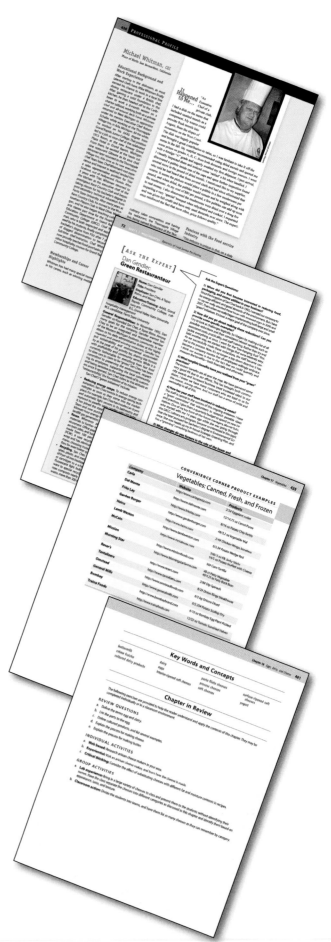

ACKNOWLEDGMENTS

The development and production of a text manifests itself from conception through completion. All during the process, transformations occur within the manuscript that result in, what the editors and author hope will be, a better-finished product. Such was the case with this book.

I would like to acknowledge the many people and companies who took interest in this project; their involvement helped me to focus my efforts on the essence of modern food service purchasing. In particular, I would like to thank the following individuals; I am certain the result is a superior book because of their contributions:

The entire staff, faculty, and student population of the Secchia Institute for Culinary Education at Grand Rapids Community College for their interest in and support of this project. In particular Randy Sahajdack, Mike Kidder, Angus Campbell, Dale Vandenburg, Bob Monaldo, Mike Whitman, Luba Petrash, and Joel Boone for their involvement. It is a pleasure to come to work every day with such a talented and committed group of colleagues.

Ralph Fischer, James Spilka, and Mercedes Rios at Meijer for their yeoman efforts in providing me magnificent products to photograph. Bob Sullivan and Jon Novak at The Plitt Company of Chicago for their outstanding seafood and use of their weekly quote sheet. Mary Powers and Robert Kowalewski and the staff at The Grand Rapids Brewing Company for allowing us to film in their wonderful brewpub. Keith Pell and Bob Eichinger at Gordon Food Service for their timely assistance and use of GFS products and information. Melissa's World/Variety Produce of Los Angeles, whose generous use of their photo library helped our search for useful images. Steve Doyle at King Milling in Lowell, Michigan, for his help with milling flours. Karen and Bill Garlough at My Chef Catering for use of several forms and graphics. Ron and Tom Prominski at 20th Century Market for providing great charcuterie products for the book, and Burdick Packing Company for their use of a weekly quote sheet. The permissions department of John Wiley & Sons, Inc. for use of materials from the *NAMP Meat Buyer's Guide*. Kameel Chamelly at Martha's Vineyard of

Grand Rapids who allowed us to set up a remote photography studio in his business so that we may have unrestrained access to a wealth of beverages. Ana Maria Olmos for her help with Oaxacan-made chocolate and mescal. SYSCO Food Service of Grand Rapids, Randy Ruiter, and Art Davis in particular, for their cooperation in the production of this book.

Chef Charles Carroll, CEC, AAC, who graciously agreed to honor this text by writing the Foreword. His exemplary career as Executive Chef of Houston's world-class River Oaks Country Club, a seven-time Culinary Olympic chef, and successful young author is remarkable. His generous praise for my book was most gratifying, and I am proud to count him as a friend.

Brother Herman Zaccarelli, CSC, whose enormous talent for revealing insights about people and the food service industry has been inspirational. Herman's early interest in my career, lifelong friendship, and continued support of this project has been very meaningful to me.

The many other celebrated food professionals I was honored to profile either in the text or at the end of each chapter. These people elevate this book, and indeed our entire food service industry, every day. Their dedication, tenacity, raw talent, and understanding of this industry are to be admired and respected. I value their friendship and continued support of my work.

The team at Delmar/Cengage Learning of Clifton Park, New York, for their care, guidance, and production of the text; I am indebted to them for their sustained faith in my work, specialized contributions, and capable support. I particularly would like to thank my Acquisitions' Editor Jim Gish, whose unwavering commitment to quality shared my vision for the final product; Managing Editor Larry Main and Director of Learning Solutions Sandy Clark for their continued support of my writing career with Delmar/Cengage Learning; Nicole Calisi, the Product Manager who steadfastly shepherded my manuscript through development and production; Wendy Troeger, Production Director, and Kathryn Kucharek, Senior Content Project Manager, for their Herculean efforts in the layout and design of the finished product. I'd like to make special recognition of Casey Kirchmayer, who, as the Art Director, was responsible for the design of this text. It takes a real visionary to pull together a color palette and design strategy for a text with so many diverse features. I'd like to thank the Marketing Department, including Scott Chrysler, Marketing Coordinator, Kristin McNary, Senior Marketing Manager, and Wendy Mapstone, Executive Marketing Manager, for their comprehensive promotion of the text; plus all of the other wonderful staff at Delmar/Cengage Learning who work so diligently to make things happen. It takes an army of talented individuals to bring a book to fruition; they were all vitally important to the process.

The reviewers, who both applauded my efforts and challenged my concepts, provided many excellent suggestions and ideas for improving the text:

Mike Artlip, CEC, CCE, CHE
Director of the School of Culinary Arts
Kendall College, Chicago, IL

Beth Augustyn, MA
Adjunct Faculty
Metropolitan Community College, Omaha, NE

David S. Bearl
Program Coordinator
First Coast Technical College, St. Augustine, FL

Greg Forte, CEC, CCE, AAC, MS
Director of Education
Orlando Culinary Academy, Orlando, FL

Dean Louie, CHE
Chef Instructor
Maui Culinary Academy, Kahului, HI

Rob Lucier, CEC
Associate Instructor/Culinary Purchaser
Johnson & Wales University, College of Culinary Arts, Providence, RI

John R. Moonen
Online Facilitator
Art Institute – Pittsburgh, Pittsburgh, PA

James Taylor, MBA, PHD
Assistant Professor, Program Director Hospitality Management
University of Mississippi, University, MS

And Randy Van Dam, whose expert photography continues to make my texts come to life; it was another great experience to work with him.

Lastly, I would like to thank my entire family who allowed me the enormous measure of time to devote to this project. They are generous and caring, and certainly my most treasured gift.

Robert Garlough

Contents

PART I: PROCUREMENT: DYNAMICS OF FOOD SERVICE PURCHASING 3

CHAPTER 1 The Purchasing Function: An Overview 4

CHAPTER 2 Food Laws and the Market and Distribution Systems 32

PART IV: POSTSCRIPT: LOOKING AHEAD 561

 CHAPTER 21 **Postscript: Futurist Thoughts on Food Service** 562

PART I

Procurement:
Dynamics of Food Service Purchasing

CHAPTER

1

© iStockphoto.com

The Purchasing Function: An Overview

"No nation was ever ruined by trade."
BENJAMIN FRANKLIN

After reading this chapter, you will be able to:

◎ Describe commerce.

◎ Outline the purchasing function.

◎ Analyze the optimal goals of selection and procurement.

◎ Describe the desired attributes and knowledge required of a buyer.

◎ Describe a storeroom policies and procedures manual, and explain content that may be included.

◎ Differentiate among the various types of sellers and how to best work with them.

◎ Distinguish among the various purchasing options and contracts available to buyers.

◎ Identify the benefits of a healthy buyer–seller relationship.

Introduction

Purchasing for food service operations involves wide-ranging skills and broad product knowledge, much of it unique to this industry. It is more than merely exchanging payment for goods or services rendered. To procure goods and services of the optimal quality at the optimal time and in a cost-effective manner, the buyer must be competent in many diverse areas of the profession. Purchasing for food service involves both the selection and procurement of goods and services from a global marketplace that changes frequently.

This chapter will outline the skills one must possess and the relationships one must maintain to function effectively as a purchasing agent in food service. The material in this chapter, and in this book, applies to everyone in the food service purchasing industry, whether buying for a small start-up business like a Texas rib shack, procuring products for a giant Las Vegas hotel, or serving as vice president of purchasing for a national restaurant chain. This chapter provides a foundation for learning trade and food service commerce.

Historical Perspectives in Trade

Archeological evidence shows that early humanoids hunted and gathered their food. They gathered grains, fruits, roots, and mushrooms and hunted animals for food. Later, they began to plant seeds—the beginning of agriculture. As more people ate food grown by farmers, cities began to develop, and populations increased.

Trade was another early human interaction. Most prehistoric people traded goods and services with neighboring tribes. Food is now traded all around the world thanks to modern transportation. Modern restaurant owners and chefs are not restricted to local foods or the local growing seasons. Some countries now import most of their food from other places, and other countries export most of what they grow or produce.

Trade is an exchange of goods or services. Trade is voluntary; both the seller and the buyer must agree to the transaction. **Commerce** is another word for trade, and a market is a place where people make trades. Bartering, the first form of trade, is where one party gives the other goods and then receives goods in return. Earlier civilizations used bread, pigs, seashells, whale's teeth, cattle, cocoa beans, and salt for bartering (see Figure 1.1). When currency was developed, buying became separate from selling. Currency is any object with an intrinsic value—such as paper money, coins,

1.1 **Using salt for bartering**

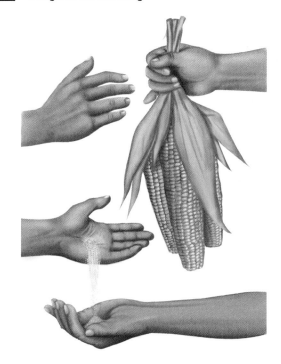

and credit cards—recognized by both the seller and the buyer as legal tender. With currency, a seller does not have to wait for a buyer with specific goods to trade. This made trading easier for both the buyer and the seller.

The Goals of Selection and Procurement

To work as a chef, food buyer, or purchasing agent, one must understand the two primary purchasing functions involved in these positions: selection and procurement. **Selection** can be defined simply as choosing from among many alternatives. A buyer must determine the eligibility and suitability of a product or service, taking into account many considerations. In food service operations, this is sometimes called a specification, or spec. Eventually, the spec becomes a detailed description of what the buyer wants to purchase. Selection only occurs when there is choice, but fortunately, in this modern world, we almost always have many alternatives from which to choose.

For example, the selection of a tomato product for use in a recipe can appear almost limitless. However, the buyer should have certain qualities in mind for the ingredient, and these will guide the selection process. If this ingredient is going to be for a recipe that is on a static menu, for example, then the tomato product must be regularly available with little cost fluctuation. Whether it is to be left raw and whole or stewed with other ingredients are examples of considerations that aid the buyer in the selection process. The goal is to identify and select the most appropriate product that best meets the needs of the enterprise.

Once a product has been selected, the buyer must find the best source for procurement. **Procurement** is the systematic exchange of payment for goods or services between the buyer and the seller. A buyer should identify all available sellers that might carry the ingredient and then conduct further research to determine the best supplier to use. The buyer and seller must then agree to the terms for the sale and delivery before procurement can take place.

AN OPTIMAL GOAL

Optimal purchasing is central to the buyer's role. Optimal purchasing considers all of the variables in the selection and procurement processes and chooses the product that best meets the needs of the operation, neither more nor better than is needed, nor less.

The goal is to sustain the operation's competitive status, maintain an adequate supply of storeroom wares, and obtain the lowest possible serving cost while ensuring the most appropriate quality and minimizing the company's product investment. **Optimal purchasing** matches the specific characteristics of the product to the specific needs of the business. Considerations that are often evaluated include:

- Product characteristics or attributes
  - Taste, texture, appearance
  - Quality grade and wholesomeness
  - Consistency
  - Availability
  - Packaging
  - Quantity
- Supplier characteristics or attributes
  - Price

- Minimum purchases required for delivery
- Delivery schedule
- Sanitation/condition of supplier's warehouse or processing facility
- Dependability

For example, even though beef tenderloin is readily available on the market, it is not the optimal product for chicken-fried steak sold at a truck-stop diner. The most expensive, or highest quality product is not always appropriate for the needs of the business. On the other hand, customer expectations at an haute cuisine restaurant where ticket averages exceed $100 per customer require premium-quality foodstuffs. This is an example of product use: the buyers match the product attributes as dictated by the recipe to the available products in the market.

The Buyer

The role of the buyer is best illustrated by an organizational chart. Smaller businesses (see Figure 1.2)—such as independent restaurants, country clubs, bakeries, bars, and catering businesses—operate differently from hotels, hospitals, the military, or restaurant chains (see Figure 1.3).

In the former, someone from the management team often serves as the buyer, as well. In restaurants and clubs, the chefs generally do all of the buying. These are considered **line positions**, as they are directly involved in the food production or service. In catering businesses, bars, and bakeries, the owner–operators often wear the buyer's hat. If they are also involved in food production or sales, then they are also considered line supervisors. There is no hard-and-fast rule, but workload is often distributed in that manner with these types of operations.

Larger organizations, such as hotels, hospitals, and restaurant chains, often employ individuals who purchase products on behalf of the organization. Because of the quantities

1.2 **Organizational chart of a small restaurant**

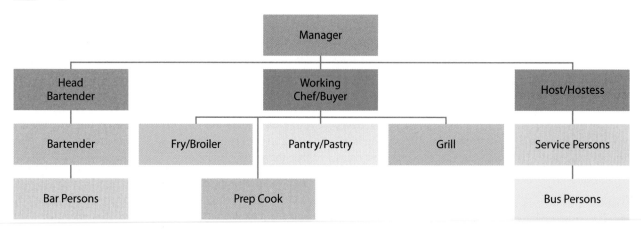

1.3 Organizational chart of a larger hotel food service operation

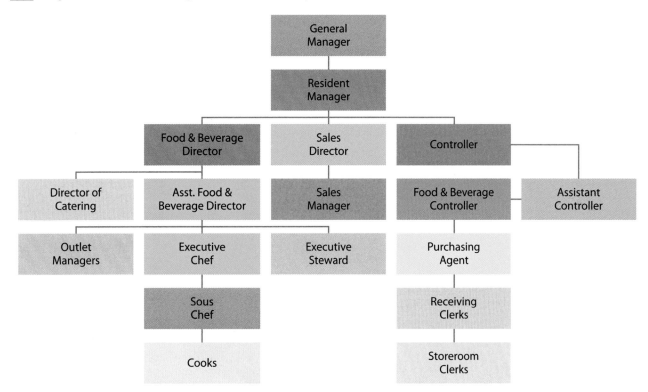

involved, a dedicated, full-time buyer can bring effective procurement processes and greater efficiency to a company, which translates into product cost savings. The benefits gained by having such a position must be weighed against the personnel costs in employing one. These positions are considered **staff positions**, as they work in support of others who are directly involved in food production or sales.

REQUIRED ATTRIBUTES AND KNOWLEDGE

Buyers come from varying backgrounds. Some have been successful in other enterprises. Others have recently come into money and wish to invest in a restaurant. Still others have worked their way up through the ranks of the food service industry.

In any case, there are certain attributes and skills that a buyer must possess to be highly successful. Beyond the obvious initiative, organizational ability, and honesty, the purchasing staff must also possess the following qualities: *ethical standards, conceptual skills, communication skills, mathematical skills, computer skills, market awareness*, an understanding of the *laws of commerce*, and *product knowledge*.

Ethical Standards

Ethics is the study of morality, what is right or wrong. Storeroom managers, food buyers, chefs, kitchen mangers, and food and beverage directors will always have temptations placed before them. They work with food, alcohol,

and money—items desired by most mortal men and women. Purchasing agents are required to maintain high moral and ethical standards that place them, and the company, beyond reproach. Opportunities will arise where these standards will be tested, and the ethical buyer must resist them. Clear guidelines for behavior can aid the buyer in maintaining professionalism, which is paramount to job success.

Many professional organizations, such as the Pennsylvania Restaurant Association, have developed **codes of ethics** for their memberships. As members of these organizations, the operators seek to elevate themselves and their businesses through proper and responsible practices. A code of ethics is based on the belief that principles should govern an organization's employees. All goals of the organization, and the decisions made by management and staff, should be guided by these values. A code of ethics should include statements that affirm a commitment to:

- Fair prices and good value.
- Good food and good service.
- Good health and welfare of employees and customers.
- Fair treatment of employees.
- Honest relationships with purveyors.
- Honest relationships with the community.
- Respect for the environment.

There are many organizations for buyers and sellers that work to elevate the ethical and professional standards within their own industry, including restaurant associations, chef associations, and supply management organizations.

Conceptual Skills

Buyers must be able to see the whole enterprise, how the various functions of the organization depend on one another. Buyers must be able to see how changes to one function will affect all of the other functions. And buyers must be able to see the relationships between the business and its place in industry. A well-informed buyer should know how her actions affect the community, political, social, and economic forces of the nation. This concept is commonly referred to as **conceptual skills**.

Food service buyers should try to understand how the product will be used and anticipate any constraints it would put on the food preparation staff. Understanding the application of the product will help the buyer make good judgments.

 Historically, chefs have frequently been hired as both sales representatives for food brokers and as buyers for large food service establishments, because of their profound understanding of food service operations and product application.

Communication Skills

Buyers need to have balanced communication skills. They must possess the ability to listen to the needs of the stakeholders of their operation, including the preparation staff, accounting staff, receiving and storing staff, and owners. Additionally, they must be able to articulate these needs succinctly to purveyors. Proper attention paid to communication will result in happier employees, fewer errors, and more efficient operations.

Mathematical Skills

Ever since prehistoric humans made their first trade, math has been an integral part of commerce. With the advent of calculators, and now computers, math has become easier—easier but no less important. Math is basic to buying, receiving, storing, and issuing—all of the primary functions of storeroom personnel.

Although machines can assist with computations, humans—who are prone to error—operate these machines. An error in math directly correlates to an error in money and, later, profit. It is vital to the operating and fiscal health of the business that all storeroom personnel demonstrate a high degree of competency in basic math.

Computer Skills

Computers have permeated our lives in virtually all areas of business, and accordingly their use is widespread in storeroom operations. Primary functions of computers, since their very onset, include data storage and computations. Such is the heart of inventory control.

Before computers were widely used in food service, operators had two choices. Either they tediously tracked their inventory on stock file cards (Figure 1.4), or they didn't even bother to maintain records, as it seemed like too much work.

Today, computers are integrated throughout all modern food service operations (Figure 1.5). Storeroom employees must be able to perform the basic functions of word processing, database entry, and spreadsheet operations. As there are numerous proprietary systems designed for food service and storeroom operations, prospective employees are expected to possess only a basic understanding of computer operations. Most establishments anticipate having to train new employees on the customized software that they use.

1.4 **Storeroom clerk working with old-fashioned storeroom card file**
Photo Courtesy of Robert Garlough

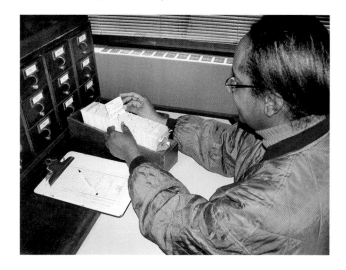

1.5 **Buyer using computerized inventory system**
© Randy Van Dam 2008

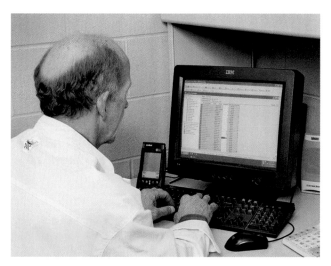

Market Awareness

Contrary to the old adage, in food service, what you don't know *will* hurt you. Successful businesses avoid threats and take advantage of opportunities. A successful buyer must possess a broad understanding of the marketplace, both local and national, and both domestic and foreign. Understanding the market is half the battle in staying competitive.

Laws of Commerce

Inherent in all forms of business are the rules and processes to which all participants are expected to adhere. In food service, as in other areas of commerce, there are established laws that govern the course of business. It is incumbent upon the buyer to be aware of such laws and to be vigilant to their practice. These laws are discussed at length in Chapter 2, "Food Laws and the Market and Distribution Systems."

Product Knowledge

Although most of the skills a buyer must possess are transferable from one profession to another, a food service buyer must additionally possess an in-depth understanding of food products. Storeroom managers and buyers can be trained in all of the requisite skills, and that includes food knowledge. However, this requires the buyer's devotion to learning, an intense interest in food, and a commitment to the profession.

Exposure to food products, in all their forms, is necessary for a buyer to learn the trade. To truly comprehend the vast array of products available, a buyer should visit dairy farms, slaughterhouses, coffee plantations, aquaculture ponds, and orchards. A buyer should make trips to bakeries, fish processing plants, butcher shops and charcuteries, cheesemongers, herb gardens, and flourmills. And a buyer should spend time at trade shows, farmer's markets, and food distributor's warehouses. In addition to learning about food, buyers should study textbooks and attend seminars to learn about the profession. They should join professional organizations and meet others who perform similar job functions. Food buyers should always be willing to learn more about their profession.

However, short of that, buyers can focus on the needs of their business's menu. They can interview their production staff and bookkeeper to get a sense of what they are looking for. They can look through the phonebook or search the Internet for a list of purveyors and set up meetings to learn about the available sellers. They can request samples of products for their chefs to evaluate. Remember, purchasing is all about the selection and procurement of product.

STOREROOM POLICIES AND PROCEDURES

Before the food service enterprise opens to the public, it must find suitable purveyors with whom to conduct business. But before the company holds its first meeting with the potential sellers, the food service operator should develop a **policies and procedures manual** for operating the storeroom. Although small operators might view this effort as a lot of unnecessary work, its dividends are always paid down the road. As Peddersen (1981) writes, "The *Guide to Purchasing*, of the National Association of Purchasing Management, declares that no purchasing manager has an excuse for not having at least an informal statement of purchasing policy and a collection of purchasing procedures" (p. 35).

Most failures in business are because of insufficient research and planning. Operators often fail to realize the real costs associated with establishing or maintaining their business, and they fall short in anticipating problem areas. Storerooms are rife with opportunities for problems, so management must organize and monitor them carefully. By having access to a comprehensive policies and procedures manual at the beginning, employees understand what is expected of them.

The policies and procedures manual provides a starting point for the purchasing staff (see Figure 1.6). Like all operating documents, the policies and procedures manual should be considered a living document, and it should be revised as better procedures and common sense become evident. All thriving businesses are able to adjust to new procedures and change with the times. Yet they all still maintain quality standards for their products and procedural standards for their employees. Peddersen (1981) suggests some of the following questions be addressed in a storeroom policies and procedures manual:

1. Which signature is required on a requisition?
2. What are the Purchasing Department's responsibilities and authority to challenge need or specifications?
3. Who may initiate or maintain contacts with suppliers or potential suppliers?
4. What are the criteria for supplier selection?
5. When is competitive bidding required?
6. Who takes part in negotiation?
7. Who may commit funds for supplies and equipment? What limits, if any, are there to this authority?
8. What authority or responsibilities does Purchasing share with other departments?
9. What is the policy on cooperative purchasing arrangements?
10. Are their limits on sales calls?
11. Who handles requests for samples or literature?
12. What are the limits on accepting gifts or entertainment from suppliers?
13. What rules govern potential conflicts of interest?
14. Will the Purchasing Department make personal purchases for employees and staff members?
15. In what committees or organizations should Purchasing be represented? (p. 37)

1.6   **Buyer reading a policies and procedures manual**
© Randy Van Dam 2008

The Seller

The seller is a vitally important factor in the business equation. To be an effective buyer, one must establish mutually satisfying relationships with a variety of **purveyors**. All too often chefs and business owners view the sellers as the opposing force, begrudging them their respect and fair profit in the marketplace. Such behavior is both unwarranted and shortsighted.

Sellers must exist in order for buyers to have product availability. When sellers are successful, they are able to broaden their products and services. When they are not, buyers have lost an option or resource. The adage "competition breeds success" plays well in food service. When businesses are successful, particularly as purveyors, there are more companies from which to choose. And, because there is competition, they must keep their pricing competitive in the market. Food service operators should welcome sellers into their offices to learn of their products and services. That being said, there are proper steps to follow when selecting purveyors.

SELECTING SELLERS

One of the most important functions that a chef, kitchen manager, food and beverage director, purchasing agent, or owner can perform is the proper selection of sellers. Whether in a small resort community, mid-American city, or bulging metropolis, the selection of purveyors can have a huge impact on the well-being of the food service operation.

A surly attitude when dealing with purveyors is counterproductive and foolish. The food service community is like all other professions; people within the community congregate. Reputations, both good and bad, are often made at one place of employment and carried on to future jobs. All too often, new working chefs anxious to earn their title treat others unfairly and with disrespect. This type of behavior might play well with a handful of celebrity chefs, but no one else tolerates such self-indulgent behavior. Doors are shut to those who don't respect others; sellers select their customers as much as buyers select their purveyors.

Sourcing: Finding the Purveyors

It is not difficult to start a list of purveyors with which to do business. Whether taking over an existing food service operation or starting a new business, the new chef must be open minded when developing a list of potential purveyors.

There are several methods for researching food service resources. Some suggestions include:

- Review the advertisements and listings in the telephone directory
- Contact the local chef's or club manager's association
- Call other chefs or managers in the area to introduce yourself
- Search the Internet for listings of food service distributors and e-vendors
- Talk to a local grocer
- Talk to a local food service equipment dealer

There are usually a variety of purveyors available that specialize in such products as meat, produce, and dairy, as well as larger food service distributors that sell both dry and refrigerated goods. Additionally, many suppliers service only locally based customers while a handful service the broader region or the entire country.

E-MARKETS

The marketplace is constantly evolving, and bricks and mortar no longer can bind it. Numerous new, as well as established, businesses have embraced the Internet as their storefront. However, according to Neef (2001), "Nearly 80% of organizations that have rushed to establish Web sites for online retailing have failed to invest in the purchasing and distribution systems that make delivery of their products possible" (p. 3).

Business-to-business (B2B) e-commerce uses the Internet to buy and sell food items. In the past few years, it has become an important way to do business. According to Neef,

- B2B e-commerce has replaced *business-to-consumer* e-commerce as the fastest growing area of e-business in the economy.

- E-procurement is the most important area of development in the B2B e-commerce area.

- E-procurement will fundamentally restructure the way in which an organization purchases goods.

- E-procurement is coming, but for most companies their online procurement capabilities are still limited to occasional and uncoordinated shopping online for office materials (p. 2).

Many smaller or boutique e-vendors have entered the food service marketplace, bringing national or international awareness to their specialty products. In addition, large distributors like Gordon Food Service offer the benefits of electronic ordering (GFS *Plus*) from their warehouses.

LOCAL SUPPLIERS

Local suppliers tend to be those who specialize in highly perishable goods, such as produce and seafood. They generally purchase their goods directly from the source, or marketplaces close to the source, and act as intermediaries. They purchase what you need and make it available to you when you need it for a slight profit.

Other local suppliers can be the growers or producers themselves, such as dairies, egg producers, fish farmers, herb farmers, bakeries, and cheesemongers (Figure 1.7). These suppliers tend to deal directly with the buyers and exchange useful information that helps each achieve its goals. The buyer must seek out these opportunities if her company allows direct purchases.

1.7 **Local supplier delivering products to a restaurant**
© Randy Van Dam 2008

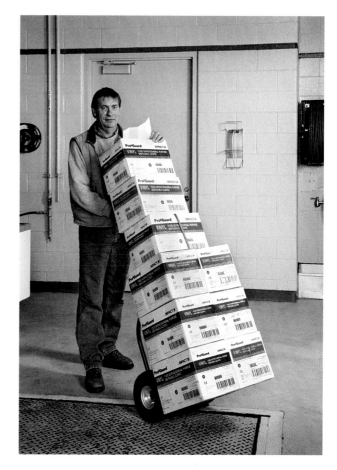

People, Places, Things

Hillary Clinton and the Farm-to-Fork Initiative

Senator Hillary Clinton organized a movement, beginning in 2006, to promote economic growth and viability for the farmers and food producers of New York State. The initiative was named Farm-to-Fork, and the goal was to broaden the market places and distribution networks of locally grown New York State produce by working with area school systems, restaurants, food retailers, and farmer's markets.

NATIONAL DISTRIBUTORS

There are several very large **food service distributors** that service either particular regions of the country (Figure 1.8) or the entire country (Figure 1.9). **Broadline** distributors have a wide range of products: They can sell everything that a food service establishment needs. They distribute goods from centrally located warehouses that often service multiple state areas.

The Introductory Meeting

There are many criteria to be considered when selecting purveyors, not the least of which is the sales representative. Typically, sales representatives do not attend introductory meetings, which are often held with area sales managers before a sales representative is assigned.

Yet the buyer should request that the sales representative attend the introductory meeting. As most sales associates are paid largely on the commission of their sales, it is in their own best interest to develop mutually beneficial relationships with their customers. It is important that the sales representative fully understand the needs and values of the buyer. Hearing that information secondhand from a sales manager can taint the message.

The following questions and strategies should be considered when first meeting with a potential supplier's representative:

- When setting up the meeting, establish the length of time for the meeting. It generally should not exceed 1 hour for the benefit of both parties.

- Hold the first meeting at the buyer's food service operation. If warranted, a second meeting to inspect the purveyor's facilities should be held at its location.

- Ask the potential purveyor to bring a printout of its product listing. Purveyors usually can comply, but rarely do they include pricing for their products. Pricing levels are generally negotiable based on volume and other factors and are closely guarded by the sellers.

- Ask purveyors if they can provide samples. This is common, particularly when the product is both fresh and narrow in scope. Meat purveyors, cheesemongers, bakeries, egg farmers, fish farmers, and produce and herb farmers often bring samples.

- Discuss the following:
  - The buyer's philosophy of business, relative to honesty, quality, service, consistency, and dependability
  - The seller's philosophy of the same issues
  - Pricing structures and methods of payment including extension of credit and C.O.D. discounts
  - Where the sellers get their products, for example:
    "Who are your suppliers?"
    "How do you get your products that you sell?"
  - Potential delivery days and times, for example:
    "I need deliveries between 7 a.m. and 9 a.m., or between 2 p.m. and
    3:30 p.m. Can you guarantee to deliver within these time periods?"
    "On which days do you deliver in my area?"
    "Can you deliver to me every other day?"

- Sales representative services, for example:
  "How frequently do you want to meet?"
  "I can only meet in the mid-mornings; can you call on me then?"
  "Can we set up established meetings: dates and times?"
  "My time is really tight. Can we keep our sales meetings to a half hour?"
  "If I get in a bind for an important event, can you personally run a product out to me?"

- Driver services, for example:
  "I intend to inspect, count, and weigh my deliveries each time. Will your driver wait patiently as I do so?"
  "Will your drivers deliver the product to inside our walk-in coolers? If not, where?"

- Truck sanitation, for example:
  "Are all of your delivery trucks refrigerated?"
  "How frequently do you clean the inside of your delivery trucks?"

- Rejection of product and credit memos, for example:
  "How do you handle product refusals or returns?"
  "Does your driver issue credit memos?"

- If interested in a purveyor's services, request a tour of its facilities.

- Obtain a credit application from the seller so you can order on credit.

Remember, the purveyor is in sales and is interested in putting the best foot forward at the introductory meeting. It is wise to remind the purveyor that your discussion has implications for many months, and potentially years, ahead. Honesty and integrity are principal to a healthy relationship, and the buyer should expect the quality level of both product and service to remain high long into the relationship.

> **BUYER'S NOTE** *Be wary of shifts in product quality or price increases after several months of service by a purveyor. Although not common, some unscrupulous purveyors attract new business by quoting lowball prices for premium products. After several months, when they believe the relationship is well established, they increase prices or reduce the quality of the product to make a better profit.*

Inspecting the Purveyor's Facilities

The failure of a supplier to maintain adequate sanitary standards can irrevocably damage the hard-earned reputation of a food service establishment. In other words, bad news travels fast when someone gets food poisoning. Although the fault may not lie primarily with the food service operator, the public rarely knows or cares when the damage originates with a supplier.

To protect the alimentary health of their clients, concerned buyers should take it upon themselves to inspect the purveyor's production and warehouse facilities when possible. This inspection can help the buyer

1.8 **Gordon Food Service services area map**
Courtesy Gordon Food Service

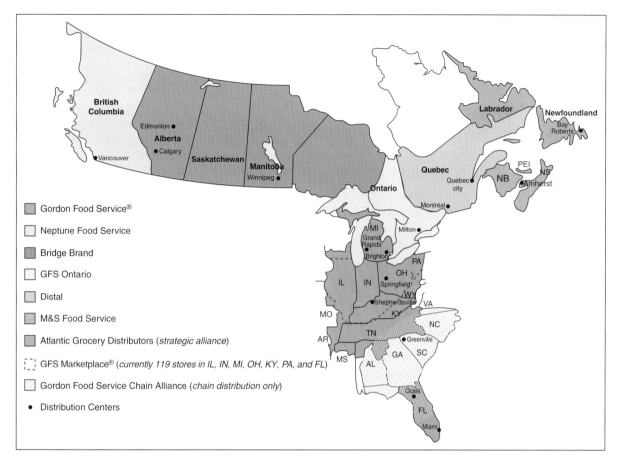

1.9 **Sysco Food Services services area map**
Courtesy SYSCO Food Services of Grand Rapids

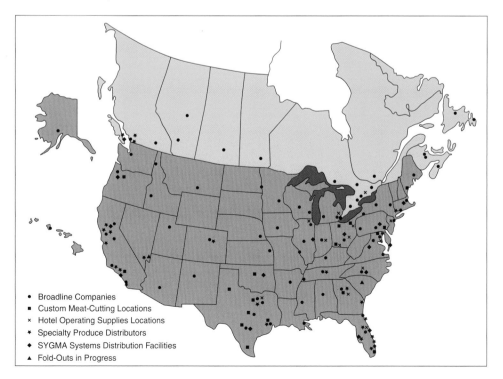

decide between two potential suppliers, particularly when product pricing seems unrealistically low from one of the sellers. Buyers should never gamble with the health and reputation of the business, particularly to save a few cents.

Establishing Purchasing Options and Contracts

Before selecting a purveyor, buyers should inquire about the variety of purchasing options available. Some sellers will allow, or even encourage, a less formal method of purchasing while other purveyors prefer a formal arrangement, clearly identifying all pricing structures and services in a negotiated contract. This difference might lie in the nature of the buyer's business, whether it is a midsized independent restaurant or a large state-run university, for example. It might also be determined by the nature of the buyer's position within the company (see Table 1.1).

Should the buyer be (a) a purchasing agent involved in centralized purchasing for multiple food service units, there is a greater likelihood for formal arrangements, compared with the (b) buyer working for a smaller, independent operation. The chance for error of a greater magnitude

warrants extra effort by both parties. A third scenario includes (c) **cooperative buying**, where people form a democratically controlled business organization to achieve a common economic end. Cooperative members realize hefty savings by buying directly from the source in massive quantities.

As Spears (1999) writes, "Purchasing negotiation is the art of arriving at mutual agreement with suppliers by means of bargaining on the essentials of a purchasing contract, such as specifications, quality assurance, price, payment terms, and delivery schedules. As such, the effectiveness of purchasing negotiation depends largely on a buyer's ability to establish bargaining strength" (p. 485).

Above all, knowledge is king. Understanding the options available is the best means of achieving optimal purchasing. Those arrangements that are flexible can benefit either the buyer or seller, as is also the case with inflexible arrangements. Oftentimes, the decision comes down to how much risk the operator is willing to bear, and how much effort the operator is willing to expend.

PURCHASING SERVICE AND MAINTENANCE CONTRACTS

"Know thyself" is a good premise when considering service and maintenance contracts. Most businesses, no matter their size or resources, recognize the need for outside

People, Places, Things

Gordon Food Service

The year 1897 marked some great adventures in history: S. A. Andree's Polar Expedition in a hot air balloon, the great Klondike Gold Rush, and production of Marconi's new invention, the radio. Another adventure, although not on quite as grand a scale, also began in 1897 . . . the birth of Gordon Food Service (GFS). It was in 1897 that 23-year-old Isaac VanWestenbrugge, a Dutch immigrant, borrowed $300 from his older brother Martin and started his business delivering butter and eggs in Grand Rapids. With headquarters in Grand Rapids, Michigan, today GFS is the largest privately held food service distributor in North America. With over 100 years in the food service business, Gordon Food Service is still family owned and committed to its customers and employees. This philosophy and commitment have given over 30,000 customers in ten U.S. states and throughout Canada access to more than 14,000 GFS and nationally branded, specialty, and exclusive products.

TABLE 1.1 Formal and Informal Purchasing Methods Comparison Matrix

Method of Purchasing	Primary Business Structures	Required Information	Advantages	Disadvantages
Business 2 Business	Smaller to larger businesses	Product Specs	Wider access to boutique vendors	Online procurement capabilities are still limited
Competitive Quotes	Smaller clubs, restaurants, caterers	Detailed product specs	Vendors must compete; best/lowest purchase price	Poorly written specs may result in inferior products
Daily Quotes	Smaller to larger businesses	Minimum information	Good for ordering highly perishable products; flexible	Time consuming
Sealed Bid Buying	Institutional, hotels, large properties	Detailed product specs; estimate of annual needs	Guaranteed lowest bids; time savings	No price fluctuations with sales
Cost-Plus and Prime Vendor Purchasing	Clubs, hotels	General knowledge of total product needs	Generally lowest available price	Generally limited selection; no competition
Standing Order	Institutional food service, bakeries, coffee shops	Good forecasting of future needs	Maintains par stock levels; time saving; favorable service	No flexibility
Informal Buying	Small independents	General knowledge of products	More flexible; requires less effort to purchase	Goods are not competitively priced
Volume Buying	Large chains, hotels	General knowledge of product needs; product specs	Stockless inventory	Possible storage fees; must take deliveries
Drop Shipment	Smaller to larger businesses	Minimum information	Does not require product storage; good for Internet purchases	Delivery charges can be high
Hedge Buying	Large chains, hotels	Product specs; estimate of total needs	Possibility for significant lower prices	Very risky—possibility for paying higher prices or getting unwanted stock

help. In addition to contracting for food and supplies, food service operators must also enter into contracts with other service providers, whether because of a lack of technical expertise, a lack of equipment, a lack of time, or a lack of interest. Thus, the need to *know thyself* becomes essential.

Unfortunately, in today's modern and litigious society, the days of the handshake sealing the deal are all but gone. It might still exist among the owners of their own enterprise, but rarely does it exist among corporate-owned companies.

Food service operators often enter into contracts for the following services:

- **Pest control.** Pest control is mandatory in food service. It is a highly specialized service, and it is unlikely that the typical food service manager would have the requisite knowledge to perform the tasks. Food service operators are required to be proactive with pest control. There are nationally recognized companies (often franchised by a local owner), corporate-owned companies, and independents all competing for the buyer's contract. Each must be considered on its own merits. Considerations include the training and

knowledge of the individual servicing the account, the quality of time spent and commitment to servicing the account, and the strength and quality of chemical agents used. Whichever company is used, it is absolutely critical to have a professional pest control company under monthly contract.

- **Waste removal and recycling.** Modern food service operators can reduce their need for garbage removal by using garbage grinders and garbage disposals. They also can be environmentally conscious by separating their recyclables, such as nonfood cardboard, glass, and metals, from other trash. Trash removal companies will supply closed Dumpsters of various sizes, depending on the needs of the operation. Most food service operators wish to contract for daily removal to minimize pests and unwanted odors. Operators should request that their Dumpsters be rotated on a regular basis and replaced with clean and sanitized units with working lid closures when necessary.

- **Cleaning.** In addition to cleaning the windows, restrooms, bars, dining areas, entrance ways, and kitchens daily, food service establishments also have specialty cleaning needs, such as exhaust hoods, tile and vinyl floor waxing, deep cleaning and degreasing, carpets and upholstery, and concrete or blacktop cleaning. The operator should assess its own willingness and ability to perform each of these duties. In reality, when these services are not contracted, they are also often placed on the back burner, and the facility quickly shows the wear and tear of use.

- **Facility maintenance and remodeling.** Maintenance is typically an ongoing need of most operations. Whether painting the kitchen, recarpeting the dining room, changing locks, or installing alarm systems, the list seems to go on and on. Many operators employ a handyman, often a retired individual who has a broad range of skills and the interest in part-time employment. Other times, operators must use the services of professionals who are contracted for specific tasks in which they are trained.

- **Groundskeeping and plowing.** Before the public ever enters a business, they evaluate the facility from the outside. It is paramount, with the vast competition that exists in the marketplace today, to be proactive about the facility's appearance. If operators are unable to maintain their own landscaping and parking lots, they must contract out the services to a dependable provider.

- **Equipment maintenance.** Equipment maintenance can be arranged in either of two ways. The traditional way is to call an equipment repair company, as needed, when something breaks. The other way is to enter into **service contracts** with companies that agree to perform preventative maintenance on the equipment, as well as fix it whenever it breaks for an agreed-upon period of time. This is often expensive for the buyer, but it provides peace of mind for important equipment, such as point-of-sales machines.

- **Equipment rental.** Oftentimes it is necessary, or more cost effective, to rent equipment rather than to buy it. When caterers are starting out, they tend to rent vans, chafing dishes, complete table settings, and even warming carts. As they grow, caterers can afford to purchase some of their own equipment but continue to rent as larger parties or busy months require. Restaurants, clubs, and hotels also rent equipment for enormous or unusual events. Some companies used to rent computer equipment because it was so costly and changed so rapidly. But as the cost of computers has dropped significantly, and their capacity has grown exponentially, it has become standard for companies to purchase, rather than rent, computers.

- **Laundry and linen supply.** Virtually every food service company, except hotels that operate their own laundry facilities, needs the services of a linen company. Depending on the location of the food service establishment, there are usually only a limited number of linen suppliers in the area. If the business decides to rent from a linen service, it should consider the following: overall cost of the service, charges for lost or damaged goods, length of service contract, ability to cancel the contract, scheduled delivery times, and variety and quality of options.

- **Bookkeeping, auditing, and check writing.** Most companies need the services of an outside auditing company, even if they can maintain their own books. Small and midsized companies usually also need bookkeeping services to print employee paychecks, bill the accounts receivables, and pay the accounts payable. Auditing companies also help to prepare the monthly financial statements, when given sales and inventory figures.

- **Legal.** Most businesses need a lawyer from time to time to advise them on legal matters relative to the business. Lawyers charge by the hour, so companies should have their paperwork in order and their needs specific when meeting with lawyers. Most operators can save themselves a lot of money by being organized and efficient and by asking good questions about the law's expectations of business.

- **Insurance.** Liability, property, hazard, and commodity insurance are a commodity, as much as any other product on the market. Operators should require insurance companies to submit quotes for contracts, and management should review the contracts annually.

- **Utilities.** Utilities such as electric and natural gas are also a commodity, and savvy owners and buyers can negotiate contracts for utilities in advance with brokers.

- **Advertising and promotion.** Most companies advertise, whether in newspapers, in the Yellow Pages, on billboards, in trade magazines, or on the Internet. Food service operators should find a means to measure the return on their investment. With the high cost of Yellow Pages ads and the many companies that provide competing services, it is important to consider the target market for the ads and how much flexibility one has to change the content.

- **Flowers and plants.** Although not a requirement for doing business, plants and flowers help to transform stark environments into friendly places of commerce. Some businesses contract with plant rental services to maintain plants, often rotating them out due to limited sunlight in some spaces.

- **Vending machines.** Vending machines have modernized over the decades, although their purpose remains essentially the same: to provide food service in locations or at times when other forms of food service are impractical. Some operators choose to own or rent the machines and stock them personally while most others use vending companies that pay a commission on the sales of the machine. There are national vendors like Service America Corporation, Canteen, and ARAMARK, which provide full-service vending, as well as privately owned vending companies in most metropolitan areas. Some suggest that a formal bid process be used for these services.

INFORMAL BUYING PRACTICES

Informal buying is often practiced by smaller operations where the chef or owner also does the buying. Although the practice is quite common, it rarely yields the savings that are realized through more formal systems of purchase. In effect, the buyers ride the market and wait until they need the goods before they order. That being said, operators practice informal buying because:

- It takes little time away from the production needs of the operation.
- Sales are volatile, and the quantities needed for a product vary daily.
- Purchasing seasonally available goods is important to the buyer.
- There are only one or two sources available for the items.
- The market is unstable, and prices fluctuate.
- The need is urgent, and the immediate receipt of goods is important.
- The size of the business is too small to warrant a formal process of purchasing.
- The business struggles with cash flow and must limit its purchases.
- The purveyor has placed the business on a C.O.D.-only arrangement because of late bill payments.

To maintain the best cost advantage possible, the buyer should still perform **competitive buying** practices. Competitive buying is when the buyer solicits quotes, either orally or written, from various sellers and compares them to find the lowest price. By contacting at least two suppliers to request daily pricing of perishable goods, such as produce, fish, and meats, the buyer is still able to practice competitive buying. If it is a large order, it might make economic sense to split the order between two purveyors. However, if it is a small order, it likely makes the most sense to purchase the products from the one purveyor whose total price is the lowest. Oftentimes, purveyors have minimum order requirements to cover delivery costs, so in those instances the buyer cannot split the order among multiple vendors.

 As a matter of practice, chefs and food service managers will often alternate purchases among multiple vendors to maintain good working relationships with their sellers. Failure to buy from one vendor could result in the loss of that source as well as the ability to keep the other vendor's prices competitive.

In contrast to competitive buying is **single-source buying**, where the buyer simply orders from one source with the hope that the price and quality are good. This method is obviously not preferred and generally underserves the needs of the operation, unless it is done by negotiated contract. Unless the product is unique and only available from a single source, or a contact has been negotiated that guarantees lower prices, it reflects a lazy and careless attitude on the part of the buyer, and management should not tolerate it.

FORMAL BUYING PRACTICES

Larger food service operations that are able to justify the payroll costs of storeroom staff uniformly engage in formal buying practices. Tax-supported, publicly held institutions such as prisons and universities usually are required to use competitive bidding processes. Hotels and restaurant chains, though not mandated by state laws, also engage in the bidding process. There are several methods of formal purchasing; they include *bid buying*, *cost plus fixed-fee buying*, *volume buying and warehousing*, *prime vendor contracts*, *long-term contracts*, *and hedging*. The negative and positive aspects of these methods are depicted in Table 1.1.

Bid Buying

Bid buying is used in competitive buying to compare the price quotations from several vendors seeking the buyer's business. Buyers can take bids by telephone, by fax, by e-mail, by sealed bid, or in person. Moreover, bids are either fixed, where the seller and buyer agree to a price for a set period of time, or daily, where the prices can vary on a daily basis.

Fixed bids are often used by larger organizations, such as universities, hospitals, and restaurant chains, which buy large quantities of perishable and nonperishable items over a long period of time. The buyers prepare **bid request forms**, as illustrated in Figure 1.10, which contain product specifications, estimated quantities, and a specified period of time. Purveyors are invited to complete the request forms and submit them to the buyer. **Sealed bids** are submitted to the company by a specified deadline and then publicly opened by the buyer. Contracts are then awarded, generally to the lowest bidders.

A **daily bid**, also known as **daily quotation**, is often used for perishable items that have only a few days' shelf life. Daily bids are often made over the phone, by fax, or by e-mail. The chef arranges a system with her supplier to obtain the daily quotes and places orders accordingly.

Whether using daily or fixed bids, buyers select vendors by either **line-item bidding** or **bottom-line bidding**. Line-item bidding involves selecting the vendor that quotes the lowest price for a single product. (Sometimes

1.10   Sample Bid Request Form

Date   *Purchasing Agent's Name*
                                                          Contact Information_____

The *name of business* will receive bid quotations for our annual purchase of *name of product category,* until *time* and *date.* Interested vendors must review the attached list of Vendor Requirements, and address these requirements, as needed, as part of their bid submission.

- Master Bid Document
- General and Special Bid Conditions
- Payment and Delivery Structure
- Vendor Warranty
- Required Product Specifications

All bidders must sign and date this cover letter receipt, acknowledging their understanding of the terms as outlined in the Vendor Requirements documentation. This signed certificate must be included with all other required bid documents. Failure to sign and submit this form may be considered grounds for disqualification.

_____   _____
Vendor's Company Name   Vendor Street Address

                                              _____
                                              City   State   Zip Code

_____   _____
Submitted by   Title   Date

---

bidders will choose to bid only on part of the request form.) Each item on the buyer's list is compared line by line, and the contract is awarded for only those items with the lowest quoted prices (see Figure 1.11). However, as mentioned earlier, oftentimes purchase minimums must be met to receive free delivery from the vendor. According to Gunn (1992), "the typical wholesaler needs a guarantee of a $600.00 minimum-order to realize a return on investment" (p. 32).

Bottom-line bidding, nicknamed the "all-or-nothing approach," requires the bidders to bid on all items on the request form. The prices from each potential vendor are totaled, and the supplier with the lowest combined total is awarded the entire contract. This process is practical for both parties: the buyer saves time, and the seller saves on delivery costs.

Cost Plus Fixed-Fee Buying

When a company negotiates a contract for **cost plus fixed-fee**, as shown in Figure 1.12, it agrees to purchase most of its products from one broadline or full-line food service distributor for a fixed markup beyond the seller's actual costs. The markup can be a set monetary amount or a percentage of the purchase price. The benefit is mutual:

the seller is guaranteed a large sale on a regular basis, and the buyer gets rock-bottom pricing without having to engage in daily competitive buying. With the spiraling costs of transportation, it is very advantageous for purveyors to maximize their deliveries to buyers. Similarly, with escalating labor costs and staff shortages, it is also often advantageous for food service operators to consolidate their time spent on buying and receiving.

Volume Buying and Warehousing

Volume buying and warehousing, sometimes referred to as "stockless purchasing," involves contracting for large quantities of singular products over an extended period of time. It requires the buyer to purchase a product in advance and then take multiple deliveries of the product over a negotiated length of time. The seller may charge the buyer a storage fee, which must be weighed against the savings incurred. However, storage charges are not always applied, particularly if the entire product is delivered within 30 days.

Oftentimes food distributors promote "show specials" during their fall or spring food shows. Buyers can negotiate the minimum quantity required for purchase and take delivery over several weeks after the show. This practice

1.11   Sample Comparative Bid Analysis

Bid Order Sheet Comparative Analysis

Delivery Date:	Order	Vendor #1		Vendor #2		Vendor #3	
Item & Description		Bid	Cost	Bid	Cost	Bid	Cost
Individual Invoice Total:							

is quite common, and it benefits the buyer who knows her own volume needs. For example, if the buyer has tracked her company's usage of 6-ounce chicken breasts per month, she might purchase 100 cases as a show special at $8 off per case. The buyer has saved her company $800 with this single-volume purchase.

Prime Vendor

A **prime vendor** contract, as illustrated in Figure 1.13, is similar to a cost plus fixed-fee contract. Rather than be contractually restricted to only one vendor, an establishment can make prime vendor arrangements with several purveyors. Sellers achieve prime vendor status by agreeing to sell their products at a set price, often based on cost plus fixed-fee. Prime vendor arrangements can be made with full-service or specialty suppliers.

Long-Term Contract

Long-term contracts are based on fixed or accelerated prices. Similar to the *volume buying and warehousing method*, this contract makes the supplier responsible for purchasing the

product and then having it available as needed. The buyer must forecast her company's needs, and if the quantity is sufficient to gain the seller's interest, the two will enter into a long-term contract. In this scenario, the buyer needs to make payment only upon receipt of each delivery, and the seller bears all storage costs.

Hedging (Forward Buying)

Hedging is a method of purchasing that often entails considerable risk to the buyer. Also known as "forward contracting" or "forward buying," hedging is the practice of investing in products that are forecasted to increase in price. However, if the price falls, the buyer is committed to purchasing products at above-average prices.

This practice is beyond the sensibilities of most businesses and is only practiced by large-volume operators that have sophisticated purchasing systems and the expertise to study the futures market. However, any operator can read the *Wall Street Journal* and *Produce Green Sheets* to learn about what's happening in the marketplace and its effect on the future prices of their products.

1.12   Sample Cost Plus Contract

XYZ Food service Company will offer (*your business*) competitive pricing through a Cost Plus Program. XYZ Food service Company will maintain the overall markup of the product category.

Product Category	Markup
Grocery	
Frozen	
Protein	
Meat	
Poultry	
Seafood	
Disposables	
Dairy	
Produce	
Tabletop	
Cleaning Powder	Agreed Upon Contractual Pricing
Beverage Systems	Agreed Upon Contractual Pricing
Ready-to-Drink Beverages	

The above markup structure has been based on the following information: average order size ( ), number of proprietary items ( ), terms ( ), commitment level (%), and number of deliveries per week per unit ( ).

When (*your business*) contracts with vendors for individual pricing, documentation verifying this information should be forwarded to the Contract Administration Team for implementation. XYZ Food service Company requests that a reasonable amount of time, seven to ten (7-10) business days, be allotted to execute new pricing. The XYZ Food service Company cannot back-date pricing contracts if they are received after the date they go into effect.

Pricing for the Cost Plus Program is firm for one (1) fiscal month. Exceptions include meat, poultry, seafood, produce, dairy, and some oils. These items will be quoted on a weekly basis. Uncontrollable market conditions may necessitate price adjustments mid-week. You will be notified of those occasions when they occur.

Pricing on cleaning products and dispensed beverages will be based upon mutual agreement. This pricing is locked in for a period of one (1) year. Please see your Chain Manager for information regarding dispensed beverage and cleaning product programs.

All pricing programs are contingent upon (*your business'*) agreement to purchase X% of total goods from XYZ Food service Company in the categories we have the ability to service. Prices are applicable to full cases.

This pricing excludes all additional costs that may be incurred by XYZ Food service Company in the course of our relationship with (*your business*). This includes any sponsorship or donations XYZ Food service Company may provide to (*your business*) as outlined in this contract.

1.13   Sample Prime Vendor Proposal

Thank you for allowing XYZ Food service Company the opportunity to act as the preferred vendor for (*your business*). We are confident that the service and support we have to offer will meet and exceed your needs throughout the duration of our relationship.

Recognizing (*your business'*) need for cost-effective pricing coupled with outstanding service, XYZ Food service Company has developed this proposal with the purpose of meeting these needs. Our desire to providing a competitively priced product teamed with superior service is unsurpassed.

As you consider XYZ Food service Company as your primary vendor, please take into account the following—these are just a few of the benefits we offer our customers.

- Easy access to various business reports
- Internet-based ordering
- A nutrition resource center to provide nutrition and ingredient information staffed by eight registered dieticians
- Our on-site quality assurance lab is a rarity in the food service distribution industry
- Electronically track product shipping and delivery
- Marketing consultants to help you improve your business
- Annual food shows

XYZ Food service Company will offer the following ordering and delivery schedules.

Next Day Deliveries
If you place an order Monday through Thursday, you will receive your order the next day. Orders placed on Friday will be delivered on Monday.

Skip Day Deliveries
There will be one (1) working day between the day you place the order and the day the order is delivered. The following schedule outlines Skip Day ordering:

Order Day	Delivery Day
Monday	Wednesday
Tuesday	Thursday
Wednesday	Friday
Thursday	Monday
Friday	Tuesday

Two Day Lead (TDL) Delivery Items
Certain slower moving items are only available on a skip day basis. These are referred to as TDL items. These items are not available to add to your order and will be listed on the front page of your XYZ Food service Company order guide for quick reference.

Additions to Your Order
To ensure that your delivery reaches you in a timely manner, we request that you limit additions to your order when possible. Any adds must be phoned in by 11:00 AM Eastern Time on the day prior to the day that the order is delivered. We will make every effort to accommodate your request; however, additions cannot always be accepted because of limited space on our trucks. If our truck is filled to capacity, the XYZ Food service Company representative will alert you at the time of the call, or will notify you as soon as they are informed of the issue by our transportation department.

As you review and evaluate this proposal, please feel free to direct all inquiries to:

XYZ Food service Company
1234 Main Street
Anytown, USA 12345

The Buying Process

The buying process occurs only after the food service establishment has planned the menu, determined quality and quantity of ingredients needed to produce the menu, written product specifications, determined price ceilings for products, determined appropriate stock levels, and identified approved purveyors. Once the owner and chef have completed these tasks, the buyer can begin her job of selection and procurement. The buying process involves three major steps: *identifying the need*, *planning for the purchase*, and *making the purchase*.

IDENTIFYING THE NEED

Identifying the need is primarily a mathematical function of the job. It requires constant communication with the production staff, and perhaps the sales staff, and a daily accounting of stock levels. The buyer's primary responsibility is to maintain an adequate level of stock to meet the production demands of the staff. Failure to have either the proper ingredients or quantity of ingredients is highly detrimental to the business. As the old adage goes about the street vendor, "you can't sell produce off an empty cart."

Methods have been established to help the buyer maintain sufficient stock. According to Warfel and Cremer (2005), "It is unfair to expect a food buyer to know exactly what is needed by operating departments and how much of it to buy. In fact, it would be unwise for the buyer to ignore the chef and operating department heads" (p. 54). Most businesses create a list of all of their needed supplies and foodstuffs. Each ingredient is crosschecked to determine its multiple uses within different recipes, and a minimum quantity is established that must be on hand at all times. This quantity is known as a **safety stock**. Various methods for determining proper stock levels and ordering amounts are discussed at length in Chapter 8.

Determining Stock Levels

When establishing an inventory, it is best to divide the products by their nature, perishable and nonperishable (see Figure 1.14 and Figure 1.15). Nonperishable items are often purchased in bulk, such as case lots, and have a longer **shelf life**. They are much easier to buy and store, and they can often be purchased from multiple full-service or broadline vendors.

Nonperishables are purchased more frequently, as needed, because of their short shelf lives. Ideally, the chef and buyer will create forms or commodity lists for each type of perishable, grouping them by the purveyor's product line. For example, separate lists should be created for dairy, produce, seafood, meats, poultry, and bakery.

In some large operations, such as a hotel, the chef is expected to prepare a daily list of all perishables needed for use over the next day or two. This list usually includes meats, fish, and poultry. The buyer, based on banquet sales contracts and established par stock levels, projects other fresh ingredients such as produce and bakery products.

According to Virts (1987), a system for determining the quantity of perishable products may include the following steps:

1. Determine normal usage rates. For example, in a normal two-day purchasing period, the operation typically purchases a specific amount of selected items: pounds of fresh meat, fresh poultry fryers, cases of lettuce, and other perishable products.
2. Consider whether additional quantities are needed for special catered events.
3. Determine the amount of each item currently in inventory.
4. Deduct that amount from the normal usage rate to calculate the quantity to purchase.
5. Make adjustments as necessary for holidays, special events, or other factors unique to the order period. (p. 64)

PLANNING FOR THE PURCHASE

After the tentative need has been determined, the buyer must consider other factors before placing the order. The most important factor is the rate at which the operation uses the items. In addition to quantifying how much of a certain product is used between deliveries, the buyer must consider the lead-time quantity for each item. This number represents the amount of units deducted from inventory between the time the reorder has been placed and the time the product actually arrives.

In some remote locations, such as resorts, purveyors might make only one delivery per week. The buyer must be able to accurately project her needs, without needlessly overbuying. This lead-time quantity is not to be confused with the safety stock levels, which should be available at all times. This safety level ensures a continuation of services in the event of damaged goods or late deliveries.

The buyer compares the quantities needed with that on hand, and prepares an order sheet. As discussed previously, the buyer can place the order in a formal or informal manner; however, the buyer must also consider the urgency of the products. Most of the time, with proper planning, emergencies can be avoided. Unfortunately, there are times when products are needed immediately, and the buyer must consider her options for obtaining the product.

MAKING THE PURCHASE

After a buyer has selected and approved suppliers from which she can buy on credit, a smart buyer will also identify retailers in the area that carry the products

1.14 **Commodities List of Perishables**

Hotel La Bocana
Commodity List of Perishables
Date: _____

Category: Dairy	On Hand	Par Stock	Order Qty	Acme Dairy	GFS	Kingma	SYSCO
Milk, 2%, 4-Gal							
Milk, Whole, 4-Gal							
Milk, Whole, 24-Pt							
Half & Half, 12-Qt							
Heavy Cream, 12-Qt							
Sour Cream, Lite, 6-Qt							
Yogurt, Plain, 6-Qt							
Butter, Print, Unsalted, 36-1#							
Butter, Print, Salted, 36-1#							
Butter Reddies, 90 ct, AA, 15#							
Butter Chips, 90 ct, AA							
Cheese, Asiago, 2.5 #							
Cheese, Bleu, Danish, 10#							
Cheese, Bleu, Crumbles, 5 #							
Cheese, Brie, 8 oz							
Cheese, Brie, 1#							
Cheese, Camembert, 1 #							
Cheese, Cheddar, Sharp, 10#							
Cheese, Cheddar, Mild, 10#							
Cheese, Gouda, 8 oz							
Cheese, Jack, 1#							
Cheese, Mozzarella, 2%, 10#							
Cheese, Mexican Blend, 3#							
Cheese, Parmesan, Fresh, 10#							
Cheese, Provolone, 10#							

1.15   Commodities List of Nonperishables

Hotel La Bocana
Commodity List of Non-Perishables
Date: _____

Category: Canned Fruits	On Hand	Par Stock	Order Qty	GFS	Sam's	SYSCO	US Foods
Applesauce, Natural, 72-4 oz, SYSCO							
Fruit, Mixed Cup, in Jce, 36-4 oz, Dole							
Fruit, Tropical Salad Mixed Cup, 36-4oz, Dole							
Grapefruit Sections, Asst, L/S, 12-5 IPM							
Orange, Mandarin, Jce, 6-#10,							
Peach Halves, L/S, 6-#10, GFS							
Pear Halves, W/P, 6-#10, SYSCO							
Pineapple, Sliced in Jce, 6-#10, Dole							
Pineapple, Tidbits in Jce, 6-#10, GFS							
Pineapple Chunks in Jce, 6-#10, Dole or GFS							

her business uses. Unfortunately, someone else's lack of planning can become the buyer's emergency. Buyers have a variety of methods and sources for obtaining goods. These include *the purchase order and blanket purchase order, standing order, daily order, drop shipments, ordering C.O.D., cash and carry, farmer's markets and retail grocers,* and *bartering.*

Regardless of the method the buyer chooses to order the supplies, the buyer should create an order record and make it available to the receiving personnel. Oftentimes, buyers work from custom-made **buyer's order forms**. These forms are created and separated by the nature of their contents, such as by seafood, meats, dairy, produce, and dry goods. As demonstrated in Figure 1.16, buyers often work with several vendors that supply the same types of product, so there will be a column for each vendor on the form. These completed order forms, indicating the vendor and expected delivery date and time, should be placed in a secure location, such as in an "Orders Placed" binder or on a clipboard in the buyer's office, for easy reference by the receiving staff.

The Purchase Order

A **purchase order (P.O.)** (see Figure 1.17) is a form issued by the buyer and sent to the purveyor. The P.O. includes the names of the items, the quantities, and the prices for the items that will be purchased. The buyer will include a P.O. number and the shipping and billing address.

Purchase orders are legal documents that communicate the buyer's intention. Because a purchase order clearly spells out the conditions for the sale, it protects both the seller and the buyer. If the buyer refuses to pay, the seller can sue for the moneys using the P.O. as evidence. If it is a large or complicated purchase, a seller may request that a buyer create a P.O. so that both parties understand the transaction. An invoice, which is the receipt for the items delivered, is another legal document that will reinforce the terms of the purchase order. The buyer can match the purchase order to the invoice to make sure that all of the items were delivered.

BLANKET PURCHASE ORDERS

A standard purchase order is usually used for companies with whom the buyer does infrequent business. If buyers plan to frequently purchase products or services from a seller over time, they often establish a **blanket purchase order**. This type of purchase order allows the buyer to purchase a certain amount of goods, usually indicated by a dollar amount, within a given time period. This speeds up the purchasing process as a separate P.O. is not needed for each transaction. The buyer merely needs to call her purveyor on the phone, send an electronic order, or submit a formal bid request to place an order with the company. As items are purchased, the seller will invoice the buyer for goods received. If needed, a "not-to-exceed" dollar amount can be added to the blanket P.O. to control the amount of spending.

1.16 Sample Buyer's Order Form for Multiple Produce Vendors

The Heritage Restaurant Buyer's Order Form						
Food Category: Dairy						
Item Description	Low-level Par	SYSCO	Jones Dairy	Crystal Dairy	Kraft	
PC: 13582 Milk, whole, 6-gal dispenser	5 each					
PC: 13576 Milk, skim, 10 oz	66 each					
PC: 13563 Milk, choc., 10 oz	136 each					
PC: 13542 Milk, butter, 10 oz	1 each					
PC: 13921 Cheese, ched., 10 lb/blk	½ blk					
PC: 13933 Cheese, sliced, Am., 3-lb stack	5 stacks					
PC: 13979 Cheese, Swiss, 10-lb loaf	½ loaf					
PC: 13961 Cheese, cream, 3-lb loaf	½ loaf					
PC: 13987 Cheese, parm., 5-lb pail	½ pail					
PC: 13995 Cheese, brie, 2-kg wheel	1 wheel					
PC: 13906 Cheese, prov., 8-lb loaf	¼ loaf					
PC: 13981 Cheese, mozz., 5-lb loaf	¼ loaf					

1.17 Order Guide for Gordon Food Service: GRCC Tech Center

Purchase Order

P.O. Number	:	O0011122
Order Date	:	4/1/2009
Expected On	:	4/3/2009
Ordered For	:	Kitchen
Ordered By	:	Chris Smith
Ordered From	:	

522 Stonewell Ave
Austin, TX 77022

Phone	:	713-555-2909	Contact	:	Martin Carter
Fax	:				

Comment   :   Sample Only

Item Name	Item Code	Quantity	Unit	Price	Total	Notes
Additive Rinse Aid 3x-RA 2/77oz Ecolab	4677912	1.000	4/1gal	$116.15	$116.15	
Additive Rinse Aid 3x-RA 2/77oz Ecolab	7746183	1.000	CS2CT	$115.90	$115.90	
Ecolab-Apex Detergent Hand Pot & Pan	4527487	1.000	CS2CT	$ 78.28	$ 78.28	
Ecolab-Apex Power Plus	4589628	1.000	CS4CT	$ 80.40	$ 80.40	
Ecolab-Apex Presoak	4526794	1.000	CS3CT	$ 89.04	$ 89.04	
Ecolab-Apex Rinse Add	4589693	1.000	CS2CT	$179.04	$179.04	
				Total:	$658.81	

Blanket purchase orders are very common among food service operators and allow for the immediate request and delivery of goods or services.

Standing Orders

If the buyer needs to purchase repetitive, specified services or items from a single supplier, the buyer can initiate a **standing order (S.O.)** to obtain more favorable pricing or service through volume commitments. This allows a business to quickly request delivery of goods and services, and it avoids the nuisance and cost of multiple purchase orders. The S.O. is limited to a certain amount for the entire year and does not represent a free license to buy goods or services not specified on the requisition.

A common practice for coffee shops, universities, convenience stores, and other food retailers is to maintain standing orders with dairies and bakeries. These businesses can usually forecast their usage with enough accuracy—relative to the sales of soft drinks, doughnuts, bagels, and milk—to establish an S.O. for daily delivery.

Daily Orders

The **daily order** is quite common among smaller, independent operators, as well as businesses that employ full-time buyers. In most cases, buyers ask purveyors to submit price quotations in advance, oftentimes weekly, so buyers can do comparative buying. Some purveyors are reluctant to quote prices more than 24 hours in advance, and it might be for good reasons such as market volatility.

In any case, the chef, owner, or designated buyer will review her commodity lists and contact the seller by the established means (online, by fax, by phone, and so on). Daily orders are placed and debited from the blanket purchase order that has been established. The goods are generally delivered within 24 hours, and the invoice is mailed later.

Drop Shipments

A **drop shipment** is a slightly different method of purchasing goods. In this instance, the seller does not have the item, or enough of the item, in stock. The seller arranges with the wholesaler or the manufacturer of the item to deliver it directly to the buyer. The wholesaler invoices the seller, who then in turn invoices the buyer. The seller will increase the price on the second invoice to cover the costs of the transaction.

Drop shipping can occur when the order quantity is more than what the seller normally carries in its store or when a buyer purchases items from a smaller store or website.

Bartering

Bartering is not limited to the remote areas of the country; it can be practiced by the most upscale of eateries. Magazines publishers, advertisers, and graphic designers commonly barter their services for dining privileges at a fine-dining restaurant. Because both businesses trade in marked-up labor, with a fraction of supply costs involved, meals can be exchanged for ad space or artwork. This is a particularly useful strategy for new businesses that are cash strapped and looking to fill their dining rooms.

 Bartering and trade-outs may be illegal or have tax consequences in some states. It is advisable to consult a tax attorney before entering into such an arrangement.

Buyer–Seller Relations: A Win–Win Approach

Not so long ago, many in business likened the negotiation process to war. Books on negotiations frequently used battlefield analogies. Meetings were seen as confrontations, where discussions needed to be held in an adversarial manner. Strategies were taught on how to win the battle and, ultimately,

the war. Only one side was meant to be victorious: the buyer. That was wrong then, and it remains wrong today.

Relationships between buyers and sellers should be mutually beneficial. As the adage goes, "It is much easier to conduct business with someone who is running toward you, rather than running away from you." With a win–win approach, both parties consider their relationship to be advantageous, and future relations are both sought after and encouraged. The buyer who believes she received value from the seller will seek further trade with that seller, and similarly the seller will seek business with that buyer if she received both respect and due profit from the last deal.

The lesson is simple. Buyers need sellers; sellers need buyers. Both deserve the opportunity to conduct business in a professional, courteous, and profitable manner. Otherwise, move on. If both parties don't walk away from a negotiation as winners, then the process has failed.

CONDUCTING SALES MEETINGS

Essential to maintaining a win–win relationship is the ability to conduct regularly scheduled sales meetings that satisfy both the buyer and the seller (Figure 1.18). As the personal productivity of both the buyer and the seller is crucial to her own success, neither party should unfairly monopolize the other's time. These meetings should be established in advance, allowing both parties to set sufficient time aside, with the least amount of interruption permitted. Most meetings can be productive if scheduled to last between a half hour and an hour. Beyond that, time is often spent on non-work-related discussions. That is fine if both parties agree, but often it can drain on one or the other's patience.

1.18 **Buyer holding sales meeting with seller in storeroom office**
© Randy Van Dam 2008.

Upon the selection of the approved sellers, the buyer should identify how frequently she wishes to meet with the sales representative and agree on specific days and times for the meetings. Additionally, the buyer should indicate what information she will be seeking from the sales representative and query what type of additional information might be available, should she desire it. Generally, this includes product searches and substitutions, plus information on new developments that may be of interest to the buyer.

Under no circumstances should buyers allow sellers (more often, potential sellers) to drop in without an appointment expecting to have the buyer's full attention for more than 1 or 2 minutes. It is advisable for buyers to post a sign outside their office indicating that all salespeople must have appointments.

The Negotiation Process

One of the greatest attributes a buyer can possess is the ability to **negotiate** a purchase with skill and diplomacy. Some consider it the single most important measure to being a successful buyer. As Shapiro et al. write in their book, *The Power of Nice: How to Negotiate So Everyone Wins-Especially You*, "The best way to get what you want is to help the other side get what they want" (2001, p. 249). Paquette writes in *The Sourcing Solution*, "The ability to negotiate is a skill set requiring training and experience, and it is one that a good buyer must use effectively on a daily basis" (2004, p. 141). To create a win–win strategy to negotiations, the buyer should consider the following elements:

- **Create partnerships.** Future business negotiations are about building long-term relationships.

- **Know the needs of all parties.** Your job as a successful buyer and negotiator is to understand the needs of the person across the table from you.

- **Know thyself.** Your needs may be different from those of the seller. The seller's greater need might be to gain, or increase, market penetration by landing your account, while you seek favorable pricing.

By understanding the needs of both parties, you are much more likely to create a strategy of success for both businesses. The skill lies in trading something of value to obtain something of value. Paquette also suggests using the following strategies in the negotiation process:

- Never make the first concession.

- Make your first concession a reasonable one.

- Make each subsequent concession smaller, less reasonable.

- Don't be afraid to ask the question. It may get answered.

- Find creative solutions.

- Recognize that good deals lead to more good deals (and vice versa).

- Know the terms.

- Keep written notes.

- Understand performance issues. (2004, p. 149)

SUPPLIER PERFORMANCE EVALUATION

Evaluations should be designed to provide information to management that will aid in their decision-making abilities. Although all information can be useful, supplier performance evaluations should seek specific information. Both the *product* and the *process* should be evaluated. Consider the following criteria for your own evaluation instrument:

- Identify the short- and long-term goals for your organization.

- Identify the specifications for your needed products.

- Look at which suppliers and products you want to evaluate.

- Develop a cross-functional team (such as including the owner, chef, accounting staff, receiving staff, and sales rep) with various suppliers and management's assistance to identify the functional priorities of the storeroom that should be evaluated.

- Define the most important factors to evaluate: price, quality, delivery time, consistency, sales representative, and other services.

- Weigh each criterion (in relation to the others).

- Determine a rating scale.

- Review the instructions for completing the evaluation for clarity and effectiveness.

- Have other buyers, outside the team, evaluate the system and criteria.

- Review completed evaluations with management.

ETHICAL AND PROFESSIONAL STANDARDS AND PRACTICES

It is up to management to establish and articulate the ethical and professional standards of the organization. Additionally, management must clearly lead by example when it comes to ethical and professional behavior. They must also insist upon this behavior from those with whom they conduct their business activities.

Both buyers and sellers must pledge to conduct their business honestly and ethically, whenever or wherever their business is conducted. It is vital that both parties be honest, responsible, trustworthy, and respectable. Neither side should sacrifice its reputation or sound business judgment. Sellers and buyers should not engage in illegal or unethical behaviors. Any short-term advantage or profit gained unethically will result in a long-term failure for the company and its agent.

Company management, such as the food and beverage director and executive chef, may not benefit personally from the financial gains of the company. No conflict of interest can be permitted, including bribes, kickbacks, or other unauthorized benefits that affect purchasing decisions. All company officers including buyers, chefs, food and beverage managers, dining room managers, and bar managers should avoid tips or bonuses. They should also avoid presents, trips, or entertainment tickets that would influence their purchasing decisions.

Van P. Atkins, CEC, AAC

Place of Birth: San Francisco, California

Courtesy Van Atkins.

Educational Background and Work Experience

Van Atkins is one of the country's preeminent chefs, having led the kitchens in some of America's largest and most celebrated hospitality properties. As with most accomplished chefs, he started by washing dishes and prepping foods in several establishments, learning from everybody for whom he worked. After schooling at Boise State University, Chef Atkins graduated from The Culinary Institute of America in 1974. He moved to Las Vegas and eventually became the executive chef of the Tropicana Hotel. Chef Atkins later became the executive chef of the famed Hilton Anatole Hotel, the largest and most complete convention resort hotel in the Southwest, situated on 45 acres outside of Dallas, Texas. Wishing to return to his hometown of San Francisco, Chef Atkins then became executive chef of the Westin St. Francis Hotel, a legendary San Francisco landmark. Always the ambitious chef, Atkins returned to Las Vegas to run the many kitchens of the famed Caesars Palace Hotel, owned by one of the world's leading gaming companies. Later, when Luxor called, he responded by becoming the opening executive chef of the iconic pyramid hotel and casino, establishing the storeroom and kitchen operations for the mega-resort. After several more years at its helm, Chef Atkins accepted the position of corporate executive chef for the L. J. Minor Corporation. Today, Chef Atkins is the senior director of business development and corporate executive chef for Custom Culinary, one of the leading providers of authentic culinary flavor systems in the food service and food processing industries.

Memberships and Career Highlights

Chef Atkins is a member of the American Culinary Federation, where he is a certified executive chef. He is also a member of the Research Chefs of America. Chef Atkins is a well-sought-after speaker and chef consultant, presenting at trade shows and culinary schools across the United States and abroad. Atkins recently returned to Dubai as a featured presenter at the CHEF seminar, held at the InterContinental Hotel. The

It Happened to Me...

"I was the Executive Chef at Caesar's Palace and we had an outdoor catering party for 18,000. It was the grand opening for the now famous Forum Shops at Caesars. Even though the Forum Shops are connected to Caesars, we had to load up the equipment and food onto 2 eighteen-wheeler refrigerated trucks and drive them to the site. You can imagine how much food was needed for this elaborate, heavy hors d'oeuvre party for 18,000 people.

"The day before the event we started to preload the refrigerated trucks. On the day of the function, we discovered that one of the refrigerated trucks had malfunctioned and froze everything that we had stored on board. Needless to say, we had to put everything into overdrive to replace all of the products! The party went off without a hitch and was hailed a success by all. From that moment on, however, we put temperature monitors on any refrigerated trucks we used for catering."

CHEF seminar, which aims to strengthen awareness of American food products, was held in conjunction with the U.S. Agricultural Trade Office and the Southern U.S. Trade Association (SUSTA). For his lifetime of culinary achievements, Chef Atkins was elected as a Fellow of the American Academy of Chefs, and the Honorable Order of the Golden Toque, an international honor society limited to 100 living chefs. However, with all of his success and notoriety, including being asked to interview for the position of White House chef in 1987, Chef Atkins still considers his mentoring of young men and women to be his greatest achievement.

Passions with the Food Service Industry

"What gives me the greatest pleasure in our business is to help others to grow. I still also thoroughly enjoy cooking and managing others in their jobs and the camaraderie of being with other chefs throughout the world. I've always said I have one of the greatest jobs in the country. I get paid to help chefs succeed in their jobs! I also enjoy the fact that we never stop learning. Wow, what a business!

Advice to a Chef or Buyer

"Always compare 'apples to apples.' Be on the lookout for new products, as manufacturers are making new products every day that are superior to the products of yesterday. Be sure to read the ingredient label on products. If you don't know what certain ingredients are, ask somebody who does. When possible, try to buy locally, and get to know your sources like the farmers, ranchers, and fishmongers."

(Note: The Forum Shops at Caesars have expanded three times since then, and it is per square foot the most profitable shopping center in the United States.)

Key Words and Concepts

bid request form	cooperative buying	line positions	sealed bid
blanket purchase order	cost plus fixed-fee	long-term contracts	selection
bottom-line bidding	daily bid	negotiate	service contracts
broadline vendor	daily order	optimal purchasing	shelf life
business-to-business (B2B) e-commerce	daily quotation	policies and procedures manual	single-source buying
buyer's order forms	drop shipment	prime vendor	staff position
code of ethics	ethics	procurement	standing order (S.O.)
commerce	fixed bids	purchase order (P.O.)	trade
competitive buying	food service distributor	purveyor	volume buying and warehousing
conceptual skill	hedging	safety stock	
	line-item bidding		

Chapter in Review

The following exercises are provided to help the reader understand and apply the contents of this chapter. They may be completed individually or in a classroom environment.

REVIEW QUESTIONS

a. Identify at least five attributes required to be a modern buyer.

b. Identify at least five important product characteristics to consider when buying.

c. Identify the various forms of formal and informal buying, and describe when each method would be appropriate to use.

d. Identify at least eight attributes that would be desirable in potential vendors.

INDIVIDUAL ACTIVITIES

a. **Web based:** Research different vendors that service your area, and find at least one vendor for each type of food used by a full-service restaurant.

b. **Experiential:** Attend a food show in your area, and speak with different purveyors at their booths.

c. **Critical thinking:** Consider why a food service operator would choose to use a formal system of buying over an informal system.

GROUP ACTIVITIES

a. **Lab experience:** Set up a series of mock sales meeting interviews, where students practice interviewing potential vendors.

b. **Classroom action:** As a class, outline the sections to a storeroom policies and procedures manual for a fictitious business. Afterward, divide the class into subgroups to develop each section.

CHAPTER

2

Food Laws and the Market and Distribution Systems

"Perfect freedom is as necessary to the health and vigor of commerce as it is to the health and vigor of citizenship." PATRICK HENRY

After reading this chapter, you will be able to:

◎ Explain the flow of goods through the market, or distribution, channel.

◎ Identify the major sources from which food and products originate.

◎ Describe the various intermediaries used in delivering food and products to food service operators.

◎ Distinguish among the different values added in the distribution channel, including form, time, place, and information.

◎ Define the different forces affecting the distribution channel, including economic, political, ethical, legal, technological, and intangible.

◎ Explain the function and business of the market.

◎ Identify and discuss the various laws and agencies involved in protecting consumers and the food service industry.

◎ State the purpose of the Organic Foods Production Act of 1990.

◎ Explain the Nutrition Education and Labeling Act.

Introduction

In Chapter 1, we covered trade and how it takes place in a market. **Markets** are where sellers and buyers come together to buy and sell goods or services. Normally, property is sold. **Property** is any good that is owned by someone. It can also refer to an object that someone controls or the right to own something. These concepts are known as "rights of ownership" within the laws of commerce.

This chapter explores the marketplace and the laws that govern it. Accepted social and business practices, along with written codes of laws, have existed since quill pens were put to parchment paper. The informed buyer should have a broad knowledge of the complex marketplace and layered distribution systems, along with an understanding of the legal systems of regulatory control that protect the buyer's and seller's interests.

2.1 The marketing channel

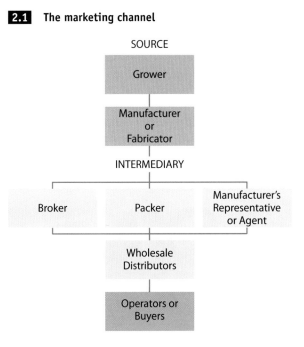

Marketing Channel

A buyer acquires his foodstuffs through the exchange of goods in the **marketing channel**, which is also referred to as the **distribution channel** (see Figure 2.1). The flow of goods through the marketing channel involves several facets, including the *sources*, *intermediaries*, and *markets*, before the buyer acquires the goods. Each component contributes a unique function to the process of ownership exchange.

SOURCES

Sources are where things begin within the flow of goods. Products originate from three major sources that supply wares to the food service industry. These sources include the *growers*, *manufacturers*, and *fabricators*.

- **Growers (producers).** Growers are the ranchers, farmers, and fishermen who produce foods directly from the land or

seas. Some growers sell their products directly to the food service operators, such as with egg farmers, fishermen, or herb farmers. Others sell their raw food to manufacturers or fabricators who use them to make new value-added products. These value-added products are then sold through distributors to food service operators.

- **Fabricators (processors).** The fabricator is responsible for the many forms of food available to the buyer. Fabricators take raw food or other raw materials and process them further, such as processing whole poultry into portions, making cheese, or fabricating cans from sheets of tin. "The food supply in the United States is marketed not only by quantity, but also by quality, variety, and convenience (Potter, 1986, p. 15)."

- **Manufacturers.** Manufacturers create new products by combining goods from growers or fabricators. For example, manufacturers take fruit from the farmers, process it into cocktail, and then package it in cans for sale to intermediaries as canned fruit cocktail.

INTERMEDIARIES

Intermediaries serve as the middlemen between the sources and the food service operators or buyers. Sometimes the intermediaries function as consultants to buyers. They offer product advice regarding certain brands or model numbers. Examples of consulting intermediaries include kitchen designers and building architects.

Other intermediaries are directly involved in the distribution of the goods. **Distribution** is vitally important in the flow of goods. As Virts (1987) writes, "Distribution is the means by which products are transferred in the marketplace, moving in turn through a series of intermediaries from the source (grower, manufacturer, or fabricator) to the hospitality operation" (p. 13). Examples of common intermediaries include *wholesale distributors*, *brokers*, *manufacturer's representatives*, *manufacturer's agents*, *importers*, *dealers*, and *leasing companies*.

- **Wholesale distributors (merchant wholesalers).** **Merchant wholesalers** are distributors that purchase products from various sources, provide storage, resell them at a profit, and deliver them to the buyer's business. They are the companies responsible for transferring (selling) the goods obtained from the growers, manufacturers, and fabricators to the consumer. They may be further classified as *broadline, full-line,* or *specialty*.

  - **Broadline.** Broadliners distribute a "broad line" of products. They commonly sell a large selection of food, nonfood supplies, and restaurant equipment.
  - **Full-line.** Full-line distributors are wholesalers that sell both food and nonfood supplies.
  - **Specialty.** Specialty wholesalers concentrate on specific categories of products, such as charcuterie items, seafood, and kitchen equipment.

- **Brokers.** **Brokers** are independent sales and marketing representatives who contract with growers, manufacturers, and fabricators to both sell and conduct local promotional programs with distributors, suppliers, and food service operators. They are in business for themselves and generally broker for several different sources that sell noncompeting categories of product. Brokers do not own the products they represent, do not set the selling price, and rarely carry an inventory; they work with local buyers who need their category of product and are paid commissions by the sources (growers, manufacturers, and fabricators).

- **Manufacturer's representatives.** **Manufacturer's representatives**, also known as *commission houses*, differ from brokers in that they carry products in inventory, set the local price for those products, and usually deliver them directly to the buyer. Like brokers, they generally represent several different lines of products from non-competing sources.

People, Places, Things

The Largest Broadline Distribution Companies

There are many local suppliers in most communities that specialize in a limited variety of products, such as seafood, dairy, and produce. Therefore, buyers often have to turn to larger companies for a broader selection of foods. Following is a list of large regional or national broadline distributors that carry a comprehensive selection of both dry and refrigerated goods.

Food Services of America (FSA)	http://www.fsafood.com
Golbon	http://www.golbon.com
Gordon Food Service (GFS)	http://www.gfs.com
J & B Wholesale	http://www.jbwhsle.com
Performance Food Group (PFG)	http://www.pfgc.com
Reinhart Food Service	http://www.reinhartfoodservice.com
Seneca Foods	http://www.senecafoods.com
SYSCO	http://www.sysco.com
U.S. Food Service	http://www.usfoodservice.com
Zanios Foods	http://www.zaniosfoods.com

- **Manufacturer's agents.** Manufacturer's agents differ from representatives in that they virtually always work directly for only one manufacturer or fabricator. They earn a commission on all sales of the company's products in the geographic region in which they operate.

- **Importers.** Importers bring the product into the country from another part of the world and sell it through a system of licensed wholesale distributors. Examples of imported products include foreign-made wine, sausage, and cheese.

- **Dealers.** Food service equipment dealers are similar to distributors in that they usually buy food service equipment from the primary sources and then resell it at a profit.

- **Leasing companies.** Retailers of food service equipment, such as point-of-sale systems and ice machines, often offer lease-to-own options as an alternative to outright purchasing of their product lines.

Value Added in the Distribution Channel

Intermediaries add value to the products being purchased. They supply a service that the operator deems worthy of additional cost to the product, as the buyer cannot or will not perform the same service for himself. These added values include *form*, *time*, *place*, and *information* (see Figure 2.2).

- **Form value.** The desired form of a product is one of the greatest values to the buyer. For example, rather than buying whole chickens that must be processed to obtain their breasts (and then dealing with how to use up the remaining parts of the bird), the buyer can buy cases of specific-sized chicken breasts. They will cost more per breast than if fabricating them from whole birds, but there is no waste, uneven sizes, or labor costs, with which to contend.

- **Time value.** Time is another valuable commodity in food service operations. It is advantageous to the buyer to have what is needed only slightly before it is needed. To buy food too far in advance only serves to tie up money in inventory, create crowded storage conditions, and allow unnecessary deterioration or spoilage. Instead, the seller should bare the cost of storage and have foods available when the buyer needs them.

- **Place value.** Having the products delivered to the buyer's place of work is a custom most operators expect, if not

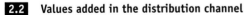
2.2 Values added in the distribution channel

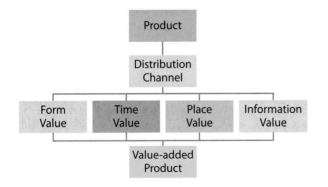

require. Because distributors have to pay for trucks, fuel, and delivery drivers for the distributors, they pass along these costs to the buyer as hidden "value-added costs." However, with the cost of deliveries having risen sharply in recent years, many sellers now require minimum purchase amounts be met before they will deliver without added delivery fees.

- **Information value.** More and more distributors are trying to distinguish their companies from their competitors by providing consulting services to their important customers. Many distributors employ corporate chefs, marketing personnel, and accountants who provide "free" information to help their customers improve their operational profits. Assistance with recipe development, free samples, promotional products, menu design, cost analysis, and promotional fliers are commonplace today among many intermediaries. The cost of these services is hidden in the price of the products being sold to all customers.

Forces Affecting the Distribution Channel

Free markets have no governmental restrictions on labor, goods, services, and capital. In a free market, goods can move freely across borders without interference or trading restrictions. However, in the complex world of global trade, there are many forces that can prevent an item from entering the market. Anything from torrential rains to drought, from civil war to labor strikes, and from environmental restrictions to seasonality can all affect the supply of products on the international, national, and local levels.

An experienced buyer constantly monitors the activity that might affect the availability and price of his needed food and supplies. Forces affecting the distribution system include *economic*, *weather*, *political*, *ethical*, *legal*, *technological*, and the *intangible* (see Figure 2.3).

- **Economic forces.** In the market system, prices adjust to meet **supply and demand**. If there are more buyers than goods, the price will rise, or demand will decrease, or the seller will make more of an item. The buyer's interest in certain goods is based on the good's perceived value to the buyer. Generally, when something is in short supply, its perceived value is heightened and its selling price is higher. Conversely, when something is commonplace, its perceived value is low and so is its selling price. However, some buyers set limits to what they will spend on any object. The seller's price must not exceed what the buyer is willing to pay. Thus, supply and demand affect the economics of the marketplace.

- **Weather.** Unusual weather can destroy crops. Because most produce (and feed for livestock) is grown in certain areas of the United States, one storm can wipe out an entire crop. This affects the sale of both the raw item and any product that is made from it. For example, if a frost hits Florida, all citrus crops such as oranges, grapefruits, lemons, and limes are damaged, and products such as orange juice, lemonade powders, and key lime pies will be in limited supply until new crops are available.

- **Political forces.** Political action committees (PACs) and lobbyists seek support from their elected government

2.3   Forces affecting in the distribution channel

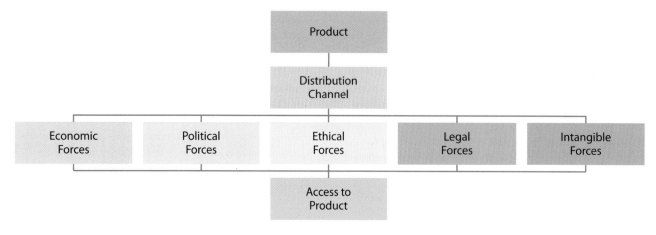

officials to help their clients prosper in business. For example, if the U.S. government places a high tariff on imported beef from South America, then it must be sold at a higher price in the U.S. marketplace. U.S. cattle ranchers benefit if the high tariffs cause a decrease in the demand for imported beef. Conversely, if produce is allowed to come from Chile or Mexico, which is cheaper because of longer growing seasons and lower labor costs, then U.S. farmers are forced to accept less for their products in the U.S. marketplace. Another, but different, political force is government restrictions, such as U.S. restrictions on the species of fish permitted for harvesting, as well as

People, Places, Things

Fair Trade Certification

Fair trade certification empowers farmers and farm workers to lift themselves out of poverty by investing in their farms and communities, protecting the environment, and developing the business skills necessary to compete in the global marketplace. Fair trade is much more than a fair price. Fair trade principles include:

- **Fair price.** Democratically organized farmer groups receive a guaranteed minimum floor price and an additional premium for certified organic products. Farmer organizations are also eligible for pre-harvest credit.

- **Fair labor conditions.** Workers on fair trade farms enjoy freedom of association, safe working conditions, and living wages. Forced child labor is strictly prohibited.

- **Direct trade.** With fair trade, importers purchase from fair trade producer groups as directly as possible, eliminating unnecessary middlemen and empowering farmers to develop the business capacity necessary to compete in the global marketplace.

- **Democratic and transparent organizations.** Fair trade farmers and farm workers decide democratically how to invest fair trade revenues.

- **Community development.** Fair trade farmers and farm workers invest fair trade premiums in social and business development projects like scholarship programs, quality improvement trainings, and organic certification.

- **Environmental sustainability.** Harmful agrochemicals and genetically modified organisms (GMOs) are strictly prohibited in favor of environmentally sustainable farming methods that protect farmers' health and preserve valuable ecosystems for future generations.

Source: Courtesy TransFair USA.

what areas people are allowed to fish. The Stubbs Bill, for example, reduced the yearly quota for tuna by nearly half.

- **Ethical forces.** As discussed in Chapter 1, the personal ethics of both the buyer and the seller is an important factor in business. Some unscrupulous buyers will require kickbacks or other incentives before conducting exclusive business with sellers. In the United States, this practice is not proper, nor defensible. However, it is common in the United States for vendors to offer holiday gifts to buyers or to support the buyer's company golf outing, for example. This activity is not illegal, and many owners often recognize it as a standard business practice.

- **Legal forces.** Over the years, suppliers have persuaded government to enact laws that ensure fair and level competition in the U.S. marketplace and minimum safety

standards for food processing facilities. Also from time to time, for various political reasons, the government enacts laws that prevent suppliers from doing business with specific countries. For example, Cuban cigars may not be purchased for sale in the U.S. marketplace.

- **Technological forces.** In recent years, technological discoveries and improvements have affected every aspect of food production: from planting, irrigating, harvesting, and holding to processing, packaging, labeling, and transporting. Additionally, the food itself is undergoing biotechnological changes as it is being engineered, preserved, and processed very differently from only a few years past.

- **Intangible forces.** The attitudes of the buyers and consumers also have an impact on the distribution channel. As buyers react to various marketing promotions, health risks, technological advances, and environmental concerns, their influence will be felt in the marketplace. Trends, both upward and downward, often affect the price and availability of products based on supply and demand.

BUYER'S NOTE

TransFair USA, a nonprofit organization, is the only independent, third-party certifier of fair trade products in the United States and one of twenty members of Fairtrade Labeling Organizations (FLO) International. TransFair's rigorous audit system, which tracks products from farm to finished product, verifies industry compliance with fair trade criteria. TransFair allows U.S. companies to display the Fair Trade Certified label on products that meet strict fair trade standards. Fair trade certification is currently available in the United States for coffee, tea and herbs, cocoa and chocolate, fresh fruit, sugar, rice, and vanilla.

Source: Courtesy TransFair USA.

MARKETS

About 50 years ago, fresh food marketplaces fell out of favor and were replaced by large, all-encompassing super-markets. In the past two decades, these giant supermarkets (often referred to as "hypermarkets") have grown to include hardware, housewares, garden supplies, electrical and plumbing supplies, and furniture. You can still find

People, Places, Things

A Nation of Farmer's Markets

There are over 4,000 farmer's markets across the United States. Several publications identify the finest among them, with the following markets often considered among the best.

Dane County Farmer's Market; Madison, Wisconsin

Ferry Plaza Farmer's Market; San Francisco, California

Union Square Greenmarket; New York, New York

Boulder County Farmer's Market; Boulder, Colorado

Crescent City Farmer's Market; New Orleans, Louisiana

Portland Farmer's Market; Portland, Oregon

Santa Fe Farmer's Market; Santa Fe, New Mexico

Salt Lake City Farmer's Market; Salt Lake City, Utah

Sunset Valley Farmer's Market; Austin, Texas

Green City Market; Chicago, Illinois

fresh food marketplaces in countries like France or Spain, or in some U.S. cities, like the Ferry Plaza Farmer's Market in San Francisco. Though supermarkets still dominate, renewed interest in locally harvested or produced food has caused farmer's markets to spring up in many towns and cities.

In addition to 4,000 farmer's markets now operating in the United States, there are numerous small farmers around the country who work directly with their local food service community. Also, large produce farms like the Chef's Garden in Milan, Ohio, operated by the Jones family, and Earthbound Farms of Carmel Valley, California, cater to chefs and restaurateurs around the country interested in specialty produce.

The Functions of the Market

A free market, with little or no governmental oversight, has four main functions:

- The exchange of information
- The exchange of money and ownership
- The exchange of goods
- The place or location where the exchange takes place

THE BUSINESS OF THE MARKET

Economics is the study of markets and how people behave when they are trading. A market can be any place where the buyer and seller interact, including face to face, via mail, or over the Internet. The following "new-age" markets have gained popularity in recent years by appealing to the interests of some segment of buyers.

- **Farmer's markets.** Any local government can arrange a farmer's market, where farmers sell their products directly to the public. While this is not a new way to sell produce, it has become more popular in the past few years. Markets have increased 111 percent in the past 10 years, with more than 3,700 markets in the United States.

- **E-commerce retailers.** E-commerce is the sale of goods and services over the Internet. The entire sales cycle, including payment, may be done online.

- **Group purchasing organization (GPO).** A GPO is a group of people who work together to buy goods and services. By pooling their purchasing powers, they can negotiate better pricing. GPOs may be funded by the vendors or the individual members. Fees may be set as a percentage of their purchases. Participation in a GPO may be voluntary, or levels may be set by the GPO leadership.

- **Wholesale clubs.** Wholesale clubs, often referred to as "box stores," are retail businesses that often require membership for admission and sell food products and supplies at deep discounts to both consumers and food service operators. While wholesale clubs offer a limited array of food service products, they are capturing a growing share of retail purchases by operators.

- **Food-buying clubs (community-supported agriculture).** Community-supported agriculture (CSA) is a means of supplying fresh food directly from the farm. Members of the CSA clubs support their local farmers by paying a lump sum advance for a "seasonal share" of the harvest. Whatever the farmer is able to produce is divided among the shareholders as it becomes available. Farmers can count on a reliable cash flow and a steady market for their products. The food is often organically grown, according to the personal philosophy and abilities of the local farmer.

U.S. Code, Federal Agencies, and Food Laws

The United States has various agencies that regulate the supply of food. For updated copies of these rules and legislation, contact your congressperson. You can also review the **U.S. Code**, which is a compilation of laws up to January 1996.

U.S. DEPARTMENT OF AGRICULTURE (USDA)

The **U.S. Department of Agriculture (USDA)** was founded in 1862 to meet the needs of farmers who needed seeds and information on crops. Today, this department is in charge of several programs, including:

- Inspection and safety of all meat, poultry, and egg products.

- Research in human nutrition and suggested daily requirements for vitamins, minerals, and protein.

- Opening markets for U.S. agricultural products in other countries. It also helps to get food to needy people in other countries.

- The Supplemental Nutrition Assistance Program (SNAP) (formerly called the Food Stamp Program); the National School Lunch Program; and the Women, Infants, and Children (WIC) program.

- Ensuring safe drinking water to rural communities in the United States.

Food Safety and Inspection Services (FSIS)

The **Food Safety and Inspection Services (FSIS)** is a division with the USDA. This department ensures that commercial meat products, poultry, and egg products are wholesome and correctly packaged and labeled.

There are two separate departments. The first department inspects the meat and poultry, and the second one grades them. Inspection is *mandatory* while grading is *voluntary*. If a company wants its products graded, it must pay for this service.

USDA INSPECTIONS

The FSIS inspects all raw meat and poultry products that cross state lines and monitors state inspection programs for meat that is sold within the state border. These state inspections must meet the requirements as set in the 1967 Wholesome Meat Act and 1968 Wholesome Poultry Products Act. If a state ends its program, the FSIS will take over the program. The FSIS also inspects products for export out of and import into the United States.

The FSIS works with other departments in the USDA to accomplish these tasks. Some of the other departments include the Food and Drug Administration and the Environmental Protection Agency.

When the inspection programs began 100 years ago, most meat was slaughtered and consumed locally. There were very few processed items. Now most meat is processed in high-volume plants and then is shipped across the country to wholesalers. Over time, inspections have changed. Earlier inspections checked animals for communicable diseases and processing plants for sanitary conditions. Now most animals are raised in closely supervised farms, and they have been genetically bred to avoid disease. Today, FSIS is more concerned with microbiological and chemical contamination of the meat products. Inspections are now based on scientific tests and statistical sampling.

Within the past decade, more processing plants are following the newer rules on pathogen reduction and Hazard Analysis and Critical Control Points (HACCP). HACCP is an encompassing philosophy that emphasizes safe handling of food from the farm to the stomach. HACCP is discussed in more detail in Chapter 7. These newer rules minimize the presence of harmful bacteria by maintaining correct temperatures. To remind cooks and other food handlers, the USDA requires that safe-handling instructions (see Figure 2.4) be on all raw or partially cooked meat and poultry products.

Certain animals are not commercially viable, such as buffalo, rabbit, reindeer, elk, deer, and antelope. Inspection of those animals for wholesale and food service

2.4 Example of USDA safe-handling instructions
Courtesy United States Department of Agriculture USDA.

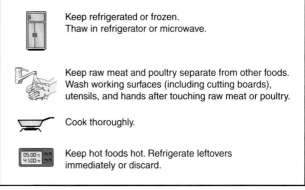

Safe Handling Instruction

This product was prepared from inspected and passed meat and/or poultry. Some food products may contain bacteria that could cause illness if the product is mishandled or cooked improperly. For your protection, follow these safe handling instructions.

Keep refrigerated or frozen. Thaw in refrigerator or microwave.

Keep raw meat and poultry separate from other foods. Wash working surfaces (including cutting boards), utensils, and hands after touching raw meat or poultry.

Cook thoroughly.

Keep hot foods hot. Refrigerate leftovers immediately or discard.

use is covered by the Agricultural Marketing Act. The Secretary of Agriculture has the authority to make sure that the product is marketable. The FSIS allows these animals to be processed in meat plants, provided that the on-site inspector knows the species and the carcass can fit on the equipment in the building. Businesses that process these unusual animals can pay an hourly fee for the inspections.

All meat that is inspected by the FSIS has a round purple stamp on the carcass and major cuts. Further cuts such as steaks do not have the stamp on the meat, but the stamp is on the box or the package. The stamp includes a plant number so that meat can be traced back to a certain facility. This stamp is made from a food-grade vegetable dye and will not harm anyone who consumes it. Figure 2.5 shows several common variations of the stamp.

People, Places, Things

Meat Inspection Services Act

In 2006, the Food Safety and Inspection Services agency celebrated the 100th anniversary of the Meat Inspection Services Act of 1906. This law mandated the inspection of all live animals intended for later consumption, carcasses, and processed products. It also set the minimum sanitary conditions for slaughtering and processing (see Figure 2.6).

2.5   USDA inspection stamps

Courtesy United States Department of Agriculture USDA

| Inspection Mark on Raw Meat | Inspection Mark on Raw Poultry | Inspection Mark on Processed Products |

USDA GRADING

Inspection of meat is mandatory, but grading is voluntary. When meat is graded, a federal grader will check for tenderness, juiciness, and flavor of the meat. For poultry, the grader will check for full flesh and that it is free of defects. The USDA Agricultural Marketing Service oversees grading, and companies that use this service must pay for the grading.

USDA grades are standardized across the nation. This means that a Choice Grade meat is the same no matter where it comes from. The grader will stamp the carcass with the grade, as shown in Figure 2.7, but it will not be visible on any retail cuts. The grade will be on the box or the package. According to the Truth in Labeling Law, the meat in the box must match the grade symbol. The different grade levels will be discussed later in Chapters 13 and 14.

2.7   Grade stamp on hanging sides of lamb

© 2006 Delmar Cengage Learning.

LABELING AND CONSUMER PROTECTION STAFF (LCPS)

This department in the USDA focuses on protecting consumers from misbranded or adulterated meat, poultry, and egg products.

ORGANIC FOODS PRODUCTION ACT OF 1990 (AMENDED JANUARY 2004)

Congress passed the federal **Organic Foods Production Act** in 1990. It regulates the guidelines for organic food production, certifies the owners, and monitors the crops for chemical contamination. It also screens organic imports.

The term *organic* typically describes food that has been cultivated or processed without the use of chemicals, including synthetic fertilizers, insecticides, artificial coloring or flavoring, and additives. Natural pesticides and fertilizers are permitted. In some states, however, *organic* simply refers to pesticide-free crops and chemical-free animal feed and water. There is no consistent regulation of organic food production across all states. This means that organic food can have chemical cross-contamination from wind, shipping, and water supply.

The National Organic Program (NOP) under the authority of the USDA is an attempt to address these issues. This regulation established national standards for the growing and production of organic foods The law includes the following provisions:

> To be sold or labeled as an organically produced agricultural product under this chapter, an agricultural product shall:
>
> Have been produced and handled without the use of synthetic chemicals, except as otherwise provided in this chapter
>
> Except as otherwise provided in this chapter and excluding livestock, not be produced on land to which any prohibited substances, including synthetic chemicals, have been applied during the 3 years immediately preceding the harvest of the agricultural products
>
> Be produced and handled in compliance with an organic plan agreed to by the producer and handler of such product and the certifying agent
>
> Courtesy USDA-NOP.

COUNTRY OF ORIGIN LABEL (COOL)

On March 16, 2009, the USDA implemented a law that requires retailers to put labels on various commodities, detailing where the commodity was raised, slaughtered, and processed. The rule applies to muscle cuts and ground beef, veal, lamb, chicken, goat, and pork; perishable agricultural commodities such as fresh and frozen vegetables and fruits; ginseng; and peanuts, macadamia nuts, and pecans. For fish and shellfish, the label must also specify whether it was wild caught or farm raised.

2.6 **A Timeline: 100 Years Since the Federal Meat Inspection Act (FMIA)**
Courtesy United States Department of Agriculture (USDA), Food Safety and Inspection Service (FSIS)

- **1905: *The Jungle***

  Upton Sinclair's book *The Jungle*, a vivid portrait of intolerable human cruelty and unsanitary conditions in a turn-of-the-century American meatpacking factory, caused public outrage and led President Theodore Roosevelt to call for government regulations of the food industry. This laid the groundwork for the passage of the Federal Meat Inspection Act.

- **1906: Federal Meat Inspection Act**

  The Meat Inspection Act was signed into law on June 30, 1906. It mandated inspection of live animals, carcasses, and processed products as well as improved sanitary conditions for slaughter and processing. After the act became law, the Meat Inspection Division (MID), responsible for inspection and enforcement of the act, grew from 981 inspectors in 1906 to 2,290 inspectors in more than 700 establishments by 1907.

- **1910: Bureau of Animal Industry Lab Research Center**

  The Bureau of Animal Industry (BAI), a predecessor of FSIS, opened a research center in Beltsville, Maryland. BAI was responsible for meat inspection research within the Meat Inspection Division of the U.S. Department of Agriculture (USDA).

- **1942: Laboratory and Sampling Structure**

  In May 1942, the structure of the Laboratory and Sampling section of the Meat Inspection Division was established. This section of the MID consisted of seven laboratories around the country that would be responsible for scientific testing of meat and meat products for foreign substances, excess water, and pollution of the water being used in processing. The laboratories were also responsible for developing new testing methods.

- **1957: The Poultry Products Inspection Act**

  Following World War II, there was tremendous growth in the poultry industry and the desire for ready-to-cook and processed poultry products. In response, in 1957, Congress passed the Poultry Products Inspection Act, which mandated inspection of poultry products in any area designated by USDA as a major consuming area, such as metropolitan localities.

- **1958: The Humane Methods of Slaughter Act of 1958 and 1978**

  Signed into law in August 1958, the Humane Methods of Slaughter Act requires all livestock in the United States be slaughtered humanely, except for kosher, halal, and other religious slaughter. Twenty years later, the Humane Methods of Slaughter Act of 1978 was enacted. This act amended the FMIA by requiring that all meat inspected by FSIS for use as human food be produced from livestock slaughtered by humane methods in accordance with the Humane Methods of Slaughter Act of 1958.

- **1967–1968: Wholesome Meat and Wholesome Poultry Products Acts**

  The Meat Inspection and Poultry Products Inspection Acts were amended to give the USDA authority to control movement of unfit meat and meat products and to require poultry products in interstate and foreign commerce to meet federal inspection standards. They also extended the department's authority regarding meat and poultry products in intrastate commerce.

- **1970: The Egg Products Inspection Act**

  This act was passed in December 1970. It mandates continuous inspection of liquid, frozen, and dried egg products. This act is still in force, and it covers all eggs except those used by food manufacturers, institutions, and retail markets.

- **1977–1981: Reorganization and New Responsibilities**

  In March 1977, the Food Safety and Quality Service (FSQS) was formed out of the USDA's Animal and Plant Health Inspection Service (APHIS) and was assigned the responsibility for meat and poultry product inspection and administration of the quality grading for agricultural products. In June 1981, USDA reorganization shifted quality grading responsibilities to the Agricultural Marketing Service, and the FSQS became the Food Safety and Inspection Service (FSIS).

- **1993: Nutrition Labeling of Meat and Poultry Products**

  In January 1993, FSIS published final regulations regarding nutrition labeling to permit voluntary nutrition labeling on single-ingredient, raw meat, and poultry products and to establish mandatory nutrition labeling requirements for all other meat and poultry products.

- **1994: Testing for *E. coli* O157:H7**

  In October 1994, FSIS declared $E.\ coli$ O157:H7 an adulterant in raw ground beef products in response to a 1993 outbreak, which resulted in 400 illnesses and four deaths. The FSIS began testing raw ground beef for $E.\ coli$ O157:H7. The testing program continues to monitor for the presence of $E.\ coli$ O157:H7 at ground beef establishments and at retail.

- **1996–2000: Hazard Analysis and Critical Control Point Systems**

  A landmark rule issued by FSIS in July 1996 focuses on the prevention and reduction of illness-causing pathogens on raw products by requiring Hazard Analysis and Critical Control Point (HACCP) systems and sanitation standard operating procedures in FSIS-inspected establishments. All establishments are required to develop a HACCP plan to ensure the safety of their products. Implementation of HACCP/PR (HACCP/Pathogen Reduction) began in January 1997 and was completed in more than 6,000 federally inspected and 2,100 state-inspected meat and poultry plants in January 2000.

- **1999: Testing for *Listeria monocytogenes***

  Listeria monocytogenes is a problem with processed meat and poultry products. Several virulent strains, which caused severe illness and deaths, led the FSIS to warn establishments to reassess their HACCP plans in terms of Listeria monocytogenes. The FSIS began testing ready-to-eat (RTE) products for this pathogen.

- **Present Day: Protecting Public Health and Ensuring a Safe and Secure Food Supply**

  FSIS's main mission is to protect food throughout the food chain. It ensures that all meat, poultry, and egg products are safe and wholesome for human consumption.

CODEX ALIMENTARIUS COMMISSION (CAC)

This department within the FSIS works with the United Nations to encourage fair international trade in food, without sacrificing the health or economic interests of consumers. The Codex Alimentarius Commission, during its 2009 international meeting in Rome, moved to improve the worldwide food safety and health of consumers by adopting more than thirty new international standards, codes of practice, and guidelines to improve (World Health Organization, 2009).

FOOD AND DRUG ADMINISTRATION (FDA)

The **Food and Drug Administration (FDA)** is a department within the U.S. Department of Health and Human Services. This department is responsible for regulating food and food labels, including the nutritional labels found on many products, among other responsibilities.

The Bioterrorism Act of 2002

After September 11, 2001, Congress passed the Public Health Security and Bioterrorism Preparedness and Response Act in 2002. This act, known as the **Bioterrorism Act of 2002**, has five parts. Title III of the act deals with the safety and security of the nation's food and drug supplies while Title IV deals with drinking water and supplies. Congress delegated responsibility for Title III to the Food and Drug Administration.

Food Labeling

In July 2003, the FDA clarified rules concerning health claims on packaged food, supplements, and over-the-counter drugs. Prior to this change, there had to be "significant scientific consensus" before a product could be labeled with a health claim. Now companies are permitted to post health claims using a hierarchy based on the certainty of the claims. The more scientific evidence that supports a claim, the stronger the wording allowed on the label.

FAIR PACKAGING AND LABELING ACT (1966)

The **Fair Packaging and Labeling Act (FPLA)** applies to labels on consumer and wholesale foodstuffs. All labels must include:

- The name of the product
- The name and location of the manufacturer, packer, importer, or distributor
- The quantity (weight or volume) of the item in both metric and standard U.S. measurement units

The act is still in effect today, although there have been requests by companies to change the measurements to metric only. This would help U.S. food manufacturers to export items without creating new packaging.

NUTRITION LABELING AND EDUCATION ACT (1994)

This act requires that all packaged food products have nutritional labeling on the boxes. Certain items such as fresh meat, fresh produce, and fresh vegetables do not have to be labeled. Restaurants and other food service operations do not have to provide nutritional labels on the dishes they create unless ordered by local law.

The act requires that the remaining food products, whether sold in a grocery store or through a wholesaler, must meet the following requirements on their package labels:

- The label must be distinct and follow the current labeling guidelines.
- The label must include the information on protein, fat, saturated fat, carbohydrates, fiber, sugar, and any other significant nutrients, in both grams and as a percentage of the Daily Values.
- The label must include all ingredients listed in descending order by weight.
- The manufacturer must base the calculations on a normal or usual standard portion size so that similar products can be compared.
- If the manufacturer wishes to claim that the product is "low fat" (or any of the other common health claims), the item must fall within specific nutritional levels to make that claim.
- If it is a juice product, the label must show what percentage of the product is from fruit juices.
- The information on the label must be complete enough that consumers or purchasing agents can be assured that the item will meet their nutritional needs.

Food labeling regulations change frequently. The FDA posts updates on the requirements and guidelines for nutritional claims on its website. Figure 2.8 shows a current nutrition label style.

FEDERAL FOOD, DRUG, AND COSMETIC ACT

The **Food, Drug, and Cosmetic Act (FDCA)** (as amended through 2004) is a series of laws passed by Congress, starting in 1938, with amendments through the present time. This act gives the FDA authority to oversee the safety of food, drugs, and cosmetics. This act also allows the FDA to regulate food additives, ensuring that they will not harm consumers. The FDA supervises the manufacturers' testing of these additives, and, if approved, the FDA will issue regulations concerning their use in food products.

As defined in section 201 (s) of the federal FDCA the FDA defines *food additive* as "any substance, with the intended use of which results directly or indirectly, in its becoming a component or otherwise affecting the characteristic of the food." Food additives are used to extend shelf life, retard the growth of mold or bacteria, and increase the satisfaction or taste of a food item. Some food additives that were in use before a 1958 amendment to the act are allowed

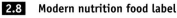

2.8 Modern nutrition food label
Courtesy of the U.S. Food and Drug Administration.

Nutrtition Facts
Serving Size ½ cup (114g)
Servings Per Container 4

Amount per serving

Calories 90   Calories from Fat 30

	% Daily Value*
Total Fat 3g	**5%**
Saturated Fat 0g	0%
Cholestrol 0mg	**0%**
Sodium 300mg	**13%**
Total Carbohydrate 13g	**4%**
Dietary Fibar 3g	12%
Sugars 3g	

Protein 3g

Vitamin A 80%	•	Vitamin C 60%
Calcium 4%	•	Iron 4%

Percent Daily Values are based on a 2,000 calorie diet. Your daily values may be higher or lower depending on your calorie needs:

	Calories	2,000	2,500
Total Fat	Less than	65g	80g
Sat Fat	Less than	20	25g
Cholestrol	Less than	300mg	300mg
Sodium	Less than	2,400mg	2,400mg
Total Carbohydrate		300mg	375mg
Dietry Fiber		25g	30g

Calories per gram:
Fat 9 • Carbohydrate 4 • Protein 4

for use under the "generally recognized as safe" (GRAS) exemption. All other additives created after this time are subject to scientific testing and FDA approval.

This act also applies to genetically engineered and modified foods. They are regarded as "food additives" and are subject to the same scientific scrutiny before they can be sold in the market or used as an ingredient in other food items. All genetically modified foods sold in the United States are subject to this process.

FOOD ALLERGEN LABELING AND CONSUMER PROTECTION ACT OF 2004 (FALCPA)

FALCPA—a 2004 amendment to the FDCA—requires that any food containing a "major food allergen" must say so on the nutritional label. If the food item normally does not contain a major food allergen but is processed in a factory that does work with a major food allergen, then this information must be on the label as well. The major food allergens that must be stated on labels include milk, eggs, fish, crustaceans including shrimp and lobster, tree nuts including almonds and pecans, peanuts, wheat, and soybeans. Any derived product from these ingredients (for example, butter) must have the parent allergen label present. This law was passed so that consumers with food allergies, who can have reactions to minute particles of the item, could safely choose food without the allergens. Currently, restaurants and other food service operations are not required to label dishes with the allergens; rather, they should train the front of the house staff to address any questions from customers.

U.S. FEDERAL TRADE COMMISSION (FTC)

The **Federal Trade Commission (FTC)** is an independent agency of the U.S. government. Its principal mission is to protect consumers and eliminate anticompetitive business practices. **Consumer protection** includes all government regulations that protect the interests of consumers, enabling them to freely choose products that meet their needs. The FTC requires businesses to disclose detailed information about their products, especially if they are selling foods that could imperil public health or safety. In October 2009, the FTC voted to require Web advertisements to be more accurate in their product representations. The goal was to target advertisers who misrepresented the benefits of their products by requiring the sellers to report typical results noted by consumers.

UNIFORM COMMERCIAL CODE (UCC)

The **Uniform Commercial Code (UCC)** is a series of laws that regulate sales and other commercial transactions, especially for goods and services that cross state lines. This code regulates processing checks, notes, and other commercial papers. It also distinguishes between merchants, or people who are in the business of buying and selling, and consumers, who are not. These laws do not affect food companies specifically but create the structures in which they sell and buy goods.

ENVIRONMENTAL PROTECTION AGENCY (EPA)

The **Environmental Protection Agency (EPA)** was created in 1970 to protect human health and the environment. The EPA is responsible for researching and setting national standards for different environmental programs, and the states are responsible for monitoring and enforcing them. The EPA does not deal with food directly, but its regulations affect the drinking water supply and the use of fertilizers on commercial farms and additives in animal feeds.

Gene D. Hall

Place of Birth: Hastings, Michigan

Educational Background and Work Experience

Gene Hall didn't start out in the food service industry. Rather, he went to school for data processing, as it was then called. His real food service training was on the job, in a series of restaurant manager positions. Proving he had a knack for the industry and in business management, Hall eventually rose to the position of general manager of a regional restaurant chain. After proving highly successful in sales for that company, he was promoted to director of franchising. Hall's skills in training and sales were put to the test when he became the sales manager for two different food service equipment dealerships, each with equipment sales in excess of $50 million. Eventually, Hall's ambition to run his own company was rewarded, and today he is a partner in HRI, Inc., a highly successful independent marketing agency for food service equipment, located in western Michigan.

Memberships and Career Highlights

Hall has enjoyed great success as a manufacturer's agent, receiving dozens of sales achievement awards from the manufacturers his company represents. Hall is ServSafe certified and a Certified Food Service Professional (CFSP), as well as an active member of Manufacturers Agents for the Food Service Industry (MAFSI). He also has been a dynamic supporter, and long-time member, of the Advisory Committee for Hospitality Education Department at Grand Rapids Community College.

Passions with the Food Service Industry

"I am very passionate about helping create functional and profitable work spaces in new or remodeled food service establishments. The difference between functional and aggravating can be as small as one or two pieces of kitchen equipment programmed in the wrong place, or specified incorrectly for the function intended.

It Happened to Me...

"I was called to demonstrate several pieces of equipment at a new high school in southwest Michigan. It was July, and the new facility was due to begin operation in late August.

I arrived at the site about the same time the food service director arrived. She walked around the kitchen in astonishment, asking rhetorical questions such as 'What am I going to do with this?' 'Why do I have a 60 gallon steam jacketed kettle when a 20 gallon would be sufficient?' 'Where is my tilting skillet?' Before starting the demonstrations we sat down and discussed her obvious dismay. I asked her if she had been involved in the planning, design, specification, and procurement of the equipment, and she said no. The school business manager had a relationship with a local architect who designed the kitchen within the school's budget. She was assured the project would be designed to her needs, but her needs were never discussed. My observation was that the equipment was adequate for function, and the design was proper for getting the food from storage to preparation to cooking to serving. The missing element was the food service director's menu planning for the school year. Several pieces of equipment were either wrong or not specified and thus never purchased for her new menu. The life lesson I learned is to try to encourage all chefs, kitchen managers, and food service directors to be involved in the decision process from the kitchen design to the equipment specifications, to the actual procurement of the equipment . . . on projects in which I am involved."

A properly designed and specified space should work smoothly from the first hour of operation until menu changes necessitate workspace changes. It is deeply satisfying to see a project that I have been involved in operate the way it was intended."

Advice to a Chef or Buyer

"Formal food service education and experience prepares a chef or facilities manager to purchase the food and supplies necessary to profitably operate an establishment. The need to purchase kitchen equipment will arise sooner or later. The wrong choice of equipment could be devastating both financially and operationally. There are sources to help make the correct decision, and I advise all food service managers to network with the following groups of people to help make an intelligent purchasing decision:

1. Food service equipment consultants.
2. Independent or factory manufacturer's agents.
3. Food service equipment dealers."

Key Words and Concepts

Bioterrorism Act of 2002

brokers

community-supported agriculture (CSA)

consumer protection

distribution

Environmental Protection Agency (EPA)

fabricators

Fair Packaging and Labeling Act (FPLA)

Federal Trade Commission (FTC)

Food and Drug Administration (FDA)

Food, Drug, and Cosmetic Act (FDCA)

Food Safety and Inspection Services (FSIS)

intermediaries

manufacturers

manufacturer's agents

manufacturer's representatives

market

marketing channel (distribution channel)

merchant wholesalers

Organic Foods Production Act

property

sources

supply and demand

Uniform Commercial Code (UCC)

U.S. Code

U.S. Department of Agriculture (USDA)

Chapter in Review

The following exercises are provided to help the reader understand and apply the contents of this chapter. They may be completed individually or in a classroom environment.

REVIEW QUESTIONS

a. Identify the four major forces that affect the market distribution system, and describe how they affect the marketplace.

b. Identify the four values added to products in the market distribution system, and give examples for each.

c. Identify the different types of intermediaries, and explain their function.

d. Identify the different forms of inspection, and discuss their purpose.

INDIVIDUAL ACTIVITIES

a. **Web based:** Research the USDA on the Internet, and discover its different departments and what services they perform.

b. **Experiential:** Find a local farmer's market or CSA in your area, and visit it to see how it is run and what products it sells.

c. **Critical thinking:** Consider what Abraham Lincoln meant when he called the USDA the "people's department."

GROUP ACTIVITIES

a. **Lab experience:** Distribute a selection of various packaged food products, and have the students evaluate their nutrition food labels.

b. **Classroom action:** Discuss the different laws that exist to protect the buyer, and discuss why they are important.

Image copyright Vitaliy Minsk, 2009. Used under license from Shutterstock.com

Practical Considerations for Buying Decisions

"History celebrates the battlefields whereon we meet our death, but scorns to speak of the plowed fields whereby we thrive; it knows the names of kings' bastards but cannot tell us the origin of wheat. That is the way of human folly."

HENRI FABRE

After reading this chapter, you will be able to:

- Identify the seasonal factors that affect the availability of foodstuffs.

- List the factors that affect the market and its influence on product availability.

- Give different examples of distribution centers.

- Identify and compare five factors that affect food palatability.

- Discuss the importance of product specification in maintaining consistency of ingredients.

- Identify three healthful considerations for handling foods.

- Describe the RAFT project and its mission to preserve indigenous American foods.

- Recall organizations such as the Monterey Bay Aquarium, WWF, and the Marine Stewardship Council, and explain their efforts to protect endangered species.

- Define two contrasting methods for studying a culture.

- Summarize the influence of religion, lifestyle, and ecology on food service.

Introduction

It is the role of scientists to gain knowledge through systematic observation and analysis. *Social scientists* consider people and the social phenomena, while *anthropologists* study the characteristics and customs of humans. *Political scientists* analyze and debate the principles, organization, and methods of government. *Economists* explore factors that affect the production, distribution, and consumption of wealth. They work with *agronomists* to study the science and economics of crop production (Figure 3.1). *Biochemists* study the life processes in plants and animals while the study of *macrobiotics* helps to prolong our lives through healthful dietary practices. Meanwhile, *ecologists* deal with all living organisms and their relationship to the environment.

All of these scientific studies combine to reveal the immense and complex nature of food in our world. Chefs and restaurateurs, both professional and student, should take considerable measure to learn about the issues affecting food, its production, its distribution, and its consumption. This text seeks to create awareness in its readers. Its goal is to present information in a politically neutral manner and to refrain from serving as a platform for any personal beliefs held by the author, whether by the inclusion or exclusion of topics contained herein.

This chapter was included as a means of balancing the scientific study of food with other responsible considerations. For the individual food service professional, it is intended more to raise questions than to provide answers. Practical considerations are raised over this

3.1 **Dr. John Beasley, Jr., professor and Extension Services peanut agronomist, University of Georgia**

Photo Courtesy Robert Garlough

and the following chapter—Chapter 4, "Modern Applications of Food Science"—while moral and business decisions are left to the reader.

Availability

Probably the most important factor to consider when choosing a food ingredient is its availability. Effort spent in the balancing of flavors, textures, colors, and cost is wasted when the focus of this effort is unattainable. Before any other question is asked, or decision made, the reliable availability of the ingredient must be determined. There are several factors that affect ingredient availability; chief among them are *seasonality*, *market regulations and influences*, and *distribution*.

SEASONALITY

Some foodstuffs are considered "seasonally available." That is, the food is grown or raised only during a specific period of the year. Generally speaking, climate and soil conditions have the greatest impact on plant life, while the birthing season dictates animal and seafood production.

In an effort to increase food production and lengthen the availability of produce and protein resources, scientists and other specialists have learned how to extend the growing season and effectively transport food from farther away. Additionally, they have created the artificial means to raise meat, fish, and fowl and to grow produce while obtaining exact specifications of size and weight.

Local Crops versus Outsourced

In most parts of our country, we experience a growing season limited by the climatic conditions of the region. Warmer areas important to growing produce include such states as Florida, Texas, and, most important, California. Northern states, albeit colder and with shorter growing seasons, include New York, Ohio, Illinois, Indiana, Wisconsin, and—second only to California in varieties produced—Michigan. Whether north or south, east or west, each state has a limited natural growing season. For years, growers have used "hot houses" and "gassing rooms" to extend the growing season and to artificially manipulate the ripening of produce.

Additionally, the advent of refrigerated transports has allowed for the safe distribution of meat, produce, and frozen foods from across the country and around the world (see Figure 3.2). No longer are we limited to the availability of produce or meats from our local farmer or slaughterhouse; we have access to a world market. Produce from Chile and New Zealand can be imported during our winter months. However, this expanded market comes with a cost. Does the lettuce grown in the

Refrigerated truck

© Randy Van Dam 2008

fields of a foreign country meet the equivalent sanitary standards of our local farmers? Are gassed tomatoes as sweet as field grown, vine ripened? Should we follow the philosophy of the **Slow Food Movement** by supporting our local farmers and designing our menus around what food is in season?

Consumers are driving demand for farm-fresh food, says Dan Barber, chef and co-owner of Blue Hill at Stone Barns in New York's Hudson Valley. "We're no longer in a '60s hippy back-to-earth mode. Companies like Whole Foods have created a modern public consciousness with actions like putting up pictures of farmers and listing provenance of food." The face of the farmer is lost when you phone only one food supplier and order everything at once, says Barber. "The national food suppliers are dumbing down the economies of scale. They can't provide the story of the people, the place, and the food" (Grossman, 2007, p. 14).

Aquaculture and Lot Feeding

Prior to the 1970s, fish and shellfish were considered an inexhaustible source of protein for most of the world's population. Then, in the next two decades, the fishing stock collapsed, causing the destruction of the commercial fishing fleets. Several fish species including salmon and rainbow trout were not available in consistent sizes or numbers to regularly offer them on menus at a consistent price.

To solve this problem, **aquaculture** was born. Aquaculture is a commercial farm that raises oysters, clams, trout, salmon, and other seafood. The fish are raised in giant net pens in the ocean, as shown in Figure 3.3. Artificial colors are added to the feed so that the flesh is the same color as wild species. Nearly one-third of all seafood is now raised in aquaculture ponds.

 Scottish ocean salmon farm

Photo Courtesy Robert Garlough

People, Places, Things

Slow Food Movement

In response to the plan of the global fast-food giant McDonald's Restaurants to build a unit near the iconic Spanish Steps in Rome, an activist from Bra, Italy named Carlo Petrini launched the first branch of the Slow Food Movement in Barolo, Italy in 1986. The movement went international in 1989, and now there are 100,000 members located across five continents. The goal of the Slow Food Movement is to protect artisan foods and food products, promote sustainable agriculture, educate consumers about food and wine, and to preserve the food and dining traditions of

Meanwhile, on land, beef, turkey, and chicken have been lot fed for years, thereby limiting their exercise and increasing their bulk. Hormone shots have also been used to stimulate muscle and tissue growth, enlarging specific parts of their body structure. Some argue against the practice, citing differences in texture and taste. Others note the benefits of raising seafood in aquatic beds that are regulated and generally toxic free—a concern of many who consume raw seafood. Still other consumers and chefs have moral objections and health-related concerns.

MARKET REGULATION AND INFLUENCES

Buyers must consider the various food sources, which are referred to as markets. The markets can be classified as to the type of food sold, location of the market, and channels of distribution involved. Additionally, the buyer must be aware of the four main functions performed in the marketplace, as first discussed in Chapter 2, "Food Laws and the Market and Distribution Systems." These include:

- The exchange of information between the seller (who often is also the grower) and the buyer
- The exchange of ownership, upon financial transaction between the seller and the buyer
- The exchange of goods between the seller and the buyer
- The location for the exchanges and transactions to occur

There are several external variables that can have a substantial impact on the free flow of goods within the market. They include *business practices*, *legal aspects*, and *governmental policies*.

Business Practices

A large number of federal regulations control general business practices, including marketing. In 1887, Congress passed the Interstate Commerce Act, governing the shipping of goods between states. Recent court cases have extended its provisions to control commerce within a state. In 1914, the Federal Trade Commission was created to promote fair business and trade practices, including prohibiting false or misleading advertising, reducing competition that restricts trade, and preventing unprofessional practices in the market.

Legal Aspects

Court decisions help build a framework in which legal buying practices must occur. Many buying and selling transactions are legally binding, so it behooves the buyer to become cognizant of the law relative to this area. Chapter 2 discusses these various laws in detail.

Governmental Policies

There are many external forces that greatly influence the market's performance and the flow of goods. Policies of the Treasury, Federal Reserve, United States Department of Agriculture, and other agencies of the U.S. and world governments move markets one way or another. For example, the U.S. requirement for nutritional labeling on packaging has had an influence on consumer buying habits, and the battle still looms over the labeling of **genetically modified foods**, also known as genetically modified organisms, or GMOs (see Figure 3.4a and Figure 3.4b). More examples include trade embargoes, balance-of-trade policies, import and export tariffs, and other federal government policies

3.4a **Sweet corn seed research sign in a field (genetically modified food)**
Photo Courtesy Robert Garlough

3.4b **Papaya labeled as "non-GMO"**
© Randy Van Dam 2008

affecting the availability and price of imports. This topic was also covered in Chapter 2.

DISTRIBUTION

Distribution is the circulation of goods in the marketplace. It tends to be more extensive in larger metropolitan areas, where the demand for goods and services is greater. Those cities and areas with the best transportation infrastructure—including truck, rail, air, and water—have the best distribution systems. As mentioned in Chapter 1, there has been a resurgence in open food markets, as shown in Figure 3.5, in most of the major cities, including New York, San Francisco, Paris, and Barcelona. As these markets gain popularity, they receive support from local governments.

Mercat de la Boqueria, pictured in Figure 3.6, was recognized as the Market of the Year in 2005 at the Sixth

3.5 **One of the many produce shops at Rungis**
Photo Courtesy Robert Garlough

3.6 **Shopping for fruit in *La Boqueria***
Photo Courtesy Robert Garlough

Congress of Public Markets, celebrated in Washington, D.C. The award highlighted the contribution La Boqueria has made to the social advancement, economic development, and environmental health and well-being of Barcelona.

Palatability

For food to be **palatable**, it must be pleasant or acceptable to the taste or mind. Generally, we identify five sensory properties of food when evaluating our foodstuffs. These include:

- Odor or aroma
- Appearance
- Temperature
- Flavor, a combination of odor and taste
- Texture, or "mouth feel"

Consistency

Consistency is a requirement that most chefs have for their ingredients. For a recipe to be reproduced to the same standard of appearance, taste, yield, and cost, the ingredients must be consistent each time. Failure to use the same specification of ingredient invites opportunities for error. Costs, cooking times, and plate presentation are all affected when the foods used to make a dish are inconsistent.

STANDARDS OF SPECIFICATION

A specification, which is discussed further in Chapter 6, "The Ingredient Process," is a written statement of standards that a chef requires of a food. Generally, chefs design recipes so the end product will look and taste a certain way. The specification is meant to ensure that the product provides the desired physical characteristics—such as appearance, aroma, taste, texture, and mouth feel—every time it is prepared.

Practicality and Suitability

Certainly one of the more pertinent considerations the food service operator will make is the practical and otherwise suitable application of the foodstuff. Practicality encompasses many considerations, from preparation to holding properties. Generally, the suitable nature of the food is determined after experimentation and practice. Chefs tend to be open to the use of new products but are content to use products that are tested and have performed well in the past. Having trust in the product that it will suitably perform and result in the final preparation as planned is paramount to the decision.

Healthful Considerations

It is the responsibility of the food service operator, as it has been since the days of the Sumerians, to protect the alimentary health and well-being of its customers. Chefs and food service operators must fully understand the products with which they work; failure to do so could put their customers and staff in harm's way. It is essential for food service operators to consider all elements of health and food safety that might have an impact on the meal. These include, among others, *nutritional*, *biochemical*, and *sanitary considerations*.

NUTRITIONAL

Food's primary purpose for all plants, animals, and humans is its **nutritional value**. Simply stated, food is the fuel of the body and mind. It nourishes and enables organisms to live and grow. The nutritional integrity of the food product should be protected in the processing and preparation of the

3.7 **Nutritional labels on assorted packaging**
© Randy Van Dam 2008

ingredient (Figure 3.7). Even though food items are incorporated into recipes and plate presentations for their taste, texture, or appearance, their nutritional contribution must not be overlooked.

BIOCHEMICAL

Biochemistry is the study of the chemical processes within plants and animals (Figure 3.8). This area of study focuses on the properties of substances and the chemical reactions that occur when they are exposed to heat or the chemicals in other food items. Biochemistry also includes the study of hybrid plants and genetically modified foods.

People, Places, Things

International Market of Rungis

The *Marché d'Intérêt National de Rungis* (or International market of Rungis), located just less than 6 miles (9 kilometers) south of Paris in the commune of Rungis, is the world's largest wholesale food market. It opened in 1969, when it was relocated from Les Halles in Paris, where it started as a fish market outside the palace walls of King Louis VI. The pride of France, Rungis has 1,500 acres of vendor stations, and all the products are delivered fresh every day. They are not allowed to remain on premise overnight for sale at Rungis the next day. Open only to professional chefs and retailers, the market offers wholesale prices. In 2002, during one of my international culinary study tours to France, I was able to lead a group of culinary arts majors on a tour through Rungis with the aid of a local chef and restaurateur. On that day, we were among 25,000 buyers from across Europe. As an example of the volume sold at Rungis, 60 percent of all of France's fruit and produce is exchanged in this market.

3.8 **Food scientist looking through a microscope**

Photo courtesy Robert Garlough

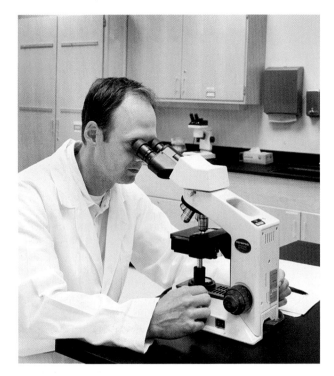

3.9 **Food stored correctly in a walk-in cooler**

© Randy Van Dam 2008

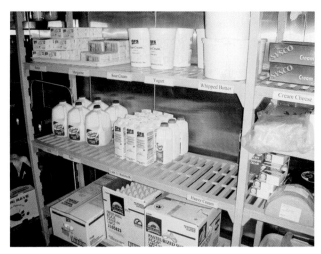

Chefs must always be vigilant to handling food properly, whether by refrigerating foods at proper temperatures or by cooking foods sufficiently to kill the harmful bacteria (see Figure 3.9). Preventing cross-contamination of foods and bacteria during the preparation process is an overarching goal in food protection. Additionally, it is incumbent upon the food service professional to purchase food only from reputable sources and to store it safely and properly.

SANITARY

History is rife with anthrax, salmonella, infectious hepatitis, perfringens, and botulism outbreaks. Haphazard handling of food and supplies has resulted in most of the health disasters related to food service operations. **Foodborne illnesses** can be caused by *chemical*, *physical*, or *biological* contaminants.

Cleaning compounds are examples of *chemical contaminants* that can be carelessly mixed with foods to poison them. *Physical contaminants* include rat feces, rodent hair, lead paint chips, rusted containers, glass, and other types of foreign matter not naturally found in food. *Biological sources* account for the majority of foodborne illnesses. In addition to the natural toxins found in certain plants (mushrooms and green potatoes, for example), the microorganisms called **pathogens** cause more than 95 percent of all foodborne illnesses.

Food manufacturers in the United States are now required to develop and observe **Hazard Analysis and Critical Control Point (HACCP)** checklists to ensure safe and sanitary procedures are followed throughout the entire production process. Most hospitals and other large food service operations elect to develop their own HACCP checklists. Smaller independent food operations, such as family-owned restaurants, often do not create HACCP checklists as the law does not presently require that they do so. Whether required by law, or not, HACCP checklists should be prepared by all food operations. The U.S. Food and Drug Administration maintains a Center for Food Safety and Applied Nutrition with useful information on HACCP.

Ethical and Ecological Considerations

Of the countless decisions a chef or manager ponders, many are financial while others are societal. Food service operators need to consider the ethical nature of their decisions and how they affect society and the environment shared by the organization. As Spears (1999) writes, "Ever since the Watergate scandal resulted in the resignation of a U.S. president, the public, businesses, and professions have become sensitive to what is and what is not ethical and to the standards by which people are measured" (p. 121).

ETHICAL STANDARDS

As discussed in Chapter 1, food service operators must constantly maintain ethical behavior to meet the highest professional standards that the general public expects. A conscious decision by management to establish ethical standards of behavior for the operation and its staff is critical to meeting these expectations. Truthful menu descriptions, product labeling, attention to food sources

[ASK THE EXPERT]

Nahid Sistani
Professor

Name: Nahid Sistani

Title: Associate Professor

Employer: Alabama A&M University

Education/Training: PhD, RD, LD

Awards/Recognition: Outstanding Teacher Award, awarded by School of Agricultural and Environmental Sciences, Alabama A&M University; and Outstanding Service Award, presented by International Student Association

General Responsibilities: Teaching and research

Ask the Expert Questions:

1) Relative to nutrition, what changes have occurred with the dining public over the past 10 years?
There has been an increasing prevalence of consumers dining in restaurants across the United States.

As food eaten away from home comprises an increasingly significant portion of total energy (calories) intake, the nutritional quality, particularly in terms of nutrient content and preparation methods, is becoming more of a concern (French et al., 2001). Although there is limited data analysis on food items in restaurants, research indicates that food sources away from home, such as in restaurants, are higher in energy and fat content compared to at-home foods (Kant & Graubard, 2004; French et al., 2001). Indeed, studies indicate that the fat content of meals in restaurants exceeds nutritional guidelines.

Another area that presents challenges to healthy eating when dining out is the portion sizes in restaurant. Portion sizes have been increasingly more significant at restaurants (French et al., 2001). When dining at restaurants, consumers may be underestimating their portion sizes, as well as food intake. Evidence suggests that people have trouble accurately estimating portion-size information, especially as the portion size increases (French et al., 2001). Similarly, portion size has an effect on food consumption. Studies reveal that, when portions are doubled in size, the consumption of many foods, such as pasta, generally increases by 18 to 25 percent (Wansink, 2004).

However, increasing public awareness of the importance of nutrition to health and wellness has also motivated commercial food service operators to consider the nutritional quality of menu selections. Consumer awareness has increased as a result of the relationship of diet to chronic diseases such as heart disease, stroke, cancer, and diabetes. Therefore, food service managers cannot afford to ignore customer demand for nutritionally adequate menu offerings. Many food service establishments are positioning and marketing nutrition to consumer demand and to gain a competitive edge. Because of consumer interest in nutrition, there has been an increase in requests for more healthful items, and as a consequence chefs are being trained to meet these needs. Many culinary institutions' curriculum includes nutritional preparation for their students. They are even offering specific training in nutrition concepts and principles for food service professionals. Also, many food service operations have either a registered dietitian on staff or as a consultant on nutritional aspects of menu planning.

2) What benefits can a food service operator realize by working with a registered dietitian or nutritionist?
Remember the dieter's plate? For many years, it usually came with cottage cheese, several pieces of fruit, and a few crackers. These days, restaurants have a lot more to offer consumers concerned about calories, cholesterol, fat, and other nutrients that may help reduce their risk of certain diseases. Menus now may carry items ranging from low-fat, low-calorie tacos to full-course meals featuring seafood or chicken dishes that are low in sodium and fat, and high in fiber and vitamins A and C. Restaurants boast about their nutritionally modified dishes with symbols, such as a big red heart signifying that the dish fits in with a diet that is consistent with general dietary recommendations, or with claims such as "low fat," "light," or "heart healthy." By working with a nutritionist or dietitian at the local or national restaurant level, a food service operator can benefit from the advice of a registered dietitian or nutritionist to assign actual nutrition values for each product; offer variations in serving sizes; learn preparation techniques; advise ingredient substitutions; conduct product testing; facilitate sources of supply, as well as regional and seasonal differences; and aid in eliminating trans fats in preparation.

3) How has the role of buyer changed in the past 10 years?
The appetite toward buying foods and beverages based on ethical and green issues such as labor treatment, eco-friendliness, fair trade, sustainable agriculture, grass-fed/free-range, biodegradability/recyclability, or charitable concerns has been escalating.

Another issue facing the role of a buyer is the local food movement; chefs and consumers are requesting fewer "food miles," the distance a food travels from the farm to the table. This is related not only to concerns over the environment but also to concerns regarding flavor/nutrient losses, supporting local farmers, and reduced chemical preservation.

4) What changes do you foresee in the role of the seller over the next 10 years?
In order to maintain long-term success, the seller must take on an evolved role that is less sales and more consulting. They should help you buy the best product for the menu application. When you purchase food products from a supplier, you will be paying for the products but also for the value additive information and service that the seller provides. As a buyer the expectation will also be that the seller can provide you with the ethical, environmental, and nutrition-related information about the products.

5) How is technology used in food service today relative to menu development, ordering, receiving, storing, inventorying, issuing, and cost controls? Please provide examples.
Computer-based training delivered via the Web or proprietary Internet sites is expanding knowledge in the workplace. About 85 percent of Fortune 1000 companies have significant e-learning initiatives under way, and we can expect to see the same trend in food service.

(continued)

The National Restaurant Association Educational Foundation even has several online courses, such as ServSafe Food Safety Training and ServSafe Manager Certification. Online food service systems have benefited from technological advances with the introduction of development software and new methods for menu preparation, ordering, receiving, storing, and inventorying. Various menu design software programs are available that can be implemented and used easily by restaurant managers to develop professional menus.

San Diego–based Cambridge Investments operates 60 Arby's and 5 Baja Fresh stores (http://www.docstoc.com/docs/9099015/The-Restauran). They use SCI's (System Concepts, Inc) Web-based purchasing and inventory management system, FOOD-TRAK, to handle the complex purchasing requirements and tracking of key inventory items. These stores also use MenuLink to evaluate managers' produce purchasing, test proposed recipes and pricing changes, and compare actual to expected food usage. The menu management function is used to determine what offers work best, so that coupon building may be directed toward those items. Since MenuLink use began, food costs have dropped 2 percent and labor costs have also dropped (Terry, 2002).

These systems are excellent and will be utilized more frequently in the future. Food service technological advancements will improve productivity, cut costs, reduce training time, and create operational efficiencies.

6) What changes or trends will occur in food service relative to product safety, selection, and availability in the near future?

The World Health Organization (WHO) reported that, in 2005, 1.8 million people died from diarrhea diseases attributed to contamination of food and drinking water.

WHO introduced the *Five Keys to Safer Food Preparation* also in order to provide more detail on the reasoning behind the suggested measures. For an electronic copy of WHO's *Five Keys to Safer Food Manual*, see http://www.who.int/foodsafety/consumer/5keysmanual/en.

The core message of the *Five Keys to Safer Food* preparation are: 1) keep clean; 2) separate raw and cooked; 3) cook thoroughly; 4) keep food at safe temperatures; 5) use safe water and raw materials. The poster has been translated into more than 40 languages and is being used to spread WHO's food hygiene message throughout the world.

7) Please provide your advice to a chef, buyer, or food service manager relative to the role and responsibility of buying in food service?

Chefs and food buyers, through their purchase habits, send a strong message to producers, suppliers and others in the system about what they think is important. Food cost and, more recently, nutritional quality have always influenced consumer habits. The challenge now is sending a strong message that environmental quality, sustainability, and social equity issues should also be considered in shopping decisions. Beyond the role and responsibility of buying, chefs and food service managers, by practicing proper purchasing, handling, preparation, and careful storage, cannot only reduce waste and save money but also inspire quality standard setting in the industry. Food service mangers also need to educate and train the food service staff to incorporate simple waste prevention and recycling programs—procedures that will eliminate waste. I advise buyers to take back boxes for reuse or recycling and to hold suppliers accountable to stock products that are eco-friendly choices; packaged in ways that reduce waste. Food service managers should even visit the grower's/producer's operation to make sure of food safety practices. I advise purchasing from local sources as the priority when it comes to responsible buying. It helps support local economy and family enterprises, enhances the environment, and usually makes for healthier, better tasting food.

People, Places, Things

The Marine Stewardship Council

The Marine Stewardship Council (MSC) was founded by Unilever, the world's largest buyer of seafood, and the World Wildlife Fund in 1997. Since 1999, it has operated as an independent organization that has brought together a vast coalition of over 100 organizations in more than twenty countries. The goal of the MSC is to create an international standard for managing environmentally responsible fisheries and sustainable seafood practices. It uses a label to denote seafood products that are produced by those operations engaged is and production methods, accurate portioning, adherence to sanitary practices, and lawful and professional business practices are just some of the behaviors expected of food service operators.

ECOLOGICAL CONCERNS

Essentially, **ecology** is the branch of biology that deals with the relations between living organisms and their environment. Our planet is an ecosystem, a community of plants and animals. Areas related to ecology are broad and far reaching. They include conservation in its many forms and environmental protection. As citizens of the world, we must consider our impact on the local, regional, national, and international bionetwork.

Chefs are decision makers, who base their decisions on a variety of criteria. Ecologically minded considerations, such as recycling, can help to preserve the environment and protect our natural resources (Figure 3.10). Chapter 4 further discusses aspects of ecology relative to food production and sustainability.

Endangered Species

Government agencies continually update lists of animals considered to be endangered species. An **endangered species** is one that has very few animals left or is threatened by environmental issues or predators. If the animals or plants are not protected, then they could become extinct. Most countries have laws protecting endangered species. Endangered species are not usually available for consumption.

There are several organizations that work with chefs to bring awareness to the food service industry and its customers. The Monterey Bay Aquarium publishes a Seafood Watch

3.10 **Separated recyclables**
Photo courtesy Robert Garlough

list online (http://www.seafoodwatch.org), outlining which seafood stocks are depleted from overfishing or contaminated by pollution. In 2006, the aquarium started advising forty-four restaurants, nearly all of them on the West Coast. It has since printed more than 22 million wallet-size guides based on the watch list for regional use), and it also runs an annual conference. The Blue Ocean Institute and the Oceans Alive organization also produce similar pocket seafood selectors that are available for food service operators to distribute to their customers. The Marine Stewardship Council (MSC) seeks to harness consumer purchasing power to promote environmentally responsible stewardship of the ocean's renewable food sources.

Roughly one in three U.S.-managed fisheries is already overfished, according to the advocacy group Environmental Defense. According to the National Oceanic and Atmospheric Administration Fisheries Service, per-capita annual U.S. seafood consumption rose from 14.8 pounds in 2001 to 16.2 pounds in 2005; more than half of that was eaten in restaurants.

Food service operators must be proactive in their selection of seafood for their menus. For example, at the Oceanaire Seafood Room in downtown Washington, Executive Chef Rob Klink stopped serving Patagonian tooth fish (a.k.a. Chilean sea bass) in 2002, despite his customers' demands for the fish. He opted to serve Alaskan sablefish instead, due to their similar qualities, and when swordfish stocks plunged worldwide, he chose Hawaiian wahoo. Klink joins thousands of other chefs and food service operators in trying to create a mutually supportive relationship with the oceans.

RENEWING AMERICA'S FOOD TRADITIONS (RAFT) PROJECT
To promote the diversity of America's edible plants and animals, American Livestock Breeds Conservancy, the Center for Sustainable Environments, Chef's Collaborative, Cultural Conservancy, Native Seed/SEARCH, Seed Savers Exchange, and Slow Food USA created RAFT in 2005. Under the auspices of Slow Food USA, this group works to document, preserve, and celebrate America's foodstuffs.

RAFT aims to:

- Create a comprehensive catalog of indigenous edible plants and animals.

- Document which foods and recipes are underused and are at risk for extinction.

- Determine which foods and animals can be restored to regular uses.

The first project that this group completed was a comprehensive report on America's endangered foods. RAFT created a list of more than 700 plants and animals, from different apple varieties to shellfish. The group identified the status of the plant or animal, its normal location or habitat, and its cultural and historical information.

RAFT is doing this for four reasons:

- **Ecological benefits.** By maintaining and increasing the plant and animal diversity, we can maintain and support healthy ecological relationships. This will help increase resistance to pests and diseases and ensure food security.

- **Gastronomic benefits.** Maintaining a wide variety of plants and animals will ensure a variety of textures, flavors, and aromas for different foodstuffs.

- **Cultural benefits.** Preserving the traditional knowledge and sustainable production of culturally significant foods prevents them from becoming extinct.

- **Health and nutrition benefits.** Eating a wide variety of foods has been known to prevent or mitigate such chronic diseases as diabetes and heart disease.

Social, Economic, and Cultural Influences

Food service operators should strongly consider any social, economic, or cultural influences that might affect the buying habits of the consumer, particularly the operator's own customer base. As individuals, we are personally involved in and aware of our own culture; however, this intimacy might bias our ability to completely understand another's culture. Understanding another's culture and cuisine requires a willingness to go beyond one's own cultural boundaries.

There are two contrasting theoretical methods in which a culture may be observed. The **emic approach** is from the viewpoint of an insider, someone who lives among the people to gain an understanding of the culture. The more common is the **etic approach**, which employs the viewpoint of an outsider to the culture (see Figure 3.11). This can be difficult because habits and food choices may appear illogical to an outside observer but can be clearly understood by the insider. **Cultural relativity** must be the goal, to understand a culture within the context of that culture, without the filters and biases of the observer affecting her observations.

Consumers are often attracted to the culinary specialties of a geographic region. Boiled lobster in Maine, clam chowder in Boston, grilled wahoo in Hawaii, pork barbecue in Memphis, fajitas in Texas, gumbo in Louisiana, and grits in Georgia are common requests among tourists. Chefs often seek to incorporate at least some indigenous ingredients and cooking methods reflective of their gastronomical region when designing their menus (see Figure 3.12). Locally influenced dishes provide an insight into the cultural fabric of any region or country, and visitors often wish to share in this greater understanding.

RELIGIOUS

According to Pamela Kittler and Kathryn Sucher, in their book *Food and Culture in America*, "the function of religion is to explain the inexplicable and thus to give humans a sense

3.11 The text's author Robert Garlough and students from his international Cuisine and Culture Study Tour, with Cablocos in the Amazon

Photo Courtesy Robert Garlough

of control over a chaotic world" (1989, p. 19). Because of its nutritional contributions and its ability to sustain life, food has always been an important element in religious rituals and customs. These customs and beliefs sometimes dictate the type of foods certain religious groups may consume or even times of the day in which food and drink may be consumed. Respect for these customs by offering selections that fall within the range of religious acceptability is both appropriate and good business.

LIFESTYLE

Studying consumer microeconomics will help the food service operator understand not only the economy but also the buying habits of the customer. **Lifestyle** is strongly tied to personal wealth and available time, and the savvy food service operator must understand the standard of living of her clientele (Figure 3.13). The style of dining, including menu choices and service needs, must match the way of life of the end user.

AVAILABLE EQUIPMENT

Recipes are developed around menus, and menus are often developed around the available equipment. In an ideal world, chefs and buyers would not have to consider kitchen equipment when developing menus, but this rarely happens, and the selection is generally limited when a chef or manager opens her own restaurant. The rest of the time, chains will dictate equipment (and menus, too), or the chef will work in an established business with a preexisting kitchen. Sometimes equipment can be replaced, or workable solutions can be

3.12 **An example of a regionally inspired menu from New Orleans featuring traditional foods**

Lunches

		*With Meat
Red Beans and Rice	$3.50	$4.95
White Beans and Rice	$3.50	$4.95
Green Lima Beans and Rice	$3.00	$4.95
Crowder Peas and Okra and Rice	$3.00	$4.95
Mustard, Collard or Cabbage Greens and Rice	$3.00	
Spaghetti and Meat Balls	$4.95	

*Meats available with above lunches

Fried Chicken Livers with gravy, Meat Loaf, Turkey Necks or Wings, Smothered Pork Chop, Baked, Fried, Stewed Chicken, Smoked Sausage

Po-Boys

Shrimp	$5.95
Fish	$4.95
Oysters	$5.95
Ham	$4.50
Smoke Sausage	$3.95
Hot Sausage	$4.00
Roastbeef	$4.50
Meat ball	$4.50

Dinner

Baked, Stewed or Fried Chicken	$6.96
Fried Fish Plate	$8.95
Seafood Combination Platter	$12.95
Crawfish or Shrimp Etouffe	$9.95
Jambalaya	$6.95

Greens: Mustard, Collard, or Cabbage
Beans: Red, White, Green, Lima, or Crowder Peas with Okra

Soups | Cup | Bowl
Gumbo | $3.50 | $4.50
Turtle Soup | $2.95 | $3.50

Desserts
Bread Pudding
w/Praline Sauce | $3.00
Cheese Cake
w/Praline Sauce | $3.00
Sweet Potato Pie | $3.00

3.13 **Customers enjoying good service**

© Randy Van Dam 2008

found using mobile equipment. However, money is a factor with either of these alternatives.

It is vital to take stock of the available equipment when developing a menu. Each recipe should be evaluated according to the equipment required. Also, chefs need to spread the preparation and finishing work around the kitchen to be sure no station is overburdened. To do this, it is wise to evaluate the menu according to its methods of cookery and equipment it requires using a "needs matrix," as shown in Table 3.1.

Profitability

Other than the few food service operations that exist due to the generous, almost philanthropic nature of their owners or benefactors, most businesses must operate for profit. As the reality of these words ring true at the end of every month,

TABLE 3.1   Menu/Equipment Needs Matrix

Menu Item	Primary Method of Cookery	Secondary Method of Cookery	Primary Equipment Needed	Secondary Equipment Needed
Shrimp bisque	Simmering		Range	
Onion soup	Simmering	Cutting	Range	
Minestrone soup	Simmering	Washing	Range	Sink
Shrimp salad	Boiling	Washing	Range	Sink
Caesar salad	Washing		Sink	
House salad	Washing		Sink	
Veal marsala	Sauteing		Range	
Strip steak	Grilling		Char-broiler	
London broil	Broiling		Char-broiler	
Filet Mignon	Grilling		Char-broiler	
Prime rib	Roasting		Alto-sham	
Veal chop	Grilling		Char-broiler	
Shrimp scampi	Sauteing		Range	
Seafood platter	Deep frying		Fryer	
Linguini	Simmering	Sauteing	Range	Range
Lamb rack	Roasting		Oven	
Osso bucco	Braising		Range	Oven

upon review of the monthly profit-and-loss statement, chefs and buyers are traditionally challenged to reduce variable costs—food and labor generally being the highest of these controllable costs.

The pressures to remain financially solvent are often strong enough to force chefs and buyers to compromise. Their goal to use organics might have to wait. Their desire to use only seasonal foods might be unrealistic. They might have to incorporate some pre-prepared foods into their menus. To some, these accommodations are easy; to others, the compromises could be reason enough to resign their position. Each food service professional must decide what cause she will support, what principles she must follow.

What's important is doing it knowingly and with proper consideration of the facts.

Jim Miller, CEC, AAC, CFSP

Place of Birth: Cleveland, Ohio

Educational Background and Work Experience

Jim Miller has worked in the food service industry ever since he could hold a job. He started out as an apprentice with Carrie Cerino's Ristorante in North Royalton, Ohio, at 15 years of age. Miller continued to work in both the restaurant and the bakery in Brecksville, Ohio, through high school and on into culinary school. He held several positions, such as line cook and banquet chef. A stellar student, Miller was an honors graduate in high school and was inducted into the National Honors Society in 1972. In culinary school, he again graduated with honors, this time from The Culinary Institute of America, in 1976. Miller was named the Most Outstanding Student from among a class of 500 graduates. Chef Miller then went to work for Interstate United Corporation from 1976 to 1983. He worked as a chef manager and eventually became the regional manager, working with contract feeding for business and industry, health care, and school food service. Chef Miller left that position in 1983 to become corporate chef for Cres Cor in Cleveland, Ohio. A longtime employee, Chef Miller is now its national accounts manager, serving the mobile solutions equipment needs of food service customers across the country.

Memberships and Career Highlights

Miller joined the Cleveland Culinary Association of the American Culinary Federation (ACF) in June 1976 as a junior member. He is still a member after more than 30 years in the industry. Always an active member, he has served as apprenticeship chair, vice president, and two-term president of the local ACF Cleveland chapter. He is currently serving on its board of directors in an advisory position. Chef Miller was initially certified by the ACF in 1983 and today remains certified as a Certified Executive Chef (CEC), believing that ongoing education is critical for professional chefs. His commitment to his chapter was recognized when he was named its Chef of the Year in both 1986 and 1991. I

Courtesy Jim Miller

It Happened to Me...

"The names, dates, and location have been omitted to protect the 'not-so-innocent' in my story:

Let's just say that I and another eager young chef faced a new challenge of outfitting a large banquet facility that would seat 9,600 customers at a time, plus employee feeding for thousands of meals per day, on three shifts. Obviously, the key here was to invest the time and effort to create definite and clear specifications up front to avoid many headaches and disappointments later. The carpenters have a phrase for this: 'measure twice and cut once.'

We had to order a lot of products, and, as usual, it had to be done fast with many last-minute additions and corrections needed. When you order equipment, of course you need to consider the menu first and last but you must also consider the volume of food, the weight of the food, and the type of employee skill levels that may be operating the equipment. We had not ordered the best of mobile racks; in fact, we bought some economy-welded racks for our operation. It turned out that we were replacing them within the first few months as angles were breaking off with the weight of overloaded pans of meat, baked potatoes, etc. We did not save any money, as we had to buy new racks that were heavier duty that would hold up to the transient work force that was very rough on the equipment.

Not all equipment is manufactured equally, even though they may look similar or even have the same number of shelves. It is like two glasses of milk. One glass could be 2% and the other whole milk. They may look alike, but they are not. Sit down and write out your needs/specifications on the item, and do not be swayed to settle for less. Not all stoves, deep fryers, or broilers have the same BTUs and may not recover fast enough to cook properly. You never have time to wait with the customer out front. You will be the person responsible for the output of your kitchen, not the salesman that just left the lovely brochures. Ask questions and decide for yourself, based on your needs. If possible, ask to test a piece of equipment before buying. Many manufacturers have some type of program.

Again, at the beginning, consider the finish. I urge you to search for quality and good value in your purchasing. The lowest price item is usually the lowest for a reason. Do not risk your reputation, job, or someone else's health/injury to find out. Ask other culinarians, like stewards or buyers, about their brands and models that work well. You will save yourself a lot of grief, both in the short time and in the long run. It is like finding a good wine: once you do, stick with it as long as you can and enjoy. Bon Appetite!

(continued)

In 1996, he became a founding member of the Research Chefs of America. He is both a member of the National Advisory Board for the School Nutrition Association and a member of the culinary advisory board for the University of Nevada, Las Vegas. Chef Miller's achievements have been recognized by being elected as a Fellow of the American Academy of Chefs and as a lifetime member of the Honorable Order of the Golden Toque, an international honor society limited to 100 living chefs.

Passions with the Food Service Industry

"My greatest joy in working in this industry is its diversity of venues. I have had the great fortune to be exposed to, and work in, many different market segments. Consider the diverse feeding requirements of stadium/arena feeding, correctional, airline food service, hotel banqueting/room service/employee feeding, universities and colleges, School Lunch and breakfast programs, the corporate world of B&I (business and industry) and the restaurateurs. We have a myriad of independent and chain restaurants that serve every ethnic type of food imaginable, from BBQ to French, Tex-Mex to Asian, Italian to seafood specialties. What a great variety of tastes and preparations in which we can get lost. The common thread is always people and food. What a wonderful, social business we have!"

Advice to a Chef or Buyer

"When searching for that correct piece of food service equipment, always do your research. Start your inquiries with colleagues, other chefs that may have used a certain brand and have had success (or failures) and are willing to share their experiences. Just ask, and you will be surprised just how quickly people will be to praise or criticize products based on their actual experiences. Whether the product is large or small, do your networking, and, in turn, they will inquire from you in the future. One thing that I have learned over the years is that most purchasing actions are not unique; the type of problems, cuisines, cooking techniques, and even personnel are similar no matter what the market segment may be. The odds are that someone else has had the same situation that you face, and their willingness to share personal experiences may help you to save time and money."

Key Words and Concepts

aquaculture

biochemistry

consistency

cultural relativity

distribution

ecology

emic approach

endangered species

etic approach

foodborne illnesses

genetically modified foods

Hazard Analysis and Critical Control Point (HACCP)

lifestyle

nutritional value

palatable

pathogens

Slow Food Movement

Chapter in Review

The following exercises are provided to help the reader understand and apply the contents of this chapter. They may be completed individually or in a classroom environment.

REVIEW QUESTIONS

a. Discuss the Slow Food Movement and its goals.

b. Discuss the benefits of modern transportation systems, as they relate to the availability of out-of-season products.

c. Discuss the four main functions performed in the marketplace.

d. Discuss the two contrasting theoretical methods by which a culture may be observed.

INDIVIDUAL ACTIVITIES

a. **Web based:** Research RAFT, and discover the different foods that are on America's Endangered Foods list.

b. **Experiential:** Create a HACCP plan for food that enters your home or work kitchen.

c. **Critical thinking:** Compare and contrast the different factors that affect palatability.

GROUP ACTIVITIES

a. **Lab experience:** Divide the class into eleven groups, and assign each one a different region of the country to use in developing regional recipes.

b. **Classroom action:** Discuss the problem of extinction as it relates to American foods. Identify actions that students and food service professionals can undertake to help sustain all food species.

CHAPTER

4

Image copyright Vitaliy Minsk, 2009. Used under license from Shutterstock.com

Modern Applications of Food Science

"When food, in the minds of eaters, is no longer associated with farming and with the land, then the eaters are suffering a kind of cultural amnesia that is misleading and dangerous." WENDELL BERRY

After reading this chapter, you will be able to:

- ◎ Summarize the philosophy of ethics.

- ◎ Define food composition.

- ◎ Relate food to Maslow's Hierarchy of Needs.

- ◎ Define GAIN, and explain its function.

- ◎ Describe hydroponics and its uses for tourism and food service operations.

- ◎ Compare and contrast the advantages and disadvantages of aquaculture.

- ◎ Define biotechnology and its application to food science.

- ◎ Explain genetically modified organisms.

- ◎ Identify common food allergens and their impact on food and nutrition labeling.

- ◎ Define food irradiation, and discuss its application.

- ◎ Explain cultural heritage and its potential relationship to tourism and food service.

- ◎ Summarize ecology and its relationship to biodiversity and monocultures.

- ◎ Explain sustainable agriculture.

- ◎ Analyze conservation as it relates to food service.

- ◎ Define organics.

Introduction

In her highly regarded textbook *Foods: Experimental Perspectives,* Margaret McWilliams writes, "An educated and thoughtful public capable of separating emotion from scientific truths with a sound science base is essential if progress is to be made toward producing the optimum food supply to meet the needs of the entire world's people" (2001, p. xiii). It is the intent of this book, and in a large way this chapter, to present topical information that might contribute to the reader's understanding of selection and procurement in a global marketplace. In doing so, this chapter strives to expose the reader to scientific subjects that are often both innovative and controversial. It is the author's hope that their inclusion will stimulate the readers' thinking and invoke discussion in the classroom.

Chefs and food service managers have an ethical responsibility as providers of nourishment, comfort, and entertainment to evaluate the modern applications of food science. They must consider nutritional, environmental, social, and scientific data—while at the same time pragmatic—when making decisions that affect their customers' food choices. In her article "Shape Your Culinary Footprint: Do Chefs Have a Debt to Consumers and the Planet?" Jody Shee writes: "Chefs are an important link in the planet's food supply: They plan menus, choose ingredients, work with purveyors, prepare food and oversee the disposal of culinary waste. Approaching these tasks with responsibility and humility makes a chef's contribution to society soar above the offering of a delicious meal" (2006, p. 14).

Ethics and Food in Modern Society

The field of **ethics** involves creating and defending the concepts of right and wrong behavior. The study of ethics requires a study of conflicts of interest, values, and ways to solve situations. Most modern philosophers divide the field into three categories: metaethics, normative ethics, and applied ethics.

Metaethics is the study of where our ethical principles come from and how they influence a person's behavior. Normative ethics regulate right and wrong behavior as determined by a society. Normative ethical guidelines for a food service purchasing agent were described in Chapter 1.

Applied ethics involves examining the controversial topics within an industry. In food service purchasing, some topics such as biotechnology and food irradiation might need guidance from applied ethical guidelines.

Mepham (1996) wrote in *Food Ethics,* as the first lines in a collection of essays on ethical issues linked to food: "None of us can avoid being interested in food. Our very existence depends on the supply of safe, nutritious foods. It is then hardly surprising that food has become the focus of a wide range of ethical concerns" (p. xi). Buyers who purchase the food and supplies, and the chefs who use them, are constantly challenged by ethical considerations. It is imperative that the buyer, manager, and chef establish a strong moral compass to help them steer through the ethical minefields inherent in decision making. As Zaccarelli (2007) writes:

> For those in leadership positions, it isn't possible to demonstrate high standards of integrity *most* of the time. They must be displayed all of the time. An individual's credibility only rises to the lowest occasion on which others observed it, not the highest. Because that is true, it is important to understand that the positive examples leaders seek to demonstrate must be displayed consistently and on every occasion in which they are observed (p. 29).

Food Composition

According to Wendell Berry, one of the foremost spokespersons on sustainable agriculture, in the United States "eating is an agricultural act" (1990, p. 145). There is a direct line from the garden to the table, where what is prepared and consumed is first grown or raised. The chef must consider the **food composition** in its entirety, not only its organic or inorganic composition, but also its pedigree.

Foods contain a variety of chemical molecules that are joined in different ways. Some appear to be homogenous in their composition, such as the potato, with its outer skin and starchy core. Others are more complex, like the cross section of an orange, which reveals a network of seeds, pulp, membranes, juice and layered skin (see Figure 4.1). The chemical substances in most foods include water, fats, carbohydrates, and proteins (including enzymes). Additionally, acids, minerals, vitamins, flavoring agents, and pigments contribute to the makeup of the ingredient.

To understand the proper handling and preparation of each ingredient, we must recognize the nature of its composition. As well, we must understand the transformations that occur when an ingredient is mixed, blended, cooked, or refrigerated.

Cross sections of an orange and a potato

© Randy Van Dam 2008

An ever-present preoccupation of humans, food in all its forms has been the focus of study since *Homo erectus* could distinguish between plant and animal. Food has forever been at the center of science, as it is essential for our survival as a species. Eminent psychologist Abraham Maslow placed the need for food, along with clothing and shelter, as the most basic of all human needs. In **Maslow's Hierarchy of Needs**, as shown in Figure 4.2, he suggested that people must achieve food stability before significant focus can be directed toward other areas of want.

As centuries and civilizations have come and passed, each has contributed to the discovery and attainment of food supplies. Curious and adventurous, common folk and notable scientists alike have steadily advanced the greater understanding of food for the benefit of their contemporaries and future generations.

Advancements in Food Science and Technology

Things don't just happen overnight. Although pedestrian, this worn expression truly reflects the scientific development of food and its related technology throughout the ages. Each society has experienced its own great advancements, built on earlier experiments.

FOCUS: COMBATING WORLD HUNGER

A prominent issue in the food service industry is making sure everyone eats enough to survive. Individuals need different amounts of nutrients depending on their sex, age, body size, climate, and activity level. Women need additional nutrients during pregnancy and lactation. Most people need at least 2,100 kilocalories per day for a healthy life.

The United Nations has set, as one of its Millennium Development Goals, a goal of reducing the number of hungry

4.2 **Maslow's Hierarchy of Needs**

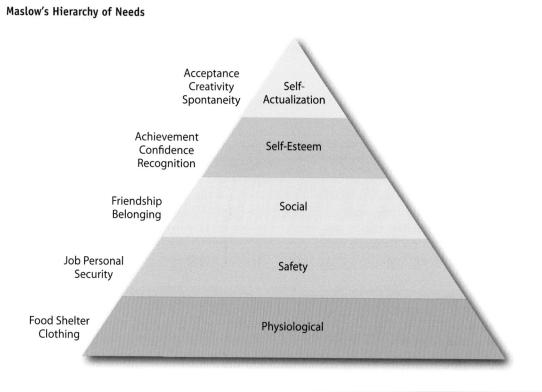

people by half within the twenty-first century. During the past 25 years, the United Nations has made tremendous strides in slowing famine and reducing the number of hungry people to 791 million—a decrease of almost 20 percent over the period (www.unicef.org/mdg).

While starvation is decreasing, the number of chronically famished is increasing in developing countries. The number of undernourished people—those who have some food but not enough for a healthy lifestyle—has also increased over time. Undernourishment is present in under-developed, transitional, and developed countries, making it difficult to eliminate.

Current estimates indicate that one of every seven people do not have enough food on a daily basis to lead a healthy and active life (http://one.wfp.org/country_brief/hunger_map/facts.html). This lack of food is one of the main risks to health worldwide. John F. Kennedy once said, "The war against hunger is truly mankind's war of liberation." Several countries have been increasing food supplies via alternative methods, such as hydroponics, aquaculture, and biotechnology. As a result, global efforts have concentrated on the following areas: *providing nutrition, hydroponics, aquaculture,* and *biotechnology.*

Providing Nutrition

In *The History of Food*, Maguelonne Toussaint-Samat wrote, "It would be sad if the history of food were to end with the word FAMINE" (1992, p. 5).

The **Global Alliance for Improved Nutrition (GAIN)** was created to combat vitamin and mineral deficiency. Nutritional deficiencies can cause learning difficulties, birth defects, compromised immune systems, blindness, and death. GAIN is a leadership hub allying different organizations that are committed to ending these deficiencies.

GAIN was launched by the UN General Assembly in May 2002 and was incorporated a year later as a Swiss Foundation. With money from various charitable organizations, GAIN disburses funds to developing countries to build food markets and fortify foodstuffs made within the area. In the past few years, GAIN has increased vitamins and minerals in food products across the world.

On a local level, food service buyers and chefs can promote nutrition and wellness for their clientele by proper selection, procurement, and preparation of foodstuffs. They can design menus to match consumer tastes, financial demands, and nutritional values.

TECHNOLOGICAL ADVANCES IN FOOD PRODUCTION

During the past few decades, food scientists have been working on increasing agricultural yields. Several of the most promising methods include *hydroponics, aquaculture,* and *biotechnology.*

Hydroponics

Hydroponics is the process of growing and cultivating plants without using soil. Many ancient civilizations, including the Incas, Egyptians, Aztecs, and Babylonians, have used hydroponics for centuries. Hydroponics uses water as a medium to grow the plants and is especially valuable for fresh vegetables in areas with little arable land. Some areas such as Hawaii and the West Indies use hydroponics to support the local population and tourists staying in hotels located on former farmland.

Many argue that hydroponic farming will be the means by which we, as citizens of this earth, will survive. Some suggest that increasing ultraviolet radiation; decreasing fresh water supplies; increasing erosion and soil degradation; increasing resistance to chemical treatments of insects, rodents, and plant diseases; and changing weather patterns will lead to increased use of hydroponics. For example, tomatoes grown in a hydroponics farm can yield 150 tons per acre. A 1,300-acre plot could grow enough tomatoes to feed everyone in Canada each year. Figure 4.3 shows a typical hydroponic system used in a modern kitchen, while Figure 4.4 illustrates the basic design elements.

4.3   **Hydroponics garden in a kitchen**
© Randy Van Dam 2008

4.4 **Drawing of hydroponic system**

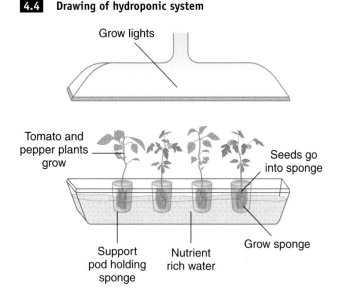

Grow lights

Tomato and pepper plants grow

Seeds go into sponge

Support pod holding sponge

Nutrient rich water

Grow sponge

Aquaculture

Aquaculture, as discussed in Chapter 3, is the act of farming fish in a specially constructed or contained environment. The farmer will artificially fertilize the eggs and then place the eggs in a large net or pen in the ocean or lake. The fish are fed on food pellets, and nets across the top protect the fish from other predators. As they grow, their lack of movement means that the fish have a greater percentage of muscle and weight than their cousins in the wild.

Aquaculture, has existed for millennia and was used in China around 2500 BC. The current boom started in the late 1960s-early 1970s after overfishing caused price inflation. Aquaculture has exploded in the past few decades in response to overfishing. Aquaculture also helps manage the supply for high-demand fish and shellfish that are hard to catch in the wild.

Fish farming is a large component of aquaculture and is becoming an increasingly larger part of the commercial fishing industry. Most aquafarmers consider the biology of the species, the feeding needs, water temperature, and containment systems as key components of their farms. Today, catfish, tilapia, trout, crawfish, oysters, shrimp, salmon, and tropical fish for aquariums are commonly grown.

Aquaculture does have some drawbacks. Most of the fish are genetically altered for quick growth. If they escape into the wild, they could alter the survival of their wild cousins. Also, the water in the farm becomes contaminated with fish feces and unconsumed food, and that has to be removed or the larger body will be contaminated with excess nitrogen, which would damage the viability of the fish in the farm.

Biotechnology

According to Bennion and Scheule (2004), "The FDA has developed a food **biotechnology** policy for foods derived from genetically modified plants. This policy is science-based

and reflects the FDA's understanding that changes in food composition can be accomplished using new genetic engineering techniques" (p. 107). Biotechnology is used to produce plants with disease and drought resistance and animals with leaner meat. It is also used to increase the flavor profile and the nutritional values of food items.

The International Service for the Acquisition of Agri-Biotech Applications reported a record 13-percent increase in global biotech crop plantings in 2006, compared with 2005. Most of the 10.3 million farmers involved were subsistence farmers. In 2006, Argentina, Brazil and the United States were the top three countries growing biotech crops, which included mostly soy (www.okspecialtyfruits.com/mb-industry-growth-statistics.php).

FOCUS: HUMAN HEALTH AND FOOD SAFETY

Great advancements have been made in the areas of human health and safety. Scientific study of food and nutrition, and related governmental policy, has recently focused on the following areas: *food engineering and GMOs, cloning farm animals, food and nutritional labeling, food allergens, growth-enhancing hormones, and food irradiation.*

Food Engineering

Genetically engineered foods, also known as "biotech foods," are foods that have been genetically modified by humans. Genetic engineering is done to increase yields, increase resistance to diseases, and longer lengthen shelf lives. There is some controversy about genetically engineered foods, and some people will not eat them. Chefs must carefully consider their target clientele if they offer genetically engineered foods.

GENETICALLY MODIFIED ORGANISMS (GMOS)

Genetically modified organisms (GMOs) is another term for foods that have been altered or genetically enhanced in a laboratory. Today, food scientists take the recombinant DNA (rDNA) and transfer this material from one plant or animal to another. Later, the food is planted on conventional farms. This is done to enhance a natural process within the plant. For example, tomatoes may be genetically modified to resist softening, so that the fruit can travel long distances without spoiling.

Not everyone is convinced of the benefits of genetically altered foods, and some have reservations over their safety. In August 2001, hundreds of anti-biotechnology activists in France destroyed two major test sites for genetically modified corn owned by the Monsanto Corporation. The activists claim that the GMOs are the unsafe products of greedy multinational businesses. Others feel that GMOs should be labeled to alert buyers to their pedigree. The worldwide debate over GMOs can be summarized with a quote from Lucretius, a Roman philosopher: "One man's meat is another man's poison."

Cloning Farm Animals

In 2006, the Food and Drug Administration (FDA) tentatively concluded that milk and meat from cloned farm animals was safe for human consumption. That made the United States the first country to allow the sale of cloned meat to the public. A January 2008 report by FDA scientists concluded that milk and meat from cows, pig, and goat clones and their offspring are as safe for the consumer as noncloned animals. When challenged by critics over the ethics of its decision, the FDA reported that food safety is its responsibility, not ethical issues related to food. This ruling remains controversial in the minds of many, as cloning is still in its infancy and the long-term effects are unclear.

Food Labeling

As mentioned in Chapter 2, the U.S. government adopted the **Food Allergen Labeling and Consumer Protection Act (FALCPA)** in 2006. The act is designed to help consumers easily identify safe and unsafe foods. As mentioned earlier, this law requires that common allergens present in the foods be included on the label. The law does not differentiate between regularly grown foodstuffs and items that have been genetically modified. Therefore, current labeling laws do not require identification of products that have been genetically modified. However, some states do have laws requiring an additional label, such as that for growth hormones in milk.

Currently, unless the genetically modified foods are significantly different from their regular counterparts, no labeling is required (unless required by local laws). This will continue to be a hotly debated topic. In Europe, the policy is slightly different. All genetically modified foods must be labeled as such, as illustrated in Figure 4.5.

4.5 **Biotech warning label**

This product is produced from GMOs

Food Allergens

As mentioned in Chapter 2, food allergies are life threatening for some people. Items sold in grocery stores or packaged for wholesale must have the allergen warning on them. Chefs and other managers should remember that most allergens are introduced to foods early in the food manufacturing cycle. There is opportunity for cross-contamination within the kitchen as well.

Although not law at this point, food service operators could, one day, have to provide warnings on their menus for recipes that include the eight most common allergens. Note the example of an allergen warning label on the loaf of bread pictured in Figure 4.6. Chefs and managers must always be concerned about the safety of their staff and customers, and they should consider introducing these warnings even before law requires them. At the least, they should be aware of the potential for cross-contamination through storage or preparation.

Growth-Enhancing Hormones

Growth-enhancing hormones were introduced in the 1950s. Growth hormones are natural steroids such as testosterone and progesterone, which are added to the feed of beef and milk animals. Currently, growth hormones are banned in the European Union but are allowed in the United States.

Growth hormones are commonly added to the feed when beef cattle are finishing their growth period. They are used to increase the feed conversion ratio (pounds of feed to pounds of weight gained by the cow), increase the weight of the cow, and increase the lean meat content of an animal. Growth hormones can add up to 90 pounds to each cow, resulting in a higher yield of usable and sellable meat. This extra meat per cow is an important part of the profitability of the American meat industry.

Currently, this is a common practice, and meat produced this way does not have to be labeled as such. But there is some concern that people who eat growth-hormone meat might suffer adverse effects, including early puberty and disrupted sexual development. As our understanding of how these hormones affect people develops, the industry might need to change its opinions on the subject.

Food Irradiation

Food irradiation is a technique that reduces disease-causing germs in food. The food items are exposed to high levels of radiant energy, which penetrates the food and kills the microorganisms without raising the temperature of the food and destroying its qualities. Food irradiation significantly reduces the presence of these organisms, which can cause foodborne illnesses.

The food does not retain the radiation, and the nutritional content and the characteristics of the food remain the same. The FDA requires that all food that has been irradiated carry the international symbol of the **radura** and display the statement "treated with radiation" or "treated by irradiation" on the packaging. Figure 4.7 shows the food irradiation symbol.

FOCUS: CULTURAL HERITAGE

Cultural heritage is the parts of our society that we want to keep, appreciate, and pass on to future generations. Cultural heritage items and traditions, such as serving turkey on Thanksgiving, have special meanings to individuals or groups. Most geographic regions have indigenous foods that are prepared and served at certain times of the year.

Tourism draws on cultural heritage. Most tourists want to see things and eat foods that they normally cannot experience in their home region. Farming and preparing these foods can have a significant effect on the local

4.6   **Allergen warning on NLEA Nutrition Facts Label**
© Randy Van Dam 2008

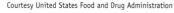

Nutrition Facts	Amount/Serving	% DV*	Amount/Serving	% DV*	*Percent Daily Values (%DV) are based on a 2,000 calorie diet. Your daily values may be higher or lower depending on your calorie needs.
Serving Size 1 Slice (35g)	**Total Fat** 1g	**2%**	**Total Carbohydrate** 18g	**6%**	
Servings Per Container 16	Saturated Fat 0g	**0%**	Dietary Fiber 1g	**6%**	
	Trans Fat 0g		Sugars 8g		
	Cholesterol 0mg	**0%**	**Protein** 3g		
Calories 90	**Sodium** 120mg	**5%**			
Calories from Fat 10	Vitamin A 0% • Vitamin C 0% • Calcium 4% • Iron 6%				
	Thiamine 4% • Riboflavin 2% • Niacin 2% • Folic Acid 0%				

	Calories:	2,000	2,500
Total Fat	Less than	65g	80g
Saturated Fat	Less than	20g	25g
Cholesterol	Less than	300mg	300mg
Sodium	Less than	2,400mg	2,400mg
Total Carbohydrate		300g	375g
Dietary Fiber		25g	30g

INGREDIENTS: WATER, WHOLE GRAIN WHEAT FLOUR, RAISINS, WHEAT FLOUR, HIGH FRUCTOSE CORN SYRUP, YEAST, WHEAT GLUTEN, SOYBEAN OIL, CINNAMON, SALT, CONTAINS 2% OR LESS OF THE FOLLOWING: SUGAR, RAISIN JUICE, SOY LECITHIN, CORN CEREAL, MALTED BARLEY FLOUR, WHEAT FIBER, FOOD STARCH, VANILLA, CARAMEL COLOR.

PK-300-0207   DIST. BY MEIJER DISTRIBUTION, INC., GRAND RAPIDS, MI 49544

ALLERGEN INFORMATION: MANUFACTURED ON THE SAME EQUIPMENT THAT ALSO PROCESSES HAZELNUTS AND SESAME SEEDS. THIS PRODUCT CONTAINS WHEAT AND SOY INGREDIENTS.

4.7   **Radura symbol**
Courtesy United States Food and Drug Administration

economy. Local food service operations can help this trend by serving foods that are native to their region and that are grown and produced by local farmers and fishermen.

FOCUS: ENVIRONMENTAL PROTECTION

Environmental protection should be considered when making purchasing decisions. Purchasing foods that contribute to deforestation, pollution, and extinction of animals and plants should be avoided. As food service professionals and citizens of the world, we must be cognizant of the ramifications of our decisions and habits. Environmental protection is an attitude, a commitment to preserve and, if possible, renew the natural resources we so freely enjoy. It is important to realize the impact each person and business can have on the environment and the food it bares. In an essay published in *The Journal of Gastronomy*, venerable chef, owner, and food activist Alice Waters (1989) wrote:

> I have always believed that a restaurant can be no better than the ingredients it has to work with. As much as by any other factor, Chez Panisse* has been defined by the search for ingredients. That search and what we have found along the way have shaped what we cook and ultimately who we are. The search has made us part of a community—a community that has grown from markets, gardens, and suppliers and has gradually come to include farmers, ranchers, and fishermen.

> It has also made us realize that, as a restaurant, we are utterly dependent on the health of the land, the sea, and the planet as a whole, and that this search for good ingredients is pointless without a healthy agriculture and a healthy environment.

Environmental protection includes the study of *ecology*, *biodiversity*, *monocultures*, *sustainable agriculture*, *conservation*, and *waste reduction*, and *organics*.

   Chez Panisse *is Alice Water's restaurant in Berkley, California.*

Ecology

A Kashmiri proverb reminds us, "We have not inherited the world from our forefathers. We have borrowed it from our children." **Ecology** is the branch of science that studies the interactions between living things and their physical environment. **Biodiversity** is increasing the available plants and animals in an area so that they will exist and mutually support each other's growth. Each ecosystem benefits from biodiversity and the protection of the local fauna and animals. A healthy ecosystem protects a region from natural disasters or helps with the speedy recovery from one.

BIODIVERSITY

Long before Al Gore's award-winning documentary on global warming, *An Inconvenient Truth*, David Orr wrote this passage in his 1991 article, "What Is Education For?":

> If today is a typical day on planet Earth, we will lose 116 square miles of rainforest, or about an acre a second. We will lose another 72 square miles to encroaching deserts, as a result of human mismanagement and overpopulation. We will lose 40 to 100 species, and no one knows whether the number is 40 or 100. Today the human population will increase by 250,000. And today we will add 2,700 tons of chlorofluorocarbons to the atmosphere and 15 million tons of carbon. Tonight the Earth will be a little hotter, its waters more acidic, and the fabric of life more threadbare (p. 52).

In the past few years, the level of biological diversity has been decreasing. The World Wide Fund for Nature maintains a Living Planet index which tracks and records the existence of 4,000 species of birds, fish, reptiles, amphibians, and mammals annually. Their records indicate land based species declined by 25 percent while marine species fell by 28 percent, and freshwater species declined by 29 percent between 1970 and 2007 (www.enn.com/wildlife/article/36390). As food purchasing agents, it is prudent to seek foodstuffs that are not in danger of becoming extinct to save the stock for future generations.

MONOCULTURES

Traditionally, farmers grew crops and raised livestock on the same farm. This helped the local ecosystem because they rotated the crops and animals on different fields. They also rotated the crops grown each year, so that fields that were depleted by the growth of corn, for example, could rejuvenate after a planting of beans or peas. The dung from the livestock could remain on the fields, increasing the soil quality for the subsequent crops. Farms could remain productive for generations using these methods.

Monoculture is the practice of growing the same crop on the same fields year after year, as shown in Figure 4.8. Farmers who do this need additional chemicals for pest controls and extra fertilizers to increase the soil quality. As time goes on, more chemicals and fertilizers are needed to produce the same yield. If several farmers on adjacent lands grow the same crops, then there is the risk that the local vermin will become resistant to the chemicals and easily destroy the crops.

4.8 **Monoculture cornfield**
Photo Courtesy Robert Garlough

Sustainable Agriculture

In his preface to the collection of essays published in *Our Sustainable Table*, Robert Clark begins, "Good farming means good food; anyone who cares about good food has a stake in good farming and in methods of food production, processing, and distribution that accord with the long-term health and sustainability of farmers, farming communities, and the land upon which they—and we—depend" (Preface).

Sustainable agriculture is a series of steps that help provide high yields without destroying the soil or decreasing the productivity. Farmers who follow this philosophy use crop rotation, plant cover crops, and use natural predators such as ladybugs to control insects and pests. Sustainable agriculture minimizes the use of chemicals, pesticides, and chemical fertilizers on farms.

During a presentation to a group of culinary educators in Chicago, celebrated chef-owner Michael Foley of Printer's Row spoke on the subject of U.S. agriculture and climatic changes, predicting that "by 2040, we'll see a totally new seasonal calendar" (2003).

Sustainability is not limited to the land. Managers and chefs also appreciate the need for marine sustainability, conservancy, and political action. Between 1998 and 2000, the conservation groups Sea Web and the Natural Resources Defense Council ran a campaign called Give Swordfish a Break, persuading more than 700 U.S. chefs and three major cruise lines to stop serving North Atlantic swordfish. In response, Clinton Administration officials closed swordfish nursery areas in U.S. waters and pushed for stronger international management rules. The fish recovered: in 1998, swordfish supplies were down to 65 percent of sustainable levels; by 2002, they were up to 94 percent (Eilperin, 2007).

CONSERVATION

Managers and chefs, and other food service operators, can influence the food habits of consumers. When humanity possesses the will to effect change, it can be a productive force for good. During certain periods in our history, conservation and family farm plots freed up enough food to feed the military and send to other countries. By conserving food, more is available for use by customers.

WASTE REDUCTION

Approximately 20 percent, or 137 million tons, of food is wasted each year. Some of this waste is left in the fields or orchards, but more of it is lost during manufacturing, storage, transportation, and final preparation in a home or restaurant. If everyone could purchase what is needed and use it before it goes bad, it would decrease the amount of food in garbage dumps.

Although most chefs prefer to use seasonally available fresh produce, food service operators should explore the increased conversion of excess fresh produce to healthy processed foods, in an effort to improve waste reduction of precious foodstuffs. Chefs should continue to use those foods that are in season and locally available, but they should concurrently consider the use of properly preserved, nutritionally viable foods that are not seasonally available.

Organics

The concept of organic farming is anything but new. Until the 1940s, virtually all fruits and vegetables were organically grown, and all livestock were hormone free. The use of laboratory-produced fertilizers was essentially non-existent. "The Earth neither grows old, nor wears out, if it be dunged," wrote Lucius Junius Moderatus Columella in his poem De Re Rustic, in 4 B.C.

The term *organic* refers to how the food is produced. Organic farmers usually follow sustainable agriculture rules. The use of chemical pesticides and fertilizers is not allowed. The food is minimally processed and packaged to maintain its integrity. Artificial ingredients, preservatives, and irradiation are not allowed. If an item is produced according to United States Department of Agriculture (USDA) organic standards, then it can have an organic label on the packaging.

The U.S. public has become increasingly aware of **organic** foods, and their sales have grown. Natural and organic products are among the fastest growing segments in the industry. American shoppers spent more than $51 billion on natural and organic products in 2005. According to a March 2007 article in *Time* magazine, "nearly a quarter of

4.9 **USDA certified organic symbol**
Courtesy United States Department of Agriculture (USDA)

American shoppers now buy organic products once a week, up from 17% in 2000" (Cloud, p. 43).

The implementation of a National Organic Program in October 2002 also contributed to increased sales. Since passage of the Organic Foods Protection Act of 1990, which mandated an organic foods certification program, the USDA has been working with related groups to develop and enhance the program. Currently, this program is still in its infancy, and there are annual revisions and comments on the laws. The USDA has established guidelines for what constitutes organic food, and the agency certifies only those products that meet the guidelines (see Figure 4.9).

Sustainability and Greening Initiatives

Many food service operators around the country have taken initiatives to "green up" their businesses. In May 2008, the National Restaurant Association (NRA) launched its "Conserve: Solutions for Sustainability" initiative to support its member companies, as well as the nation's almost 1 million food service locations, in becoming more sustainable businesses. The NRA's Conserve Web site provides a broad array of resources, including educational reference materials and opinions expressed by interested NRA members, on promoting sustainability at the operator level (Tork USA, 2009).

Although "greening" has become a trendy topic in recent years, many in the restaurant industry have been environmentally focused for years. In 1990, the Green Restaurant Association (GRA) was formed as a nonprofit national environmental organization. They certify restaurants as being "Green Restaurants" based on specific environmentally friendly conservation practices.

The following are recent initiatives that chains and independents across the United States have undertaken:

- Restaurant Eve in Alexandria, Virginia, (where a five-course dinner sells for $105), owner Cathal Armstrong raises hundreds of worms that eat some of the restaurant's organic waste. Worm castings are used as fertilizer in the vegetable garden behind the restaurant.

- *Ted's Montana Grill* uses 5.6 million paper straws per year, instead of plastic.

- *Subway's* napkins are made from 100 percent recycled paper. Subway figures its 4 billion recycled napkins save 147,000 trees annually.

- All new *Starbucks* stores built in the United States after 2010 will be green buildings certified by the U.S. Green Building Council, a nonprofit independent group that certifies buildings that meet minimum green standards. (Horovitz, 2008)

[ASK THE EXPERT]

Dan Gendler
Green Restauranteur

Name: Dan Gendler

Title: President

Employer: San Chez, A Tapas Bistro, and Mezze

Education/Training: AAAS, Grand Rapids Community College, culinary arts
B.S., Grand Valley State University, hospitality management
M.S. candidate, Ferris State University

General Responsibilities: In November 1992, Dan Gendler co-founded *San Chez, A Tapas Bistro*. Among many goals for the company, Gendler wanted San Chez to be an integrated and responsible member of the Western Michigan business community. In addition to his daily administrative duties at the highly regarded and award-winning restaurant, Gendler has put sustainability and environmental accountability at the peak of his priority list, sharing top honors with profitability and community service. While it is currently fashionable for everything from fast food to slow cars to claim to be "green," San Chez has been committed to preserving the environment, respecting its employees, supporting the local community, and being sensitive to the unique needs of its customers since it opened. San Chez refers to this attitude as "restaurantship," the foundation of its mission.

San Chez's "green initiatives" include:

- **Reducing energy usage.** To reduce energy consumption, San Chez invests in energy-saving technologies as soon as they come into the marketplace. For example, San Chez has installed air dryers and automatic light sensors in its bathrooms and replaced its paraffin table candles with LED lights. It has joined the state's Consumer's Energy Green Team and now purchases nearly 50 percent of its kilowatt-hour energy from "green" sources such as landfill gas generators and wind power plants.
- **Reuse.** Whenever possible, San Chez reuses materials to further reduce its impact on the environment. Office paper for internal use is reused on both sides, and San Chez only purchases paper made from 100 percent post-consumer waste (PCW). It uses recyclable foil instead of plastic wrap and has eliminated bottled water from the menu, choosing instead to install filters and purifiers for even better quality water.
- **Recycling.** San Chez recycles 45,000 pounds of glass, plastic, and metal per year; turns 44 gallons of fryer oil into biodiesel weekly; donates used toner cartridges to a school for recycling; and sends fluorescent light bulbs and old computer hardware to special recycling centers. Plus, San Chez now composts nearly all pre- and post-consumer waste, more than 200 tons each year.

Ask the Expert Questions:

1) When did you first become interested in reducing food, packaging, and excess utilities in your business?
Since the inception of San Chez back in 1992, I wanted our company to be energy efficient and good stewards of the environment. But I have to say we really attacked these issues with renewed vigor in 2000 and 2001. That's when we really began implementing both large and small "green" initiatives. It's been a major goal of the company ever since.

2) How did you go about making these reductions? Can you provide some specific examples?
I try to look at challenges logically. So I began by making a list of all possible reductions and then considered related variables such as associated costs, practicality, and staff training. Rather than try and tackle everything at once, I went for the "low-hanging fruit" first. Said another way, we started with things that were relatively easy. As we successfully made these reductions, the staff became central to the process. Now, it's no longer a top-down directive; it has become a company mantra that all employees willingly embrace. I think our success is due to the fact that we could quantify and measure the benefits—both financially and otherwise.

3) What tangible benefits have you realized from your "green" practices?
The known benefits are all over the map. We have garnered some very good PR due to our efforts. This has brought both community awards and increased business (read increased sales) to our doors. I know we have many customers who are loyal to us for this reason, among others. And our staff has a sense of pride and ownership in all of this.

4) How has your staff been involved in reducing waste?
The staff is central to the success of this ongoing endeavor. I have a "green committee" that volunteers to research possible ideas and practices. I give them a quarterly budget to spend on new initiatives. One of my key front-of-the-house managers, Marnie Suhr, who started with me 14 years ago while she was going through the GRCC culinary arts program, became so interested in this topic that she later pursued her bachelor's degree in Environmental Science. She now heads up my in-house Strategic Greening Plan, and has a "greening" consulting business of her own.

5) What changes do you foresee in the role of the buyer and food service operator over the next 10 years relative to "green" practices?
For things to change, buyers must gain awareness to the possibilities. And then they must set the demand from their suppliers. Suppliers will provide new products if companies create the demand.

6) What changes or "green" trends will occur in food service relative to product selection, availability, and packaging in the near future?
I'm happy to say that a lot is already happening. I think sustainability will become a part of our everyday thought process and behavior. We'll emphasize the 3 R's of reduce, reuse, and recycle, and we'll look at buying more locally.

7) Please provide your advice to a chef, buyer, or food service manager relative to the role and responsibility of buying in food service.
Start! Start now! It's okay, even better, to start slowly and deliberately so what you do works well. This process requires changing long-engrained habits for most people; it can't be done overnight. You must prioritize, assign an annual budget (because saving often requires spending), and stick to it.

Michael L. Minor, CEC, AAC

Place of Birth: Harbor Beach, Michigan

Educational Background and Work Experience

Mike Minor learned many things from his parents, but at the top of the list were the value of an education and that luck was the by-product of hard work. Minor started working at the Kellogg Center Hotel, on the campus of Michigan State University, when he was 15 years old. After graduating from Lansing Sexton High School in 1966, he went to Lansing Community College to study hospitality management while continuing to work at the Kellogg Center as its head baker. Minor served in the Vietnam War as the chef for the commanding general of the 199th Infantry Brigade, Suan Loc, Vietnam (1969–1970). After his tour was over, Minor was fortunate to be accepted as an apprentice at the famed Greenbrier Hotel in White Sulphur Springs, West Virginia. He graduated at the top of his class in 1973 and moved to Williamsburg, Virginia, to become the sous chef of the Williamsburg Inn. Chef Minor then moved to South Carolina and became the executive chef for the Deering-Milliken Research Corporation Guest House from 1974 to 1976, while also taking business-related courses at the University of South Carolina. Chef Minor then returned north to join the family business established by his father, the L. J. Minor Corporation, a leading manufacturer of food bases and sauce concentrates. In 1979, Minor was promoted to the position of plant superintendent, a position he held for five years until he became vice president of professional services for the L. J. Minor Corporation. Ten years later, Nestlé USA Food services Division purchased the company, and Minor became director of culinary services. Chef Minor retired from Nestle in 2003 and opened a successful company with his nephew that was soon purchased by Custom Culinary, where he is now the director of culinary services.

Memberships and Career Highlights

Minor received the U.S. Army Accommodation Medal for his service in Vietnam, his first of many medals. In 1980, Chef Minor traveled to Frankfurt, Germany, and competed in the Internationale KochKunst-

Courtesy Michael L. Minor

It Happened to Me...

"I was working as the Production Manager for the L. J. Minor Corporation. We had been researching new methods of manufacturing food bases using a different type of machine that would not only chop cooked meat but mix the final product as well. We tested this method using the exact machine we were considering, which was in a sausage plant owned by a friend. All of the tests were positive, so the decision was made to purchase the machine. The General Manager of the company, Mike Zelski, and I found a new machine at the Food Processor Show in Chicago at a very good show price of $80,000, which was about a $40,000 savings. We called my father and he said, "If you're sure this is the right machine, and you've done all your homework, go ahead with the purchase." We bought the machine only to find out we didn't have enough electric power in the entire plant to run the machine, nor a space to put it in. It ended up costing the company roughly $100,000 to install a new transformer that would provide the electric power necessary to run the machine. We also had to complete a room specifically designed to accommodate the machine. Once the machine was installed, it did greatly improve our productivity and product quality. However, the lesson learned in this purchasing decision was that there is more to selection and procurement than sometimes meets the eye. I never took into consideration all of the ways making this purchase would impact our manufacturing plant, and its incremental costs. We were lucky because this whole event had a positive ending, but be sure before making any purchase, large or small, that you do your research first … and always look for the hole in the doughnut."

Ausstellung (Culinary Olympics), where he earned a gold medal. He returned to the Culinary Olympics in 1984 and led a team of eight chefs to win the Grand Gold Medal. In 1986, Minor was awarded an honorary PhD in Culinary Arts from Johnson and Wales University, and later he received the prestigious Herman G. Rusch Humanitarian Award from the American Culinary Federation. He is a member of the American Culinary Federation, a member of the Institute of Food Technologists, and a founding member of the Research Chefs of America. For his many achievements, he was named a Fellow of the American Academy of Chefs and elected to the Honorable Order of the Golden Toque. In 1997, Michigan State University created the Michael L. Minor Master of Science in Food Service Management Degree,

the first food service degree program to carry an individual's name. However, even after all the accolades, Minor says that his greatest achievement was his marriage to Edwina in 1969. Luck is the by-product of hard work.

Passions with the Food Service Industry

"The greatest pleasure in the food industry is producing a quality product that will be enjoyed and appreciated by your customer. It is really no harder (and takes no more energy) to make an excellent product than it is to make something mediocre.

Teaching young culinarians about all of the products, services, and changes in today's food service industry is something

(continued)

else that I thoroughly enjoy. The tastes and trends of the dining public are ever changing, and we have to learn to change as new trends develop."

Advice to a Chef or Buyer

"When purchasing products, the first consideration is: does the product add quality and value to my establishment? If the answer is yes, then I research several companies that produce the product … along with their methods of production, raw materials, manufacturing practices, and the people you deal with. All of these criteria have to meet my expectations before I make a purchasing decision. Price is always a factor, but I always remember what my father, Dr. Lewis J. Minor, used to say, 'Quality is remembered long after the price is forgotten.'"

Key Words and Concepts

biodiversity

biotechnology

cultural
heritage

ecology

ethics

Food Allergen Labeling
and Consumer
Protection Act (FALCPA)

food composition

food irradiation

genetically engineered foods

genetically modified
organisms (GMOs)

Global Alliance for
Improved Nutrition
(GAIN)

hydroponics

Maslow's Hierarchy of
Needs

monoculture

organic

radura

sustainable agriculture

Chapter in Review

The following exercises are provided to help the reader understand and apply the contents of this chapter. They may be completed individually or in a classroom environment.

REVIEW QUESTIONS

a) Discuss Maslow's Hierarchy of Needs, and its application to modern food purchasing.

b) Discuss modern applications of hydroponics, aquaculture, and biotechnology as they relate to the available foods.

c) Discuss the cost–benefit of aquaculture as it relates to ecology and modern food service.

INDIVIDUAL ACTIVITIES

a) **Web based:** Research modern advancements in food science and technology.

b) **Experiential:** Research the marketplace to evaluate the availability of irradiated foods. (Look for the Radura symbol.)

c) **Critical thinking:** Consider how ethics affect modern food service.

GROUP ACTIVITIES

a) **Lab experience:** Bring samples of organic fruits and vegetables into the classroom or lab and compare them with their nonorganic counterparts. Compare quality factors like size, color, texture, and flavor, along with their price differences.

b) **Classroom action:** Discuss GMOs and their impact on global food service.

PART II

Purchasing Management: Mastering the Storeroom Function

CHAPTER

5

© iStockphoto.com

Measuring and Packaging for Preservation, Sale, and Distribution

"The technical progress of industry has been a reflection of our ability to apply increasingly accurate methods of measurement to material things."

LOUIS RUTHENBURG

After reading this chapter, you will be able to:

◎ Compare and contrast the methods used in food preservation, and discuss their application.

◎ Identify the methods by which fruit and vegetables can be packed.

◎ Explain the difference between *cold smoking and hot smoking*.

◎ List the various utensils used in measuring dry and liquid ingredients.

◎ Evaluate the differences in balance beam, mechanical, and digital scales, and discuss their applications in food service.

◎ Name the various packaging materials used in food service.

Introduction

Since the earliest times, people have used methods for **preserving foods**, such as salting, brining, drying, and smoking, so they could safely store their food for later consumption. Explorers such as Columbus, Magellan, Cook, Lewis, and Clark all used these methods to carry their food long distances during their travels. Later, refrigeration, canning, and drying foods helped modernize the process.

Unlike people in the past, modern food service operators have a great variety of fresh and shelf-stable products from which to choose. They can purchase local meats, fish, cheeses and produce, or foods from distant lands, perhaps even from another hemisphere. And they can buy the food in various forms: large or small, fresh or frozen, dried or smoked, canned or vacuum sealed, whole or in pieces; the choices are limitless. Depending on the requirements of their businesses, chefs can find almost any product to suit their needs.

A solid understanding of modern packaging is paramount to the role of the food service operator. Chefs and buyers both need to understand the many methods of preservation to know what effects these processes have on the foods as well as the advantages. Additionally, they need to know how foods are measured and packaged for purchase and distribution. All of this information will allow chefs and buyers to speak the language of the seller.

The Advantages of Food Preservation

People have been preserving foods in jars and bottles for ages. Archeologists regularly uncover shards of pots and other food storage devices in which many cultures would store their harvest for the lean and cold times that followed. Food preservation has played a significant role in our social and cultural history. According to Sue Shephard (2000):

> Food preserving helped make it possible for our nomadic ancestors to settle down in one place and build agrarian communities where they could live in reasonable confidence that they would not go hungry through the variable seasons and the many other difficulties that nature might throw at them. Food preserving also made it possible for some of our ancestors to travel, taking their food with them as they journeyed over long distances to explore unknown places, confident, if they could find no fresh food, that their portable provisions meant they would not starve. (p. 15)

Preserved foods provide the following benefits:

- Preserving foods while they are in season is less expensive than using out of season foods.

- Chefs can offer unique, custom-made products as signature items.

- Food that is processed directly from the field usually retains a higher level of vitamins and minerals than crops that travel many miles before they are used.

- It is convenient to have the preserved food on hand.

- The preserving agents enrich and add to the flavor of the food.

As this text will illustrate, there are many ways that food can be preserved. The following methods are discussed in this chapter: *commercial and kitchen canning, vacuum packaging, freezing,* and an assortment of *drying methods.*

THE ADVANTAGES OF CANNING

In the modern kitchen, it makes sense to capture the freshness and quality of foods while they are at their peak. To that end, preservation has become an important part of kitchen philosophy. There are many advantages to using canned products, such as:

- Canned fruits and vegetables are packed at their peak of harvest, which means they are packed at their peak nutrient value and quality.

- Every food can is hermetically sealed, which prevents contamination.

- They have long shelf lives.

- Dry storage is cheaper than refrigeration or freezing.

- Canned goods are usually cheaper than the other forms.

- Canned goods are appropriate for some recipes.

History of Canning Food

Canning dates back to the late eighteenth century when Napoleon offered a prize for developing a reliable and easily transportable method of food preservation. Nicolas Appert won the prize by putting food in airtight glass containers and then heating the containers to prevent spoilage. Later, an Englishman, Peter Durand, modified the technique, using unbreakable tin containers. A few years later, the first commercial canning factory was opened in England. Initially, lead was used to seal the cans, which leached into the food and caused illness and death. Because of that, canned food had a reputation as being dangerous.

As time went on, explorers and, later, military experts looked again at canning. They solved the lead problem, and canneries opened in the United States and other countries. Later, Louis Pasteur discovered microorganisms in the cans that caused spoilage. He found that heating or pasteurizing the food would kill the microorganisms, and the food would be safe. See Figures 5.1a-5.1g to view the kitchen-made canning process.

5.1a   **Typical utensils used for kitchen-canning**
Figures 5.1 a–g © Randy Van Dam 2008

5.1b   The canning jars are first sterilized in boiling water.

5.1c   Heated food, such as strawberry jam, is ladled into the sterilized jars.

5.1d   The rim of the jar is carefully wiped clean to create a good seal.

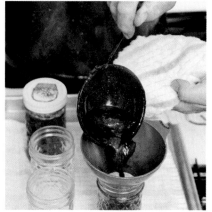

5.1e   The jars are carefully submerged under the boiling water to process for at least 15 minutes.

5.1f   After they are removed from the water bath, using a finger to test if a vacuum has formed inside the cooled jars.

5.1g   The jars are labeled to identify their contents and date of production.

Commercially Processed Canning

Canning hasn't changed much since its inception. Food is heated to temperatures high enough to destroy microorganisms and then packed into airtight containers and sealed. The food in the containers is heated under steam and pressure. The length of time and the temperature for the processing depends on the ingredients in the can, including the food's acidity, density, and heat transfer rates. The goal is to minimize the time in processing while retaining flavor and nutrition. Once a can is sealed, the food should be safe for consumption for approximately 2 years as long as the can is not damaged. Canned food does not need preservatives to keep the food safe. Cans are now made from 100 percent recycled steel and come in a wide range of sizes. (See Figures 5.2 and Tables 5.1 and 5.2.)

Sometimes the food must be processed before it is canned. Fruits and vegetables might need to be pitted or peeled, and the stems are removed. Food may be chopped or sliced for customer convenience. Seafood is usually deboned and shelled. Also, meats and fish are usually cooked prior to canning so that they will fit in the can.

> **BUYER'S NOTE** *When bacteria and microorganisms grow, they normally produce a gas that will cause the can to bulge. Never eat food from leaking, bulging, or damaged cans. Never eat food from containers that squirt liquid when opened. Do not eat any food that has an abnormal odor or appearance.*

> **BUYER'S NOTE** *Most locales ban the sale of items canned in a restaurant or food service kitchen. If a chef or owner has an original food item he wishes to sell, then he should contact a local canning facility to can the sauce or menu item. Then, this item can be sold or used in the kitchen.*

5.2 **Assorted can sizes**
© Randy Van Dam 2008; Courtesy Gordon Food Service

TABLE 5.1 **Commercial Can Sizes**

Can Size/ Number	Approximate Volume of Food	Approximate Weight of Food	Approximate Content in Milliliters	Number of Cans per Case
No. 1 picnic	1 1/4 cups	10 1/2 to 12 ounces	311 ml	24 or 48
No. 211 cylinder	1 1/2 cups	12 ounces	355 ml	24, 36, or 48
No. 300	1 3/4 cups	14 to 16 ounces	400 ml	24, 36, or 48
No. 303	2 cups	16 to 17 ounces	440 ml	12 or 24
No. 2	2 1/2 cups	20 ounces	590 ml	12 or 24
No. 2 1/2	3 1/2 cups	27 to 29 ounces	843 ml	12 or 24
No. 3	5 3/4 cups	51 ounces	1360 ml	12
No. 5	7 cups	56 ounces	1650 ml	12
No. 10	3 quarts (12–13 cups)	6 1/2 pounds to 7 pounds and 5 ounces	3070 ml	6
Gallon	4 quarts (16 cups)	128 ounces	3800 ml (3.8 L)	4 or 6

TABLE 5.2 Common Can Sizes and Their Appropriate Contents

Size	Weight	Cups	Servings
1/4	4 oz		1
3/8	6 oz		1
1/2	8 oz		2
1 picnic	10 1/2 oz		2–3
211	12 oz		3–4
300	13 1/2 oz		3–4
303	15 1/2 oz		4
2	20 oz		5
2 1/2	28 1/2 oz		7
3	33 1/2 oz		8
3 cylinder	46 oz		10–12
5	56 oz		14
10	103 1/2 oz		25

THE ADVANTAGES OF VACUUM PACKAGING

Vacuum packing (sealing) is a way to prolong the life and freshness of food. Vacuum packing removes atmospheric oxygen and moisture, making it hard for bacteria and other microorganisms to grow. For example, potato chips are normally packaged in vacuum-sealed bags to protect the chips from breaking and to prevent staling. Vacuum packaging is popular in commissary or hub kitchens because the food can be cooked in the main kitchen, vacuum packed, and then shipped to satellite kitchens.

The vacuum sealer can be either a floor unit or tabletop appliance (see Figure 5.3a and Figure 5.3b), which is used to remove the air and then seal the bag by pressing two heated strips on the bag to melt the plastic together. Most sealers have optional attachments that can seal jars, canisters, and bottles. Vacuum sealing is normally used to store dry food items such as coffee, nuts, cheeses, and smoked fish.

(BUYER'S NOTE) *Your local health department might regulate vacuum sealing, so it is important to contact this office for guidance.*

Modified Atmosphere Packaging (MAP)

A large number of foods are adversely affected by normal atmospheric conditions, particularly humidity and oxygen. These items include fresh and processed meat, fresh and dried fruit, vegetables, nuts, crackers, and fish. Oxygen supports the growth of bacteria on the surface of the meat, particularly under warm temperatures.

5.3a **Floor model vacuum processor**
© Randy Van Dam 2008

5.3b **Tabletop vacuum processor**
© Randy Van Dam 2008

Modified atmosphere packaging (MAP) is similar to vacuum sealing in that the air in the package is removed, but with MAP an additional gas is added. This gas prevents the oxygen degradation that normally happens when food is exposed to air. Some gases such as carbon dioxide may be added to retard the growth of bacteria in the stored foods.

There are a wide variety of vacuum-sealed and gas-flushed options. Fresh chicken can be bagged and placed in a box with a modified atmosphere. Fresh red meat, especially the primal and subprimal cuts, can be packaged for easy transportation. Sliced items that could quickly dry out, such as pepperoni and salami, are normally packaged with a gas. Fresh produce such as lettuce mixes are frequently packaged in **Cryovac® Barrier Bags** bags.

BUYER'S NOTE Local health departments might ban the use of MAP in food service operations, so an owner should check local food codes before using this process.

THE ADVANTAGES OF FREEZING FOODS

Freezing food is another easy and cost-effective method for preserving food. Most foods, including both raw ingredients and finished products, can be frozen. Because commercial packers freeze fruits and vegetables near the fields, frozen foods can be as nutritious as fresh-picked ones. Freezing works by stopping the chemical and biological process that allows microorganisms to flourish. Other advantages of freezing food include:

People, Places, Things

Current Food Code Requirements for Cooling

Current Food Code requires food to cool to 70°F within 2 hours, then from 70 to 41°F within 4 more hours. How can this be done? Quick-chill methods are the accepted practices for cooling food quickly. Ice bathing food, use of ice wands, or storing food in shallow layers are a few of the methods that will facilitate quicker cooling of food. Ice bathing is a process where a stockpot of hot food is placed into ice water. Ice wands are filled with water, frozen, and then used to place into hot food. Combining these methods, ice bathing while stirring food with an ice wand, provides very effective cooling for soups and sauces. When cooling in the walk-in cooler, keep food containers shallow and uncovered in the coldest part of the cooler, where there is good air circulation. Use of metal pans is recommended to transfer cold to the food. Food should never be placed in a reach-in or preparation refrigerator to cool. This equipment is designed only to hold cold food cold, not to cool hot food. During the cooling process, stirring or rotating food also quickens food cooling.

Courtesy DuPage County Health Department

- Food is prepared at the convenience of the cook or the production schedule.

- Like foods such as roasts can be cooked at the same time and then frozen, saving energy costs.

- Individual portions can be frozen for later use.

- Leftovers can be frozen and then used later as part of a planned meal.

- Special menu items such as no-salt dishes can be prepared in quantity and frozen as single servings for later use.

- Recipes that are complicated with many steps can be doubled or tripled and the extra portions frozen. This will save the kitchen production time.

Rapid, or blast, chilling has been used in the United States since the 1950s as a means of preserving food and preventing food poisoning. In 1974, France passed a law requiring food to be rapidly chilled to 50°F within 2 hours or less after cooking, or to freeze to 0°F within 4 hours. Standard walk-in coolers cannot achieve this rapid cooling, so companies like Irinox, Advance Energy Technologies, Alto-Shaam, and Delfield developed specially designed units. Though not currently a law in the United States, it is possible that the Food and Drug Administration (FDA) and United States Department of Agriculture (USDA) could require rapid chilling of cooked foods in the not-too-distant future.

Preparing to Freeze

Most foods, with the exception of fresh lettuce or elaborately iced desserts, can be frozen. If the chef is not sure how freezing will affect an item, then he should freeze a small portion and then thaw it to make sure the quality is acceptable. Cooked foods should be slightly undercooked before freezing, as the reheating process will complete the cooking. All foods should be frozen as soon as possible. Food that is held at room temperature before freezing risks contamination and loss of flavor, color, texture, and nutritional levels.

After cooking food that is to be frozen, it is necessary to cool the food as rapidly as possible to at least 60°F (15°C). The safest way to do this is to place small containers of the prepared foods in a sink of ice water. The containers should be set on supports so that the water circulates within the sink. (see Figure 5.4a) Change the water frequently, or run cold water around the pan. When the item's temperature is below the sanitation safety zone, package and freeze it immediately. For liquid items such as soups, stews, or sauces, an ice wand can be inserted into the pot to cool it down (see Figure 5.4b)

> (BUYER'S NOTE) *Do not place glass or ceramic containers in ice water as they may break.*

Packaging for Freezing

Most kitchens purchase frozen foods, but occasionally they freeze their own surplus goods, particularly when they've

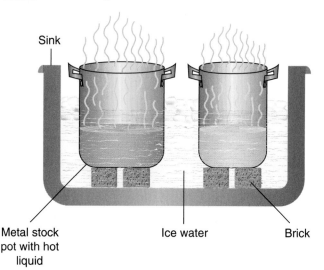

5.4a **Food cooling in a sink filled with ice water**

Sink

Metal stock pot with hot liquid

Ice water

Brick

5.4b **Ice wand inserted into hot liquids**
© Randy Van Dam 2008

purchased too much food and need to store it before it goes bad. For example, a restaurant might order food for a banquet and then later have the estimated count drop, creating a need to freeze and store food for later use.

Food should be packaged before storing in the freezer. Ideally, the quantity in each package should correspond to an issuing amount or enough for one serving at a time. This will make it easy for the cook to take out what is needed, as food should not be thawed and then refrozen. Remember, once frozen food thaws, it tends to spoil faster than fresh items. Make sure each item is labeled with the name of the item and the date that it was frozen. Before packaging, consider the following information.

- The packaging material should keep the air out and moisture in. Make sure that the container is moisture or vapor resistant or the food will dry out.

- Waxed papers, household aluminum foil, and commercial cartons such as for cottage cheese and deli salads are not moisture-vapor resistant, and if you use these, the food will dry out.

- Make sure the size is large enough to hold enough food for one day's production or for one portion of an item. If the food item is liquid, make sure there is enough head room for expansion.

- Select containers that can stack and pack easily. Reusable containers normally cost more, but they can be washed and reused. Make sure that the containers meet local health code regulations.

- Rigid containers such as those made from aluminum, plastic, or heavily waxed cardboard are good for fruits, vegetables, cooked foods, and liquids.

- Flexible containers such as cellophane bags, heavy aluminum foil, plastic film, polyethylene, or laminated paper are good for firm foods with irregular shapes such as chicken, meat, and baked goods. Bags can be used inside cartons for additional protection against moisture loss.

- Cheap packaging materials are not cost effective. Normally they will not protect the food from freezer burns or moisture loss.

FREEZING FRUITS

Excess in-season fruit can be frozen for later use, but most establishments purchase fruit that was frozen near the fields. This fruit retains most of its nutrients. Frozen fruit is available as whole berries or sliced or chopped for other fruits.

TYPES OF PACK

Fruits are frozen by large packing houses, boutique farm operations, and food service operators in much the same way. The most common packing methods include the following:

- **Sugar pack.** Sugar is sprinkled over the fruit and gently mixed. It then sits in the bowl for a few minutes to draw out the juice, and then it is frozen immediately. (See Figure 5.5a.)

- **Syrup pack.** Sugar is dissolved in lukewarm water until the solution is clear. It is then cooled and ascorbic acid is added. The syrup covers the fruit, and then it is frozen. Corn syrup is sometimes used instead of straight syrup or honey. (See Figure 5.5b.)

- **Dry pack.** Food is packed in containers, sealed, and frozen. This is a good method for small whole fruits that do not need sugar.

- **Tray pack.** Fruits, often berries, are spread over a large tray and frozen.

- **Other unsweetened packs.** Some fruits may be packed in water, unsweetened juice, or pectin syrup.

5.5a **Adding sugar to whole strawberries before freezing**
© Randy Van Dam 2008

5.5b **Adding syrup over fresh-sliced peaches before freezing**
© Randy Van Dam 2008

FREEZING VEGETABLES

Most vegetables are available in a frozen form. Like frozen fruits, frozen vegetables retain their flavor and nutrients. Most vegetables are **blanched**, or briefly immersed in boiling water or steam so that they are not tough when used.

Some vegetables, such as green onions, lettuce and other salad greens, radishes, and raw tomatoes, do not thaw well after freezing.

Most frozen vegetables are cooked without thawing. The only exception is corn on the cob, which needs partial thawing before cooking. Check any quantity food cookbook for techniques on cooking vegetables.

FREEZING MEATS

Commercially packaged frozen meats from reputable wholesalers can go directly into the freezer without any changes to the packaging. However, fresh meat must be wrapped and packaged before it is frozen. The kitchen staff should use special freezer wrap with moisture-resistant barriers to prevent moisture loss. The meat should be bagged to prevent freezer burns. One suggested method using butcher paper is as follows (see Figure 5.6):

1. Use a piece of paper that is at least three times the size of the piece of meat.

2. Place the meat in the center of the paper.

3. If needed, separate individual servings of meat (burgers, chops) with a piece of freezer paper so that they will easily separate.

4. Bring two edges of the paper together, above the meat. Fold down a half inch and then in 1-inch folds until the paper is up against the meat.

5. Press the wrap down to force the air out of the package.

6. Fold the ends over and seal the edges carefully with freezer tape.

7. Label the meat with the name of the product, distributor, case number, and date it was frozen.

5.6 Steps for wrapping meat in freezer paper

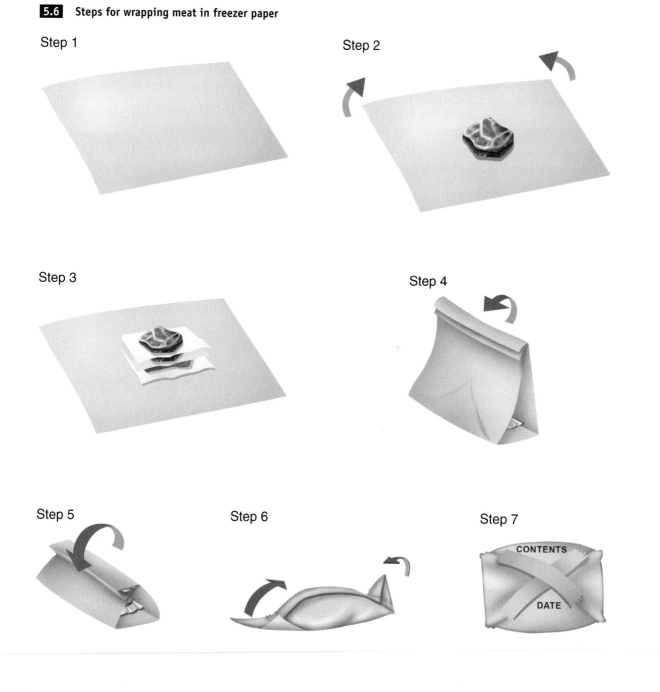

Step 1

Step 2

Step 3

Step 4

Step 5

Step 6

Step 7

CONTENTS

DATE

THE ADVANTAGES OF DRYING FOODS

Food drying is another ancient method of preserving foods. In warm, dry climates, the food is placed on racks in the sun until it is dried. In colder or more humid climates, drying is done in ovens or hot boxes. When food is dried, the moisture is taken out of the product so that microorganisms cannot grow. Dried foods can be consumed as is, or they can be reconstituted by adding water. Dried foods will not have the same appearance, taste, or nutritive value of fresh foods, but there are many advantages, including:

- Dried food last much longer, if properly stored.
- Dried foods keep well and take up less space than canned or frozen foods.
- Dried foods have a unique texture that adds appeal to menu items.
- Very little equipment is needed to dry food.
- Drying food is a great way to use up surplus goods.

Methods of Drying

Over the centuries, several dependable drying methods have been used. Not much has changed with these methods, although technology continues to improve the process. These machines are available to both the home cooking enthusiast as well as the commercial food service operator. In either case, the cost is relatively low. The common methods of drying include *dehydration, sun-drying, oven-drying,* and *air-drying.*

DEHYDRATION

Dehydration is the process of removing water from food products. All methods of drying use some form of dehydration to dry out the food. Commercial producers use dehydration to make packaged soups, coffee, tea, and most spices.

SUN-DRYING METHOD

Sun drying is an ancient method whereby food such as tomatoes and olives are placed on racks in the sun, while wind circulates around them. This system uses natural draft dryers, as illustrated in Figure 5.7. Some other foods, like coffee beans, are spread over a flat, dry surface (such as a large concrete slab) and allowed to dry. This only works with bright sunshine, low humidity, and constant temperatures of about 100°F (37.8°C).

Sun drying is a slow process; it can take weeks to completely dry out the food. While the food is drying, it might need tenting and screens to protect it from pests and

5.7 Natural draft dryer

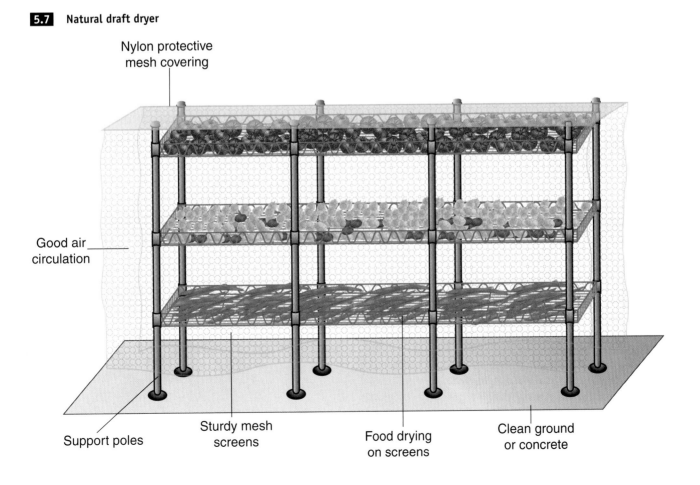

Nylon protective mesh covering

Good air circulation

Support poles

Sturdy mesh screens

Food drying on screens

Clean ground or concrete

inclement weather, and it might need to be regularly turned. Sun drying is not as sanitary as other methods of drying, and the food should be checked before using for insects, dust, and droppings.

OVEN-DRYING METHOD

Oven drying is the simplest method of drying food, as it requires almost no special equipment except for what is already available in a commercial kitchen. It tends to be a lot faster than sun drying and is generally more reliable. The only drawback to oven drying is the small amount that can be dried at one time. However, if the food is dried daily for freshness, it meets a chef's needs very well. As drying foods takes so much time, oven space must be carefully allocated. One of the best times to dry is overnight, when the space is not at a premium. To achieve consistent results, chefs should follow some basic guidelines:

- Set the oven to the lowest possible setting, and preheat to 140°F (60°C). Some ovens might run at this temperature with just the gas pilot lit.

- An accurate reading is very important, so you should check the temperature with a reliable thermometer.

- Arrange the food on trays with a half-inch (1.25 cm) gap between the items (see Figure 5.8).

- Do not overfill the oven, as this will slow the drying process. No more than four trays at a time should be used.

- Try to keep the oven slightly ajar during the drying process to allow humidity to escape.

- Encourage airflow by using the oven fan or by placing a fan close to the oven.

- If possible, rotate the trays for even drying.

AIR-DRYING METHOD

Food-drying machines come in all shapes and sizes, and they are a very reliable way of producing large quantities of dried food. They tend to operate at lower temperatures, often around 125°F (52°C), thus taking a little longer to dry than a commercial oven. However, these dryers are well ventilated and tend to dry products more evenly and with a more consistent result.

Preheat the dryer to 125°F (52°C), and place the food evenly spaced on the racks.

Stack the racks in the dryer and gradually increase the temperature to 140°F (60°C) until the food is completely dried (see Figure 5.9).

Methods for Drying Ingredients

Any ingredient that has moisture can be dried. The following ingredients are some of the more commonly dried foods.

DRYING HERBS

Growing and drying herbs has gained popularity in the commercial kitchen as an inexpensive way of keeping a dependable supply close at hand. For the best result, use only the young tender leaves that are more flavorful and aromatic when dried. When picking the herbs for drying, some important factors include:

- Cut the stalks when the leaves are mature.

- Use only the leafy tops and flower clusters for drying.

- Avoid leaves from the bottom of the stalk as they are not as fragrant as the top leaves.

- Remove all dead and discolored leaves.

5.9   **Mango and apple slices drying in a food dehydrator**
© Randy Van Dam 2008

5.8   **Tomatoes drying in an oven on a silpat**
© Randy Van Dam 2008

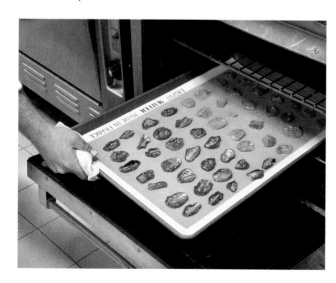

- Rinse carefully with cold water to wash off dust and dirt.

- Dry completely with paper towel.

When air-drying herbs, here are some suggestions:

- Tie a bunch of the picked herb together by the stems.

- Place the bunched herbs into a ventilated brown bag and tie shut, making sure the herb does not touch the sides of the bag.

- Hang the bag in a warm, dry, airy room or attic. Herbs will dry in 1 to 2 weeks.

- Alternately, pick the leaves and dry them on a tray in a warm, dry, airy place away from direct sunlight.

When drying in an oven, it is important that the oven be used solely for drying at that time. It should be done at an appropriate time when no one can interfere with the drying process.

- Place the clean, fresh leaves in a single layer on the racks.

- There should be at least 1 inch (2.5 cm) around the edge of the racks and between the herbs so that the air can circulate freely.

- Place in an oven set at 130°F (54°C).

- Keep the oven door propped open slightly for ventilation and to control the heat. Drying will take 2 to 4 hours.

Careful storage of the herbs is important to ensure the best quality. Use the following method:

- When the leaves are dry, shake them from the stems.

- Crush the leaves at this point; however, keep in mind that whole herbs retain their flavor longer than crushed or ground herbs.

- Store dried herbs in small airtight containers away from direct light.

DRYING VEGETABLES

Virtually all vegetables can be dried successfully in the kitchen, especially when cut small and used as garnitures for finished salads and appetizers (see Figure 5.10). Remember to always start with fresh, mature produce that is very ripe and ready to eat. When selecting vegetables for drying, there are several factors that the chef should consider:

- Harvest only what you can dry at one time.

- Wash off the dirt, and cut out the bad spots.

- Cut, slice, or chop the vegetables as desired, but note that thin pieces will dry faster than thicker ones.

- Blanch the vegetables before drying.

- Vegetables can be salted or sprinkled with herbs before drying.

- Spread the vegetables in thin layers on the trays. Make sure there is enough space for air to circulate.

- Dry strong-odor vegetables separately from other items.

5.10 **Assorted dried vegetables**
© Randy Van Dam 2008

DRYING FRUITS

When drying fruits, choose only those that were recently harvested. They should be fully ripened, naturally sweet and flavorful, and be of the same high quality that would be served at the table. Proper sanitation and cross-contamination preventions should be of the utmost importance. All fruits will need some kind of pretreatment before drying. Consider the following when drying fruit:

- Wash the fruit well, removing any leaves or dirt.

- Discard any bruised, overripe, or otherwise damaged fruit.

- Remove the unwanted parts of the fruit such as pits, seeds, stones, and cores.

- The skin can be left on the fruit: it will help support the shape of the fruit when sliced and also add a nice splash of color.

- Fruits that have a waxy skin such as plums and cherries should be blanched to remove the skin. To do so, score or crack the skins, plunge the fruit into boiling salted water, and then refresh them in an ice bath immediately. This will loosen the skin so it can be removed easily and quickly. Drain this fruit well on absorbent towels as soon as it is peeled.

- Oxidation or discoloration can occur with some light-colored fruits. If this is not stopped, it can damage the texture, flavor, aroma, and aesthetic qualities of the fruit. This darkening is due to a chemical reaction on contact with air and can be checked by the use of an antioxidant.

- Ascorbic acid diluted in water (2 teaspoons per cup for apples and 1 teaspoon per cup for other light-colored fruits) will keep fruits white during drying.

- Do not soak fruits in water before drying because the fruits will absorb the water, and this slows down the process.

- Arrange the fruits in a single layer, spaced a half inch (1.25 cm) apart, on the racks for drying.
- The length of drying time will depend on the size of the fruit pieces and the method used to dry them.

Smoking Foods

Humans have been smoking food since ancient times, probably unwittingly at first. Our ancestors commonly hung their "kill" in the rafters of their timber, straw, or stone dwellings to prevent wild animals from running off with it and also to preserve the meat through air drying. It was also common at the time to build fires in the center of these lodgings. The smoke from these fires would swirl upward and envelope the hanging meat. Chimneys were not common, and the smoke would become trapped under the sod roofs. The "blackhouses" of Scotland get their name from the soot that coated their walls and ceilings.

This is likely how the practice of smoking meat began, once it was discovered that the smoked foods lasted longer and remained in better condition. And, probably just as important, the smoke improved the taste of the otherwise unseasoned and possibly rancid meat. Once realized, smoking meats and seafood became a common method of preservation, helping to provide meat, fish, and other food for the long dark winter months (Figure 5.11).

In modern times, the smoking process still involves the same basic steps: brining, salting, or somehow curing the food; air drying it; and then smoking it slowly over a smoldering fuel source. The smoke settles on the food and forms a film called the **pellicle**. This film covers the skin and settles in the pores, penetrating the food. This gives the food its smoky flavor and kills bacteria, yeast, and other molds. The smoke also prevents oils and fats within the meat from going bad. The process extends the product's shelf life—but only to a point. Smoking is now primarily used to impart a pleasant taste and color to the food, as well as to enhance the natural flavors. The equipment and methods used to smoke food have changed dramatically as technology has progressed, and the demand for smoked products has risen.

SMOKING EQUIPMENT

The most primitive smokers were simple, enclosed vessels or rooms through which air could flow freely. This enabled the smoke to continually generate, and the heat within the chamber could be controlled. They tended to last for years, and the person operating them had an intimate knowledge of the process and knew exactly how to produce the best results.

Today, there are a host of machines available for smoking, and they all have their own procedures for use, generally according to the manufacturer's instructions (see Figure 5.12). Although it would be impossible to write about them all, this section will offer some common guidelines for and general insights into the process of smoking foods.

5.12 **Filled smoker in use**

5.11 **Food being smoked over an open fire**

UNDERSTANDING THE ELEMENTS INVOLVED IN SMOKING

The smoking chamber can be made from almost anything and comes in many shapes and sizes; however, there are some very important elements to keep in mind when choosing one (see Figure 5.13).

- The chamber should be of the appropriate size for the quantity of product.

- It should have the ability to hang smoke sticks and to receive small and large sheet pans or screens for supporting resting products.

- It should have easy access for loading, with a solid, well-sealed door.

- It should have effective dampers for releasing moisture and smoke.

- The dampers control the flow of smoke and can affect the color of the finished product. There should be a draft control at the base of the chamber to work with the damper and to create the flow of air. The dampers should be easy to operate and have the ability to stay wide open or shut, or any point in between, as required.

The heat source can be wood, peat, pellet, gas, or electric. It must work dependably, and it should have accurate and reliable temperature gauges and controls so as to monitor the cooking process properly. The heat source does not have to double as the smoke source, and often it works in conjunction with a smoke source.

The smoke source can be exterior to the food chamber and heat source where it is more versatile and controllable. It should have the capabilities for both cold smoking and hot smoking. The smoke source should be fitted with a fan to allow for a controlled flow of smoke, enabling it to produce a consistent amount of smoke for a consistent length of time. The fan also enables the chamber to be used for cold smoking as the heat source can be turned off independently.

The humidity control allows for a greater range of products that can be smoked, including dried and semi-dried sausage and meats that have to be very carefully monitored. If the chef is working with a large quantity, it is sometimes better to do this drying process in a separate air-controlled room that will draw the moisture out and control the relative humidity. The ideal conditions for this drying process are between 45°F and 55°F (7.2°C and 12.8°C) with a humidity of 70 to 72 percent.

The type of fuel used will affect the flavor of the product, so it should be carefully selected (see Table 5.3). Certain foods can be paired with specific woods to complement the flavors; these pairings are also represented in Table 5.3. A combination of hardwoods, such as oak, alder, and mesquite, generally provides the best results for smoking. Fruit woods, such as cherry and apple, contain a lot of tar compounds

5.13   **Drawing of parts to a smoker**

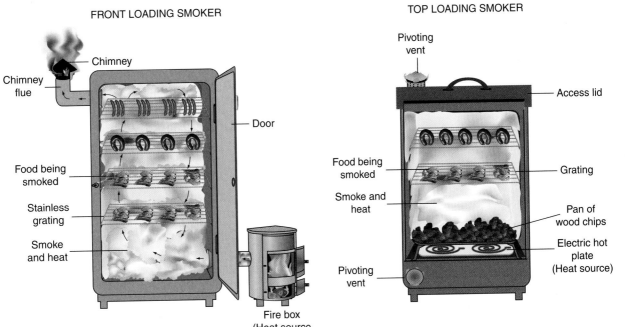

FRONT LOADING SMOKER

Chimney
Chimney flue
Door
Food being smoked
Stainless grating
Smoke and heat
Fire box (Heat source with hardwood)

TOP LOADING SMOKER

Pivoting vent
Access lid
Food being smoked
Smoke and heat
Grating
Pan of wood chips
Electric hot plate (Heat source)
Pivoting vent

TABLE 5.3   **Common Fuels Used in Smoking**

Type of Fuel	Type of food	Strength	Soaking	Flavor
Fruit woods: peach, apple, cherry	Poultry, game, pork, and salmon	Mild	30 minutes	Sweet
Pecan wood	Turkey, goose, and salmon	Delicate; dark color	1 hour	Delicate pecan flavor
Alder wood	Salmon, trout, swordfish, fish roe, chicken, and pork	Medium to mild, good color	1 hour	Wood smoke flavor
Mesquite wood	Beef, duck, lamb, and some strong fish	Medium; more delicate than hickory	1–2 hours	Sweet, delicate flavor
Hickory wood	Hams, bacon, turkey, beef ribs, and any pork cut	Strong, smoky	1–2 hours	Strong, pungent, and smoky
Grapevine	Fish and delicate poultry and game	Very delicate	30 minutes	Light and slightly fruity
Spices	All foods (should be added to wood as a flavor enhancer)	Smolder only for a delicate taste	30 minutes	Light and slightly fragrant
Air-dried peat	Oily fish, especially herring, mackerel, and salmon	Smolder only for delicate flavor and color	No soaking	Rich peaty aroma with good coloring qualities

and should be used sparingly or in combination with hard-woods. Soaking the dried wood well, prior to its use, helps to give a colder smoke and a much better final product. Soaked rice, tea leaves, spices, specialty woods, dried fruit skins, dried peat, and plant leaves are some examples of fuel alternatives used throughout the world (see Figure 5.14).

COLD AND HOT SMOKING

There are two methods of smoking food: **cold smoking** and **hot smoking**. As their names suggest, cold smoking is done

 5.14   **Peat being cut and stacked on a Scottish moor**
Photo courtesy Robert Garlough

without heat, and hot smoking is done with heat. Cold smoking merely imparts a smoke flavor and color without increasing the internal temperature of the food, allowing it to remain raw if desired. Hot smoking raises the internal temperature of the product and helps to cook the food.

Cold smoking is done by controlling the flow of smoke from the smoke generator, preferably located on the outside of the chamber, and blowing the smoke over the food with the heat source switched off. Alternatively, the heat source can be left on if the food is placed between two layers of ice on pans, thus preventing the heat from getting to the food. The time and amount of smoke differs by recipe and needs to be carefully watched.

Hot smoking is done by controlling the heat and application of smoke over a long period of time, allowing the food to cook and the smoke to penetrate evenly.

> BUYER'S NOTE   *Wood chips should be soaked for at least 30 minutes before using. Put the food on the grill and then add the chips directly to the charcoal for a stronger flavor.*

The Need for Measuring

Measuring is the process of calculating the amount of an ingredient by using a standard measurement device, such as a measuring spoon, measuring cup, or measuring utensil. The quality of the food in any dining facility can be controlled to a great extent by the strict adherence to the recipes. Ingredients inaccurately weighed and measured may yield unsatisfactory products or shortages in inventory. Assigning responsibility for weighing and measuring ingredients to properly trained personnel reduces the possibility of using incorrect amounts.

To produce consistent products of high quality, chefs and storeroom managers must know the sizes and yields of all pans, measures, ladles, and other equipment used in preparing and serving the food. The provision of proper and adequate equipment, including measuring equipment, is a responsibility of the supervising chef.

HISTORY OF MEASURING WEIGHT AND VOLUME

Over the centuries, **systems of measurement** were based on a local unit such as a king's thumb or by making containers the size of a fist. While these units were useful in the local markets, they could not be used by merchants trading in different markets. As time went on, these units became **customary units**, which were standard across a country or at least within a region.

At the end of the eighteenth century, King Louis XVI of France asked his leading scientists to create a standardized system of measurement that could replace all of the different systems that were in use. This group produced the metric system, which managed to survive the French Revolution and was adopted in many different countries. Now, the metric system is used in most countries except the United States. Because it is so prevalent worldwide, most food is packaged in metric units as well as standard U.S. measurements.

> **BUYER'S NOTE** *A meter is one ten-millionth of the length of the earth's meridian along a quadrant (the meridian through Paris from pole to the equator), and a liter weighs 1 kg and measures 1 dm³. Later, the Celsius measurement for temperature was derived from this system.*

Laws to Regulate Measurement

Laws were originally developed to prevent fraud in measuring items. Back then, they would compare a measurement used to a standard. Now most units of measurement are scientifically defined and are confirmed by international treaties. In the United States, commercial measurements are regulated by the National Institute of Standards and Technology (NIST), a division of the Commerce Department. Internationally, these standards are maintained by the *Bureau International des Poids et Measures* (BIPM) in Paris. This body works to ensure worldwide uniformity of measurements among the 51 nations that have agreed to this treaty. The BIPM ensures that the calibration is the same for every country.

SCALES

A **scale** is a device used to measure the weight of an object. **Weight** is the measurement of an ingredient's mass or the level of gravity that is acting on the ingredient. Solids such as food, or occasionally liquids, are measured according to their gravitational force on the scale. Modern scales come in three general varieties, as shown in Figure 5.15, and each is used in food service.

- **Balance beam.** This is still one of the most accurate means of measuring weight. The desired weight is placed on one arm of the scale, and the ingredients are added to the other side until they balance. Balance beam scales are still used in open markets and in baking.

- **Mechanical or spring.** This scale is less accurate but does measure close enough for most culinary work. This scale has a calibrated spring that moves linearly as weight is added to the pan. Spring scales are available as table units or hanging units, making them more practical for day-to-day kitchen work.

- **Electronic (digital).** The digital scale can be either a floor model used for weighing large quantities at receiving or, more commonly, as a tabletop unit used for scaling ingredients during issue or food preparation. Digital models usually measure in ounces and pounds, as well as grams and kilograms. They have tare buttons that allow users to subtract the container's weight. As their price has become more reasonable, their accuracy and flexibility make the digital scale the tool of choice in modern food service establishments, particularly with bakeries and formal storeroom operations.

The proper and consistent use of scales is essential to portion control in both the storeroom and production kitchen, and it is possibly the most important tool available to the receiving clerk. Operators must not neglect their use in favor of visually estimating weight.

5.15 From left to right, spring-loaded mechanical scale, electronic digital scales, and balance beam scale
© Randy Van Dam 2008

MEASURING TOOLS

A variety of special utensils, designed to gauge ingredients in other ways, are also available. Measuring tools are used to quantify the volume of either liquid or dry ingredients (see Table 5.4). Measuring spoons and cups can be single slide measures. Semi-soft ingredients, such as butter or shortening, can be measured with sliding canisters. Each tool is typically created to assist the measuring process in a unique and efficient manner. Examples of sizes include:

- **Measuring spoons.** These are available in a variety of sizes and materials (see Figure 5.16a). The smallest sets of spoons measure a smidgen, a pinch, and a dash. Other sets contain U.S. customary measures: teaspoon (tsp) and tablespoon (tbsp) measures of 1/8 tsp, 1/4 tsp, 1/2 tsp, 3/4 tsp, 1 tsp, 1 1/2 tsp, 2 tsp, 2 1/2 tsp, and 1 tbsp. They also come in metric (milliliter, or ml) sizes: 0.6 ml, 1.25 ml, 2.5 ml, 3.75 ml, 5 ml, 7.5 ml, 10 ml, 12.5 ml, and 15 ml.

- **Measuring cups.** These are available as either dry or liquid measures:

  - Dry measures generally include 1/8, 1/4, 1/3, 1/2, 1, and 2 cups in U.S. measures, or 30 ml, 60 ml, 80 ml, 120 ml, and 240 ml in metric units (see Figure 5.16b).

  - Liquid measuring cups can range from 1 teaspoon, or 5 milliliters, to 16 cups, or 3.8 liters. The smallest cup measures 1 to 6 teaspoons, or 5 to 30 milliliters. Medium-sized cups hold U.S. measures of 1 to 2 cups, 1 to 4 cups, or 1 to 8 cups. Large measures hold 1 quart to 4 quarts. For metric measures, the sizes come in 100 to 500 ml, 100 ml to 1000 ml (1 liter), or 100 ml to 2 liters (see Figure 5.16c).

- **Measuring ladles.** Ladles are used to portion and serve gumbos, stews, soups, sauces, gravies, salad dressings, and other liquids or semi-liquids. The most common ladles come in 1- to 12-ounce sizes (see Figure 5.16d and Table 5.5).

5.16a **Assorted measuring spoons**

Figures 5.16 a–d © Randy Van Dam 2008

5.16b **Assorted dry measures**

5.16c **Assorted liquid measures**

5.16d **Assorted scoops and ladles**

TABLE 5.4   **Dry and Liquid Measure Equivalents**

Dry Measuring Equivalents
1 tablespoon = 3 teaspoons = 15 ml
1/8 cup = 2 tablespoons = 30 ml
1/4 cup = 4 tablespoons = 50 ml
1/3 cup = 5 1/3 tablespoons = 75 ml
1/2 cup = 8 tablespoons = 125 ml
2/3 cup = 10 2/3 tablespoons = 150 ml
3/4 cup = 12 tablespoons = 175 ml
1 cup = 16 tablespoons = 250 ml

Liquid Measuring Equivalents
1 cup = 8 fluid ounces = 1/2 pint
2 cups = 16 fluid ounces = 1 pint = 1/2 quart
4 cups = 32 fluid ounces = 2 pints = 1 quart = 1/4 gallon
8 cups = 64 fluid ounces = 4 pints = 2 quarts = 1/2 gallon
16 cups = 128 ounces = 6 pints = 4 quarts = 1 gallon

TABLE 5.5 Ladle Sizes and Measures

Ladle Size	Part of a Cup
1 ounce	1/8
2 ounce	1/4
2 2/3 ounce	1/3
4 ounce	1/2
6 ounce	3/4
8 ounce	1
12 ounce	1 1/2

TABLE 5.6 Scoop Sizes, Weights, and Volume Capacities

Scoop Size Number	Volume (U.S. Customary)	Approximate Weight (U.S. Customary)
6	2/3 cup	5 ounce
8	1/2 cup	4 ounce
10	3 fluid ounce	3 to 3 1/2 ounce
12	1/3 cup	2 1/2 to 3 ounce
16	1/4 cup	2 to 2 1/2 ounce
20	1 1/2 fluid ounce	1 3/4 ounce
24	1 1/3 fluid ounce	1 1/2 ounce
30	1 fluid ounce	1 ounce
40	7/8 fluid ounce	7/8 ounce
60	1/2 fluid ounce	1/2 ounce

- **Measuring scoops.** Standard-sized food scoops or dippers are used to serve specific-sized portions of semi-solid or solid foods, such as cole slaw, cottage cheese, mashed potatoes, and ice cream (see Figure 5.16d). Recipes for schools, restaurants, and other commercial food service establishments refer to these standard scoop sizes. Scoop sizes are determined by the number of level scoops that it will take to fill a quart. For example, a number 8 scoop produces eight half-cup portions from one quart, and a number 16 scoop produces sixteen quarter-cup portions from one quart. Table 5.6 lists the various scoop sizes and their equivalent measurements in terms of ounces, milliliters, or grams.

Commercial Packaging Options

Packaging has changed over the years. In earlier times, most kitchens used glass or tin to keep food safe. Later, metallic and plastic containers were developed. Packaging is normally used for several purposes, including:

- Providing a barrier against dirt and other contaminants.
- Preventing loss of moisture from leakage.
- Protecting food from physical and chemical damage, as well as damage from air and sunlight.
- Protecting food from insects, vermin, and rodents.
- Helping employees transport food around the kitchen.
- Motivating customers to purchase the foodstuffs (for products they can see) and providing cooking and nutritional information.

PROPERTIES OF PACKAGING MATERIALS

Each packaging material has certain properties that make it more suitable for specific food products.

TYPES OF PACKAGING

As mentioned earlier in the chapter, there are several different types of packaging available to a restaurant owner or manager. Normally, the types of packaging are divided into three categories:

- **Flexible packaging.** This is packaging that can expand to hold the product and move with the person carrying it. One example of flexible packaging includes the plastic or paper bags used to carry home to-go orders (see Figure 5.17a).
- **Semi-flexible packaging.** This packaging is mostly rigid but has some flexibility. Some examples include cereal boxes and the soft foam plastic for cookies, crackers, and other soft foods (see Figure 5.17b).
- **Rigid packaging.** This packaging does not expand or move with the product. Examples include crates, bottles, and metal cans (see Figure 5.17c).

 Flexible packaging
© Randy Van Dam 2008; Courtesy Gordon Food Service

5.17b Semi-flexible packaging

Figures 5.17b–.18b © Randy Van Dam 2008

5.18a Leaves used in wrapping foods

5.17c Rigid packaging

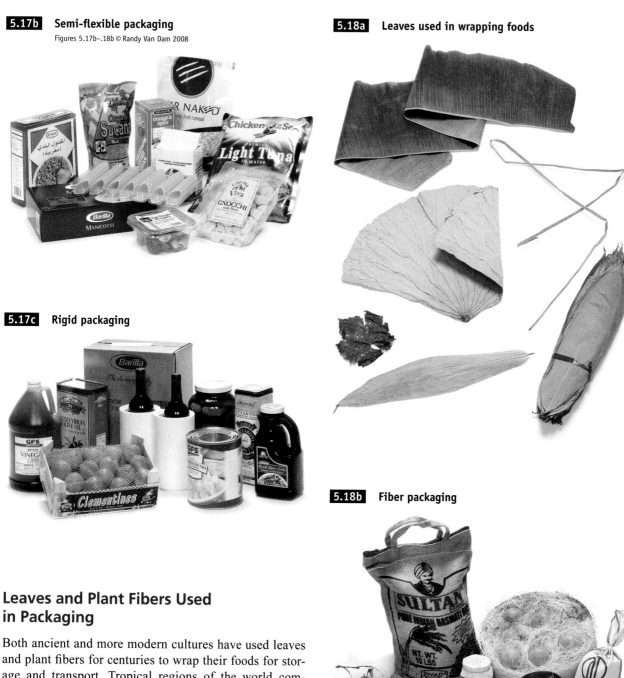

5.18b Fiber packaging

Leaves and Plant Fibers Used in Packaging

Both ancient and more modern cultures have used leaves and plant fibers for centuries to wrap their foods for storage and transport. Tropical regions of the world commonly use banana and plantain leaves, and vegetable fibers such as jute, raffia, and yucca, to wrap assorted food products. Mediterranean regions use grape leaves, while Asian regions favor bamboo leaves to wrap both raw and cooked foods. Although both inexpensive and biodegradable, they can be impractical as they fail to protect the food against moisture, oxygen, and microorganisms (see Figures 5.18a and 5.18b).

Paper Used in Packaging

Paper and cardboard have been widely used for over 100 years, and may be the oldest form of flexible packaging. Although plastic gained ground in its broad use for food packaging, the

biodegradable benefits of using paper packaging have caused its resurgence (see Figure 5.19).

Glass Used in Packaging

As an ancient form of rigid packaging, glass has been used in modern times for more costly ingredients and those

5.19 **Paper and cardboard packaging**
© Randy Van Dam 2008; Courtesy Meijer, Inc.

5.20 **Glass packaging**
© Randy Van Dam 2008

 5.21 **Mustard in earthenware packaging**
© Randy Van Dam 2008; Courtesy SYSCO Food Services of Grand Rapids

5.22 **Metal packaging**
© Randy Van Dam 2008; Courtesy SYSCO Food Services of Grand Rapids

requiring the flavor and aroma protection provided by glassware. Glass is also considered a higher-quality container, and is preferred for its visual benefits (see Figure 5.20).

Earthenware Used in Packaging

Earthenware containers are still used worldwide, as they have been for centuries, although their use has lessened in favor of glassware during the last several decades. Glazed pots and crocks have been used since ancient times to store oil, wine, and fruit, while unglazed crocks were used for cheese curds. Today, certain charcuterie products, such as pate and whole grain mustard, are the most commonly used ingredients packed in earthenware crockery (see Figure 5.21).

Metals Used in Packaging

Metal is now widely used for storing raw foods in cans, such as vegetables and fruits, as well as the use of aluminum foil for wrapping foods (see Figure 5.22).

 BUYER'S NOTE *Acidic foods, such as tomatoes and citrus fruits, can degrade aluminum foil wrapping and containers.*

Plastics Used in Packaging

Although plastics have existed for nearly 200 years, their use for storing foods is the most recent of the storage materials discussed in this chapter.

Modern packaging designs commonly use recyclable and recycled plastics, but the search for other reuse functions continues (see Figure 5.23).

Wood Used in Packaging

Wood has been used for centuries in food service, from cutting boards and tabletops to packaging, storage, and shipping. Because wood is an absorbent and porous material,

5.23 **Plastic packaging**
© Randy Van Dam 2008

5.24 **Wood packaging**
© Randy Van Dam 2008

the hygienic properties of wood are disputed. Furthermore, wood is said to be more difficult to clean and sanitize than other materials.

Results from recent research and development studies show, however, that wood has good hygienic properties.

Good manufacturing quality, good handling practice, and proper sanitation treatments still make wood a suitable material for most applications in the food service industry (see Figure 5.24). However, operators must review their local health codes for the final determination.

William A. Lyman, CEC, AAC

Place of Birth: Minneapolis, Minnesota

Educational Background and Work Experience

Growing up in suburban Minneapolis, Bill Lyman's friend helped him get his first high school job at the Central Avenue Café. Besides his dishwashing and floor-mopping duties, Lyman peeled, cut, and blanched potatoes for French fries. (Lyman was from an era when commercially frozen French fries weren't available, and dishwashers made their own soap from old fryer shortening and lye.) Lyman left his cook's helper job after graduating from high school in 1950 to butcher chicken and fish for a talented French chef at the Minikahda Country Club. Lyman earned $150 a month working 10 1/2 hour days, six days a week. But his real pay came in the foundation that was built while preparing haute cuisine at a prestigious country club. After a stint in the military, Lyman continued to build his career with cook's and chef's positions in a few small hotels and by taking a few summer classes at The Culinary Institute of America, then located in New Haven, Connecticut. Chef Lyman eventually accepted the position of research and development chef for General Mills in 1966, one of the country's first R&D chefs. Lyman worked with soy proteins as a meat replacement with items like Baco-Bits. He later accepted a similar position with the Litton Microwave Oven Company, when microwave ovens first came into prominence. That position led Chef Lyman to become the developmental manager of Cook Chill Systems for the Cryovac Division of the W. R. Grace company—at the time, the foremost leader in food packaging systems. After 11 years, he was promoted to vice president of research and development for Grace Culinary Systems. Now retired from W. R. Grace, Chef Lyman continues working as an industry consultant setting up USDA-approved Cook-Chill facilities for major food service manufacturers around the United States and abroad.

Memberships and Career Highlights

After traveling to Frankfurt, Germany, in 1964 to observe the Internationale Kochkunst Ausstellung (Culinary Olympics), Lyman was given the opportunity on short notice to compete as an independent. Always the positive thinker, Lyman took the chance and worked 72 hours straight

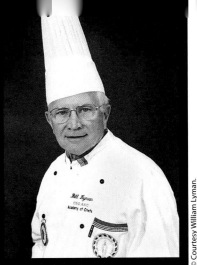

© Courtesy William Lyman.

It Happened to Me...

"Through all these years, I started my cooking career as a green-horn high school kid flipping burgers at a short order restaurant, and finished many years later as an executive chef in the consulting business, training employees to produce food in large batches for packaging equipment.

If I were to give someone advice based on my life experiences, I would say get your education. In the early years working in the food industry, I had no formal culinary education. A friend told me that the Culinary Institute of America had a summer short course so I spent two months at the CIA in New Haven, Connecticut, working with the finest instructors. They taught me the basics of cooking and baking so that I could move on to more challenging positions.

Every time I visit a culinary school in the United States, I'm amazed how well the students are prepared for chef positions when they graduate. The only way I was able to learn through many years was to observe, and then jump in to do the job. How fortunate these young men and women are to have great instructors and accredited schools to prepare them for their career in the food industry."

to earn himself a bronze medal. That kind of "can-do" attitude has proven to be Lyman's hallmark. He is always willing to help others in their careers. Keenly interested in culinary colleges, Chef Lyman has been a visiting chef-lecturer to many schools and served as the chairman of the Accrediting Commission for the American Culinary Federation. He is still an active member of the Research Chefs of America (RCA) and the American Culinary Federation (ACF). For his lifetime contributions to the food service industry, Lyman was named a Fellow of the American Academy of Chefs and serves as Grand Commander of the Honorable Order of the Golden Toque, an international culinary honor society limited to 100 living chefs.

Passions with the Food Service Industry

"My passion for working in the food industry started so many years ago as a fry cook in a local restaurant. It was just a job for a teenager wanting to make a few extra bucks! I soon found the joy of preparing food was a gratifying experience. Working in restaurants and country clubs with exceptional chefs, many foreign-born, taught me the skills I needed to move

ahead in the food industry field. Eleven years as a research chef at General Mills and five years at Litton Industries strengthened my interest in the commercial side of food preparation. My greatest opportunity came when Cryovac, which was a division of W. R. Grace, employed me to start working in the Cook Chill System. I spent seventeen years in the preparation and packaging of cook chill foods in large commissaries and production facilities. Part of this time was with Grace Culinary Systems using only Cook Chill production for chain restaurants and wholesale food manufacturers."

Advice to a Chef or Buyer

"I would advise a chef or food service manager to employ talented young people as apprentices who have graduated from one of the many fine culinary arts schools. It's also important for chefs and managers to attend the various trade shows for information on the latest ingredients, equipment and technology that is available. Use the technical support available to you through your suppliers.

Purchasing agents should not forget quality when trying to reduce costs for the facility. The most popular sales person may not be the one with the best product."

Key Words and Concepts

---

blanched	food drying	pellicle	systems of measurement
canning	freezing food	preserving food	vacuum packing (sealing)
cold smoking	hot smoking	rigid packaging	weight
Cryovac® Barrier Bag	measuring	scale	
customary units	modified atmosphere packaging (MAP)	semi-flexible packaging	
flexible packaging	oven drying	sun drying	

Chapter in Review

The following exercises are provided to help the reader understand and apply the contents of this chapter. They may be completed individually or in a classroom environment.

REVIEW QUESTIONS

a. Identify and describe the different methods of packing fruit.

b. Describe the steps in canning prepared foods according to the boiled water bath method.

c. Discuss the difference between hot and cold smoking and when each method is most appropriate.

d. Identify the various types of food scales, and determine their best uses.

INDIVIDUAL ACTIVITIES

a. **Web based:** Research Cryovac® Barrier Bags and their uses.

b. **Experiential:** Line up different-sized cans, and practice identifying them by their can number and volume capacity.

c. **Critical thinking:** Identify all forms of flexible food packaging, and consider which is best for use with the foods listed on a sample menu.

GROUP ACTIVITIES

a. **Lab experience:** Prepare some cooked foods, such as chutney, applesauce, salsa, and jam, and then can them using the boiled water bath method.

b. **Classroom action:** Identify twenty different types of food, and discuss how they may be packaged differently for preservation or sale.

© iStockphoto.com/ Vetta Collection

The Ingredient Process

"For the things of this world cannot be made
known without a knowledge of mathematics."
ROGER BACON

After reading this chapter, you will be able to:

- ◎ Identify the various considerations made when planning a menu.

- ◎ Define standardized recipes, and identify the type of information contained in writing the recipe.

- ◎ Explain the purpose of product specifications, and list the characteristics that can be used to describe the product.

- ◎ Illustrate the considerations made in conducting quality analysis.

- ◎ Summarize the ABC analysis method and its benefits to operators who conduct them.

- ◎ Describe how yield cost analyses are performed.

- ◎ Evaluate the use of convenience foods, and the concept of make-or-buy analysis.

- ◎ Relate the different blind tests that buyers perform when evaluating products, including drain weight, taste and texture, and size and count.

Introduction

Ingredients are the central focus of the buyer, and the process of selecting the most beneficial products for the operation involves many considerations. Favorable purchasing means matching the specific characteristics of the ingredient to the specific needs of the business. As stated in Chapter 1, the buyer's ultimate goals are to sustain the operation's competitive status, maintain an adequate supply of storeroom wares, obtain the lowest possible serving cost while ensuring the most appropriate quality, and minimize the company's product investment.

To accomplish these goals, the buyer must follow a sequential and deliberate process—the "ingredient process"—with input from all departments within the operation and as well as outside sources. This chapter discusses the steps involved in identifying the most appropriate ingredients to purchase for a food service business.

Waste and overtime labor costs are the primary reasons for going out of business. Whether a manufacturing plant that has too high a scrap rate or a restaurant that is inefficient with its food purchasing and production methods, no business can withstand the mismanagement of time and ingredients. The success of the food enterprise depends on the effective control of its ingredient process.

Planning the Menu

With most food service operations, the process of ingredient selection begins with the menu. In fact, creating the menu is one of the first activities to be completed when planning or designing a food service operation. To plan the menu, upper management must consider *target markets, consumer demand, required contribution margins, available staffing and skills, seasonality and availability of foodstuffs, available equipment and facilities,* and finally the *preferences of chefs, owners, and operators.*

- **Target markets.** The first consideration when planning the menu is to clearly identify the target market. The target market is the customer base that will primarily support the business.

- **Consumer demand.** The second consideration is the wants and needs of the potential customer base. By analyzing local and national consumer trends and considering customer surveys, operators can plan a menu that will be well received by the consumer. Customers will frequent the food service operations that meet their menu and service expectations. Whether offering quick-service, family, or fine dining, menus must be designed to address anticipated consumer demand.

- **Required contribution margins.** Menu options, and their individual pricing strategies, must be constructed to meet required profit margins. A profit margin is the percent of sales remaining after expenses have been satisfied. Profitability is the mandate of all operators, and menus are the tools for creating the necessary sales.

- **Available staffing and skills.** The employees' skill level is important to consider when planning the menu. It is unwise to plan a menu that is beyond the abilities of its staff to prepare in a consistent manner.

- **Seasonality and availability of foodstuffs.** The consistent availability of ingredients, including their potential for fluctuations in cost and quality due to seasonal influences, must be thoroughly researched before deciding on the menu.

- **Available equipment and facilities.** When menus are developed for established food service operations with existing kitchen facilities, the available equipment must be analyzed (see Figure 6.1). Each piece of equipment is designed for one or more methods of preparation or cookery. Menus must conform to the available equipment, or the additional cost of new equipment must be added to the overhead.

- **Owner, operator, or chef preferences.** Oftentimes, chefs and owners allow their personal preferences to influence menu creation. All owners should take advantage of their chef's knowledge, but it should not be the final consideration in menu planning.

Market Research

Once the buyer has identified the product needs for the food service operation, she must begin to conduct market research. **Market research** involves methodically gathering data and then analyzing the results. Market research can be used to investigate potential ingredients, customers, and suppliers. Market research also helps chefs find new ingredients and vendors.

Market research helps owners and managers make decisions about their recipes and ingredients based on accurate data. Following is a list of questions that a properly designed market research study can answer.

- What is going on in my local market, the regional market, and the national market?

- What are some of the new food trends?

- What are consumers saying about products in the market?

- Who are the competitors that use these products?

- What are my needs and the needs of my customers?

- What are the most important needs of my customers?

6.1 **Equipment Analysis for Menu Development**

Location	Equipment	Potential Cooking Methods
Pantry		
	2-door freezer	
	4-door freezer	
	Reach-in cooler	
	2-bay prep sink	
	8-ft work table	
	Slicer	
	Food processor	
	20-qt mixer/grinder	
Cooking Battery		
	Walk-in freezer	
	Walk-in cooler	
	16-range burners	
	2-drawer broiler	
	4 under ovens	
	2 convection ovens	
	Steamer	
	3-bay fryer	
	16-ft work table	
	Steam table	
Bakery/Pastry		
	60-qt mixer	
	30-qt mixer	
	Food processor	
	Stackingdeck oven	
	12-ft work table	

- Are those needs being met by my current ingredients or recipes?
- Where can I find these new ingredients?
- Can my normal vendors obtain these ingredients?

If the market research indicates that a menu item will not be popular, or ingredients are not available, then the dish must be modified or dropped.

BUYER'S NOTE — *In other areas of business, market research also applies to gathering information about competitors and consumer preferences.*

Recipe Development

Recipes are the foundation of production management and storeroom operations. When developing recipes, the chef or kitchen manager must meet the menu expectations of the customers while also meeting the profitability demands of the operation. Yet the chef or kitchen manager also must design the menu with other less apparent, but still important, needs of the business in mind. These needs might include cross-utilization of product due to limited storage space, minimal variety of dishware to plate the food, and limited ingredients because of seasonal fluctuations in price or quality.

Skilled chefs can design recipes and menus that use the ingredients in advantageous ways. As the ingredients are the biggest variables in any recipe, considered and clever use of these ingredients can be a major benefit to the business, including the storeroom operation.

CROSS-UTILIZATION

The benefits of **cross-utilization**, where both raw and pre-pared food products are used in multiple fashions, are seen many areas of the kitchen, including procurement, inventory management, cash flow, and food production. The ability to use the same product specifications for items like sausage, chicken breast, shrimp, and cut vegetables helps to reduce inventory while streamlining food production and decreasing the overall costs of procurement.

[ASK THE EXPERT]

Phillip Lopez
Professional Food Service Buyer

Name: Phillip Lopez

Title: Director of Procurement

Employer: River Oaks Country Club

Background and General Responsibilities:
Phil Lopez gained many of his foundational skills with inventory control as an applied mathematics major at the University of Houston. He gained a well-rounded understanding of country club operations while serving as the assistant beverage manager, kitchen manager, and purchasing manager over a 10-year period at the Houston Country Club. In 2006, after various jobs in food and equipment sales and marketing, Lopez joined the staff at Houston's prestigious River Oaks Country Club as the director of procurement. River Oaks is considered one of the nation's top ten country clubs and does nearly $10 million in food and beverage sales annually. As the director of procurement, Lopez developed, implemented, and now maintains the centralized system of purchasing. He implemented a computerized inventory system that integrates the club's purchasing, receiving, inventory, and cost reporting systems. Lopez is also working with club management to develop and monitor a 5-year capital budget process.

Ask the Expert Questions:

1) How has the role of buyer changed in the past 10 years?
Knowledge of product. Today's buyer is held accountable for more product knowledge than ever before—from pricing, to ingredients, to availability. Chefs are getting more creative and demanding, and buyers need to know where to source different products from and in a timely manner. Ten years ago, chefs would tell the buyer what to buy and from where to buy it. Buyers are now more of a partner with chefs, bringing new items, helping to create the product specification list.

2) What changes do you foresee in the role of the buyer over the next 10 years?
I see the role of buyer becoming an area of specific training. If managers knew more about what it takes to order, receive, store, distribute, and inventory various items, they could be of much greater help to any operation.

3) What changes do you foresee in the role of the seller over the next 10 years?
More and more vendors are producing "main supplier" programs. With the larger vendors acquiring smaller companies (i.e., produce), I see more of these full-service programs being used. These programs allow audits when requested, allowing the transparency needed for both sides. This creates true business partnerships.

4) How is technology used in food service today relative to ordering, receiving, storing, inventorying, issuing, and cost controls? Please provide examples.
Technology is used in many computer programs that help the buyer in many ways; the one I am most familiar with (use) is FoodTrak. It helps us to create shopping lists, Purchase Orders, inventory lists (with which a buyer can also have a perpetual inventory, based on what has been received and what has been issued). The program can also give you sales prices based on your budgeted food cost (this is done by being able to input recipes into the program and having your actual cost of the recipe). FoodTrak also aids our accounting department. We can input GL accounts for each item, making sure that items are charged to the correct cost center (helping with cost controls as well).

5) What changes or trends will occur in food service relative to product selection and availability in the near future?
The consumer always dictates change. With consumers becoming more and more educated about food, I think the demand for healthier, smaller portioned, and well-balanced meals will be commonplace, if not already here. For example, some quick-service places are offering fruit with kids' meals. This demand will necessitate increased availability. For example, I can remember not too long ago when "spring mix" salad greens were a special order; now everyone stocks it.

6) What concerns or predictions do you hold for the global marketplace? What issues, such as source identification, GMOs, crop sustainability, endangered species, seasonality, buying local versus outsourcing, and increased transportation costs will become even more relevant in the near future?
With the media keeping a close eye for and ready to report the next "XYZ" product causing "ABC," I believe manufactures will volunteer better source certificates. Food service has to be able to supply these products in order to survive. Buying local is nice for the community, but it can increase your food cost. Speaking for larger food service operations, I do not think transportation fees will become more relevant. I believe the economy will be back and transportation costs not being a factor.

7) How do you see your role in relation to the production areas and staff?
As a mentor. It is my job to help educate the staff as to what goes into bringing a product in, the price point of A vs. B (with some staff, this also leads into the selling price as well), the need for maintenance of an item (help them think of replacement cost), and the general cleanliness of the area(s).

8) Please provide your advice to a chef, buyer, or food service manager relative to the role and responsibility of buying in food service?
Understanding! I am reminded of an old proverb: *Tell me and I will forget, show me and I will remember, involve me and I will understand.* With the buyer, chef, and food service manager understanding each other's job (time permitting, maybe work in each department awhile) the whole operation runs much smoother. I have always been one to ask questions. This helps my understanding of what will be done with the product once it arrives. But this is also a chance to ask how the product will be care for (maintained).

WRITING STANDARDIZED RECIPES

Standardized recipes require the measured use of tightly specified ingredients prepared and cooked in a consistent manner. They are written to ensure regularity in costs, preparation, appearance, taste, and yield. When standardized recipes are used, the product served to the customer has the same quality and quantity each and every visit. Standardized recipes promote food cost control, as the ingredients can be tracked and expanded to serve a specific number of guests. One reason that chain restaurants and hotels are statistically more profitable than independent operations is their commitment to standardization and consistency. Many independent operators, whether run by a family or an investor group, have traditionally been lax in their use of standardized recipes.

Standardized recipes generally contain certain information that is beneficial to the operator's purchasing and food production staff, such as *recipe identification code, recipe name, ingredients, weights and measures, directions for preparation, yield, portion size, cost per ounce/serving* (optional), and *food cost percentage* (optional) (see Figure 6.2).

- **Recipe identification code.** An alphanumeric code is used to catalogue the recipe in the operator's computerized or manual recipe file system. It is often cross-referenced by menu category, meal period, method of cookery, or main ingredient.

- **Recipe name.** The name of the recipe as it appears on the menu.

- **Ingredients.** The ingredients are listed by order of use in the recipe. The ingredient name is first, followed by any descriptions, such as *shrimp, 21/25* count, or *onion, minced.*

- **Weights and measures.** Often recipes are written by weight and volume measurements. Weighing ingredients is a more accurate method, while using volume measure is easier for less skilled employees. Baked goods recipes are always written with weight measurements. Modern recipes are also commonly written in both U.S. customary and metric measures, in separate columns.

- **Directions for preparation.** The directions are written in procedural order of preparation. They also identify the mixing methods, number and size of pans, cooking temperature and time, and the directions for serving.

- **Yield.** The total yield is given by volume or by number of servings.

- **Portion size.** The size of the portion to be served, either by weight or volume, must be identified in order to determine portion yields and cost.

- **Cost per ounce/serving.** Calculating the cost is optional, as it may vary as ingredient prices fluctuate. However, to stay within budget, recipes should be costed out on a routine basis. The operator should calculate the cost of the recipe, serving cost, and, if applicable, the cost per ounce.

- **Food cost percentage.** Operators like to keep an eye on their higher and lower margin items. Some computer programs that link recipes to actual and current ingredient costs allow the operator to establish a "maximum allowable food cost percentage." Should ingredient costs escalate, the software sends a warning notice to the operator.

Identifying Product Needs

After an operation creates the menu and writes the recipes, the next step is to identify the ingredients according to their intended use. This is done to determine possible cross-use in the menu and to lay the groundwork for writing ingredient specifications down the road. To make purchasing easier, ingredients are categorized by type of product. For example, seafood is listed separately from meat, and produce is listed separately from dry goods, helping buyers to itemize and quantify their product needs.

THE ABC ANALYSIS

Most food service establishments want to minimize the amount of inventory on their shelves and in their refrigerators and freezers. Dollars tied up in inventory are not available for payroll or new equipment. Additionally, inventory that stays on the shelves risks spoiling or pest infestation. **ABC analysis** is an analysis of inventory designed to increase the number of turns, or the number of times in a week or a month that a particular food item is used up, to minimize inventory on the shelves. Because the average food service establishment can have hundreds or thousands of different items in its inventory, using the ABC method is a great way to keep track of them.

"A" items are the most expensive, or they are items crucial to an establishment's menu and concept. "B" items are the mid-priced inventory items, while "C" items are the cheapest. Figure 6.3 shows an analysis based on costs. In the average operation, "A" items will take up 50 to 60 percent of the inventory dollars, but they comprise roughly 20 percent of the items on the shelves. "B" items make up 30 to 40 percent of the inventory dollars and account for 30 to 40 percent of the items. "C" items make up a minimal amount of dollars, but can account for up to 50 percent of the inventory items on the shelves. Using a steak house as an example, a steak would be an "A" inventory item, the baked potato a "B" item, and the straw a "C" inventory item. By actively managing the "A" items, a manager can decrease the total dollar amount of purchases. If sales allow, reducing the purchase of one or two "A" items will have a bigger impact than reducing all of the "C" items. Just make sure that the "A" items are not reduced to a point where customer orders cannot be fulfilled.

The ABC system has a variety of other benefits, as well. It can also be used to design an inventory verification scheme.

6.2 **Standardized Recipe Card**

Recipe Name: _____   Recipe ID: _____

FORECASTED YIELD: _____   PORTION SIZE: _____   NUMBER OF PORTIONS: _____   PORTION COST: _____

INGREDIENTS:	INGREDIENT CODE:	ACTUAL: WEIGHT	MEASURE	INGREDIENT COST:

TOTAL COST: _____

FOOD COST PERCENTAGE: _____

PREPARATION METHODS:	ORDERING/NOTES/EQUIPMENT NEEDS:
	Place Photograph Here

6.3 Example of ABC Analysis

Category A Products (combined 50–60% of inventory dollars expended)

Product	Percent of Purchases	Supplier(s)
Fresh meats	24%	Ajax Meats, Burdick
Fresh seafood	19%	Plitt, Superior
Produce	15%	Kingma's, GFS, SYSCO

Category B Products (combined 30–40% of inventory dollars expended)

Product	Percent of Purchases	Supplier(s)
Cheese	10%	Baldwins, Midwest
Desserts	9%	East End Pastries, Nelson's
Dairy	9%	Baldwins, Frank's
Dry Goods	8%	SYSCO, GFS

Category C Products (combined 5–10% of inventory dollars expended)

Product	Percent of Purchases	Supplier(s)
Spices and Herbs	3%	SYSCO, Schreiber
Misc. specialty products	3%	

"A" items should be counted frequently, possibly nightly or weekly. "B" and "C" items can be inventoried monthly. The ABC system can also be used to write ingredient specifications. Some operators will write a spec for all of the "A" and "B" items without worrying about the "C" items, as the time and effort to create specs for minor products is not justifiable, in their minds. And the ABC analysis can aid the buyer in focusing on those purchases that cost the most. For example, if a company spends 28 percent of its purchase dollars on seafood, 26 percent on meat, and 22 percent on produce, then it behooves the buyer to focus much of her attention on acquiring those three categories.

Product Evaluation and Selection

As discussed, it is the buyer's responsibility to source products for the food service operation. Usually, chefs have a general knowledge of the products with which they wish to work.

Additionally, most chefs like to expand their repertoire of recipes and broaden their familiarity with new and different products. This passion for learning translates well to the dining public, as consumers also look to enlarge their dining experiences. To stay competitive, chefs and buyers must find the best available products. This process is known as product analysis. To encourage purchase of their products, vendors commonly provide free samples for potential customers to evaluate. The most common forms of analysis include the *quality analysis, value analysis, make-or-buy analysis,* and *yield cost analysis.*

QUALITY ANALYSIS

Essentially, "quality" is a perception about an object, person, or experience. It may be personal, or it may be shared by a broader group of individuals. Quality is difficult to quantify by weight or count, but it is measurable. Chefs and buyers can measure the quality of an ingredient by its *nutrition and health value, freshness, appearance, aroma, taste, texture,* and *consistency.*

- **Nutrition and health value.** With the current emphasis on proper nutrition and healthful practices, products are often evaluated in that context. Those that are nutritious and healthful are commonly equated to being of high quality.

- **Freshness.** Society equates freshness to quality. Even though canning and freezing processes have been refined, the public views items that are "fresh" to be of the highest quality. Buyers use this factor for determining the age and condition of products, and their potential shelf life.

- **Appearance.** As the adage goes, "people eat with their eyes." Oftentimes, customers cannot get past the appearance of a food item to sample its flavors and texture. Buyers use appearance as a means to judge the acceptability of a product by the customer. Bruising, blemishes, discoloration, and the lack of symmetry might all be causes for concern, depending on the product's application. Items that will be stewed or pureed do not require the visual appeal of center-of-the-plate foodstuffs.

- **Aroma.** Aroma can be a useful barometer for evaluating the ripeness or age of a product. This is useful when judging the quality of seafood, meat, fruits, and cheeses; aroma is indispensable to the trained buyer.

- **Taste.** Taste is perhaps the most important consideration when evaluating quality. A pleasant or appropriate taste is essential. Chefs are generally very particular about taste and will forgo many other quality considerations in deference to taste.

- **Texture.** Texture has become more important to chefs in modern times, as they recognize the necessity of appealing to the customer's senses. The texture characteristics of different ingredients can affect their perceived quality.

- **Consistency.** Consistency is highly valued by chefs. It is important when developing standardized recipes that the ingredients be consistent in flavor and taste, and often in size, yield, and color. Recipes are created with these specific characteristics in mind; ingredients that are inconsistent are worrisome to chefs and often are eliminated from standardized recipes. They can be used on seasonal menus or as daily specials, but often they are disregarded for long-term application.

To further determine a product's quality, certain tests are performed on a selection of ingredients to draw comparisons between like items. A series of **blind tests**, also known as **can cuttings**, are performed to compare similar items, often from competing suppliers (see Figure 6.4, page 106). The buyer generally coordinates the blind tests, preparing samples by removing labels or known marks of identification to eliminate any preconceived impressions. The buyer will code each can to help identify the samples after the tests are completed. To be accurate, the samples must be from cans or containers of comparable size.

The executive chef, sous chef, garde manger chef, banquet chef, pastry chef, owner, or any other member of the staff whose opinion is valued by the executive chef are gathered to evaluate the similar products without knowledge of their brand or source. Common methods for evaluation include the *drained weight test; count and size test;* and *taste, texture, and appearance test.* The results of the tests are recorded on an evaluation form, which is prepared in advance by the buyer and lists each coded product being sampled.

- **Drained weight tests.** The **drained weight test** is used to determine the **servable weight** of ingredients generally co-packed in cans, pouches, or tubs with a protective packing medium. These items, such as string beans, stewed tomatoes, sliced peaches, Mandarin oranges, or Kalamata olives, are separated from their packing medium by draining the can through a sieve. The weight or volume of the **packing medium**, which can be salted water, natural juices, heavy syrup, or oil, is measured separately from the weight or volume of the product. The test is repeated for all comparable items to rank the products by their servable weight (see Figure 6.5a and Figure 6.5b).

- **Count and size tests.** The count and size tests are used to determine the actual number of items in containers of comparable size. Oftentimes, there is a wide discrepancy between brands of like canned products. One vendor's number 10 can of medium pitted black olives often contains a noticeable difference in count and size from another brand's product. The cans are opened, and the contents are poured into clean trays, preferably white plastic, for examination by each person. The items in each tray are counted, and their count is recorded on the evaluation form. Broken pieces and any other related observations are also recorded (see Figure 6.6).

- **Taste, texture, and appearance tests.** Oftentimes, the public can be biased by price or brand name. Taste, texture, and appearance tests, performed blindly, are an important tool in determining quality without the influence of brand names. After the items have been examined for count and size, the evaluators should taste them. Each product should be analyzed for its overall taste and texture. For example, some black olives have a strong brine taste, while others do not. Some have softened textures, while others seem woody.

Each test score is tabulated, and a winner is determined based on its quality factors. However, in many cases, quality is not the only consideration. Price and the product's value to the operation must also be measured.

VALUE ANALYSIS

Simply stated, value refers to the relationship between price and quality. Like quality, value is also a perception, but it is easier to measure. After the quality assessment has been conducted, the buyer reveals to the chef the actual brand names and prices of each item tested. Then the quality and price of the products are evaluated to determine their value.

It is easy to decide to purchase an item whose quality ranking is highest and whose price is lowest. After that, it becomes more difficult to choose a product. For example one company might choose to purchase a mid-priced item among highest quality grades. Another company might choose a lower graded item with a lower price. Some companies will purchase the highest quality items no matter the cost. The business must resolve the overall value of each item it commits to purchase.

In value analysis, the buyer must also consider the "value" of the packaging and if the product is available in more economical quantities, such as in bulk versus portion-controlled. Other than keeping quality, packaging does not generally affect quality. Therefore, some purchasing decisions may be based on the need for certain-sized containers.

6.4 **Blank Blind Test Product Evaluation Form**

Product Samples	Color	Texture		Length	Defects	Flavor/Hold Time	Total Score	Comments
	Variations? Sugar?	**External** Crisp? Dry? Oily? Tough?	**Internal** Dry? Mealy? Hard? Hollow?	Uniformity Shorts Slivers	Rot Disease Damage			
PRODUCT A		Woody						
Score	3	2		3	3	3	14	
PRODUCT B		Firm				Sweet		Superior product
Score	4	4		3	4	4	19	
PRODUCT C		Mushy				Sweet		Acceptable product
Score	3	3		3	4	4	17	
PRODUCT D		Woody			Broken pieces			
Score	2	2		3	2	3	12	
Additional Comments:					**Product Description:** Generic Name: Black Olives Packing Size: Large, pitted			

Evaluator's Name: Smith

Score Key : 4 Excellent
3 Good
2 Fair
1 Unacceptable

6.5a Drain weight test on a can of olives
© Randy Van Dam 2008.

6.6 Chef evaluating the count and size of black olives
© Randy Van Dam 2008.

MAKE-OR-BUY ANALYSIS

A third major analysis performed on ingredients depends on whether the operation plans to make its own products from scratch or to purchase them from an outside source. One of the fundamental considerations that chef-managers give to the selection of menu items, and the ingredients necessary to create them, is the **make-or-buy decision**. Managers, chefs, and buyers always have to consider the sourcing of their ingredients and in what finished state of preparedness they are purchased. Sometimes it is better for the operation to fabricate ingredients; other times it makes more sense to buy items pre-made. If the decision is made to purchase ready-made products, then

6.5b Drain Weight Test Form

Product Samples	Combined Starting Weight	Weight of Packing Medium	Weight of Drained Product	Comments
PRODUCT A Brand:_____				
PRODUCT B Brand:_____				
PRODUCT C Brand:_____				
PRODUCT D Brand:_____				
Additional Comments: **Evaluator's Name:**_____			**Product Description:** **Generic Name:**	

6.7   **Make-or-Buy Analysis Form**

Scratch-Made Product

Product Rating Scale	Portion/Unit Size	Appearance	Consistency	Taste/Flavor	Labor Cost	Food Cost	Total Cost	Total Rating Score
Puff pastry sheets								
Pizza skin	12 oz							
Soft roll	1.6 oz							
Hard roll	2 oz							
Baguette	12 oz							
Hoagie roll								
Fruit Danish								
Coffee cake	16 oz							
Brownie								
NY cheesecake								
Pecan pie								

Purchased Convenience Product

Product Description	Brand Name	Portion/Unit Size	Appearance	Consistency	Taste/Flavor	Labor Cost	Food Cost	Total Cost	Total Rating Score
Puff pastry sheets									
Pizza skin									
Soft roll									
Hard roll									
Baguette									
Hoagie roll									
Fruit Danish									
Coffee cake									
Brownie									
NY cheesecake									
Pecan pie									

Product Rating Scale

Ratings Score	Appearance	Consistency	Taste/Flavor
1	Not appealing	Very random	Poor
2	Manufactured	Somewhat random	Fair
3	Fairly appealing	Generally uniform	Good
4	Artisan	Very consistent	Excellent

the establishment should have a blind taste test, as mentioned previously. Figure 6.7 illustrates a sample analysis worksheet to determine the make-or-buy decisions for baked goods.

Evaluating Convenience Products

Convenience foods are any food items on which some preparation has already been performed, prior to purchase. As Pavesic and Magnant (2005) write, "Some or all of the production steps to bring the particular product to that level of readiness are performed outside the restaurant by the processor" (p. 105). Their cost, taste, appearance, and consistency are easier to evaluate than those made from scratch.

Conveniences, or ready-prepared products, have grown exponentially in the retail and commercial marketplace. Every category of product, from beverages to desserts, has seen tremendous growth in convenience foods, both in sales and in the breadth of varieties available. As Marcia Wade wrote in a 2005 article:

> The overwhelming theme of the "2005 Prepared Foods R&D Trends Survey: Culinary and Food Service Product Development Trends" is that manufacturers should provide greater consistency in the products they offer food service operators, while helping these customers lower their overhead costs.

The 2009 Trend Forecast from *Prepared Foods* emphasized "the use of exotic fruits and fresh, soothing flavors with a touch of spice to jazz up their new products" (Prepared Foods e-flash, 2008).

According to Steve Jilleba, corporate executive chef for Unilever Foodsolutions, "Convenience items have changed in that the customer is demanding more quality and bolder flavors. They're looking for natural ingredients and strong, fresh flavors" (Interview, NRA Show, 2008).

YIELD COST ANALYSIS

The last form of ingredient scrutiny is known as the yield cost analysis. The purpose of a **yield cost analysis** is to determine the **edible portion cost (EP cost)**, which is also known as the serving portion cost (SP cost) or plate cost, of a recipe. The data required for this calculation are the purchase price of the ingredients and their edible yield. Yield is defined as the amount of product that should result from the recipe. **Yield** can also be defined as the amount of useable product available after processing.

Most recipes contain ingredients that require processing, such as trimming or preliminary cooking, that will result in shrinkage. When items are initially purchased, their weight is known as the **as-purchased weight (AP weight)**, and their cost is known as the **as-purchased cost (AP cost)**.

People, Places, Things

Conducting Professional Can Cuttings

A can cutting is a quality examination, often sponsored by a vendor, where a specific product from a variety of companies, brands, and quality grades is evaluated. A typical can cutting might be one carried out by the corporate chef of a chain of Italian restaurants seeking to identify the most appropriate canned plum tomato product for a signature sauce. A can cutting is an important management tool that is used to identify the most appropriate product for a particular menu application, for example, stewed tomatoes or whole peeled plum tomatoes for making a tomato ragu.

When conducting a can cutting, it is important to be consistent so that a comprehensive and objective evaluation is made, and to record the examination for later use. Most food service professionals use a variety of forms: some simple, others highly specific and detailed. When developing a form for your operation, it is important to consider the factors most relevant to the canned product you are evaluating and its menu application. Common factors recorded on the can-cutting form include color, texture, drained weight, taste, uniformity, smell, and noted defects. Other information may include vendor, case price, edible portion (EP) cost, portion size, nutritional considerations (such as sugar and sodium levels), and written comments. Two common food service terms used to evaluate canned food products are edible portion (EP) and as purchased (AP). In the example of a canned whole pear product, the entire unopened can would be the AP weight, and the drained edible pear would be the EP.

After an item has been trimmed, peeled, or precooked, its weight or volume decreases, and resulting in a higher EP cost and lower **edible portion weight (EP weight)**. For example, after removing the wilted outer leaves and core from a head of lettuce, the remaining useable lettuce costs more per ounce (EP cost) than the original cost per ounce for the entire head of lettuce (AP cost), as depicted in Figure 6.8.

To account for the shrinkage, chefs and buyers should conduct a yield cost analysis on all menu items that require processing to determine their true cost per portion. Calculating yield will also help the buyer better determine quantities needed for production and storage. According to Pavesic and Magnant (2005), "Over time, the chef or owner will discover the optimum size to purchase that results in the highest yield and least amount of waste" (p. 108).

Take the following example of a yield cost analysis:

Case of iceberg head lettuce (@ $18.00/case)
48 lbs Weight of lettuce and packing case
−2 lbs Weight of packing case
46 lbs AP weight of head lettuce

The EP weight of the lettuce is determined by multiplying the AP weight by the yield percentage. For example, let's assume the yield percentage for head lettuce is 72 percent, after the core and wilted outer leaves are removed.

46 lbs AP weight of lettuce
× 72% Yield percentage of lettuce
= 33.12 lb EP weight

6.8 **Comparing the weight of AP lettuce to EP lettuce**
© Randy Van Dam 2008

The AP cost per pound is determined by dividing the AP cost by the AP weight. The EP cost per pound is determined by dividing the AP cost by the EP weight.

For example:

$18.00 a case / 46.00 lbs (AP weight) = $0.391 per lb
(AP cost)

$18.00 a case / 33.12 lbs (EP weight) = $0.543 per lb
(EP cost)

People, Places, Things

Upper-Crust Convenience

"It's not your grandfather's TV dinners," to take a line from a well-known automobile advertisement. Convenience foods have exploded in recent years, and their quality has matched their imagination. Following are examples of several companies that offer upper-crust convenience products and flavorings available through broadline or specialty distributors, such as Chefex, an upscale division of SYSCO.

- **Willie Birds Turkeys**—Smoked turkey breast, boneless smoked duck, and chicken breast

- **Todhunter Foods**—Wine reductions

- **Terra Spice**—Dried fruits and vegetables, dried mushrooms and truffle oil, specialty spice blends

- **Primal Essence**—Culinary spice extracts

- **Perfect Purée**—Frozen fruit and vegetables purées

- **Pastry Star**—Broad varieties of fruit coulis

- **Ciao Imports**—Fresh frozen pastas filled with ingredients such as truffles and Gorgonzola

- **Charlie Trotter**—A line of natural sauces, salmon, and duck leg confit

- **Boyajian**—Chili infused olive oil, basil-infused olive oil, garlic-infused vinegar, maple-infused vinegar, ginger-infused vinegar

- **BliS**—Barrel-aged maple syrup, wild-caught American sturgeon–smoked caviar, sake-cured trout roe, smoked salt

Butcher's Yield Tests

In times past, most large clubs and hotels had their own butcher shops where sides and quarters of hanging meat were brought in on rails, and taken to walk-in coolers to **dry-age** before fabrication. Staff butchers would cut up the chicken, veal, lamb, beef, and pork to the specifications of the chef de cuisine and chef garde manger. As Garlough and Campbell (2006) write, "Menus were painstakingly written to utilize all of the primary cuts, lesser cuts, by-products and trimmings. Bones were used for stock and fat was turned to tallow or roux" (p. 31).

Nowadays, chefs usually buy primal cuts, boxed meat, and precut portions that are **wet-aged**. The decision whether to purchase precut portioned veal scallops or whole legs of veal to be broken down and portioned by the staff is important and usually well considered by the chef. To decide which is most cost efficient, chefs perform a **butcher's yield test** (see Figure 6.9). The test evaluates the cost of the staff cutting their own portions (including the resultant by-products of trim, bones, and fat) or buying the product pre-portioned. It is a classic make-or-buy decision. When establishments choose to cut their own meat, which of course only applies to establishments that have chefs trained to do so, the banquet and garde manger chefs are often called upon to turn the trimmings into profitable appetizers, sausages, pâtés, and other forcemeats.

A butcher's yield test will also reveal three important cost considerations: the yield percentage, the EP cost, and the cost factor multiplier. The yield percentage is used to calculate how much product needs to be ordered. The amount to order is calculated by multiplying the number of guests times the portion size and dividing the total by the yield percentage:

$$\frac{\text{Number of guests} \times \text{portion size}}{\text{Yield percentage}}$$

$$= \text{Order quantity}$$

The cost factor multiplier is useful for determining new EP costs when AP costs change, without having to perform a new butcher's yield test. The cost factor multiplier is determined by dividing the new EP cost by the AP cost. For example, in Figure 6.9, the AP cost is $3.45 per pound. The new cost per pound, after fabrication, is $4.39 per pound. Dividing 4.39 by 3.45 yields a quotient of 1.27. In this example, 1.27 is the cost factor multiplier. It is expressed as:

$$\text{New AP Cost} \times \text{cost factor multiplier} = \text{New EP cost}$$

Writing Product Specifications

Once the chef and buyer have established the quality and value standards for their products, they begin to create the written **product specifications**. Product specifications, also known as purchase specifications, help to ensure that quality standards are met. As Kotschevar and Donnelly (1998) write,

"A specification is a statement of all the factors required in a product to satisfy a purchase need" (p. 50). Products specifications typically include product information that can be validated upon delivery and that can be communicated clearly between the buyers and the sellers.

Specifications serve as an anchor around which the purchasing function revolves. They are often referred to as "the heart of purchasing." And it has been shown that, when good, clear specifications are written, lower prices and higher quality are obtained. Buyers work with three forms of specifications: the *internal, external,* and *general conditions.*

- **Internal.** Also known as the *menu specification*, the internal specification is used within the food service operation. Buyers and chefs should clearly identify the portion size, method of cookery, handling directions, and plate presentations in their product specifications.

- **External.** The external product specification is derived from the internal specification. External specifications are written to clearly describe products to purveyors, and are often sent to potential vendors for their bid quotes. They ensure that all vendors are bidding on the exact same item and not offering lesser products to the buyer at lower prices.

- **General conditions.** The general conditions (specifications) describe the business factors and considerations involved in bidding on products, as required by the buyer. This section includes delivery locations and times, billing instructions, and related information.

It is suggested that the food service operator create a product specification reference guide for the buyer and receiving personnel. The reference guide will aid the buyer in clearly stating the product specs to the sellers, and receiving personal will know what to look for when receiving deliveries. Table 6.1 illustrates many categories and descriptors used to construct written specifications.

THE SPECIFICATION FORM

Specifications can be written in many ways and in different formats. No matter how they are written, they generally include much of the same information (see Figure 6.10), such as:

- **Generic product name.** The simple name of the product without any brand or processing information, such as *sliced peaches* or *ground beef.*

- **Product specification reference guide code.** The unique alphanumeric code used to catalogue the product into the food service operation's product specification reference guide.

- **Brand name.** Often, buyers prefer to use a specific **packer's brand** or private label brand name, as they indicate an acceptable level of quality. A packer's brand system is that company's grading system, often used in lieu of the government's federal quality grade. Examples include the Sysco brand levels of quality: *SYSCO Supreme, SYSCO Imperial, SYSCO Classic* and *SYSCO Reliance,* and *SYSCO Natural.* Or the buyer may prefer a specific brand such as *Heinz Ketchup* only.

6.9 **Butcher's Yield Test**

Item Veal leg   **Specification** 334 B   **Condition** _____

Other Remarks Fresh _____

Date Received _____ **Weight at Receipt** 42 lb   **No. of Pcs.** 1 _____

Purchased Price per Pound $3.45/lb   **Total as Purchased Cost** $144.90

Date of Test _____ **Weight at Time of Test** _____ **No. of Pcs.** 1 _____

Supplier _____ **Fabricating or Cutting Instructions** _____

Results of Test:

Credits	Weight	Percentage of Total	Value per Pound	Extension
Usable trim	4 lb	9.5	$4.49	$17.96
Bones	7 lb	16.6	$1.05	$7.35
Fat	3.5 lb	8.3	$0.20	$0.70
Shrinkage	0	0	0	0
Cutting loss	2 lb	4.8	$3.45	$6.90
TOTAL CREDITS	16.5 lb	39.2		$32.91

			AP Cost	$144.90
			Less Credit	$32.91
Yield of Fabricated Product		42 − 16.5 = 25.5	Cost of Fabricated Product	$111.99
Percentage of Total		60.8%		
Cost per Pound		$4.39		
Cost Factor (new/old)		4.39/3.45 = 1.27		

Additional Comments: _____

_____

_____

Signature

NOTE: Show percentages of all products to total. Indicate reasons for loss or gain in total weight, such as shrinkage through storage or cutting loss or added material as may occur in ground beef, etc.

TABLE 6.1 Specification Category Matrix and Descriptor Terms

Descriptor	Fresh Fruits	Canned Fruits	Fresh Vegetables	Canned Vegetables	Meat	Seafood
Flavor	X	X	X	X	X	X
Color	X	X	X	X	X	X
Texture	X	X	X	X	X	X
Tenderness		X				
Firmness	X		X			
Maturity	X		X	X		
Count						
Absence of Defects	X	X	X	X	X	X
Appearance	X	X	X	X	X	X
Uniformity of Size	X	X	X	X		
Symmetry	X					
Clearness of Syrup		X				
Syrup Density		X				
Cut	X		X			
Style				X		
Drained Weight		X		X		
Marbling					X	
Size	X				X	X
IMPS					X	

6.10   Sample Product Specification Form

Exact Ingredient Name: _____

Unique Product Code Number: _____

Supplier (Sources): _____

Recipe Use(s): _____

_____

Size (weight/count info): _____

Grade (if appropriate): _____

Packer's Brand (if appropriate): _____

Place of Origin: _____

Package Size: _____

Type of Package: _____

Preservation / Processing Method: _____

Form (if appropriate): _____

Color (if appropriate): _____

Degree of Ripeness (if appropriate): _____

Acceptable Substitute: _____

Cost Limitations: _____

- **Supplier catalogue code.** This is the code used by the supplier to list the product in its sales catalogue, such as the broadliners SYSCO or Gordon Food Services. Also, the North American Meat Processor's Association has identified specific food service cuts in its publication, **The Meat Buyer's Guide**. These codes describe the exact trim dimensions and weight ranges for each cut of beef, lamb, veal, pork, chicken, turkey, duck/goose, and game birds. Examples include *109* beef rib, roast ready; *189A* beef loin, tenderloin, full, side muscle on, defatted; *416A* pork spareribs, St. Louis style.

- **Intended use of the product.** It is helpful to the buyer to know all of the intended uses for the product in case substitutions need to be made. The intended use also affects the preferred type of packaging.

- **Packaging form.** Buyers need to specify how they want their products packaged, as this affects the weight, preservation method, shelf life, freshness, and portion size, among other considerations. Examples include *#10 can* of ketchup, *glass bottled* ketchup, *plastic squeeze bottled* ketchup, and *portion controlled* (PC) ketchup.

- **Market form.** The market form indicates how an item is processed before it is packaged. Examples include *shredded* carrots, *individually quick frozen* (IQF) raspberries, *dried* parsley flakes, canned *in oil* tuna, and *fresh ground* beef.

- **Size.** Buyers must be specific about packaging or portion sizes to best meet the needs of the operation. Examples

include *6-ounce, double-lobe* chicken breast, *10-ounce* bottle, and *16/20* shrimp.

- **Acceptable trim.** The acceptable trim measures the maximum amount of acceptable waste allowed in a product upon receipt. This specification is often used with fresh produce like lettuce, carrots, and pineapple.

- **Grade.** The U.S. Department of Agriculture (USDA) provides quality measurements or indicators known as USDA grades. As the program is voluntary, it is wise for the buyer to list the USDA grade "or its equivalent" as the spec. Examples include the eight quality grades for beef: USDA Prime, Choice, Select, Standard, Commercial, Utility, Cutter, and Canner.

- **Color.** Some products vary in color, which might influence the buyer's choice. Examples include *green* beans, *brown-shelled* eggs, and *white* asparagus.

- **Place of origin.** The origin is where the product is grown, caught, or raised. Examples include *Florida* oranges, *Copper River* salmon, *Alaskan* king crab, and *New Zealand* lamb.

- **Acceptable substitutes.** Although not desirable, operators may elect to identify reasonable substitutions to use when the primary ingredient is unavailable, such as substituting *beefsteak tomatoes* for *best boy tomatoes.*

- **Price limitations.** There are times when the cost of certain ingredients can become so prohibitive that it is best to restrict their ordering. For example, *fresh blackberries must not exceed $4 per pint. If the price is more than that, then the sales representative must contact the buyer for further instructions.*

Candy Wallace

Place of Birth: Chicago, Illinois

Educational Background and Work Experience

Candy Wallace is a force to be reckoned with. Starting out in Chicago, Wallace worked in a variety of food service positions until she finished her bachelor's degree in political science from the University of Maryland. With her sights set on the political arena, she worked on Capitol Hill in Washington, D.C., as a staff associate for a member of Congress. As a political staffer, Wallace was invited to many of the receptions and parties at the international embassies, the White House on occasion, and the Beltway circuit, all the while gaining exposure to many exciting international cuisines. Her boss bragged about Wallace's prowess in the kitchen, having first tasted her food at a holiday party. The congressman hosted a huge reception at his home in Virginia, with the food designed and prepared by Wallace—an event that became a popular annual affair. Chef Wallace's services as a weekend caterer in Washington, D.C., were launched, and Taste! Of Washington, D.C., was born. Taste! thrived for 4 years, until she accepted an offer to work for the congressman and his family as a private chef. Wallace held this position until the congressman retired and returned to his home state, after which time she went to work for an international food company back in Chicago. Working in restaurants part-time on the weekends while still working in marketing and advertising, Wallace found that she was more at home behind a stove than behind a desk. Since that time, she hasn't looked back on corporate America. After a series of successful positions as a private chef in Chicago and Los Angeles, Chef Wallace became the chef of the Yugoslavian Village Restaurant in Burbank, California, chef-owner of Taste! Of Los Angeles, and chef-owner of The Serving Spoon in San Diego. Today, Candy Wallace is the executive director of the American Personal & Private Chef Association, helping others to reach their dreams of self-employment through work as personal or private chefs.

Memberships and Career Highlights

Chef Wallace is a member of the American Culinary Federation (ACF), the International Association of Culinary Professionals (IACP),

Courtesy Candy Wallace

It Happened to Me...

"Operating as a personal chef or a private chef means that you are purchasing supplies and cooking for one client (or family) per day, so you are not a large enough account to be purchasing from a wholesale food purveyor in bulk, unless you are also catering for those clients. Clients and levels of service vary widely, since clients may be busy, time-pressed single professionals or two-income professionals with children. They may also be high profile clients, or clients with specific medical challenges, or even seniors with discretionary income who choose to remain independent and in their own homes who do not choose to dine out each night.

Clients are different, as are their needs and desires. The service you provide may be anything from fine dining to simple, fresh family fare, but the promise you make to the client is that you will be preparing palate specific meals from all fresh components on a regular basis, whether it be daily by a private chef or weekly by a personal chef.

Your word to your client as a private or personal chef impacts your employment and reputation, and that is a direct impact on your bottom line. I learned that I needed to touch and select each component of the meals I prepared for my clients through this example:

I was tasked to prepare an Italian themed event for 800, for a high profile client. I decided to use one of the wholesale food companies in town that had been courting me and that promised quality, convenience, and timely delivery. They also said they could beat the prices I was paying at the sources I was currently using while matching their quality of product. My thinking was, 'Wonderful, I don't have to run all over town this time sourcing all of my needs for this dinner, I can have it delivered from one source and possibly save some money.' BIG mistake!

I had requested that the delivery include 15 pounds of fresh basil, so it would be fresh and beautiful for the event. I opened the cases upon delivery, and found all of the basil was rotten. When I called the company looking for a solution, they were unwilling to help me resolve the problem in a way that would save the day. To compound the problem, I had ordered petit veal shanks for osso bucco and specified they all be the same size. HA! They varied from 1 inch in diameter to 6 inches in diameter, and the company once again did not feel compelled to make good on their promise of consistency in the size of the shanks. The result was my going back to my personal relationships with purveyors I can count on. Consistency of quality and accountability are direct contributors to my profitability as a personal chef.

I recently did a dinner for a client that involved shrimp and 80 lobsters. My fishmonger not only added 2 extra lobsters per set poundage, but they allowed me to put on a jacket and net and go in the back to select my own lobsters. In addition, they cut and packaged the live lobsters per my instructions without question. My cheese vendor had no Parmesan for me that day, but sent her husband out to a colleague's store and delivered it to my client's home in order to keep her word to me.

KNOW your sources and develop relationships that contribute to the quality and profitability of your business."

(continued)

the Women Chefs & Restaurateurs (WCR), and Les Dames d'Escoffier. Among her many honors, Wallace received the prestigious Award of Excellence for Businessperson of the Year in 2003 from the International Association of Culinary Professionals (IACP) at its conference in Montreal. The award was presented in recognition of her contributions to the industry through the creation and professional development of the personal chef segment of the food service industry. In 2004, she was invited to write a textbook for aspiring professional personal chefs for John Wiley & Sons. In May of 2006, Wallace was invited to represent the food service industry at a conference in London that addressed the growing global concern created by the breakdown of the family dinner. She spoke about the contributions that personal and private chefs make daily to the quality of their clients' lives and the assistance they provide in bringing families back to the table so parents can teach their children social skills, conversational skills, negotiating skills, cultural rituals, and the healthy eating patterns necessary to thrive in today's world. However, Wallace feels her greatest achievement was the validation of the personal chef career path by the ACF at the 2002 National Convention where then-President Chef Edward Leonard, CMC, AAC

"officially recognized and endorsed the personal chef career path on behalf of the largest organization of professional chefs in the Western Hemisphere." It is now part of the ACF Certification program.

Passions with the Food Service Industry

"As a personal chef, I have actually replaced 'Mom' or 'Grandma' in some of my busy clients' kitchens. Making a contribution to my clients' well-being and quality of life is almost as important as the palate specific meals I design and prepare for them. As a personal chef, I have the honor to make a huge contribution to my clients' well being through the preparation of delicious, healthy meals, but also by contributing to their wellness through stress reduction, introduction of more time into their busy lives, and on occasion even bringing families back to the table so that parents can instill skills and information in their children that will serve them well in future life. I am a professional who is paid to do her three favorite things in life: shop, cook, and nurture."

Advice to a Chef or Buyer

"Personal chefs are small business owners, so they are not purchasing in bulk like most of the food service industry. Many of our sources are retail operations since we are shopping daily for our clients. Good relationships with purveyors can pay off for self-employed personal chefs in several ways.

When I realized I had spent more than $50,000 in one grocery store alone in one year in support of my personal chef clients, I contacted each of the purveyors I used in my daily service and asked if they would like to discuss finding a way to say 'thank you' to a good client.

My butchers, fishmongers, produce vendors and grocers and specialty stores all agreed that client loyalty should be recognized and rewarded. In some cases that 'thank you' translated into a rebate of a percentage of dollars spent in that establishment, which contributed directly to the profitability of my business. In other cases, it manifested in additional services such as my butchers and fishmongers prepping for me at no additional cost. Since time is money, that was also a savings for me.

Knowing that you can consistently count on your purveyors to supply the freshest, finest components for your clients' dining experience at a reasonable fee is peace of mind, and also contributes to the bottom line of your business."

Key Words and Concepts

ABC analysis

as-purchased cost
(AP cost)

as-purchased weight
(AP weight)

blind tests

butcher's yield test

can cuttings

convenience foods

cross-utilization

drained weight test

dry-age

edible portion cost
(EP cost)

edible portion weight
(EP weight)

make-or-buy decision

market research

packer's brand

packing medium

product specifications

servable weight

standardized recipes

The Meat Buyer's Guide

wet-age

yield

yield cost analysis

Chapter in Review

The following exercises are provided to help the reader understand and apply the contents of this chapter. They may be completed individually or in a classroom environment.

REVIEW QUESTIONS

a. Identify the considerations that must be made when planning the menu, and give examples for each.

b. Identify the elements that are essential to writing a standardized recipe.

c. Identify the elements that are essential to writing a product specification.

d. Identify as many products as possible whose AP price is the same as their EP price.

INDIVIDUAL ACTIVITIES

a. **Web based:** Research meat vendors in your area to determine if anyone sells dry-aged beef. Try to visit the location where it is being aged.

b. **Experiential:** Create a standardized recipe format, either on paper or electronically, that you might use in your food service operation.

c. **Critical thinking:** Evaluate a convenience food product, and determine when the product would be appropriate for use, and when not.

GROUP ACTIVITIES

a. **Lab experience:** Obtain at least four different samples (more is better) of five different foods, such as: Mandarin oranges, large black olives, cut green beans, sliced peaches in syrup, and kernel corn. Be sure the cans are of the same size and volume, the contents are labeled the same, and they are of different brands. Using a different *product evaluation form* for each category of food, record the name of each brand on the form, along with its price. Assign a letter to identify each different can, and then mark each can's side with its corresponding letter after removing the paper wrapper/label. This form will become the instructor's *master product guide*. Repeat this process for all categories, until a master guide is created for each type of product. Divide the class into five evaluation teams, or as many different categories of food available, and issue them blank product evaluation forms. (Each team will evaluate only one food category.) Ask the student teams to complete the form by conducting various blind evaluations, include the *drained weight test; count and size test; and taste, texture, and appearance test* for determining the overall item with the highest quality. Ask the students to rank their choices from best to worst product, and then reveal the brand name and cost of these items using the master product guide. Discuss the price/value relationship of each product.

b. **Classroom action:** Conduct a make-or-buy discussion, after having the students complete several *butcher's yield tests,* given imaginary weights and prices.

CHAPTER

7

© Randy Van Dam 2008

The Storeroom

"Put all good eggs in one basket and then watch that basket."

ANDREW CARNEGIE

After reading this chapter, you will be able to:

- ◎ Relate the storeroom as a service provider.
- ◎ Describe the organization of staffing, as it applies to food service operations.
- ◎ List the different positions employed in storeroom operations.
- ◎ Define the different categories of employees, including line and staff, and exempt and nonexempt.
- ◎ Identify common features found in receiving docks.
- ◎ List common files kept in the buyer's office.
- ◎ Describe common features found in dry and refrigerated storage.
- ◎ Identify the various types of shelving used in dry and refrigerated storage.
- ◎ Explain storeroom sanitation.
- ◎ Describe the use of herb gardens, hydroponics and live seafood tanks.
- ◎ Compare the three R's: reduce, reuse, and recycle.

Introduction

A properly managed storeroom is crucial for a business's financial success. Because storerooms are the central repository for all of the goods in the establishment, a well-run storeroom will help kitchen employees complete their work in a timely manner. If the storeroom is not run properly, then the inventory lists will not be accurate, and food will not be available when the kitchen staff needs it. This means that the establishment, as a whole, is unlikely to achieve high profits or satisfied guests.

This chapter will illustrate the best practices for staffing and maintaining the storeroom. It must be noted, however, that many well-run storerooms exist without employing extra staff solely dedicated to buying, receiving, storing, and issuing. In many smaller restaurants and clubs, the chef or manager will take the primary, or consolidated, role in managing those functions. That being said, the information contained in this chapter, and indeed in the whole text, can apply to any sized establishment.

The Storeroom as Service Provider

Most kitchens are set up in a similar manner: food and supplies flow through the restaurant in well-established patterns. The storeroom is the central hub, and then food moves out of the storeroom, like spokes on a wheel, to the different sections of the kitchen (see Figure 7.1). A well-run storeroom provides quality food at a reasonable cost to the establishment and in a timely manner for the kitchen. In a sense, a storeroom can be considered a service provider, with the kitchen and the front of the house as its customers. And, like any well-run restaurant, the storeroom should have the food available in the right quantities at the right time. If food supplies are supposed to be available for production by 8 a.m., and they don't arrive until 11:30 a.m., then the production staff is dissatisfied, often resulting in poor service to their customers.

Complementary to the service function of issuing food in a timely manner is the informed selection and procurement by whoever does the buying. If the operation employs a purchasing agent, then this individual must also be the eyes and ears of the chef in the marketplace. New or better products are frequently entering the market, and buyers need to stay abreast of these developments. The buyer (whether chef, manager, or dedicated purchasing agent) is the conduit through which ingredients flow.

7.1 **The storeroom: hub of operations**

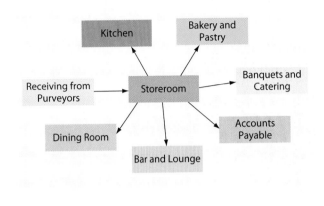

Organization of Staffing

For the storeroom to be thorough in research, efficient in service, and methodical in practice, the storeroom must be organized properly—both in facilities and staffing. Food service operations, like all businesses, arrange their staff according to traditional **organizational charts**, with both vertical and horizontal lines of authority and responsibility (see Figure 7.2).

Those positions involved in the actual production or service of the food service operation, whether paid by the hour or by salary, are known as line positions, as first discussed in Chapter 1. They are directly in the business's line of work. Examples of line positions include the dishwashers, prep cooks, bakers, servers, and bartenders. Those who support the workers, or enable them to perform their work, are known as staff positions. Staff workers sustain the line workers and are seldom seen by the customers. Examples of staff positions include bookkeepers, maintenance, and storeroom staff.

The storeroom staff, whether supervised by the owner, executive chef or food and beverage director, is scheduled primarily around the needs of the food production staff. No matter the size or complexity of the operation, staff must be available to receive, store, and issue the products as needed.

That being said, labor laws must be followed, and labor costs must be controlled. Food and labor costs are the largest controllable costs of the organization, and the storeroom is central to their control. (Refer to Chapter 9 on cost controls.)

Staffing will depend on the size of the operation. Small establishments that purchase less than $750,000 a year typically have the chef or manager do the ordering, and then the cooks or other employees help put away the stock. When purchasing levels reach $5 million or more, then most likely there will be a dedicated manager and staff for purchasing and receiving. For establishments that lie between these two figures, there might be one or two people with full- or part-time purchasing, receiving, and issuing responsibilities.

7.2 **Hotel organizational chart**

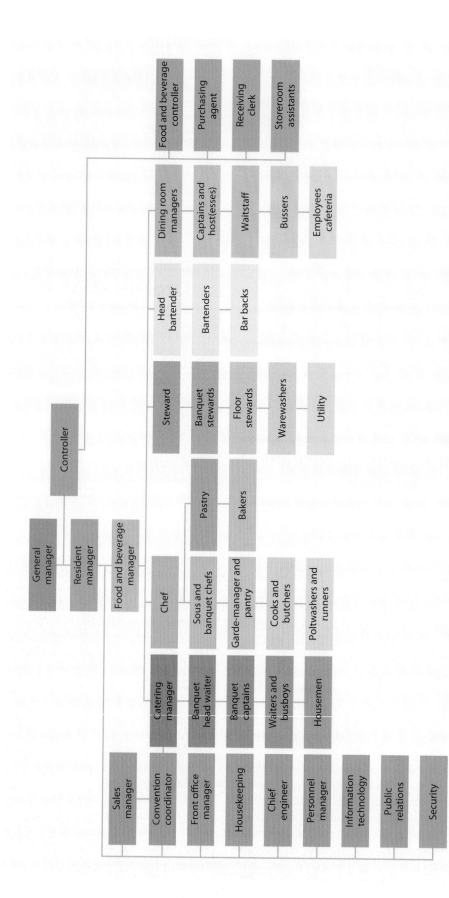

In many small and midsized food service operations, owners and chefs perform the duties of storeroom buyers, and cooks often receive and store the food and supplies.

LABOR LAWS

The Department of Labor enforces the **Fair Labor Standards Act (FLSA)**. This act sets the federal minimum wage and overtime pay standards. Employees who fall under its provisions must be paid at least the prevailing minimum wage rate and receive time and a half for working more than 40 hours a week. FLSA does not require businesses to offer vacation days, severance, sick leave, or paid holidays. Employees who fall under this law are normally considered **nonexempt employees**.

Exempt employees are not covered under (exempt from) FLSA provisions, especially the time-and-a-half regulation. Normally, exempt employees are paid a salary, and they are expected to work the hours needed to complete their responsibilities. To exempt an employee from the overtime provisions, the owners must show that this position meets certain requirements, which vary depending on the type of exemption. An exempt employee cannot be paid by the hour.

FLSA does include other provisions. All establishments must have a standard 7-day work week and cannot move overtime hours to a subsequent week with fewer hours. FLSA requires that actual hours worked count toward the 40-hour limit, and a company may allow vacation or sick time as part of the calculation.

Finally, states can, and do, pass laws that go beyond the FLSA guidelines. Some states and cities will have a higher minimum wage rate or may require overtime after 8 hours of work per day. Some states will also regulate hours worked or equipment used by minors. The higher standard is the one that needs to be followed, and if an owner has any questions, he should seek legal advice.

 Wages are generally tied to skills required versus labor pool available. The manager needs to budget for the related employment costs (i.e., taxes, retirement, and insurance) in addition to the hourly wages paid.

PERSONNEL FILES

Every restaurant should maintain records on its employees. While FLSA does not require a particular form to be used, the establishment should keep certain identifying information along with the hours worked and the wages earned. The following information should be kept for each employee:

- Employee name, which should match the name on the employee's Social Security card, and an employee number or symbol if used for payroll records.
- Address and other contact information
- Birth date, if younger than 19
- Gender
- Position(s) held at this establishment
- Hours worked each day and each week
- Details on how the employee is paid

People, Places, Things

The Fair Labor Standards Act (FLSA)

The Fair Labor Standards Act (FLSA), which prescribes standards for the basic minimum wage and overtime pay, affects most private and public employment. It requires employers to pay covered employees who are not otherwise exempt at least the federal minimum wage and overtime pay of one-and-one-half-times the regular rate of pay. For nonagricultural operations, it restricts the hours that children under age 16 can work and forbids the employment of children under age 18 in certain jobs deemed too dangerous. For agricultural operations, it prohibits the employment of children under age 16 during school hours and in certain jobs deemed too dangerous. The act is administered by the Employment Standards Administration's Wage and Hour Division within the U.S. Department of Labor.

Courtesy: U.S. Department of Labor.

- The hourly wage rate for each position that the employee holds at the establishment

- Total daily or weekly earnings

- Total overtime earnings for the week

- Any additions (such as a bonus pay) or deductions (such as taxes, insurance, or other legally required deductions)

- Date the paycheck was issued and the pay period that it covered

This information must be kept for each pay period and is used for tax forms at the end of the year.

The I-9 Form

All U.S. employers must complete a **Form I-9** for each person they hire. This form must be completed as soon as the person is hired and must be retained on the premises. All employees, including citizens and noncitizens, should fill this form out. The employer must verify the eligibility of the employees and make copies of any documents that the employee shows for verification. See Figure 7.3, which includes a list of acceptable documents on the back of the I-9 form.

COMMON STOREROOM POSITIONS AND DUTIES

In smaller operations, like catering companies and small and midsized restaurants, the owner, manager, or working chef usually also function as the storeroom manager and buyer. Kitchen staff, such as the sous chefs, line cooks, dishwashers and prep cooks, assist with the receiving and storing duties. The storeroom is usually left open to the kitchen staff to obtain their products as needed.

In larger operations like high-volume restaurants and smaller hotels, the executive chef also serves as the storeroom manager but often with the assistance of a part-time storeroom assistant who helps with the buying and inventorying the items. Often the kitchen staff is still involved in receiving and issuing the products.

In very high-volume operations with multiple outlets, such as hotels, hospitals, culinary schools, and local independent chains, there are several positions commonly assigned to the storeroom (see Figure 7.4). These positions include the *storeroom manager, buyer, receiving clerk, and storeroom assistants.*

- **Storeroom manager.** The **storeroom manager**, also known as the *stockroom manager*, supervises and coordinates the activities of all storeroom employees, including the ordering, receiving, storing, inventorying, issuing, and delivering of the food, materials, supplies, tools, and equipment. The storeroom manager is primarily responsible for the layout of the stockroom, including both the dry and refrigerated storage areas. The storeroom manager oversees the buying process,

including determining stock levels, inventory turnover, and product delivery schedules. The manager advises the storeroom employees on how to store the items and on the proper procedures for issuing the stock. The manager is also responsible for conducting regular storeroom inventories, maintaining written records, and helping to determine food costs for each outlet served by the storeroom. To perform these functions, the manager must have a broad understanding of food, supplies, and food service operations, including quality grades, potential vendors, commodity laws, market forces, and bookkeeping.

- **Buyer.** The **buyer** is often the "face of the food service operation" to the purveyors. Buyers are the people who meet with the supplier's sales staff or local growers. The buyer is primarily responsible for the purchase of all food, beverages, and supplies for the different outlets of the food service operation. The buyer also purchases durable goods such as kitchen tools and equipment, tables and chairs, and tabletop china and glassware. Additionally, buyers arrange most company leases, such as the linen and uniform service, and they may negotiate contracts for outside services such as pest control and kitchen exhaust hood cleaning. The buyer develops the product specifications in concert with the executive chef and ensures that the storeroom maintains quality standards and financial parameters. Buyers are generally second in command in the storeroom and in training to become a storeroom manager.

- **Receiving clerk.** The **receiving clerk** is primarily responsible for the receipt and storage of all food items and equipment received by the food service operation. It is the receiving clerk's responsibility to inspect all products being delivered and to determine if they match the product specifications. They also weigh, count, and inspect the products for appropriate quality and quantity, as ordered by the buyer. Often, the receiving clerk has access to copies of all purchase orders and product specifications. The security of the received items is under the control of this individual, who places them in their designated dry and refrigerated storage locations. The receiving clerk must ice-down fresh poultry and seafood or weigh individual portions of meat and seafood for tagging. The receiving clerk might also assist in conducting inventories and issuing products for the manager and is often in training to become a buyer.

- **Storeroom assistants.** **Storeroom assistants** perform a wide variety of tasks, including helping to portion items purchased in bulk, such as cheese and nuts; picking items for issue; and assisting during inventory. They are responsible for maintaining the sanitation of the storeroom facilities, including mopping the coolers and washing the sinks. Storeroom assistants are often in training to become receiving clerks.

7.3 **Form I-9, front and back sides**

Federal Register/Vol. 73, No. 243,/Wednesday, December 17, 2008/Rules and Regulations   76515

OMB No. 1615-0047; Expires 06/30/09

Department of Homeland Security
U.S. Citizenship and Immigration Services

**Form I-9, Employment
Eligibility Verification**

Read instructions carefully before completing this form. The instructions must be available during completion of this form.

ANTI-DISCRIMINATION NOTICE: It is illegal to discriminate against work-authorized individuals. Employers CANNOT specify which document(s) they will accept from an employee. The refusal to hire an individual because the documents have a future expiration date may also constitute illegal discrimination.

Section 1. Employee Information and Verification *(To be completed and signed by employee at the time employment begins.)*

Print Name Last	First	middle Initial	Maiden Name

Address *(Street Name and Number)*	Apt #	Date of Birth *(month/day/year)*

City	State	Zip Code	Social Security #

I am aware that federal law provides for imprisonment and/or fines for false statements or use of false documents in connection with the completion of this form.

I attest under penalty of perjury, that I am (check one of the following).
☐ A citizen of the United States
☐ A noncitizen national of the United States (see instructions)
☐ A lawful permanent resident (Alien #) _____
☐ An alien authorized to work (Alien # or Admission #) _____
until (expiration date, if applicable-*month/day/year*)

Employee's Signature	Date *(month/day/year)*

Preparer and/or Translator Certification *(To be completed and signed if Section 1 is prepared by a person other than the employee)* I attest, under penalty of perjury, that I have assisted in the completion of this form and that to the best of my knowledge the information is ture and correct.

Preparer's/Translator's Signature	Print Name

Address *(Street Name and Number, city, State, Zip code)*	Date *(month/day/year)*

Section 2. Employer Review and Verification *(To be completed and signed by employer. Examine one document from List A OR examine one document List B and one from List C as listed on the reverse of this form, and record the title, number, and expiration date, if any, of the document(s).)*

	List A	OR	List B	AND	List C
Document title	_____		_____		_____
Issuing authority	_____		_____		_____
Document #	_____		_____		_____
Expiration Date *(if any):*	_____		_____		_____
Document #	_____				
Expiration Date *(if any):*	_____				

CERTIFICATION: I attest, under penalty of perjury, that I have examined the document(s) presented by the above named employee, that the above listed document(s) appear to be genuine and to relate to the employee named, that the employee began employment on *(month/day/year)* _____ **and that to the best of any knowledge the employee is authorized to work in the United State. (State employment agencies may omit the date the employee began employment.)**

Signature of Employee of Agricultural department	Print Name	Title

Business or Organization Name and Address *(Street Name and Number, City, State, Zip Code)*	Date *(month/day/year)*

Section 3. Updating and Reverification *(To be completed and signed by employer)*

A. New Name *(if applicable)*	B. Date of rehire *(month/day/year)* *(if applicable)*

C. If employee's previous grant of work authorization has expired, provide the information below for the document that establishes current and employment authorization.

DocumentTitle:_____ Document#:_____ ExpirationDate*(if any)*_____

I attest, under penalty of perjury, that to the best of my knowledge, this employee is authorized to work in the United States, and if the employee presented document(s), the document(s) I have examined appear to be genuine and to relate to the individual.

Signature of Employer or Authorized Representative	Date *(month/day/year)*

(continued)

7.3 (*continued*)

76516 Federal Register/Vol. 73, No. 243,/Wednesday, December 17, 2008/Rules and Regulations

LIST OF ACCEPTABLE DOCUMENTS
All documents must be unexpired

LIST A	LIST B	LIST C
Documents that Establish Both Identity and Employment Authorization	Documents that Establish Identity	Documents that Establish Employment Authorization
	OR	AND

LIST A	LIST B	LIST C
1. U.S. Passport or U.S. Passport Card	1. Driver's license or ID card issued by a State or outlying possession of the United States provided it contains a photograph or information such as name, date of birth, gender, height, eye color, and address	1. Social Secutiry Account Number card other than one that specifies on the face that the issuance of the card does not authorize employment in the United States
2. Permanent Resident Card or Alien Registration Receipt Card (Form I-551)		
3. Foreign passport that contains a temporary I-551 stamp or temporary I-551 printed notation on a machine-readable immigrant visa	2. ID card issued by federal, state or local government agenices or entities, provided it contains a photograph or information such as name, date of birth, gender, height, eye color, and address	2. Certification of Birth abroad issued by the Department of State (Form FS-545)
		3. Certification of Report of Birth issued by the Department of States (Form Ds-1350)
4. Employment Authorization Document that contains a photograph (Form I-766)	3. School ID card with a photograph	
	4. Voter's registration card	4. Original or certified copy of birth certificate issued by a state, county, municipal authority, or territory of the United States bearing an offifical seal
	5. U.S. Military card or draft record	
5. In the case of a nonimmigrant alien authorized to work for a specific employer incident to status, a foreign passport with Form I-94 or Form I-94A bearing the same name as the passport and containing an endorsement of the alien's nonimmigrant status, as long as the period of endorsement has not yet expired and the proposed employment is not in conflict with employment is not in conflict with any restrictions or limitations identified on the form	6. Military dependent's ID card	
	7. U.S. Coast Guard Merchant Mariner Card	5. Native American tribal document
	8. Native American tribal document	
	9. Driver's license issued by a Canadian government authority	6. U.S. Citizen ID Card (Form I-197)
	For persons under age 18 who are unable to present a document listed above	7. Identification Card for Use of Resident Citizen in the United State (Form I-179)
6. Passport from the Federate States of Micronesia (FSM) or the Republic of the Marshall Islands (RMI) with Form I-94 or Form I-94A indicating nonimmigrant admission under the Compact of Free Association Between the United States and the FSM or RMI	10. School record or report card	
	11. Clinic, doctor, or hospital record	8. Employment authorization document issued by the Department of Homeland Security
	12. Day-care or nursery school record	

Illustrations of many of these documents appear in Part 8 of the Handbook for Employers (M-274)

7.4 Large hotel storeroom organizational chart

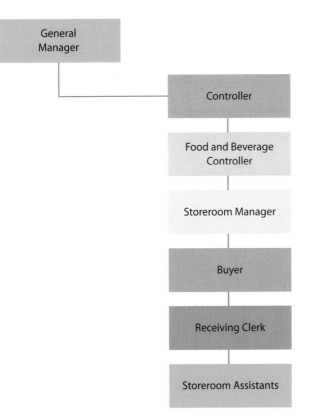

- General Manager
- Controller
- Food and Beverage Controller
- Storeroom Manager
- Buyer
- Receiving Clerk
- Storeroom Assistants

Organization of Facilities

The storeroom should be organized with safety, sanitation, and efficiency in mind (see Figure 7.5a and Figure 7.5b). A manager should address the following:

- There should be enough room in the dry, refrigerated, and freezer sections to store the type and quantities needed.
- All of the areas should be kept clean and free of clutter. There should be enough aisle space to allow access to the products and to use a hand cart.
- The shelves and bins should be labeled so that each item has its own spot and employees can easily find the products.
- Any equipment needed for reaching items such as stepladders, carts, and stools should be kept near the storerooms but out of the way.
- The rooms should have enough lighting so that employees can easily see all of the products.
- Doors should be wide enough to allow carts and pallets to pass through.

All storerooms should be designed for the productivity of the staff, and for safe and secure storage of the products (see Figure 7.6). Among the many considerations are the following:

- Storerooms should be separated from the main food preparation areas. There should be a wall or secure fencing

7.5a A well-organized dry storeroom

© Randy Van Dam 2008

7.5b A well-organized walk-in cooler

© Randy Van Dam 2008

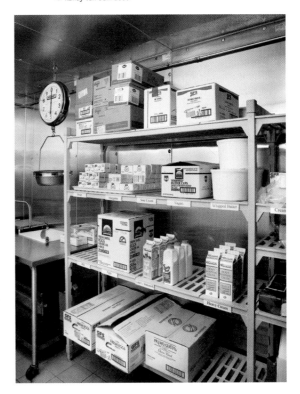

7.6 **Well-designed facilities**

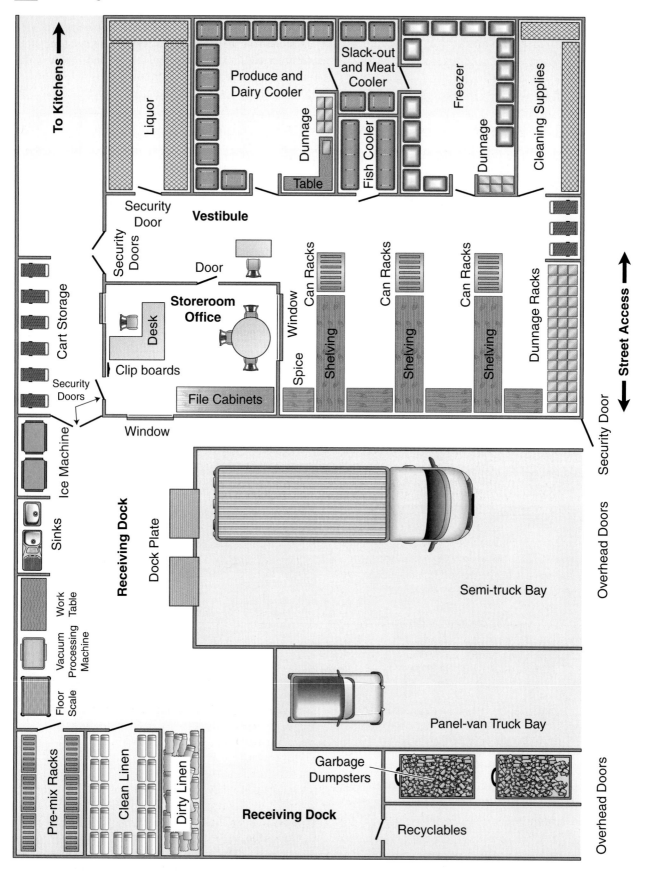

that controls access to the room but allows air circulation. This will help discourage theft while allowing for a quick review of the contents of the room. This helps the person completing the receiving paperwork.

- The storeroom facility should be located near receiving and production. Ideally, it is located between the receiving docks and the main production kitchens, with the buyer's or receiving office accessible and within view.

- Proper maintenance of the temperatures in the dry and refrigerated storage areas is essential. Air compressors for the coolers and freezers generate a lot of heat and should be vented to the outside.

- Dry storage areas for bakery products, particularly bags of flour, should be free of electrical panels or other electrical boxes, as they could spark and start a fire. Additionally, these boxes should be placed in an area where they can be accessed by outside contractors for service.

SPACE REQUIREMENTS

Traditionally, owners and upper management tend not to provide extensive space for areas they perceive only as support services. It is believed these spaces don't generate revenue, directly or indirectly. Therefore, with the high cost of real estate and construction, it is understandable that owners want large dining rooms and bars. After all, the more customers an establishment can serve, the higher the potential revenues. Kitchens and storerooms are normally smaller for this reason, as they are considered a drain on profits.

It is up to the chef and storeroom manager to demonstrate the importance of the kitchen and storeroom as a profit center, not a drain on the revenue. The kitchen and storeroom require adequate space to provide proper support. There is a direct correlation between the needs of the business and the ability of the storeroom to meet those needs. If the storerooms are too small, then the establishment will have to increase the number of orders per week to serve the estimated customers.

The size of the storeroom is related to the nature of the business it serves. According to Scriven and Stevens (1989), "for restaurants and clubs, the following guidelines can be used for dry storage area requirements" (p. 7):

- 100–200 meals per day: 120–200 square feet
- 200–350 meals per day: 200–250 square feet
- 350–500 meals per day: 250–400 square feet
- 500–1,000 meals per day: 300–650 square feet

These indicators are meant for informal dry storerooms, with no offices or other uses, for smaller operations. For larger businesses, which probably have multiple food outlets, Warfel and Cremer (2005) write,

Whether the requirements are based on cubic feet per hundred covers served per day, the dollar volume of business, or the size of the kitchen area and, thereby, the dining area, the final decisions are always tied to the volume of business expected and the distance to and adequacy of the market to be used. (p. 131)

A common rule of thumb in architecture and design is to allocate a percentage of the total space available for the entire facility. Often 10 to 12 percent is allocated for the needs of the storeroom operation, including dry, refrigerated, and freezer. For example, if the property is 50,000 square feet, then 5,000 to 6,000 square feet of that space should be designated for storage.

Some state and county health departments use a formula to calculate dry and refrigerated storage areas: a half a square foot is multiplied by the number of meal periods and the seating capacity. For example:

100 seats × 3 meal periods (lunch, dinner, late night) × 1/2 sq ft = 150 sq ft

This would require a facility to dedicate 150 square feet of dry storage and 150 square feet of refrigerated storage.

RECEIVING DOCK

The receiving dock is the gateway to the food service operation for most food, supplies, and equipment. It should be designed with both delivery and receiving functions in mind. The locations of food service operations are not always ideal for receiving goods. In mega-cities like New York, Los Angeles, Boston, and London, where real estate is very expensive, receiving is done through basement elevators that open onto city sidewalks. Some restaurants do not have a receiving dock but rather a back door through which deliveries are made. The space available and the cost of building a receiving dock can be prohibitive to these operations.

However, when space and money are not as limited, large organizations like hospitals, corporations, colleges, and hotels always design and build receiving docks for their operations. For these locations, certain features and equipment are designed into the receiving spaces, such as:

- **Flexible loading docks.** The delivery trucks that service food service operations vary in size and height. Some trailer heights differ by as much as 18 inches. Broadline distributors use semi-tractor trailers to deliver their supplies, and they use a *dockplate* (see Figure 7.7) to even out the distance from the truck to the dock. Additionally, many purveyors use smaller trucks and vans to make their deliveries, which are much lower than the traditional dock height of 4 to 5 feet. The ramp for a delivery van should be sloped no greater than a 1:12 ratio, allowing for easy maneuverability of delivery carts and dollies. Ideally, large food service operators can build delivery docks and ramps that are practical for both styles of truck.

7.7   **A truck backed against receiving dock with dockplate**
© Randy Van Dam 2008

7.8   **Chef pushing flat-bed cart into walk-in cooler**
© Randy Van Dam 2008

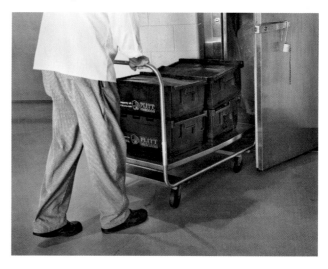

7.9   **Clerk weighing fish using floor scale**
© Randy Van Dam 2008

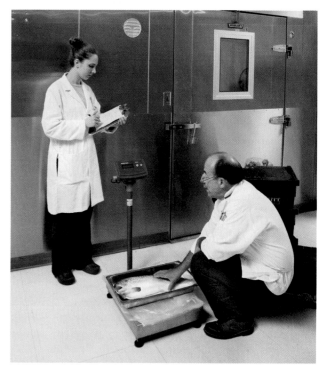

- **Flexible overhead lighting.** The insides of trucks are not lit, making it difficult to see within the truck bed. With sufficient lighting in the loading dock, staff can easily read the paperwork. The use of lighting on retractable cord reels can help in these situations.

- **Cleaning equipment.** A mop closet near the receiving dock is handy for cleaning the dock, especially after a spill. Additionally, including power washers and compressed air to clean carts, hood screens, and cooking equipment on the back dock helps to keep the kitchen clean. This equipment should be kept separate from the main receiving dock area for Hazard Analysis and Critical Control Point (HACCP) reasons.

- **Carts and hand trucks.** Most items that come through the receiving dock are packaged in cases, sometimes on pallets, for ease of transportation and handling. Clerks usually need the assistance of flat carts, two-wheel dollies, and sometimes motorized hand trucks to transport the heavy volume of product that comes through their docks (see Figure 7.8). All carts should be located near the dock.

- **Scales.** Meats, seafood, poultry, and produce need to be weighed upon receipt, using large floor or table scales (see Figure 7.9). Some loading docks have a nearby room in which they weigh and repackage nuts, coffee, and cheeses into smaller portions.

- **Sinks.** The receiving clerk will need to wash down fresh whole chickens and fish upon receipt and then ice them for storage. Also, occasionally the storeroom will need to thaw items under running water, when there is not

enough time to slack out slowly under refrigeration (see Figure 7.10a and Figure 7.10b). There should be a sink for this purpose located adjacent to both the receiving dock and preparation areas.

- **Ice machine.** An ice machine and buckets should be nearby so that fresh seafood and poultry can be iced when they are received.

- **Refuse and recyclable dumpsters.** The receiving dock is often also the location of the refuse containers. Some operations make it their policy to transfer all produce,

which arrives in cardboard, into plastic bins while still on the loading dock. This step is meant to be a preventative measure against pest infestation, as cockroaches occasionally accompany produce boxes. Again, all garbage and container storage should be located away from the food receiving areas per HACCP guidelines, but having them nearby makes recycling discarded cardboard or other items easy.

- **Returnable-recyclable container storage.** Many states have returnable-recyclable laws that require bottle deposits be paid on beer and carbonated beverage purchases. Most operations have a dedicated storage room for empty returnables. This room should be near a sink so that the bottles can be rinsed out before they are stored.

- **Pest control devices.** As the receiving dock is the portal to the food service storeroom and production facilities, it is important that a strong defense against pests be mounted right at the dock. Consider placing rodent traps, forced air curtains, and bug zappers, along with monthly pest control treatments.

- **Soiled linen storage.** Used and soiled linen generally needs to be stored near the loading dock, when linen service

is contracted with rental companies. Either a designated storeroom or staging area for linen carts must be made available (see Figure 7.11).

- **Pre-mix beverage and keg storage.** Most operations use pre-mix or post-mix carbonated beverages and keg systems for their dispensed beverages. They are frequently designed near the receiving dock for the sake of convenience.

BUYING AND RECEIVING OFFICE

The location of the buying and receiving office is very important to the overall function and security of the buying and receiving process. In large hotels, the storeroom is often located below ground, even though the receiving dock is frequently at ground level. This situation is not ideal. To the extent possible, operators should always try to locate their storeroom facilities as close to receiving as possible to aid proper receiving, security, and holding temperatures for their products.

When that is not possible, the next best option is to have a small receiving office located adjacent to the receiving

7.11 **A well-organized linen storeroom**
© Randy Van Dam 2008

7.12 **Chef pulling an invoice from a drawer file**
© Randy Van Dam 2008

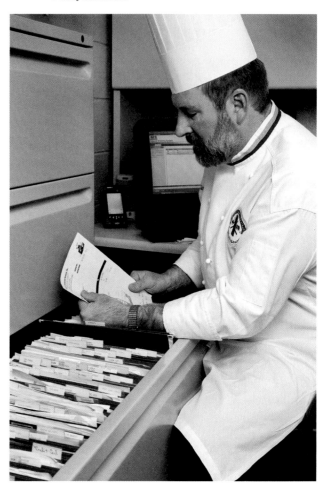

dock. However, the chef or buyer's office must be accessible, if not adjoined, to the storeroom. Ideally, the receiving dock and storeroom are located near each other, with the buying and receiving office located between them.

File Systems

Besides the location, the *organization* of the office is also vital to the success of the operation. It is incumbent on the chef or buyer to organize the product specifications, purchase orders, requisitions, invoices and inventories on behalf of the business entity. In addition, the chef or buyer must have the maintenance files, product catalogues, and equipment catalogues available for easy access. The following items need to be organized by the chef or buyer:

- **Accounts payable files.** The manager, chef, or buyer should keep separate files for each company from which he purchases goods or services. The person receiving deliveries must be trained to place all signed delivery receipts or invoices into the file (Figure 7.12). The manager or chef should enter the charges into a computerized file, making it easy to later calculate and analyze monthly, quarterly, and annual purchases by product category. The actual receipts and any other

delivery paperwork should be sent to the accounting department for payment and reconciliation with the wholesaler's statements.

- **Product specifications.** Chefs and buyers must identify product specifications for each ingredient, as discussed in Chapter 6, "The Ingredient Process," and keep them readily available for reference in buying and receiving.

- **Product catalogues and source guides.** Chefs and buyers must make it a priority to gather information about all ingredients available to them. Even after menus are established, recipes are written, and ingredients are identified, chefs must constantly create new recipes for daily specials and revised menus. Periodically, these catalogues should be culled for oldest publications.

- **Equipment and supply catalogues.** Food service operations use a variety of tabletop supplies, small wares, and large equipment to run their businesses. Owners and chefs need to have access to equipment and supply catalogues for reference.

- **Maintenance files.** Equipment such as computers, dish machines, ventilation hoods, and floor mixers require periodic maintenance to keep them operating at optimal performance levels. Often, companies will enter into service agreements for regular maintenance checks to keep the equipment working properly. Additionally, some equipment will need occasional repair or parts replaced, necessitating a service call by a licensed food service equipment technician. All of these documents should be organized for easy access.

- **Requisitions and pick-slips.** With formal storeroom operations, authorized department heads use requisitions to obtain their supplies. The requisition can either be a paper document completed by the department head or a virtual document submitted electronically. The storeroom staff will print a **pick-slip** to use in collecting the requisitioned items from their storage locations. The purchasing manager reviews the slips and compares them to the inventory on hand. If there is a question about the need for an item, it may be returned to the department head for clarification or justification before it is filled. The requisition slips should be filed according to each customer, for use in calculating the food cost for that department.

It is also helpful to have past requisitions available in case questions arise regarding shortages or other concerns.

- **Inventories.** For the operation to determine its storeroom values, periodic physical counts must be done to compare to the perpetual inventory. The chef or buyer should keep these forms on file as well as send a copy to the accounting office.

In addition to the hard files, the modern chef or buyer should organize virtual files on an office computer, ideally a laptop for optimal portability. The following computer files should be established and maintained daily, if not done automatically by one of the many inventory software programs available for the food service industry:

- **Accounts payable.** If the establishment does not have a computerized accounting program, then a chef can create a spreadsheet with the days of the month down the first column and the name of each vendor heading the other columns. The storeroom manager or receiving clerk should post all daily delivery invoices (see Figure 7.13) to their appropriate accounts, thereby maintaining a running balance of all deliveries, both by company and as an aggregate of the business.

7.13 **Sample Computerized Accounts Payable Template**

	Invoice 317500						
Vendor:	1008	King's Desserts				POSTED	
Invoice no.:	317500	265 Meyer Lane Naperville, IL					
PO:		Terms: Net 30 Delay 25					
Description:	Inventory						
Amount:	2,604.38	Invoice Date:	18 Apr 07	Period:	4	2007	
Paid:		Due Date:	13 May 07	Disc. %:			
Owing:	2,604.38	Discount Date:		Discount:			

	Amount	GL Account	Sub 1	Sub 2	Sub 3	Name
▶	2,434.00	1200	10	1		Inventory - Frozen Pies -East
	170.38	1195	10	1		GST Receivable - Frozen Pies -East

OK Cancel

- **Issues and sales by department.** It is very important for chefs to know their daily, weekly, and monthly cost of food and food cost percentages. A simple chart can be used to track issues and sales. Each internal "customer" of the storeroom, such as the restaurant or bakery, is listed as a heading. Their daily issues are recorded as are their internal and external sales. Another column that divides the food costs column by the sales column to calculate the food cost percentage. To-date costs and sales figures are totaled at the bottom, giving an aggregate computation for the month (see Figure 7.14).

- **Inventory values.** To speed up the inventory process, the chef or buyer can create a template with the inventory names and storage locations. This spreadsheet would have column headings for the products, their count, their current price, and their extended value (which is determined by multiplying the current price by the current count). See Figure 7.15. The rows should include all of the products listed in the same order that they are arranged

in the storerooms and coolers, not alphabetically. Most software packages will allow the operator to arrange the inventory by location for counting and then later alphabetically for locating specific items. If possible, the counts should be entered directly into the computer or a handheld device when they are received to avoid errors when the data is entered into the program.

- **Program compatibility.** If the establishment uses a food service inventory program, it should interface with the accounts receivables program to transfer invoice information quickly. These programs should provide inventory counts, ingredient and recipe costs, and nutritional information.

Right-To-Know Information

To inform all hospitality employees about potentially harmful chemicals they might encounter in the workplace, the federal, state, and municipal governments have instituted

7.14 **Sample Computerized Issues and Sales Template**

Monthly Departmental Issues and Sales
Month: _____ Year: _____

Day	Restaurant			Bakery			Banquets			Coffee Shop		
	Issue Costs	Sales	FC%	Issue Costs	Sales	FC%	Issue Costs	Sales	FC%	Issue Costs	Sales	FC%
1												
2												
3												
4												
5												
6												
7												
8												
9												
10												
11												
12												
13												
14												
15												
31												
Total to Date												

7.15   Sample Computerized Inventory Template

Date: 1/15/2010   InvenTech Software
Time: 4:24 PM   Inventory On-Hand
                                     Grouse Mountain Grill
Inventory Date:
12/15/2009
Beverage Room

Item	Cost/ Unit	Unit(s)	Open	Purchases	Sales	In Stock	Actual	Theoreti- cal Usage	Shrink- age	Start Date
drink "Gato- rade"	$0.41	can(s)	$7.41	$25.00	$28.83	$6.59	$6.59	$28.83	$-	11/30/2009
drink "Snapple"	$0.44	bottle(s)	$7.07	$53.00	$55.21	$4.56	$4.56	$55.21	$-	11/30/2009
juice "Kerns"	$0.30	each	$1.20	$18.00	$11.40	$7.80	$7.50	$11.70	$0.30	11/30/2009
juice "Knud- sen's"	$0.50	bottle(s)	$16.50	$42.00	$48.00	$10.50	$10.00	$48.50	$0.50	11/30/2009
juice "Ocean"	$0.37	each	$2.20	$33.00	$20.54	$14.67	$14.67	$20.54	$-	11/30/2009
juice "Tropi- cana"	$0.56	bottle(s)	$6.17	$37.00	$35.88	$7.29	$7.29	$35.88	$-	11/30/2009
juice "V-8"	$0.68	bottle(s)	$6.77	$92.00	$80.50	$18.27	$18.27	$80.50	$-	11/30/2009
juice "V-8" 46 oz	$1.75	can(s)	$17.50	$42.00	$29.75	$29.75	$28.00	$31.50	$1.75	11/30/2009
juice apple	$2.54	bottle(s)	$7.62	$330.01	$317.31	$20.31	$20.31	$317.31	$-	11/30/2009
juice pineapple (lg)	$1.25	can(s)	$11.25	$30.00	$31.25	$10.00	$10.00	$31.25	$-	11/30/2009
juice pineapple	$0.28	can(s)	$1.69	$9.00	$5.62	$5.06	$5.06	$5.62	$-	11/30/2009
juice tomato (sm)	$0.30	bottle(s)	$4.50	$24.00	$25.20	$3.30	$3.30	$25.20	$-	11/30/2009
pop assorted	$7.25	case	$3.63	$58.00	$54.38	$7.25	$7.25	$54.38	$-	11/30/2009
pop gin- ger ale	$8.83	case	$8.83	$53.00	$44.17	$17.67	$17.67	$44.17	$-	11/30/2009
syrup assorted	$26.00	box(es)	$32.50	$130.00	$136.50	$26.00	$26.00	$136.50	$-	11/30/2009
water "Evian"	$8.00	case	$8.00	$160.00	$24.00	$144.00	$144.00	$24.00	$-	11/30/2009
water "Geyser"	$0.63	each	$8.19	$70.00	$76.88	$1.25	$1.25	$76.55	$-	11/30/2009
water "Pel- legrino"	$13.50	case	$27.00	$270.00	$13.50	$283.50	$270.00	$27.00	$13.50	11/30/2009
water club soda	$1.27	liter(s)	$25.89	$190.01	$173.54	$41.80	$41.80	$173.54	$-	11/30/2009
water tonic	$0.80	liter(s)	$7.20	$40.00	$45.60	$1.60	$1.60	$45.60	$-	11/30/2009
			$211.12	$1,706.02	$1,258.06	$661.17	$645.12	$1,273.78	$16.05	

Right-To-Know regulations for all companies. These regulations require manufacturers of these chemical agents to provide their food service customers with Material Safety Data Sheets (MSDS). For example, when food service operators purchase a case of dish machine soap, its MSDS accompanies the box. Operators are then required to assemble all of the MSDS sheets for products they use and to make the sheets available for their staff. If needed, MSDS sheets can be found on the manufacturer's websites.

Fresh fish	32°F (0°C)
Live shellfish	30°F to 41°F (−1°C to 5°C)
Meat and poultry	32°F to 41°F (0°C to 5°C)
Dairy products	35°F to 41°F (2°C to 5°C)
Eggs	40°F to 45°F (4°C to 7°C)
Fruits and vegetables	Ranging from 32°F to 50°F (0°C to 10°C)
Freezer storage	0°F to 10°F (−18°C to −12°C)

Refrigerated Storage

7.16 **Work table and hanging scales in a cooler**
© Randy Van Dam 2008

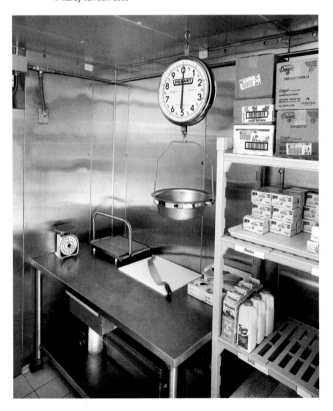

Refrigeration was one of the greatest technological achievements of the modern era. Most food products need to be kept at particular temperatures and humidity levels to keep them from spoiling. In most operations, due to limited cooler space, most refrigerated foods are stored together between 34°F and 38°F (1°C and 3°C). However, operations that purchase large quantities of meat, seafood, produce, and dairy items often have dedicated walk-in coolers for each category. The recommended temperature guidelines for refrigerated and frozen products, as identified by the National Restaurant Association Educational Foundation (NRAEF), are:

If possible, when ordering new doors for walk-in coolers and freezers, door windows should be included in the equipment specifications. Windows deter theft and reduce the opening of doors for inspection, thereby letting less air out and reducing electricity costs. Hanging clear plastic curtain strips inside the entrance to the coolers and freezers also helps to keep the cold air in. When space allows, placing a work table and scales inside a cooler, as shown in Figure 7.16, can aid employees in handling the perishable foods safely and efficiently. The compressors for these units should be located outside of the kitchen area so that the hot air from the compressors does not recirculate into the kitchen.

People, Places, Things

The 2-Degree Rule

In cooperation with Foley Fish of Boston, researchers have quantified the negative effects that lesser refrigeration has on seafood. Their findings show that, for every 2 degrees Fahrenheit that fish are stored above 32°F (0°C) in a 24-hour period, the fish deteriorate an extra day's worth. For example, if freshly caught fish is stored at 36°F, after 24 hours it will be like it has been stored for 72 hours at 32°F. This illustrates the importance of icing down fish upon receipt and their quick production

EQUIPMENT NEEDS FOR STORAGE AREAS

The equipment needs for coolers and freezers are somewhat different from dry storage areas. A dry storage room needs certain commercial stockroom equipment. For decades, many operations successfully used wooden shelving, painted with washable white paint, and balance beam scales to run their operations. However, modern food service establishments have many more options available to them.

Storage in colder areas has some special considerations. Items in this area must be able to withstand the cold temperatures and humidity, so wooden items are not suitable; stainless steel is preferred. Following is a list of equipment that is commonly used in dry and refrigerated storage areas:

- **Shelving.** All shelving must meet local sanitary codes. Ideally, the shelving should be modular, with standard shelf and leg lengths. The company should purchase shelves made for food service applications, such as Cambro, instead of generic products that are from home-improvement centers. The best shelving for refrigeration is made from durable plastic or stainless steel that has been coated with vinyl to keep from rusting (see Figure 7.17). The shelving should be erected no higher than 6 1/2 feet, with a minimum of 6 inches between the bottom shelf and the floor. The shelves should be between 18 and 24 inches deep, with 16 to 18 inches between each row. A combination of solid shelving and wire shelving is recommended, depending on a product's need for air circulation (wire) or support and drainage protection (solid). New designs allow portions of the shelves to be conveniently removed for cleaning in pot sinks or dish machines. For the dry storage areas, chrome-coated or galvanized metal and Formica-covered or painted wooden shelving is still acceptable in most localities, because they are washable, nonporous, and bacteria resistant. However, stainless steel shelving is preferred by operators and health departments alike for their long-term durability and adjustable design. Shelving in dry storerooms should be flexible to allow for maximum use of the space. The adjustable shelving can be wall mounted (see Figure 7.18a and Figure 7.18b) but is traditionally used freestanding (see Figure 7.18c). It is practical to purchase shelving that is available in different shelf lengths and widths, and that can be assembled with varying heights between the shelves. The object is to select shelving that can accommodate varying numbers and sizes of cans and boxes.

- **Wall racks.** Wall racks are used to store specific items with specific shapes or sizes, such as spice containers (see Figure 7.19). Normally, these are available from the distributor or manufacturer.

- **Can racks.** Many fruits, sauces, and vegetables are packaged in large commercial cans and shipped in cases. To help with their storage, and to expedite their use, most

7.17 Washable and adjustable plastic shelving in cooler
© Randy Van Dam 2008

operators employ the use of can racks for storing "broken" or opened cases, as shown in Figure 7.20. Can racks are found within the dry storage areas, not the refrigerator or freezer sections. Some establishments will load a day's worth of cans onto a can rack and then wheel it into the kitchen for use that day.

- **Dunnage racks.** Dunnage racks are used for stacking cases of products that the operation uses in high volume, such as frozen cases of bread dough, frozen cases of snap-n-bake cookies, or frozen cases of chicken breasts. In the dry storage, dunnage racks are used to hold cases of canned goods or bagged items such as flour (see Figure 7.21). They are similar to a pallet, but they are designed for use within a food service facility and for easy cleaning.

- **Scales.** In some kitchens, scales are used within the coolers or storerooms to measure out smaller portions of products. The smaller amounts are then issued to different chefs within the operation. Figure 7.22a and Figure 7.22b show scales in use.

- **Work table.** If the staff portions and bags smaller amounts from bulk storage, then a stainless steel table is a handy addition to the storage areas. The table will generally have plastic food bags, product tags, and portion scales.

7.18a Wall-mounted adjustable shelving

Figures 7.18a–.20 © Randy Van Dam 2008

7.18b Mounting bracket

7.18c Dry storeroom with traditional adjustable shelving

7.19 Wall spice rack

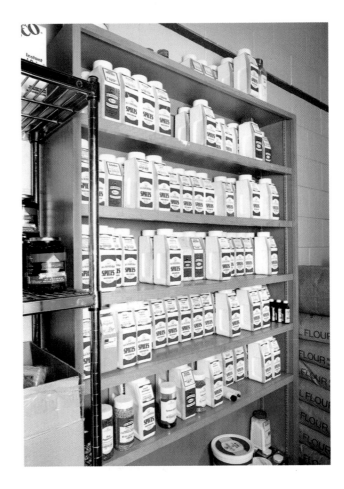

7.20 Can racks

7.21 **Dunnage racks loaded with flour bags**

© Randy Van Dam 2008

- **Sinks and drain tables.** In high-volume operations that feature fresh seafood or poultry, some companies will opt to locate a drainage sink inside the cooler instead of near the receiving area. The drainage sink is used to keep the perishable products chilled while washing and re-icing the product and while applying seafood tags.

- **Vacuum processing equipment.** Some storeroom clerks and chefs use vacuum processing equipment to package raw portioned products such as steaks and fish fillets. Others use it to package cheese, nuts, and dried fruits and vegetables, as shown in Figure 7.23.

- **Thermometers and alarms.** Wall-mounted and portable thermometers are used to maintain proper refrigeration. If possible, alarms can be used to alert the storeroom staff to temperature fluctuations. Newly developed systems not only sound an alarm on the outside of the cooler and in the storeroom, but they also have the ability to be remotely monitored by computer 24 hours a day.

REACH-IN REFRIGERATION TEMPERATURES

Although most storeroom operations use walk-in refrigeration, reach-in refrigeration is sometimes used for smaller storage needs. For example, chocolate is best stored between 57°F and 61°F (14°C and 16°C), which prevents the butter in the chocolate from blooming in

7.22a **Clerk using a mechanical hanging scale**

© Randy Van Dam 2008

7.22b **Clerk using an electronic portion scale**

© Randy Van Dam 2008

7.23 **Clerk using vacuum processing machine to package portioned cheese from bulk**

© Randy Van Dam 2008

warmer temperatures. Cheese is best stored at 45°F (7°C) and is highly susceptible to absorbing odors from other items with which it is stored. Reach-in refrigerators can be adjusted to these temperatures, thereby providing the optimal storage conditions. Reach-in refrigerators are perfect for use within the kitchen where the cooks need access to cold food items on a regular basis. Smaller units can be installed under work tables.

> BUYER'S NOTE *Different state and local health codes might restrict the use of vacuum processing equipment to locations that have HACCP plans in place or sterile refrigerated facilities, such as meat fabrication rooms. Chefs and managers should check with their local health departments.*

STORING FOOD AND PAPER TEMPERATURES

As with refrigerated storage, the dry storeroom should have proper control over air circulation, temperature, humidity, and light. Whereas all potentially hazardous foods require refrigeration somewhere below 40°F (4°C), dry goods, canned goods, and paper products have no storage temperatures or humidity levels mandated by the health department. Yet dry and canned goods stored in cool, dry environments generally fair better and are less

prone to spoilage and bug infestation. It is recommended that storeroom temperatures be kept between 50°F and 70°F (10°C to 21°C) and the relative humidity be kept at 50 to 60 percent.

Storeroom Layouts

Storerooms should have a practical layout for the benefit of those who need their supplies. The following is a list of useful tips in organizing food and paper goods:

- Before placing items in storage, develop a room layout for the space using graph paper:
  - Line the available walls with freestanding shelving. In the dry storage area, make sure to leave room for wall racks, wall shelves, and dunnage racks.
  - Create rows of freestanding shelving, extending from the entrance of the storeroom to the opposing wall. Be sure to allow sufficient space between rows for the storeroom staff to access products.
  - Design overhead lighting to illuminate the shelf products. Check with the local health department to determine minimum levels of lighting required.
  - Design a separate lockable storeroom within the main storeroom for liquor storage, unless beverage personnel require direct access.
- If there is sufficient space, allow 16 to 18 inches between shelves. If space is limited, narrow the distances between shelves to accommodate specific can sizes or frozen case sizes. In either case, as required by the health department, leave at least 6 inches of unobstructed space beneath the lowest shelf to allow for easy cleaning.
- If space is available, select shelving that is between 18 and 24 inches deep, depending on the products it will hold.
- Group items by category, such as bakery supplies, paper goods, canned vegetables, pasta, oils, or seasonings. Store like items together in the freezers and coolers.
- Store glass products and other breakables close to the floor.
- Store items that weigh more than 30 pounds at waist level, and store lighter items on the upper shelves.
- Use dunnage racks for storing items that are issued in bulk.
- Each product should have its own address. Create row and shelf labels for easy location of the products. These labels should be in holders on the front of the shelves to facilitate physical inventories, and they can include barcodes for easy counting with a handheld device.
- If needed, some shelves can be designated as overflow storage where additional items needed for large banquets can be stored until used.
- Allow adequate storage space for all items, even when they are out of stock.

STORING BEVERAGES

Beverages can be stored in a variety of cool room or refrigerated locations. However, it is very important that they are stored at consistent temperatures and rotated regularly for freshness. According to the National Restaurant Association Educational Foundation (NRAEF, 2007), "Beverage alcohols can evaporate and develop offensive odors and flavors. Some can change composition, are sensitive to temperature, or cannot easily be preserved once opened (if at all)" (p. 63).

The following scenarios are the most common for storing beverages:

- **Canned and bottled beverages.** Canned and bottled, also known as RTD (ready to drink) beverages include juices, water, mixes, beer, and soda. Canned and bottled products are susceptible to spoilage by excessive heat and, therefore, must be stored in temperatures below 70°F (21°C) for any extended period of time. All canned and bottled products have a limited shelf life, although they may range anywhere from a few months to several years. It is important to purchase only what can be rotated out on a regular basis. The following spaces are the most common storage areas for canned and bottled beverages:

  - **Dry storeroom.** Some operations choose to store their canned and bottled beverages along with their other products in the primary storeroom. These products do need extensive storage space, though, so a separate room may be warranted.

  - **Cage.** A cage may be either a fixed location or a portable unit used for transporting issued products to remote locations. For ease of construction and minimal cost, a section of the room or alcove is typically fenced off with screening and a gate. Approved staff can have access to the beverages as needed.

  - **Cooler.** If space permits, canned and bottled beverages are stored under refrigeration for both security and desired serving temperature. The ideal refrigerated temperature for beer, mineral water, and soda is 40–45°F (4–7°C). Special coolers are available from beverage distributors for use in customer service areas.

- **Wine.** There are some restaurants that have invested thousands of dollars to have an extensive wine list. Not only is a carefully developed wine list a drawing card for well-healed clientele, it is also an effective and proven method for generating high sales dollars. This asset must be preserved under the right conditions.

  - **Cellars.** Cellars are often created to provide the ideal conditions for storing and aging wine. The correct storing temperature for wines is between 50°F and 60°F (10°C and 16°C). Most sommeliers prefer to keep the wines at 55°F (13°C). At lower temperatures, wines cease to age, and at warmer temperatures, wines age prematurely. Storing wines at room temperature (70°F or 21°C) hurries the maturity process, rapidly aging the wine. For longer periods of time, wine should be stored in the following manner:

    In dark, well-ventilated and insulated spaces
    Temperature controlled between 50 F and 60°F (10°C and 16°C)
    On racks or in bins with no vibration or movement
    Stored horizontally, to keep their corks moist, with label facing upward
    *Using **bin tags** to identify and catalogue the wine (see Figure 7.24)*

  - **Cage.** Wine cages are sometimes used to securely transport issue wine and also to secure wine within a walk-in cooler or dry storage area.

  - **Cooler.** Although wines should not be stored in temperatures outside of 50–60°F (10–16°C) for very long, it is quite acceptable and practical to store wines in a cooler: the best temperature between 40°F and 45°F (4°C and 7°C). Most wines are served chilled, and walk-ins offer security and speed of cooling, particularly in volume banquet situations. The wine is chilled for only a short period of time. The correct serving temperature varies for each type of wine. The following temperatures are considered ideal:

    White and rosé wines—chilled 45–55°F (7–13°C)
    Most red wines—chilled 60–65°F (16–19°C)
    Very good red wines—room temperature of 70°F (21°C)
    Sparkling wines—chilled to 45°F (7°C)

- **Distilled spirits.** Distilled spirits are a popular choice among certain groups of customers. In recent years, the public has chosen to spend more money on higher quality beer, wines, and spirits. Microbrews, exotic martinis, mojitos, and margaritas have grabbed the attention of the new generation, and distilleries have responded with new flavors and tastes.

  - **Liquor storeroom.** Liquor and other distilled spirits represent a sizeable investment in stock, and they are also a popular item to steal. To protect this investment, most operators construct a separate room to store their unissued distilled spirits, known as the *liquor supply room* (see Figure 7.25). In restaurants and nightclubs, this room could be located behind the main lounge bar. In smaller operations, even the owner's office can serve as the liquor storeroom. Ideally, it is a separate locked space under the control of the storeroom staff, or, in the absence of a storeroom staff, a manager. To prevent theft, open bottles of liquor should not be stored in the same room with unopened bottles, so that lesser brands cannot be poured into empty premium liquor bottles. Partial bottles are kept at the bar. If the establishment has temporary bars, such as those for banquets, then there should be a separate storage area for open bottles.

  - **Cage.** In addition to fixed cages (Figure 7.26a), many businesses use portable cages to store and transport issued stock in a secure manner (see Figure 7.26b). They are often assembled from liquor stock and then issued to service or bar personnel for use in remote banquet bars.

7.24 **Wine Bin Tag**

BIN CARD _____

Date: _____   Product: _____

Balance Brought Forward: _____   Bottle Size: _____

**Paste
wine
label
here**

DATE	IN	OUT	TOTAL ON HAND

7.25 **Liquor supply room**

© Randy Van Dam 2008

- **Beverage systems.** These mechanical systems dispense soda, water, and liquor. They can be as simple as a soda gun or as sophisticated as a computerized liquor system that makes drinks. The liquor for these systems should be kept in a locked room, much like stored bottles.

- **Kegs.** Draft beer, wine, root beer, and ciders can be stored and dispensed in kegs that are dispensed either by hand drawing the draft beer, or with CO_2. The kegs are stored under refrigeration during use and until they are replaced (see Figure 7.27). The ideal temperature is between 40°F and 45°F (4°C and 7°C).

- **Pre-mix.** In pre-mix sodas, the syrup and water is combined and sold in bags or canisters. The CO_2 is in the container, and a dip stick activates the bubbles. Pre-mix systems are usually less expensive than post-mix. Vendors will generally provide and install fountainheads, as shown in Figure 7.28, when using their products.

- **Post-mix.** Also known as bag-in-box, the soda syrup is in bags or canisters and is mixed with carbonated water at the time of service, as shown in Figure 7.29. This produces a "fresher" soda, and it is still cheaper for operators than bottled or canned products. But it does require the operator to have a CO_2 tank and a syrup pump on the premises. The syrup and water travel to the gun in plastic tubing, so the closer the system is to the guns or machine, the easier it is to keep the system clean.

Fixed beverage cage

Figures 7.26a–.28 © Randy Van Dam 2008

7.26b **Portable beverage cage**

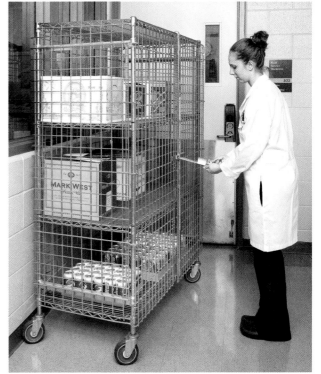

7.27 **Keg system**

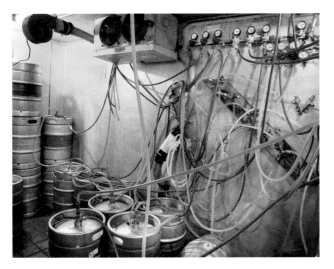

7.28 **Pre-mix fountainheads**

deposit. The cans and bottles should be cleaned before they are stored to avoid insect contamination.

STORING RETURNABLE BEVERAGE CONTAINERS

Some states require a deposit on containers in which carbonated beverages are sold, so recycling is not only an environmentally responsible act but a mandatory business practice. Operators must store returnable containers until they are returned for the

STORING CHEMICAL SUPPLIES

To protect the integrity of the products, and the health of the general public, health codes require operators to store their cleaning supplies and chemicals separately from their food. Ideally, this should be a separate room, but some local codes will allow a designated section in the dry storage area. Some cleaning supplies are sold in concentrates and must be mixed with water before use. Other chemical companies

7.29   **Post-mix bag-in-box rack**

© Randy Van Dam 2008

will supply an operator with racks and dispensing equipment for mixing and storing the chemicals. Bulk supplies such as 5 gallon buckets of dishwasher sanitizer must be stored near the equipment. Cleaning supplies, whether for pot sinks, dish machines, ovens, or floors, are important and often expensive parts of the operation, and they must be regulated by the storeroom staff. These items should be issued as needed and carefully managed like all other assets of the business.

STORING LINEN AND SUNDRIES

Food service operators who choose to have their staff wear uniforms, including side towels and aprons, or use linen napkins and tablecloths in their dining rooms generally have two choices: own and wash, or rent. Many larger operations, such as hotels, spas, and resorts, operate their own laundering facilities. In these cases, the buyer's responsibility is often limited to identifying sources for the initial purchase of linens or uniforms (to be analyzed by other department heads). The in-house laundry then manages the stock levels and will inform the purchasing department when more linens are needed.

The other option is to rent the linens, towels, aprons, and uniforms. It is the responsibility of the buyer to source the products and the responsibility of the chef, owner, or dining room

manager to make the selections. The buyer is then responsible for ordering and storing the various linen supplies, as needed. When linens are rented, the supplier will stop by on a regularly scheduled basis to pick up dirty linens and replace them with clean ones. Normally enough items are left to last several days.

Each location stores and issues products differently. Some places store the table linen and napkins in closets where the table service staff has direct access, or it is controlled by the dining room supervisor. Other businesses keep everything under the direct control of the storeroom staff, which only issues products by requisition. It is best to note that all linen is expensive to rent, and management must enforce proper controls. Hourly staff tends to be cavalier and wasteful with linen.

Table linen is traditionally sorted, folded, and packaged by size and color. Facilities for clean linen should be organized with sufficient shelving to also separate the product according to size and color, with each shelf space labeled for easy inventory. Additionally, sufficient pipe rod must be available to hang chef jackets, table skirting, and wall drapes as required by the operation.

Soiled and clean linen should be kept in separate locations. Linen bags and carts should be made available to all remote kitchens and dining spaces that generate soiled linen, with directions to sort used table linens from soiled side towels. Additionally, delivery personnel should never be allowed to have unsupervised access to clean linen storage facilities.

STORING SMALL WARES AND EQUIPMENT

In addition to food, cleaning supplies, disposables, and linen, storeroom managers purchase tabletop supplies, glassware, flatware, and china for their operations. Most operations purchase these products from specialty distributors or special order them from their broadline distributors. Normally, delivery for these items takes longer than for foodstuffs, so the buyer must keep a careful eye on the stock. The benefit of using common tabletop supplies is having them almost always available, as needed. Additionally, commonly available product lines tend to be less expensive than special order products. But if the establishment wishes to have a unique tabletop, special ordering may be the only way to go.

It is best to have enough tabletop supplies available for a minimum of two and a half times the seating capacity of all dining and banquet facilities. Operators should also store an additional half times the seating capacity for immediate backup. This cushion gives operators time to purchase additional tabletop supplies and small wares when they are on sale, or when the company is in a position to make purchases. Back-up items should be stored separately and not placed into service unless needed. If items are taken out of the back-up storage, the purchasing manager should be alerted. Having extra items in circulation can lead to careless handling and emergency buying.

Seafood Tanks

Today, seafood is delivered to locations far from where it was caught, providing operators the access to fresh fish, shellfish, and crustaceans. Not every restaurant can use fresh seafood, depending on their target market and other considerations. The use of commercial **live tanks** provides the opportunity to offer freshly killed fish and shellfish to the clientele, providing both the quality and the *appearance of freshness* that comes with live products being on site. These holding tanks vary in size, with the largest ones (upwards of 330 gallons) able to hold up to 200–250 pounds of lobster, 150 pounds of catfish, or 100 pounds of trout for approximately one week, and are often placed in the lobby for customers to see (see Figure 7.30). The live product will only survive for a brief amount of time in captivity and must be rotated with freshly delivered product. The buyer must determine the volume needs of the operation and order accordingly to prevent an abundance of dead fish or lobsters.

The tanks must be cleaned regularly, both manually and through the use of chemicals, and the water temperature must be monitored. Although manufacturers of modern tank systems have made great advancements over the past several decades, they still require effort to balance the volume of live product, light, chemicals, feed, and water temperature when maintaining a system.

Hydroponics

As first discussed in Chapter 4, "Modern Applications of Food Science," hydroponic farming is simply growing plant life in nutrient-rich solution, without the presence of soil. It generally occurs in tightly controlled environments such as hydroponic greenhouses. If an establishment has a hydroponic garden, the storeroom staff must manage the growth and harvesting of the herbs and vegetables.

7.30   **Lobster tank**
© Randy Van Dam 2008

People, Places, Things

Making the Lobster Run

I've worked in two different haute cuisine restaurant operations that had live tanks to hold fresh seafood. The first was

rainbow trout, where I worked as a saucier in the mid-1970s. The other was in Jacksonville, Florida, where I was the executive chef of an upscale restaurant and nightclub in 1980. I used to make late-night trips to the Jacksonville airport every Tuesday to meet a Delta Airlines flight from Boston. I would receive five Styrofoam boxes of live Maine lobsters, covered in seaweed and wet newspapers. I personally went to the airport because the lobsters represented a lot of money, and I wanted to inspect each delivery for freshness; if the lobsters weren't lively, I would refuse to accept them, which I needed to do once in a while at the beginning. My supplier in Boston, who wasn't interested in losing money by sending me listless "sleepers," noted my personal attention to receiving. After refusing a few containers, my purveyor began sending me better product. While I was at the airport, my kitchen staff would cook all of the remaining lobsters left in the tank, which we would use for Lobster Americaine or bisque for the tourist clientele, who otherwise loved looking at the tank of live lobsters while waiting to be seated. The maintenance staff would clean the tank, and it was ready for my new delivery of live lobsters by the time I returned from

Herb Gardens

Culinary herbs are fresh or dried leaves used in foods for their flavor value. Although not always widely known, there are hundreds of these plants that can be raised and used for this purpose. Using both traditional and hydroponic gardens, many restaurateurs have chosen to raise their own herbs (see Figure 7.31) or to get fresh herbs from local growers. Buyers should explore the possibilities of working with area farmers for the benefit of both businesses.

In addition to their traditional use in prepared dishes, culinary herbs can be made into value-added products such as herbal teas, savory and sweet jellies, fresh cheeses, flavored butters, chutneys, and sauces. Modern chefs must consider ways of extending the use of these products to bring excitement and interest to their menus.

7.31   **Chef harvesting from an outdoor herb garden**

© Courtesy of Pat Yost Gardens 2008

Storeroom Sanitation

As with all other areas of the modern food service operation, the storeroom must be maintained with the highest sanitation standards. Immediately upon receipt, all supplies become assets of the company. To keep those assets in their optimum condition, they must be handled properly and stored in ideal conditions with a focus on proper sanitation. As Labensky and Hause (2007) write,

> **Sanitation** refers to the creation and maintenance of conditions that will prevent food contamination or food-borne illness. Contamination refers to the presence, generally unintended, of harmful organisms or substances. Contaminants, or hazards, can either be *biological, chemical,* or *physical.* When consumed in sufficient quantities, food-borne contaminants can cause illness or injury, long-lasting disease or even death. (p. 20)

Some potential sanitation issues include:

- **Biological hazard.** Storeroom employees should make sure that cross-contamination does not occur so as to prevent disease-causing microorganisms, such as bacteria, yeast, and mold, from entering the food in significant numbers.

- **Chemical hazard.** Storeroom employees should make sure that the food is not contaminated by chemicals stored on the premises.

- **Physical hazard.** Storeroom employees should make sure that food is protected from foreign particles, such as wood chips, metal shavings, and glass shards.

SANITARY PRACTICES

According to the Centers for Disease Control and Prevention (CDC) there are approximately 76 million food-related illnesses in the United States each year. Most of these incidents can be traced back to poor food handling by food service employees.

Generally speaking, most microorganisms and other contaminants cannot travel by themselves. Instead, they are carried by humans, rodents, and insects. **Cross-contamination** is when safe foods come into contact with harmful organisms or substances, often by contact with human hands, cutting boards, work surfaces, or chef's knives.

This form of contamination can occur, for example, when a storeroom clerk uses a side towel to clean a cutting board and knife that was used to portion fish and then wipes a dish counter dry with the same towel. Subsequently, a cook places heads of lettuce on the contaminated counter, which will later be cut for salad. See Table 7.1 for a list of several foodborne diseases or organisms and the foods commonly associated with them.

The following steps should be followed to prevent cross-contamination:

- Employees should wash their hands each time they enter the kitchen and before they handle foods.

- Employees should wash their hands each time they work with different potentially hazardous food categories.

- Employees should wear single-use gloves each time they handle foods that will not be cooked or sanitized. They should change gloves frequently.

- Employees should wear gloves, or use tongs or disposable wrapping material, to handle foods used for immediate use.

- Employees should properly sanitize all work surfaces, including cutting boards, sinks, and tabletops.

TABLE 7.1 Characteristics of Food Infections and Intoxications

Disease/Organism	Foods Involved	Control Measures
Botulism	Low-acid canned foods, meats, sausage, fish	Follow proper canning procedures; cook foods properly
Campylobacter juni	Raw milk, eggs, poultry, raw beef, cake icing, water	Cook foods properly; prevent cross-contamination
Clostridium perfringens poisoning	Meat, poultry, and other foods held at room temperature	Cool foods immediately after cooking; hold hot foods above 135° F
Escherichia coli 0157:H7	Ground beed, raw milk, chicken	Cook meat properly; no cross-contamination
Listeriosis	Vegetables, milk, cheese, meat, seafood	Cook foods properly; prevent cross-contamination; use standard sanitary practices
Salmonellosis	Meat, poultry, and egg products; milk products	Cook thoroughly; prevent cross-contamination; use standard sanitary practices
Staphylococcus poisoning	Custard- or cream-filled baked goods, ham, poultry, dressing, gravy, eggs, potato salad, cream sauces, sandwich fillings	Refrigerate foods; use standard sanitary practices
Yersiniosis	Unpasteurized milk, contaminated water, pork, other raw meats	Cook foods properly; prevent cross-contamination; use standard sanitary practices

- Employees should use different color-coded cutting boards to prepare meats, poultry, seafood, and produce.
- Employees should properly sanitize all small wares used for preparing foods.
- Employees should discard soiled side towels and aprons in linen bags, as needed.

FOOD DETERIORATION

Deterioration begins immediately upon food being harvested or manufactured. How well it is handled after being received at the establishment determines its ultimate value to the consumer. As Reed (2006) writes, "Satisfactory methods of handling foods are designed to overcome the two major causes of food deterioration:

- Chemical changes within the food that result in loss of quality and reduction in nutrient value.
- Spoilage organisms (mold, yeast, bacteria) that get into the food and produce undesirable or even dangerous effects." (p. 153)

The receiving staff must be vigilant about placing perishable foods in refrigerated storage as quickly as possible. And, conversely, foods for issue must be kept at proper temperatures right up until they leave the storeroom. Storeroom employees must be vigilant about keeping foods outside the **temperature danger zone** as much as possible. Most bacteria that cause foodborne illnesses multiply rapidly at temperatures between 70°F and 125°F (21°C and 52°C), so the temperature danger zone refers to the broad range of temperatures between 41°F and 135°F (5°C and 57°C), as shown in Figure 7.32. By storing foods outside of the temperature danger zone, bacteria's ability to flourish is dramatically reduced.

BUYER'S NOTE Use clear storage containers with tight-fitting lids that can be labeled, such as Lexon, to preserve and protect products in the storeroom and coolers.

The internal temperature of foods may not be allowed to stay within that range for more than 2 hours to be safe. Foods allowed to remain within those ranges for any extended length of time provide optimal conditions for bacterial growth, as shown in Figure 7.33. When bacteria are transported from one location to another, there is a *lag phase* in their initial growth, and they are slow to expand. This period is followed by a sharp increase in bacterial growth, known as the *log phase*, until they reach a point where they can no longer expand, known as the *stationary phase*. Bacteria then decline to grow (*decline phase*) because the product is saturated, as there is no more food, space, or moisture available to support them.

Quality Loss and Spoilage

When foods deteriorate, often chemical adulterations become evident in the foods, such as softening, darkening, or discoloration. These chemical changes also result in some loss of flavor and nutritional value. These preliminary changes do not always necessitate the disposal of the product or fear of causing illness if used.

7.32 **The temperature danger zone**

Boiling point
at sea level

Cooking temperatures
destroy most vegetative
bacteria forms.

Bacteria growth prevented;
however, many survive.
Survival depends on length
of time at these temperatures
and the bacteria type.

Minimum
holding
temperature
for hot foods

Bacteria growth

DANGER ZONE
41°F(5°C)—135°F(51°C)
Rapid growth of bacteria.
May be toxin production.
Do not keep foods in this
temperature range for more
than 2–3 hours total.

Bacteria growth very rapid
at 60°F(16°C)—120°F(48°C)

Maximum
holding
temperature
for cold foods

Bacteria growth

Freezing
point

Refrigeration temperatures.
Bacteria growth is very slow.

Freezing temperatures stop
bacteria growth; however,
many bacteria survive.

Optimum
freezer
storage
temperature

7.33 **Bacterial growth curve chart**

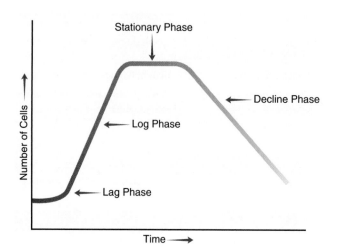

possess these microorganisms, each with their own characteristics and effects:

- **Bacteria.** Bacteria will grow in all low-acid foods. They also grow in bland foods like vegetables and poultry but not in tart foods like pickled products and fruits. Some bacteria are not harmful, although some can cause illness to varying degrees. Bacteria can be detected by a glossy sheen on the surface of meats, poultry, and seafood, or when food cans become bulged.

- **Yeasts.** Yeasts grow best in liquid or semi-solid foods that are tart or high in sugars. Yeast acts on the sugars to form carbon dioxide and alcohol. Bulges in raw foods or canned goods and yeasty odors are evidence of the CO_2. The alcohol also adds a fermented flavor to the food.

- **Mold.** Molds are aerobic, requiring air to thrive. For this reason, molds only appear on the surface of tart and bland foods. As molds mature, they tend to form yellow, green, white, or black patches on their host foods. Generally considered undesirable (except in certain cheeses and corn), molds give off musty tastes and odors.

All foods that show signs of contamination from one of these sources must be discarded.

HACCP

To ensure that foods remain safe and sanitary during all phases of their handling, many food businesses institute a **Hazard Analysis and Critical Control Point (HACCP)** system. As Lachney (2002) writes,

> Hazard Analysis and Critical Control Point is not an approach to food safety, it *is* food safety. Instead of attempting to track down the "guilty" food that made

However, foods that show changes in color, smell, and texture will begin to spoil within days. This once again reinforces the need for operators to purchase only the amount of fresh foods they can safely use within a few days and to properly rotate all other preserved foods in storage.

Spoilage is best detected by off-odors and slimy surface textures that quickly lead to food that is unfit for human consumption. Various bacteria, yeasts, and mold, which are omnipresent in nature, create spoilage. All untreated foods people sick, HACCP focuses on *preventing* food safety problems *before* they ever occur. HACCP does this by assessing the risks associated a food product or process, and then establishing necessary steps needed to control the risk. (p. 1)

To implement the process, the food service professional must evaluate his food operation according to the seven HACCP principles, developed by the National Advisory Committee on Microbiological Criteria for Foods (NAC-MCF) (see Figure 7.34).

From its early application in the 1960s, led by NASA engineers to create a system that would ensure a safe food system for their astronauts, to its adoption by FDA's Food Code, HACCP has become part of our industry's fabric. As Lachney continues:

> Today, HACCP is becoming the mainstay of the food industry. Its future will permeate all types of food operations (e.g. crops production and harvest, raising stock, fishing, transporting/storing/preparing foods). In essence, from the farm or from the sea, to the dining room table or to the hospital bedside, HACCP will ensure safe food. HACCP is here to stay. (p. 2)

Chefs, managers, and storeroom operators must assess their handling of all foodstuffs, from receiving through sale to the customer, to ensure safe handling and storage.

7.34   **HACCP System Flowchart**

HACCP INSPECTION DATA FLOW DIAGRAM

EST.NAME:	PERMIT NO.:	INSPECTOR:
DATE:	TIME IN: AM/PM	TIME OUT: AM/PM

Record all observations below-tranfer violations to Inspection Report
FOOD TEMPERATURES/TIMES/OTHER CRITICAL LIMITS
Use Additional Forms If Necessary

FOOD	1	CRITICAL LIMIT	2	CRITICAL MIMIT	3	CRITICAL LIMIT	4	CRTITICAL LIMIT
STEP								
A. SOURCE								
B. STORAGE								
C. PREP BEFORE COOK								
D. COOK								
E. PREP AFTER COOK								
F. HOT/COLD HOLD								
G. DISPLAY/ SERVICE								
H. COOL								
I. REHEAT								

OTHER FOOD TEMPERATURES OBSERVED   Use steps from above for location

FOOD	TEMP.	STEP	FOOD	TEMP.	STEP	FOOD	TEMP.	STEP

(Adapted from the 1999 FDA Model Food Code.)

Environmental Concerns

Recycling has become a major component of waste reduction, in a growing effort to reduce trash and restore our natural resources. In addition to reducing waste, many containers and packaging materials can be reused or recycled (hence the three R's: *reduce, reuse,* and *recycle*).

Items such as batteries, plastics, papers, cardboard, glass, and metal can be separated, reserved, and redistributed to local reusing and recycling companies by storeroom personnel (see Figure 7.35). An establishment can take other measures too, for example, by purchasing fresh or frozen vegetables, there will very few cans for recycling

At this point, recycling is largely voluntary. Generally, it is not practiced for any economic benefit but rather out of concern for the environment and recognition of personal and business responsibility to recycle. However, some operators find recycling is not currently cost effective. It is expected that recycling will become more commonplace as related costs decrease or societal pressures and consumer expectations grow.

7.35 **Recycling containers with various recycled products**

Photo courtesy Robert Garlough

[ASK THE EXPERT]

Allan J. Kramer, R.S.
Registered Sanitarian

Name: Allan J. Kramer, R.S.

Title: Supervising Sanitarian, Environmental Health Division

Employer: Kent County Health Department, Michigan

Education/Training: Bachelor of science, with an emphasis on environmental health from Grand Valley State University

General Responsibilities: Kramer supervises ten general sanitarians and one plan reviewer. Together, they are responsible for inspecting the food production facilities and practices of 2,2150 entities involved in the preparation and consumption of retail food. Their sites include schools, hospitals, restaurants, country clubs, hotels, food commissaries, catering kitchens, department stores, mall and retail food outlets, churches, and vending sites. Essentially, any location that prepares or sells prepared food to the general public falls under their jurisdiction. For a site to receive a license to prepare and sell food, the County Health Department sanitarians must inspect the facilities to ensure that they adhere to the guidelines set forth by the Food and Drug Administration's (FDA) Food Code.

Ask the Expert Questions:

1) How does a food service operator receive approval for its kitchen facilities?
When a new food service facility is being built, or an existing facility undergoes a major renovation, they are required to submit their construction plans to our office for review and approval. This must be done prior to the commencement of any construction, or they run the risk of having to rebuild any area that doesn't meet the code requirements. These areas include plumbing; mop, hand and pot sinks; water heater capacity; refrigeration and dry storage; employee support space; along with floor, wall and work surfaces. Our office provides Plan Submittal Instructions to the operators, providing steps for submitting their construction drawings for review. Additionally, the operator must complete an extensive Plan Review Application that requires answers to specific operating policy and procedure questions. The two documents are then reviewed by our office and discussed extensively with the applicant before any license will be granted.

2) After a food service facility is up and running, what areas do you consider critical during your periodic follow-up inspections?
After a place has been opened and operating, we make periodic inspections to ensure they remain compliant with the food code. Of course any area that can be of immediate or potential danger to the general public is of concern to our office. Specifically, we look at storage and prep areas to determine the potential for cross-contamination of raw and cooked food items, as well as chemical storage. This includes proper rotation and dating of stock. We inspect the perimeter area surrounding the facility for signs of rodents, including the Dumpster and door sweeps. We look for rodent rubs along the walls, trails, and droppings. Our inspectors observe the storeroom and preparation staff for proper personal hygiene and sanitation practices. We also inspect their cleaning practices, storage practices, and inquire into the sourcing of food supplies to ensure product safety. All walls, floors, and work surfaces must be smooth, non-absorbent and easily cleanable.

3) What problem areas do you often observe?
Some older establishments continue to add reach-in refrigerators in lieu of a larger walk-in cooler. Reach-ins cause excessive heat in the prep areas, and poor circulation of refrigerated air around the food; premature spoilage often results. Too much heat producing equipment can create an imbalance in the air being exhausted. All equipment must be NSF approved, and of commercial design and quality. Some operators try to get by on home-style kitchen equipment. Also, if an area is not easy to clean, then it often is not cleaned. Surfaces must remain smooth and non-porous to be sanitary. Also, we like to see 18-inches of shelf space, or a physical barrier such as a wall, between stored food and chemicals. Additionally, we like all food kept stored off the floor in both dry and refrigerated storage areas.

4) Please provide your advice to a chef, buyer, or food service manager relative to the role and responsibility of buying in food service?
Operators should view their local environmental health departments as concerned partners, and as a reliable resource. Rather than view health department inspectors as adversaries, operators should realize our role is to ensure food safety for the general public. To do so, we provide food service operators with sanitation guidelines so they may operate their businesses within the Food Code as established by the U.S. Food and Drug Administration.

Michael Kidder

Place of Birth: Hastings, Michigan

Courtesy Michael Kidder

Educational Background and Work Experience

Michael Kidder knew he wanted to be in the food business ever since he could hold his first paying job. Kidder loves to work with his hands, and, besides toying with trucks and snowmobiles, he finds great satisfaction in the physical requirements of his daily responsibilities as operations coordinator for the Secchia Institute for Culinary Education (SICE) at Grand Rapids Community College (GRCC). In high school, Kidder worked as a cook in a local family restaurant famed for their barbecued ribs. Because of his passion toward anything he pursues, Kidder quickly rose to become the kitchen manager at Sam's Joint. Kidder enrolled in the culinary arts program at GRCC, where he also worked as a receiving clerk for its food service storeroom operation. After graduating from GRCC in 1991 with an AAAS degree in culinary arts, and earning the department's Director's Award for his outstanding student performance, Kidder became the P.M. sous chef for Applause Catering and Pietro's Ristorante. When GRCC expanded both its food service and culinary education facilities, Kidder was recruited to return to GRCC in the position of storeroom buyer. He eventually rose through the ranks to become the storeroom manager, overseeing the daily purchasing, receiving, storing, and issuing of the Secchia Institute's 1,400 different products in inventory. As the department continued to expand, Kidder's duties also grew. He now works as the college's operations coordinator for the Secchia Institute for Culinary Education and is responsible for overseeing the purchasing for, and maintenance of, all kitchen and dining facilities including all food, supplies, linen, furniture, and equipment; managing the kitchen stewards; and coordinating the SICE's popular seminar program for nonprofessional culinary enthusiasts. Kidder continues to stay abreast of developments in the industry and regularly attends trade shows and takes continuing education classes.

Memberships and Career Highlights

Kidder is an active member of his local chapter of the International Food Services Executives Association, earning certifica-

It Happened to Me...

"When I first started working in the food service storeroom at Grand Rapids Community College, I was told a story about how a local international corporation known for their philanthropic deeds purchased an historic hotel in our downtown back in 1979. They closed the property for 2 years while they renovated the existing rooms and added a 27-story tower of guest rooms to the property. The new hotel owners retained the services of an individual who had been working for many years at the hotel, in the capacity of sous chef, to become the new head food buyer. The management recognized the necessary value of product knowledge required to run a successful food service storeroom operation.

And when they were in the process of purchasing all new tabletop supplies, linen, and furniture . . . they wisely included the local sales representatives and their companies in the purchases. With the enormous orders for new products, the owners easily could have arranged to skip the middleman in order to save several million dollars by purchasing directly from the factory. But the company knew the value of developing a mutually supportive relationship with its vendors. They understood that over the long term, the hotel would benefit from having developed a strong rapport with its suppliers. The Amway Grand Plaza Hotel is now the only five star and five diamond property in Michigan. I learned about that specific value from my first storeroom supervisor, who learned about it from the author of this book. And now I can attest to the wisdom in his advice, because my college and the SICE receives great service from people who feel they are partners in our department's success."

tions as both a Certified Food Manager (CFM) and Certified Food Executive (CFE). He is also very supportive of the various activities coordinated between the college's SICE and the different professional hospitality organizations, such as the International Taster's Guild annual International Wine Judging, which occurs at GRCC. Kidder and his staff are responsible for coordinating the receiving, storing, and issuing of nearly 2,000 wines entered in the annual competition from around the globe. He also enjoys the challenge of helping to source the many unusual ingredients needed for the SICE's international culinary competition known as "the Nation's Cup." Kidder assists with many annual charitable fundraising events, including the local American Culinary Federation's *Feast for*

Kids dinner, and *Soup's On*, a local charity event to benefit the homeless.

Passions with the Food Service Industry

"Working at a culinary school and seeing the students develop personally and professionally over the 2 to 3 years that they are here is the BEST! It's great to see the focused ones get even better and the undecided ones find the direction to which they are looking. I never get tired, because they bring so much energy to this place."

Advice to a Chef or Buyer

"Whether you are a chef, manager, or buyer, you need to stay true to your vendors once you establish a relationship

(continued)

with the few that you work with the most. Their service to you pays off ... the late afternoon call when your back is against the wall and you need something by dinner service; it's priceless. Customers expect quality food and timely service from their dining experiences, and chefs expect no less from their storerooms and suppliers. To make that happen, vendors must want to provide you with their best service.

Buying is a profession that requires constant attention to details and nurturing of relationships. Wherever your path leads, take it seriously and put in the necessary effort to be considered a professional."

Key Words and Concepts

bin tag

biological hazard

buyer

chemical hazard

cross-contamination

deterioration

dunnage rack

exempt employees

Fair Labor Standards Act (FLSA)

Form I-9

Hazard Analysis and Critical Control Point (HACCP)

live tanks

nonexempt employees

organizational charts

physical hazard

pick-slip

receiving clerk

recycling

Right-To-Know regulations

sanitation

storeroom assistants

storeroom manager

temperature danger zone

Chapter in Review

The following exercises are provided to help the reader understand and apply the contents of this chapter. They may be completed individually or in a classroom environment.

REVIEW QUESTIONS

a. Identify and discuss which positions in a large restaurant, club, or hotel would be exempt and which would be nonexempt.

b. Discuss the use of live tanks and when they are practical, or not.

c. Explain the value of a properly organized storeroom.

d. Describe the different ways in which a storeroom can prevent contamination and breaches of sanitation protocol.

INDIVIDUAL ACTIVITIES

a. **Web based:** Research recycling companies in your area, and find out which service commercial food service operations.

b. **Experiential:** Find a hotel in your area that operates a formal storeroom operation, and ask to tour the facilities. Interview the storeroom manager to learn about what he does.

c. **Critical thinking:** Create a storeroom cooler on paper. Organize the spaces as if this was the only cooler a restaurant had to store all of its in-use inventory, as well as raw goods. Identify specific locations for dairy, produce, meats, and seafood, and how they would be held and stored.

GROUP ACTIVITIES

a. **Lab experience:** Start an herb garden or hydroponic garden in your kitchen or support spaces for a readily available source for fresh herbs and peppers. Note: Check with your local health department regarding applicable codes.

b. **Classroom action:** Examine all of the shelving in your coolers and dry storage areas. Determine if they are being used properly and meeting the needs of the operation or if they can be improved upon, inexpensively.

CHAPTER

8

© iStockphoto.com

Receiving, Storing, and Issuing

"Let all things be done decently and in order."
CORINTHIANS

After reading this chapter, you will be able to:

- ◎ Evaluate the receiving process and the responsibilities associated with receiving products.

- ◎ Explain the use of a product specification reference guide and the buyer's order form.

- ◎ Describe product inspections, discrepancies, product rejections, and credit memos.

- ◎ Summarize the storing process, and compare the formal control methods, including ABC analysis, par stock method, mini-max method, and economic order quantity.

- ◎ Define formal and informal issuing.

- ◎ Describe the use of storeroom requisitions and purchase requisitions.

- ◎ Explain the differences between a physical inventory and a perpetual inventory.

- ◎ Identify the hardware and software used with computerized inventory systems.

- ◎ Describe the methods used to determine inventory valuation, including FIFO, LIFO, weighted average, actual cost, and latest purchase price.

- ◎ Apply the use of ingredient rooms as they relate to inventory management.

Introduction

Once the food service operator orders products for the establishment, the responsibility lies with the kitchen or storeroom staff to receive, store, and issue them properly. That responsibility begins the moment the chef or receiving clerk signs the delivery copy of the bill. From that moment forward, the food service operation must view those goods as perishable assets of the business and take every needed measure to store and protect them as they would a bundle of cash.

This chapter discusses the important precautions food service operators must take to guard against theft and product deterioration during the receiving, storing, and issuing processes, while accounting for the products in storage. Additionally, this chapter discusses the diverse methods available to a food service operator in issuing the products to the different departments while exercising proper order and control of the storeroom. Chapter 7 discussed the layout of the storage areas, as well as the necessary temperatures and equipment needed for the storeroom, so those topics will not be addressed here.

The Receiving Process

Nowhere else in the food service operation can the operator exercise greater control than at the receiving dock. It is at this location that the legal, financial, and physical responsibility for the product is transferred. Once the product has passed from the hands of the vendor to the hands of the buyer, the buyer has very little leverage to receive a credit or a return. Because the product is now in the hands of the operation, there is very little incentive, other than to keep the customer's business, for a vendor to issue a credit.

Recognizing that hundreds of thousands, if not millions, of dollars' worth of equipment, supplies, food, and beverage pass through the receiving dock every year, management should establish strict policies and procedures for this area. In many operations, both large and small, receiving is left to an hourly employee who has received little training for the position. Even with a receiving department, the receiving manager might be pressed for time and quickly delegate the job of receiving a shipment to a less qualified member of staff.

The function of the receiving department is crucial in terms of cost, accuracy, and quality control. This responsibility should not be left to someone who is untrained and uninterested in the job. The receiving department's duty is to verify the delivered order, which is done by:

- Inspecting the product for quality.
- Inspecting the wholesomeness of the product.
- Counting the cases to make sure the number matches the order (see Figure 8.1a).
- Confirming the order matches established product specifications (see Figure 8.1b).
- Obtaining any credit memos, if applicable (see Figure 8.1c).
- Checking the math calculations (see Figure 8.1d).
- Properly storing the products (see Figure 8.1e).
- Filing the paperwork immediately (see Figure 8.1f).

Remembering the "three Q's of receiving" when taking deliveries can help ensure an accurate and successful transaction every time:

- **Quality.** Be sure that the quality of the product meets the specifications and expectations of the operation. Make sure that all items in the case are inspected for wholesomeness and freshness.
- **Quantity.** Count, weigh, or measure the products to confirm that the amount ordered is the amount received. Make sure that the case count matches the invoice count and that it is the same quantity ordered.
- **Quote.** Confirm that the quoted price received when the products were ordered is the same price being charged upon delivery. Immediately note any discrepancies and contact the vendor for a credit.

PRODUCT INSPECTIONS

The hours that the receiving dock is open for deliveries is one of the first important considerations to make when establishing the policies and practices for the business. The kitchen would like to have the goods available, in their freshest condition, when they are first needed. The receiving staff is interested in having the deliveries made when the dock is open and when a trained receiving clerk (or other trained employee) is available to receive the delivery (see Figure 8.2).

This requires communication and planning on the part of the management team right from the beginning. As discussed in Chapter 1, the chef or buyer must select suitable purveyors who can provide deliveries on acceptable days and at acceptable times for the operation, though the operation might also need to adjust planned work schedules to accommodate some deliveries. Once the purveyors and the buyer agree on delivery times, it is recommended that a "Receiving Hours of Operation" sign be posted by the receiving dock entrance to remind drivers of this decision. All too often, a sales staff will promise specific services to

8.1a Inspecting the product for quality, wholesomeness, and count

Figures 8.1a–f © Randy Van Dam 2008

8.1b Confirming the order matches established product specifications

8.1c Obtaining a credit memo

8.1d Checking the math calculations

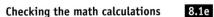

8.1e Properly storing the products

8.1f Filing the paperwork immediately

8.2 Delivery truck driver unloading stock while receiving clerk inspects the products

© Randy Van Dam 2008

their customers but fail to communicate those expectations to their own delivery staff. But an operator must also understand that vendors normally route their trucks based on the delivery with the highest profit. Operators can ask for broad times, but narrow windows such as "only between 8:00 and 8:30 a.m." might be logistically impossible. Also, operators must understand that even if the delivery is scheduled during their window, weather and traffic conditions might prevent a timely drop off.

Even with the best of planning, exceptions must be made. Warfel and Cremer (2005) write: "Even if there is a regular schedule for the receiving office to be open and for most deliveries to be made, some deliveries may be made before the receiving office is open. The receiving clerk should work out specific instructions for that person in the food department who will be signing for such deliveries and checking on the shipment" (p. 109).

Although some operations spend little time checking in their stock, it is not recommended to forgo this right and responsibility. Professional drivers and sales staff quickly analyze each customer by its business practices.

If a food service operation establishes itself as a company that cares about the products it receives, the driver will inform the seller, and the seller will raise its own standards to meet the buyer's expectations. The driver doesn't want to defend her company's poor quality products to the receiving clerk, and neither person wants to be put in the situation of returning bad merchandise.

One of the most important responsibilities the receiving agent holds is to protect the interests of her business by conducting efficient, but thorough, inspections of all received products. This process should be done politely and with respect to the driver's time and delivery schedule. Rarely is it appropriate or necessary to be confrontational to the delivery personnel, nor is it justifiable for the driver to hurry the receiving clerk while she is performing her product inspections. Merchandise inspections are a normal part of the buyer–seller relationship. The receiving clerk is charged with verifying the order, which includes inspections of *specification, quality,* and *quantity.*

> **BUYER'S NOTE** *It is also advisable to post an "Hours of Operation" sign and a "No Sales Meetings without Prior Appointments" sign outside the chef or buyer's office.*

Reviewing Specifications and Orders

When a delivery is made, the receiving clerk must first verify that the delivered goods were actually ordered in the first place.

Sometimes, drivers mistakenly deliver items to one customer that were ordered by another. To prevent this problem, the buyer should create a buyer's order form, as discussed in Chapter 1 (see Figure 1.18), for the receiving clerk to reference. The buyer should place the completed form in a binder, in a drawer, or on a clipboard for access by all receiving personnel when the goods arrive. The receiving clerk can then compare the delivery statement to the buyer's order form and note any discrepancies in specification, count, or weight.

Next, the receiving clerk must verify that the delivered goods meet the specifications of the establishment. As discussed in Chapter 6, the business should have previously determined its product specifications and communicated them to the vendor. Ideally, the business should create a product specification reference guide, which contains specifications for all of the products it purchases, assembled in a three-ring binder or posted on the office wall. The buyer and receiving clerk should review this guide regularly and when necessary.

BLIND RECEIVING

The process of **blind receiving** puts an extra level of responsibility on the receiving clerk. With this system, the delivery person brings only a list of the items in the shipment. The receiving clerk will count and weigh everything that arrives

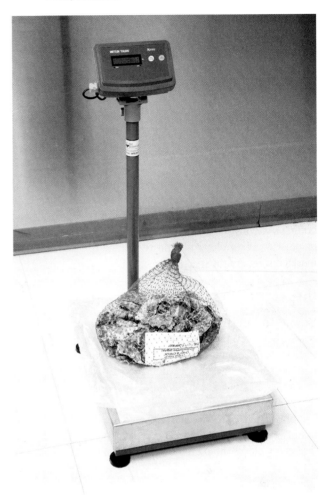

8.3 Bag of shellfish being weighed
© Randy Van Dam 2008

and record the data on the receiving check sheet (Figure 8.3). The purveyor must send its full invoice, complete with the purveyor's counts and weights, directly to the accounting office. The accounting office then compares the receiving clerk's check sheet with the invoice from the purveyor and verifies that all is as billed and prices were charged are as quoted. Although this system seems beneficial to the food service operator, the practice is seldom used because of its cumbersome and labor-intensive procedures.

Some establishments accept deliveries in the middle of the night, when there are no personnel on the premises. Known as a **key stop**, or drop stop, the driver has a key to the establishment (and to coolers and freezers) and then places the goods in designated places. With this type of delivery, the driver should be instructed to leave the invoice in a designated spot, and then, in the morning, the receiving personnel will fill out a blind receiving form. If there are any discrepancies, the receiving department will call the purveyor and the accounting department in the food service establishment.

Inspecting the Quality

All receiving personnel should be properly trained by the chef or kitchen manager to make determinations of quality. It should not be assumed, or even expected, of an untrained individual to have the same food knowledge of the chef, who has had years of education and experience. Therefore, a chef must properly train receiving clerks to evaluate the quality of meats, poultry, seafood, dairy, produce, and dry goods. Ideally, the chef or kitchen manager will initially work alongside the receiving clerk (see Figure 8.4), pointing out the quality factors of each type of product, before the clerk is allowed to receive products on her own.

Although the concept of quality seems purely subjective, both consumers and governmental regulating bodies agree that its traits can be measurable. Factors such as freshness, color, size, consistency, and taste can be measured and evaluated. Receiving clerks should be trained to look for these marks during their inspections.

Inspecting the Quantity

Quantity measurements are much easier than quality evaluations; however, they are not to be ignored or taken lightly. Products are commonly sold by count, weight, or packaged lots. Whether by the each, pound, kilogram, dozen, lug, case, or can, products must be counted or weighed during the receiving process (see Figure 8.5). To facilitate ordering and shipping, most products are packaged for ease of transport but also in quantities that are practical for the buyer's use. Receiving clerks should remove the lids on the cases and any

8.5 Recently received containers of produce
© Randy Van Dam 2008

8.6 Receiving clerk weighing meat with delivery driver looking on
© Randy Van Dam 2008

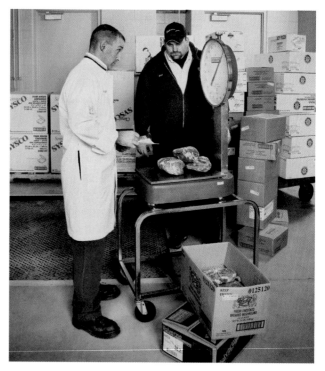

8.4 Chef training a receiving clerk to inspect fish
© Randy Van Dam 2008

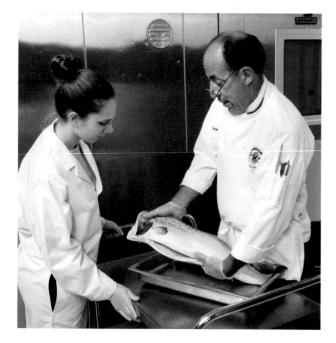

ice or packing material before weighing the products. Large scales are often located at the back dock for quick access (see Figure 8.6). The receiving clerk will also inspect the quality of the meat or fish at this time.

Some food items, like whole fish or sub-primal cuts of beef, will have a different weight for each piece. In large operations that manage formal storerooms, after the delivery has been formally inspected and accepted, the receiving clerk weighs each whole fish or sub-primal cut. The clerk

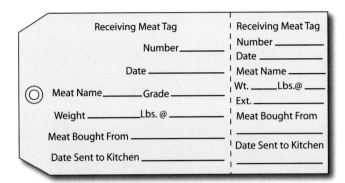

8.7 Sample meat tag

then applies an individual **weight tag** (sometimes called fish or meat tags) to each item (see Figure 8.7). The tag is also designed to track product weights, that correspond to their weight upon receipt, as they are issued. For example, when the storeroom issues three whole tenderloins, the clerk removes one side of each tag and attaches them to the pick-slip. The issued meat's weight is recorded and deducted from the perpetual inventory, while its appropriate cost is charged to the department. The meat is issued with the other half of the weight tag still attached, for the benefit of the department that ordered the meat.

PRODUCT DISCREPANCIES

In some instances, substitutions or mistakes are made in the quality, weight, or count of delivered items. Receiving clerks must always be vigilant to human deception, mistakes, or poor judgment. Chapter 10, "Security Issues with Vendors, Employees, and Customers," discusses some of the ways in which vendors and employees can create discrepancies to their own advantage.

It is the right and responsibility of the receiving personnel to ensure their business receives what it has ordered and pays only for what it receives. Anything less is irresponsible behavior. The clerk has the right to professionally question the quality and quantity of any products being delivered. It is precisely at this moment when objections should be raised.

Oftentimes, the receiving clerk will immediately contact the buyer or chef to determine what she wishes to do. Chefs might accept an inferior product or lesser count when they feel pressured by the needs of production. When this happens, the chef should call the supplier and express concern about the insufficient quality or amount. Ideally, a mutually respectful relationship exists and neither party exhibits unprofessional behavior. Chefs and receiving clerks also have the right to reject the inferior product, sending it back with the delivery truck. When this happens, the receiving clerk must record it on the invoice so that a credit can be granted.

Rejection

Failure to accept a delivery is known as a **product rejection**. When a product fails to meet the quality standards of a food service establishment, the operator has the right to reject the delivered product *before signing acceptance of the delivery*. Usually, the occasional rejection of product by a receiving clerk is no cause for alarm by either party. However, if the vendor feels the buyer is being unreasonable or the buyer feels the vendor is inconsistent in its quality, then either party has the right to terminate the business relationship except where a long-term contract is in force.

A vendor does not have to accept a rejected product once a buyer has signed the delivery statement. At that point, legally, it becomes the property of the buyer. However, most vendors do have a credit procedure in place that allows for a sales representative or the driver to return and verify the condition of the items. If the representative or driver does agree to a credit, then the product will be returned to the vendor. These credit policies are used to keep the customers satisfied.

 As discussed in previous chapters, building a strong relationship based on mutual respect between buyers and sellers is important in conducting business in a nonadversarial manner.

CREDIT MEMO

When the buyer's receiving agent has rejected a product and it is being reloaded onto the vendor's delivery truck, a **credit memo** for the returned product's value must be issued (see Figure 8.8). A delivery slip or statement always accompanies the delivered products, and when the receiving clerk accepts the products, the clerk signs the two-part form. The clerk retains one copy, and the other goes with the driver. The driver's copy is sent to the vendor's accounting office, where a weekly, monthly, or semimonthly invoice is billed to the buyer's business, requesting payment based on previously agreed upon terms, such as cash, 7 days, 14 days, or 30 days.

As the invoice was prepared in advance of the delivery, the statement must be revised to subtract the value of the rejected item. The vendor's driver issues the credit memo, noting that the statement is to be adjusted (credited) equal to the rejected items' value. The driver typically indicates the reason for the credit, such as "tomatoes were too ripe for customer." Some vendors will have the driver note the credit on the invoice and then send a formal copy of the credit memo at a later time. Both the driver and the receiving clerk staple their copies of the credit memo to their own copies of the signed delivery statement and file them accordingly. The receiving clerk should make sure that the bookkeeper knows that a credit is expected for that invoice.

8.8 Sample Credit Memo

Credit Memo

Sold To: _____ Date: _____

Customer Number: _____

Invoice Number: _____ Invoice Date: _____

Instructions:

☐ Pickup Order Only

☐ Pickup and Credit Order

☐ Credit Only

ITEM	PRODUCT CODE	QUANTITY	PACKAGE	PRICE	AMOUNT

Reason for Credit: _____

_____

_____

_____

Delivery Driver Signature: _____ Date: _____

Receiving Clerk: _____ Date: _____

[ASK THE EXPERT]

Jennifer Booker
Culinary Educator

Name: Jennifer Booker

Title: Program Director and Instructor, Culinary Arts Program

Employer: Grayson Technical Education Program

Education/Training: University of Tulsa, bachelor of arts in organizational communications/business;

The University of Oklahoma–Okmulgee, associate of culinary arts

Le Cordon Bleu-Paris, Certificate Base du Cuisine

General Responsibilities: As program director, in charge of the Culinary Arts Program, Booker is a very busy person. In addition to her daily teaching responsibilities in both lectures and lab classes, Booker handles curriculum development and student recruitment. She works as a mentor for students in the Skills USA/FCCLA competitions and as the Hot Foods Team coach. As department head, Booker is primarily responsible for the program's purchasing and receiving duties.

Ask the Expert Questions:

1) In your role as a culinary educator, which areas do you emphasize as being the most important with storeroom operations?

Price versus quality. You generally get what you pay for. If you want a fresh or prepackaged product that will yield a quality plate, you must be willing to pay for it. This is not to say that you should only use ultra-expensive items or that only expensive items are quality. What it means is that you must know your product. Students should get into the habit of checking every box that is delivered to their establishment—every time. Don't assume that because the order was in good shape the last ten times it was delivered that it will be in good shape every time. Remember once you sign for it, it's yours. Check your product. Buyers must also pay close attention to the amount of inventory on hand. If there is too much inventory in stock, it will perish. If too

little, the establishment must pay extra money for rush orders and additional delivery days.

2) What problem areas do you warn them about relative to the role of buyer?

Buyers should be aware that the quality, amount per unit and price may, and often will change without any prior notice. Be sure to check your product; every box, every time! Know where your products come from. Consumers are more knowledgeable about the origin of their food than ever before and often base their dining choice on where the food prepared at that restaurant comes from. Not all food imported into the United States is raised or grown under the same guidelines as that same product would be here. As a result, your clientele will often ask where their meal comes from and as the Buyer, Restaurant owner, or Chef, you must know. Once your quality product has arrived, it must be stored properly. This job falls under the role of the Buyer. Proper climate control and product rotation (FIFO) is a huge part of extending a product's shelf-life.

3) What changes or trends will occur in food service relative to product selection and availability in the near future?

In a way, the role of the Buyer has come full circle. Although almost all products are available all year round, it doesn't always mean it is of the best quality. It is no longer enough to simply press a computer key or pick up a phone and place an order. Just because watermelon is available in December, that doesn't guarantee its quality. The Buyer must be aware of not just where the product comes from, but how it was transported, how long the trip and in what condition the product started that journey. Locally grown produce, more organic products, herbicide-free, pesticide-free, hormone-free, free-range poultry and eggs, and grass-fed beef; all of these products are fast becoming very popular among consumers and in high demand. As the buyer, you must keep current with what's popular; be it a fad or a food service trend. This is where having a personal relationship with your local purveyors becomes an invaluable trait. This will ensure that you know what's in season, what's available, where your order is from, and how it was raised.

4) Please provide your advice to a chef, buyer, or food service manager relative to the role and responsibility of buying in food service?

One of the most important roles of any food service operation, if not the most important, is that of the Buyer. The Buyer must be very aware of pricing and cost controls. Mismanagement of the purchasing department often ends in the failure of the entire establishment. To avoid this, the Buyer should assist with costing, and there should be a very close relationship between the Chef, Buyer, and Food Service Manager, with all three acting as a team to get the best products at the best price. Ultimately, remember that it is impossible to produce a quality dish without the knowledge of how to locate, purchase, and store quality products.

MAINTAINING STATEMENT FILES

The receiving clerk should always immediately file a copy of the vendor's signed delivery statement (see Figure 8.9). Some businesses also like the receiving personnel to attach the completed buyer's order form to the delivery statement, validating that the form was cross-referenced during receiving. The original invoice should go to the bookkeeper for payment.

Ideally, a separate file exists for each vendor the buyer uses. The clerk might receive several deliveries every day, and a structure must be in place to organize the delivery statements by individual purveyor. This is done for two reasons. First, the buyer or chef should be recording the delivery total into her own computer or ledger sheet to track daily expenses, by purveyor. Second, some vendors will send a monthly report of all deliveries made to the food service

8.9 **Sample Signed Delivery Statement**

INVOICE DATE & NUMBER			PAGE		SP
03 12		24748	1		
1972	11204	40	3		SB
ROUTE	ACCOUNT	LOAD	STOP	SEG.	

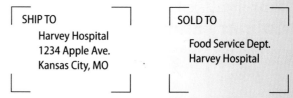

SHIP TO
Harvey Hospital
1234 Apple Ave.
Kansas City, MO

SOLD TO
Food Service Dept.
Harvey Hospital

SPECIAL INSTRUCTIONS:
PO 58372 WED AM

DUP INV. DOCK OFF HARVEY AVE.

QUAN	CNTR.	DESCRIPTION	PACK	SIZE	PRICE	EXTENSION	PROD. CODE
3	CS SB	FRUIT COCKTAIL	6	10	14.59	43.77	02931
12	CS SB	PEACH AMB Y C SLICED	6	10	13.04	156.48	04119
1	CS SR	APPLE RINGS SPICE RED	6	10	13.20	13.20	02089
5	CS SR	ORANGES MANDARIN	6	10	21.63	108.15	36822
12	CS SR	PINEAPPLE JUICE	12	46 oz.	6.48	77.76	18614
3	CS SB	PINEAPPLE 115/120 MAY	6	10	17.62	52.86	06445
	CS SR	PINEAPPLE CHUNKS XHS	6	10	15.39	STOCKOUT	3
2	CS SG	PIMENTOS BROKEN IMP	24	28 oz.	32.02	64.04	37770
1	CS SR	STRAWBERRY PIE FILLING	6	10	23.83	23.83	07641
3	CS SB	PEARS BART SLICED	6	10	15.72	47.16	05595
1	CS SR	LEMON PIE FILLING RTU	6	10	17.76	17.76	03616
1	CS SR	APPLE PIE FILLING RTU	6	10	18.28	18.28	00083
4	CS SB	CHERRIES BING PITTED	6	10	25.28	101.12	01545
1	CS SR	CHERRY PIE FILLING	6	10	22.75	22.75	01743
3	CS SR	KUMQUATS 70/75	12	5	27.76	83.28	03590
3	CS SR	BEANS GARBANZO	6	10	9.60	28.80	08896
2	CS SR	PLUMS PRUNE DIETETIC	6	10	13.01	26.02	16287
3	CS SR	BEEF INST BOUIL PKT	6	100	16.49	49.47	33779
3	CS SR	CHICKEN INST BOUIL PKT	6	100	16.49	49.47	33797
TOTALS ***	AMT.	$1504.37 PROCESSED FOODS					

	TOTAL WEIGHT	PLEASE PAY		TERMS
	3814	→ THIS AMOUNT	$1504.37	NET

DUPLICATE INVOICE
NOTE: ALL SHORTAGES AND DAMAGES MUST BE NOTED AT TIME OF RECEIPT.

Received by: _____ JQ Smith _____   Date: ____ 9/06/09 ____ establishment. It should be the practice of the food service operator to validate these totals by comparing them to the delivery statements, less any credit memos. Mistakes can happen, and it is not unusual to be billed for items not received. If a food service establishment does not receive a monthly report, then it can call the vendor's customer service and request that one be sent.

The Storing Process

After the product has been ordered and received, it must be stored properly until needed for production. It is in the **storing** process, as much as during production, that money can be lost, whether by carrying excessive inventory, improper handling of perishables, deterioration of product, or inaccurate bookkeeping procedures. The processes of inventory management and inventory valuation are both critical to the fiscal health of the business.

Once received, inspected, and accepted, the products must be immediately stored to preserve and protect them. Oftentimes, delivery drivers will wheel perishable goods from their refrigerated trucks directly into the refrigerated coolers of the storeroom. This helps preserve the freshness of the perishables and aids the clerk in immediately storing the deliveries after they are inspected. Yet all too often in busy operations, food is left unattended on receiving docks, leaving it open to theft or deterioration. Businesses must promote a policy of immediate storage and control.

INVENTORY MANAGEMENT

Simply stated, **inventory management** is the process of controlling the inventory volume until it is to be issued. A manager or chef cannot effectively order products without counting and controlling the inventory. Cost figures and period accounting cannot be accurate unless physical inventories are conducted on a regular basis. As Schmidgall, Hayes, and Ninemeier (2002) write in *Restaurant Financial Basics*:

> Two accounting concerns involve controlling the quantity and assessing the value of products in storage. Both directly affect the profitability of the restaurant. If, for example, the quantity of products in storage is excessive, cash flow can be affected (cash is tied up in inventory), the chance for spoilage increases (which requires additional purchases to compensate for products that have been purchased but from which no revenue was generated), and opportunities for employment theft increase. By contrast, when inadequate levels of inventory are maintained, there is an increased chance of **stockouts**, which can result in employee frustration, guest dissatisfaction,

and increased food costs if, for example, replacement products must be purchased at retail market prices (pp. 243–244).

Chefs and managers will institute systems of control to address these accounting concerns. These systems can be either informal or formal and are usually dictated by the inventory volume required by the operation or the number of revenue centers (food outlets) obtaining their supplies from the storeroom.

Shelf Life

Care should be taken to manage the inventory according to its shelf life. Perfectly good food, which becomes an asset of the company upon its receipt, will become a financial loss if left to spoil. To manage the shelf life, the storeroom manager must consider the quantity of product on hand, the length of time it is in storage, the temperature in which it is stored, and how it is packaged. A product such as chicken can arrive frozen, fresh, or individually vacuum packed. Each of these packing types has different shelf lives and storage needs.

Informal Systems of Control

Controls can only exist when access to inventory is restricted. The more restricted the access, the lesser chance for theft or error and the greater likelihood for fiscal accuracy.

Perhaps the most commonly used system of control is the informal system. Informal systems are common in most independent and smaller chain restaurants and hotels. They use informal controls as they do not have enough products in house to support the added cost of dedicated storeroom personnel. Informal systems normally consist of check sheets that employees use when they remove items from the storeroom. Additionally, certain restrictions are usually put in place, such as only allowing managers or trusted employees to have a key to the storeroom. Because these systems are informal, they vary from establishment to establishment. But most systems should include some sort of requisition or pull system as well as par levels for most items.

Formal Systems of Control

A formal system of control involves both a system of tracking issues and the staff to do this. The formal system is generally only implemented in larger food service operations that have multiple food outlets and a need by management to separate out the food costs for each operation.

These formal storeroom operations often employ multiple full- or part-time employees to purchase, receive, store, and issue products. Requests for products from the storeroom are made with a storeroom requisition, a formal document that can be used to trace issues and determine food costs for each outlet.

The formal system is preferred by working chefs, who are often delighted to have staff who can focus their full attention on purchasing, receiving, and taking inventory, as these tasks can take many hours each week. The problem lies in the cost of staffing, and only those operations that can justify the savings offered by diligent buying and accounting accuracy, or operations that purchase an extraordinary amount of product each week, can employ storeroom staff.

Quantifying Amounts to Purchase

Whether a business uses the formal or informal system of control, it generally uses some system for quantifying amounts to purchase. The buyer must develop a system for knowing when and how much product to order. These methods include *ABC analysis, par stock method, mini-max method, Levinson approach,* and *economic order quantity.*

ABC ANALYSIS

ABC analysis, which was discussed in Chapter 6, allows an operator to prioritize the products on which it spends the most. To employ the ABC analysis method, an operator must create a list of all items in inventory, along with their average costs and annual usage quantities. Average costs are multiplied by the quantities used to determine the total annual purchase dollars spent per item. The items are then divided into three categories based on their annual purchase amount. Those items demanding the most purchase dollars are categorized as A-list items, those items with the least dollars spent are on the C-list, and those in the middle are on the B-list.

The A-list items are either high-cost or high-volume items that can be easily identified and monitored for control. These products deserve the most attention because a change in their cost or usage will affect inventory values and cash flow. Researching alternative purveyors or seeking sales or quantity discounts for these items can benefit the operation greatly. Conversely, ordering fewer of these items at a time when discounts are not available is a certain method of reducing inventory values and tying up less money.

PAR STOCK METHOD

Some establishments maintain a small, dry storeroom containing a "partial stock" near the main kitchen for access by the kitchen staff. In this room, the chef or kitchen manager maintains a **par stock** of the most used items. This method reduces the number of trips necessary to the main storeroom while maintaining a certain level of security. It also prompts reordering of those frequently used products.

MINI-MAX METHOD (SAFETY STOCK METHOD)

Some food service operators maintain their inventory levels by determining the optimum level of product they need to meet the needs of their operation without overstocking. They do this by establishing their minimum and maximum (mini-max) inventory levels. The minimum is normally the lowest amount of product that must be on the shelf during a normal order cycle. Safety stock is how much is needed during a normal ordering period. The maximum inventory level consists of the **safety stock** plus the correct ordering quantity, or how much is used within an order period. There are several mathematical formulas and software programs that can determine the safety stock, minimum levels, and maximum levels for a product.

> The mini-max method is often confused with the par stock method of holding inventory. Remember a mini-max system has designated levels for each item. A par stock is simply stock items kept in the kitchen.

> This is the most commonly used method of maintaining proper stock levels in independent restaurants, clubs, and small hotels. Maintaining proper par stocks and mini-max inventories contributes greatly to successful purchasing.

THE LEVINSON APPROACH

Charles Levinson first devised this ordering method and later wrote about it in his text *Food and Beverage Operation.* The process is designed to help buyers determine the correct time to order and the correct order size. It involves accepting the supplier's delivery schedule and ordering protocols. (On average, most merchandise is ordered weekly.) Prior to ordering, the buyer must closely approximate the product to be used between deliveries, following these steps:

a. Estimate how many guests will likely be served, known as the *estimated guest count*, using historical data.

b. Project the number of each item to be sold based on the estimated guest count, known as the *projected sales*, using historical data.

c. Calculate the raw weight of each ingredient required for the projected sales.

To calculate the raw weight, the buyer must determine the portion factor (PF) and the portion divider (PD) for each ingredient.

- The PF is calculated as follows:
  PF = 16 ounces / Ingredient weight (for one serving, in ounces)

- The PD is calculated as follows:
  PD = PF × Ingredient yield percentage

The ingredient yield percentage is the percent of an ingredient that can be served. Oftentimes, ingredients such as fish are purchased head-on, with skin and skeleton. These elements may be deemed unusable and must be removed prior to portioning. So, following this example, only 70 percent of a salmon filet is servable.

Calculate the amount to order, known as the *order size*, for all items by dividing the *customer demand* for a product, also known as *popularity index*, by the portion divider.

Order size = Customer demand/ PD

(Adjust this order size if necessary to account for special events or stock on hand.)

For example: The business serves 300 portions (customer demand) of salmon filet per week.

Ingredient	Serving Size	Yield %
Salmon filet	12 oz.	70

PF = 16/12 = 1.33
PD = 1.33 × 70% = 0.931
Order size = 300/0.931 = 322.23 lbs

ECONOMIC ORDER QUANTITY

In some limited instances, very large food service operators must consider the added costs associated with receiving, stocking, and inventory control. The total annual cost of restocking inventory product directly depends on the number of times it is ordered in a year. To decrease these costs, orders should be placed as seldom as possible by ordering larger quantities. However, operators cannot place too large of orders or they risk incurring holding costs, theft, or spoilage.

The calculations to determine the benefits of this method can be daunting. As Spears (1999) writes:

> The **economic order quantity** (EOQ) concept is derived from a sensible balance of ordering cost and inventory holding cost. The **ordering cost** is defined as the total operating expenses of the purchasing and receiving departments, expenses of purchase orders and invoice payment, and data processing costs for purchasing and inventory. **Holding cost** is the total of all expenses in maintaining an inventory: the cost of capital tied up in inventory, obsolescence of products, storage, insurance, handling taxes, depreciation, deterioration, and breakage (p. 156).

 This issue is of little consequence to most food service operators, but it can be an important calculation for large food service operations. Holding costs also are important if a chain maintains its own commissary system.

CONDUCTING INVENTORIES

One of the main goals of any storeroom is to maintain inventory accuracy, which is when the correct product with the correct quantities is located where it should be in the storeroom. And the records of the establishment should reflect that number. Most establishments will tolerate minor differences such as a lost onion or an additional potato. These differences, called variances, should be investigated if the records differ significantly from what is on the shelves.

To obtain accurate cost figures for the food service operation, the staff must, at a minimum, conduct periodic physical inventories to determine the costs of goods used. Larger, or more technically sophisticated, food service operations will also conduct perpetual inventories on a more regular basis. The perpetual inventory values are then compared with the physical inventory values to determine the differences, if any, which could indicate security or shrink issues.

Smaller operations that carry minimal inventories, such as quick-service restaurants, often conduct their inventories on a weekly, if not daily, basis. Larger, more complex operations with hefty inventories and heavy production schedules will do a formal inventory once a month or quarterly. As a rule of thumb, the more often a physical inventory is done, the more accurate the records. Note that this formal inventory should not be confused with the check that is done before an order is placed with a sales representative. This quick inventory is done simply to verify product on the shelf before making an order.

Operators have a choice as to whether they wish to consider the value of inventory considered "in use," or the raw product that is in the kitchen and available for production. This is also referred to as **food in service**. Generally, this product consists of many partial containers of spice, foil, flour, liquids, and other staples. Most chefs and managers either choose to ignore the value of this stock or assign it a fixed dollar amount, as it remains relatively consistent from one accounting period to the next. Nearly all operators consider only canned goods and staples not yet issued, plus all cases of meat, poultry, and seafood. These high-cost items can directly affect the value of inventory and are simple enough to inventory quickly. A chef or owner can pick any of these methods, but the same method should be used each period.

Physical Inventories

Physical inventories (also known as periodic or actual) are, as the name suggests, done physically in the storeroom and coolers. They require a complete accounting of all items still in inventory and not issued as part of the in-use stock. Generally, the storeroom is closed to issues during this time, which could take several hours. The physical inventory might best be planned for the early morning, mid-afternoon, or close of business.

The storeroom and accounting staffs, if they exist, will do the inventory. If not, it is best to have the owner, manager, or sous chef, with the help of a few hourly employees, complete the task. Ideally, if the chef or kitchen manager is responsible for maintaining a specific food cost, it is best to have another individual conduct the inventory to preserve the integrity of the process. In publically held companies, the Sarbanes-Oxley Act (SOX) requires a separation of those who place order and those who verify orders so that stockholders can have confidence in the ultimate financial statements.

The person conducting the inventory will have a printed form, or computerized spreadsheet, that lists all of the items, broken down by categories of products. The form should match the physical layout of the rooms for quicker counting (Figure 8.10). The bulk of the process is simply counting the number of units of each item. After everything is counted, the count is multiplied by the unit cost, as determined by the method of valuation. For this reason, spreadsheet software loaded onto laptop computers work well for conducting inventories (see Figure 8.11).

 Requiring more than one individual to conduct physical inventories is a prudent means of establishing checks and balances during the inventory process.

Perpetual Inventories

A **perpetual inventory**, also known as a virtual inventory, is a count of the stock that is supposed to be on the shelves in the storeroom. A perpetual inventory is constantly maintained and adjusted each time product is added or removed from the available inventory. Perpetual inventories are typically used in establishments that run a formal storeroom operation or that have available staff to undertake the recording process. Establishments that accept government commodities, such as schools, must maintain a perpetual inventory of those items. Although some storeroom operators used to use file card systems to record the perpetual inventories, all modern food service operators use computers with database and spreadsheet software to track their inventory values.

Perpetual inventories are compared with the physical inventories, which still must be taken periodically to determine the

8.10   **Sample Inventory Check Sheet**

Inventory Check Sheet					
Food Category: Dairy					
Item and Description	Storeroom Location Code	Opening Inventory	Closing Inventory	Usage	Value
PC: 13582 Milk, whole, 6-gal dispenser	C-3A	2			
PC: 13576 Milk, skim, 10 oz	C-3A	24			
PC: 13563 Milk, choc., 10 oz	C-3A	16			
PC: 13542 Milk, butter, 10 oz	C-3A	8			
PC: 13921 Cheese, ched., 10 lb/blk	C-2B	2			
PC: 13933 Cheese, sliced, Am., 3-lb stack	C-2B	4			
PC: 13979 Cheese, Swiss, 10-lb loaf	C-2B	1			
PC: 13961 Cheese, cream, 3-lb loaf	C-2B	5			
PC: 13987 Cheese, parm., 5-lb pail	C-2B	3			
PC: 13995 Cheese, brie, 2-kg wheel	C-2B	2			
PC: 13906 Cheese, prov., 8-lb loaf	C-2B	1			
PC: 13981 Cheese, mozz., 5-lb loaf	C-2B	6			
PC:					
PC:					
PC:					
PC:					

Chef and storeroom staff conducting physical inventory with laptop and bar code scanner

© Randy Van Dam 2008

cost of goods. Those operators that maintain perpetual inventories will conduct the physical inventories less frequently and then make periodic adjustments to their accounting figures. Normally, the accounting value of the stock is determined by the physical count, whereas the perpetual inventory provides important historical data about the quantity of each item.

INVENTORY RECORD SYSTEMS

Maintaining an inventory record system requires a compilation of inventory quantities and values, which are periodically updated by the operator. These records can be part of an inventory book, when using a manual system, or in a dedicated storeroom inventory database, when using a computer. The record will contain certain details for each product carried in the storeroom, such as:

- Stock item number
- Storage location code
- Product description
- Product specifications
- Approved brand names
- Approved purveyors
- Packaging information
- Recipe number cross-reference

- Average monthly consumption
- Mini-max levels
- Quantities ordered
- Quantities on hand
- Unit costs

Maintaining an inventory record system yields numerous benefits to the operator, including:

- It provides a record of what products the business requires.
- It improves the accuracy of the inventory process.
- It facilitates historical analysis of inventory.
- It helps with statistical analysis of purchases, including creating the ABC analysis.
- It provides a description and specification of each product that the business uses.
- It lists all purveyors that the company uses.
- It matches the ingredients to the recipes in which they are used.
- It provides a price history for each product.
- It details product usage over a specific period of time.
- It makes the inventory process easier.
- It allows the operator to calculate the fiscal inventory.
- It provides important fiscal data for determining food cost values.

BUYER'S NOTE *Every establishment should conduct physical counts on a regular basis. This is used to determine the value of the inventory. The difference between the physical count and the balance in the perpetual inventory is called* ***shrinkage****. This figure represents goods that were not on hand and were not sold. Shrinkage normally occurs from spoilage, theft, inaccurate counts or math, poor bookkeeping, and poor issuing practices. If the shrinkage amount is nominal (less than 2 percent of the total value of the goods), then it is added to the cost of goods sold. If it is much higher than that, it is subtracted as a loss. Operators must investigate high levels of shrinkage and initiate procedures to prevent reoccurrence.*

Written

Before the advent of computers, businesses relied solely on manual inventory systems to manage their stock levels and determine their inventory values. To this day there are numerous retailers, some in food service, who elect to continue to use manually recorded systems to calculate their perpetual inventory and fiscal inventory. These operators record their entries on ledger sheets or stock cards that can be custom designed or purchased from a business supply store (see Figure 8.12).

Each time an inventory item is either received by the storeroom (usually from a delivery) or issued to a member of staff, its

8.12 Example Stock Inventory Form

Stock Inventory Record

Product Name: _____   Product Code: _____

DATE	RECEIVED / ISSUED	ON HAND	DATE	RECEIVED / ISSUED	ON HAND	DATE	RECEIVED / ISSUED	ON HAND

transaction must be manually recorded on the designated "count of stock" form or card in the inventory book or file system.

The benefits of a manually recorded system over a computerized system are worth considering. They include ease of organization and use and limited cost. The disadvantage is that it is a time-consuming method that requires frequent counts to reconcile the cards with the inventory on the shelves.

Computerized

A computerized inventory system contains all of the information in the manual system, yet it has the added capacity to provide countless reports that show cost or inventory information depicted in a variety of formats over limitless time frames (see Figure 8.13). Some useful reports that a computerized system can generate include:

- Costs by daily, weekly, monthly, quarterly, biannual, or annual purchases
- Costs by category of expenses, such as meat, seafood, dairy, produce, or liquor
- Costs by individual purveyor
- Quantity of usage of specific ingredients over any period of time
- High and low costs of a product over any period of time

INVENTORY SYSTEM HARDWARE

There are many different computer hardware systems available to a food service operation. Most chefs will work with a desktop personal computer, a laptop, or a personal digital assistant (PDA), as shown in Figure 8.14. There are many different brands available, and the hardware purchased should match the requirements of the inventory software that is being run on it.

INVENTORY SYSTEM SOFTWARE

It is strongly suggested that the operator create an electronic spreadsheet for conducting the physical inventory, complete with at least the following information:

- Product codes
- Product names
- Brand names
- Storeroom location codes
- Unit costs

The spreadsheet can be updated as needed with new product information. The chef can simply take a laptop or PDA into the storeroom to conduct the inventory, and the calculations are immediately updated. Historical data can also be collected, and sales figures can be automatically integrated with the cost of goods figures, upon the completion of the inventory.

In addition to operators making their own spreadsheets, there are numerous commercial software packages that interface recipe, costing, and ingredient information with "back of the house" financial packages. These management tools can be used for inventory management, recipe costing, and menu sales analysis. Most point-of-sale and food service management programs will have this module available to their customers.

VALUING INVENTORY

Every business that holds an inventory of goods and supplies, which are considered part of its assets, must determine a method for valuing that inventory. To create a balance sheet for the company, the business must first determine the value of its assets.

All accounting systems require some recognized system to be consistently employed from one accounting period to the next. The following systems of inventory valuation are most commonly used in food service operations:

- **FIFO.** The first in, first out (FIFO) system requires the operator to use the oldest products held in inventory first, then the next oldest, and so forth. The assumption is that those items left in the storeroom, during the time the value

8.13 **Computerized Inventory Report**

Date: 6/27/201X
Time: 3:57 PM

Extensions
GRCC

Extensions Date: 6/11/201X

HED Storeroom

Can Rack 104

Item	Cost	Units	Quantity	Extension	Prior Qty
Sauce, marinara	$3.06	#10 can	5	$15.30	5
Sauce, nacho cheese	$8.78	#10 can	6	$52.65	5
Sauce, nacho cheese	$52.65	case		$0.00	
Sauce, pizza	$5.67	#10 can	3	$17.00	5
Sauce, pizza	$34.00	case		$0.00	
Sauce, spaghetti	$7.24	#10 can		$0.00	0
Sauce, spaghetti	$43.44	case		$0.00	
Sauce, Swedish	$40.68	case		$0.00	5
Sauce, Swedish	$40.69	case		$0.00	5
Sauce, Swedish	$4.52	#5 can	5	$22.60	5
Sauce, Swedish	$4.52	#5 can	5	$22.61	5
Sauce, sweet n' sour	$5.08	#5 can	1	$5.08	3
Strawberries, sliced	$5.87	#5 can	5	$29.35	2
Strawberries, sliced`	$35.22	case		$0.00	
Tomato juice	$17.90	case		$0.00	
Tomato juice	$1.99	#5 can	11	$21.88	2
Tomato paste #10	$5.25	#10 can	1	$5.25	1
Tomato paste #10	$31.50	case		$0.00	
Tomato puree	$3.53	#10 can	5	$17.67	5
Tomato puree	$21.20	case		$0.00	
Tomato sauce	$3.08	#10 can	3	$9.23	3

is calculated, should be considered among those most recently purchased in their category. The value assigned to those items in stock is then based on the most recent purchase price. Remember, this is for inventory evaluation purposes only—all products should be rotated so that the oldest is used first regardless of which method is used to value the inventory.

- **LIFO.** The last in, first out (LIFO) system assumes the reverse of the FIFO method and uses the value of those items held the longest in inventory. It does not require that the newest items be issued first in food production, but rather it is only a method of accounting. Because it does not match physical use of the product, this is not a popular method to value the inventory.

- **Weighted average.** This method of valuation takes the average cost of the same items currently held in inventory. The inventory value is calculated based on the total quantity of like products purchased at different unit prices

times the average cost of purchase. The average price is weighted according to the quantity of products available in inventory that are purchased at each price.

- **Actual cost.** This system considers the actual price that was paid for each item held in inventory. When possible, the operator will often write the cost on the individual unit's packaging at the time the product is first received. The inventory value is the sum of these individual unit costs. It is important to keep competing sales forces from seeing these prices.

- **Latest purchase price.** This method uses the latest purchase price in valuing the ending inventory of all goods. This method is frequently used as it is very easy to do. This has the same net effect on the inventory value as the FIFO system without regards to inventory rotation.

Whichever valuation method is chosen, it should be used consistently within the operation. Changing the valuation method will significantly affect inventory figures and food cost.

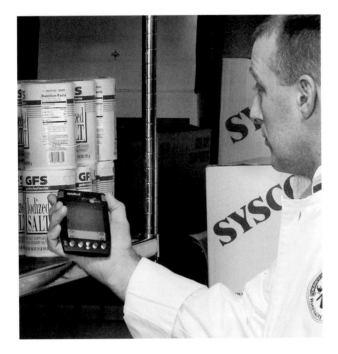

8.14 Personal handheld device being used to scan inventory

© Randy Van Dam 2008

FIXED ASSET INVENTORY

In addition to tracking the flow of consumable or liquid assets (such as food, supplies, and beverages), some companies create methods for tracking their fixed assets. These items, such as office equipment, laptop computers, vehicles, and furniture, are counted as part of a company's fixed assets and must be accounted for on the balance sheet.

There are several ways that assets can be tracked. Some places will use a metal bar code on all of the larger assets. This allows a bar code reader to verify that the item is where it needs to be. For larger, more permanent assets, such as a walk-in, bar codes are not needed as they are difficult to steal.

Other items that cannot be bar coded are handled differently. The easiest method for storing and inventorying glassware is to place them in stackable glass racks designed to hold their appropriate size and shape. Plates can also be stored in portable "chip-rack" carts or dish crates. Silverware is more tedious to count and is frequently separated by type and then counted and weighed to establish a fixed number per dozens. For example, sixty (five dozen) teaspoons might weigh 6.3 pounds. Operators simply weigh their teaspoons, and other flatware, for a fairly accurate count.

The Issuing Process

The **issuing** process is the last opportunity the food service operator has to direct the raw assets of the business. While properly recorded and safely held in inventory, food and supplies retain their monetary value. However, they are also not earning revenue through customer sales and actually add to the lost opportunity and holding costs associated with excess purchased inventory. They must be issued into production to recoup their purchase price and earn a profit for the business.

INFORMAL ISSUING

The issuing process takes one of two methods; informal or formal. With the informal, or uncontrolled, method, it is believed that all stock leaves the storeroom and is put directly into production. Production records or sales figures cannot always verify this assumption. However, it remains a common practice among many independent and chain operations that the storerooms are open to the kitchen staff, who are allowed to freely enter the room when needing supplies. The chef might keep the room locked except during times of pre-prep, when products are most often needed for production. The storeroom is sometimes located in a basement below the kitchen or in a room close to the receiving door. In either case, it is often subject to theft if not controlled properly. According to Feinstein and Stefanelli (2005):

> Some operations with no specific storeroom person manage to have excellent product costs with open storerooms. These firms, however, limit storeroom entry to persons who are under close, continuous supervision. Commonly, these firms maintain minimal stocks so that pilferage is more noticeable to supervisors. In some cases, only small "working storerooms" are open to employees, and large storerooms that are used to stock the working storerooms are accessible only to a limited number of management personnel. (p. 341)

One disadvantage of the **informal issuing** system is its lack of separation of costs. This is not a problem for the restaurant, bakery, or caterer that sells its products via one retail outlet. These operations generally maintain one or two line items for revenues and the same for expenses. The blending of product costs does not warrant extra effort to separate them, and they can determine their food costs and profit with acceptable accuracy. But for larger establishments, informal issuing can be problematic.

A second concern is the business's lack of control over the products' usage. The restaurant must assume the food was used during production, but it cannot otherwise trace its whereabouts without specific efforts to do so.

If the establishment does not have a dedicated storeroom manager, then the following steps to reduce work hours and increase control are suggested:

- Lock up the storeroom, and require staff to obtain the key from a supervising kitchen manager or chef.

- Require staff to conduct an inventory of in-use supplies to determine their needs for the next day's production.

- Have the kitchen manager or chef personally issue the needed supplies at the beginning of the shift.

- Create a reorder form, and record issues when taking them from the storeroom.

- Reduce deliveries and paperwork by purchasing most food and supplies from one or two distributors, if it is possible to obtain preferential pricing and maintain the quality levels desired.

- Ask the owner, manager, or assistant manager to do the receiving and quality checks, if trained properly by the chef. Separate the ordering and receiving duties.

- If space permits, store expensive delivery items in the locked storeroom or protein cooler, and send the other supplies to in-use inventory.

- Liquor, wines, and other alcoholic products must always be stored separately from other inventory products. Other beverages should also be stored separately from both the liquor and the food.

- Track daily usage of expensive items, and then compare them to sales.

FORMAL ISSUING

With **formal issuing**, or controlled issuing, the buyer purchases goods on behalf of all outlets within the food service operation. The goods are then, essentially, sold at cost to each outlet within the operation. The process of releasing products from the storeroom into production is controlled by requisitions. These forms are used to request products needed for immediate daily production. The products may come from any part of the dry or refrigerated storeroom.

Each item issued is weighed and counted to determine its food cost, and then it is recorded as an expense to a specific area of production. As formal storeroom operations are generally only found in larger operations that have multiple food outlets and revenue centers, such as hotels and hospitals, their benefit to the overall operation is enormous. Formal storeroom operations provide immediate information on daily and periodic food cost by revenue center, as well as combined product volumes and inventory levels.

DIRECT ISSUES

When products are issued immediately into production from the receiving dock without going through storage, those items are called **direct issues**. They should be recorded in the storeroom's inventory so as to chronicle the product for historical purposes and for balancing the storeroom's financials; nevertheless, this practice is not absolutely required. The product's expenditure, however, must be charged to the cost center to which it is issued. Failure to do so would artificially improve the food cost of that area by providing free product for sale, while robbing the storeroom of its proper reimbursement.

Product Requisitions

Product requisitions, also known as **storeroom requisitions** (or storeroom "reqs"), are the forms used to identify the foods that the chef needs for that day's production (see Figure 8.15a and Figure 8.15b). When compiled, either by computer program or paper document, they serve as a shopping list to be filled by the storeroom. The person completing the requisition generally keeps a copy for her own records and sends the original on to the storeroom staff.

Although there are differences among storerooms, there are not many differences among the requisitions used by hotels, hospitals, military food service, culinary schools, or restaurant chains. Although most places create their own forms, each typically contains the following information:

- Name of cost center or person completing the requisition (requesting the product)

- Date requested for product delivery/availability

- Unique product code

- Product name

- Quantity/amount desired

- Quantity/amount issued (to be completed by the storeroom staff)

- Cost (to be completed by the storeroom staff)

Every company has its own policy regarding when requisitions are due to the storeroom. Some places allow requisitions to be delivered with little or no lead time required, while other places demand a minimum of 24 hours notice.

Purchase Requisitions

Purchase requisitions are internal documents used in businesses that have formal storeroom operations. Staff who need equipment not normally carried by the storeroom, such as chocolate tempering machines or dough sheeters, complete purchase requisitions that detail the specifications of the desired equipment (see Figure 8.16). These forms allow the chef to communicate her exact needs to the operation's buyer, as a matter of record, and they allow the buyer to seek budgetary approval from the owner or general manager prior to purchase.

THE INGREDIENT ROOM

Ingredient rooms are not common in most food service operations, but they are often employed in large institutional operations such as military or health care facilities to control waste and promote safe food handling. Ingredient rooms, which act as a way station between the storeroom and the production kitchens, are used to weigh, measure, and then assemble food for the day's recipes. The ingredients for the recipes are placed on carts or containers and then delivered to the kitchen for final cooking.

8.15a **Example of Standard Storeroom Requisition**

Date Ordered _____   Credit Department _____

Department _____   Charge Function _____

Date Needed _____   Date of Function _____

Customer Code No. _____   Customer Name _____

Product Class	Product Type	Product Description	Item Description	Unit Pack	Quantity Ordered	Quantity Received

White – Storeroom   Yellow – Kitchen   Pink – Accounting

8.15b   **Example of Par Stock Requisition**

Date _____   Requisition Number _____

Time _____   Department _____

Prepared by _____   Priced by _____

Delivered by _____   Extended by _____

Received by _____   Approved by _____

Item Description	Product Code	Par	On Hand	Order	Price		Extension	

TOTAL .... $

White – Purchasing   Yellow – Originator   Pink – Accounting

8.16 **Example of Purchase Requisition**

Date _____   Requisition Number _____

Time _____   Department _____

Prepared by _____   Priced by _____

Delivered by _____   Extended by _____

Received by _____   Approved by _____

Item Description (include model number)	Quantity	Price		Extension	
TOTAL .... $					

White – Purchasing   Yellow – Originator   Pink – Accounting

Stafford T. DeCambra,
CCE, CEC, CCA, AAC
Place of Birth: Oahu, Hawaii

Educational Background and Work Experience

Growing up in Oahu, Stafford DeCambra was like any other islander from Hawaii; he loved surfing, climbing volcanic rock, and hiking through the lush vegetation—and he was proud of his Hawaiian culture. With an early interest in food service, DeCambra worked in a variety of properties for a few years after high school before leaving the island and heading off to culinary school. After earning his AOS at the Culinary Institute of America, Chef DeCambra returned to his island to work in a variety of culinary positions. Eventually, in 1989, Chef DeCambra became the executive chef of the Kona Surf Resort and Country Club in Kailua-Kona, Hawaii. While there, his SS James Makee Restaurant, featuring Hawaii's Pacific Rim cuisine, received Triple A's 4 Diamond Award. Concurrently, DeCambra worked for a few years as executive chef for the Hawaiian Island Gourmet Company, where he was responsible for all culinary operations for a full-service catering company that combined Hawaii regional cuisine with international flavor. He left those two positions in 1993 to become senior executive chef of American Classic Voyages Company, responsible for complete galley operations for three different cruise ships, serving 2,000 passengers. He was directly responsible for the on-board development of all culinary personnel, budgets, menu planning, payroll, food cost control, maintenance, and sanitation of the vessels. In 2001, Chef DeCambra left the cruise company to move to Choctaw, Mississippi, and the Pearl River Resorts, Silver Star Casino and Hotel, where he quickly became the resort's corporate executive chef in charge of an operation with food and beverage revenues exceeding $48 million. Chef DeCambra later moved to Atmore, Alabama, to become executive chef of the new $245 million Wind Creek casino operated by PCI Gaming Authority. Wind Creek is a 17-floor, 236-room hotel, with four restaurants and an innovative cooking studio and culinary classroom under the direction of Chef DeCambra.

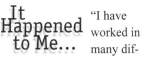

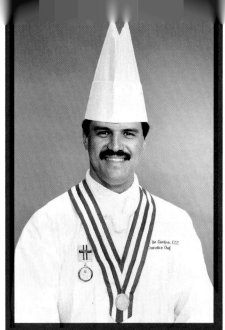

Courtesy Stafford T. DeCambra

"I have worked in many different food service operations from small free-standing single units; to hotel operations with multiple theme restaurants; to mega cruise ships with large volume feeding operations; to managing resort destination operations with multi-unit food service operations ranging from coffee bars, to cafes and bistros, to theme specialty restaurants, and to white cloth fine-dining operations that can generate in access of $48M in total food sales. (Again, I'll stress the importance of purchasing controls as one of the most valuable areas of cost control that can help or hinder your bottom line, and I'll share a story with you.)

In starting my previous position as the Resort Corporate Executive Chef for the Pearl River Resort in Choctaw, Mississippi, and after moving into the Deep South from Hawaii, I experienced a real learning curve. My initiation of understanding the customs, traditions, people and cuisine was new and very exciting; and I enjoyed the Southern charm and hospitality that was genuinely offered to me. As the Resort Corporate Executive Chef, in 2002, I was in a position to open a new casino with 550 rooms and six new food service restaurant operations for Pearl River Resort. Already in existence were another casino with 600 rooms, an additional seven food service operations on this destination resort, not to mention a golf club, water park, and multiple fast food operations.

I can honestly tell you, in the south, there are certain menu items that are staple traditions with their cuisine; and in the south it's fried chicken and fried catfish, no matter where you go. The procurement of catfish and fresh chicken are in my 'top 10' most important items to watch, and knowing past history of the usage of these products makes it is somewhat easy to gauge and project for production. It also helps greatly with costs that pertain to the operating budget(s). Well, after a great opening and four months of operating the new casino (with its six new food service restaurant operations), I realized that my cost for purchasing fresh chickens were starting to exceed my projections by 3 percent. What made matters worse, it was also happening at my pre-existing casino operation. I immediately checked my catfish purchases, in relationship to cost and production, and found them to be in line (in comparison with my existing operating casino).

During a delivery of fresh chickens, I did a random 'on-site receiving inspection' with my current Warehouse/Storeroom Manager at my pre-existing casino operation. During this inspection, I began to look closely at each case of fresh chickens. I checked for freshness, and I also decided to randomly weigh some of the cases, comparing the unit cost and weight compared to

(continued)

Memberships and Career Highlights

Along the way, his affable personality, competence in the kitchen, and strong leadership skills drew the attention of many admirers. Among his numerous awards and accomplishments, DeCambra was named his American Culinary Federation (ACF) chapter's Chef of the Year three different times, in two states. He also won the ACF Regional Chef of the Year honors in two different regions, in 1995 and 2006. Among his most coveted honors, Chef DeCambra received the ACF National Chef Professionalism Award in 2004 and the national ACF Humanitarian Award in 2006. In 2007, Chef DeCambra was elected as the vice chair for the American Academy of Chefs. In addition to being a Fellow of the American Academy of Chefs and member of the American Culinary Federation, Chef DeCambra is a member of European World Master Chef's Society, the Confrerie de la Chaine des Rottisseurs, and Les Toques Blanche International. As an individual competitor at the 2008 Internationale Kochkunst-Ausstellung held in Erfurt, Germany, Chef DeCambra earned two bronze and two gold medals in culinary salon competition.

Passions with the Food Service Industry

"For me, the true beauty of my craft is in my personal passion for the Culinary Arts. "I love to cook. I am always curious to learn more about food every day, and I thrive on the intensity of the fast pace and pressure in the kitchen. The challenge to be creative and produce exceptional products, I adore. As a nationally recognized Chef, I have attributed my interest in regional and different ethnic cooking to my local upbringing in Hawaii. I guess I would be among the so-called 'new generation' of Hawaiian Chefs, creating my own interpretation of the fresh, spicy and exciting flavors of my native Hawaii.

the vendor invoice. Overall, it was close with some of the case weights, but others were not quite matching up. I found the weight of the ice (that is used to keep the fresh whole chickens chilled to the proper temperature) was also included in the case weight on the invoice. I then began the task of removing the crushed ice from the case and getting the weight of the crushed ice. Then I began to weigh the fresh chicken seeking its total weight. Well...You do the math!

I headed to the new casino operation and guess what? It was totally identical. To make a long story short, this issue was addressed with the supplier and vendor. And it was resolved immediately. I did not accuse, or even hint that I suspected foul play. As a Chef, I feel it is honorable to support the local economy as much as possible, especially knowing that I am in the position to do so. However, it was a humbling experience for my storeroom manager and me, as we had not been following correct receiving procedures.

Moral of the story: Be sure to set-up established Specifications and Standards. Monitor, and follow-up randomly, on established receiving procedures for accuracy and control. And don't be afraid to investigate concerns or issues that can help contribute to the 'bottom line.'"

With a lust for traveling, I draw inspiration from the different cultures that abound, and I first turned to the flavors of Southeast Asian cuisine. I focused on the local ethnic dishes from Japan, China, Thailand and Vietnam, while learning first hand in those countries. My determination, hard work and the instinct to follow my dreams made me no stranger to cooking. Additionally, my obsession for travel and native cuisine, while working through various international chefs exchange programs, has afforded me the opportunities to work in Jamaica and Tahiti, all the while sharing my passion for the cuisine of the Hawaiian Islands. I love the versatility found in the Culinary Arts; it is contagious, it is very rewarding, and I truly love being part of this industry."

Advice to a Chef or Buyer

"Purchasing controls are one of the most valuable areas of cost control that can help or hinder your 'bottom line.' As the Resort Corporate Executive Chef, product specifications and standards are the first line of defense after my menu development

is finalized. They set the quality standards that my internal and external customers understand and acknowledge, which ultimately establishes my expectations for getting and receiving quality products in all my operations. Be sure to watch your produce and protein products thoroughly. These high cost and highly perishable products need to be constantly monitored and controlled, daily. Quality can waiver, and prices in today's market are volatile. The best advice that I can give a chef or buyer in managing food operations, either small or large, is to watch your 'top 10' purchases. You will see what I mean once you make this part of your daily active role as a chef or buyer. You will see how just these few products truly affect your 'bottom line.' When you are in a position like I am, with revenues in excess of $48M a year, I practice due diligence by monitoring my 'top 25' purchases on a weekly basis. I follow market flows and trends, and the effect it has on the operation. I do what needs to be done to keep my purchasing and cost controls in line for optimum return and corporate revenues."

Key Words and Concepts

---

actual cost	formal issuing	LIFO	shrinkage
blind receiving	holding costs	ordering cost	stockouts
credit memo	informal issuing	par stock	storeroom requisition
direct issues	ingredient room	perpetual inventory	storing
economic order quantity (EOQ)	inventory management	physical inventory	weighted average
	issuing	product rejection	weight tag
FIFO	key stop	purchase requisition	
food in service	latest purchase price	safety stock	

Chapter in Review

The following exercises are provided to help the reader understand and apply the contents of this chapter. They may be completed individually or in a classroom environment.

REVIEW QUESTIONS

a. Explain the need for product inspection when receiving.

b. List the receiving checks that should be undertaken for delivered products.

c. Identify the different methods used for valuing inventory.

d. Describe the different systems used by buyers to determine appropriate quantities of product to order.

INDIVIDUAL ACTIVITIES

a. **Web based:** Create an inventory format, using spreadsheet software, that could be used to track physical or perpetual inventories.

b. **Experiential:** Ask to observe a receiving clerk while the clerk meets with a delivery driver, and watch as the clerk receives, inspects, and stores the products.

c. **Critical thinking:** Compare and contrast formal and informal issuing, and consider when each system is appropriate for use.

GROUP ACTIVITIES

a. **Lab experience:** With the cooperation of a large food service operation, such as a hotel or culinary school, allow each student to participate in the entire receiving, storing, and issuing process. Have the participants perform each function, under the guidance of the paid staff, in order to fully comprehend the process.

b. **Classroom action:** With the cooperation of a large food service operation, such as a hotel or culinary school, allow each student to participate in taking the physical inventory, under the guidance of the paid staff, in order to fully comprehend the process.

Cost Control Measures for Food Service Operations

"Profitability is the sovereign criterion of the enterprise."

PETER F. DRUCKER

After reading this chapter, you will be able to:

- ◎ Define the Siamese twins of management.
- ◎ Summarize the importance of control systems and quality management.
- ◎ Clarify the use of financial statements, including income statements, balance sheets, cash flow, and operating budgets.
- ◎ Define fixed, variable, conversion, and common costs.

- ◎ Outline the purpose of production reports.
- ◎ Relate the concept of food cost and the Forty Thieves.
- ◎ Summarize inventory management and the benefits of controlling inventory.
- ◎ Explain how to calculate food and labor costs.
- ◎ Describe how to make payroll calculations.
- ◎ Perform break-even analysis and the method used for graphing.

Introduction

Food service operators need controls in place to measure their organization's performance and to compare it to established quality standards for operation. Cost control measures are an essential part of management and are vital to successful storeroom operations.

This chapter includes the primary measures that food service operators should take to monitor their staff's performance and manage their business's revenues and expenses. Effective cost control measures are crucial for all stations and departments within a food service operation, from the delivery door to the business entrance. As Pavesic and Magnant (2005) note:

Cost control is more than just computing percentages and ratios; it involves making decisions after the information has been compiled and interpreted. ... Therefore, a more complete definition of cost control can be explained by citing its purposes, which are:

1. To provide management with the information necessary to make day-to-day operational decisions.

2. To monitor the efficiency of individuals and departments.

3. To inform management of what expenses are being incurred, what incomes are being received, and whether they are within standards or budgets.

4. To prevent fraud and theft by employees, guests, and purveyors.

5. To be the basis for knowing where the business is going, not for discovering where it has been.

6. To emphasize prevention and not correction.

7. To maximize profit not minimize losses. (p. 9)

The savvy food service operator must have a strong system of *planning* and *controls*, known as the **Siamese twins of management,** to ensure the business accomplishes its goals. *Planning* is creating a view of the future through budgets, projections, and production systems. *Controls* are the systems set up to make sure that the plans are carried out. As Garlough and Campbell (2006) state, "This system of planning and controlling generally results in an efficient and well-trained staff producing food within budget" (p.13).

Using Other People's Money

Historically, storerooms were considered a drain on the business. Storerooms lost money because they were inefficiently managed. Products were purchased but not issued or used because of deterioration, theft, or poor controls. However, in today's economy and global marketplace, the purchasing function has become much more proactive in contributing to the fiscal health of a food service organization.

As the banking industry has ably demonstrated for centuries, there is profit to be made by using other people's money. Bankers have made fortunes for their establishments by borrowing the collective deposits of many of their customers at a low interest rate and then lending it to other customers at a higher rate. The modest difference between the two interest rates results in a healthy profit for the bank, when compounded by numerous transactions. The more deposits their customers make, the more loans the banks can grant and, therefore, the more profits they can earn.

Similarly, food service operators can improve their bottom-line profitability by efficient methods of purchasing, stock management, and cost controls. By maintaining a minimal yet sufficient amount of stock purchased with the free credit from their suppliers and turning it quickly, food service operators can sell their goods days before the bills are due. This use of other people's money can result in a substantial profit for the operator when the money is wisely invested and compounded over time. The longer the terms, such as 7 days or 30 days, the more opportunity the establishment has to sell the food before paying for it. At the very least, paying bills on time before interest charges accrue guarantees a reduction in costs.

Additionally, money can be made by efficient methods of procurement. Under normal circumstances, operators determine their recipe costs and menu prices based on everyday food costs. But when the purchasing agent is able to take advantage of volume or promotional discounts by accurately forecasting the establishment's product needs and thereby reducing the recipe's food cost, then the business will see additional profit.

The Importance of Control Systems

There is a clear and evident need for control systems in all aspects of food service operations. Controls, or systems of measure, are necessary to gauge the progress of the business toward obtaining its goals. Companies use controls to measure day-to-day revenues and expenses, customer and employee satisfaction, and other criteria against established standards. Successful food service operations control the various costs associated with the business. No chef or food and beverage director can remain in business without first establishing, and then maintaining, a comprehensive system of cost controls.

In their text on cost controls, Dittmer and Keefe (2006) write:

The **control process** consists of four steps:

1. Establish standards and standard procedures for operation.

2. Train all individuals to follow established standards and standard procedures.

3. Monitor performance and compare actual performances with established standards.

4. Take appropriate action to correct deviations from standards. (p. 64)

The Importance of Quality Standards

The perception of quality, although subject to personal opinion, can be identified and measured according to a preset list of agreed-upon standards. These **quality standards** are an important tool for gauging a company's progress. Without established standards, and a system to measure their attainment, a company has no barometer by which to make their business decisions (see Figure 9.1). The quality of each meal should be measured against these guidelines each time it is served.

Evaluating Performance Using Financial Statements

There are four primary **financial statements** that food service operations use to manage and control their finances: *income statements, balance sheets, cash flow statements,* and *operating budgets.* Each report has a separate purpose, and, collectively, their use gives the operator insight into the business's performance.

MANAGING BY INCOME STATEMENTS

Perhaps the most important financial management tool is the **income statement**, also known as the **profit and loss statement (P&L)**, which is a detailed listing of the revenue and expenses for a given time, known as an **accounting period**. The level of detail on the report can vary, depending on the needs of the operator, although its format is typically standardized. Most food service operators choose to use the **Uniform System of Accounts for Restaurants**, developed

 Sample quality standard
Courtesy USDA

United States Standards for Grades of Fresh Asparagus

Grades

§51.3720 U.S. No. 1

"U.S. No. 1" consists of stalks of asparagus which are fresh, well trimmed, and fairly straight; which are free from decay and free from damage caused by spreading or broken tips, dirt, disease, insects, or other means.

(a) Size. Unless otherwise specified, the diameter of each stalk is not less than one-half inch.

(b) Color. Unless otherwise specified, not less than two-thirds of the stalk length shall be the color of the lot.

(c) Tolerances. In order to allow for variations incident to proper grading and handling, the following tolerances, by count, are provided as specified:

  1. For defects. Ten percent for stalks in any lot which fail to meet the requirements of this grade other than for trimming, including therein not more than 5 percent for defects causing serious damage: **Provided,** That not more than one-fifth of this latter amount, or 1 percent, shall be allowed for stalks affected by decay.

by the National Restaurant Association. In its seventh edition, as of the writing of this text, the Uniform System is designed to include all forms of revenues and expenses common to food service operations. The basic formula for the income statement is:

$$\text{Revenues} - \text{Expenses} + \text{Gains} - \text{Losses} = \text{Income}$$

Revenues are the money received when a meal is served. **Expenses** are the costs associated with purchasing the ingredients, preparing and serving the food, and with keeping the building open. *Gains* are any money received from other sources such as interest, sale of equipment, or dividends. *Losses* are any money that is gone from the business, such as money paid because of damage to equipment.

 Nonoperating activities *include any gain or loss on company investments, the operating profit or loss of any business subsidiary, and any accounting changes required to conform to revised accounting principles.*

The P&L is best understood by dividing it into three sections: *gross profit, operating expenses,* and *nonoperating expenses*—listed in order of most controllable to least controllable from a manager's point of view. As noted in Figure 9.2, the gross profit section consists of *sales, cost of*

sales, and *gross profit.* In a food service establishment, these would include food and beverage sales and the costs of the items sold. These revenues should be analyzed on a daily basis by a chef, kitchen manager, or the general manager of the establishment. The operating expenses section covers *operating expenses* and *operating income,* which would include repairs and maintenance. These are less predictable to control. The nonoperating expenses section includes *interest* through net profit/(loss). Because interest to creditors and income taxes are predetermined, and generally not subject to change, they are likely beyond the manager's control.

Designing income statements that show previous years' figures is an excellent means by which to measure performance. At a minimum, the P&L should show both the current year and the prior year, and their percentage differences. Some P&Ls show 3 years' worth of figures (see Figure 9.2), while others go back five years. The longer the view, the easier it is to spot trends and anomalies. It is recommended that P&Ls be

9.2   Sample 3-year Income Statement

Benham's Bistro
Income Statement
For the Years Ended December 31, 20X1, 20X2, 20X3

	20X3	20X3	20X2	20X2	20X1	20X1
Sales:						
Food	$600,000	69.9%	$630,000	69.2%	$670,000	68.9%
Beverage	258,000	30.1%	281,000	30.8%	302,000	31.1%
Total	858,000	100.0%	911,000	100.0%	972,000	100.0%
Cost of Sales:						
Food	225,000	37.5%	250,000	39.7%	265,000	39.6%
Beverage	63,000	24.4%	68,000	24.2%	74,000	24.5%
Total	288,000	33.6%	318,000	34.9%	339,000	34.9%
Gross Profit:						
Food	375,000	62.5%	380,000	60.3%	405,000	60.4%
Beverage	195,000	75.6%	213,000	75.8%	228,000	75.5%
Total	570,000	66.4%	593,000	65.1%	633,000	65.1%
Operating Expenses:						
Payroll	234,000	27.3%	245,000	26.9%	261,000	26.9%
Employee benefits	38,000	4.4%	40,000	4.4%	51,000	5.2%
Direct operating expenses	42,000	4.9%	45,000	4.9%	49,000	5.0%
Music and entertainment	2,000	0.2%	2,000	0.2%	2,200	0.2%
Marketing	19,000	2.2%	20,000	2.2%	21,000	2.2%
Utilities	26,000	3.0%	28,000	3.1%	31,000	3.2%
General and administrative services expenses	27,000	3.1%	29,000	3.2%	32,000	3.3%
Repairs and maintenance	13,000	1.5%	13,000	1.4%	14,000	1.4%
Occupational costs	38,000	4.4%	40,000	4.4%	43,000	4.4%
Depreciation	24,000	2.8%	25,000	2.7%	26,.000	2.7%
Total operating expenses	463,000	54.0%	487,000	53.5%	530,200	54.5%
Operating income	107,000	12.4%	106,000	11.6%	102,800	10.6%
Interest	30,000	3.5%	30,000	3.3%	30,000	
Net profit before income tax	77,000	8.9%	76,000	8.3%	72,800	
Income tax	23,000	2.7%	23,000	2.5%	22,500	
Net profit	$54,000	6.2%	$53,000	5.8%	$50,300	

constructed for each month and then aggregated by quarters and years. Better reports include "to date" columns that show activity as it occurs *to date*. Smaller operations that carry little stock and offer limited menus, such as quick-service restaurants, can perform daily or weekly P&L computations. With this information, a company can quickly make changes that will help its business. Other income statements will show a comparison of actual figures to the projected or budgeted figures. This format helps the establishment stay on track.

MANAGING BY BALANCE SHEETS

For a business to know its financial health, it must draw a comparison between its **assets** and **liabilities**. Assets are the things that the company owns. Assets are the permanent fixtures—including equipment, bowls, knives, and plates—that are used over and over again to produce what is sold. Liabilities are the money owed to creditors. Liabilities are different from expenses, as expenses are normally paid within the year; liabilities are paid over many years. The **balance sheet** shows a company's assets and liabilities and the difference between these two figures (see Figure 9.3). The balance sheet shows the value of the assets and the liabilities on a specific date, and it serves as a "snapshot" of the financial conditions on any particular date.

Normally, a balance sheet shows the assets, liabilities, and the shareholder equity or net worth. The **current assets**, such as equipment, are listed first, followed by the long-term assets, such as land and buildings. Liabilities are

People, Places, Things

An Example of Evaluating Performance

In 1988, my brother and sister-in-law decided to apply their experiences from corporate America to start their own business, and they embarked on new careers as retail deli-bakery and specialty food operators. Their initial concept was to offer upscale home meal replacement food items, including entrees, fine salads, charcuterie products and cheeses, fresh baked muffins and cookies, and assorted specialty food items to the high-income households of the western Chicago suburbs. Additionally, the business provided off-premise catering and sold upscale gift baskets, using the store's various food products. With successful backgrounds in marketing and promotion, and with the assistance of myself and other knowledgeable family members, a business plan was established. The facility was designed, the menus and recipes written, operating procedures established, and a retail and kitchen staff hired. They established the business in a 4,700-square-foot retail space in a high-traffic strip mall in Naperville, Illinois.

The business grew slowly but never reached the projected sales as estimated in the business plan. (Two large local grocery chains also decided to offer similar products just after they had opened.) Each aspect of the business was continually evaluated for its contribution to total sales and gross margin performance using P&L statements, and they eventually decided to change the focus of the business. They used a series of measurable standards to determine that the off-premise catering portion of their business was more profitable and was yielding higher sales volumes than the retail operation. Additionally, the business could relocate to a much larger facility in a light industrial park location that was leased at one-third the square foot cost of the old location, as the catering business no longer needed a high-traffic retail presence. The shift to catering proved wise, and the company, *My Chef, Inc.*, has enjoyed both consistent growth and profitability for more than 20 years under their leadership. Had there not been a system in place for evaluating performance back then, and still today, the company might have folded years ago.

Note: The U.S Chamber of Commerce named My Chef, Inc. the national 2007 Small Business of the Year.

9.3 Sample Balance Sheet

Campbell's Tavern
BALANCE SHEET
October 31, 20XX

ASSETS

CURRENT ASSETS

CASH CHECKING	$782	
CASH PAYROLL	2,500	
CASH MONEY MKT.	10,000	
TOTAL CASH		13,282
AMEX REC.	25,120	
VISA/MC REC.	10,500	
HOUSE ACCOUNTS	15,000	
PREPAID EXPENSES	10,000	
		60,620

INVENTORY

FOOD	20,000	
WINE	200,000	
LIQUOR	35,000	
BEER	7,000	
OTHER BEV.	5,000	
TOTAL INVENTORY		267,000
TOTAL CURRENT ASSETS		340,902

FIXED ASSETS

FURNITURE AND EQUIPMENT	215,000	
LEASEHOLD IMPROVEMENTS	1,000,000	
	1,215,000	
ACCUMULATED DEPRECIATION	(140,000)	
NET FIXED ASSETS		1,075,000

OTHER ASSETS

SECURITY DEPOSITS	20,000	
LIQUOR LICENSE	5,100	
ARTWORK	75,000	
TOTAL OTHER ASSETS		100,100
TOTAL ASSETS		**1,516,002**

LIABILITIES AND STOCKHOLDERS' EQUITY

CURRENT LIABILITIES

CURRENT PORTION ST DEBT	$175,000	
ACCOUNTS PAYABLE	150,000	
ACCRUED WAGES	20,000	
ACCRUED INCOME TAXES	5,000	
ACCRUED PAYROLL TAXES	15,000	
GIFT CERTIFICATES PAYABLE	16,000	
TOTAL CURRENT LIABILITIES		381,000
NOTES PAYABLE LT PORTION		600,000
TOTAL LIABILITIES		981,000

STOCKHOLDERS' EQUITY

CAPITAL STOCK	1,000	
PAID IN CAPITAL	199,000	
RETAINED EARNINGS	75,000	
NET INCOME	260,002	
TOTAL STOCKHOLDERS' EQUITY		535,002
TOTAL LIABILITIES AND STOCKHOLDERS' EQUITY		**$1,516,002**

listed the same way with those that are due soon listed first, followed by the ones that are due later. The Shareholder's equity section is the difference between the two:

Assets – Liabilities = Owner's (shareholder's) equity/net worth

The net income (or losses), as indicated by an income statement, is included in the owner's equity section. This figure, called retained earnings, is a cumulative sum of all of the net incomes and losses since the business opened. Other line items in the owner's equity section include goodwill, stock, and dividends.

Balance sheets are prepared for the benefit of shareholders to see how their investment is doing. They are also prepared for banks when a business is seeking a loan, so that banks can confirm the fiscal health of the business, often using current or **fixed assets** as collateral for the loan.

MANAGING BY CASH FLOW

It is often said in business that cash is king. When buyers have readily available cash, they are often able to make better purchases than when using credit. The goal of every entrepreneur is to make payroll, meaning the business needs to have sufficient cash on hand to pay current debts. Failure to make payroll is often the first sign of a business in trouble, one that has **cash flow** problems.

Cash flow is the comparison between cash that is readily available and the bills that are due in the near future. The goal is to have more money coming in than going out. Most managers plan their cash flows, mapping out when cash should come in and go out. **Accounts receivable** are money owed to the business, such as from credit cards or customers who receive monthly bills from the establishment. **Accounts payable** are the money that the restaurant owes and should be paying out within the next few weeks. Most managers watch the difference between the payables and receivables (see Figure 9.4). If money is not coming in fast enough, then the purchasing manager might be limited in what he can purchase.

Most restaurants have seasonal influences that affect their cash flow. Normally, certain costs such as rent are the same each month, but revenues experience dramatic swings. Catering businesses and resorts often experience these huge changes to their P&Ls from one month to the next. For backup during these lean periods of negative cash flow, owners will often secure **bank lines of credit**. It is common for small and midsized companies to use bank lines of credit to cover their check payments and to protect their credit status.

The **statement of cash flows** is the financial report that shows incoming and outgoing monies over a certain period of time. This report ties together the information from the income statement and balance sheet by explaining all of the differences in their respective accounts. The statement is divided into three sections: First is operating, or the monies associated with the operations of the food service establishment. Next is financing, which shows the monies associated with loans, stocks, or owner's draws. Third is investing, which is all monies associated with investments held by the establishment, such as interest on the checking accounts. Normally this statement is used by managers to plan their bill payments (see Figure 9.5).

Accounts Receivable

An accounts receivable refers to a charge that has been billed to the customer but not yet collected. It represents money due the business for services performed. In food service, a receivable could be an invoice sent to a customer after a party was catered or credit card payments due from the bank. In accounting terms, they are considered an asset, because all accounts receivable are converted to cash.

Accounts Payable

Accounts payables is money owed to vendors and other purveyors when assets or goods are purchased on an open account. This is money spent by the food service establishment to purchase the food and other items needed for service. A common example is the money owed to a food service distributor when the food is purchased on credit. Accounts payable are listed in the liabilities section of the balance sheet.

> BUYER'S NOTE
> A telltale sign that a business is in trouble is when its accounts payable are growing faster than its accounts receivable, which can result in bills going unpaid.

MANAGING BY OPERATING BUDGETS

In addition to using quality standards, businesses must also use **operating budgets** to achieve their financial goals. Stated in dollar terms, operating budgets forecast the estimated expenses that a business must incur to achieve estimated sales revenues. By extension, the operating budget indicates the expected profit for a specific period of time. It is a clear financial plan that must exist to evaluate performance. Operating budgets are simply income statements prepared for a future date (see Figure 9.6).

Owners or general managers create operating budgets each year for the new year's projected business. The operating budgets are normally prepared using historical information from previous budgets and other financial documents, coupled with any foreseen changes in sales and costs. Operating budgets can measure any period of time, from one day to one year or more. Typically, budgets are projected for periods of one year but are divided into months and quarters. As many businesses are cyclical, with seasonal fluctuations in sales, budgets are more useful when they cover shorter periods of time, such as by the month.

The purpose of an operating budget is to measure performance—to be sure the business is achieving its sales goals within an expected range of expense. Comparisons are made between the projected (*budgeted*) amounts and percentages, and the *actual* numbers achieved. If the budget was created properly, all other financial concerns will be met if the business stays within budget and meets its projected revenues and expenses. Remember, the establishment should stay within both the dollar and percentage values to be a useful tool for the managers.

9.4 **Sample Cash Flow Quarterly Comparison**

Olmos Food Corporation
Quarterly Cash Flow Statement

	06/30/09	06/30/08	06/30/07	06/30/06
Cash flow from operations, investments, and financial activities				
Net income (loss)	8,168	9,993	7,829	7,346
Depreciation/amortization and depletion	1,186	1,439	1,084	1,536
Net change from assets/liabilities	0	1,046	-231	0
Net cash from discontinued operations	0	0	0	375
Other operating activities	5,272	3,319	5,827	4,165
Net cash from operating activities	14,626	15,797	14,509	13,422
Property and equipment	-1,109	-891	-770	-1,103
Acquisition/disposition of units	-4	-1,063	0	0
Investments	-1,632	-5,259	-10,075	-7,631
Other investing activities	0	0	0	0
Net cash from investing activities	-2,745	-7,213	-10,845	-8,734
Uses of funds				
Issuance (repurchase) of capital stock	-635	-4,366	-4,572	-5,821
Issuance (repayment) of debt	0	0	0	0
Increase (decrease) short-term debt	0	0	0	0
Payment of dividends and other distributions	-1,729	-857	0	0
Other financing activities	0	0	0	235
Net cash from financing activities	-2,364	-5,223	-4,572	-5,586
Effect of exchange rate changes	27	61	2	-26
Net change in cash and equivalents	9,544	3,422	-906	-924
Cash at beginning of period	6,438	3,016	3,922	4,846
Cash at end of period	15,982	6,438	3,016	3,922

Revenue

Sales are considered the company's **revenue**. Revenue results from the exchange of products and services for cash or its equivalent. Most food service establishments separate out the different revenue categories such as food, beverage, vended products, services, room rental, and merchandise. Each item should be identified on its own income line and then combined as total revenue.

Prime Costs (Expenses)

Prime costs are the food ingredients and the labor needed to transform them into a dish. In most restaurants, prime costs are a combination of the *cost of goods sold* and *payroll*. Table 9.1 shows some customary percentages in this industry for businesses that specialize in food sales (restaurants) over beverage sales (bars). Please note: these percentages

are rough guidelines, and the type of format, level of service, and make-versus-buy decisions affect the possible ranges.

Although Table 9.1 shows some common percentages, each restaurant is different. A seafood house could have a high food cost but a lower payroll cost while a pasta restaurant might have a low food cost but larger payroll cost. Most food service establishments aim for a prime cost of 60 to 69 percent of sales. If the figure is closer to 60 percent, then there is more money available to pay fixed costs, which results in higher profits for the establishment. Never use the financials from one establishment as the absolute model for another. Fixed costs can vary considerably from one business to the next, and variable costs will also change based on the nature of the business.

Though the prime cost ratio may vary from restaurant to restaurant, if it is more than 69 percent at any establishment on a regular basis, odds are the owner is losing money. If this happens for a short period of time, such as the slow season, and the owner has set aside money to cover it, then there should not

9.5 Sample Cash Flow Statement

Monaldo's Seafood
Statement of Cash Flows
For the Year Ended December 31, 20XX

Net cash flow from operating activities:		
Net income		$96,000
Adjustments to reconcile net income to net cash flows from operating activities:		
Depreciation	$60,000	
Gain on sale of investments	(10,000)	
Decrease in accounts receivable	4,000	
Increase in inventory	(2,000)	
Increase in accounts payroll	800	
Increase in accrued payroll	600	
Decrease in income taxes payable	(1,000)	52,400
Net cash flow from operating activities		148,400
Investing activities:		
Sale of investments	$5,000	
Purchase of investments	(15,000)	
Purchase of equipment	(40,000)	
Net cash flow used in investing activities		(50,000)
Financing activities:		
Payment of long-term debt	$(22,000)	
Dividends paid to stockholders	(38,000)	
Net cash flow in financing activities		(60,000)
Net increase in cash during 20XX		38,000
Cash at the beginning of 20XX		20,000
Cash at the end of 20XX		$58,000

Supplementary disclosure of cash flow information

Cash paid during the year for:		
Interest	$32,500	
Income taxes	$27,000	

be a problem. Smaller establishments such as ice cream stands or hot dog carts can handle a prime cost of 70 to 72 percent, as they have relatively few equipment needs or fixed costs.

Fixed, Variable, Conversion, and Common Costs

Most operators divide their expenses into categories for easy tracking. *Fixed, variable, conversion*, and *common costs* are all part of the average food service operation, and each has its own definition and manner of control.

These expenses all have their own unique relationship to sales. They are often reported as a percentage of sales, by dividing each cost figure by sales.

FIXED COSTS

Fixed costs, also called "overhead," remain the same regardless of how many customers are served or the total revenue

9.6 **Sample Restaurant Budget**

Benham Bistro
Annual Budget
For the Year Ending December 31, 20X1

	20X1	20X1
Sales:		
Food	$600,000	69.9%
Beverage	258,000	30.1%
Total	858,000	100.0%
Cost of Sales:		
Food	225,000	37.5%
Beverage	63,000	24.4%
Total	288,000	33.6%
Gross Profit:		
Food	375,000	62.5%
Beverage	195,000	75.6%
Total	570,000	66.4%
Operating Expenses:		
Payroll	234,000	27.3%
Employee benefits	38,000	4.4%
Direct operating expenses	42,000	4.9%
Music and entertainment	2,000	0.2%
Marketing	19,000	2.2%
Utilities	26,000	3.0%
General and administrative services expenses	27,000	3.1%
Repairs and maintenance	13,000	1.5%
Occupational costs	38,000	4.4%
Depreciation	24,000	2.8%
Total operating expenses	463,000	54.0%
Operating income	107,000	12.4%
Interest	30,000	3.5%
Net profit before income tax	77,000	8.9%
Income tax	23,000	2.7%
Net profit	$54,000	6.2%

TABLE 9.1 **Customary Prime Costs for Restaurants**

Food cost	18% to 40%
Wine cost	4% to 15%
Liquor cost	4% to 15%
Beer cost	4% to 10%
Other beverage costs	5% to 12%
Labor cost	20% to 35%

for the period. In the short run, line items like property insurance, loans, and rent are considered fixed costs. Fixed costs are known in advance, do not change with sales, and are expressed in dollar amounts. Kitchen managers have virtually no ability to lower fixed costs, as they are usually negotiated when the business is opened. Managers and chefs can really only influence variable costs, whereas owners tend to focus on fixed costs.

VARIABLE (CONTROLLABLE) COSTS

Variable costs change depending on the number of customers served or dollars in revenue collected. Every additional customer will cause a corresponding increase in these costs. Some examples of variable costs include the labor to prepare the meals, the ingredients, the table linens, and the to-go packaging. The exact amounts of these costs are not known in advance, although they can be estimated from the budgets. The chefs and managers, with careful purchasing and adherence to portion controls, can influence these costs.

 Owners and general managers battle to lower fixed costs, while buyers and chefs battle to lower variable costs. Said another way, fixed costs are renegotiated annually, while variable costs are renegotiated daily.

CONVERSION COSTS

Conversion costs are the sum of direct labor and the business overhead. They are the costs associated with converting raw foods into finished goods. Included in these costs are the raw food, disposables, direct labor, equipment loans, rent, and utilities. They do not include any costs associated with sales.

COMMON COSTS VERSUS DIRECT COSTS

A **common cost**, or **joint cost**, is a cost that is common to several areas of the establishment but cannot easily be traced to each individually. Many conversion costs can also be considered common costs. For example, salaried staff, equipment costs, rent, and utilities are joint costs incurred by all departments in a food service operation, and they cannot easily be assigned to a specific area. Common costs are also used to calculate overhead costs that must be considered when pricing the menu. Some examples of common costs include the spices, fryer oils, and seasonings used to prepare many items on the menu. Because it is difficult to ascertain which menu item used up the most oil, it is normally considered a common cost.

Direct costs are those that can easily be assigned to a product. They include the raw food, direct labor, and supplies used in the food item's production. This expense is vitally important when calculating recipe costs and when pricing the menu.

Evaluating Performance by Other Management Tools

In addition to the traditional financial instruments that are common to most businesses, the food service industry employs management tools that may be considered unique to this industry. The following are examples of commonly used evaluations in food service.

MAKE-OR-BUY DECISIONS

With all of the ready-to-eat foods available in the marketplace today, the food service operator has many make-or-buy decisions to make. Ready-to-eat foods might meet an establishment's needs at a lower cost, but they should only be used if they meet the operation's quality standards and customer expectations.

Ready-to-eat foods will have a higher food cost but a lower labor cost. As previously discussed in this chapter, the prime costs of virtually all food service establishments are their food and labor costs. Together, these generally represent the largest costs of doing business, and they are interrelated. For example, a restaurant might choose to purchase par-baked rolls, requiring no labor to prepare them. The per-unit food cost is somewhat higher than that of rolls made from scratch, but the labor costs are lower. If the combined food and labor cost of the scratch-prepared roll is per-unit comparable to the ready-prepared roll, then the operator must decide which is better for his operation—to make or buy. Operators typically consider many factors—including ease of preparation, storage versus production space, staffing and skills, product consistency, and uniqueness—when making this decision.

Food buyers must research what suitable products are available in the marketplace and make this information known to the chef, kitchen manager, food service director, or owner. Oftentimes, make or buy is a group decision, with several managers and chefs evaluating the products.

PRODUCTION REPORTS

Garlough and Campbell (2006) write that **production reports** (see Figure 9.7) "serve three primary purposes, including (1) control, (2) communication, and (3) calculation. As an instrument of control, the production report is used to record the activity surrounding all prepared menu items" (p. 39).

The contemporary concept of production management in food service parallels the modern systems used by the manufacturing industry. Both take raw materials and fabricate them to the specifications and needs of their customers. Although the shelf life of food products is shorter than that of most other goods, the stages of production and the overall management concerns are comparable.

A quality product is within the ability of most operations, if the owners and management staff are willing to provide the environment and leadership to make it happen.

Food Costs and the Forty Thieves

The vigilant food service operator must learn to control the financial bottom line by controlling the products' flow through the operation. Production reports are useful tools in combating the "forty thieves of food cost," as presented first in a magazine article written for *Cooking for Profit* by Robert C. Petrie, back in 1972, and later reprinted in *SPECS: The Food service and Purchasing Specification Manual*. Although originally written many decades ago, its lessons are still relevant today. The following points are just some of the means by which money can be lost, and profits not realized, when control measures aren't enacted in all departments of the operation:

A. Purchasing
  1. Purchasing too much
  2. Purchasing for too high a cost
  3. No detailed specifications—quality, weight, type
  4. No competitive purchasing policy
  5. No cost budget for purchasing
  6. No audit of invoices and payments

B. Receiving
  7. Theft by receiving personnel
  8. No system of credits for low quality, damaged merchandise, or goods not received
  9. Lack of facilities and/or scales
  10. Perishable foods left out of storage

C. Storage
  11. Foods improperly placed in storage (e.g., fats, eggs, milk near strong cheese and fish)
  12. Storage at wrong temperature and humidity
  13. No daily inspection of stored goods
  14. Poor sanitation in dry and refrigerated storage areas
  15. Prices not marked in storeroom
  16. No physical or perpetual inventory policy
  17. Lack of single responsibility for food storage and issues

D. Issuing
  18. No control or record of foods issued from storeroom
  19. Permitting forced or automatic issues

E. Pre-Preparation
  20. Excessive trim of vegetables and meat
  21. No check on raw yields
  22. No use of end products for production of low cost meals

Sample Production Report

Food Production Sheet

Day:

Date:

Customer Count:					
Menu Item	Portion Size	Quantity to Prepare	Quantity Actually Prepared	Quantity Left Over	Quantity Used

Comments:

F. Production

23. Overproduction! Overproduction! Overproduction!

24. Wrong methods of cooking

25. Cooking at wrong temperatures

26. Cooking too long

27. No scheduling of foods to be processed (too early, too late)

28. Not using standard recipes

29. Not cooking in small batches

G. Service

30. No standard portion sizes

31. No standard size utensils for serving

32. No care of leftovers

33. No record of food produced and leaving production area

34. Carelessness (spillage, waste, cold food)

H. Sales

35. Food taken out of building

36. Unrecorded sales and incorrect pricing; "not charges" or cash not turned in

37. No food popularity index or comparison of sales and inventory consumption

38. No sales records to detect trends

39. Poor pricing of menu items

40. Employee meal costs; overproduction or unauthorized meals (pp. 19-20)

MENU ENGINEERING

Menu analysis is recording the sales history of all menu items sold, and evaluating both the item's contribution to profit and customer appeal. As the menu is the primary means of soliciting revenue through customer sales, it is crucial to the operation that the menu be developed with deliberate and considered forethought. The crucial question is, "How does the selling of this menu item help us achieve success?"

Menu engineering is a way to achieve this success (see Figure 9.8). It is used to create a menu that is both profitable to the operation and acceptable to the customer. It considers both financial gain and customer demand. Several variables are generally considered when analyzing a menu, including:

- Food cost percentage
- Contribution margin
- Goal value
- Popularity
- Selling price
- Variable expenses
- Fixed expenses

Menu engineering classifies each menu item according to its popularity index (sales volumes) and profitability index (low food cost). Menu classifications may include:

- **Mainstay.** These menu items are very popular but not very profitable. They are often considered signature dishes and remain on the menu to help maintain volume sales (high sales volume, high food cost).

- **Winner.** Winners are both popular and profitable. These are the favorites of management (high sales volume, low food cost).

- **Loser.** Losers are soon to be vanquished from the menus and replaced with items that are better sellers or more profitable, or both. Just be careful: if you banish all of your losers at once, then menu items in the mainstay and under-repair categories might slip into the loser category (low sales volume, high food cost).

9.8 **Sample Menu Engineering**

A	B	C	D	E	F	G	H	I	J	K	L
Item	# Sold	Mix % (rounded)	Volume Mix Category	Sell Price	Food Cost	Contribution Margin	Total Revenue	Total Food Cost	Total Cont Margin	Cost Category	Classification
1. Veal patty	170	5.6	LOW	$5.95	$2.10	3.85	1011.50	357.00	654.50	LOW	Under Repair
2. Veal liver	450	15.0	HIGH	$6.25	$2.60	3.65	2812.50	1170.00	1642.50	LOW	Winner
3. Burger plate	350	11.7	HIGH	$4.50	$1.25	3.25	1575.00	437.50	1137.50	HIGH	Mainstay
4. Meat loaf	380	12.7	HIGH	$4.95	$1.55	3.40	1881.00	589.00	1292.00	HIGH	Mainstay
5. Salmon cakes	80	2.7	LOW	$6.10	$3.00	3.10	488.00	240.00	248.00	HIGH	Loser
6. Reuben plate	410	13.7	HIGH	$5.50	$1.80	3.70	2255.00	738.00	1517.00	LOW	Winner
7. Steak sand	290	9.7	HIGH	$5.85	$2.45	3.40	1696.50	710.50	986.00	HIGH	Mainstay
8. Chili dog	320	10.7	HIGH	$4.85	$1.60	3.25	1552.00	512.00	1040.00	HIGH	Mainstay
9. Burrito plate	440	14.7	HIGH	$5.25	$1.50	3.75	2310.00	660.00	1650.00	LOW	Winner
10. Club sand	110	3.7	LOW	$4.95	$1.60	3.35	5445.00	176.00	368.50	HIGH	Loser
Totals	3000								10,536 ÷ 3000 = 3.51 (Average CM)		
									AVE CM = 3.51		

*Key

C = B ÷ 3000
D = 7% > High
7% < Low
G = E−F

H = B × E
I = B × F
J = B × G

K = Contribution greater than Average CM (3.51)
(if CM is greater than 3.51 = Low Risk)
(if CM is lesser than 3.51 = High Risk)

Mainstay : High volume, High Cost
Winner: High volume, low Cost
Loser : Low volume, High Cost
Under Repair: Low volume, Low Cost

- **Under repair.** These menu items are confusing to management. They experience low sales volumes but are profitable. This predicament often causes management to "repair" them in an effort to improve sales volumes. Normally, these items need a marketing intervention to fix poor menu placement, overpricing, or a poor value perception (low sales volume, low food cost).

Controlling Inventory

If food cost figures are not in line with the budgeted figures, then the operator should start doing a weekly inventory. The managers should look at the requisitions carefully to make sure that items are not being over-ordered. Chapter 8, "Receiving, Storing, and Issuing," illustrated several methods to control the amount of product ordered and issued. Another popular method is to restrict purchases to a certain percentage of sales. If the owner has forecasted sales of $50,000 for the month and the average food cost percentage is 40 percent, then the chef can only order $20,000 of food that month.

CALCULATING INVENTORY TURNOVER

The rate at which the inventory of a business "turns over," or replaces itself, is often a sign of efficiency and effective purchasing. Because of the perishable nature of most food products, it is better to "turn" the inventory on a regular basis. The formula for average inventory value is as follows, and it can be calculated after each time the inventory is taken.

$$\text{Average inventory value} = \frac{\text{Opening inventory value} + \text{closing inventory value}}{2}$$

Inventory turnover is a ratio that shows how often the inventory is replaced. The formula for turnover is:

$$\text{Turnover} = \frac{\text{Issues}}{\text{Average inventory value}}$$

Another version of the formula is

$$\text{Turnover} = \frac{\text{Cost of goods sold}}{\text{Average inventory value}}$$

If an establishment has a wide variety of inventory levels because of their seasonal nature, an average inventory may be substituted for closing inventory in the average inventory value calculation. Also, the first formula for turnover is used more often, but the second version is used if the restaurant records its issues at market value instead of cost (see Figure 9.9 for a sample turnover calculation using the monthly cost of goods).

Once the turnover ratio is calculated, it should be compared to industry averages and historical data. A low turnover rate means that sales are low, or there is excess inventory on the shelves. A high ratio means increased sales or

9.9 **Sample Calculations for Inventory Turnover**

Calculations for Inventory Turnover Using Summary of Monthly Cost of Goods For the Year 20XX	
January	$37,600
February	37,000
March	35,300
April	31,000
May	29,200
June	27,000
July	28,300
August	35,000
September	36,400
October	40,200
November	45,000
December	50,800
	$432,800 Total yearly cost of goods (Issues)

| Opening Inventory January 1, 20XX $17,000 | + | Closing Inventory December 31, 20XX $20,200 | = | $\dfrac{37,200}{2}$ | = | Average Inventory Value 18,600 |

$$\frac{\text{Issues}}{\text{Avg. Inventory Value}} = \frac{\$432,800}{\$18,600} = 23.27 \text{ Turnovers of Inventory Value}$$

low inventory levels. The goal is to have enough goods on the shelves to cover the forecasted business before the next delivery. If there is too much inventory on the shelves, then money is tied up and not available for use elsewhere in the restaurant. If the restaurant has to decrease its menu prices, then it might run into financial trouble. According to Feinstein and Stefanelli (2005):

> The normal food turnover is between 20 and 25 times a year on the average. This means that it takes about two weeks for all foods to move from the receiving dock to a customer's stomach; for liquor, the turnover is between 7 to 10 times per year. But since there is no generally accepted rule-of-thumb inventory turnover figure in the hospitality industry, an operation must decide what represents a good turnover figure for its business. (p. 141)

It should be stressed that conducting inventories more frequently provides better and timelier information to the operator. Inventory turnover values can also be computed on a monthly basis.

CALCULATING FOOD AND BEVERAGE COSTS

Food costs are the costs associated with producing all of the menu items. This cost includes the cost of the meat, dairy, fruits, vegetables, breads, and all other ingredients. If the items are served with disposable paper products, some establishments will include them into the cost of food as well. Other places do not. Either method is fine as long as it is done consistently.

If the organization provides employee meals or food for promotions, these actual costs must be deducted from the cost of food to arrive at the actual cost of sales.

Beverage costs are the costs of the alcoholic and nonalcoholic beverages and their associated food garnishes and disposable paper products. In some states, the alcoholic and nonalcoholic beverages are tracked separately, as they are taxed at a different rate from the food sales.

Food and beverage costs are also called the **cost of goods** which is calculated using the following formula:

$$
\begin{aligned}
&\text{Beginning food inventory} \\
&\underline{+ \text{ Food purchases}} \\
&= \text{Foods available for sale} \\
&\underline{- \text{ Ending food inventory}} \\
&= \text{Cost of food}
\end{aligned}
$$

To calculate the cost of beverages, simply substitute the beverage inventories and purchase figures.

Food cost percentage (FC%) is the ratio of the cost of food to sales. It is the percentage of sales needed to cover the food cost of the item. The lower the food cost percentage, the lower the cost of the food for that item. Higher food cost percentages may mean more expensive prices or a greater ratio of ready-to-use foods in the storerooms. The formula is:

$$\frac{\text{Total food cost}}{\text{Total sales}} = \text{FC\%}$$

For example, let's assume that a small cheese tray at the Deluxe Hotel costs $40 for the food on the tray. The tray sells on the banquet menu for $130. The food cost percentage is:

$$\$ 40 \,/\, \$130 = 0.307, \text{ or } 30.7\%$$

If the hotel reduces the cost of the food by $2, then the food cost percentage would change to:

$$\$38 \,/\, \$130 = 0.292, \text{ or } 29.2\%$$

Food cost percentage is lowered when the cost of the item decreases or the sales price increases. The percentage increases if the cost of the food increases or the sales price decreases. This is a great management tool to measure menu performance, but it does not include the volume of sales or the profit earned by the menu item.

Once a food cost percentage is determined, managers can use it to gain other information. For example, a target sales price can be calculated by dividing the food cost by the target food cost percentage. Using the same figures as before:

$$\$40 \,/\, 0.307 = \$130.29$$

Or a targeted food cost can be calculated by multiplying the sales price by the food cost percentage. Using the same figures:

$$\$130 \times 30\% = \$39 \text{ or approximately } \$40$$

If you use the food cost percentage to determine menu prices, then you need to pay attention to seasonal fluctuations in the prices of the item.

Using Sales Analysis for Determining Food Cost Percentage

Normally, the purchasing agent does not set menu prices, but it is his responsibility to inform management of fluctuating prices in commodities so that menu pricing can be adjusted. The price of berries in the wintertime can be double the summer season price. Shrimp, salmon, and even beef fluctuate with availability and demand. Evaluating sales by menu item is essential to determine not only what to charge, but also what should—and should not—be on the menu.

One way to make a sales analysis is to tabulate the number of portions served for each item over a period of time. The period of time should be no less than 1 week, but it does not need to exceed a month. To illustrate, let us use a 1-week period and a menu of 50 items.

Step 1. Tabulate the number of sales of each item for 1 week.

Step 2. Multiply the total of each item by its selling price (1,700 soft drinks at $1.50 each = $2,550).

Step 3. Add the totals for each of the 50 menu items from Step 2 together. This grand total should equal the total sales dollars for the week.

Step 4. Divide each of the totals in Step 2 by the grand total from Step 3. The quotient of this division is the percentage of the total sales dollar represented by each item—in other words, their contribution percent to sales. (Example: If soft drink sales are $2,550 and grand total sales are $25,500, then soft drinks represent 10 percent of total sales.)

Step 5. Multiply the number of each item sold (from Step 1) by the item's food cost (1,700 soft drinks at $0.21 food cost = $357.00 total food cost).

Step 6. Add the totals of the food costs from Step 5 together. This figure will be less than your total food cost (from inventory) for the week because of food items used that are not part of the menu item food cost (cups, lids, straws, etc.). Divide this total rough food cost by the actual total food cost (from inventory).

Example: Rough food cost at $728.75 is divided by actual food cost at $765.00 = 95.3 percent

The difference of 4.7 percent (100.0 percent − 95.3 percent) should be added to the food cost of each menu item. This is done by multiplying each Step 5 figure by 1.047. This grand total should equal the actual food cost (soft drinks: $0.021 × 1.047 = $0.022).

Step 7. Divide the food cost of each item by its selling price. The result of this division is the food cost percentage of that item (soft drinks: $0.22/$1.50 = 0.1466 or 14.7 percent).

Step 8. Divide the total food cost from Step 6 by the grand total sales from Step 3. The result of this division is the average food cost percentage for all items.
Example: $765 (total food cost)/$2,550 = 0.30 or 30 percent.

Many food inventory software programs and POS systems can create this form for you.

Reducing Costs

There are several ways to reduce the cost of goods sold or other costs associated with conducting business. Based on the menu, there are five control tools an operator can use in determining standard food and beverage costs:

1. Standard purchase specifications
2. Standard recipes
3. Standard yields
4. Standard portion size
5. Standard portion costs

A few methods to help lower food costs and related expenses include:

- **Raise menu prices.** Raising prices "appears" to be the easiest way to make more profit, but in reality there is an art to pricing competitively. The public has demonstrated time and again, in many retail areas, that there is a limit to what it is willing to pay for a product. An owner needs to make sure that the menu prices match the ambiance and clientele of the establishment.

- **Provide proper training.** The staff is most often the key to quality and cost controls. They must be cognizant of control procedures and follow them as directed.

- **Reduce product quality.** This is a slippery slope that should be approached with caution. People often forget the price and only remember the quality. Some items such as straws can probably be substituted for lesser brands without incident, but substituting grades of meat will be noticed by the customers.

- **Price the high cost percentage items accordingly.** Look for the places where the most money can be saved with your menu items. If an item has a high food cost, it should be priced higher than other menu items. If it does not sell at the higher price, it should be removed from the menu.

- **Recost standardized recipes.** If it has been some time since the recipes have been checked for their cost, it might be time to recheck these figures. With the newer inventory software programs, the recipes can be recosted on a daily basis.

- **Update inventory values.** Be sure to keep the inventory values up to date. Again, an inventory management program will help with this.

- **Control portion sizes.** Sometimes portions are larger than they need to be. Watch the dish room and see how much comes back on the plates, and talk to the wait staff to see which items are most often taken home in "doggy bags." All standardized recipes should have a standard serving size, and the manager should check that the right utensils are being used for service.

- **Minimize waste in the kitchen.** Track waste. Don't let anyone throw anything away without it being recorded.

- **Spot-check prep staff.** Make sure the precut portions weigh what they are supposed to weigh.

- **Link the chef's pay to a pre-set food cost percentage.** Set up an incentive deal for the chef. To do this, chefs need full access and control of related costs. Just make sure that the bonus program does not sacrifice quality for results and has allowances for extraordinary situations such as the dramatic increase in the price of a key item.

- **Set up purchase order systems.** Purchase order systems dissuade random and impulsive purchasing habits by careless buyers.

- **Check the use of convenience foods by employees.** Some convenience foods, such as canned tomatoes and bottled apple juice, are used in virtually every commercial food service operation. They have become cost effective and are available year-round. Also, some convenience foods like soup and sauce bases have proved important to kitchens that cannot make their own stocks from scratch. However, it is important to consider the cost-benefit of all convenience foods.

- **Organize the storage room, and keep inventory to a minimum.** Oftentimes reducing the amount of inventory on hand can prevent waste. When there is less in the cupboard, it is easy to see what is there.

- **Purchase based on a budget.** Adhering to a tight budget requires a certain discipline on the part of the buyer. It's helpful in controlling cash flow, and it often inspires creativity and cost-consciousness in the staff.

 Always be mindful of quality. If quality is sacrificed because of a limited budget, this should be discussed with management.

- **Use trade-outs.** Labor-intensive businesses like advertising agencies and radio stations will often consider the use of trade-outs for their services: the *value* of meals could be exchanged for the *value* of advertisements.

 As discussed in Chapter 1, it is advisable to investigate the legalities of using trade-outs, due to tax implications.

- **Look for discounts.** One very common way to save money is through the use of **discounts**. The following are the most common forms of discounts:

  - **Opportunity buys.** Sometimes vendors have products they need to unload quickly, at significant discounts, normally because they ordered too much. If it is a product that the establishment can use, then it might be a good opportunity to purchase it at a reduced price.

  - **Brand incentives.** Some manufacturers privately label their own line of products (such as SYSCO Supreme, Imperial, and Classic) and can sell their own brands at greater discounted prices than national brand products. Just make sure that the private label is comparable to the national brand. If the private label is substituted for the national brand on a regular basis, then the chef should have a talk with the manufacturer's sales representative.

  - **Volume discounts.** Volume buying is based on the total dollars spent with a company for a variety of products, versus the quantity of any one particular item. Establishments that buy the bulk of their food items from one vendor are normally eligible for this reduced pricing.

  - **Quantity discounts.** Different from volume buying, this discount is given for buying a large amount of one particular item. If an establishment has one or two key ingredients, such as a 6-ounce portioned frozen chicken breast, then it should ask its vendors for a quantity discount on this item.

  - **Cash discounts.** Cash is always preferred, as opposed to allowing customers to defer payment. Discounts of up to 2 percent may be given to cash-paying customers. Each vendor will have its own policies on cash discounts; however, if a restaurant has outstanding bills or pays bills on credit late, then it will not receive a cash discount.

- **Promotional discounts.** Companies will sometimes provide advertising dollars or promotional products to offer incentives to the buyers. The company will give the establishment a rebate or a discount on the products that it uses, or give the establishment money for mentioning the brand on the menu.

- **Introductory discounts.** When sellers want customers to try their new products, they will often provide products for free or at discounted rates for a trial period.

- **Damaged goods discounts.** Occasionally goods, such as equipment, are damaged in shipping or during their production. Buyers might be able to get discounts on items that are still functionally solid but cosmetically damaged. Do not accept damaged goods discounts on food items, especially canned goods.

- **Trade-show discounts.** As a general rule, vendors will offer trade-show discounts to their buyers if they purchase certain items within a limited time period. Also, sometimes buyers will offer discounts on display or showroom equipment.

Standardized Recipe and Portion Costs

It is virtually impossible to realize a consistent profit from menu items that are not prepared with standardized recipes. As first discussed in Chapter 6, a standardized recipe is a customized recipe developed by the food service establishment describing exactly how the dish is to be prepared, including specifications of the ingredients, necessary tools and equipment, the time and personnel involved, and ideally a picture of the item, as desired for service.

A standardized recipe includes:

- The name of the recipe
- Recipe ID number
- The yield, including weight or volume
- Portion size
- Specific ingredient information, including form, size, quality, packaging, and quantity
- Preparation methods, including methods of cookery, time, temperature, and holding procedures
- Equipment needs, including tabletop and production
- Plate presentation information, accompanied by a digital photograph of the "plate-up"
- Ingredient and recipe cost information
- Ingredient and recipe nutrition information

The following twelve steps are useful in developing a standardized recipe:

1. Talk through the process with those involved in daily food preparation. Find a recipe that would likely be appropriate for the business.

2. Check if the business has the necessary tools and equipment. Will it be feasible to prepare, or do new purchases have to be made?

3. Cost it out:
   - Is it feasible for the market?
   - Is it worthwhile to produce (profitable, unique, appealing)?
   - Or is it a loss leader?

4. Try it out in its original format.
   - Does it taste good? Does it match the target market?
   - Evaluate: appearance, tenderness, texture, flavor, and overall quality

5. Convert the recipe to a standard size, specifying portion size, yield, and the number of portions.

6. Have someone else make the converted recipe.
   - Evaluate again: Does it still have the desired quality characteristics? Some recipes do not work well in large quantity.

7. Make any desired or necessary changes.

8. Make the batch/converted recipe several times:
   - Is it consistent?
   - Are the flavors and other characteristics the same?
   - Is it functional to produce in this size?

9. Put into the standardized recipe format of the business.

10. Have the preparation employees prepare (re-create) it according to the standard format.
    - Evaluate, adjust, change, or clarify directions.

11. Train the preparation staff to follow the directions exactly as written.

12. File for future application, or begin using.

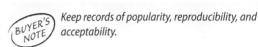 *Keep records of popularity, reproducibility, and acceptability.*

All recipe costs must be calculated prior to menu pricing. The establishment should use a standardized recipe cost form, preferably on a computerized spreadsheet, for every menu item it offers (see Figure 9.10a and Figure 9.10b). The most efficient method is to create a computerized file of all standardized recipes used by the company and to periodically update their costs with current pricing. Some computer software on the market now interfaces the storeroom database with the recipe database, which automatically updates all recipe costs as ingredient costs change.

When a business uses standardized recipes with product specifications that yield consistent quantities, the business maintains portion costs. These recipes must have portioning systems that yield consistent numbers of portions. If little fluctuation occurs in the cost of the raw goods, then the portion costs should remain consistent.

9.10a **Sample Manually Written Recipe Cost Sheet**

Recipe Cost Sheet			
Recipe Number _____ Recipe for _____ Total Yield _____ Usage _____		Page _____ of _____ Date Priced _____ Number of Servings _____ Portion Size _____	
AMOUNT/UNIT	**INGREDIENTS**	**UNIT PRICE**	**EXTENSION**
		TOTAL COST	$
		PORTION COST	$

9.10b Sample Computerized Recipe Cost Sheet

RECIPE COST INFORMATION							
Recipe Name:			Recipe Desc: Beef Stroganoff		Author:		Yield: 50
Serving Size: 4 oz ladle			Prep Time:		Cook Time:		
Vendor Code	**Item Code**	**Analysis Code**	**Description**	**Amount**	**Unit Cost**	**Cost**	**Cost per Portion**
GFS	443689	CHM08	Beef Dcd Stew-ready 85% lean 4-5# Ke	8.50 lb	$2.66	$22.61	$0.452
GFS	113271	HLS58	Margarine Sld 30-1# GFS	6 oz	$0.03	$0.16	$0.003
GFS	547336	11282A	Onion Spanish Jumbo 5-10# P/I	1 lb	$0.44	$0.44	$0.009
GFS	170895	11143	Celery Stalk 24 Sz 6ct Markon	1 lb	$0.74	$0.74	$0.015
GFS	225037	TS053	Spice Pepr Blk Reg Grind 16z Trde	2 tsp	$0.04	$0.08	$0.002
GFS	130885	BFF51	Base Bf Lo Sod 12-1# Lego	2.33 tsp	$0.25	$0.58	$0.012
GFS	111111	97010	Water	7 cup	$0.00	$0.00	$0.000
GFS	227528	BSM04	Flour H&r A/p 2-25# GFS	6 oz	$0.02	$0.10	$0.002
GFS	111111	97010	Water	1.50 cup	$0.00	$0.00	$0.000
GFS	109843	FN002	Sauce Worcestershire 4-1gal Frenc	0.25 cup	$0.00	$0.00	$0.000
GFS	119024	GIO05	Mushroom Stems & Pcs Dom 6-10 GFS	1 qt	$3.16	$3.16	$0.063
GFS	113721	HLS58	Margarine Sld 30-1# GFS	2.50 oz	$0.03	$0.07	$0.001
GFS	534331	BMD09	Sour Cream Lite 4-5# Cntryfr	2.75 cup	$0.50	$1.38	$0.028

	Food Cost	**Selling Price**	**Markup**	**Cost**
Portion	30%	$1.95	$1.37	$0.59
Total		$97.70	$68.39	$29.31

Plate Costs

Plate costs go beyond the "center of the plate" menu item; they include the costs of all of the items appearing on the same plate. For example, let's assume a restaurant includes vegetables and starches with all entrées. These items are not sold á la carte or individually. As these items are included on the plate, the cost of these items must be considered in the overall pricing of each entrée.

Garnishes, au jus for prime rib, melted butter for lobster, chutney for pork roast, and mint for lamb are often made available to the guest for no "extra charge." Yet their costs must be accounted for in the plate cost (see Figure 9.11). Quick-service establishments, among others, factor into their plate costs the enormous quantities of paper disposables and condiments their customers use. If the menu item must be served on disposable paper products, that cost must be added to the plate costs.

For items whose cost is hard to calculate, such as parsley sprigs, it may be easier to add a percentage of the menu price to the costs. Some companies call this the "Q-factor," or spice cost.

CALCULATING LABOR COSTS

Labor costs are all of the monies paid to employees to run the business. They include the direct wages, taxes, and benefits accrued to the employee. Normally, salaried employees' payroll expenses are separated from the hourly, as the former is a fixed cost, and the latter is a variable cost.

Labor costs tend to be the biggest challenge to food service operators trying to stay within budget. Labor costs are often more difficult to identify initially for individual menu items without conducting time studies. However, after a few days of preparing these items, most chefs can streamline their work and organize their production schedules for optimum efficiency. Labor costs are generally calculated by identifying the wages (and sometimes related benefits) of employees for a specific period of time. Upper management generally dictates the desired labor cost percentage and then assigns the staffing responsibility to the executive chef. Changes in minimum wage laws, the availability of skilled labor, and variances in the productivity of individual employees all can have a tremendous impact on labor costs.

9.11 Sample Plate Cost Sheet

Recipe Plate Cost Sheet

Menu Item: _____ Date Cost Calculated: _____

Amount/Unit	Plate Elements	Unit Price		Extension	
	Protein				
	Vegetable				
	Starch				
	Sauce				
	Other				

Total Cost $

The **labor cost percentage** (LC%) is the relationship between labor costs and sales. It is the percentage of sales needed to prepare the menu items and sell them to the customers. The labor cost percentage is calculated by dividing the cost of labor by sales.

$$\frac{\text{Total labor cost}}{\text{Total sales}} = \text{LC\%}$$

Using the cheese tray example from earlier in this chapter, suppose it costs the hotel $24 in labor costs to prepare it. The tray sells to the customer for $130. The labor cost percentage is:

$$\frac{\$24}{\$130} = 0.184, \text{ or } 18.4\%$$

If the hotel reduces its labor cost by $4, then the percentage would drop to:

$$\frac{\$20}{\$130} = 0.153, \text{ or } 15.3\%$$

In most hotel, banquet, and catering situations, and often in some restaurants, management is able to forecast sales for a given period, based on historical data and contracted events. In an effort to control labor costs, they will provide specific labor budgets to their food and beverage managers, managing chefs, and department heads and instruct them not to exceed the prescribed limits. The desired labor cost will be met if the forecasted sales are met.

The skill is in balancing fixed labor costs with variable labor costs, while meeting the production needs of the operation and payroll needs of the staff. The following scenario reflects how the fluctuation of sales affects available money for hourly labor.

In most cases, chefs are able to average their labor costs over a month's time. Note in the scenario depicted in Table 9.2 that the total monthly sales equal $224,000 with $44,800 available for the monthly labor budget. As long as the chef spends, on average, no more than $11,200 per week in labor, he will meet the desired labor cost budget. One note on this method: If there is a big day, such as Mother's Day, or a series of events, then the labor might be higher than normal. If this is noted in the labor sheets, then the establishment has a record of the reason for the overage. However, the chef's ability to manage the staff's productivity is paramount in achieving labor cost goals.

Calculating Payroll

Hourly employees are paid their standard wages until they exceed 40 hours in a workweek. Additionally, they receive a variety of benefits that cost their employer a percentage of the their income. Most employers will add up the total labor costs for the hourly employees and then divide the dollar amount by the number of hours worked. If employees receive bonuses based on work performance, then that dollar amount is added in as well. Figure 9.12 show an example of payroll calculations.

The employer, on behalf of the government, must withhold taxes from the employees' earned income. The following deductions are often withheld from employees:

- **Income tax:** Federal and state income taxes are deducted from each paycheck based on the number of exemptions that the employee claimed on his W-4 form.

- **Social Security (FICA):** All employers must deduct a percentage of income from each paycheck to go to Social Security. This percentage is based on the check amount, and the company is required to match the contribution of each employee. Employees' Social Security numbers are used to identify employees when this money is sent to tax officials.

TABLE 9.2   Available Monthly Labor Cost Budget

Calculating Labor Cost Projections					
Scenario: Management has told you to maintain a monthly labor cost of 20 percent of sales. They project the following sales; how do you schedule your hourly staff?					
	Week 1	**Week 2**	**Week 3**	**Week 4**	**Month to Date**
Rest. Sales	25,000	25,000	29,000	28,000	107,000
Banquet Sales	30,000	21,000	34,000	32,000	117,000
Total Sales	55,000	46,000	63,000	60,000	224,000
Desired Labor Cost	X 0.20	X 0.20	X 0.20	X 0.20	X 0.20
Weekly Ave. Labor Cost	11,000	9,200	12,600	12,000	44,800

Weekly Fixed Labor Costs:	
Executive Chef	$1,300
Sous Chef	1,100
Banquet Chef	800
Total Fixed Labor Costs	$3,200

9.12 Sample Payroll Calculation

Payroll Budget Estimated Worksheet

Week of January 13, 20XX   **Department** Kitchen

Date prepared 1/6/20XX   **Prepared by** Kitchen Manager

Name	Position	Rate of Pay	Scheduled Hrs	Scheduled Overtime	Total Earned
Joe Smith	Cook	$9.50	37.5		$356.25
Jane Jones	Cook	$8.50	40	4	$391.00
Eric Brown	Cook	$8.50	22.5		$191.25
Sam White	Sal Pantry	$6.50	14.5		$94.25
Emily Green	Sal Pantry	$6.15	40	6	$301.30
Don Black	Dishwasher	$6.15	27		$166.05
Leslie Little	Diashwasher	$6.15	15		$92.25
Total			203.5	10	$1,592.40

Allowance for Social Security, Medicare, Federal and State Unemployment Taxes: Total Hourly Wages $1,592.40 x Rate 1.12 =	$1,783.04

EMPLOYEE MEALS
Note: could be added to or subtracted from the payroll according to management's policy.

		Estimated Number of Meals	Cost	
	Total	24	$3.00	$72.00

TOTAL (Wages & Meals)					$1,855.04
Estimated Sales for Week					$10,000.00
Estimated Payroll (Labor) Cost Percentage for Week					18.55%
Payroll (Labor) Cost Percentage Goal					18.00%

BUYER'S NOTE *It is easier to stay within prescribed labor cost budgets during busy periods of business, compared with slower periods. As management salaries are fixed, their cost remains constant no matter the need for staffing. More sales bring in more dollars to compensate for hourly labor costs.*

- **Voluntary deductions:** These are deductions authorized by the employees and include transfers to savings programs, charitable donations, child support, health insurance, life insurance, and other benefits offered by the company.

Some establishments process their own payroll with the help of computer software programs while others hire companies to provide payroll and bookkeeping services.

Break-Even Analysis

Break-even analysis, also known as **cost-volume-profit (CVP) analysis**, is used to evaluate how much sales is needed to cover the expenses of an establishment.

The break-even analysis is a management tool that can aid food service managers in examining the relationship among various revenues, costs, and the sales volume. A break-even analysis will allow the manager to determine the sales revenue necessary at any desired profit level. This analysis is often employed when considering a capital investment, such as an expansion of the business (construction costs), or when acquiring expensive equipment or delivery vehicles. The food service operator can safely estimate the sales necessary to cover the costs of construction or acquisition, also known as **desired profit.**

CALCULATING THE BREAK-EVEN POINT

The **break-even point** is the volume of sales (S) needed to cover total costs (TC) (see Figure 9.13). When sales are at the break-even (BE) point, all expenses are paid, but the profit is zero dollars. There is no loss, but there is also no profit. As Dittmer and Keefe (2006) wrote:

> When sales reach a level sufficient to cover all variable costs (VC) and all fixed costs (FC), with an additional amount left over, that amount is obviously profit. Moreover, because contribution margin must go to cover fixed costs until break-even is reached, after break-even is reached, the contribution margin becomes profit. The importance of the contribution margin in food and beverage management cannot be overemphasized. (p. 90)

From a formula standpoint, the equation would read as follows:

$$\text{Break-even} = \text{Fixed cost dollars} / \text{gross margin percentage}$$

As discussed earlier, fixed costs are known. Most establishments know their mortgage payments, salaries, and loan payments in advance. The gross margin percentage is calculated from the income statement by dividing the gross margin by sales.

Although somewhat theoretical, break-even analysis is a useful management tool. It not only can be used to determine the point at which sales equal costs, but, as Pavesic and Magnant (2005) suggest, it can also provide insight into the following:

- The amount of sales needed to realize a predetermined profit
- The impact on break-even if fixed or variable costs are increased
- The impact on break-even if fixed or variable costs are decreased
- The point where it would be better for the operator to close the door for a slow meal period or day, because costs are not covered enough to remain open
- The number of customers that need to be served at a specific check average to achieve a particular sales level
- The sales level required to pay for any planned purchases or remodeling
- The number of additional customers that need to be served at discounted prices to achieve break-even
- The impact on break-even if menu prices are adjusted
- The break-even for any specific meal period, time of day, day of week, week, month, or year (p. 51).

Purchasing managers can use the break-even point to aid them in their purchasing decisions. If the purchases are too high for the period, then the purchasing manager has to slow down his purchases. If it is going to be a busy period, then the manager can increase his purchases.

9.13 Break-even graph

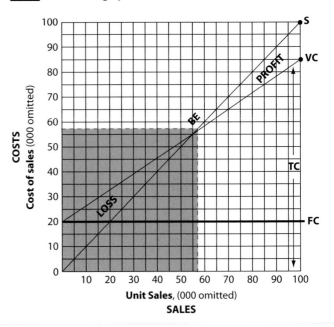

William C. Garlough

Place of Birth: Watertown, New York

Educational Background and Work Experience

After Bill Garlough graduated from Boston University in the mid-1970s, he was asked at every job interview why he majored in philosophy. "After all," they'd say, "what good is a bachelor's degree in philosophy?" His response: "Others were taught to memorize and regurgitate facts; I was taught to ask why, and then choose the path that is right for me." He's been blazing a path ever since! After getting his feet wet in sales and marketing with a few smaller companies, Garlough eventually moved up to Fortune 100 companies. His first commercial experience with food was as a product manager for Borden Inc.'s Food Division. He left Borden to take the national director of sales and marketing position with Jacobs Suchard's Imported Products Division. After exceeding sales and profit goals year after year, Garlough and his wife, Karen, found they wanted to leave their corporate jobs to start their own business. Even though their work allowed them to travel the world and enjoy its diversity of food and culture, they were ready for new challenges. In 1988, with a little help from family, they opened My Chef, Inc., in Naperville, Illinois. As discussed earlier in this chapter, the concept was initially for *home meal replacement* as part of a retail deli-bakery specialty food store. Garlough wore many hats, including that of chief financial officer (CFO) for the company, and to this day he still oversees the purchasing responsibilities. After a few years of sluggish growth and with a constant eye on the P&L statement, Bill and Karen Garlough made the daring leap to off-premise catering. Now, based in a 14,000-square-foot facility with a staff of 58 employees, My Chef Catering has proved to be a storied success in suburban Chicago, garnering them both personal satisfaction and national praise. Although he actively served as the president for the local Rotary Club and continues to serve as president of My Chef Catering, Garlough has found time for another personal cause: as a Level One Certified Sommelier, by the Court of the Master Sommeliers, Garlough now writes newspaper columns in which to share his love of food and wine.

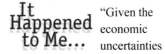

It Happened to Me...

Courtesy William Garlough

"Given the economic uncertainties of the mid 1980s, I left corporate America to live the life of a small business owner. I traded national programs and exposure for a more localized lifestyle. I believed I would have more control of my destiny.

What I did not properly appreciate was that my new business needed tight cost controls to achieve this dream. During the initial start-up phase, I wore many hats. I delegated the business's food and packaging purchasing responsibilities to the new Executive Chef, without sufficient purchasing guidelines. It was more convenient for this new employee to purchase almost everything from one distributor. He also utilized a local produce supplier who was more than happy to bring out one to two cases of fresh produce for a price. Unfortunately, this led to high food costs and a poor financial picture. Given that we kept a close eye on our P&L, we quickly corrected these procedures.

Over the years, I have employed some chefs that were cost conscious and others that were apathetic to this important area. My advice to an aspiring chef is to pay close attention to purchasing guidelines, as it is a major indicator as to whether you are company minded and a team player, or more short-sighted. Cost controls are a key ingredient to a food service business's success. Successful businesses provide their customers with a quality experience that meets or exceeds their expectations. To afford and accomplish this, an eye for cost controls is mandatory."

Memberships and Career Highlights

A few of the company's recent accolades include the Business Ledger's 2005 Award for Business Excellence, Jaycees 2005 Distinguished Service Award (Business Category), Greater Aurora Chamber of Commerce 2006 Small Business of the Year, the Naperville Area Chamber of Commerce 2006 Overall Small Business of the Year, and the winner of the U.S. Chamber of Commerce Blue Ribbon Award for 2006—one of only sixty companies in the United States to be recognized. The following year, in 2007, My Chef Catering was named the national winner of the U.S. Chamber of Commerce's Small Business of the Year award. Garlough is an active member of the Naperville Chamber of Commerce, and, with his ability to grow a company from scratch, My Chef Catering now has the resources to donate to more than 100 charitable causes, a responsibility Bill and Karen Garlough take to heart. Recognized for his many community efforts and organizational prowess, Garlough was named the Rotary Club of Naperville's Rotarian of the Year for 2004–2005.

Passions with the Food Service Industry

"There are two main reasons why the food industry is important to me. First, food is a necessity of life. I am proud to be associated with the food industry that demonstrates compassion for others through numerous charity benefits and product donations. Second, food and wine pairings are one of life's true pleasures. The world is full of a wide array of culinary tastes and styles waiting to be discovered."

(continued)

Advice to a Chef or Buyer

"In order for a business to be successful, it must offer quality products relative to its price points that return an acceptable gross profit margin. To accomplish this, the business must have in place and adhere to strict cost controls. We receive weekly bids from two or more large food service distributors to ensure our core items are competitively priced. We also purchase some high-end items from specialty distributors, such as imported meats and cheeses, but we are constantly mindful that our prices more than cover our costs. In our business, we strongly believe that we must always maintain a high level of quality, which means we don't always make the same profit margin on each event. But, unless it's for a charitable cause, we always make a fair profit."

Key Words and Concepts

accounting period	conversion costs	food cost	prime costs
accounts payable	cost of goods	food cost percentages	production reports
accounts receivable	cost-volume-profit (CVP) analysis	income statement	profit and loss statement (P&L)
assets	current assets	issued	quality standards
balance sheet	desired profit	joint cost	revenues
bank lines of credit	direct costs	labor cost	Siamese twins of management
beverage cost	discounts	labor cost percentage	statement of cash flows
break-even analysis	expenses	liabilities	Uniform System of Accounts for Restaurants
break-even point	financial statements	menu analysis	
cash flow	fixed assets	menu engineering	
common costs	fixed costs	operating budget	variable costs
control process		plate costs	

Chapter in Review

The following exercises are provided to help the reader understand and apply the contents of this chapter. They may be completed individually or in a classroom environment.

REVIEW QUESTIONS

a. Identify the four primary financial statements used by businesses to manage and control their finances, and distinguish their use from one another.

b. Identify the different deductions that may be on a paycheck, and distinguish between those that are company paid and employee paid.

c. Explain the twelve steps used in making a standardized recipe.

d. Identify and describe the five tools used to develop standardized food and beverage costs.

INDIVIDUAL ACTIVITIES

a. **Web based:** Research different Internet sources to find examples of financial statements that would be useful to model when establishing your own business's statements.

b. **Experiential:** Go to the accounting office of a retail business and ask to see how it organizes its accounts receivable and accounts payable.

c. **Critical thinking:** Identify the many ways an operator can change the food costs of menu items.

GROUP ACTIVITIES

a. **Lab experience:** Using a variety of common ingredients and prepared foods, determine the plate costs for a sample dinner plate. Try to reduce the plate's costs without diluting its appearance or quality/value perception by substituting different ingredients.

b. **Classroom action:** Create several scenarios of fictitious food service operations, identifying their monthly fixed costs, variable cost percents, and desired profit. Have students practice calculating to find break-even.

© iStockphoto.com

Security Issues with Vendors, Employees, and Customers

"Every life is a march from innocence, through temptation, to virtue or vice." LYMAN ABBOTT

After reading this chapter, you will be able to:

- ◎ Describe the different forms of supplier error and dishonesty, including various sales scams, product substitutions and shortages, and inventory theft by delivery personnel.

- ◎ Illustrate the different forms of employee dishonesty, including product substitutions, fraudulent invoices, kickbacks, and theft.

- ◎ Identify security problems in purchasing, receiving, storing and issuing.

- ◎ Explain behaviors that could indicate employee dishonesty.

- ◎ List methods for protecting your customers from being harmed by other guests.

Introduction

Food service operators can be deceived by their own employees, their suppliers, or both. Too often, workers do look for opportunities to steal money, expensive food, alcohol, or equipment. They can pad their timecards with hours of phantom labor or even work in collusion with unscrupulous vendors for mutual benefit. Sellers can seek to gain advantage over the buyer's business by sending less than billed (short) weights, sending inferior products, or overcharging for the delivered products.

Food service operators must be vigilant to the many ways their businesses can lose money or prestige at the hands of their own employees or sellers. Although not all losses are intentional, this chapter focuses on the various methods by which people can challenge the security of a food service entity. The operator must implement a comprehensive series of procedures to prevent such misappropriations from occurring. As Feinstein and Stefanelli (2005) write:

> The heightened interest in security that is found in the food service industry can be attributed to at least four factors: (1) hospitality operators find it increasingly difficult to pass on security losses to the consumer in the form of higher menu and room prices; (2) in general, the public has become more security conscious; (3) the cost of insurance coverage has skyrocketed; and (4) a good deal of unfavorable publicity has focused on the hospitality purchasing function. (p. 352)

Supplier Error and Dishonesty

Although most purveyors operate their businesses in a principled manner, some sellers might try to obtain profits through dishonest measures. There is a distinct difference between vendor error and vendor deception. **Vendor error** is unwittingly sending products or invoices that have problems with their pricing, quantity, or quality. **Vendor dishonesty** is purposely misleading the buyer by delivering inferior products, shorting the deliveries by weight or count, or billing for products neither sold nor ordered.

SALES SCAMS

In modern times, companies are more susceptible to sales scams. Whether by telephone, fax, e-mail, PDA, Blackberry, or mail, buyers are inundated with bogus sales offers. Normally, the sales representatives will contact people outside of the buyer's office, as buyers are generally more informed about

such scams. Items sold include generic-branded products, "knock-offs" of expensive brand-name products, poor-quality office supplies, and equipment with high service charges. These items are sold at a higher price for lower quality goods.

Backdoor Selling

When a vendor has difficulty getting its products into an operation, often because the buyer shows little interest in the items, the vendor will sometimes approach a chef or cook. Bypassing the buyer, and going directly to an individual who will use the product is known as **backdoor selling** (see Figure 10.1). Although this is not illegal, "most operations seek to avoid backdoor selling because it can negatively affect an operation's bargaining position and the price the operation pays for products" (NRAEF, 2007, p. 23). All food service establishments should have a written policy concerning which employees may speak to sales representatives. Also, even if chefs are asked not to deal directly with purveyors, the purchasing agent should still consult with the chef about purchasing decisions. Chefs might have a preference in purveyors that should be taken into consideration.

PRODUCT SUBSTITUTIONS AND SHORTAGES

It is not unusual for sellers to mistakenly substitute one product for another or to accidentally forget to include products in the deliveries. In both cases, the mistakes are made at the warehouse while the products are being assembled or the delivery trucks are being loaded. The sellers do so without intent of deception and with no desire to defraud their customers.

 **Salesperson giving product to chef**
© Randy Van Dam 2008

A second situation, this time intentionally deceitful, is for the seller to knowingly substitute items of lesser quality or to short deliveries with the intention of making an unearned profit. The receiving clerks should take note of short deliveries that occur on a regular basis.

INVENTORY THEFT BY DELIVERY PERSONNEL

Outside agents can deplete the inventory as much as those who work inside the business. **Inventory shrinkage** can sometimes, though rarely, be attributed to unscrupulous sales or delivery staff stealing from their customers, generally without the knowledge or approval of their employers.

For example, once the careless or trusting receiving personnel inspect the delivered goods, the dishonest drivers will casually remove items from the delivery. Or items such as clean linen that has already been formally received and stored can often be removed with the soiled linen, as shown in Figure 10.2. The driver will then sell the items to other operations and pocket the profits. A third, and somewhat common, method is when the delivery driver removes items such as citrus fruits from a case and then attempts to sell them for cash someplace else.

BUYER'S NOTE *Outright dishonesty by suppliers or drivers is not common, but it has happened to more than one food service operation. Good control systems help to keep honest people honest.*

People, Places, Things

Less Than He Bargained For

Years ago, I interviewed for the position of executive chef of a large fine-dining restaurant and nightclub in northern Florida. This operation sat approximately 340 between the two main dining rooms, 300 in two additional banquet rooms, and about 120 more in the multi-tiered lounge. It was open for lunch and dinner 6 days a week. At the time, I was happily working as a chef-instructor in a culinary school in St. Augustine. But after our first son was born, I needed to make more money to pay for the new house we had just purchased. Chef

positions paid better than teaching positions, if you could get into the right place.

I was also the apprenticeship coordinator for the local chapter of the American Culinary Federation, and one of my apprentices who was working as the banquet chef at that restaurant told me he thought the chef was going to be fired because of his high food cost. After the banquet chef spoke to the owner on my behalf, I received a call and was asked to come for dinner. During the dinner with the owner, I agreed to come back the next night and sit at the bar to watch the operation, incognito of course. I also asked to be allowed into the kitchen after the executive chef was gone to carefully look over the situation. Advice: *Never* take a position without first looking at the working conditions!

During our discussions, I asked for $6,000 more in salary than the owner wanted to pay me. He told me that he could not afford the extra money to pay my asking salary. However, I showed him how he could: During my walk through the kitchen, storeroom, and its several walk-in coolers and freezers, I noticed something peculiar about the prime rib. It still had the back strap, feather bones, and extra exterior fat. The owner thought he was getting 109A beef rib, roast-ready, special prime rib, but in fact he was getting 107 beef ribs. The restaurant was paying $3.25 a pound for about 2 1/2 pounds of unwanted bone, gristle, and fat per rib roast. That equals $8.13 per rib, and at 50 ribs per week, the restaurant was paying $21,000 a year more than it should have. The chef was fired (he was going anyway), and I got the job, including my extra $6,000 in salary.

Moral of the story: Read the specs on the food you buy, and make sure you get what you are paying for.

10.2 **Delivery driver hiding clean, wrapped lines under the dirty linen**

© Randy Van Dam 2008

Employee Error and Dishonesty

Handling food and alcohol, whether as a buyer, receiving agent, or stockroom manager, requires a high standard of ethics. Although dishonest suppliers have several means of deceiving unsuspecting customers, dishonest employees have even more opportunities to abuse their employer's trust because they have better access to the products.

SECURITY PROBLEMS IN PURCHASING

Security problems can originate during the purchasing function. Operators must institute procedures that prevent opportunities for theft and pilferage. The following examples are methods by which operators can protect their businesses:

- The functions of buyer and bookkeeper (accounts payables) should never be performed by the same individual. If they were, this person could create fake invoices and then "pay" them, pocketing the money. No person other than the general manager or owner should have control of more than one of these functions: ordering, receiving, billing, or payment authorization.

- Owners or chefs must approve, in writing, all emergency purchases. If there are many emergency purchases in a short period of time, then the ordering quantities should be reviewed.

- Owners or upper management should document all cash paid out and require receipts for all purchases. Owners should insist that all purchases be paid by check. If the buyer needs to purchase items at Sam's Club or another warehouse, then the owner can use the Internet to look up the order and then send the employee with the exact change for the purchase.

- All invoices must be marked "paid" upon their payment to suppliers and filed with a copy of the payment check.

- Owners and chefs should periodically review the names of all companies to whom payments are made and verify their existence. There should be a list of authorized purveyors with which the company does business on a regular basis.

- No payments should be allowed to go to post office boxes unless the authenticity is verified from several sources.

- Owners or upper management should employ an independent accounting firm to conduct periodic audits of storeroom purchases.

- Electronic locks and security web cams should be installed in all receiving and storage areas.

- The same individual should not perform both buyer and receiving clerk duties. Otherwise, this person could "order" items and then "receive" them, and then manipulate the payment process.

- Receiving clerks should be given sufficient time and authority to properly perform their duties.

- Employee parking should be a safe distance from the kitchen and storeroom entrances. No employees should be allowed to park near the trash Dumpsters. If there are safety issues with leaving the building after dark, then management should escort employees to their cars.

- A member of management should be present when all trash is removed from the building. If allowed by local trash regulations, the establishment should use clear plastic bags and a solid waste reducer.

- If the purveyor requires cash payments for deliveries, then the owner should pay the driver directly and request a receipt.

Fraudulent Invoices

There are two principal scams involving falsified or **fraudulent invoices** to customers. The first version is padding invoices. Costs for products that were never shipped, nor received, are added to month-end invoices and sent to unsuspecting buyers. Often they are slipped in undetected and paid by the buyer. This can be avoided by verifying all deliveries.

Another security issue involves a conspiracy between a seller and a company's bookkeeper. In this case, a seller occasionally sends a false invoice for products never shipped, nor received, and the bookkeeper pays the invoice. Similarly, a seller sends a duplicate invoice to a co-conspirator bookkeeper who pays both invoices. In both cases, they split the payments for their own benefit.

A different type of invoice scam involves paying invoices from fictitious companies. Someone, such as a buyer or bookkeeper from a hotel, country club, or multimillion-dollar catering business, establishes a dummy company and bank account that sends invoices for products or services never delivered. The bookkeeper mails payments to the dummy company's post office box (Figure 10.3).

Reciprocity

Owners or upper management can sometimes put the buyer into an ethical quandary when agreements of **reciprocity** are made with suppliers. Reciprocity is a symbiotic relationship between a supplier and a food service establishment (see Figure 10.4). The problem comes when purchases are made even when they're not advantageous to the company. As Coltman (1990) writes:

> A supplier may allow its sales representatives to eat in the purchasing company's restaurant and charge their meals to the supplier's business on condition that the purchasing company reciprocates by buying most or all of its needed products from that supplier. This practice limits the purchaser's ability to shop around because the reciprocating supplier is automatically given the business. (p. 26)

Management should establish a policy on reciprocity that does not violate laws or cause ethical dilemmas. If the food service establishment and the supplier are too entwined, then it might be difficult to change purveyors.

People, Places, Things

Telltale Signs of Possible Theft

There are a variety of telltale signs that point to possible theft by the staff. Management must be vigilant to all areas of control and realize that anyone can be tempted to steal, even long-term employees, friends, or relatives. The following questions should be considered when examining the possibility for theft.

(**Note:** Answers in the affirmative do not necessarily mean theft is occurring.)

- Is any employee overly friendly with one of your supplier's delivery or sales personnel?

- Is any employee overly friendly with a regular customer?

- Has any employee recently incurred extensive personal or family medical bills without a known means to satisfy them?

- Has any employee displayed spending habits or a lifestyle beyond her known ability to pay?

- Does any employee have a dependence on drugs or alcohol?

- Does any employee repeatedly ask for an advance on her paycheck?

- Is any employee overextended with debts?

- Are you at a loss as to why your restaurant is not making a profit?

- Is any employee requesting to be reassigned to work in cashiering, storeroom purchasing, storeroom receiving, or accounts receivable, which doesn't make sense given her background or career aspirations?

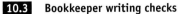

10.3 Bookkeeper writing checks

© Randy Van Dam 2008

10.4 A group of salespeople socializing at a bar

© Randy Van Dam 2008

SECURITY PROBLEMS IN RECEIVING

Errors do occasionally occur when delivering food to an establishment. Mistakes do happen, and receiving clerks must perform their duties consistently and faithfully, even with trusted purveyors.

Allowing receiving personnel to accept deliveries without proper examination can create security problems. Establishments must keep a written record of all orders as a reference for inspecting deliveries. The record, known as the purchase order, must be compared with the delivery invoice for accuracy of weight and count. Additionally, the specifications of goods received should be compared with those ordered.

Inventory Substitutions

Additionally, sellers can bribe or offer kickbacks to food service employees, such as receiving clerks, to accept lesser quality products than were ordered. Overpaying for inferior merchandise adds unnecessary costs for the company, but using lesser quality products also costs the company's reputation in the eyes of its customers. Managers should occasionally check that the products they ordered are what were received.

Kickbacks

Sellers may offer the buyer or receiving clerk, or others involved in the company's purchasing or receiving responsibilities, a **kickback**. A kickback is a payment in cash or other product meant to influence the purchasing decisions. Normally kickbacks are given to increase sales or number of cases delivered. One example of a kickback is when the buyer from a large business orders 400 pounds of frozen shrimp at $8 per pound (worth $3,200) but receives a lesser amount. The seller may deliver only 350 pounds (worth $2,800), although the receiving clerk intentionally confirms that 400 pounds were received. The seller gives the receiving clerk half the difference in value ($200) and keeps the other half.

Another example is when the buyer pays $10 per pound for that same 400 pounds of shrimp ($4,000), even though the buyer knows comparable quality shrimp is available for $8 per pound ($3,200). The seller pays the buyer half the difference ($400) and keeps the other half.

In addition to terminating employees who are found guilty of such practices, management should also **blackball** those guilty sellers from doing any future business with the firm.

SECURITY PROBLEMS IN STORING

Access to inventory must be limited. As Pavesic and Magnant (2005) write, "Control over inventory and storage areas can take place without full- or part-time storeroom personnel. Control is greatly enhanced when inventory (count) is taken on a regular basis and storage areas are kept clean and organized" (p. 305). The inventory should be arranged conveniently and logically for easy access and inventory, with the oldest products rotated forward on the shelves. Each item should have only one location, and the physical inventory records should mirror the arrangement of products in the storage areas. Items that are formally counted and methodically recorded tend to be measured more accurately.

When storeroom personnel rely solely on their own eyes and ears to control costs, they cannot account for other people entering the storeroom, with or without their knowledge. Storage areas must limited to those whose job requires access to supplies. Restricting admittance to inventory through one door also helps to monitor activity, as well as using magnetic security cards to enter, as shown in Figure 10.5. A proper locking system on access doors is paramount. There are several locking systems available, and some of them can be connected to digital cameras for added security.

Inventory Theft by Staff

When left unregulated or unguarded, stock may be stolen by any number of employees (see Figure 10.6). According to the National Restaurant Association, "It has been estimated that the food service industry loses 3 to 8 percent of its gross sales due to internal theft and close to twenty billion dollars a year owing to theft and cash mishandling" (p. 87).

Food service operators need to evaluate their procedures to ensure no opportunities exist for theft of inventory. The following list reflects important questions and procedures to consider:

- Is there more than one set of keys to the storerooms, refrigerators, and freezers?

- Are spare storeroom keys secured in a locked cabinet when not in use?

- Does a storeroom employee keep the keys from one day to the next?

- Are employees required to sign out keys in a logbook?

10.6 **Cook putting Cryovac-wrapped tenderloin in a backpack**

© Randy Van Dam 2008

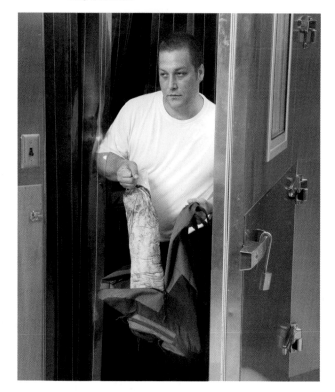

10.5 **Person using security card entry system to enter doorway**

© Randy Van Dam 2008

- Are two signatures required for acquiring keys (by the person requesting the keys and the clerk who issues them)?

- Are the kitchen keys left out in the open, such as hanging on a hook, during work hours?

- Are designated hours of operation for the storeroom consistently maintained?

- When the storeroom needs to be opened during off hours, is there a member of management present?

- Does the buyer frequently leave the place of business during work hours?

- Are other employees, beyond the storeroom staff, allowed to enter the dry or refrigerated storage facilities unsupervised?

- Do salespeople or delivery drivers have access to the storage areas?

- Do salespeople or delivery drivers help with stock placement or inventory?

- Is a written requisition required for all issues?

- Does the issuing clerk add items to the deliveries, which are reputedly called in and requested by the kitchen, without getting authorized signatures?

- Are bartenders issued bottles of liquor without any formal record of the request and issue? There should be an issue tag or receipt for each bottle.

- Is there a policy in force on employee meals? Are employees allowed to prepare their own meals while at work?

- Are front-of-the-house employees allowed to enter the kitchen unsupervised to make emergency food withdrawals?

- Does an employee make frequent trips to the bathroom, locker room, parking lot, or dumpster without good reason?

- Are employees seen passing packages off to friends or relatives?

- Does the back door have an alarm that sounds when opened?

The best deterrent to theft is a vigilant management team employing practical and purposeful control systems.

Employees are less likely to steal from employers when opportunities are limited. Restricting right of entry to storage areas is the primary defense against product loss due to theft. Conducting unannounced inventories and audits of the books are also good methods for deterring employee-induced shrinkage, as the potential to be caught is greatly heightened.

The second best deterrent to theft is letting the staff know, upon their initial training, that procedures are in place to detect theft and to identify the potential thieves. The use of electronic locking systems and security cameras can be very effective in reducing, if not eliminating, inventory theft. Most people are honest, and good systems of security help keep them honest.

People, Places, Things

One for the Road

At that same restaurant where I interviewed for the executive chef position, I sat at the bar in the main lounge on my second night of scouting the operation, before accepting the position. I arrived early in the evening, before the restaurant had filled, to observe the service and bar staffs. This particular restaurant had three service stations for the waitstaff, located throughout the two main dining rooms. Each station was designed to have the waitstaff plate their own soups, salads, bread, and nonalcoholic beverages for service, rather than have the kitchen staff plate them. The kitchen merely restocked their stations when the servers ran low on product. Presumably, this was done to speed up service. I watched

with interest, as the waitstaff all arrived to start their shift. Virtually every server made himself or herself a free beverage, large salad, soup, and bread before starting his or her side work. Over the course of one evening's dinner shift, more than 18 waitstaff prepared their own meals at the expense of the chef's food cost!

Also at this particular business, they had a large liquor storeroom behind the main lounge's long bar. The head bartender had a key, as did the owner and the food and beverage manager. There was a smaller second bar located at the opposite end of the restaurant, out of view from the front bar, which functioned as a service bar for both the banquet and dining room servers. During the course of the evening, I watched as a server approached the front bar's head bartender to request a bottle of dark rum, reportedly for the back bar. In reality, as I discovered by discreetly following the server with his ill-gotten bottle of rum across the dining room floor, the server headed to the parking lot to conceal the stolen bottle in his car. The back bar never asked him to get the bottle! And, during that same evening, I watched as another bartender occasionally worked out of an open cash drawer, making change for cash payments by customers without actually ringing up their sales. The result was that the bartender's cash in the drawer far exceeded what the register tape would show. Presumably, this bartender was going to pocket the excess cash after counting down the drawer at the end of the shift. The restaurant's waitstaff and bartenders were looting this business at every turn. Three weeks after I started as the executive chef, the owner fired the food and beverage manager, too. I ended up with both jobs, until leaving the restaurant to start the Culinary Arts program at Grand Rapids Community College in 1980.

Moral of the story: Most people are honest, but it helps to keep them that way by removing temptations and instituting procedures that safeguard valuable assets.

Inventory Value Padding

Inventory value padding involves intentionally overstating the monetary value of the products held in inventory. The value can be misrepresented in one of two ways. One version involves altering the ending inventory dollar value to mislead management into believing a lower food cost is achieved. A chef or food and beverage director may do this to "earn" a bonus, or to keep her job, in the short term. As the following formula illustrates, adding the values of the beginning inventory and purchases, and then subtracting the ending inventory determines the cost of foods sold. If the ending inventory is purposely increased, then the cost of foods sold will go down. This is an easy way to change the numbers on paper to a manager's advantage.

> Beginning inventory + purchases
> = Total food available − Ending Inventory
> = Cost of foods sold

Another method of padding the value is to substitute lower priced products for more expensive and generally superior products that were purchased by the business. This can occur when the products are left in an open storeroom where security is slack. The employee switches the products and then either consumes them or sells them for a profit.

SECURITY PROBLEMS IN ISSUING

Sometimes problems can occur during the issuing process. Chefs might order their supplies using the normal requisitioning system only to have some of the expensive items diverted by an issuing clerk. It is important that station chefs check-in their received storeroom supplies, comparing their requests with the actual deliveries.

Preventing Tampering

Tampering or altering a product to make it dangerous for consumption is a potential threat to the industry. Products can be tampered with at any point during the food production: from the farm to the plate. Accidental food tampering can include foodborne illnesses such as *E. coli*, which can be found in meats and fresh produce. Food service establishments should make sure that they are buying food from reputable dealers, and they should buy products with a locally sound reputation.

The following are only some of the methods by which an operator can help to maintain a safe and secure food service company:

1. Know your suppliers. Take a tour of their facilities to make sure they are clean and secure.
2. Make sure that your employees only purchase items from the approved suppliers.
3. Inspect all cases for signs of damage or tampering. If a master case is broken open, then check all of the internal containers as well.
4. Control access to the food storage areas and the kitchens.
5. Keep the exterior of the building well lit.
6. Check the ventilation system, and make sure that it is cleaned on a regular basis.
7. Keep fresh foods covered while in the storerooms or refrigerators.
8. Make sure that the storerooms are well lit.
9. Make sure chemicals are kept locked in their own storage areas.
10. If you have a self-serve concept, such as a buffet, make sure that an employee monitors it and removes and disposes of any food items that are suspect.

Charles Carroll, CEC, AAC,

Place of Birth: St. Johnsbury, Vermont

Educational Background and Work Experience

It would be difficult to imagine that Charles Carroll would end up doing anything other than working in the hospitality industry. After all, he spent his childhood working in his family's Rabbit Hill Country Inn, located in Waterford, Vermont. And on top of that, both his father and brother are also chefs. However, one very important part of Carroll's training was the time he spent working at the Balsams Grand Resort Hotel in Dixville Notch, New Hampshire. After working as an apprentice under Chef Phil Learned for 2 years, Carroll attended the Culinary Institute of America to receive his AOS degree in Culinary Arts. Upon leaving the CIA, he returned to the Balsams as sous chef and apprenticeship coordinator, positions he considered very important to his education. During his time at the Balsams, Chef Carroll became very involved in culinary salon competition, eventually earning medals at the prestigious Internationale KochKunst Ausstellung (Culinary Olympics) in Germany. Carroll later became executive chef of the Balsams and in due course moved to Rochester, New York, to become the executive chef of the Oak Hill Country Club. Today, Chef Carroll is the executive chef of the celebrated River Oaks Country Club in Houston, Texas, where he continues to exhibit his exemplary leadership and culinary skills.

Memberships and Career Highlights

Among his many accomplishments, including being a member of seven U.S. Culinary Olympic Teams with more that 70 national and international awards, including the title of Best in the World Cold Salon, Culinary Olympics 2000, Chef Carroll was named the 2005 ACF Central region Chef of the Year. As an active member of the American Culinary Federation (ACF), Chef Carroll has received three ACF Presidential Medallions from three different ACF presidents in three different decades. He is president of LeNôtre Culinary Board of Trustees, a member of Les Chaine de Rotisseurs, and secretary treasurer to the Escoffier Society of Houston. One of Chef Carroll's professional goals was reached

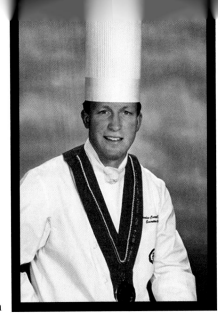

Courtesy Charles Carroll

It Happened to Me...

"I was working at a very busy, high-revenue property and was having fluctuating food cost issues. I combed every idea I could think of to try and find out why our food cost was so sporadic. I checked invoices; I personally checked in the food; I followed it to production and cut down on all the waste I could find; cross-utilized all food on all the menus; tracked the inventory and hospitality giveaways; made sure to get credit on all employee dining; managers signing food chits for all complimentary food; I even made sure to get credit from all the bars' requisitions for fruit and sodas, bottled water, and so on. I still could not find out why the food cost was floating.

I kept checking the invoices, and they all made sense. I had a suspicion that my purchasing agent was less than honest, but I could not catch him ever doing anything wrong. As a matter of fact, whenever I asked anything of him, he usually delivered very quickly, sometimes scary-quick. But I did have a problem with him constantly leaving the property and working his scheduled hours. Every time I addressed him about it, he had some halfway good excuse, like we always needed something last minute that he had to go and pick up. I told him that I wanted to know when he was leaving and when he was coming back. He constantly had a problem with this. So I would write him up.

I started digging in more to the inventory and the prices he used. Every month he would not update the prices; therefore, the inventory would never be accurate. I would write him up again until finally, one day, I had to let him go.

Three weeks later, I got a phone call. You're not going to believe this when I tell you. It was from a construction worker who was working about five miles away. It was the month of December at the time. The construction worker wanted to know if the "Meat Guy" was going to come around because the holidays were coming and they wanted to place their order.

I almost fell out of my chair. I said, 'Yah, he is coming. What do you guys need this week?' He placed an order of about $1,000.00 worth of meat. I almost passed out on the spot! I told him I would be right down with the order. I went down and met the guy. When he saw me coming, he knew there was trouble. But the way I saw it, my theft problem was not the construction guy's fault. The purchasing agent told him that the property knew of the program.

So, how was he doing it? How could he get all that beef, have my property pay for it and me not know anything about it? Well, the purchasing agent would go to the meat purveyor to order, and pick up, a "hot shot" order (a last-minute order) even though I sent letters to all purveyors insisting that all hot shot orders had to be signed by me. However, to get around my directive, the

(continued)

when he published his first book in 2007, *Finding Time to Be Great: Leadership Lessons from a Chef*. Even after all of these accomplishments, perhaps his most important honor was when he was inducted into both the Academy of Chefs and the Honorable Order of the Golden Toque with his father.

Passions with the Food Service Industry

"I have been blessed with a wonderful career. I am so fortunate to have worked at the properties that I have. They have been all very supportive in whatever I wanted to do or accomplish. Because of their support, I have been able to be active in many organizations and Culinary Olympic Teams, all of which expanded my culinary knowledge and horizons. My biggest passion always has been building culinary teams. I love mentoring young professionals, prepping them throughout their career and watching them get their first Executive Chef position. I love young kitchens full of

purchasing agent forged my signature, picked up the meat, went to the job site, sold it for cash, and passed the invoice directly to accounting...complete with my forged signature! I would have no opportunity to ever see the "false hot shot" invoices. Accounting could not tell the difference, because they routinely picked up the signed invoices from their mailbox, anyway.

So there you have it, a great lesson that I paid for, that you have just learned for free."

life and ready to chew off the end of a table to excel in our field. I thrive on building the perfect kitchen atmosphere where young people can grow."

Advice to a Chef or Buyer

"Everyone is going to tell you to buy the best products you can, and to buy correctly during the seasons. What I would like to encourage you to do is to develop a passion for knowing where your products come from. Learn what goes into developing it. Visit as many venders' properties, farms, distributors, and plants as you can.

Seeing these properties firsthand will burn an image into your head every time you place an order. Some tours will solidify your confidence, or defer your decision in placing the order with them. If you're not doing the ordering, make sure you walk the storeroom every day to be sure everything is being properly handled. Be sure to personally check all invoices at the end of the day. And by all means, be certain the accounting department doesn't pay any invoice without your signature; this will ensure nothing is coming in the back door that you do not approve."

Key Words and Concepts

---

backdoor selling	inventory shrinkage	kickbacks	vendor dishonesty
blackball	inventory value padding	reciprocity	vendor error
fraudulent invoices			

Chapter in Review

The following exercises are provided to help the reader understand and apply the contents of this chapter. They may be completed individually or in a classroom environment.

REVIEW QUESTIONS

a. Discuss the ramifications of a bartender working from an open cash register drawer.

b. Discuss *kickbacks* and how they may occur within a business.

c. Discuss *fraudulent invoices* and how they may occur within a business.

d. Identify and discuss all of the signs that an employee may be stealing from an operation. Discuss how management should respond, considering the rights of the employee and the responsibility of management.

INDIVIDUAL ACTIVITIES

a. **Web based:** Research different lock companies and security camera systems for possible use in storerooms and receiving docks.

b. **Experiential:** Walk around a food service operation and look for the ways security could be breached. Develop a list of ideas that could be used to prevent employee or vendor theft.

c. **Critical thinking:** What steps would you take if you thought a friend or relative might be guilty of some form of theft or product substitution?

GROUP ACTIVITIES

a. **Lab experience:** Have each student interview a chef or storeroom manager regarding his or her experiences with security problems. Combine all of these experiences, and develop a "Case Studies in Food Service Security" manual for reference by the students.

b. **Classroom action:** Discuss all of the methods by which employees and vendors could steal from a business, and then create policies or procedures that would prevent those activities from happening.

PART III

The Commodities:
Developing Product Knowledge

Image copyright Elena Elisseeva, 2009. Used under license from Shutterstock.com

Herbs, Spices, Minerals, and Flavoring Agents

"Men have traveled, as they have lived, for religion, for wealth, for knowledge, for pleasure, for power and the overthrow of rivals. Yet no very profound acquaintance with Haklut's book is needed to discern, as he clearly discerned, the single thread of interest running through all these pilgrimages. The discovery of the new Western World followed, as an incidental consequence, from the long struggle of the nations of Europe for commercial supremacy and control of the traffic with the East. In all these dreams of the politicians and merchants, sailors and geographers, who pushed back the limits of the unknown world, there is the same glitter of gold and precious stones, the same odour of far-fetched spices."

SIR WALTER RALEIGH

After reading this chapter, you will be able to:

◎ Explain the differences among herbs, spices, and minerals.

◎ List commonly used herbs, spices, and salts.

◎ Identify global sources for herbs, spices, and salts.

◎ Describe common herb and spice blends.

◎ List commonly used oils and their applications.

◎ Describe the process for making infused and flavored oils.

◎ Explain the smoke point of oils.

◎ List commonly used vinegars and their applications.

◎ Summarize the process for making infused and flavored vinegars.

◎ Define condiments as flavoring agents, and give examples.

Introduction

People have been using spices since before 50,000 BC. Early humans had discovered that leaves, roots, and bark could be added to meat in the fire pits. They would wrap meat in leaves, infusing the food with flavor. In ancient times, most people used spices that were available in their local area. Later, as trade developed, spices were traded over long distances. Because of the many miles between their origin and the courts of Europe, spices were rare and expensive, normally used sparingly for food, perfumes, and medical use. Early explorers such as Marco Polo increased the demand for spices with their descriptions of the flavorful food. Later, English, Dutch, Spanish, and Portuguese traders created the spice routes from the Far East to Europe. Then the Americans started importing their own spices from Asia, creating several millionaires in the food service industries.

Product Identification

Herbs are the leaves of shrubs and nonwoody or herbaceous plants. Most herbs originated in mild climates such as in Italy and France. In the United States, herbs can be grown outdoors in the summer and then kept indoors in the winter. Most herbs are used for flavoring foods, teas, and occasionally for medical purposes. Herbs can be dried or used fresh. They are normally sold in whole, ground, or crushed forms.

Spices come from roots, barks, buds, seeds, berries, or the fruit of tropical trees, plants, and shrubs. Spices are normally stronger than herbs and are used in smaller amounts. Spices can be used as food flavorings and medicine, but they are not normally used as a tea. Some spices can also act as preservatives within a dish.

Minerals are crystals formed by different geological processes. Minerals are mined from the earth or produced by evaporating water. Salt is the edible mineral that most people are familiar with.

Flavoring agents are artificial or natural substances that are added to enhance the flavor of the spices or to add flavor to neutral food items. Food manufactures often add them while processing the food. Most restaurants do not use them in their day-to-day operations.

Herbs

Herbs have long been prized for their medicinal properties. Most herbs have natural antioxidant properties, vitamins, and other nutritional values. When purchasing fresh herbs, you should pick brightly colored stems, and you should not use wilted or dusty herbs. Use the herbs immediately after purchasing them, or, if they have to be held, wrap them in a damp towel and place them in a sealed container for up to 5 days. Herbs can also be dried, as mentioned in Chapter 5. The following is a list of some popular varieties.

Basil. Basil is a member of the mint family and has a pungent aromatic flavor. There are several types of basil, including lemon, clove, cinnamon, and anise, and the leaves taste like the name of their variety. Basil is used in Italian dishes and pesto. (See Figure 11.1.)

Bay leaf. Also known as laurel or bay laurel leaf, it is a spicy herb from the Mediterranean area. It is used in Italian, French, Turkish, and Moroccan cooking. Fresh bay leaves are rare; the dried form is more readily available. Bay leaves are used in meat dishes, and the whole leaf should be removed after cooking. (See Figure 11.2.)

Chervil. Chervil is also known as cicily or sweet cicily. It is a member of the parsley family, but the leaves are lacier than the regular variety. Chervil is popular in French cooking and as an ingredient in *fines herbes*.

Chives. Chives are a member of the onion family. They have a very mild flavor and can be used to add heat to egg and potato dishes. The flowers are edible and can be used in salads. (See Figure 11.3.)

Cilantro. Cilantro is a member of the parsley family. It is also called *Chinese parsley* or *coriander*. Its flavor is peppery with a soapy aftertaste. It is used extensively in Latin American, Asian, and Caribbean cooking. (See Figure 11.4.)

Dill. Dill, or dill weed, is an herb that is used in dressings, potato dishes, and pickles. The herb is used in dishes, while the seeds are used for pickling. Dill's flavor fades with cooking, so it is better when added right before serving. (See Figure 11.5.)

Marjoram. Marjoram is a member of the mint family and is related to basil and oregano. It is similar to oregano, but the flavor is sweeter and milder. Marjoram and oregano are interchangeable in most recipes. It is frequently used in Italian, North African, French, and Middle Eastern cooking. (See Figure 11.6.)

11.1 Basil

Figures 11.1–11.6 © Randy Van Dam 2008

11.2 Bay leaf

11.3 Chives

11.4 Cilantro

11.5 Dill

11.6 Marjoram

Mint. Mint is an herb with more than 30 species. Spearmint and peppermint are the two most popular flavors. Mint has a spicy bite with a cool aftertaste. (See Figure 11.7.)

Oregano. Oregano is a member of the mint family with bright green leaves. Oregano is available fresh in the summertime. Another variation is called Mexican oregano, and it is sold dried. Oregano is popular in Italian, Greek, and Mediterranean cooking. (See Figure 11.8.)

Parsley. Parsley is a common herb available fresh almost year-round. The two main varieties are flat leaf (Italian), which has a strong flavor, and curly leaf, which has a milder taste and is a popular garnish. Parsley is used in Italian, French, and Middle Eastern cooking. (See Figure 11.9a and Figure 11.9b.)

Rosemary. Rosemary bushes are related to pine trees. The needles of the plant are clipped from the bushes and used to flavor dishes. The stalks are woody and can be used as skewers. Rosemary is popular in Mediterranean cooking. (See Figure 11.10.)

Sage. Sage leaves are furry, so this herb is normally sold in a ground or chopped form. Rubbed sage has the furry top coat removed. Sage has a spicy bite and a unique flavor. It is a popular ingredient in sausages and stuffings. (See Figure 11.11.)

Savory. Savory has a taste that is a cross between mint and thyme. Summer savory is milder than the winter variety. Both varieties are available on a regular basis. Savory is added to stews and meat dishes.

Sorrel. Sorrel looks like spinach and has a tangy flavor that increases when it gets older. Sorrel is a great addition to salads. It can also be ground or chopped and added to meat dishes.

Tarragon. Tarragon has small leaves with an anise flavor. Tarragon is very strong and can overwhelm other spices. It is a key ingredient in béarnaise sauce and French cooking. (See Figure 11.12.)

Thyme. Thyme has more than 20 varieties, each named after the dominant flavor of the herb. It is used to flavor meats and in French cooking. It is also an ingredient in *bouquet garni* and *herbes de Provence*. (See Figure 11.13.)

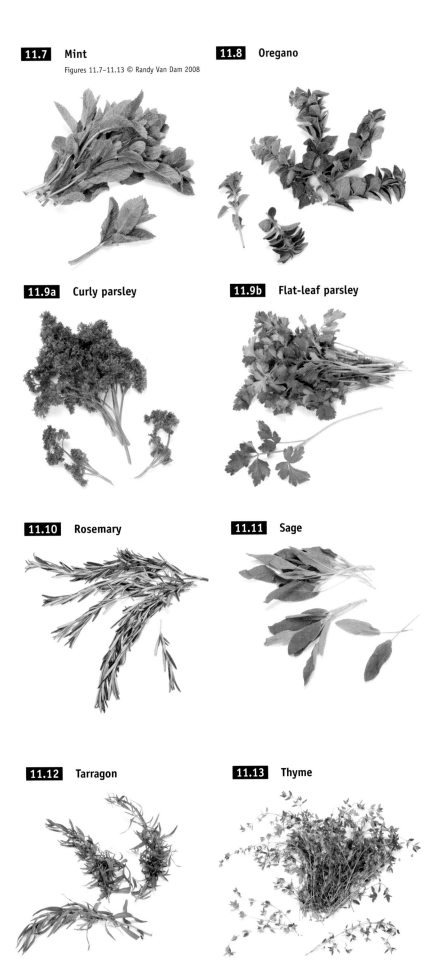

11.7 Mint

Figures 11.7–11.13 © Randy Van Dam 2008

11.8 Oregano

11.9a Curly parsley

11.9b Flat-leaf parsley

11.10 Rosemary

11.11 Sage

11.12 Tarragon

11.13 Thyme

Spices

Spices, for the most part, have a more intense flavor than herbs. The following is only a representative list of the numerous spices available to the professional chef.

Cinnamon. Cinnamon is the inner bark of a tropical evergreen tree. While there are many different varieties, the two commercial varieties are *Cinnamomum cassia* and *Cinnamomum zeylanicum*. Cinnamon originated in Sri Lanka but can grow in any tropical region. The trees are kept small and pruned to produce more branches. The harvesters use special knives to peel the bark from the tree. It is then cleaned and left to dry. As it dries, it curls into rolls, which are sold as cinnamon sticks. Most cinnamon is ground and sold in that form. (See Figure 11.14.)

Galangal (galingale, Siamese ginger). This member of the ginger family has a spicy hot ginger flavor. It is used in Thai cooking and in Asian dishes. Galangal can be substituted for ginger, but the taste is stronger. (See Figure 11.15.)

Ginger. Ginger is a knobby root or rhizome with a spicy, unique flavor. Ginger can be purchased fresh either in a young or mature form. Older ginger must be peeled. Whole ginger is used in Asian cooking. The other form is ground, which was first sliced, then dried, and then ground. This form is used in sauces and desserts. Fresh ginger and the dried forms are not always interchangeable, but check the recipe to make sure. Fresh ginger roots must be stored in a cool, dark place. (See Figure 11.16.)

Horseradish. Horseradish is a root, long known for its bitter taste. Horseradish is sold fresh or grated. Grated horseradish must be kept in the refrigerator. Horseradish is used in condiments, dressings, and sauces where a sharp bite is desired. (See Figure 11.17.)

Lemongrass. Lemongrass looks like scallions but has a lemony taste and tartness. It is used in Thai and Vietnamese cooking. This spice is only available as a fresh herb and should be kept in the refrigerator. (See Figure 11.18.)

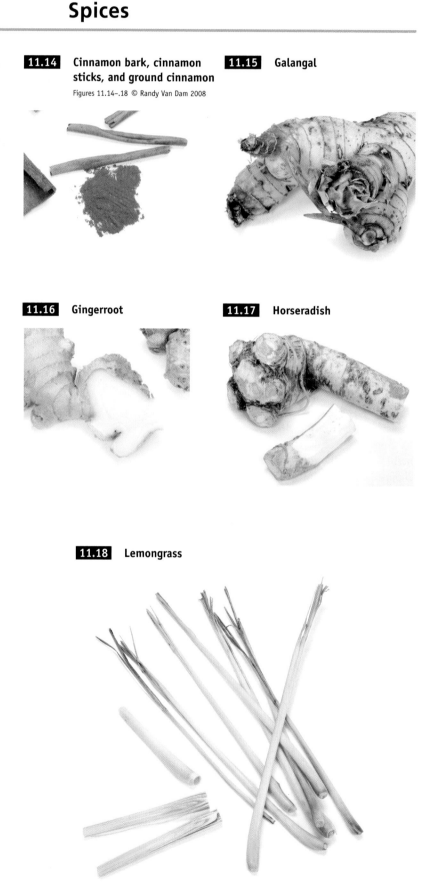

11.14   **Cinnamon bark, cinnamon sticks, and ground cinnamon**

Figures 11.14–.18 © Randy Van Dam 2008

11.15   **Galangal**

11.16   **Gingerroot**

11.17   **Horseradish**

11.18   **Lemongrass**

Mace and nutmeg. Nutmeg is the seed of a tropical ever-green tree while mace is the dried covering of the seed. Both are sold in the ground form. Mace and nutmeg are normally interchangeable in recipes. They are used in sauces and desserts. (See Figure 11.19.)

Mustard seed. Mustard seeds are seeds from Asian bushes. Brown seeds come from one species of the bush while white seeds come from another. Brown seeds normally have more of a bite than the white ones. The whole seeds are used in pickling, chutneys, and some sauces. The seeds are also ground into powder, which can be used to flavor meats and sauces. Ground mustard powder is mixed with water or other liquids to create the condiment mustard. (See Figure 11.20.)

Parsley root. Parsley root is a beige root from a parsley plant. It tastes like a carrot. Parsley root is used in stocks and soups. The leaves can be used like any fresh parsley. (See Figure 11.21.)

Peppercorns. Peppercorns are the berries from the *piper nigrum* bush. Most peppercorns are grown in India, Indonesia, Brazil, and Malaysia. Pepper is the most traded spice and is used in virtually all cuisines. Peppercorns are sold by their color. Green peppercorns are harvested early. If they are allowed to dry, they turn black. White peppercorns are harvested when ripe. Peppercorns are ground into pepper. There are several grinds available, including fine, coarse, and restaurant grade. Restaurants often purchase

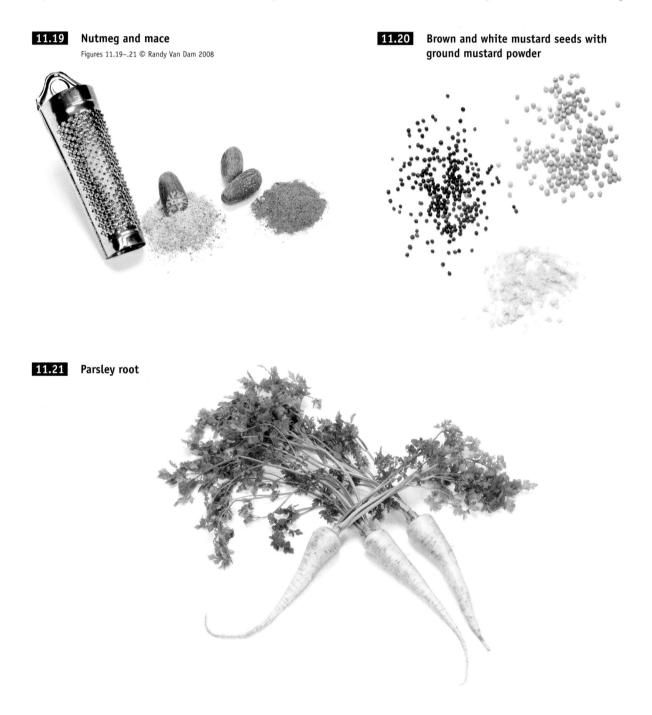

11.19 Nutmeg and mace

Figures 11.19–.21 © Randy Van Dam 2008

11.20 Brown and white mustard seeds with ground mustard powder

11.21 Parsley root

both the ground pepper and whole berries for recipes. (See Figure 11.22a, Figure 22b, and Figure 22c.)

Poppy seeds. Poppy seeds come from poppy plants. They are available in white, black, or blue. Poppy seeds are used whole but can be ground.

Sesame seeds. Sesame seeds are the seeds from the sesame plant. They are sold by color, with white and black as the dominant colors. Sesame seeds are sprinkled on breads and rolls. They may also be toasted and added to sauces, salads, or as a garnish. They can also be ground to a paste to make dressing and dips. (See Figure 11.23.)

Saffron. Saffron, the stamens of the *saffron crocus* flower, is a rare and expensive spice. Each flower is picked by hand, and then the stamens are removed. Saffron is sold by the stamen or thread, or in a ground form. The threads do need to be reconstituted by soaking in water before they are used. While there is no substitute for the flavor of saffron,

turmeric is used to add the golden yellow color to some dishes. (See Figure 11.24.)

Star anise. Star anise is used frequently in Chinese cooking. The spice comes from the seeds in the star-shaped pod. The seeds are dried and then used whole or ground into a powder. Star anise adds a licorice flavor to main dishes and meats, and it is an ingredient in five-spice powders. (See Figure 11.25.)

Tamarind. Tamarind is the sticky pulp wrapped around small seeds of a bean pod. Tamarind has a sharp sour taste and can be used in recipes where a sharp taste with some body is needed. It is used in condiments and sauces. It is often sold in blocks in Asian food shops. (See Figure 11.26.)

Vanilla bean. There are many varieties of vanilla orchids, but most are used for perfumes. Only two species are used for food production: Bourbon and Tahitian. Tahitian vanilla pods are more fragrant and must be imported to

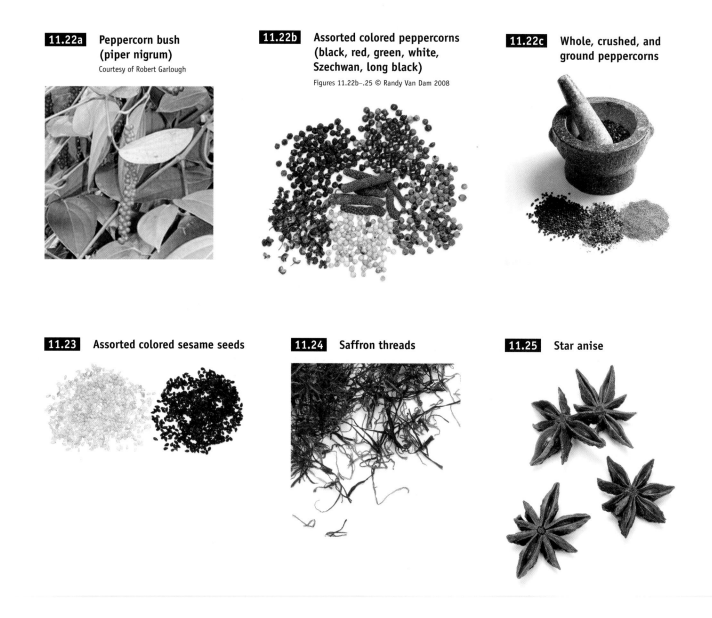

11.22a   **Peppercorn bush (piper nigrum)**

Courtesy of Robert Garlough

11.22b   **Assorted colored peppercorns (black, red, green, white, Szechwan, long black)**

Figures 11.22b–.25 © Randy Van Dam 2008

11.22c   **Whole, crushed, and ground peppercorns**

11.23   **Assorted colored sesame seeds**

11.24   **Saffron threads**

11.25   **Star anise**

11.26 Tamarind pods and seeds

Figures 11.26–.29 © Randy Van Dam 2008

11.27 Vanilla bean

11.28 Wasabi powder

the United States. Bourbon vanilla is more common and is frequently imported from Mexico at a cheaper price. Vanilla can be sold as pods. The cook must split the pod open and then scrape the seeds out. Vanilla pods are used to infuse the vanilla flavor into puddings, dessert fillings, frostings, and sauces. Vanilla is also available as a liquid extract. The vanilla pods are soaked in a pure food-grade alcohol base. Once the base soaks up the flavor, water is added to dilute the solution. This form of vanilla is used for cakes and other baked desserts. (See Figure 11.27.)

Wasabi. Fresh wasabi root is only available in Japan. In the United States, it is sold as a ground powder or a paste. Wasabi is very spicy and adds heat to food. (See Figure 11.28.)

STORAGE AND HANDLING

Fresh herbs and spices will only last a few days. They should be purchased in small quantities, just enough to make it to the next delivery. The dried forms of whole herbs and spices, on the other hand, last a long time and can be successfully stored in the kitchen. The crushed and ground versions from commercial spice manufactures do not last as long as the dried, whole versions. Therefore, some establishments will buy the dried, whole spices and then crush or grind them as needed.

Herbs and spices can be ground or crushed with a mortar and pestle, with a rolling pin in a plastic bag, or with a spoon and a cup. You can also use electrical spice grinders and food processors. Because the flavor evaporates quickly, these ground spices should be used as soon as possible.

Commercially ground spices and herbs should be checked for freshness at least once a quarter by smelling them. If they lack their distinctive aromas, they should be discarded. Spices should be purchased in small quantities so that they can be used before the flavor is lost. There are four factors that affect the quality of spices:

- **Light:** Colored spices should be protected from light. They should be stored in dark containers clearly labeled and can be transferred to smaller containers for use in the kitchen.

- **Humidity:** Dried spices and herbs will attract water. All spices should be stored in cool, dry places to prevent moisture from infiltrating them.

- **Oxygen:** The essential oils will oxidize or dissipate when exposed to atmospheric oxygen. Spice containers should have tight covers and only be opened for measurement.

- **Heat:** Heat will also dissipate essential oils. If dried spices are needed on a hot line, then they should be issued in small containers and checked on a daily basis.

MARKET FORMS

These types of spices are used either whole or in various processed forms (see Figure 11.29). The major forms are as follows.

Whole. Whole spices can be simmered in sauces, soups, and stews. They are also used in pickling and relishes. Whole spices can be ground for garnishes or tableside service.

Granulated. Granulation is a process where the spices are dehydrated and then mechanically chopped into even pieces. Granulated spices have an intact cell structure and impart more flavor than the ground versions. Garlic, onion, and red pepper are the major spices that can be successfully granulated. These spices can be sprinkled on top of breads, salads, and meats where an extra burst of flavor is desired.

Ground. Ground spices are made by drying the whole herb or spice and then grinding it to a fine powder. Ground spices have a more intense flavor than the whole or

11.29 Indian spice tin

granulated varieties, but this flavor will quickly dissipate if the spices are not stored correctly. Ground spices are used in most recipes and in baking.

Extractives. Extracts are the essential oils of the herb dissolved in water, oil, or alcohol bases. They are added in their liquid form to the recipe. Extractives include vanilla extract, lemon extract, garlic oils, and mint oils.

Herb and spice blends. These are combinations of ground, granulated, whole, and extractive spices. They can be made in the kitchen or purchased commercially. Some of the common commercial blends include:

- **Chili powder:** red pepper, cumin, oregano, salt, and garlic powder
- **Curry powder:** coriander, turmeric, cumin, fenugreek seed, white pepper, allspice, yellow mustard, red pepper, and ginger
- **Poultry seasoning:** white pepper, sage, thyme, marjoram, savory, ginger, allspice, and nutmeg
- **Apple pie:** cinnamon, ginger, nutmeg, allspice, and cloves
- **Pumpkin pie spice:** ginger, cinnamon, nutmeg, and cloves

There are also seasoning blends common to particular countries. Table 11.1 identifies some of the frequently used spice blends and their countries of origin.

TABLE 11.1 Distinctive Regional or National Spice Blends

Brazil	**Meat rub spice mix:** allspice, black peppercorn, cumin, malagueta pepper, clove, ginger, coriander
Britain	**Charcuterie spice mix:** white pepper, mace, nutmeg, ginger, coriander, cayenne, sage
China	**Five-spice powder:** star anise, Sichuan peppercorns, fennel seeds, cloves, cinnamon
India	**Garam masala:** cardamom seeds, cloves, cumin seeds, nutmeg, black peppercorns, cinnamon
Italy	**Tomato sauce mix:** garlic, oregano, basil, parsley, bay leaf, white peppercorn, fennel seed
Mexico	**Chili powder:** mild chilies, oregano, cumin seeds, cayenne
South Africa	**Stewing spice mix:** mace, allspice, nutmeg, coriander, cumin, thyme, rosemary, marjoram, white pepper
USA	**Cajun spice:** garlic powder, thyme, cayenne, black pepper, onion powder, salt

People, Places, Things

Distinctive Flavor Profiles of World Cuisines

We tend to associate various flavor profiles with certain cuisines. This can be directly attributed to the herbs, spices, and flavoring agents commonly used in their foodstuffs, as well as the primary ingredients. Often, prevalent use is due to

historically available through proximity or trade. When chefs seek to imitate ethnic dishes, it is vital that they carefully adhere to the flavor profiles.

Caribbean	fresh ginger, nutmeg, ginger and allspice, fresh chilies, garlic
Mexican	coriander, cinnamon, cumin, cayenne, black pepper, fresh oregano, cilantro, fresh and dried chilies
North African	saffron, cumin, paprika, turmeric, black pepper, cinnamon, ginger
Northern Europe	caraway, cardamom, cinnamon, mustard, dill, nutmeg, bay leaf, thyme, tarragon
Mediterranean	basil, oregano, parsley, fennel seed, black pepper, mustard, cayenne, saffron, anchovies, garlic, olive oil
Chinese	five-spice powder, fresh ginger, soy sauce, fish sauce, sesame oil, white pepper
Thai	cumin, star anise, turmeric, fresh chilies, basil, cilantro, lemongrass
East Indian	cardamom, cinnamon cloves, coriander, cumin, fennel, turmeric, mustard, curry
Middle East	cloves, allspice, cinnamon, cumin, mint,

Minerals

Salt is the mineral used the most in cooking. Technically, table salt is sodium chloride, and sodium plays an important part in human fluid levels. Without salt, the liquid substances will not stay at their proper levels, and vital organs might not work the way they should. Salt is also an important part of the transmission of electrical impulses in the nervous system. Too little or too much salt can lead to health issues.

Salt is also a preservative, used in ancient times to preserve meats. While salt is now readily available and cheap, in previous centuries, it was expensive and hard to find. Salt mines were normally fought over, and international trade was often started because of a country's need to find new sources of salt.

Salt is used in cooking for several reasons, including:

- Preventing mold and bacteria growth.
- Acting as a brake for the chemical reactions produced by yeast in baked goods.
- Brightening food flavors and helping to reinforce the flavors of other spices.
- Decreasing the sourness of acids and increasing the sweetness of sugar within a dish.

TYPES OF SALT

There are many types of salt available in the marketplace. The following list identifies some of the basic types that have been traditionally used for a variety of purposes.

Canning and pickling salt. Canning salt is a "pure" salt with no additives. This salt is similar to table salt, but it does not include iodine or anti-caking additives. When these items are present in salt, they darken the pickles. (See Figure 11.30.)

Coarse salt. Coarse salt is a large grain sea salt. It does not dissolve as quickly as table salt in a stew or sauce. It can be measured with fingers and sprinkled on salads and meats. Coarse salt can be combined with a liquid to create salt crust pastes for meat and fish. (See Figure 11.31.)

Flake salt. Flake salt is made by drying sea salts until they look like snowflakes. Flake salt is very fine and dissolves quickly. It is used as a garnish. (See Figure 11.32.)

Grinder salt. This is larger chunks of salt that can be used in a salt grinder. Grinder salt is dried so that moisture won't clog the grinder mechanisms. Salt grinders should be made of ceramic or plastic as stainless steel will corrode with the salt. (See Figure 11.33a and Figure 11.33b.)

Kosher salt. Kosher salt is a regular salt that has a coarser ground. It has no additives and is used to prepare meat according to Jewish dietary laws. It is also used for pickles, pretzels, and margarita glasses. Kosher salt can also be used for pickling salt. It comes in fine and coarse grains. (See Figure 11.34.)

Popcorn salt. This is a super-fine salt for popcorn, corn on the cob, and French fries. It is designed to cling to the items. (See Figure 11.35.)

Rock salt. This is a non-food-grade salt that is normally used for icy walkways. In the kitchen, it is used for ice cream machines to cool the container. The rock salt is mixed with water and then poured into the container. (See Figure 11.36.)

Sea salt (*sal del mar, sel de mer, sale marino*). Sea salt is salt that comes from the sea. The ocean water is funneled into large trays and dried; then the salt is dried in the sun. Sea salt is available from numerous countries that border the oceans. Sea salt will contain minerals indigenous to the region from which it came. Sea salt is available in coarse and fine grinds. (See Figure 11.37a and Figure 11.37b.)

People, Places, Things

Salt from the Sea

All of the world's salt deposits are of marine origin; salt mines are simply markers for the areas where water once flowed. Sea salt is obtained either naturally by sun and wind evaporation or artificially from water evaporation pans. Unlike rock salt, it contains only 34 percent sodium chloride and is rich in trace elements. There are several types available. English sea salt comes primarily from Essex. It has a very "salty" taste and can be distinguished by its flake form. Brittany sea salt from France has a gray color characteristic of the sea floor beneath the salt marshes. With a delicate flavor, it is an exceptional salt for both kitchen and table. *Fleur de sel*, which translates literally as "flower of salt," comes from the salt marshes in Guêrande and is very rare. It is said to form only when the wind blows from the east. It is harvested many

11.30 **Canning and pickling salt**

Figures 11.30–.36 © Randy Van Dam 2008

11.31 **Coarse salt**

11.32 **Pink flake salt**

11.33a **Grinder salt**

11.33b **Plastic salt and pepper grinders**

11.34 **Kosher salt**

11.35 **Popcorn salt**

11.36 **Rock salt**

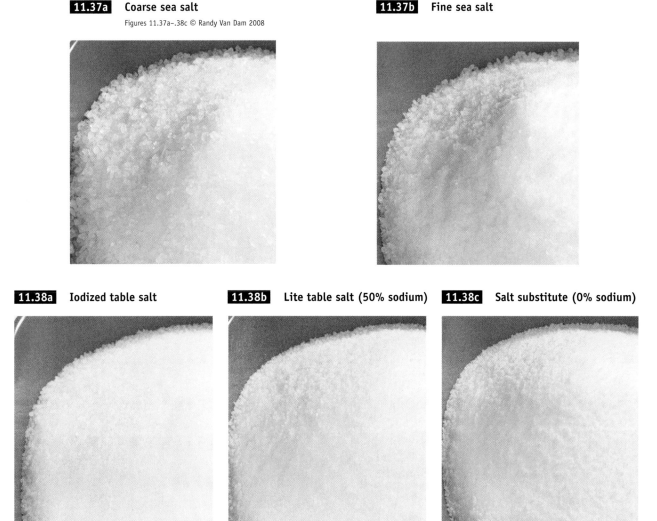

11.37a Coarse sea salt

Figures 11.37a–.38c © Randy Van Dam 2008

11.37b Fine sea salt

11.38a Iodized table salt

11.38b Lite table salt (50% sodium)

11.38c Salt substitute (0% sodium)

Table salt. Table salt is mined and then refined in factories until only sodium chloride is left. Most U.S. table salt has iodine, a nutrient most inland people need, added to it. Plain salt is available in areas located near the sea shores. (See Figure 11.38a, Figure 11.38b, and Figure 11.38c.)

While all of these different types of salt have been available for centuries, it has only been in the past few years that chefs have learned to appreciate the different types that are available. They include the following:

Black salt (Kala Namak, Sanchal). Black salt is a dark, pearly pinkish-grey mineral salt. It has a strong sulfur flavor from the mines from which it comes. It is available in very fine or coarse grains and is used in Indian cooking. (See Figure 11.39.)

Brazilian sea salt. This salt is harvested off the coasts of Brazil. It is a pure sea salt with very few minerals. It is used in salt grinders and for roasting meats. (See Figure 11.40.)

Celtic salt (French grey sea salt). This salt is harvested off the shores of Brittany, France. This salt has a high trace mineral content, and it is harvested using wooden rakes so that metal does not corrode it during the harvest. It is available in coarse, fine, and extra fine grains. It is used in French cooking. (See Figure 11.41.)

***Fleur de sel* (flower of salt, *flor de sal*).** This salt is from the Guerande region of France. It is a sea salt that forms from natural oceanic evaporation ponds. This salt has a unique flavor and is frequently used in French cooking. (See Figure 11.42.)

Grey salt (*sel gris*, Celtic sea salt). This is a light grey, almost purple salt from France. It is collected from the oceanic salt flats near the coasts. It is available in a coarse, fine, and very fine grain. (See Figure 11.43.)

Hawaiian sea salt (Alaea, Alae, Hawaiian red salt). This is a sea salt from Hawaii, which dries on the volcanic flats near the beaches. This adds iron oxide and a pink color to the salt. The taste is not as strong as regular sea salts. Hawaiian sea salt comes in a fine and coarse grain. (See Figure 11.44.)

Himalayan pink salt. This salt comes from the foothills of the Himalayan mountain chain. It is a mined salt that has picked up minerals, which give it its color. It is available in a fine grain or crystal. (See Figure 11.45a and Figure 11.45b.)

11.39 Black salt

Figures 11.39–.45b © Randy Van Dam 2008

11.40 Brazilian sea salt

11.41 Celtic salt

11.42 *Fleur de sel salt*

11.43 Grey salt

11.44 Hawaiian sea salt

11.45a Himalayan pink salt (finely ground)

11.45b Himalayan pink salt (large crystal form, before grinding)

Italian sea salt (Sicilian sea salt, *sale marino*). This is a sea salt produced in Sicily from the waters of the Mediterranean Sea. It has a higher level of minerals and less sodium chloride than regular salt. It is harvested by evaporating pans of sea water. It is available in coarse and fine grains.

New Zealand sea salt. This is a sea salt from New Zealand harvested from the Pacific Ocean. It is gathered from the salt fields near the coast. It is available in a fine grain and is used for spice blends. (See Figure 11.46.)

Organic salt. There are three institutions that certify that salt was gathered from clean ocean water and clean salt beds: Nature and Progrès (France), Bio-Gro (New Zealand), and Soil Association Certified (Wales). Organic salt must be harvested and packaged according to their guidelines.

Smoked sea salt. This is sea salt that is smoked over wood fires. This gives the salt a smoky flavor, and later the salt transfers that smoked flavor to meats, soups, and salads. It is available in fine and coarse grains. (See Figure 11.47a, Figure 11.47b, and Figure 11.47c.)

In the kitchen, all salt should be stored in a dry place to prevent it from solidifying or caking; under proper conditions, it will keep indefinitely. Do not store salt in silver salt-shakers or saltcellars because the chlorine in the salt reacts with the silver, causing a green discoloration.

11.46 New Zealand sea salt

Figures 11.46–.47c © Randy Van Dam 2008

11.47a Chardonnay oak-smoked fleur de sel

11.47b Northwest alder-smoked sea salt

11.47c Black-smoked sea salt

People, Places, Things

Making Smoked Salt

Making a basic smoked salt is an easy process. It can be made by spreading coarse kosher salt or coarse sea salt on a sheet pan and then placing it in a cold smoker (even while smoking other foods at the same time). The color of the salt will darken. Other more complex flavors can also be obtained by adding a few steps. For example, smoked chardonnay sea salt is made by first packing a dry wine barrel that previously held chardonnay wine. After a few months of storage in the cask, the salt is removed, and the barrel is broken up into firewood. The chardonnay-flavored wood is then used as the fuel with which to cold smoke the chardonnay-infused salt.

[ASK THE EXPERT]

Steve Jilleba
Flavor Expert

Name: Steve Jilleba, CMC, AAC, Flavor Expert

Title: Corporate Executive Chef for North America

Employer: Unilever Foodsolutions

Education/Training: As one of only 61 ACF Certified Master Chefs in the world, Chef Jilleba has enjoyed an extensive and varied culinary background as an executive chef in numerous hotels, country clubs, resorts, and fine-dining establishments. He also worked as a culinary instructor for the Academy of Culinary Arts. Chef Jilleba is a graduate of the Culinary Institute of America in Hyde Park, New York, and is currently a member of the American Culinary Federation (ACF), American Academy of Chefs (AAC) and World Association of Chefs Societies (WACS), among other prestigious culinary organizations. He has competed in three International Culinary Olympic events and won numerous gold medals.

Awards/Honors:

ACF Certified Master Chef

Honorary Doctorate in Culinary Arts, Johnson and Wales University

ACF Chef of the Year and Member of the Year 1999 Chicago

Regional Chef Professionalism Award Winner 2000

Regional Chef of the Year 2001

Herman Rusch Lifetime Achievement Award, Central Region

Team Manager 2004 and 2008 ACF Youth Team

#145 Distinguish Visiting Chef Johnson and Wales University

Won numerous gold medals at three International Culinary Olympics

General Responsibilities: As the National Culinary Committee Chairman for the American Culinary Federation, Chef Jilleba is a highly respected member of the organization, helping to supervise sanctioned culinary competitions nationally. Chef Jilleba was the ACF National Team Manager for 2008 National Youth Team and has been named the National Team Manager for the 2012 ACF National Culinary Team. In addition to Chef Jilleba's other achievements, for the past three years he has worked directly with the Culinary Institute of America on behalf of Unilever Foodsolutions to coproduce the *Savoring the Best of World Flavors* DVD series. Chef Jilleba has hosted the series, introducing food service chefs to the gold standards of authentic global cuisine and delivering a unique, hands-on perspective of the tastes and traditions of world cuisines.

Ask the Expert Questions:

1) How important is taste and nutrition to the American chef?

My nutritional education and past experience proved their full value as I moved toward my goal of Certified Master Chef in 1997. This is an area of the test that requires you to produce a menu with certain nutritional standards predetermined with of course the golden rule of good taste being paramount. I was able to successfully complete this portion of the exam.

2) Can chefs provide flavorful foods that are also nutritionally sound?

Nutrition became an area of focus for me in the late '80s while I was working for a hotel management group in Santa Rosa, California. As the corporate chef, I spearheaded a project to redesign their menus to feature the cornucopia of fruits, vegetables, and grains that were so plentiful in the area. Protein was designed to simply complement the dishes. This menu concept progressed to the utilization of healthier cooking techniques such as poaching, steaming, and grilling; it culminated with a dedicated spa menu that was available throughout the hotel chain. The primary focus was to create healthy nutritional options for our guests with flavor remaining still the primary fundamental rule.

This refocusing on healthy menu options became a hallmark for me throughout my career. My future employment at a hotel on the Eastern seaboard, and then later at a city club in the Midwest, both included a menu transformation to healthier menus with great flavor. While working at a Midwest private club, we took the opportunity to directly market and educate its members through the club's newsletter. The educational program included networking with the University of Iowa Hospital and Dr. Dean Ornish. We collaborated and offered two-day seminars featuring heart-health advice from Dr. Ornish, nutritional dietary consulting by University of Iowa Hospital, and a healthy cooking techniques presentation by myself.

3) What are today's customers looking for in their chef-prepared meals?

Today, as my career continues to evolve, I am the corporate chef of a global food manufacturing company. Today's customers are looking for bold flavors, good nutritional balance, and value. We take this into consideration when creating products by researching and introducing new ethnic flavors, being mindful of keeping a clean and healthy ingredient label that focuses on fruits, vegetables, grains, smaller protein portions, and, of course, taste.

Flavoring Agents

There are many different dehydrated vegetables that can be used as seasonings. Onion, garlic, sweet red pepper, mint, and mixed vegetables are available, as well as freeze-dried chives and shallots. Officially, the Food and Drug Administration (FDA) does not consider dehydrated vegetables to be spices, but they are used as such in the kitchen.

Condiments are combinations of herbs and spices with a liquid base. This category includes mustards, catsup, relish, chutneys, Tabasco, hot sauces, Worcestershire sauce, BBQ sauces, and steak sauces. These prepared items can be used as ingredients within a recipe or offered on the side to customers at the table. (See Figure 11.48.)

OILS

Oils are liquid fats from plants or animals. They are liquid at room temperature, and they are related to the solid forms such as butter, margarine, lard, and shortening. Vegetable oil is a generic term for a blend of different plant oils. The most common oils in a kitchen are corn, olive, canola, palm, soybean, and sunflower oils. Some oils may be made from nuts including walnut oil.

Oils can be flavored by adding herbs, spices, and vegetables. Normally the flavoring agent sits for some time in the oil to allow the flavor to infuse it. Garlic and onions are not used to flavor oil as they can introduce *Clostridium botulinum* to the oil.

Cold-pressed oils are made by pressing the vegetable on an expeller press; the friction of the pressing heats the oil as it is processed. Some harder nuts and seeds require additional pressure, which will increase the heat of the process. Other oils are extracted by adding chemicals that react with the vegetables to draw the oil out.

Plants with delicate tastes such as olive, pumpkin, grapeseed, flaxseed, avacado, canola, and garlic must be pressed in a temperature-controlled environment so that they do not heat up and lose their flavor.

It is important to note that Europe has strict guidelines for pressing oils, while the United States does not. Thus, it is possible for U.S. oils to be labeled "cold pressed" when they have actually been extracted by other methods.

All oils are sensitive to damage from heat, light, and exposure to oxygen. Oils should be stored in a cool, dry place and not issued until needed. If oil is needed in the hot part of the kitchen, it should be issued in small containers. Oil that has gone bad has an off smell and taste. This oil should be discarded immediately.

Refined oils with lots of monounsaturated fats can be kept up to a year in a cool, dry place. Oils with polyunsaturated fats will keep for 6 months. Virgin and extra-virgin oil can keep for about a year after opening. Unrefined monosaturated oils will keep for up to 8 months.

Smoke point is the temperature at which the oil will start to smoke (see Figure 11.49). Vegetable oils can handle higher temperatures than animal oils, as shown in Table 11.2, and are often used as **cooking oils**. When the smoke point is reached, the oil will break down and must be discarded.

 11.48 **Assorted bottled condiments**

© Randy Van Dam 2008

11.49 The smoke point of oil
© Randy Van Dam 2008

11.50 Various olive oils
© Randy Van Dam 2008

A commercial kitchen might need several types of oils (see Figure 11.50, Figure 11.51, Figure 11.52, and Figure 11.53). The different types include:

- **Avocado oil.** This oil is pressed from the pits and the flesh of the avocado fruit. It is used as an ingredient in salad dressings.

- **Coconut oil.** This is extracted from dried coconut kernels. It is used in Indian dishes and for commercial baking. It is high in saturated fats.

- **Corn oil.** This is oil extracted from corn. It is high in polyunsaturated fats and has a high smoke point. It can be used in most recipes.

- **Cottonseed oil.** This oil is from cottonseeds, and it is used to make margarine and blended cooking oils. It has a distinctive flavor and is used in Egyptian cuisine.

- **Grapeseed oil.** This oil is extracted from grape seeds and has a pale color. It does not cloud when it gets cold, so it is great for mayonnaise and blended salad dressings. It also

Types of Oils

There are many different types of oils available today. Oils should be chosen based on:

- Recipe usage (e.g., whether the food will be fried or sautéed in the oil)

- Nutritional or allergy concerns

- Flavor profile

People, Places, Things

Making Chili Oil

While most oils can be flavored cold, chili oil is best heated. Keep the heat very low, and supervise cooking; if the chilies are overheated, they will give off throat-burning fumes. You can use any oil, and you can choose milder or hotter chilies. Oils with distinctive flavors, such as Asian sesame oil, are best added after the original mixture is cooked so their flavors have the greatest effect. To make chili oil, combine 1 cup (250 ml) peanut oil and 6 Tbsp chopped dried red chilies in a shallow saucepan. Cook 10 minutes over very low heat, and then cool. When cold, add 2 to 3 tsp ground cayenne pepper and 1

TABLE 11.2 Smoke Points of Cooking Oils and Fats

Oils and Fat	Quality	Smoke Point	
Almond Oil		420°F	216°C
Avocado Oil		520°F	271°C
Butter		350°F	271°C
Canalo Oil	Unrefined	225°F	107°C
	Semirefined	350°F	177°C
	Refined	400°F	204°C
Coconut Oil	Unrefined	350°F	177°C
	Refined	450°F	232°C
Corn Oil	Unrefined	320°F	160°C
	Refined	450°F	232°C
Cottonseed Oil		420°F	216°C
Flaxseed Oil	Unrefined	225°F	107°C
Gee (Indian Clarified Butter)		485°F	252°C
Grapeseed Oil		420°F	216°C
Hazelnut Oil		430°F	221°C
Hemp Oil		330°F	165°C
Lard		370°F	782°C
Macadamia Oil		390°F	199°C
Olive Oil	Extra Virgin	320°F	160°C
	Virgin	420°F	216°C
Pomace		460°F	238°C
	Extra light	468°F	242°C
High Quality (Low Acidity) Olive Oil	Extra Virgin	405°F	207°C
Peanut Oil	Unrefined	320°F	160°C
	Refined	450°F	232°C
Rice Bran Oil		190°F	254°C
Safflower Oil	Unrefined	225°F	107°C
	Semirefined	320°F	160°C
	Refined	450°F	232°C
		510°F	266°C
Seasame Oil	Unrefined	350°F	177°C
		410°F	210°C
	Semirefined	450°F	232°C
Soybean Oil	Unrefined	320°F	160°C
	Semirefined	350°F	177°C
	Refined	450°F	232°C
Sunflower Oil	Unrefined	225°F	107°C
	Semirefined	450°F	232°C
High Oleic Sunflower Oil	Unrefined	320°F	160°C
	Refined	450°F	232°C
Tea Oil		485°F	252°C
Vegetable Shortening		360°F	182°C
Walnut Oil	Unrefined	320°F	160°C
	Semirefined	400°F	204°C

11.51 **Various vegetable oils**

© Randy Van Dam 2008

11.52 **Various nut oils**

© Randy Van Dam 2008

11.53 **Various infused oils**

© Randy Van Dam 2008

has a high smoke point so it works for general cooking. It is high in polyunsaturated fats.

- **Hazelnut oil.** This is extracted from hazelnuts and has a rich flavor. It is made in France, and, because of the price, it is normally reserved for salad dressings or marinades. It loses flavor when heated, so it should only be added at the last minute to hot dishes.

- **Olive oils.** This is oil made from olives. It is usually produced in the Mediterranean regions, although California now also produces olive oil. There are several different types of Mediterranean olive oils available.
  - **Italian olive oil.** This is oil from the Tuscany and Umbria areas of Italy. The Italian government keeps close tabs on the production of the oils and ensures the processing and manufacturing.
  - **Greek olive oil.** This is oil made in Greece. While Greece is the third largest producer of olive oil in the world, the quality tends to vary from manufacturer to manufacturer.
  - **French olive oil.** The French do not make as much olive oil as the Greeks or Italians, but the quality is very high.
  - **Spanish olive oil.** Spain is the second largest producer of olive oil in the world. It has several quality controls to make sure that only the best oils are available on the market.

- **Palm.** This is oil from the *dende* or palm nut. It has a light color and is good for salad dressings and sautéing. It does turn rancid quickly, so it must be refrigerated.

- **Peanut oil.** This is almost tasteless oil that can be used for salads, cooking, and frying.

- **Pine seed oil.** This oil is made in France from pine seeds. It is very expensive but has a distinctive flavor that is used in salad dressings.

- **Pumpkin seed oil.** This oil is made in Austria from toasted pumpkin seeds and is used for seasoning vegetables and fish.

- **Rapeseed oil (canola).** This is a general, neutral-flavor oil that can be used for frying, sautéing, and baking. It is a good all-purpose oil.

- **Safflower oil.** This oil is from the safflower and has a bright yellow color. It is the highest in polyunsaturated fats. It is another all-purpose oil that can be used in many different places in the kitchen.

- **Sesame oil.** There are several versions of this oil. The European version is light in color and is a good cooking oil. The Asian version is made from toasted seeds and has a deeper taste. The Middle Eastern seeds have a lighter flavor. This oil can be used for cooking but will add its flavor to the food.

- **Soy oil.** Made from soybeans, it is part of vegetable blend oils.

- **Sunflower oil.** This is made from sunflower seeds and is a good all-purpose oil. It is pale and tasteless, making it ideal for cooking with stronger ingredients.

- **Vegetable oil.** This is normally a blend of different oils. Each manufacture has its own proprietary blend.

- **Walnut oil.** This is oil made from walnuts. The best versions come from the Perigord and Dordogne regions of France. This is a very expensive oil, and it does not store well. Walnut oil has a strong taste, so it is best used in salad dressing and baking.

VINEGARS

Vinegar is a translation from the French *vin aigre*, which means sour wine. Vinegar is made by exposing wine with less than 18 percent alcohol to the air. Bacteria in the air will

 Barrels of balsamic vinegar in storage attic (note cloth used to cover the air holes in the kegs)
Courtesy of Robert Garlough

 Author with balsamic vinegar kegs of succeeding size
Courtesy of Robert Garlough

 **Opening in top of barrel revealing the vinegar**
Courtesy of Robert Garlough

react with the residual yeast to create a *mother*, or a thick layer of mold on the top of the liquid. The mother reacts with the alcohol to change it into acetic acid, with a remnant of the original liquid's taste. Cider, malt (beer), and rice wines can also be used to create vinegars.

The first vinegars were created naturally, but today the yeast and bacteria are carefully added to the base alcohol, and the reaction is carefully controlled. If the process is allowed to proceed naturally, all of the flavor could be lost, with a bitter residue.

Types of Vinegars

There are several types of vinegar available for food service use.

Wine vinegar. Vinegar can be made from red and white wines. Better wines will make better vinegars. Some white wine vinegar is made by adding the mother to the wine in oak barrels, which causes a second chemical reaction. This reaction takes some time, and some manufacturers heat the barrels to speed up the process, resulting in a vinegar that is not as good. Champagne makes a vinegar with a delicate flavor, while sherry makes a caramel-colored, mellow vinegar. Wine vinegars should list their brand and origin in the purchasing specifications.

Balsamic vinegar. This is made from grape juice that is aged in casks. True **Balsamic vinegar** must be aged for at least 12 years and sometimes for decades. Good balsamic vinegars from the Modena region of Italy can be used as after-dinner drinks. This vinegar is very smooth and not as harsh as other varieties.

Cider vinegar. This is made from apple cider, which is apple juice and pulp that is allowed to ferment naturally, and then the mother is added to create the vinegar. Cider vinegar

11.55 Assorted bottles of balsamic vinegars
© Randy Van Dam 2008

has a sharp, strong taste and odor, which can overpower most ingredients. It is used in salad dressing, pickles, and some specialty dishes.

Malt vinegar. This is made from malted barley left-over from beer production. Malt vinegar has a strong grainy tasted, which overpowers salad dressings. It is used for pickling vegetables, in chutneys, and as a condiment for fried fish and chips or French fries.

Spirit vinegar. This is vinegar that is distilled when the mother is converting the alcohol. Spirit vinegar is harsh tasting, too harsh for cooking. It is used for commercial pickling.

People, Places, Things

Making Balsamic Vinegar

The art of vinegar-making has been practiced for over a thousand years, with balsamic vinegar being an ever-present ingredient used by the Greeks and Romans. Made in Modena, Italy for centuries, the unfermented juice (must) of grapes, including Trebbiano, Sauvignon, and Lambrusco, is reduced over heat to approximately half its original volume. "Mother" bacteria and yeast is added to the juice causing fermentation, which turns the syrup-like "must" into acetic acid. The mixture is then aged and flavored for at least 12 years in various wooden barrels, each constructed from oak, acacia, juniper, mulberry, cherry, chestnut, and other flavorful hardwoods. The barrels are reduced in size as the mixture continually evaporates while aging. Vinegars made by this lengthy process receive DOC Modena certification, while cheaper versions of balsamic vinegar are often made in stainless barrels and aged for 6 months or more. (See Figures 11.54 and 11.55.)

11.56 **Assorted vinegars**
© Randy Van Dam 2008

Rice vinegar. This vinegar is made from rice wines. Japanese rice vinegar is mellower than the Chinese versions. Rice vinegar may be white or red and is frequently flavored with sesame, soy sauce, or other flavorings. The Chinese also make a black vinegar from sorghum sugar and grains.

Flavored vinegars. Flavored vinegars are made by adding a flavoring agent to white wine vinegar. Any vegetable, such as onions, garlic, or spices, can be added to the vinegar. The length of time the vegetable is steeped in the oil depends on the strength of flavor desired.

People, Places, Things

Making Flavored Vinegars

- **Making herb vinegar.** Place 2 oz (60 g) fresh, clean herbs in a clean jar with a clamp-top lid. Bring 2 cups (500 ml) vinegar to a boil and pour over the herbs. Seal and leave for at least 2 weeks, shaking the jar occasionally. To store, strain the vinegar into a clean jar or bottle and seal with a cork. (See Figure 11.56.)

- **Making fruit vinegar.** Any soft fruit, particularly summer fruit, can be used to enhance the flavor of vinegar. It is best to use white wine vinegar, which allows the color of the fruit to come through. Herbs and spices, such as peppercorns, cinnamon, or bay leaf, are a flavorful addition. Combine 1 lb (500 g) fresh fruit, such as raspberries, blueberries, apricots, or oranges, and 5 cups (1.25 liters) vinegar in a sterilized glass jar with an airtight seal. Leave in a warm place, for at least 4 weeks, to steep. Shake the jar occasionally. Strain the fruit and vinegar into a saucepan, pressing to extract flavor from the fruit. Add 1 Tbsp sugar, and stir to blend. Place the mixture over low heat and simmer for 10 minutes. Transfer to sterilized jars. For a more attractive presentation, add a few fresh berries or pieces of fruit. (See Figure 11.57.)

11.57   Assorted fruit and herbal vinegars

© Randy Van Dam 2008

CONVENIENCE CORNER PRODUCT EXAMPLES

Herbs, Spices, Minerals, and Flavoring Agents

Company	Website	Products
Heinz	http://www.heinz.com	12/12 oz Vinegar, Malt 4/1 gal Vinegar, Red Wine 24/5 oz Steak Sauce 57
Kikkoman	http://www.kikkoman.com	4/1 gal Soy Sauce 4/1 gal Teriyaki Sauce
Knorr	http://www.knorr.com	2/1 gal Sauce and Marinade Southwest
Kraft	http://www.kraftfoods.com	60/1.5 oz Dressings, Balsamic
Land O Lakes	http://www.Landolakes.com	4/4# Garlic Herb Spread
McCormick	http://www.mccormick.com	6/13 oz Mix, Seasoning, Chili 6/22 oz Seasoning, Mesquite 1# Spice 5 Chinese
O Olive Oil	http://www.ooliveoil.com	2/.5 gal Vinegar, Balsamic
Boyajian	http://www.boyajianinc.com	4/1 gal Vinegar, Cider Sweet
Lee Kum Kee	http://usa.lkk.com	12/7 oz Oil, Chili Hot
Wesson	http://www.wessonoil.com	3/1 Oil, Cottonseed
La Tourangelle	http://www.latourangelle.com	6/8.45 oz Oil, Truffle Block Grape Seed Oil
Fennel Pollen	http://www.fennelpollen.com	4 oz Spice, Fennel Pollen Beef/Lamb
Bombay Spice	http://www.bombayspice.com	6/8 oz Spice, Garlic Pickled

Jennifer Lewis

Place of Birth: Chicago, Illinois

Educational Background and Work Experience

Jennifer Lewis has enjoyed a career rich with opportunities for personal and professional growth. While studying fine arts at Marquette University in Milwaukee, Chef Lewis worked summers as the assistant manager for Chicago's Ritz-Carlton Hotel café. After graduating with a B.A. degree, Chef Lewis continued to work at the Ritz until she enrolled in the culinary arts program at Kendall College. Her internship through Kendall landed her a dual position in both the baking and pastry department and garde manger department of Boston's Ritz-Carlton Hotel. After graduating from Kendall College in 1989 with an A.A.S. degree in culinary arts, Chef Lewis moved to Chicago's Four Seasons Hotel to work in both the garde manger and banquet departments. Chef Lewis has held a number of other chef positions, including in garde manger and pastries departments at Chicago's famed Everest, in banquets at Chicago's Hotel InterContinental, and as owner of the Queen Bee Gourmet deli in Chicago. In addition to her chef positions, she was the import/export coordinator for T. J. Harkin Spice Company and import/export reefer coordinator for Sea-Land Services. Lewis is a chef-consultant for Amazing Edibles Catering in Chicago, an adjunct faculty member teaching baking and pastries at Kendall College, and a culinary educator teaching both baking and pastries and cooking at Lexington College.

Memberships and Career Highlights

Chef Lewis is a member of the Windy City Chapter of the American Culinary Federation (Chicago) and the International Association of Culinary Professionals. In 2002, the Illinois Department of Education certified her as a vocational education teacher of culinary arts. Chef Lewis shared her love of baking with the general public for a number of years with her monthly column, "Baking Bits," in Chicago's *Daily Southtown Press.* Her passion for teaching was honored by her peers at Lexington College when Chef Lewis was named the Educator of the Year in 2005, the same year she became a Certified Hospitality Educator. The next year, in October 2006, Chef Lewis achieved the level of ACF Certified Culinary Educator. In

2007, Chef Lewis was granted an education scholarship by the Charlie Trotter Culinary Education Foundation to assist her in the pursuit of an M.A. in education from DePaul University.

Passions with the Food Service Industry

"Many traditional chefs have not worked in 'front of the house' positions or even in other trades. My managerial and customer relations–oriented jobs have allowed me to share perspectives with my students that are somewhat unique. Food is my love, from the kitchen, yet at the same time I can help motivate students through teaching to understand the importance of food from a managerial viewpoint. Often students beginning in this industry do not see some of their early job experiences as 'long-term' assets to their careers. I try

It Happened to Me...

Courtesy Jennifer Lewis

"I had been working very hard as a line cook, banquet cook, pastry cook, and in garde manager—and feeling very burnt out. On a whim, I decided to take an offer to be involved with shipping perishable and temperature-controlled cargo known as 'reefers.' Reefers are 20- and 40-foot containers, with 90 percent of the cargo being food. I thought ... sure, I could do this!

Actually the job was very exciting with a lot of pressure from shippers, importers, and exporters. After all, shipping 40,000 pounds of beef to Japan on any afternoon was no small matter. My sanitation training came into play many times when customers tried to pull some very scary tricks—my radar would always go up: bacteria! Temperature Danger Zone!

One of my shippers was involved with spices, and I frequently worked with them on filing tariffs (in laymen's terms, filing rates) for imports to the U.S. from countries with which the customer had never done business. My specialty was South and Central America. I knew these shipping routes and tariffs well—so well, in fact, that I could file tariffs quickly and procure containers overseas even faster. Some shippers came to our company because we could move so much more product than the competition!

All of my multitasking experiences as a line cook coupled with the stress endured while working the hot line had prepared me for the erratic shipping business. Whether it was plating for 400 guests or filing rates for spice importers, I now know I can be organized and work under a lot of pressure. The epiphany I experienced was to realize that the skills that are built and the confidence that is gained through the many positions held during the course of a career become one's allies in future campaigns. It is important to take each job seriously and to realize that a fulfilling career is built over years of varied work experiences."

to bridge these life experiences, knowing that I have personally taken a variety of food experiences for use in my everyday work."

Advice to a Chef or Buyer

"Understand the 'big picture'! As you work and hold positions throughout your career, take note from where and from whom your employers purchase their food and supplies. When you are preparing food, notice the quality and consistency (or not) of the product being received. Can this purveyor meet your employer's or your own requests for timeliness ... prices ... specs? Be sure to note from where this product originates; this is incredibly important.

Chefs must be vigilant to where their products are being grown, processed, and handled.

As an importer for a spice company, my customers asked these questions every single time. Topics such as ... Quality: Did the sesame seeds "stick" to the product? Price/quantity: Could the supplier fill the order of ten 40-foot containers in 3 weeks? How long would it take to get to the customer? Believe it or not ... even if it was coming from Venezuela, the customer had time constraints. Product: Cinnamon, an important spice, but labor intensive and shipped from very remote islands. Does their product have the proper taste? These are examples of the relevant questions by customers using the product.

Listen to what is going on around you! The food business is incredibly exciting; know that you can be a contributor to a thriving and important world."

Key Words and Concepts

---

balsamic vinegar	flavoring agents	minerals	spices
cold-pressed oils	herbs	smoke point	vinegar
cooking oils			

Chapter in Review

The following exercises are provided to help the reader understand and apply the contents of this chapter. They may be completed individually or in a classroom environment.

REVIEW QUESTIONS

a. Explain the differences among spices, herbs, and minerals.

b. Describe the benefits of cold-pressing olives to make oil.

c. Discuss the smoke point of oils.

d. Identify various spices and their source countries.

e. Identify the herbs and spices that comprise the common spice blends, and identify their uses.

INDIVIDUAL ACTIVITIES

a. **Web based:** Using the Internet, research sources for buying different fresh herbs, flavoring agents, salts, flavored oils, and vinegars.

b. **Experiential:** Visit a local herb farmer and learn how herbs are grown, harvested, and dried.

c. **Critical thinking:** Identify the best oils to use for different culinary purposes, including deep frying, sautéing, pan frying, flavoring foods, and making salad dressing.

GROUP ACTIVITIES

a. **Lab experience:** Create a variety of flavored oils and vinegars.

b. **Classroom action:** Divide the class into small groups, and have the groups identify as many herbs and spices as they can remember.

CHAPTER

12

© iStockphoto.com

Bakery Supplies

"Other things are just food, but chocolate's chocolate!"
PATRICK SKENE CATLING

After reading this chapter, you will be able to:

◎ List the basic ingredients used in baking.

◎ Explain how starches gelatinize, and explain their use as thickening agents.

◎ Describe the process for incorporating cornstarch as a thickening agent.

◎ Identify and discuss the use of chemical leavening agents.

◎ Describe the parts of a wheat kernel and their functions, including the bran, endosperm, and germ.

◎ Distinguish among the varieties of wheat.

◎ Summarize the different types of flours and their uses.

◎ Identify the different types of fats and their properties.

◎ Identify the different types of sweeteners.

◎ Explain the chocolate manufacturing process.

◎ Identify the various types of chocolate.

Introduction

In addition to paying close attention to fresh meats, produce, and dairy products, buyers must pay sufficiently close attention to the dry goods they procure, as well. This chapter focuses on the thickening agents, leavening agents, flours, fats, sweeteners, and cacao products commonly used by food service operators.

Basic Baking Ingredients

Most bakery and pastry recipes use the same ingredients, only varying in ratios or different methods of preparation. The following ingredients are fundamental to most food service operations, and chefs and purchasing agents should be familiar with them.

THICKENING AND BINDING AGENTS

Thickening agents are used to bind and thicken watery substances like sauces and fillings. The process involves the **gelatinization** of starches, whereby the starch granules swell as they absorb moisture when placed in liquid and heated. Gelatinization occurs gradually over a range of temperatures (150°F–212°F, or 66°C–100°C); as the granules continue to absorb moisture, the mixture thickens. The ideal mixture should be free of lumps, have a clean flavor without a starchy aftertaste, and be of the correct consistency. There are several types of thickeners available on the market (see Figure 12.1):

Agar. Agar is derived from seaweed, and is often substituted by vegans for standard gelatin, which is made from animal tissue. It is used to thicken soups, sauces, jellies, and anmisu, a Japanese dessert.

Arrowroot. Arrowroot is a starch that is made from the maranta plant. It will thicken soups and sauces but does not clear a cloudy liquid. Arrowroot does not change the taste of sauces, which makes it handy for delicately flavored items. Arrowroot is also used to make sauces for people who are allergic to the other thickening agents.

Cornstarch. This is derived from the endosperm of the corn kernel and is frequently used in puddings, soups, and sauces. Cornstarch is readily available, and most cooks are familiar with its use. Cornstarch does tend to lump, so it must be handled properly. It is combined with a cold liquid to make a thin paste before it is added to the hot sauces. Cornstarch does breakdown if it is stirred for too long or if it is heated for long periods of time. Cornstarch will clarify cloudy soups and sauces. Some baking recipes including

12.1 Assorted thickening agents (Top row L to R: guar gum, myrrh gum, Arabic gum, xanthan gum; Bottom row L to R: fruit pectin, pearl tapioca, cornstarch, agar)
© Randy Van Dam 2008

cakes and cookies will substitute cornstarch for part of the flour. This will create a baked good that has a finer texture and crumb.

Gelatin. Gelatin, made from animal and fish bones, is available as sheets, granules, or powder. There are two types on the market: instant, which is added to the food, and the regular type, which must be soaked in water before use. There are kosher and halal-certified gelatins, which are made from specific animals or parts of animals to comply with these religious customs. Gelatin is used to thicken food and fillings, and it stabilizes temperature-sensitive items such as ice cream.

Guar gum. Also known as guaran, it is made from the guar bean shrub. It is sold as a coarse to fine powder. It is used as a binder to soak up excess water in ice creams, commercial sauces, and salad dressings. Guar gum is rarely used in a food service kitchen but is present in many commercially prepared products.

Pectin. Pectin is a thickener made from certain fruits and is used to make jelly and jam. Some fruits such as apples have a high level of pectin naturally, so very little is added during processing. Other fruits such as strawberries have very little natural pectin, so it must be added for the jam to set properly. Pectin is readily available through grocery stores and wholesalers.

Tapioca. Tapioca is granules made from the dried cassava root. It is used to make tapioca pudding, which is thickened when the granules rehydrate with the liquid. Tapioca is also used to thicken some sauces. There is a related form, called cassava or tapioca flour, which consists of the granules ground into a fine powder.

Xanthan gum. This is a commercial thickener found in frozen foods, beverages, salad dressings, and sauces.

LEAVENING AGENTS

A **leavening agent** is a substance that creates air. Later, this air is trapped by the moist flour and causes the dough to rise. Leavening agents need a reactor such as moisture, heat, or an acid to start the process. After the air is produced and the dough is larger, the dough is baked, which sets the form of the item and traps the air, creating the crumb and texture of the baked good. There are several types of leavening agents available:

- **Baking powder.** Baking powder is a fine white substance that reacts in the presence of liquid and heat, releasing carbon dioxide, which leavens dough. It is made up of a mixture of alkaline and acid salts. Baking powder was perfected toward the end of the nineteenth century, shortly after the invention of baking soda (Figure 12.2a). A crude form of baking powder was used in the United States around 1790, but it had a bitter aftertaste. The first baking powder containing cream of tartar was developed around 1835; it was a mixture of sodium bicarbonate and the residue of cream of tartar from barrels in which wine

was made. This kind of baking powder was first sold commercially in 1850. At the end of the nineteenth century, the cream of tartar was replaced with the acid salts monocalcium phosphate, aluminum sulfate, and sodium sulfate.

A much more effective leavening agent than baking soda, baking powder reacts with the wet ingredients at lower temperatures and has no aftertaste, unless an excessive amount is used. Fast-acting, slow-acting, double-action, and low-sodium baking powder are among the most widely available varieties:

- **Fast-acting baking powder** contains monohydrous monocalcium phosphate. It begins to produce carbon dioxide as soon as it is combined with liquid. Because more than 90 percent of the carbon dioxide is released within the first few minutes, dough containing fast-acting baking powder has to be prepared quickly and baked immediately to ensure that it retains the gas and rises as desired.

- **Slow-acting baking powder** is made by combining anhydrous monocalcium phosphate with sodium phosphate and aluminum phosphate, or with sodium sulfate and aluminum sulfate. The phosphate is in the form of tiny particles coated with an insoluble substance that makes them react more slowly in the presence of liquid. Most of the carbon dioxide is produced after the phosphate is heated in the oven. Because virtually no gas is produced before the dough is baked, dough made with slow-acting baking powder can be stored in the refrigerator overnight.

- **Double-action baking powder** contains two acids that react with liquid ingredients at different speeds: monohydrous monocalcium phosphate, which reacts very quickly, mainly at room temperature, and a mixture of aluminum phosphate and sodium phosphate (or aluminum sulfate and sodium sulfate), which reacts very slowly and not until it is heated in the oven. This kind of baking powder can be used with dough that has to be refrigerated before it is baked.

- **Low-sodium baking powder** contains potassium salts rather than sodium salts; it is ideal for people on low-sodium diets.

  Baking powder should be stored at room temperature, away from heat and humidity. It can be less effective if stored for a long period of time. To ensure that it is still active, pour 4 to 5 tablespoons of boiling water over 1 ½ teaspoons of baking powder. If it is still fresh, it will bubble vigorously; if it is less than fresh, only a few bubbles will form or there will be no reaction whatsoever.

- **Baking soda.** A leavening agent, baking soda is a fine white powder that consists of a mixture of alkaline salts. It has been in common use since the middle of the nineteenth century, when it revolutionized culinary

Baking powder (left) and baking soda (right)
© Randy Van Dam 2008

12.2b **Active dry yeast (left) and compressed yeast (right)**
© Randy Van Dam 2008

practices by making it easier to produce leavened baked goods. It was partially responsible for the boom in the production of commercial bakery products like cakes, cookies, and donuts. It also expanded the range of ingredients used in breads and pastries by making it possible to use flours containing less gluten and to incorporate ingredients like nuts, wheat germ, cheese, and raisins.

When dissolved in water and heated, sodium bicarbonate decomposes into sodium carbonate, water, and carbon dioxide (which is what makes dough rise). Although the residue of sodium bicarbonate can create a bitter aftertaste, the production of sodium bicarbonate can be entirely avoided by using baking soda in combination with an acid ingredient, which will transform all of the bicarbonate of soda into water or carbon dioxide. It is thus important to ensure that dough made with baking soda is sufficiently acidic.

Molasses, honey, malt, fruit or fruit juice, chocolate, cocoa, lemon juice, yogurt, sour cream, buttermilk, and vinegar are the acidic ingredients most frequently added to dough. Even when used in combination with acidic ingredients, baking soda can still create an aftertaste because it is a rather stable compound that has to be heated to very high temperatures before it will decompose.

- **Cream of tartar.** A fine white powder used as a stabilizer, cream of tartar is a by-product of the wine fermentation process. Crystals containing potassium bitartrate form on the interior walls of the barrels in which wine is fermented. The tartaric acid, produced when grapes ferment, is first isolated in the form of potassium salt. The crystals are then ground, purified, dehydrated, and reground to the powder known as cream of tartar. Since about 1835, cream of tartar has been combined with baking soda to be used as dry yeast. Cream of tartar reacts rapidly in the presence of baking soda and liquid, which makes

dough rise very quickly. However, dough that is leavened in this way begins to lose volume if it is not baked immediately; for this reason, manufacturers have developed dry yeasts containing slower-acting agents like monocalcium phosphate.

- **Yeast.** Yeast is a microscopic fungus, usually a unicellular organism that is used primarily to make bread. Scientists have identified 39 different yeast geniuses, comprising more than 350 species. The most commonly used species of yeast is *Saccharomyces cerevisiae,* which is also known as "brewer's yeast" (it is a by-product of the beer-fermentation process) or "baker's yeast."

Live yeast is sold fresh and compressed (cake), or dried (see Figure 12.2b). Dry yeast can consist of a single yeast or a mixture of several yeasts; often obtained as a byproduct of the fermentation of alcohol, it is also grown specifically for use as a raising agent. Compressed (cake) yeast is usually sold by weight and should contain 70 percent moisture. Dry yeast is available in regular or fast-acting varieties, either in grains or as a powder. Be sure to check the expiry date on the package.

Fresh compressed yeast should not be refrigerated for longer than two weeks. When stored for too long, it becomes inactive and starts to turn brown. Prolonged refrigeration can diminish its effectiveness as a raising agent. Dry yeast can be stored for a longer period of time, up to a year, if is refrigerated or stored in a cool place.

FLOURS

Flour is milled or ground wheat, rice, cereal grains, nuts, lentils, beans, or vegetables. Normally flour is made from wheat, and flour made from other substances usually has the root source included in the name, such as rye flour, buckwheat flour, and chickpea flour.

It is believed that the first coarse flour, which included the germ and bran, was made some 75,000 years ago by first roasting and then pounding the edible grains between two stones. Sometime between this early period and the beginning of agriculture (10,000 years ago), humans made the first dough from cereal flour and baked it on a heated stone, thus creating the first form of bread. In the early days, the grains were separated from the harvested ears of wheat using stones, after which they were ground by hand. Later, cows crushed the grains. The invention of the millstone and the water wheel greatly improved production, clearing the way for the art of bread making.

The Industrial Revolution gave rise to gigantic industrial mills (see Figure 12.3 and Figure 12.4). During the nineteenth century, increasingly sophisticated machines, such as steel rollers, gradually replaced millstones, which improved the grinding and pulverization operations as well as allowed for better separation of the germ and bran (see Figure 12.5a and Figure 12.5b).

In modern day roller mills, flour is produced by separating the endosperm from the other primary components of the wheat kernel and reducing it to a powdery texture. Protein quantity and baking characteristics are important considerations when selecting flour for baking.

Wheat flour has five components: fat, starches, proteins, water, and minerals. The quality of the end product depends on the flour used. There are three types of wheat flour available:

- **Hard wheat.** This wheat has smaller kernels and a higher protein and gluten count than the other two types. It is ideal for bread making as the high protein level helps the dough to form and hold its shape. The protein levels of this flour will vary depending on the variety of flour used. The two most popular are *hard red* and *hard white* (see Figure 12.6). Hard flour will have protein levels of 15 to 16 percent, which is higher than the recommended 12 percent for bread making.

- **Soft wheat.** Soft wheat has a larger kernel that is easier to break open. Soft wheat makes flour with very little protein or gluten. This is ideal for quick breads, cookies, and cakes. The protein levels range from 9 to 11 percent.

- **Durum wheat.** This is a different species from the hard and soft wheat. Durham wheat has high protein content, but it will not make a good loaf of bread. Instead, it is used to make pasta, macaroni, and noodles.

Each wheat variety has its own blend of nutrients that give it certain properties. For example, soft wheat

12.3 **King Milling flour mill**
Courtesy of King Milling

contains little gluten and is very well suited to cake making, while hard wheat has a higher gluten (higher protein) content, making it more suitable for bread making (see Table 12.1).

The baking qualities of all types of flour are improved if the flour is stored for several weeks after milling; during this aging stage, a natural process of oxidation causes the flour to become whiter. To hasten the maturing process and to control the end results, the flour industry now adds bleaching agents such as chlorine dioxide and maturing agents such as potassium bromated, depending on the type of flour. To compensate for the loss of nutrients caused by the removal of the bran and germ during milling, various vitamins (thiamine, riboflavin, niacin) and minerals (iron) are added to the flour to fortify it. This practice is mandatory for white flour in Canada and the United States.

The wheat berry consists of three parts:

- The **endosperm** (kernel) is the largest part of the grain, and it is made up of starch.

- The **bran** is a fibrous layer, which has many vitamins and minerals that feed the wheat berry.

- The **germ** is at the lower end of the berry and contains the seeds for new plants. This part of the berry has the most fat and the most vitamins and minerals. Because of the fat, it is highly perishable. (See Figure 12.7a and Figure 12.7b.)

The bran and germ are sold separately to cereal and health food companies, while the remaining midlings are used primarily as livestock feed. Refined flour and refined

12.4 **The flour milling process**
Courtesy North American Millers' Association.

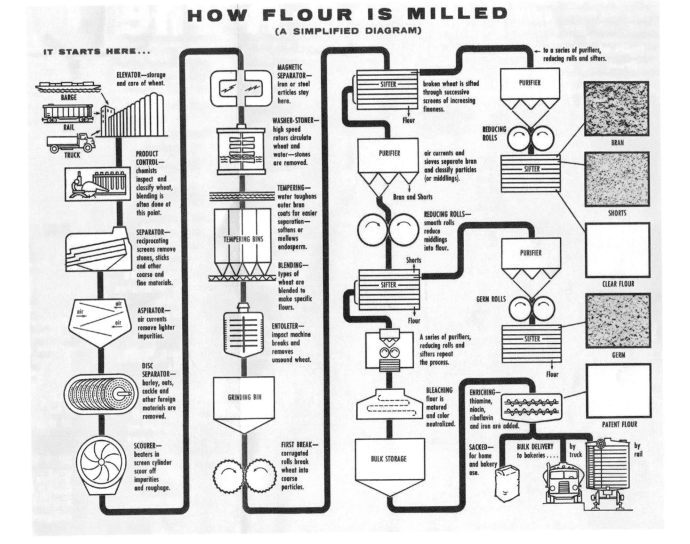

HOW FLOUR IS MILLED
(A SIMPLIFIED DIAGRAM)

IT STARTS HERE...

ELEVATOR—storage and care of wheat.

BARGE

RAIL

TRUCK

PRODUCT CONTROL—chemists inspect and classify wheat, blending is often done at this point.

SEPARATOR—reciprocating screens remove stones, sticks and other coarse and fine materials.

ASPIRATOR—air currents remove lighter impurities.

DISC SEPARATOR—barley, oats, cockle and other foreign materials are removed.

SCOURER—beaters in screen cylinder scour off impurities and roughage.

MAGNETIC SEPARATOR—iron or steel articles stay here.

WASHER-STONER—high speed rotors circulate wheat and water—stones are removed.

TEMPERING—water toughens outer bran coats for easier separation—softens or mellows endosperm.

TEMPERING BINS

BLENDING—types of wheat are blended to make specific flours.

ENTOLETER—impact machine breaks and removes unsound wheat.

GRINDING BIN

FIRST BREAK—corrugated rolls break wheat into coarse particles.

SIFTER

broken wheat is sifted through successive screens of increasing fineness.

Flour

PURIFIER

air currents and sieves separate bran and classify particles (or middlings).

Bran and Shorts

REDUCING ROLLS—smooth rolls reduce middlings into flour.

Shorts

SIFTER

Flour

A series of purifiers, reducing rolls and sifters repeat the process.

BLEACHING—flour is matured and color neutralized.

BULK STORAGE

to a series of purifiers, reducing rolls and sifters.

PURIFIER

REDUCING ROLLS

SIFTER

BRAN

SHORTS

PURIFIER

CLEAR FLOUR

GERM ROLLS

SIFTER

GERM

Flour

ENRICHING—thiamine, niacin, riboflavin and iron are added.

PATENT FLOUR

SACKED—for home and bakery use.

BULK DELIVERY to bakeries . . . .

by truck

by rail

12.5a **A pair of roller mills**
Courtesy of King Milling

12.5b **Wheat going through rollers**
Courtesy of King Milling

12.6 Different wheat berries and durum (Clockwise L to R: Hard Red Winter, Hard Red Spring, Soft Red Winter, Soft White Winter, Durum)

© Randy Van Dam 2008

TABLE 12.1 Table of Protein Content of Various Flours

Type of Flour	Protein (%)	Uses
Instant flour	2	Thickening sauces and gravies
Cake	7–9.5	Cakes
Pastry	7.5–12	Pie crusts, biscuits, cookies
All-purpose	10–13	General baking, egg pasta, noodles
Bread	12–15	Yeast bread, pasta
Durham wheat	13–14	Pasta
Whole wheat	13–14	Yeast bread
High gluten	14–15	Yeast bread, bagels
Vital wheat gluten	40–80	Added to weak flours for strengthening

flour products have better keeping qualities because, without the oily germ, they turn rancid less quickly. They are ground to a different fineness, depending on the need for the finished product. Grains are ground into a coarse product called *meal*. Continued grinding produces silky *flour*. Figure 12.8a shows the wheat kernel, cracked wheat, and wheat flour. Figure 12.8b shows corn that is first coarse meal, then medium meal, and finally flour.

There are many different types of flours available in the kitchen (see Figure 12.9a and Figure 12.9b). The most popular are:

All-purpose flour. This flour is a blend of hard and soft wheat flours. It can be used to make everything from breads to cakes, but other flours will make a better product. All-purpose flour is best for establishments that need a little bit of flour for different purposes.

12.7a **Diagram of the wheat berry**
Courtesy North American Millers' Association.

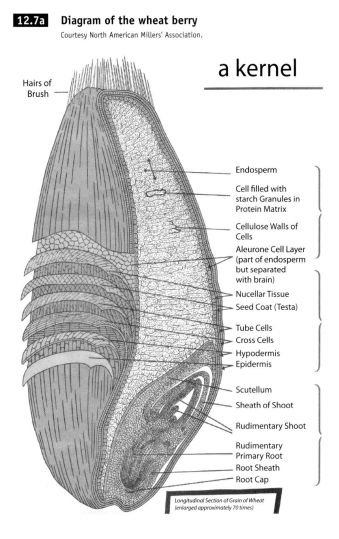

a kernel

Hairs of Brush

Endosperm

Cell filled with starch Granules in Protein Matrix

Cellulose Walls of Cells

Aleurone Cell Layer (part of endosperm but separated with brain)

Nucellar Tissue

Seed Coat (Testa)

Tube Cells

Cross Cells

Hypodermis

Epidermis

Scutellum

Sheath of Shoot

Rudimentary Shoot

Rudimentary Primary Root

Root Sheath

Root Cap

Longitudinal Section of Grain of Wheat (enlarged approximately 70 times)

12.7b **Piles of wheat bran, endosperm, germ, and whole berries**
© Randy Van Dam 2008

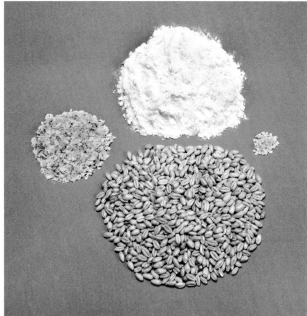

Bread flour. This is made from hard wheat and has a very high gluten content. It is used to make breads.

Cake flour. This is made from soft flour and has a very low protein and gluten content. Cake flour is highly refined and very soft to the touch. It makes a cake with a fine, tender crumb.

Gluten flour. This is high-gluten, starch-free wheat flour. It is made from high-protein hard wheat flour. Gluten flour has 45 percent gluten mixed with white or wheat flour. It is used in bread making and added to rye, barley, or oat flour to help it rise.

Graham flour. This is wheat flour made from whole wheat with an intact bran. Graham flour will have flakes of the ground bran in the flour.

Pastry flour. This is similar to cake flour, made from soft wheat with a low gluten level. The biggest difference between pastry and cake flour is that cake flour is further milled and refined.

Self-rising flour. This is all-purpose flour with a leavening agent such as baking soda added to it. Self-rising flour is used to save time when making quick breads. One cup of self-rising flour has 1½ teaspoons of the leavening agent and ½ teaspoon of salt.

Unbleached flour. Most "white" flour is wheat flour that has been chemically bleached to turn white. This chemically bleached flour makes a lighter crumb and a lighter colored product. Unbleached flour is wheat flour that is milled repeatedly to remove the bran from the flour. It is darker than white flour and is lighter than wheat flour. Because there is no additional chemical added to the flour, it has a natural wheat flavor.

Whole wheat flour. This is made by milling the entire grain (endosperm, germ, and bran). It is darker in color and has a nutty taste. Some whole wheat flours are stone ground. Whole wheat flour can be substituted for white flour in most recipes, but it will result in a darker, denser product with more flavor and nutrients. Whole wheat flour is perishable and must be stored in a refrigerator or freezer.

Refined flours should be stored in cool, dry, dark conditions, away from insects and rodents. Unrefined flours must be stored in the refrigerator or freezer to keep the fats in the grains from spoiling.

12.8a Wheat kernel, cracked wheat, and wheat flour

Figures 12.8a–.9b © Randy Van Dam 2008

12.8b Coarse cornmeal, medium cornmeal, and corn flour

12.9a Assorted wheat flours

12.9b Assorted other flours

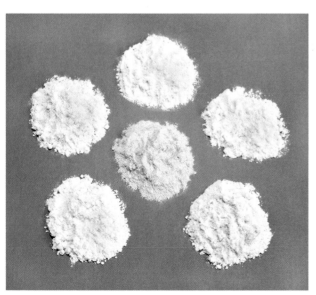

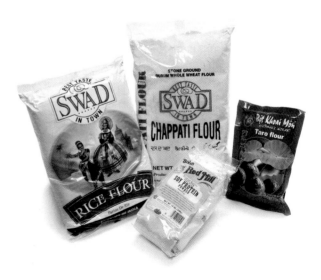

Fats

Fats have a myriad of functions in the kitchen. They add flavor, they tenderize baked goods, and they provide texture and richness. **Fats** act as a preservative (think of tuna in oil, or goat cheese packed in oil), and they are essential in most marinades. Fats are used in almost all cooking techniques, including frying, baking, roasting, pastry making, and sauce making. This category includes solid fats such as butter, lard, and margarine and liquid fats such as oils.

Before choosing a fat, you should consider the following four characteristics that will make a difference in the flavor of the final product:

- **Flavor.** Unrefined oils have the most flavor because they are pressed from the nut or seed without heat. Refined oils have very little flavor and are used when you don't want the fat to add taste to the item.

- **Texture.** Oils and fat help create the texture or crumb on the item. Fats make the pie crust flaky and the cookies tender.

- **Leavening.** Some fats will help with the leavening process. In cream puffs, the fat melts and turns into steam, which is trapped by the dough layers. In other recipes, creaming a solid fat will create pockets that the chemical leavening agent can then fill with air.

- **Tenderize.** Fat coats starch molecules, which prevents gluten from forming. This helps to make cakes, cookies, and desserts tender. To start this process, a solid fat is creamed or beaten. Later, the flour is added and combined to make a batter. Oils are not used in baking, except for quick breads that are baked immediately after mixing so that the gluten does not have time to set.

Liquid oils were covered in Chapter 11, "Herbs, Spices, Minerals, and Flavoring Agents," and the most common solid fats in baking are butter, margarine, processed shortening, and lard.

Butter

Butter is made from the cream of cows or sometimes goats. By law, butter must contain 80 percent milk fat by weight. It is made by separating the cream from the milk, and then the cream is churned or shaken until it turns into a solid. The solids are then formed into blocks (see Figure 12.10). The market types of butter include (see Figure 12.11a):

- **Salted:** This butter has a little bit of salt added to it during the churning process.

- **Unsalted:** This butter has no added salt or other flavoring agents added. The taste is tarter than salted butter. It is used

in baking for pie crusts and cakes where the additional salt affects the chemical reactions.

- **Whipped butter:** This is salted or unsalted butter that is whipped with air so that it is light and fluffy. It is packaged in tubs and is used as a spread. Normally, whipped butter is not used in baking as it is less dense than regular butter and will not work as well. Butter that is whipped in the kitchen is used as a base for frostings.

- **Butter-margarine mixtures:** These are butter products with margarine added to them. They are used as table spreads. If the fat content is high enough, they can be used for baking.

12.10 **Diagram of butter-making process**

Courtesy Professor Douglas Goff, Dairy Science and Technology Education, University of Guelph, Canada

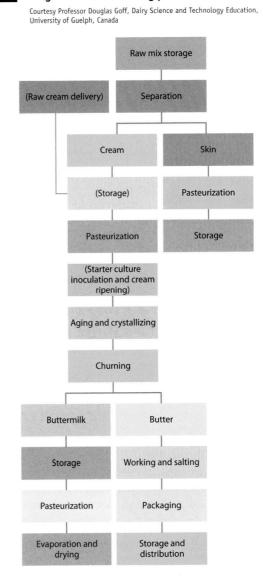

- **Cultured butter:** This is buttered made from cultured cream. Cultured cream has yeast added to it to make it tangier. Cultured butter is popular in Europe and is now available in major markets in the United States. It is used to finish sauces and for some baking.

- **Clarified butter/ghee:** This butter is melted with the milk solids separated out. It is the pure fat of the cream and remains in a liquid form at room temperature. It has a high burning point, so it can be used for sautéing and baking. It adds a nutty taste to baked goods.

Butter is rated on a scale of 1 to 100, which takes into consideration the flavor, color, salt content, and body of butter. This government scale grades the butter as AA, A, B, or C. Butter with a grade of 93 or higher is rated as AA. B and C grade products are used for commercial baking and food processing.

Butter should be kept at 40°F (4.4°C) to keep the quality and prevent spoilage. It can be stored for about 1 month. Butter can be frozen. If it is kept at 20 to 30°F (−6.6 to −1.1°C), it can be stored for up to 4 months. At lower temperatures such as −10°F (−23.3°C), it can be kept for a year.

Margarine

Margarine is any solid or soft substitute for butter. Margarine is made from partially hydrogenated vegetable oils. Margarine products cannot be labeled as "butter," but they can be called "butter substitutes." Most margarine is sold in one of the three following forms (see Figure 12.11b):

- **Hard:** This is sold in a block form that resembles butter sticks. Hard margarines normally have some animal fat or shortening in them, and they are used for baking.

- **Traditional:** These margarines are softer and can be spread on bread right out of the refrigerator. There is a wide variety of margarines in this category, some which are made from vegetable oils and some from shortening. These margarines are used for table spreads, cooking, and baking.

- **Soft:** These resemble whipped butter. They are very soft and have a high percentage of air in their composition. Soft margarines are used for table spreads. They should not be used for baking or cooking.

As mentioned earlier in the chapter, there are some forms of margarine with real butter. These blends have the taste of butter but with the lower cost of margarine. They are available in the hard, traditional, and soft forms. Additionally, for the vegan market, soy margarines are available (see Figure 12.11c). Some margarines contain trace amounts of whey, casein and caseinate, and lactose, making them unsuitable for those seeking non-dairy products. Soy margarines are considered vegan non-dairy spreads. Margarine should be stored in the refrigerator or freezer. It will keep for the same time as butter.

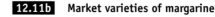

12.11a   Market varieties of butter

Figures 12.11a–c © Randy Van Dam 2008

12.11b   Market varieties of margarine

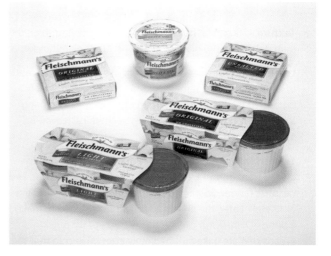

12.11c   Soy margarine

Processed Shortening

Vegetable shortening is made by forcing hydrogen atoms into unsaturated fatty acids. The result is a solid fat at room temperature. Vegetable shortening is used in baking to make crusts and can be substituted for butter or margarine in baking recipes. However, there will be a difference in the taste and texture if shortening is used instead of butter.

Lard

Lard is rendered and clarified pork fat. Lard's quality is based on the rendering process and where the fat came from. The best lards come from fat around the kidneys. Lard is normally sold after it has been bleached and processed. Some lard is hydrogenated to make it a quality product.

Lard makes very tender and flaky biscuits, pastries, and pie crusts. It can be substituted for butter in more baking recipes, but you should decrease the lard by 20 to 25 percent. It is also used for frying and sautéing. Unprocessed lard may be tied to pieces of meat to add more flavor when roasting. Depending on how much processing it has had, lard should be stored at room temperature or in the refrigerator. Check the box for storage requirements. (See Figure 12.12 for various butter and butter substitute products.)

12.12 Assorted market varieties of butter and butter substitutes (stick margarine, stick butter, whipped margarine, lard, whipped butter, vegetable shortening, and butter flavored shortening)

© Randy Van Dam 2008

Sweeteners

Sweeteners are flavors that add sweet to any item. Once rare, sugar has become the most popular food additive. Some of the more frequently used sweeteners include the following.

Brown sugar. Brown sugar is made by adding molasses to white sugar. (See Figure 12.13.)

Unrefined brown sugar. "Unrefined" sugar is really "less refined," in that it has not been completely stripped down to a pure white crystal that is all sweetness and no flavor. Unrefined brown sugars come from sugarcane and are at an intermediate processing step on their way to white sugar. This form of sugar is not readily available for use in kitchens. (See Figure 12.14.)

Coconut sugar (palm sugar). This is sugar made from the sap of the coconut palm. It has a sharper flavor with the sweet. Because it is a raw sugar, it is sold in blocks either dried or moist—with some water added. (See Figure 12.15.)

Confectioner's sugar. This is white sugar that has been ground into a fine powder. There are three levels of confectioner's sugar, including 10X (0.010 mm), 6X (0.060 mm), and icing sugar (0.024 mm). Most confectioner's sugar contains cornstarch to prevent lumps or caking. (See Figure 12.16.)

Corn syrup (Karo® syrup). This is a sweet syrup made from corn. There is a variation known as high-fructose corn syrup (HFCS) where the glucose in the corn was changed to fructose. HFCS is very sweet and very cheap, so it can be added to virtually every commercially prepared food. Corn syrup is used in making candies, desserts, and fondants. (See Figure 12.17.)

Dextrose is another form of sweetener made from corn products. It is used in commercial dressings and sauces and is not available for use in a kitchen. (See Figure 12.18.)

Golden syrup. This is a by-product of sugar refining. It is made from syrup that is left behind when the sugar crystals

12.13   **Light and dark brown sugar**

Figures 12.13–.16 © Randy Van Dam 2008

12.14   **Unrefined brown sugar**

12.15   **Coconut (palm) sugar**

12.16   **Confectioner's sugar**

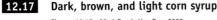

12.17 Dark, brown, and light corn syrup
Figures 12.17–.20 © Randy Van Dam 2008

are forming. Golden syrup will remain liquid and inhibits the formation of sugar crystals. It is used to make fondants and pulled candies where flexibility is needed. It is also added to hard candies to prevent sugar crystals from forming. (See Figure 12.19.)

Blue agave syrup (nectar). Originally, this was a cheap sweetener made from the by-products of tequila making. As the demand for tequila grew, this sweetener became more expensive. It is sometimes used as a sweetener for diabetics. (See Figure 12.20.)

Maple syrup. This comes from maple tree sap that has been boiled down and filtered. It takes approximately 40 gallons of sap to produce one gallon of syrup. The resultant maple syrup must reach a minimum 66 brix, meaning at least 66 percent sugar by weight with a maximum of 34 percent water. Maple syrup is produced only in eastern Canada and the northeastern United States. Canadian maple syrup has three quality levels and is classified according to its color: Canada #1, which is a light-flavored, thin syrup used as a sauce for pancakes and waffles, Canada #2, which is amber colored and a thicker syrup that is used for pancakes and baking, and Canada #3 which is the darkest form of syrup. It works best for cooking. The northeastern American states of Vermont, New Hampshire, New York, as well as Michigan, also produce excellent maple syrups. All U.S. states use the same USDA color standards, but sometimes vary their terminology (see Figure 12.21a). If the word "flavored" appears on the label, then it is artificially created from chemicals and corn syrup. (See Figure 12.21a.)

Maple sugar. This is maple syrup boiled until it crystallizes and then is poured into molds. It is sold as a candy or it may be pulverized into a powder. Maple sugar has a strong flavor and is used in baking to add a maple flavor to baked items.

12.18 Dextrose

12.19 Golden syrup

12.20 Organic blue agave syrup

12.21a **Maple Syrup Classifications Color and Grade Equivalents**

Michigan, New York, New Hampshire Syrup Grades	Vermont Syrup Grades	Canadian Syrup Grades
Grade A Light Amber	Fancy	Number 1 Extra Light
Grade A Medium Amber	Medium Amber	Number 1 Light Grade A
Grade A Dark Amber	Dark Amber	Number 1 Medium Grade A
Grade B (used for reprocessing)	Grade B	Number 2 Amber
	Commercial Quality	Number 3 Dark
Substandard Quality	Substandard Quality	Number 1 Extra Light

12.21b **Maple syrup**

Figures 12.21b–.24 © Randy Van Dam 2008

12.22 **Molasses L to R: blackstrap, robust, original (light)**

12.23 **Raw sugar**   **12.24** **Raw sugar**

Molasses (treacle). Molasses, a by-product of sugar production, is a liquid with a strong bitter aftertaste. Molasses comes in various grades, from blackstrap, which comes from the earliest stage in sugar production and is dark with a deep flavor, to lighter grades that have lots of sugar crystals and a light flavor. When using molasses, make sure you are using the right quality for the recipe. (See Figure 12.22.)

Raw sugar. This is produced during the first stage of white sugar. It is brown and has a larger grain and a nutty flavor. True raw sugar is not sold in the United States as it may contain mold, insect parts, or bacteria. Instead, raw sugar with the impurities filtered out is sold and is labeled *muscavado, turbinado,* or *demerera* sugar. (See Figure 12.23.)

Rock crystal sugar. This is huge crystal sugar made by soaking a string in sugar water. As the water evaporates, the sugar clings to the string. Later, it can be cut off the string and used as a garnish. Some rock sugar is set on sticks and is used as a swivel stick for drinks. (See Figure 12.24.)

White sugar. This is derived from the juice of sugarcane or sugar beets. As the sugar is extracted, various by-products such as raw sugar and molasses are made. Sugar is also called sucrose, table sugar, beet sugar, cane sugar, refined sugar, and granulated sugar. (See Figure 12.25.)

You should store dry sweeteners in a dry place at room temperature. Keep the sugar in bags to keep it from getting hard. Liquid sweeteners such as corn syrup and molasses should be kept in tightly sealed containers at room temperature. They can be kept in a refrigerator, but the sugar may start to crystallize.

CACAO AND CHOCOLATE

Chocolate is made from cocoa beans. Cocoa is grown in tropical climates, especially Honduras, the Caribbean, Madagascar, Sri Lanka, and Sumantra. Chocolate has many levels of quality. The lower quality chocolates are used to

12.25 **Granulated and superfine white sugar**

© Randy Van Dam 2008

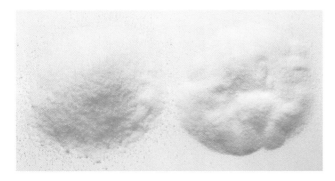

make cheaper candies while the higher quality chocolates make finer products.

All chocolate products must be labeled with their percentage of cocoa solids. The higher the percentage, the more cocoa solids are in the bar, and the more intense the flavor. A low percentage means that there are other fats in the bar. The sugar level must also be included on the label. If sugar is listed first, then the bar will be very sweet.

Chocolate is made by first picking and sorting the cocoa beans. Then they are dried, and pebbles and debris are removed. At this stage, the beans are graded. Higher quality beans have more flavor and command a higher price. After grading, the beans are roasted, which reduces the bitterness and enhances the flavor. After the beans are roasted and cooled, the beans are cracked by rolling them between hot rollers. What remains is a sticky pasted called chocolate liquor or chocolate mass. This liquor contains about 53 percent cocoa butter.

Cocoa powder is the next step in the processing. The chocolate liquor is pressed to extract the cocoa butter. What is left over is cooled, ground, and sifted as a powder. Cocoa powders still contain 10 percent to 25 percent fat. **Dutch-processed cocoa** is made by adding an alkaline to the chocolate mass before processing. This produces a cocoa that is darker and has a stronger taste.

Manufacture of Chocolate

Making chocolate bars is a complex art, mainly because the divergent physical properties of sugar and cacao make it difficult to obtain a homogenous liquor or paste. After the beans are roasted and extracted, the **conching** process is started. This is where the chocolate mass is heated and blended for as few as a couple of hours or up to 72 hours. Conching ensures that the chocolate is evenly blended. After conching, the chocolate is **tempered**, which involves heating and cooling the chocolate a couple of times. Tempering makes the cocoa butter crystals more uniform in size, and it gives the chocolate its bright color and snap sound when broken. The last step is molding, where the

chocolate is poured into molds, and then cooled and packaged (see Figure 12.26).

The many different chocolate products available on the market are defined according to their cacao content and to their added ingredients. Each country sets its own norms regulating the various types of chocolate and their composition, and methods may vary slightly from the basic process. In countries that grow the cacao beans, chocolate is often made by individuals or in small villages. Figures 12.27a-12.27g show how chocolate is made in a small chocolate shop in Oaxaca, Mexico, an ingredient integral to their food and culture. The final product is used in making mole sauces, in making hot chocolate, in baking, or eaten out of hand.

12.26 **Diagram of the chocolate manufacturing process**

Courtesy Professor Douglas Goff, Dairy Science and Technology Education, University of Guelph, Canada

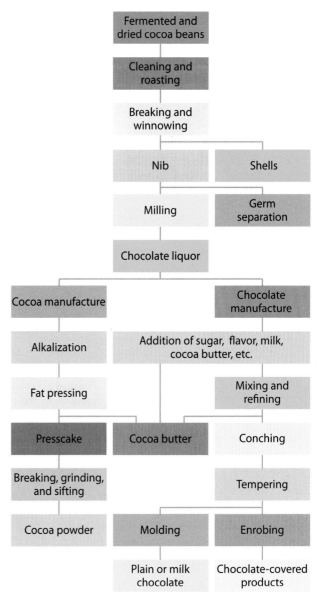

12.27a Cacao nibs and pod

Figure 12.27a-g Courtesy of Robert Garlough

12.27b Blending ingredients according to a recipe: cacao nibs, cinnamon bark, almonds

12.27c Filling the grinder hopper with the ingredient mixture

12.27d Performing the first grind (Note: ground mixture spills onto a measured amount of sugar)

12.27e Blending the ground mixture with the sugar

12.27f Performing second grind (with sugar) to form powder

12.27g Finished chocolate for sale in bulk (Note: pressure on the chocolate will cause it to melt slightly and bind)

Types of Chocolate

The quality of chocolate is as broad as the quality of wine. Some are for general purpose, while others meet a specific need. As fine chocolate is expensive, chefs should become aware of the properties of the chocolate they wish to use before making the purchase. The different types of chocolate include the following.

Chocolate liquor. As described earlier, this is the first step in the processing of the bean. This is not considered real chocolate but is sometimes sold in this form.

Cocoa powder. Also mentioned earlier, cocoa powder is the second step in the processing. It is used in baking, chocolate drinks, and truffles. (See Figure 12.28.)

Unsweetened chocolate. Unsweetened chocolate is the chocolate mass once it has solidified; it contains no sugar or milk. True unsweetened chocolate contains nothing but the chocolate liquor and cocoa butter. It has a chocolate flavor but is too bitter to be edible on its own, though it is used for baking. If the recipe does not specify unsweetened chocolate, then additional sugar should be added to compensate for the taste. (See Figure 12.29.)

Dark (noir) chocolate. This has some sugar added. Dark chocolate contains between 35 percent and 70 percent chocolate liquor. Occasionally, it contains emulsifiers. Dark chocolate can be eaten plain or used in baking and cooking. (See Figure 12.30.)

Bittersweet chocolate. This product has more chocolate liquor and less sugar than semi-sweet chocolate. Both are sometimes referred to as "couverture." (See Figure 12.31.)

Semi-sweet chocolate. This has more sugar than the dark chocolate. Semi-sweet chocolate can range from very sweet to almost bitter and can be eaten plain or used in baking. (See Figure 12.32.)

Milk chocolate. This is chocolate made with milk powder. Milk adds a rich flavor to the chocolate. Milk chocolate is great for eating and is used for some baking applications. (See Figure 12.33.)

White chocolate. White chocolate is not considered real chocolate because it does not contain any chocolate liquor. White chocolate has cocoa butter, at least 32 percent; milk; sugar; and vanilla. It has a sweet flavor and is used to make white chocolate desserts, cheesecakes, and fillings. (See Figure 12.34.)

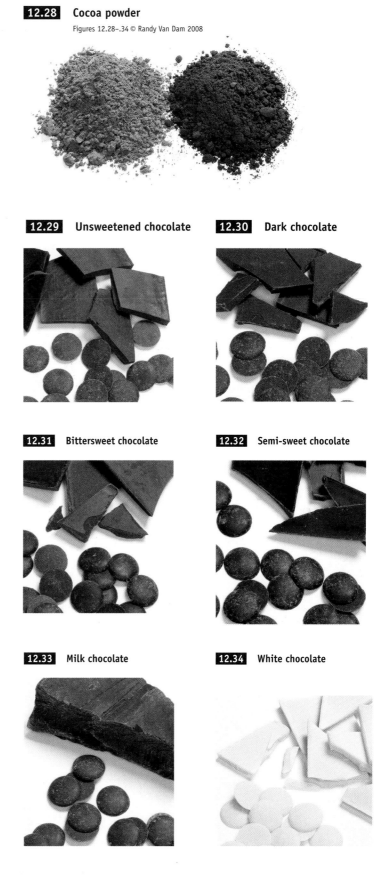

12.28 Cocoa powder

Figures 12.28–.34 © Randy Van Dam 2008

12.29 Unsweetened chocolate

12.30 Dark chocolate

12.31 Bittersweet chocolate

12.32 Semi-sweet chocolate

12.33 Milk chocolate

12.34 White chocolate

CONVENIENCE CORNER PRODUCT EXAMPLES

Bakery

Company	Website	Products
Alessi	http://www.alessibakery.com	2/56 ct Cheesecake Crusts Mini
Alpha	http://www.alphabaking.com	144/1.4 oz Dinner Rolls
Awrey	http://www.awrey.com	36 ct/6 oz Cinn Rolls Iced
Foxtail Foods	http://www.foxtailfoods.com	6/46 oz Pie Cherry NSA 6/46 oz Pie Peach NSA
General Mills	http://www.generalmills.com	6/6# Brownie Mix 6/5# Icing Mix Chocolate
Hershey's	http://www.hersheys.com	25# Chocolate Chips White
Otis Spunk-meyer	http://www.otisspunkmeyer.com	48/3 oz Bagel Plain 240/1.33 oz Dough Cookie Oatmeal
Parco	http://www.parcofoods.com	5# Cookie Chocolate Chip
Rich's	http://www.richs.com	20/16 oz Bread Ciabatta 320/1 oz Dough Bread French Stix 120/2.5 oz Dough Danish Twist 144/2 oz Dough Roll Hot Dog 15# Icing Vanilla Buttercream
SaraLee	http://www.saraleefood service.com	4/69 oz Brownie Chocolate Fudge 36/2.13 oz Roll Cinnamon
Sweet Street	http://www.sweetstreet.com	2/14 ct Cake Red Velvet
Cheesecake Factory	http://www.thecheesecakefactory.com	2/110oz Cake Chocolate Fudgy 14 ct
Elis		6/64 oz Cake Tiramisu

Joel Tanner, CEC, AAC

Place of Birth: Battle Creek, Michigan

Educational Background and Work Experience

Joel Tanner graduated from Lakeview High School near Battle Creek, Michigan, from where he later received the first "Outstanding Alumni Award." He had a few high school jobs in food service, and after graduation Joel worker for the Burdick Meat Packers as a meat cutter. This skill proved invaluable when he went on to the Culinary Institute of America, graduating in 1977. After graduation, Chef Tanner moved to Wichita, Kansas, to take the position of executive sous chef for the Wichita Club. After a few years in Kansas, Tanner returned to Michigan to become the executive chef of the Michigan Education Association Conference Center, in Battle Creek. That position led to his job as club manager of Food and Beverage for the Hastings Elks Club, in Hastings, Michigan. The L. J. Minor Corporation asked Tanner to work for them, so it was at this time that Chef Tanner began working part-time at area food shows as a corporate chef-consultant, talking about the use of convenience soup and sauce bases. Chef Tanner eventually left the Elks Club to take over as executive chef for the Battle Creek Country Club. He later was promoted to the dual position of associate manager and executive chef. Looking for a change and the opportunity to learn more about the industry, Tanner left the day-to-day kitchen to become corporate executive chef for SYSCO Food Services Inc., a position he held for many years. However, eventually the kitchen beckoned his return, and after 10 years, Chef Tanner left SYSCO to become associate manager and executive chef of the newly opened Watermark Country Club in Grand Rapids, Michigan. After a long stint with the Watermark, Chef Tanner retired. However, his retirement lasted only about two weeks, until he got calls from several food service companies looking for him to consult on their product lines and business operations. Today, Chef Tanner is the corporate chef for KeyImpact Sales and Systems, a food marketing and sales company.

Courtesy Joel Tanner

It Happened to Me...

"I was the Executive Chef at the Battle Creek Country Club, which is located in my home town and where I wanted to really make a name for myself. To do so, I worked long hours, and at the time, made all food items from scratch. Once, I was asked to cater an event for a major manufacturing company that was located in another town. They asked me to cater the event because of my reputation for preparing high-quality food, and I was willing to do so as they offered to pay a hefty sum for my services. The catering event would last for two weeks and would consist of all meals in the day, each day. As to my surprise and horror, when I made my first visit to inspect where all the food was to be prepared, I found only one stove with four burners and an oven that wouldn't even hold a full-size sheet tray. That's when I knew I was in BIG trouble!

Fortunately for me, I had never turned away any food brokers or manufacturer's reps. And that's also when I realized there were excellent food products being manufactured that I had never considered before, because I was (before then) bias against convenience foods. Now, to be sure, there were also some bad ones on the market . . . not all products met my standards then, nor do they today. However, at the time, finding the right ones gave my own culinary skills some needed training: learning how to plate, cook, and keep my food cost in line using these products, while still meeting my own high standards of quality.

With lots of hard work and after humbling myself, the event was a great success and the owners of the company were very happy. The event even came in under budget. This event taught me a lot about food and food cost, which I think took me to a higher level of understanding as a chef. It also led me to my next position in the food service field, as a Corporate Chef for the largest food distribution company in the world."

Memberships and Career Highlights

When Tanner was working for some area restaurants before going on to culinary school, he joined the American Culinary Federation (ACF), West Michigan chapter. He's been an active member ever since, serving in a variety of officer and committee chair positions and hosting annual presidential balls at his club operations. He became certified by the ACF as an executive chef (CEC), served as co-chair of the national ACF Awards Committee, and served as chair of the ACFEI Accreditation Commission. This kind of participation earned Chef Tanner an induction as a Fellow of the American Academy of Chefs in 1978, the honor society of the ACF. Chef Tanner was awarded the LP. Gen. John D. McLaughlin Trophy by the American Academy of Chefs in 1998, the first person to receive the award. He was also the ACF Central Region Chef Professionalism Award recipient in 2001, and the ACF Central Region Chef of the Year Award recipient in 2002. Chef Tanner has been actively involved in supporting the Hospitality Education Department of Grand Rapids Community College (GRCC) for many years, serving different terms as the vice chair and chair of its Advisory

(continued)

Committee. For his work in support of culinary education in west Michigan, Chef Tanner was inducted into the Hospitality Hall of Fame of GRCC in 1997. His greatest honor was to be inducted into the Honorable Order of the Golden Toque, an international honor society limited to 100 living chefs. He now serves as a director within that organization.

Passions with the Food Service Industry

"One of my greatest satisfactions is having the ability to train and teach young chefs how to produce excellent meals that address the current trends in a quality fashion, while also keeping the costs in a profitable range. This means keeping an open mind to what can be made from scratch and what time-saving items can be used. I also love looking at new menu items to help keep me current with today's trends."

Advice to a Chef or Buyer

"Always take time to look at new menu products that come into the marketplace. Don't ever say, 'I will never use that item,' especially with the labor market getting harder to fill positions and with the growing cost of labor. Some of these products might save your job, as they don't call in sick or want to go home early. These products give the chef time to be more creative in plating, allow more time for menu planning, and also help in maintaining a consistent food cost, while helping keep labor costs down. It is important to keep in mind that less expensive food items can be more labor intensive. A good chef knows how to balance the menu and prep work."

Key Words and Concepts

bran	dextrose	gelatinization	margarine
butter	Dutch-processed cocoa	germ	tempered
cocoa powder	endosperm	lard	vegetable shortening
conching	fats	leavening agent	yeast

Chapter in Review

The following exercises are provided to help the reader understand and apply the contents of this chapter. They may be completed individually or in a classroom environment.

REVIEW QUESTIONS

a. Describe the use of starches as thickening agents.

b. Identify the three main parts to a wheat kernel and the functions they play as a food source.

c. Identify different fats and the properties that distinguish them.

d. Identify different sweeteners and their properties and potential applications in baking.

e. Discuss the different flours and their applications in baking.

INDIVIDUAL ACTIVITIES

a. **Web based:** Research sources for quality chocolate, and request samples from each supplier.

b. **Experiential:** Obtain different sweeteners and fats, and perform a "blind tasting" to try to identify them.

c. **Critical thinking:** Read the ingredient listings of different packaged baked goods and determine the purpose for the flours, fats, and sweeteners selected for use.

GROUP ACTIVITIES

a. **Lab experience:** Using the same baking formula, prepare a variety of samples while substituting the type of flour used. Evaluate the final products, and compare and contrast the effects on the final product caused by the different flours.

b. **Classroom action:** Discuss a list of baking recipes and the effects of substituting different fats, flours, and sweeteners.

© iStockphoto.com

CHAPTER 13

Meats and Offal

"All normal people love meat. If I went to a barbeque and there was no meat, I would say 'Yo goober, where's the meat?' . . . You don't win friends with salad!

HOMER SIMPSON

After reading this chapter, you will be able to:

◎ Define the term *meat*, and identify the four basic animals from which meat is derived.

◎ Explain the importance of *The Meat Buyer's Guide* and IMPS system.

◎ Summarize the USDA's system for grading meat.

◎ Identify the most commonly used grades of meat for beef, veal, lamb, and pork.

◎ List the products classified as offal or variety meats.

◎ Identify the four categories of sausages.

Introduction

Meats are usually the largest part of a food service operator's food budget, representing a substantial portion of the total food cost. This chapter serves as an overview of meats and offal, including the varieties and grading systems used to measure their quality. The United States leads the world in meat production, with exports going primarily to Asia and the Middle East. Though a leader in production, the United States still imports more meat than it exports. Imported lamb and frozen beef come from Australia, New Zealand, and South and Central America. Meat products, such as sausages, come from Europe. Wherever the source, all imported meat must meet the federal government's stringent bacteriological standards and sanitary regulations.

Meats

The word *meat* is descended from earlier words that meant food. Today, the term means animal flesh that is prepared for eating. Meat includes the muscles and the fat as well as the organ meat and any product made from meat including sausage and ground beef. Meat is normally sold and categorized by the animal of origin.

Animal muscle is composed of fibers, tube-like strings that are held together by connective tissues. The texture of the fibers and composition of the connective tissue determines the tenderness of the meat. Additionally, fat content, age, and size can affect the flavor and tenderness of the meat. Meat is inspected for its "finish" (the layer of fat around the meat carcass) and its "marbling" (the flecks of fat distributed throughout the meat), and grades of quality are assigned accordingly. Each of these variables affects the overall quality of the product.

BUYING AND STORING

Working with the U.S. Department of Agriculture, the North American Meat Processors Association (**NAMP**) has created *The Meat Buyer's Guide*. This publication is considered the best source of information on the cuts available from wholesale and retail meat markets. Each animal (beef, lamb, veal, pork, by-products, and various poultry) has its own section in the guide. Each guide includes pictures of the major cuts and all products derived from that cut. Each primal, subprimal, and retail cut has a unique number, so if a buyer orders a Beef 116a, then he will receive a beef chuck roll that is boneless and contains specified muscles within the cut. Using numbers avoids confusion over local terminology and butcher preferences.

Meat distributors will use the NAMP information and institutional meat purchase specifications (**IMPS**) codes to prepare their own lists of product for sale. The distributors will generally fax or e-mail to their customers a quote sheet each week detailing the weekly prices they are offering. (See Figure 13.1.)

There are many considerations that the purchasing agent must take into account when buying meat. There are differences in the available cuts and grades, as discussed later in this chapter. And, if the menu advertises a certain grade, breed, or brand, then that will obviously dictate the type of meat needed. When purchasing meat, the buyer must also consider the amount needed and the operation's available storage. Finally, the buyer should purchase the meat that is best suited to the recipe. If the recipe calls for diced beef to be used in a stew, for example, then a Select-grade meat from the shoulder would be an appropriate cut. Using hand-diced tenderloin would be a waste, as that is an expensive cut of meat that needs a dry-cooking method. Matching the meat carefully to the recipe will ensure that the recipe has the correct taste and stays within the budget.

If meat is processed in one state and then shipped across state lines for sale or consumption, the USDA Food Safety and Inspection services must inspect it for wholesomeness. As mentioned in Chapter 2, "Food Laws and the Market and Distribution Systems," the processing plant pays for the inspection programs. Meat that will be consumed within the state falls under state inspection guidelines, which must be equal to or greater than the federal standards.

Chapter 2 also discussed the stamps that are on the meat carcasses and showed various examples (also see Figure 13.2).

USDA's Meat Grading Program

The USDA has quality standards, or grades, for beef, veal, and lamb. It also has yield grades for beef, pork, and lamb. Pork has quality grades, but because the grade levels are so close together, most chefs do not specify a certain grade of pork. The federal government developed the USDA grade standards and employs the inspectors who judge the meat. These inspectors are supervised by regional and national inspectors who check the inspectors on a regular basis. This means that Choice beef will have the same characteristics no matter where it is purchased. Graded meat will have a purple shield mark stamped on the carcass. This mark may be visible on larger cuts of meat but not on portion cuts. Figure 13.3 shows a picture of a meat stamp on a bag of Cryovac-wrapped meat.

Purchase Forms

Beef, pork, and lamb are available in many different forms. For example, if a chef wants beef ribs, then the buyer can

May-4-2010 01:27P FROM: _____   TO: _____

13.1 Quote Sheet from Meat Purveyor

CERTIFIED ANGUS BEEF PRODUCTS

Code	Product	Price
F-R16B	C.A.B. Rstd Top Round split	$3.69
C-C112A	C.A.B. Lip On Ribeye 13up	$7.29
C-C116A	C.A.B. Chuck Roll neckoff	$2.39
C-C167A	C.A.B. Peeled Knuckles	$2.69
C-C168	C.A.B. Top (Inside) Round	$2.34
C-C180C	C.A.B. 0xl BO Strip, 1/4"	$8.39
C-C189A	C.A.B. PSMO Tenderloin 5+	$11.95
C-C193	C.A.B. Peeled Flank Steak	$6.39

Other Products

Code	Product	Price
S-1173C	Portebone Steak 1" Tail	$7.70
S-1174B	T-Bone Steak 1" Tail	$7.20
S-1180A-CC	CC Bnls Strip Steak 1" Tail	$10.45
S-1184B	CC Top Butt Steak	$7.19
S-1185B-F	Sizzle Steak Ball Tip Flat	$4.89
S-1190A	Tenderloin Medallions	$6.95
S-1190A-AA	Tenderloin Steak	$18.45
B-1176KM	Kabob Meat random	$2.99
B-1176ST	Sirloin Tips	$2.79
B-135A	Diced Beef	$2.79
F-1101-5	Cubed/Swiss Steak 30x5z	$4.19
F-903P	Sliced Veal Liver 40z 10#	$3.99
P-1412	C.C. Pork Chops LP	$2.99
P-1232	AA Lamb Loin Chops	$10.95
P-1232I	NZ Lamb Loin Chops	$7.95
G-136-80	Ground Beef	$1.44
F-R112A3	Cooked Lipon Rib Eye 1/bx	$5.79
F-R170	Miniat Ckd Pot Roast 4x7#	$3.69
F-R193	Miniat Ckd Diced Beef IOF	
F-R413	Cooked Pork Loin Roast 2x8#	$3.98
C-112A-12	Lip On Ribeye 13/up PREM	$6.39
C-168-U	Top (Inside) Round	$2.09
B-185B	Ball Tips 2/up	$2.99
C-180C	AA 0xl Bnls Strip, Xtrim	$5.99
C-184-13	Top Butt 13/up	$2.74
C-184B	Cap Off CC Top Butt	$4.49
B-190-AA	PTS Tenderloin	$9.69
C-189A	PSMO Tenderloin/ Choice +	$9.95
C-193	Flank Steak	$4.84
F-134	Soup Bones 25# bxs	$.64
P-410	Pork Loin (14/18#)	$1.59
P-412B	Bnls CC Pork Loin	$6.89

Code	Product	Price
C-500	Dearborn Bone In Hams 2pc	$1.69
C-509B	Dearborn Buffet Ham	$2.39
C-509E	Pit Hams	$2.99
C-509F	Dearborn Football Ham 2pc	$2.39
F-421	Danish Back Ribs 1.75avg	$2.99
C-539T	Tick Country Bacou	$1.99
F-539A	Ossian Platter Bacon 18/22	$2.59
F-539E	Layout SS Bacon 18/22 15#	$2.59
F-570B	Bulk Pork Sausage	$1.89
F-570N2	Sausage Links, NC, 2oz	$2.29
F-570NC	Per Saus Link, NC, 1oz	$2.29
F-570P8	Peer Sausage Pats, 2oz	$2.29
F-204	AA Lamb Rack, Chine Off	$5.99
F-204F	N.Z. Frnch Lamb Rack 16/18	$10.25
F-2321	NZ Lamb Short Loin	$7.95
F-262	Imp. Lamb Shanks	$2.79
F-312	Bnls Veal Strip Loin 1x1 4pc	$10.95
F-371	Veal Eye Of Round 12#	$1.49
F-398	Veal Bones	$.99
C-PC01	**Fryers, (wogs)	$.99
F-PC200	IQF Fryers 8pc 12hd (96 pc)	$34.95
F-PC207	Chix Backs for Stock	$.39
F-PC220B	Chickens Breast Meat 40#	$1.59
F-PC224-S	Skins Chix Brst 24x4oz	$2.59
F-PC225-S	Sknis Chix Brst 24x6oz	$2.59
F-PC226-S	Skin Chix Brst 24x8oz	$2.59
F-PC228-S	Skin Chix Brst 24x8oz	$2.69
F-PC2255	5oz Flat Skins Chix Brst 28pc	$34.95
F-PC4831	George's Chix Tenders	$1.69
F-ED301	Ducklings 5#avg 6/case	
F-P53067	Semi Bnls Quail 4.5oz 24ct	$2.39
WG-6605	**Pheasant 2.25/2.50# 10pc	$1.99
C-PT103	Deli Turkey Brst/fresh 2pc	$2.49
F-PT104A	Bone In Turkey Brst, 12/16	$1.19
F-PT104BO	BO Raw T-Breast/foil wrap	
F-PT105-22	Tom Turkeys 22/26# Avg.	
F-SF110	Alaskan Follock IQF 2/4oz	$1.39
F-SF116	Walleye Filets 10/12oz 11#	
F-SF244	Sashimi YF Tuna 9/11oz 15#	
F-SF248	Grouper Filets 8/10oz 10#	$4.95
F-SF401	King Crab Legs 123/14ct 20#	
F-867CL	Italian Sausage-Rope Style	$2.49
F-874	Chorizo Sausage Links	
F-878	Dearborn Anduli Sausage	$3.09
F-02626	Hard/Genoa Salami	$3.95

Code	Product	Price
F-V1304	Vienna Ski Franks 6.0" 4/1	$36.95
F-V1318	Vienna Ski Franks 6.0" 8/1	
F-V1330	Vienna Ski Franks 5.25" 10/1	
F-V1544	Vienna Polish Fruks 6.0" 4/1	
F-V2155	Vienna Sled Italian Beef 10#	
F-V5564	Vienna Itl. Gravy Mix 40x4oz	
F-V56768	Vienna Sport Pepper 2gal	
F-V56772	Vienna Green Relish 2gal	
F-V5708	Vienna Pickles 55/65ct 5gal	
F-0706	Anduli Sausage Encrte 200x1z	
F-0720	Mini Renbens 200x1z	
F-0725	Mini Beef Wellinton 200x1z	
F-0800	Coconut Shrimp 21/25 100ct	
F-0805	Coconut Chix Tender 100x1z	
F-0807	Coconut Lobster Tl 100x.75z	
F-0842	Borsun StfMushroom 200x1z	
F-2415	Tandoori Chicken 100x.8z	
F-3631	Dragon Shrimp 100x.75z	
F-7135	BrieEmCrte/Raspbry 200x1z	
F-7252	PortobeloMushPuff 100x1.5z	
F-16813	Cocktail Springrolls 4x100p	
F-16813A	Cocktail Springrolls 1x100p	

**Denotes Specialty item. Advance ordering required.

13.2 **Federal inspection mark**
Courtesy USDA

buy precut ribs all the way up to a half carcass of beef, and then the chef can cut the ribs. The purchasing forms are very important: the same meat can have a wide range of per-pound cost based on the amount of processing that has to be done in the kitchen. The purchase forms, from most trimming to least trimming, include:

Primal cuts. Primal cuts are roughly one-eighth of the animal. In beef, they would correspond to the "arms," "legs," or "back" of the animal. Primal cuts have a low per-pound cost, but the chef must cut the meat into subprimals and steaks. Cutting on the premises will generate trim meat and extra fat, which are wasted unless they are reused in soups, stocks, or ground on the premises. If an establishment purchases primal cuts, it must have a skilled butcher chef on the premises to cut the meat.

Subprimal. Subprimals are smaller roasts, rounds, and ribs cut from a primal cut. Subprimals will have names

13.3 **Cryovac bags of meat showing meat stamps**
© Randy Van Dam 2008

such as beef rib roast or beef ribeye roll, indicating their origin in the primal. Subprimals are more expensive than primal cuts. Some subprimals will need further trimming or removal of the fat caps before use, and this can be done in the food service operation by the chef or by the meat suppliers. Subprimals can be cooked as is as roasts. They can also be cut into steaks by an experienced chef.

Portion cuts. Portion cut are steaks cut from the subprimals by the meat supplier or wholesaler. The buyer will specify the steak cut, NAMP number, grade, weight per steak, and total weight for the case. Portion cuts are the most expensive option per pound, but there is no waste or trim to worry about. Portion cuts are also popular in establishments that do not have chefs who can cut the meat.

BEEF

Beef is any meat from domesticated cows. The higher grades of beef are from animals raised for their meat, while some of the lower grades are from dairy cows that are too old for milk. Some breeds such as Angus will have meat that is tenderer than other varieties, and cuts from little-used muscles such as along the back will have meat that is more tender than the active muscles from the shoulder and leg. Meats from these cuts are more expensive, as there is only a small portion of these cuts available from one animal. (See Table 13.1 for an index of beef products and weight ranges, and see Table 13.2 for an index of beef portion cuts.)

Beef carcasses are graded in two ways:

• **Quality grade.** This is the level of flavor, fat, juiciness, and tenderness in the carcass.

• **Yield grade.** This is the amount of usable meat in the carcass.

Quality grades are based on the amount of fat flakes within the muscle. This is called marbling, and a roast with more marbling is more tender than one with less. Certain parts of the cow, such as the tenderloin, will have more marbling than, say, a shoulder cut. And each animal is different: two cows raised under the same conditions might have different levels of marbling. The quality grade is also based on the color of the meat and the age of the animal. Younger cows will grade at a higher level than older cows that have worked more muscles. The grades for beef include *USDA Prime, Choice, Select, Standard, Commercial, Utility, Cutter,* and *Canner.* (See Figure 13.4.)

USDA Prime. Prime-grade beef comes from younger cattle that are on special diets to promote the marbling. Prime beef is the smallest portion of meat available in the market and is normally sold to upscale, four-star restaurants. Some Prime meat is available through specialty butchers for retail sales. Prime beef has the most marbling and is the most

13.4a, b   **Quality grade stamps for USDA Prime, Choice, and Select**
Courtesy USDA

13.5   **Yield grade stamp**
Courtesy USDA

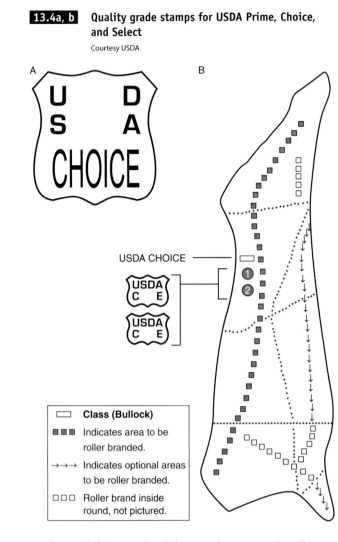

tender and juiciest steaks. Prime-grade roasts and steaks can be cooked with dry-heat methods.

USDA Choice. Choice grade has slightly less marbling than Prime, but the flavor is almost as good as prime. Choice-grade meat is readily available for most restaurants and grocery stores. Choice meat can be cooked with dry-heat methods.

USDA Select. Select beef is leaner than Choice or Prime grades and has significantly less marbling. It does not have as much juiciness as the higher grades. Most beef is sold in this grade, and it is easily obtainable from butchers and wholesalers. Only the most tender cuts can be dry cooked, and the other cuts should be marinated or cooked with a moist-heat method.

Standard and Commercial. These two grades are the lowest quality available for sale to restaurants and grocery stores. They must be cooked with moist-heat methods as there is very little marbling in the meat. Standard and Commercial grades come from older animals or dairy cows.

Utility, Cutter, and Canner. These grades are not sold to retailers or restaurants. They are instead used by food manufacturers to make ground beef, hot dogs, and other processed meat food. This grade has no marbling and comes from the oldest animals.

No-roll. Some meat companies choose not to pay a USDA inspector to grade the meat. Because this meat is not graded, it does not have a quality stamp on it, hence the term "no-roll." No-roll beef varies in quality and availability, but it is almost always cheaper than the Prime, Choice, or Select varieties. It has been inspected for wholesomeness, so it is safe for human consumption. No-roll beef is good for specials and moist-heat cooking.

Yield grades range from 1 to 5 and simply indicate the amount of usable meat from the carcass. A yield grade is only important if the establishment is purchasing carcasses or primal cuts and needs to know how much meat is available for cutting. If the establishment is buying subprimals or portion cuts, then the yield grade is not needed. (See Figure 13.5 and Figure 13.6.)

13.6 Beef skeletal chart
© 2007 NAMP, reprinted with permission of John Wiley & Sons

Beef Skeletal Chart

Location, Structure, and Names of Bones

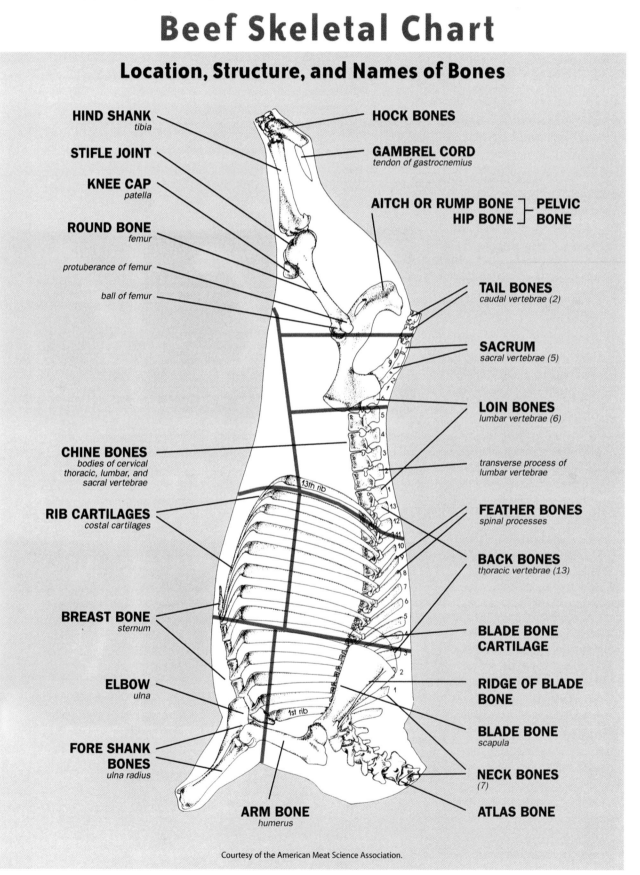

HIND SHANK
tibia

STIFLE JOINT

KNEE CAP
patella

ROUND BONE
femur

protuberance of femur

ball of femur

CHINE BONES
*bodies of cervical
thoracic, lumbar, and
sacral vertebrae*

RIB CARTILAGES
costal cartilages

BREAST BONE
sternum

ELBOW
ulna

FORE SHANK
BONES
ulna radius

ARM BONE
humerus

HOCK BONES

GAMBREL CORD
tendon of gastrocnemius

AITCH OR RUMP BONE ⎤ PELVIC
HIP BONE ⎦ BONE

TAIL BONES
caudal vertebrae (2)

SACRUM
sacral vertebrae (5)

LOIN BONES
lumbar vertebrae (6)

*transverse process of
lumbar vertebrae*

FEATHER BONES
spinal processes

BACK BONES
thoracic vertebrae (13)

BLADE BONE
CARTILAGE

RIDGE OF BLADE
BONE

BLADE BONE
scapula

NECK BONES
(7)

ATLAS BONE

13th rib

1st rib

Courtesy of the American Meat Science Association.

TABLE 13.1 Index of Beef Products and Weight Ranges

© 2007 NAMP, reprinted with permission of John Wiley & Sons

ITEM	PRODUCT NAME	SUGGESTED UPC NO.	PG*	Weight Ranges (Pounds)			
				A	B	C	D
100	Carcass	1000	11	500–600	600–700	700–800	800–up
101	Side	1000	11	250–300	300–350	350–400	400–up
102	Forequarter	1002	11	131–157	157–183	183–400	400–up
103	Rib, Primal	1003	12	24–28	28–33	33–38	38–up
107	Rib, Oven-Prepared	1171	12	17–19	19–23	23–26	26–up
109	Rib, Roast-Ready	1173	13	14–16	16–19	19–22	22–up
109A	Rib, Roast-Ready, Special	1173	14	14–16	16–19	19–22	22–up
109B	Rib, Blade Meat	1185	14	3–up			
109D	Rib, Roast-Ready, Cover Off, Short-cut	1190	14	12–14	14–17	17–20	20–up
109E	Rib, Ribeye Roll, Lip-On, Bone In	1193	14	11–13	13–16	16–19	20–up
110	Rib, Roast-Ready, Boneless	1172	15	11–13	13–16	16–19	19–up
112	Rib, Ribeye Roll	1177	15	5–6	6–8	8–10	10–up
112A	Rib, Ribeye Roll, Lip-On	1176	15	6–7	7–9	9–11	11–up
112C	Rib, Ribeye (IM)	1192	16	3–4	4–6	6–8	8–up
112D	Rib, Ribeye Cap (IM)	1185	16	Under 2	2–up		
113	Chuck, Square-Cut	1006	17	66–79	79–93	93–106	106–up
114	Chuck, Shoulder (Clod)	1019	17	13–15	15–18	18–21	21–up
114C	Chuck, Shoulder (Clod), Trimmed	1021	18	Under 12	12–14	14–18	18–up
114D	Chuck, Shoulder (Clod), Top Blade	1137	18	Under 2	8–10	10–12	12–up
114E	Chuck, Shoulder (Clod), Arm Roast	1131	19	Under 8	8–10	10–12	12–up
114F	Chuck, Shoulder Tender (IM)	1030	19	0.6–0.75	0.75–0.9	0.9–1.00	1–up
115	Chuck, Square-cut, Boneless	1010	20	54–65	65–77	77–88	88–up
115D	Chuck, Square, Perctoral Meat (IM)	1632	20	*Random*			
116A	Chuck, Chuck Roll	1028	21	13–15	15–18	18–21	21–up
116B	Chuck, Chuck Tender	1115	21	Under 1	1–3	3–up	
116D	Chuck, Chuck Eye Roll	1029	22	Under 8	8–10	10–14	14–up
116E	Chuck, Under Blade Roast	1151	22	Under 8	8–10	10–14	14–up
116G	Chuck, Edge Roast (IM)	1092	22	Under 2	2–up		
116H	Chuck, Chuck Eye (IM)	1095	23	Under 2	2–up		

* Denotes page number in NAMP *Meat Buyer's Guide.*

TABLE 13.1 *(continued)*

117	Foreshank	1633	23	7–8	8–10	10–12	12–up
120	Brisket, Deckle-Off, Boneless	1615	23	6–8	8–10	10–12	12–up
120A	Brisket, Flat Cut, Boneless (IM)	1622	24	4–6	6–8	8–10	10–up
120B	Brisket, Point Cut, Boneless (IM)	1627	24	Under 3	3–4	4–6	6–up
120C	Brisket, 2-Piece, Bonele	1616	24	6–8	8–10	10–12	12–up
121	Plate, Short Plate	1593	24	20–27	27–31	31–35	35–up
121C	Plate, Outside Skirt, (Diaphragm) (IM)	1607	24	1–2	2–3	3–up	
121D	Plate, Inside Skirt, *(Transversus Abdominis)* (IM)	1612	25	1–3	3–4	4–up	
123	Short Ribs	1599	25	2–3	3–4	4–5	5–up
123A	Short Plate, Short Ribs, Trimmed	1597	25		*Amount as Specified*		
123B	Rib, Short Ribs, Trimmed	1602	26		*Amount as Specified*		
123C	Rib, Short Ribs	1612	26		*Amount as Specified*		
123D	Short Ribs, Boneless (IM)	1604	26	1–2	2–3	3–4	4–up
124	Rib, Back Ribs	1182	26		*Amount as Specified*		
124A	Rib, Rib Fingers, Boneless	1190	27		*Amount as Specified*		
130	Chuck, Short Ribs	1124	27	2–3	3–4	4–5	5–up
134	Beef Bones	1644	27		*Amount as Specified*		
135	Diced Beef	1727	28		*Amount as Specified*		
135A	Beef for Stewing	1742	28		*Amount as Specified*		
135B	Beef for Kabobs	1724	28		*Amount as Specified*		
136	Ground Beef	1653	29		*Amount as Specified*		
136A	Ground Beef and Vegetable	1704	29		*Amount as Specified*		
136B	Beef Patty Mix	1705	30		*Amount as Specified*		
136C	Beef Patty Mix, Lean	1706	30		*Amount as Specified*		
137	Ground Beef, Special	1700	30		*Amount as Specified*		
140	Hanging Tender	1435	31		**Random**		
155	Hindquarter	1003	11	119–143	143–167	167–190	190–up
158	Round, Primal	1439	31	59–71	71–83	83–95	95–up
158A	Round, Diamond-Cut	1461	32	63–76	76–89	89–102	102–up
160	Round, Shank Off, Partially Boneless	1440	32	47–57	57–67	67–76	76–up
160B	Round, Heel and Shank Off, Semi-Boneless	1463	33	38–46	46–54	54–60	60–up

(continued)

TABLE 13.1 *(continued)*

ITEM	PRODUCT NAME	SUGGESTED UPC NO.	PG*	Weight Ranges (Pounds)			
				A	B	C	D
161B	Round, Heel and Shank Off, Without Knuckle, Boneless	1478	33	30–37	37–44	44–51	51–up
163	Round, Shank Off, 3-Way, Boneless	1442	33	41–50	50–58	58–66	66–up
166A	Round, Rump Partially Removed, Shank Off	1491	33	44–52	52–61	61–70	70–up
166B	Round, Rump and Shank Partially Off, Handle On	1493	34	44–52	52–61	61–70	70–up
167	Round, Knuckle (Tip)	1525	34	8–9	9–11	11–13	13–up
167A	Round, Knuckle (Tip), Peeled	1526	35	7–8	8–10	10–12	12–up
167D	Round, Knuckle (Tip), Peeled, 2-Piece	1578	35	5–7	7–9	9–12	12–up
167E	Round, Knuckle (Tip), Center Roast (IM)	1549	35	Under 2	2–up		
167F	Round, Knuckle (Tip), Side Roast (IM)	1463	35	Under 2	2–up		
168	Round, Top (Inside), Untrimmed	1453	36	14–17	17–20	20–23	23–up
169	Round, Top (Inside)	1455	36	14–17	17–20	20–23	23–up
169A	Round, Top (Inside), Cap Off	1454	36	12–15	15–18	18–20	20–up
169B	Round, Top (Inside), Cap (IM)	1461	36	1–2	2–3	3–up	
169C	Round, Top (Inside), Side (IM)	1571	37	Under 1	1–up		
169D	Round, Top (Inside), Soft Side Removed	1461	37	9–10	10–12	12–14	14–up
170	Round, Bottom (Gooseneck)	1443	37	18–23	23–27	27–31	31–up
170A	Round, Bottom (Gooseneck), Heel Out	1445	38	17–20	20–24	24–28	28–up
171B	Round, Outside Round (Flat)	1464	38	8–10	10–13	13–16	16–up
171C	Round, Eye of Round (IM)	1460	39	Under 3	3–5	5–up	
171D	Round, Outside Round, Side Muscle Removed (IM)	1462	39	4–6	6–9	9–12	12–up
171E	Round, Outside Round, Side Roast (IM)	1463	39	2–3	3–5	5–7	7–up
171F	Round, Bottom Round, Heel	1477	39	3–4	4–6	6–up	
172	Loin, Full Loin, Trimmed	1270	40	30–37	37–45	45–52	52–up
172A	Loin, Full Loin, Diamond-Cut, Trimmed	1305	41	35–42	42–50	50–57	57–up
174	Loin, Short Loin, Short-Cut	1278	41	14–20	20–25	25–30	30–up

* Denotes page number in NAMP *Meat Buyer's Guide.*

TABLE 13.1 (continued)

175	Loin, Strip Loin, Bone In	1285	42	11–14	14–18	18–22	22–up
176	Loin, Steak Tail	1415	43	0.6–075	0.75–0.9	0.9–1.00	1–up
180	Loin, Strip Loin, Boneless	1286	43	8–10	10–12	12–14	14–up
181	Loin, Sirloin	1282	44	16–19	19–24	24–28	28–up
181A	Loin, Top Sirloin, Bone In	1303	44	11–14	14–17	17–20	20–up
184	Loin, Top Sirloin Butt, Boneless	1298	44	8–10	10–12	12–14	14–up
184A	Loin, Top Sirloin Butt, Semi Center-Cut, Boneless	1306	45	7–9	9–11	11–13	13–up
184B	Loin, Top Sirloin Butt, Center-Cut, Boneless, Cap Off (IM)	1313	45	5–7	7–9	9–11	11–up
184D	Loin, Top Sirloin Cap (IM)	1300	45	1–2	2–3	3–4	4–up
184E	Loin, Top Sirloin Butt, Boneless, 2-Piece	1299	45	8–9	9–11	11–13	13–up
184F	Loin, Top Sirloin Butt, Center-Cut, Boneless, Seamed, 2-Piece	1428	45	6–7	7–8	8–10	10–up
185	Loin, Bottom Sirloin Butt, Boneless	1274	46	5–6	6–7	7–8	8–up
185A	Loin, Bottom Sirloin Butt, Flap, Boneless (IM)	1302	46	1–3	3–up		
185B	Loin, Bottom Sirloin Butt, Ball Tip, Boneless	1307	46	1.5–3	3–up		
185C	Loin, Bottom Sirloin Butt, Tri-Tip, Boneless (IM)	1429	47	1.5–3	3–up		
185D	Loin, Bottom Sirloin Butt, Tri-Tip, Boneless, Defatted (IM)	1430	47	1.5–3	3–up		
189	Loin Tenderloin, Full	1293	47	4–5	5–6	6–7	7–up
189A	Loin Tenderloin, Full, Side Muscle On, Defatted	1387	48	3–4	4–5	5–6	6–up
190	Loin Tenderloin, Full, Side Muscle On, Defatted	1394	48	2–3	3–4	4–up	
190A	Loin Tenderloin, Full, Side Muscle Off, Skinned	1387	48	2–3	3–4	4–up	
191	Loin, Tenderloin, Butt	1295	49	1–2	2–3	3–4	4–up
191A	Loin Tenderloin, Butt, Dafatted	1296	49	1–2	2–3	3–4	4–up
191B	Loin, Tenderloin, Butt, Skinned	1297	49	Under 2	2–3	3–up	
192	Loin, Tenderloin, Short	1386	50	2–3	3–4	4–up	
192A	Loin, Tenderloin Tails	1394	50	*Amount as Specified*			
193	Flank, Flank Steak (IM)	1581	50	Under 1	1–2	2–up	

TABLE 13.2 **Index of Beef Portion Cuts**

© 2007 NAMP, reprinted with permission of John Wiley & Sons

ITEM	PRODUCT NAME	SUGGESTED UPC NO.	PG*	*Suggested Portion Weight Range*
1100	Cubed Steak	1709	55	3–8 oz.
1101	Cubed Steak, Special	1709	55	3–8 oz.
1102	Braising Steak, Swiss	1742	55	4–8 oz.
1103	Rib, Rib Steak, Bone In	1239	56	8–18 oz.
1103B	Rib, Rib Steak, Bone In, Frenched		56	12–36 oz.
1112	Rib, Ribeye Roll Steak, Boneless	1209	57	4–12 oz.
1112A	Rib, Ribeye Steak, Lip-On, Boneless	1203	57	4–12 oz.
1112B	Rib, Ribeye Steak, Lip-On, Short-Cut, Boneless	1215	57	4–12 oz.
1112C	Rib, Ribeye (IM)	1102	57	4–12 oz.
1112D	Rib, Ribeye Cap (IM)	1180	58	4–8 oz.
1114D	Shoulder, Top Blade Steak (IM)	1144	58	4–8 oz.
1114E	Shoulder, Arm Steak	1162	58	4–8 oz.
1114F	Shoulder Tender, Portioned	1164	59	2–14 oz.
1116D	Chuck, Chuck Eye Roll Steak, Boneless (for Braising)	1096	59	4–12 oz.
1121D	Plate, Inside Skirt Steak, Boneless (IM)	1607	59	4–8 oz.
1121E	Plate, Outside Skirt Steak, Skinned (IM)	1612	59	4–8 oz.
1123	Short Rib, Bone In	1259	60	3–10 oz.
1136	Ground Beef Patties	1677	60	*Desired ounces or number per pound*
1136A	Ground Beef and Vegetable Protein Product Patties	1691	60	*Desired ounces or number per pound*
1136B	Beef Patties	1680	60	*Desired ounces or number per pound*
1137	Ground Beef Patties, Special	1694	60	*Desired ounces or number per pound*
1140	Hanging Tender Steak		61	3–10 oz.
1167	Round, Knuckle (Tip) Steak	1527	61	3–10 oz.
1167A	Round, Knuckle (Tip) Steak, Peeled	1535	61	3–10 oz.
1167D	Round, Knuckle (Tip) Steak, Peeled, Special	1549	62	4–8 oz.
1167E	Round, Knuckle (Tip), Center Steaks (IM)	1550	62	4–16 oz.

* Denotes page number in NAMP *Meat Buyer's Guide.*

TABLE 13.2 *(continued)*

1167F	Round, Knuckle (Tip), Side Steaks (IM)	1543	62	4–16 oz.
1169	Round, Top (Inside) Round Steak	1553	63	3–12 oz.
1170A	Round, Bottom (Gooseneck) Round Steak	1466	63	3–24 oz.
1173	Loin, Porterhouse Steak	1330	64	10–12 oz.
1174	Loin, T-Bone Steak	1369	64	8–24 oz.
1179	Loin, Strip Loin Steak, Bone In	1398	65	8–24 oz.
1179A	Loin, Strip Loin Steak, Bone In, Center-Cut	1399	65	8–24 oz.
1180	Loin, Strip Loin Steak, Boneless	1404	65	6–20 oz.
1180A	Loin, Strip Loin Steak, Boneless, Center-Cut	1410	66	6–20 oz.
1184	Loin, Top Sirloin Butt Steak, Boneless	1422	66	4–24 oz.
1184A	Loin, Top Sirloin Butt Steak, Semi Center-Cut, Boneless	1427	67	4–16 oz.
1184B	Loin, Top Sirloin Butt Steak, Center-Cut, Boneless (IM)	1426	67	4–16 oz.
1184D	Loin, Top Sirloin Cap Steak, Boneless (1M)	1421	68	4–8 oz.
1184F	Loin, Top Sirloin Butt Steak, Center-Cut, Boneless, Seamed	1436	68	4–16 oz.
1185A	Loin, Bottom Sirloin Butt, Flap Steak (IM)	1428	68	3–8 oz.
1185B	Loin, Bottom Sirloin Butt, Ball Tip Steak (IM)	1435	69	3–10 oz.
1185C	Loin, Bottom Sirloin Butt, Tri-Tip Steak (IM)	1430	69	3–8 oz.
1185D	Loin, Bottom Sirloin Butt, Tri-Tip Steak, Defatted (IM)	1430	69	3–8 oz.
1189	Loin, Tenderloin Steak	1388	69	4–14 oz.
1189A	Loin, Tenderloin Steak, Side Muscle On, Defatted	1389	70	3–14 oz.
1190	Loin, Tenderloin Steak, Side Muscle Off, Defatted	1394	70	3–14 oz.
1190A	Loin, Tenderloin Steak, Side Muscle Off, Skinned	1395	70	3–14 oz.
1190B	Loin, Tenderloin Steak, Side Muscle Off, Skinned, Center-Cut	1436	70	3–14 oz.
1190C	Loin, Tenderloin Tips	1392	70	*Amount as Specified*

13.7 Veal skeletal chart

© 2007 NAMP, reprinted with permission of John Wiley & Sons

Veal Skeletal Chart

Location, Structure, and Names of Bones

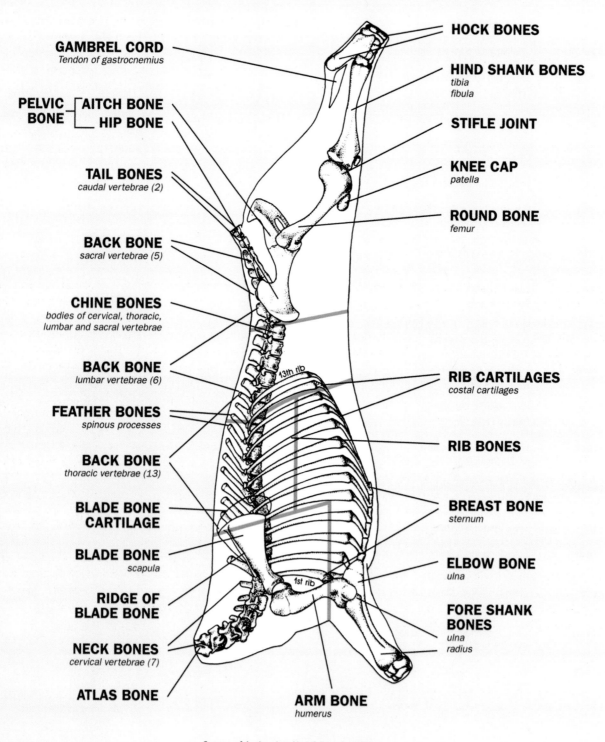

HOCK BONES

HIND SHANK BONES
tibia
fibula

STIFLE JOINT

KNEE CAP
patella

ROUND BONE
femur

RIB CARTILAGES
costal cartilages

RIB BONES

BREAST BONE
sternum

ELBOW BONE
ulna

FORE SHANK
BONES
ulna
radius

GAMBREL CORD
Tendon of gastrocnemius

PELVIC BONE
⎰ AITCH BONE
⎱ HIP BONE

TAIL BONES
caudal vertebrae (2)

BACK BONE
sacral vertebrae (5)

CHINE BONES
bodies of cervical, thoracic,
lumbar and sacral vertebrae

BACK BONE
lumbar vertebrae (6)

FEATHER BONES
spinous processes

BACK BONE
thoracic vertebrae (13)

BLADE BONE
CARTILAGE

BLADE BONE
scapula

RIDGE OF
BLADE BONE

NECK BONES
cervical vertebrae (7)

ATLAS BONE

ARM BONE
humerus

13th rib

1st rib

Courtesy of the American Meat Science Association.

VEAL AND CALF

Veal is meat from a young cow, one that is between 16 and 18 weeks of age when slaughtered (see Figure 13.7). Veal is a by-product of the dairy industry, as dairy cows can only produce milk after having a baby. The male offspring and some of the female calves are kept for about a month before they are sold for veal. The most common forms of veal include:

- **Calf.** A calf is a young cow that has not reached puberty or 9 months. Calves are older than veal calves when slaughtered. This meat is more tender than beef but less tender than veal.

- **Bob veal.** These are very young cows, slaughtered before they are 3 weeks old.

- **Special-diet veal.** These are veal calves that are fed special diets that increase the nutritional value of the meat. Most veal calves are raised on special diets.

Veal is graded based on the quality of the lean meat and the proportion of fat, bone, and lean meat in the carcass. The color of the meat is also an indicator of age: the younger the animal, the whiter their muscles. Older animals have a red cast to their meat. For quality, there are five grades: *Prime, Choice, Good, Standard,* and *Utility*. Most veal for the restaurant market is Prime, Choice, or Good, while Standard and Utility are used in processed foods. Veal meat should be gray-pink to light pink and have very little marbling or visible fat. The meat will have a velvet texture. The chops can be cooked with a dry-heat method while the rest of the cuts would benefit from marinating or moist-heat cooking. (See Table 13.3 and Table 13.4.)

LAMB

Most lamb is from animals that are less than 1 year old (see Figure 13.8). Because lamb meat can vary based on the breed of the animal, most kitchens will only buy lamb that has been graded by the USDA. There are five grades available, including *Prime, Choice, Good, Utility,* and *Cull*. The first two grades are available for restaurants and retail sales, while the other three are used for food processing.

USDA Prime. Prime-graded lamb is very tender, juicy, and has lots of flavor. This grade has marbling through the

cut so that it can be cooked with dry-heat methods such as roasting or broiling.

USDA Choice. This lamb has less marbling but is still very tender. The chops can be roasted or broiled, while some of the other cuts could use some marinating or moist heat.

Before purchasing lamb, the chef must determine the cooking method. For example, if the menu item is leg of lamb, cooked by oven roasting, then a Prime or Choice grade will be needed to retain the flavor. Any grade lower than this will dry out and become very tough when cooked with dry heat. If the recipe calls for another cut such as the breast, ribs, or shank, then the grade is not as important as the meat should be braised to keep it tender.

Mutton is meat from older lambs, those that are more than 1 year old. Mutton will be tougher than lamb, and mutton will never have a Prime grade. Cull grade is reserved for exceptionally tough mutton and is only available for food processors. Mutton is rare in the United States and must be cooked with a long, moist-heat application. (See Table 13.5 and Table 13.6.)

PORK

Pork is meat from young pigs. Over the past 30 years, pork producers have changed the pig feed, breeding stocks, and animal husbandry practices to produce a meat that is leaner, with less fat, and a sweeter taste than earlier years. These changes have helped make pork almost interchangeable with chicken in most dishes. And, today, most pork fat is trimmed from the cuts and portion meat, unless the consumer asks that it be kept on. (See Figure 13.9.)

The USDA has two grades for pork: Acceptable and Unacceptable. Unacceptable pork is not sold on the retail market but can be used by food processors. Acceptable pork is then graded for yield to determine how much can be used from the carcass.

Because pork does not have different quality grades, it should be purchased from reputable and reliable vendors. High-quality pork has only a thin layer of fat on the outside with some marbling and a grayish-pink color. The meat should be firm to the touch. Pork can be cooked by either a dry-heat or moist-heat method, depending on what part of the pig the meat came from. Pork also accepts marinades, which help to change the flavor profile. (See Table 13.7 and Table 13.8.)

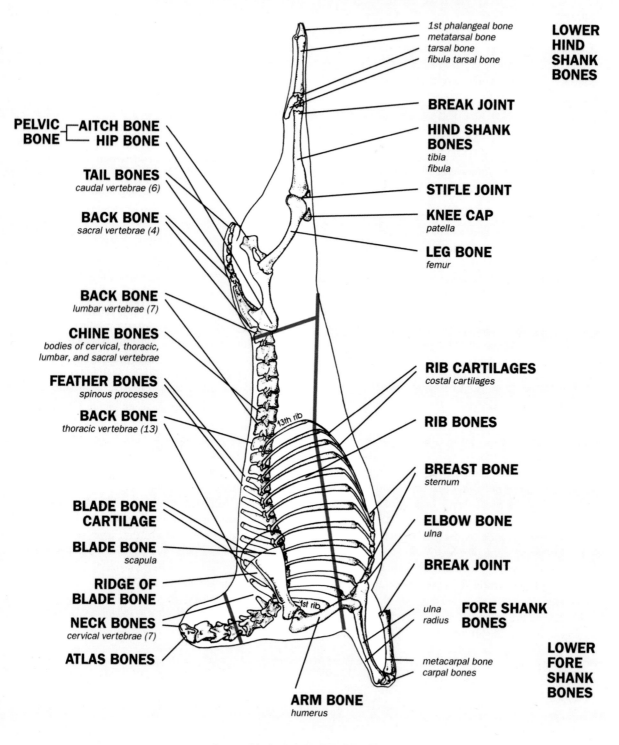

Lamb Skeletal Chart
Location, Structure, and Names of Bones

1st phalangeal bone
metatarsal bone
tarsal bone
fibula tarsal bone

LOWER HIND SHANK BONES

BREAK JOINT

PELVIC BONE — **AITCH BONE** — **HIP BONE**

HIND SHANK BONES
tibia
fibula

TAIL BONES
caudal vertebrae (6)

STIFLE JOINT

BACK BONE
sacral vertebrae (4)

KNEE CAP
patella

LEG BONE
femur

BACK BONE
lumbar vertebrae (7)

CHINE BONES
bodies of cervical, thoracic, lumbar, and sacral vertebrae

RIB CARTILAGES
costal cartilages

FEATHER BONES
spinous processes

BACK BONE
thoracic vertebrae (13)

13th rib

RIB BONES

BREAST BONE
sternum

BLADE BONE CARTILAGE

ELBOW BONE
ulna

BLADE BONE
scapula

BREAK JOINT

RIDGE OF BLADE BONE

ulna
radius

FORE SHANK BONES

1st rib

NECK BONES
cervical vertebrae (7)

ATLAS BONES

metacarpal bone
carpal bones

LOWER FORE SHANK BONES

ARM BONE
humerus

Courtesy of the American Meat Science Association.

13.9 Pork skeletal chart
© 2007 NAMP, reprinted with permission of John Wiley & Sons

Pork Skeletal Chart

Location, Structure, and Names of Bones

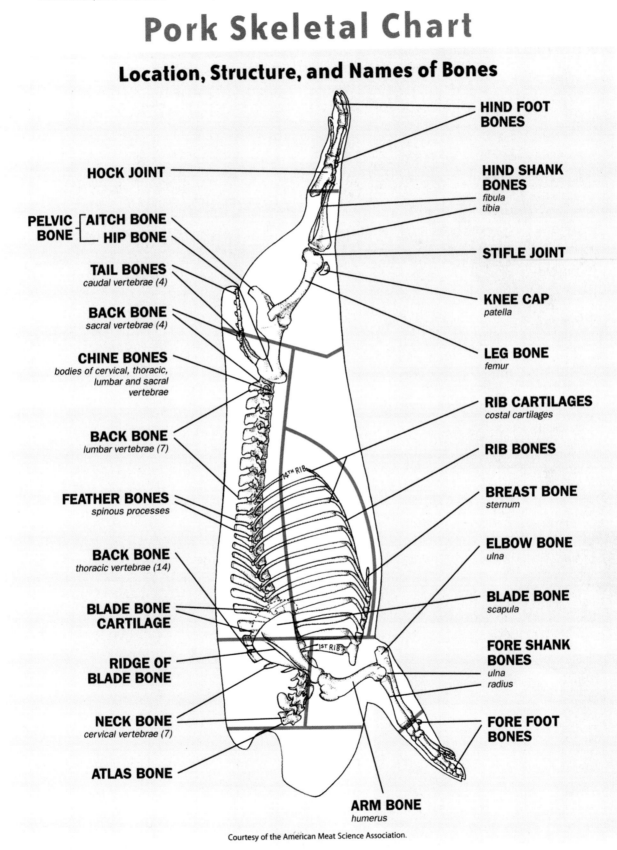

HIND FOOT BONES

HOCK JOINT

HIND SHANK BONES
fibula
tibia

PELVIC BONE — AITCH BONE / HIP BONE

STIFLE JOINT

TAIL BONES
caudal vertebrae (4)

KNEE CAP
patella

BACK BONE
sacral vertebrae (4)

CHINE BONES
bodies of cervical, thoracic, lumbar and sacral vertebrae

LEG BONE
femur

RIB CARTILAGES
costal cartilages

BACK BONE
lumbar vertebrae (7)

RIB BONES

14TH RIB

FEATHER BONES
spinous processes

BREAST BONE
sternum

ELBOW BONE
ulna

BACK BONE
thoracic vertebrae (14)

BLADE BONE
scapula

BLADE BONE CARTILAGE

FORE SHANK BONES
ulna
radius

1ST RIB

RIDGE OF BLADE BONE

NECK BONE
cervical vertebrae (7)

FORE FOOT BONES

ATLAS BONE

ARM BONE
humerus

Courtesy of the American Meat Science Association.

TABLE 13.3 **Veal and Calf Products Weight Ranges**

© 2007 NAMP, reprinted with permission of John Wiley & Sons

ITEM	PRODUCT NAME	SUGGESTED UPC NO.	PG*	Weight Ranges (Pounds)				
				A	B	C	D	E
	Carcass	2765	110	50–70	70–175	175–245	245–300	300–up
	Side	2630	110	25–35	35–87	87–122	122–150	150–up
	Foresaddle, 11 Ribs	2633	110	25–34	34–86	86–120	120–147	147–up
	Forequater, 11 Ribs	2634	110	12–17	17–43	43–60	60–74	74–up
	Hotel Rack, 7 Ribs	2655	111	4–6	6–14	14–20	20–25	25–up
	Hotel Rack, 6 Ribs	2662	111	3–5	5–13	13–19	19–24	24–up
	Hotel Rack, Chop-Ready, 7 Ribs	2656	111	1–2	2–5	5–7	7–9	9–up
	Hotel Rack Chop-Ready, 6 Ribs	2663	112	1–2	2–4	4–6	6–8	8–up
	Hotel Rack, Chop-Ready, 7 Ribs, Frenched	2664	112	1–2	2–5	5–7	7–9	9–up
	Hotel Rack, Chop-Ready, 6 Ribs, Frenched	2774	112	1–2	2–4	4–6	6–8	8–up
	Rack, Ribeye, Boneless, 7 Ribs	2657	112	0.5–2	2–4	4–6	6–9	9–up
	Chucks, 4 Ribs	2649	113	14–20	20–49	49–69	69–85	85–up
	Veal Chucks, Arm Chuck, 4 Ribs		113	14–20	20–49	49–69	69–85	85–up
	Chucks, Square-Cut, 4 Ribs	2635	113	11–16	16–39	39–55	55–68	68–up
	Chuck, Square-Cut, 4 Ribs, Boneless	2650	113	10–19	19–26	26–33	33–40	40–up
	Chuck, Square-Cut, 4 Ribs, Neck Off, Boneless, Tied	2651	114	9–17	17–25	25–32	32–39	39–up
	Chuck, Square-Cut, Clod Out, Boneless, Tied	2654	114	9–15	15–20	20–30	30–38	38–up
	Chuck, Outside Shoulder, Boneless	2636	114	2–4	4–5	5–7	7–9	9–up
	Chuck, Shoulder Clod, Boneless	2637	115	1.5–3	3–4	4–6	6–9	9–up
	Chuck, Shoulder Clod, Roast	2638	115	2–4	3–4	4–6	6–9	9–up
	Chuck Tender	2654	115	0.5–1	1–2			
	Chuck, Bladwe Portion, Neck Off, Boneless	2744	115	7–13	13–21	21–28	28–38	38–up
	Foreshank	2733	115	1–2	2–3	3–4	4–5	5–up
	Foreshank, Center-Cut	2745	116	under 1	1–2	2–3	3–4	4–up
	Breast	2728	116	3–4	4–10	10–15	15–18	18–up
	Breast with Pocket	2730	116	3–4	4–10	10–15	15–18	18–up
	Short Ribs	2745	117					

* Denotes page number in NAMP *Meat Buyer's Guide.*

TABLE 13.3 (continued)

Hindsaddle, 2 Ribs	2766	110	25–36	36–89	89–125	125–153	153–up
Hindquarter, 2 Ribs	2767	110	12–18	18–45	45–63	63–76	76–up
Loins	2768	117	6–12	12–18	18–30	30–36	36–up
Loins, Trimmed	2665	117	3–7	7–18	18–26	26–30	30–up
Loins, Block-Ready, Trimmed	2678	117	under 3	3–5	5–7	7–8	8–up
Leg	2679	118	19–27	27–68	68–95	95–117	117–up
Leg, Boneless	2680	118	8–11	11–26	26–36	36–45	45–up
Legs, Shank Off, Boneless	2684	118	7–10	10–24	24–34	34–42	42–up
Hindshank	2746	118	1–2	2–5	5–6	6–8	8–up
Veal Hindshank, Center Cut		119	1–2	2–3	3–4	4–5	5–6
Back, Trimmed	2769	119	8–13	13–32	32–46	46–58	58–up
Loin, Strip Loin, Boneless	2666	119	2–3	3–5	5–7	7–8	8–up
Loin, Strip Loin, Boneless, Skinned (Special)	2676	119	2–3	3–5	5–up		
Leg, Butt Tenderloin, Defatted	2677	120	1–1.5	1.5–up			
Leg, Butt Tenderloin, Skinned	2678	120	0.5–1	1–up			
Loin, Short Tenderloin	2673	120	0.5–1	1–up			
Leg, Top Round, (Inside), Cap On	2681	120	3–8	8–12	12–14	14–16	16–up
Leg, Top Round, Cap Off	2682	121	3–8	8–10	10–13	13–15	15–up
Leg, Bottom (Gooseneck), Heel Out	2706	121	under 2	2–3.5	3.5–5	5.5–7	7–up
Leg, Knuckle (Sirloin Tip), Cap Off, Trimmed	2703	121	under 1	1–2	2–3	3–4	4–up
Leg, Hip, Cap Off, Boneless	2698	122	under 1	1–1.5	1.5–2	2–2.5	2.5–up
Leg, Eye of Round (Leg)	2715	122	under 0.25	0.25–0.5	0.5–1	1–1.5	1.5–up
Leg, TBS, 4 Parts	2683	122	8–11	11–27	27–38	38–47	47–up
Leg, TBS, 3 Parts	2684	122	6–9	9–24	24–32	32–39	39–up
Leg, BHS, 3 Parts	2685	123	6–12	12–27	27–35	35–42	42–up
Bones, Mixed	2762	123					
Bones, Marrow	2763	123					
Flank, Flank Steak	2747	123	under 0.25	0.25–0.3	0.3–0.5	0.5–0.75	0.75–up
Veal for Stewing	2742	124					
Veal for Kabobs	2743	124					
Ground Veal	2722	124					

TABLE 13.4 Index of Veal Portion Cuts

© 2007 NAMP, reprinted with permission of John Wiley & Sons

ITEM	PRODUCT NAME	SUGGESTED UPC NO.	PG*	Suggested Portion Weight Ranges
	Cubed Steak, Boneless	2736	128	3–8 oz.
	Cubed Steak, Boneless, Special	2746	128	3–8 oz.
	Veal Slices, Boneless	2720	128	1–6 oz.
	Rack, Rib Chops, 7 Rib	2655	128	4–8 oz.
	Rack, Rib Chops, 6 Rib	2905	129	4–8 oz.
	Rack, Rib Chops, Cap Off, 7 Rib	2656	129	4–8 oz.
	Rack, Rib Chops, Cap Off, 6 Rib	2906	129	4–8 oz.
	Rack, Rib Chops, Frenched, 7 Rib	2907	129	4–8 oz.
	Rack, Rib Chops, Frenched, 6 Rib	2908	129	4–8 oz.
	Chuck, Shoulder Arm Chops	2641	130	4–8 oz.
	Chuck, Shoulder Blade Chops	2646	130	4–8 oz.
	Osso Buco, Foreshank	2747	130	2–8 oz.
	Loin chops	2669	130	4–8 oz.
	Cutlets, Boneless	2714	131	3–8 oz.
	Osso Buco, Hindshank	2715	131	2–8 oz.
	Leg, Top Round (Inside), Cap Off, Cutlets, Boneless	2692	131	1–6 oz.
	Ground Veal Patties	2725	132	2–8 oz.
	Ground Veal and Vegetable Protein Product Patties	2726	132	2–8 oz.
	Veal Patties	2727	132	2–8 oz.

* Denotes page number in NAMP *Meat Buyer's Guide.*

TABLE 13.5 **Index of Lamb Products and Weight Ranges**

© 2007 NAMP, reprinted with permission of John Wiley & Sons

ITEM	PRODUCT NAME	Suggested UPC NO.	PG*	Weight Ranges (Pounds)			
				A	B	C	D
200	Carcass	2910	80	41–55	55–65	65–75	75–up
200A	Carcass, 3 Way	2911	80	41–55	55–65	65–75	75–up
200B	Carcass, Block-Ready	2912	80	41–55	55–65	65–75	75–up
204	Rack	2941	81	4–5	5–7	7–9	9–up
204A	Rack, Chined	2942	81	2–down	2–3	3–4	4–up
204B	Rack, Roast-Ready	2951	81	2–down	2–3	3–4	4–up
204C	Rack, Roast-Ready Frenched	2945	82	2–down	2–3	3–4	4–up
204D	Rack, Roast-Ready, Frenched, Special	2946	82	1.5–down	1.5–2.5	2.5–3.5	3.5–up
204E	Rack, Ribeye Roll	2943	82	1–down	1–1.5	1.5–2.5	2.5–up
206	Shoulder	2937	82	14–19	19–23	23–27	27–up
207	Shoulder, Square-Cut	2913	83	5–6	6–8	8–10	10–up
207A	Shoulder, Outside	2938	83	3–down	3–4	4–5	5–up
208	Shoulder, Square-Cut, Boneless	2929	83	4–5	5–7	7–9	9–up
208A	Shoulder, Outside, Boneless	2934	83	2–down	2–3	3–5	5–up
208B	Shoulder, Arm Out, Boneless	2939	84	3–down	3–4	4–6	6–up
208C	Shoulder, Inside Roll, Boneless	2940	84	1.5–down	1.5–2.5	2.5–3.5	3.5–up
209	Breast	3002	84	2–down	2–3	3–4	4–up
209A	Ribs, Breast Bones Off	3008	84	2–down	2–3	3–4	4–up
209B	Shoulder, Ribs	3007	85	1–down	1–2	3–4	4–up
210	Forehank	3010	85	0.5–1	1–1.5	1.5–2	2–up
229A	Hindsaddle, Long-Cut, Trimmed	3030	85	23–29	29–36	36–41	41–up
230	Hindsaddle	3031	85	20–25	25–30	30–35	35–up
231	Loins	3032	86	6–8	8–11	11–13	13–up
232	Loins, Trimmed	2953	86	4–5	5–7	7–9	9–up
232A	Loin, Block-Ready, Trimmed	2962	87	1–2	2–3	3–4	4–up

* Denotes page number in NAMP *Meat Buyer's Guide.*

TABLE 13.5 *(continued)*

ITEM	PRODUCT NAME	Suggested UPC NO.	PG*	Weight Ranges (Pounds)			
				A	B	C	D
232B	Loins, Double, Boneless	2958	87	2–down	2–3	3–5	5–up
232C	Loin, Single, Boneless		87	1–down	1–1.5	1.5–2.5	2.5–up
232D	Loin, Short Tender-loin	2961	87	0.5–down	0.5–1	1–2	2–up
233	Legs	2964	88	6–9	9–13	13–17	17–up
233A	Leg, Trotter Off	2994	88	5–9	9–13	13–17	17–up
233C	Leg, Trotter Off, Semi-Boneless	2972	88	4–8	8–12	12–16	16–up
233D	Leg, Shank Off, Semi-Boneless	2995	89	3–5	5–7	7–10	10–up
233E	Leg, Steamship, 3/4, Aitch Bone Removed	2967	89	5–7	7–9	9–11	11–up
233F	Leg, Hindshank	2997	89	1–down	1–2	2–up	
233G	Leg, Hindshank, Hell On	2969	90	1–down	1–up		
234	Leg, Boneless	2973	90	5–8	8–11	11–13	13–up
234A	Leg, Shank Off, Boneless	2974	90	6–8	8–9	9–11	11–up
234C	Leg, Bottom, Boneless		90	1–3	2–4	4–6	6–up
234D	Leg, Outside, Boneless	2987	91	1–down	1–1.5	1.5–3	3–up
234E	Leg, Inside, Boneless	2985	91	1–down	1–1.5	1.5–2	2–up
234F	Leg, Sirloin Tip, Boneless	2989	91	0.5–down	0.5–1.5	1.5–2.5	2.5–up
234G	Sirloin, Boneless	2982	92	2–down	2–3	3–4	4–up
235	Back	3033	92	11–12	12–14	14–16	16–18
236	Back, Trimmed	3034	92	8–11	11–13	13–15	15–up
246	Tenderloin	2961	93	0.5–down	5.5–1.5	1.5–2.5	2.5–up
295	Lamb for Stewing	3016	93	*Amount as Specified*			
295A	Lamb for Kabobs	3017	93	*Amount as Specified*			
296	Ground Lamb	2998	94	*Amount as Specified*			

TABLE 13.6 **Index of Lamb Portion Cuts**

© 2007 NAMP, reprinted with permission of John Wiley & Sons

ITEM	PRODUCT NAME	SUGGESTED UPC NO.	PG*	Suggested Portion Weight Range
1200	Cubed Steaks	3013	98	2–6 oz.
1204B	Rib Chops	2948	98	2–8 oz.
1204C	Rib Chops, Frenched	2949	98	2–8 oz.
1204D	Rib Chops, Frenched, Special	2951	99	2–8 oz.
1204F	Rib Chops, Frenched, Fancy	2952	99	2–8 oz.
1207	Shoulder Chops	2918	100	2–8 oz.
1232A	Loin Chops	2955	100	2–8 oz.
1232C	Loin Chops, Single, Boneless	2957	101	2–8 oz.
1233E	Leg, Center-Cut Chops	2980	101	2–8 oz.
1234A	Leg, Cutlet, Boneless	2992	101	2–8 oz.
1296	Ground Lamb Patties	2999	102	2–8 oz.

* Denotes page number in NAMP *Meat Buyer's Guide.*

TABLE 13.7   **Index of Pork Products and Weight Ranges**

© 2007 NAMP, reprinted with permission of John Wiley & Sons

ITEM	PRODUCT NAME	SUGGESTED UPC NO.	PG*	Weight Ranges (Pounds)			
				A	B	C	D
	Carcass	3160	140	120–150	150–180	180–210	210–up
	Roasting Pig	3161	140	12–24	24–40	40–60	100–up
	Leg (Fresh Ham)	3390	141	14–17	17–20	20–26	26–up
	Leg (Fresh Ham), Short Shank	3391	141	14–17	17–20	20–26	26–up
	Leg, Hind Semi-Boneless	3400	141	14–16	16–18	18–20	20–up
	Leg, Hind Shank	3517	142	1–down	1–up		
	Leg (Fresh Ham), Skinned	3387	142	14–17	17–20	20–26	26–up
	Leg (Fresh Ham), Skinned, Short Shank	3401	142	14–17	17–20	20–26	26–up
	Leg (Fresh Ham), Boneless	3388	143	6–8	8–10	10–12	12–up
	Leg (Fresh Ham), Boneless, Short Shank, Trimmed	3406	143	6–8	8–10	10–12	12–up
	Leg (Fresh Ham), Outside	3411	143	2–4	4–5	5–6	6–up
	Leg (Fresh Ham), Outside, Trimmed, Shank Removed	3425	143	2–3	3–5	5–6	6–up
	Leg (Fresh Ham), Inside	3408	144	3–down	3–4	4–5	5–up
	Leg (Fresh Ham), TBS, 3-Way, Boneless	3426	144	12–14	14–16	16–18	18–up
	Shoulder	3180	144	8–12	12–16	16–20	20–up
	Shoulder, Outside	3213	145	8–12	12–18	18–22	22–up
	Shoulder, Inside, Boneless	3214	145	2–4	4–8	8–up	
	Shoulder, Skinned	3163	145	8–12	12–16	16–20	2–up
	Shoulder, Picnic	3168	146	4–6	6–8	8–12	12–up
	Shoulder, Picnic, Boneless	3170	146	2–4	4–6	6–8	8–up
	Shoulder, Picnic, Cushion, Boneless	3204	146	*Amount as Specified*			
	Shoulder, Pectoral Meat		147	1–down	1–up		
	Shoulder, Boston Butt, Bone In	3184	147	2–4	4–8	8–up	
	Shoulder, Boston Butt, Boneless	3185	147	2–4	4–8	8–up	
	Shoulder, Boston Butt, Boneless, Special	3205	147	2–4	4–6	6–8	8–up
	Shoulder Butt, Cellar Trimmed, Boneless	3206	148	1.5–3	3–4	4–7	7–up
	Belly	3427	148	10–12	12–14	14–18	18–up
	Fat Back	3499	148				
	Belly, Skinless	3431	148	7–9	9–11	11–13	13–up
	Belly, Single Ribbed, Skinless	3432	148	10–12	12–14	14–18	18–up
	Belly, Center-Cut, Skinless	3481	149	7–9	9–11	11–13	13–up

* Denotes page number in NAMP *Meat Buyer's Guide.*

TABLE 13.7   *(continued)*

ITEM	PRODUCT NAME	SUGGESTED UPC NO.	PG*	Weight Ranges (Pounds)			
				A	B	C	D
	Loin, Bone In	3216	149	10–14	14–18	18–22	22–up
	Loin, Sirloin End, Bone In	3330	150	4–down	4–up		
	Loin, Rib End, Bone In	3289	150	4–down	4–up		
	Loin, Bone In, Bladeless	3218	150	10–14	14–18	18–22	22–up
	Loin, Bone In, Center-Cut, 8 Ribs	3225	151	4–6	6–8	8–10	10–up
	Loin, Bone In, Center-Cut, 8 Ribs, Chine Bone Off	3227	151	4–5	5–7	7–9	9–up
	Loin, Boneless, Center-Cut, 8 Ribs	3226	152	2–4	4–5	4–6	6–up
	Loin, Boneless, Center-Cut, 11 Ribs	3231	152	5–7	7–9	9–11	11–up
	Loin, Boneless, Center-Cut, 11 Ribs, Chine Bone Off	3232	153	4–6	6–8	8–10	10–up
	Loin, Boneless, Center-Cut, 11 Ribs	3333	153	3–5	5–6	6–7	7–up
	Loin, Center-Cut, Rib End (Rack)	3266	153	7–down	7–up		
	Loin, Boneless	3224	154	6–8	8–10	10–12	12–up
	Loin, Boneless, Roast	3270	154	6–8	8–10	10–12	12–up
	Loin, Boneless, Special	3273	155	6–8	8–10	10–12	12–up
	Loin, Loin Eye		155	3–5	5–8	8–up	
	Loin, Canadian Back	3383	155	3–4	4–5	5–6	6–up
	Tenderloin	3358	156	0.5–1	1–1.5	1.5–up	
	Tenderloin, Side Muscle Off	3365	156	0.5–1	1–1.5	1.5–up	
	Spareribs	3468	159	2.5–down	2.5–3.5	3.5–5.5	5.5–up
	Spareribs, St. Louis Style	3478	159	1.5–2	2–3	3–up	
	Spareribs, Brisket Bones	3480	159	0.25–0.33	0.33–0.5	0.5–0.75	0.75–up
	Spareribs, Breast Off	3479	159	2.5–down	2.5–3.5	3.5–5.5	5.5–up
	Breast Bones	3482	159*	Under–1	Over–1		
	Shoulder Hocks	3511	156	0.25–0.75	0.75–1.5	1.5–up	
	Leg (Fresh Ham) Hocks	3516	156				
	Trimmings	3541	157				
	Pig's Feet, Front	3508	157				
	Neck Bones	3484	157				
	Loin, Back Ribs	3243	158	1.5–down	1.5–1.75	1.75–2.25	2.25–up
	Loin, Country-Style Ribs	3275	160	2–3	3–up		
	Loin, Riblet	3496	160				
	Pork for Kabobs	3496	161				
	Caul Fat	3553	161				
	Ground Pork	3433	162				

TABLE 13.8   Index of Pork Portion Cuts

© 2007 NAMP, reprinted with permission of John Wiley & Sons

ITEM	PRODUCT NAME	SUGGESTED UPC NO.	PG*	Suggested Portion Weight Range
1400	Steak, Cubed	3421	166	3–8 oz.
1401	Steak, Cubed, Special	3425	166	3–8 oz.
1402	Cutlets	3490	166	3–8 oz.
1406	Boston Butt Steaks	3186	167	4–8 oz.
1407	Shoulder Butt Steaks, Boneless	3192	167	3–8 oz.
1410	Loin Chops	3313	167	3–8 oz.
1410A	Loin, Rib Chops	3236	168	3–8 oz.
1410B	Loin, End Chops	3325	168	4–8 oz.
1411	Loin Chops, Bladeless	3326	168	3–8 oz.
1412	Loin Chops, Center-Cut	3322	169	3–8 oz.
1412A	Loin Chops, Center-Cut, Chine Bone Off	3369	169	3–8 oz.
1412B	Loin Chops, Center-Cut, Boneless	3354	170	3–8 oz.
1412E	Loin Chops, Center-Cut, One Muscle, Boneless	3379	170	6–8 oz.
1413	Loin Chops, Boneless	3374	170	3–6 oz.
1413B	Loin, End Chops, Boneless	3383	171	3–6 oz.
1438	Steaks, Flaked and Formed, Frozen	3482	171	*Amount as specified*
1438A	Sandwich Steaks, Flaked, Chopped, Formed, and Wafer Sliced, Frozen	3483	171	*Amount as specified*
1495	Coarse Chopped Pord	3465	172	*Amount as specified*
1496	Ground Pork Patties	3466	172	*Amount as specified*

* Denotes page number in NAMP *Meat Buyer's Guide.*

CONVENIENCE CORNER PRODUCT EXAMPLES

Meats and Offal

Company	Website	Products
Cargill	http://www.cargillfoods.com	20/8 oz Beef Ribeye Burger 2/5# Pork Medallions Stirfry
Farmland	http://www.farmlandfood service.com	10# Franks Beef Black Angus 4×1 32/5 oz Pork Chop Smoked
Hormel	http://www.hormelfoods.com	2/10# Bacon Smokehouse 13/17 xt 6/2# Beef Corned Sliced 3/5# Beef Barbacoa 2/5# Salami Hard
Johnsonville	http://www.johnsonville.com	10# Sausage Crumble Hot 180/1 oz Sausage Link Maple 18×1
Rich's	http://www.richs.com	4/5# Beef BBQ w/sauce
Tyson	http://www.tyson.com	2/5# Meatloaf Cooked 4/5# Tyson Beef Taco Mix
Fontanini	http://www.fontanini.com	2/5# Beef Pot Roast w/Gravy
Armour -Star	http://www.armour-star.com	10# Meatballs Beef ½ oz
Austin Blues	http://www.hormelfood service.com/brands/austin-blues.aspx	12/1.75 # Blue Pork Ribs St. Louis
Hillshire Farms	http://www.gomeat.com	2/6# Sausage Cheddarwurst 5×1
Patrick Cudahy	http://www.patrickcudahy.com	2/10# Bacon 14/18 Apple Smoked

Offal (Variety Meats)

Offal, also called *variety meats*, consists of the edible non-muscular parts of slaughter animals. **Variety meats** are generally broken down into organ meats: red offal (which includes heart, tongue, lungs or "lights," liver, and kidneys) and white offal (brains, marrow, testicles or "mountain oysters," feet, thymus or "sweetbreads," head, and tripe). Certain variety meats are more highly appreciated, such as kidneys, veal liver, sweetbreads, brains, tongue, and lamb testicles or "fries," and are thus more costly.

The main types of beef offal are tongue, liver, tripe, feet, and tail (oxtail) (see Figure 13.10a on the following page). Pork provides the greatest selection of common variety meats (see Figure 13.10b). Sheep and lamb offal consists of brains, kidneys, fries, and feet (see Figure 13.10c). Veal offal (brains, marrow, kidneys, liver, and sweetbreads) is particularly prized, given its delicate flavor. Lungs and spleen are used mainly as animal feed and historically have been eaten in times of famine. In modern times, foie gras has become the most expensive variety meat of choice.

In addition to the unusual organ meats, meat mixtures such as sausage meats and cold cuts are also classified as variety meats. Sausages are important to many international cuisines and are commonly featured during every meal period in American food service.

BUYING AND STORING

Always make sure that variety meats are very fresh, as they are much more perishable than other meats. They should have the characteristic offal color and should not be swimming in liquid. Buy about 5 ounces of raw offal for each 3 ½ ounces of cooked meat that the recipe requires (Figure 13.11).

Because the liver and kidneys filter undesirable substances found in the live animal's body, they can contain traces of heavy metals, medicines, and pesticides. However, given government control of meat products and the fact that most people consume only moderate quantities of variety meats, the risk to humans is probably negligible.

Variety meats are highly perishable and can be kept for only a day or two, in the refrigerator. Although they can be frozen for 3 to 4 months, freezing alters the flavor, texture, and appearance of most types of offal.

Buy smooth, evenly colored sausages that do not feel sticky. Dried sausage should be firm, have a pleasant odor, and be covered with a "bloom" (small white spots about the size of the head of a pin). Check the expiration date on vacuum-packed products.

Fresh or cooked sausages can be refrigerated for about 3 days and frozen for 2 to 3 months. If they are in sealed packages, they can be frozen as is; otherwise, wrap them well before freezing them. Whole dried sausages can be stored for up to 3 months in a cool, dry place. When dried sausages are very ripe, or if they have been partially or completely sliced, store them in a refrigerator and serve them within 3 to 5 days. Cover them and store them well away from foods with strong odors. Sliced cooked sausages can also be refrigerated for 3 to 5 days.

HEART

The heart is a type of red offal. Eating the heart of an animal has long been considered a symbolic gesture; in primitive societies, it was thought to bolster courage. But heart has very little importance in contemporary cuisine.

Although the heart is quite a stringy meat, it can be excellent. The hearts of calves, lambs, and chickens are the most sought after, because they are small and tender. Pig's heart is moderately tender, while ox (beef) heart is the largest, firmest, and strongest tasting (see Figure 13.12).

13.12   **Beef heart**

 13.11   **Sliced blood sausage**
Courtesy of Robert Garlough

13.10a **Diagram showing where offal, or variety meats, come from on beef**

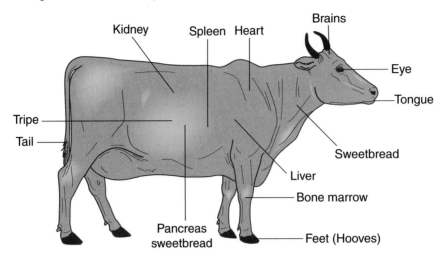

13.10b **Diagram showing where offal, or variety meats, come from on pork**

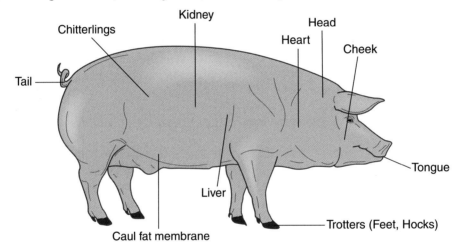

13.10c **Diagram showing where offal, or variety meats, come from on sheep**

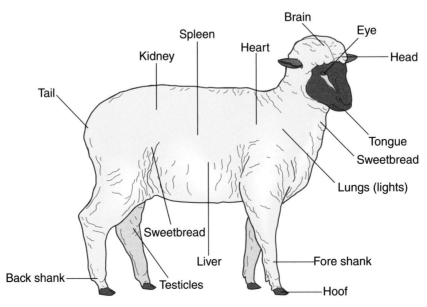

LIVER

Liver is a type of edible red offal that comes from domesticated animals, poultry, and game, as well as from certain fish (cod, monkfish, and skate). Liver from young animals is more tender and flavorful, and calf's (baby beef) liver is the most sought after. The livers of lamb, heifers, rabbits, and poultry such as chicken, duck, and geese are also renowned for their tenderness and their delicate flavor. Liver from oxen (beef), sheep, and pigs has a stronger flavor and becomes relatively pasty when cooked (see Figure 13.13).

The color of liver ranges from pinkish brown to reddish brown, depending on the species and age of the animal. Look for shiny liver with a pleasant smell; it should not be soaking in a large amount of liquid. Buy approximately 6 ounces of raw liver for each 4-ounce portion of cooked liver that the recipe requires.

Foie Gras

Foie gras is duck or goose liver that has been hypertrophied (enlarged) by force-feeding the birds; prepared and cooked with great care, it is regarded as a delicacy by food connoisseurs. The use of the term *foie gras* is regulated in several countries, including France, to avoid confusion and misleading claims. At least 20 percent of any product labeled *foie gras* must consist of fattened goose or duck liver. If the product does not meet or exceed the 20 percent rule, and it contains the livers or flesh of other animals, it should be referred to as *foie-gras pâté, terrine,* or *galantine.*

The force-feeding of geese and ducks is an ancient practice that dates back to the time of the Egyptians; they noticed that wild geese would prepare for migration by eating vast amounts of food and storing the excess energy in the form of fat in their livers. The Greeks also were known to force-feed geese with a mixture of crushed wheat and water, while the Romans used figs. Geese and ducks are now usually force-fed a gruel-like mixture of corn, lard, beans, and salt. Fattened goose livers generally weigh between 28 and 36 ounces, but fattened duck livers rarely weigh more

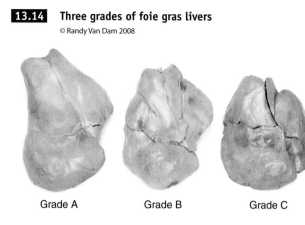

13.14 **Three grades of foie gras livers**
© Randy Van Dam 2008

Grade A Grade B Grade C

than 12 to 16 ounces. Those opposed to the force-feeding of animals contend that the practice is inhumane. Foie gras is produced in various ways: in France, force-feeding birds by means of tubes is an increasingly popular method; an alternative method is to induce bulimia in geese by destroying their ability to determine whether they are hungry, which makes it easier to force-feed and fatten them.

Foie gras is sold raw and ready to eat. It should be refrigerated the day before it is eaten; open the container 1 hour before it is to be served, returning it to the refrigerator. Run the blade of a knife under hot water, and then cut the foie gras into slices. It can be eaten with a fork or on toasted bread. Because foie gras is perishable, it can be kept refrigerated for no longer than 3 or 4 days after the package has been opened. Reseal the package carefully to prevent the foie gras from drying out or absorbing food odors. (See Figure 13.14.)

TONGUE

The tongue has a thick membrane, which should be removed after cooking (see Figure 13.15a and Figure 13.15b). Beef tongue can weigh up to 5 pounds and has a very strong taste

13.15a **Fresh beef tongue (unpeeled) in the marketplace**
Courtesy of Robert Garlough

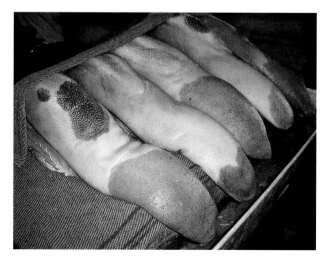

13.13 **Beef liver**
© Randy Van Dam 2008

13.15b   **Fresh beef tongue (peeled) ready for production**
© Randy Van Dam 2008

13.16   **Thalamus (sweetbread)**

as compared with calf's tongue, which is very tender. Pig and bird tongue are also available, and some fish tongue such as cod can be purchased.

Tongue can be refrigerated for 1 or 2 days, but it should be cooked as soon as possible because it deteriorates rapidly, especially if left at room temperature for a long period of time in the liquid in which it was cooked. Tongue can be frozen for 3 to 4 months.

SWEETBREADS

A **sweetbread** is the thymus gland from lambs and calves. It is a small white gland located just below the windpipe. The gland has two parts: a central lobe, which is called the heart sweetbread or kernel, and two outside lobes known as the throat sweetbread. The lobes disappear as the animal ages, so sweetbreads are only available from young stock. (See Figure 13.16.)

Sweetbreads have a delicate taste and are very perishable. They should be cooked as soon as possible, within a day or two at most. They can be blanched and frozen if needed.

BRAINS

The brains of certain slaughter animals are commonly cooked and eaten. The most delicate and sought after are those of sheep and lambs, which are very pale. The taste of calf brains, which are more highly colored, is comparable. Cow brains are firmer and red-veined, and pork brains are seldom eaten. Only purchase brains from reputable dealers who had access to the animals while they were alive and can verify where the stock came from.

Choose brains that are grayish pink, plump, pleasant smelling, and free of spots and blood clots. Buy about 4 ounces of fresh brains per serving. Brains are highly perishable; they can be kept for a day or two in the refrigerator. If not used immediately, they should be blanched in salted water with a bit of vinegar or lemon juice.

CALF KIDNEYS

Kidney is a type of red offal that comes from various domesticated animals. Pork and sheep kidneys are composed of a single lobe, while those of the calf and the ox (beef) have several. The kidneys of young animals like calves, heifers, and lambs are tender and flavorful. Pork, sheep, and beef kidneys have a strong, bitter taste and are relatively tough. Beef and lamb kidneys are dark brown, calves' kidneys are a lighter shade of brown (see Figure 13.17), and pork kidneys are a light shade of reddish brown.

Choose plump, firm, shiny kidneys of the appropriate color; they should not smell of ammonia. Because kidneys are extremely perishable, they should not be refrigerated for longer than 1 day. They can be frozen but must be used as soon as they are defrosted.

TRIPE

Tripe is made from the stomachs of cows and lambs (see Figure 13.18). Tripe is usually blanched before it is sold. Choose white or cream-colored tripe (the color depends on

13.17 **Calves' (veal) kidneys**
Courtesy of Robert Garlough

13.18 **Beef tripe**
Courtesy of Robert Garlough

the sex of the animal) that has a pleasant odor. Before cooking tripe, soak it for about 10 minutes in cold water, then rinse it, brush it to remove the fat, and slice it. Tripe can be poached for 1 or 2 hours, then sautéed or fried for about 10 minutes. It can also be blanched for about 15 minutes and then braised for 3 to 4 hours; it can be tough if not thoroughly cooked.

SAUSAGES

The Greeks and Romans were the first major producers of sausage, followed later by the Germans who refined their techniques. Sausage is an easy solution for using up leftover parts of an animal after the meat is removed. By varying the spices, meat, and casing, there are hundreds of different sausages available on the market. Each country has its own methods for making sausage, led by the Germans who make more than 1,500 varieties.

Most sausages are made from lean and fatty cuts of pork, but some sausages are also made from beef, lamb, veal, poultry, and the variety meats. There are vegetarian versions that are made from tofu, soy, and vegetable mixtures. Most sausages also contain water, fillers such as flour or milk powder, sugars, spices, and preservatives. All of the ingredients are chopped coarsely or finely, depending on the desired result, and mixed together to form what is known as the filling or stuffing, which is sometimes smoked (see Figure 13.20a).

Then the mixture is piped into a natural or synthetic casing. **Natural casings** are pork or lamb intestines while **synthetic casings** are made from collagen or cellulose (see Figure 13.19a, Figure 13.19b, and Figure 13.19c). Cellulose casings are inedible, and they must be peeled before eating. Collagen casings are edible. Today, most casings are artificial, though natural casings are used for some specialty sausages. (See Figure 13.20b and Figure 13.20c.)

> **BUYER'S NOTE** *See Table 5.5 in Chapter 5 for a list of fuels commonly used for smoking meat products.*

Types of Sausages

There are four types of sausages available on the market:

Small fresh sausages: These are either raw or cured and smoked. Some examples include Toulouse sausages, merguez, crepinettes, chipolatas, frankfurters, and breakfast sausages. Small fresh sausages can be grilled, fried, or boiled. Sausages that are dried and cured can be eaten without any additional cooking. (See Figure 13.21.)

Small cooked sausages: These are small sausages that are cooked at the plant and can be eaten as is. Some examples include cocktail sausages, Vienna sausages, and Strasbourg saveloy sausages. They can be warmed before serving. (See Figure 13.22.)

Large cooked sausages: These are large, long sausages that are too big to eat without slicing or cutting into cubes. Cooked sausages are purchased pre-cooked, and they are normally served cold. Large cooked sausages are the most common variety, and each nation has its own favorites. Some examples include Mortadella, Cambridge sausage, bologna, liver sausage, and saucisson de Paris and saucision de Lyon. (See Figure 13.23.)

Dried sausages: Dried sausages are raw but have been salted, fermented, and then dried. The fermentation transforms the sugar in the mixture into lactic acid, which helps to preserve it. Because dried sausages have no water and are very acidic, they are shelf stable with a long shelf life. Examples of dried sausage include salami, pepperoni, summer sausage, and other deli meat varieties. (See Figure 13.24a and Figure 13.24b. Also, for assorted smoked meats and sausages, see Figure 13.25.)

13.19a **Diagram illustrating where natural casings come from beef**

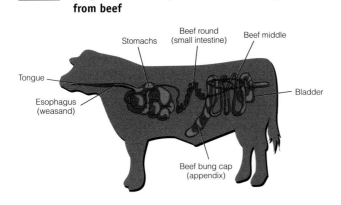

13.20a **Various sausage ingredients being mixed**

Figures 13.20a - c © Randy Van Dam 2008

13.19b **Diagram illustrating where natural casings come from hog**

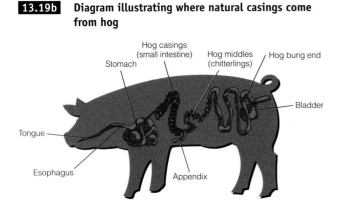

13.20b **Sausage being stuffed into casing through sausage horn**

13.19c **Diagram illustrating where natural casings come from sheep**

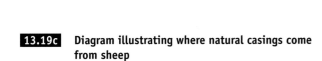
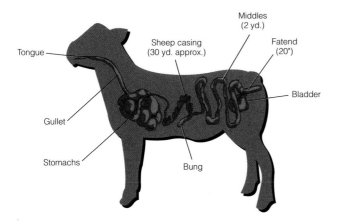

13.20c **Sausage being loaded into a smoker**

13.21 **Small fresh sausages**
© Randy Van Dam 2008

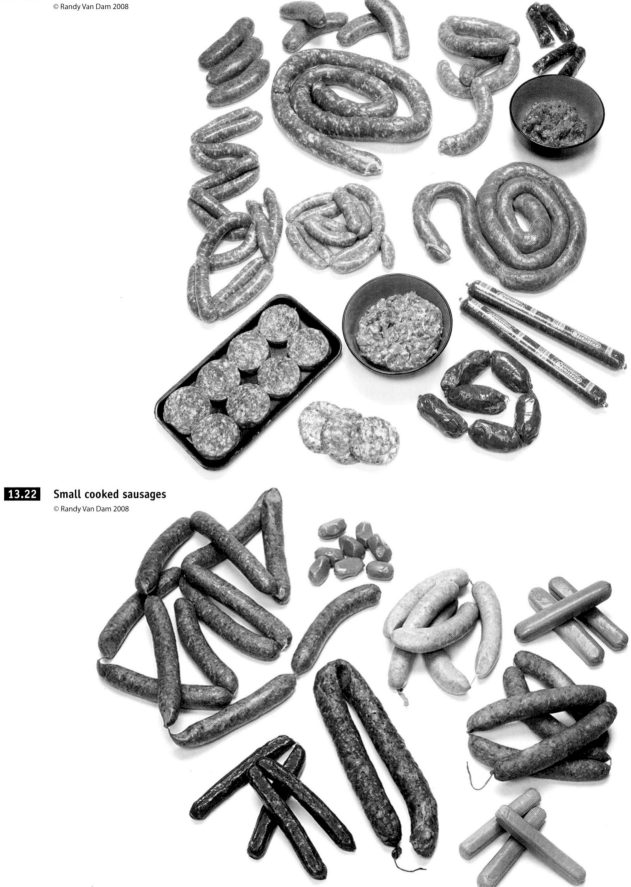

13.22 **Small cooked sausages**
© Randy Van Dam 2008

13.23   **Large cooked sausages**
© Randy Van Dam 2008

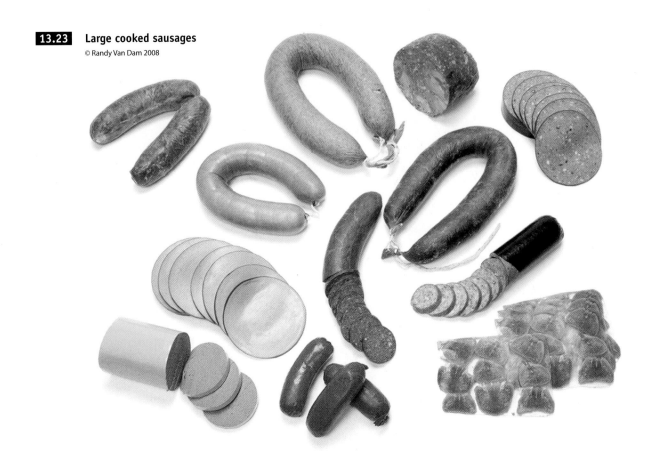

13.24a   **Dried sausages**
© Randy Van Dam 2008

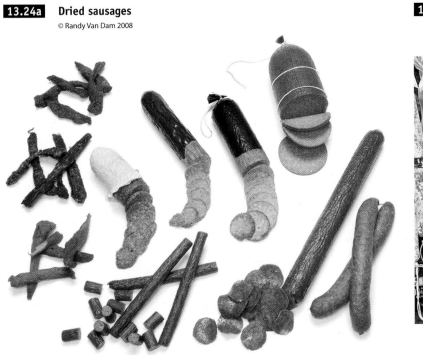

13.24b   **Dried sausages hanging in the charcuterie shop**
Courtesy of Robert Garlough

13.25 Assorted smoked meats
© Randy Van Dam 2008

13.26 **Scottish Breakfast featuring grilled blood sausage**
Courtesy of Robert Garlough

People, Places, Things

Blood Sausages

Blood sausage consists mainly of pig's blood and fat that is cooked and seasoned, then stuffed into a section of intestine. It may also contain ox, calf's, or sheep's blood. Thought to be one of the first prepared meats consumed by humans, it is mentioned in texts dating back over 5,000 years. Blood sausages are made in an infinite variety of ways; it has been suggested that in France there are as many different kinds of blood sausages as there are butchers, because the proportions of blood and fat can be varied and a broad range of optional ingredients can be added (onions, spinach, raisins, apples, prunes, chestnuts, milk, cream, brandy, semolina, crustless bread, oats, spices, and herbs). This mixture is inserted into a casing (usually the intestine of the animal), and then poached. Scottish people consume grilled blood sausage regularly, as part of their famous "Scottish breakfast." (See Figure 13.26)

TABLE 13.9   **Sausage Varieties and Origins**

Sausage	Type	Known Origin	Ingredients	Cooking Method
Andouille	Smoked	Cajun	Pork, salt, very spicy, sugar, paprika, red pepper, garlic, sage	Ready to eat
Berliner	Cured, smoked	Berlin, Germany	Pork, veal, beef chuck, dextrose, onion, salt, pepper	Ready to eat
Blood Sausage (Blood pudding)	Fresh	United Kingdom	Pig's blood, diced pork fat, onions, breadcrumbs, oatmeal, black pepper, salt	Gently saut[accent over e]
Bockwurst	Fresh	Germany	Veal, pork, milk, chives, eggs	Steam, saut[accent over e], Bake to 155 degrees F
Boerewors	Fresh	South Africa	Lean beef, pork butt, coriander seeds, red wine vinegar, pepper, salt	Steam, saut[accent over e], Bake to 155 degrees F
Bologna	Cooked, Smoked	Bologna, Italy	Cured beef and pork, garlic, salt	Ready to eat
Boudin Blanc	Fresh, delicate	France	Pork, fat, eggs, cream, bread crumbs, seasonings	Gently sauté
Boudin Noir	Precooked	France	Onions, pork fat, blood, bread crumbs, flavorings	Ready to eat; better saut[accent over e]
Bratwurst	Fresh, sometimes smoked and cooked	Germany	Pork or beef, veal, dry milk, onion, garlic, coriander, caraway, nutmeg	Steam, Fry, Grill, Bake to 155 degrees F
Braunschweiger	Cooked	Brunswick	Pork, liver, beef liver, chicken liver, salt pork, salt, dextrose	Ready to eat
Cervelat or Summer Sausage	Cured, Smoked, Semi–Dry	France	Pork, beef, garlic, mustard, mild spices	Ready to eat
Chorizo	Dry, Smoked	Spain	Pork, cilantro, paprika, garlic, chili powder, very spicy	Usually ready to eat
Genoa	Cured, Dry	Genoa, Italy	Pork, Dextrose, Burgundy wine, pepper, salt	Ready to eat
Goteborg	Smoked	Gothenberg, Sweden	Beef, pork,	Ready to eat
Hot Dogs (Frankfurter)	Cooked, Smoked, Cured	Frankfurt-am-Main, Germany	Cured beef and pork, garlic, salt, sugar, mustard, pepper	Ready to eat
Kielbasa	Fresh, Smoked	Poland	Beef, pork, garlic, pork or beef fat, mustard	Steam, Fry, Grill, Bake to 155 degrees F
Knackwurst	Precooked, Smoked	Germany	Beef, pork, lots of garlic, cumin	Ready to eat
Kolbasz (Hungarian Sausage)	Semi-Dry, Smoked	Gyula, Hungary	Pork, garlic, Hungarian paprika, allspice, cloves, salt	Steam, saut[accent over e]
Linguica (Portuguese Sausage)	Cured, Smoked	Portugal	Pork butt, onions, lots of garlic, paprika, cumin, cinnamon, vinegar	Usually ready to eat
Lyons	Dry	Lyon, France	Pork, garlic, white wine, salt	Ready to eat
Mettwurst (Schmierwurst)	Fresh, cured, smoked	Germany	Lean salt pork, beef, coriander seeds, salt	Soft, Ready to eat
Milano Salame	Dry, cured	Milan, Italy	Pork, garlic, salt, pepper, sugar	Ready to eat
Mortadella	Semi-dry, Smoked	Italy	Cubes of pork fat, pork, beef, peppercorns, garlic, anise	Steam, Fry, Grill, Bake to 155 degrees F
Pastrami	Cured, Smoked	Romania	Beef brisket, garlic, coriander seeds, dextrose, pepper, salt	Ready to eat
Pepperoni	Air-dried	Italy	Pork, beef, lots of black and red pepper	Usually ready to eat
Polish Sausage	Fresh	Poland	Pork, beef, garlic, thyme or marjoram, pork fat, pepper	Steam, Fry, Grill, Bake to 155 degrees F
Salami	Dry, Cured	Italy, Germany	Pork, garlic, salt, pepper, sugar	Ready to eat
Sweet or Hot Italian	Fresh	Italy	Sweet: garlic, sugar, anise, and fennel Hot: paprika, chile peppers, onion, garlic, fennel, parsley	Steam, Fry, Grill, Bake to 155 degrees F
Weiners	Cooked, Smoked	Vienna, Austria	Cured beef and pork, garlic, salt, sugar,	Ready to eat

HAM

The word *ham* comes from the Old English *hamm*, which means pork that comes from the hind leg of a hog. Ham made from the front leg of a hog will be labeled *pork shoulder picnic*. Turkey ham must be made from the thigh meat of turkey. Ham can be sold in fresh, cook-before-eating, fully cooked, picnic, or country varieties. George A. Hormel & Company pioneered canned hams in the United States in 1926. (See Table 13.10.) Although the term for country ham originally referred to the preparation method of curing and smoking that was practiced in the backwoods areas of Georgia, Kentucky, Virginia, and Tennessee, it now refers to the specific style of meat preparation.

Purchasing Ham

Fresh ham should have a well-marbled lean section with a firm white layer of fat. Young pork will have a grayish-pink color while older pork will be rosy. Cured hams should be firm and plump, rosy pink with a fine grain to the meat. After curing, some hams are smoked, which is done by hanging ham in a smokehouse, allowing it to absorb smoke from smoldering fires. This gives added flavor and color to meat and slows spoilage. You will mostly likely have to depend on dating codes on the ham and the reputation of the producer to judge the quality of uncut hams. (See Figure 13.27.)

Storing Ham

Ham can be stored differently according to its method of curing and preservation. It may be left at room temperature, canned, refrigerated, or frozen. It should be noted that freezer storage is for quality only. Frozen hams remain safe indefinitely.

13.27 **Parma hams hanging in drying room**
Courtesy of Robert Garlough

TABLE 13.10 **Ham Varieties and Terminology**
Source: http://homecooking.about.com/library/weekly/blham.htm

Ham Varieties and Terminology	
Aged Hams	These are heavily cured, smoked hams that have been hung to age from one to seven (yes seven!) years. They are covered in a mold, which must be scraped and washed off prior to eating.
Bayonne Ham	This French ham hails from Bearn or the Basque region, most simply cured with Bayonne salt. These are raw, uncooked hams. Aficionados enjoy raw slices on buttered peasant bread.
Boneless, Bone-in, Partially Boned	Self-explanatory. Partially boned hams have the hip and/or shank bones removed. Hams with the bone(s) left in are generally more flavorful.
Brine-Cured	The meat is soaked in brine and then smoked. This is the most common variety at standard grocery stores. They can vary widely in quality.
Canadian Bacon	A lean cut taken from eye of the loin of the middle back. It is precooked smoked meat. It is much more akin to ham than to bacon. Also referred to as back bacon in some areas.
Canned Ham	Can consist of a whole piece of meat or bits and pieces pressed together into a form and fused with a gelatin mixture.
Country-Cured	Hogs are generally fed on nuts and fruit to produce a more flavorful and tender meat. Must be cured, aged and dried at least 70 days. They are usually dry-cured in salt, then smoked over fragrant hardwoods and aged at least six months. The meat may be drier, depending on the length of aging. A mold will most likely form, which is simply scraped and washed away. Also known as country-style ham. These are also called "old hams" in Kentucky. Most country-cured hams are uncooked and need to be cooked using a special process. Check the label.

(continued)

TABLE 13.10   *(continued)*

Ham Varieties and Terminology	
Culatello	This Italian ham is cured and soaked in wine during aging. It is lean and rosy red, with a clean, delicate flavor. A popular component of antipasto platters.
Cured Ham	Pork that has gone through a variety of curing processes to preserve the meat.
Dry Curing	The entire surface of the meat is thoroughly covered with salt and then stored until the salt permeates the meat thereby preserving it.
FDA Ham Labeling	**Ham:** contains no added water and at least 20.5 percent protein after removal of fat. **Ham with natural juices:** contains at least 18.5 percent protein. **Ham, water added:** contains up to 10 percent added water, but at least 17 percent protein. **Ham and water product:** contains any amount of water (amount must be listed).
Fresh ham	Raw, uncooked port cut of meat from the hog's hind leg. Must be cooked prior to eating.
Fully Cooked	Heated to an internal temperature of 148 degrees F or above. Need not be heated prior to serving. Can be eaten right from the wrapper or reheated to an internal temperature of 130 degrees F to release a richer flavor.
Gammon	From an Old Northern French word "Gambe" for hind- leg of the pig or ham; popular in Great Britain.
Ham Portions	Halves with the center slices removed.
Injection-Curing	The process of injecting brine into the meat. This method may also be combined with other curing techniques.
Irish Ham	Belfast is famous for their pickled or brined hams, but what gives them their own unique flavor is the process of smoking over peat fires. Like country-cured hams, they must be soaked, scrubbed, simmered and then baked before eating.
Partially Cooked	Heated to at least 137 degrees F, the minimum temperature needed to kill trichina parasite. Most commercial manufacturers cook to an internal temperature of 140 degrees F. Must be cooked prior to serving.
Picnic Ham	Meat from the upper part of the foreleg of the hog, including a portion of the shoulder. It is not a true ham, but a less expensive substitute for regular ham, although less tender in texture. It is also referred to as picnic shoulder or pork shoulder. They can be fresh or smoked. Smoked picnic hams are very similar to traditional hams.
Prosciutto	Italian ham. The meat is seasoned, salt-cured, and air-dried. It is not smoked. The meat is pressed into a dense, firm texture. Parma ham is true prosciutto. Other varieties are now made in the United States. Italian prosciuttos include prosciutto cotto (cooked) and prosciutto crudo (uncooked, but cured and ready to eat). Others are named for the region in Italy in which they were made. Prosciutto is generally eaten as-is or added during the last cooking stages. Extended cooking of prosciutto toughens the meat.
Ready-to-Eat Hams	Same as fully cooked. Can be eaten right from the wrapper or reheated to an internal temperature of 130 degrees F to release a richer flavor.
Scotch Ham	Once made in Scotland, this term now refers to uncooked, boneless, mildly cured hams sold in casings.
Smithfield Ham	A variety of country-cured ham made in Smithfield, Virginia. It is coated with salt, sodium nitrate, and sugar, refrigerated for five days, salted again, refrigerated again for one day per pound of meat, washed, refrigerated for another two weeks, smoked for ten days, and then aged six to twelve months. In order to be labeled a Smithfield, the ham must be cured in the described manner within the city of Smithfield, VA. The meat is deep red in color, dry, with a pungent flavor. Considered a gourmet's choice, they are rather expensive and need to be cooked long and slow before eating.
Sweet-Pickle Curing	The meat is covered in a seasoned sweet brine, sometimes referred to as sugar-cured where brown sugar or molasses is added to the cure mix.
Urban-Style	This is the style used by commercial manufacturers to produce mass quantities, usually using an injection-curing method. Also known as city hams. The meat is less expensive because the processing is shorter and less complicated. The end result is invariably much blander in taste than country-style.
Westphalian Ham	Made from pigs fed with acorns in the Westphalia forest of Germany. It is cured and then slowly smoked over a mixture of beechwood and juniper woods, resulting in a very dark brown, dense ham with a light smoky flavor. It is considered one of the best and as such is pricey. Black Forest ham is similar.
York Ham	From England, this mild-flavored ham has delicate pink meat and must be cooked like country-cured ham before eating. It is traditionally served with Madeira Sauce.

Jean E. Clary, CEC, AAC

Place of Birth: Pony, Montana

Educational Background and Work Experience

From the ages of 8 to 14, Jean Clary worked with his grandmother in her kitchen on a ranch in southwestern Montana. It was during the 1930s and the Great Depression; there was no money, no paved roads, no electricity, no indoor plumbing. Living was very primitive and complicated, even harsh. As it was a good-sized ranch that employed ten to thirty men, depending on the time of year, there was a lot of baking, cooking, and killing and dressing of their own beef cattle, sheep, chicken, game, fish, and hogs, which Clary was privileged to learn. They had "spring houses" (made of stone, with cold spring water running into them) and were able to keep the dairy products, eggs, and meats for short periods. In summer, excess vegetables, fruits, meat, and fish were canned and stored in the fruit cellars. Smoked and cured hams, bacon, and other meats were finished in the smokehouse. It was a tremendous foundation for any aspiring chef.

However, Clary's adult life began in the service of our country, as a soldier in the U.S. Army Air Force, where he was assigned to the Inspector General's office. Upon discharge from the military, he enrolled in college at the Montana School of Mines. To help with his education and income, Clary went to work as an underground contract miner for Anaconda Copper Mining Co. in Butte, Montana, a position he continue to hold after graduation. However, after a mining accident ended his mining career, the doctors told him to move somewhere warm and dry, so Clary went to work where he knew he would be warm and never hungry.

Clary's career in food service is as remarkable as it is vast. In the kitchen, Chef Clary worked as co-owner and executive chef of the Sierra Restaurant in Lone Pine, California; as sous chef of the Alisal Ranch Resort in Solvang, California; the executive chef of the Dream Inn Hotel in Santa Cruz, California; and as the executive chef of La Canada Country Club in La Canada, California. Clary worked as the executive vice president of Southeastern Art & Culture Center (SEAC) in Kahala, Hawaii, the Thai and Chinese Art Foundation of the tobacco heiress, Doris Duke. As a hotelier, Chef Clary

Courtesy of Robert Garlough

It Happened to Me...

"I was promoted to the position of Regional Food & Beverage Director, Region VI, a corporate position at Holiday Inns, Inc. This region consisted of sixty-two high-rise hotels in Curacao, Aruba, Jamaica, Freeport and Paradise Island, Bahamas, Bermuda, plus roadside Holiday Inns in New Orleans, Georgia, Alabama, Florida, Tennessee, New England States, and New York. These inns consistently lost $3–10 million per year in the food operations, so my job was to reduce the loss . . . and possibly even create a profit. I first visited the properties, met the management, checked kitchen storage and production areas, and procured menus from each property. In less than a week of studying the menus and information that I had gleaned, I came to the conclusion that I could readily improve the food operations and guest relations by standardizing the menus with some standard edible portion cut meats. Of the sixty-two menus I had accumulated, there were at least forty different steak cuts, all varying in sizes, trim, and grade. A customer could visit any of these properties and never get the same product twice.

I set up a meeting with Kenneth Monfort, Chairman of Monfort Meats in Greeley, Colorado, to establish a standard for four different portion-cut steaks. At that time, Monfort Meats was just starting a portion meat cutting plant in Greeley, and Region VI Holiday Inns would be an appealing account. I had previously worked with Kenneth Monfort, so we met in the Greeley corporate office and over the period of about 4 days, we negotiated a contract for about $1.5 million worth of meat cuts per quarter, for one year. I went to the portion cut plant and worked for two days showing the cutters what I wanted as a New York cut, a New York steak sandwich cut, a ribeye (airline), and a top butt sirloin. We also set up the packaging and labeling so that packaged steaks, properly labeled, could fit into the reach-in refrigerator freezers of the small inns.

I worked with Region VI Director of Sales to create packaged food functions along with rooms and other incidentals. We presented our package plans to the airlines, which they loved! They immediately filled our properties with guests, and within one year, Region VI was the top profit producer in the International Holiday Inns system. I became the International #1 Food and Beverage Director of the year at the Annual International Holiday Inns Conference in Memphis, Tennessee."

was the food and beverage director of the Holiday Inn Hollywood, vice president of Hollywood-Pacific District for Holiday Inn Inc. (ten properties), and executive vice president of Region VI and corporate food and beverage director for Holiday Inn Inc. (sixty-two properties). Chef Clary left Holiday Inn to work for famed billionaire tycoon Howard Hughes, as the executive vice president and corporate food and beverage director of Hughes' Hotel-Summa Corporation (twelve hotel properties). Clary eventually left the Hughes Corporation to venture out on his own. Along with a part-

ner, he became co-owner, executive vice president, and executive chef of his own chain of restaurants, Ricardo's Mexican Restaurants, in Las Vegas. The chain grew to eight properties, until Clary decided to retire from operations. Today, Chef Clary occasionally teaches Food and Beverage at Century College in Las Vegas, serves as an accreditation specialist for the ACF Accrediting Commission, and writes the monthly newsletter for the Honorable Order of the Golden Toque.

Memberships and Career Highlights

In 1964, Chef Clary attended his first chef's convention with the American Institute of Chefs, in Oklahoma City, Oklahoma. In 1974, he helped found the Las Vegas Chapter of the ACF–Las Vegas Chefs. Also in 1974, he was named the Number One Food & Beverage Director among all 1,736 Holiday Inn International properties and inducted into the Honorable Order of the Golden Toque, an international culinary honor society limited to 100 living members. In 1978, Clary was awarded Medal #51 from the Antonin Carême Society of San Francisco. In 1988, Chef Clary was inducted into the ACF–Las Vegas Chefs Hall of Fame. One of his proudest honors was when he served as the Grand Commander of The Honorable Order of the Golden Toque from 1994 to 1998.

Passions with the Food Service Industry

"I grew up in the Great Depression, and I was very determined not to be hungry again. It was, therefore, one of the major reasons that I was eventually drawn to the kitchen. The kitchen became an arena for me to compete against myself and to self-learn the nuances of the food industry. With schooling in chemistry and physics, which play an important part in food production, this knowledge gave me an ability to analyze the processes in a very unique way and an advantage over many others."

Advice to a Chef or Buyer

"Maintain par stocks on all items on the menu: in the storeroom, freezers, and production. Plus, maintain par stocks on all non-food items, including china, glass, silverware, kitchen utensils, pots, pans, ware washing, cleaning supplies, etc. It is one of the most important parts of controlling the kitchen. Par stock for production should be allocated to appropriate hotel pans. This means using the pans to hold portions that are dated, stored, and stocked in a consistent manner. With a maximum par stock, and a minimum to reorder or produce, you will now be able to control inventory, production, ordering, buying, and storage of all products. If you establish a usage system such as FIFO (first in, first out) or LILO (last in, last out), you will reduce all waste and spoilage. It is important that waste and spoilage should be recorded: when, why, what, authorized by whom. Trash should only contain cleaned empty cans, bottles, and paper (no food). The ware-washing area should be monitored at all times for food being returned on plates. Any excess food should be investigated to see why the customer is not consuming it. There is no need to produce what the customer will not eat."

Key Words and Concepts

---

foie gras	natural casings	sweetbreads	variety meats
IMPS	offal	synthetic casings	veal
meat	quality grade	tripe	yield grades
NAMP			

Chapter in Review

The following exercises are provided to help the reader understand and apply the contents of this chapter. They may be completed individually or in a classroom environment.

REVIEW QUESTIONS

a. What are the four basic types of animals from which meat is derived?

b. Define IMPS and NAMP. Why are they so important?

c. List the four categories of sausages, and give an example for each.

d. Define the terms *offal* and *variety meats*, and give several examples.

e. Explain the term *foie gras* as it applies to offal.

INDIVIDUAL ACTIVITIES

a. **Web based:** Research sources for organic and farm-raised meats.

b. **Experiential:** Visit a meat packing plant or butcher shop, and learn how meat is processed.

c. **Critical thinking:** Create menu items and preparation processes for lesser cuts and lesser quality meats.

GROUP ACTIVITIES

a. **Lab experience:** Obtain several cuts of meat with different quality grades and marbling levels. After grilling the meat equally, have the students blindly determine the grade of the meat, based only on taste and texture.

b. **Classroom action:** Discuss the grading system for meats and how it affects the purchasing process.

CHAPTER

14

© Janet Faye Hastings, 2009. Used under license from Shutterstock.com

Poultry and Game

"Poultry is for cookery what canvas is for painting, and the cap of Fortunatus for the charlatans. It is served to us boiled, roast, hot or cold, whole or in portions, with or without sauce, and always with equal success."

JEAN-ANTHELME BRILLAT-SAVARIN

After reading this chapter, you will be able to:

- ◎ Distinguish between poultry and feathered game.
- ◎ Describe how game differs from domesticated animals.
- ◎ Explain poultry inspection and grading.
- ◎ Summarize the quality factors for carcasses and parts.
- ◎ Outline the different categories of chicken.
- ◎ List several species of furred and feathered game.
- ◎ Differentiate between hare and rabbit.

Introduction

Poultry is any domesticated edible bird. Virtually all poultry is raised for human consumption or for their eggs. When most people hear the word *poultry*, they think of chicken, turkey, and duck. Yet, in the past several years, formerly feathered game such as pheasant and quail have begun to be farm raised and are now available year-round.

This chapter will review the common poultry birds and discuss the common game or wild animals that are available for a food service operator. As discussed in the last chapter, *The Meat Buyer's Guide* contains information on poultry, including specific chapters on chicken, turkey, duck, goose, and game birds. The guide shows the different poultry birds that are available and their associated cuts and buying forms.

Poultry

Birds have been domesticated since the earliest times. More than 4,000 years ago, early inhabitants of India and Mesopotamia bred poultry for consumption. Later, the Greeks and Romans figured out how to fatten the birds for higher yields. Poultry is prized for its high protein content. Poultry has always been a popular animal, as it is easy to raise, needing local grasses for food, and is easier to transport than the larger domesticated animals, such as cows and pigs. Now, poultry is considered a staple on most food service menus.

BUYING AND STORING

Poultry is available from a variety of resources, from broadline distributors to local merchants. It is always imperative to know the supplier and to be sure the supplier adheres to the strictest sanitary procedures during processing, storing, and shipping.

You should inspect all poultry and verify the receiving temperature upon delivery. Poultry should be delivered either at freezing for fresh products (32°F) or hard frozen for frozen products (0°F or lower). Reject any product that displays any sign of mishandling or time and temperature abuse. Some of these signs include:

- Off or stale odor
- Flesh not firm to the touch with a slightly slimy feel
- Ice pack melted
- Large amounts of blood or clear fluid
- Broken boxes or torn bags

Poultry has a short shelf life and is very time sensitive. The total time poultry spends in the temperature danger zone (41°F to 135°F) must be kept at an absolute minimum. In general, only 3 days' worth of fresh poultry should be kept in the cooler at any time. Fresh poultry should never spend more than 7 days in the cooler. Vacuum-packed and frozen product has a longer shelf life, but, once thawed or opened, it should be used within 3 days. For proper storage according to Hazard Analysis and Critical Control Point (HACCP) principles, raw unprepped poultry should be stored under raw, ready-to-cook poultry. All raw products should be stored under any cooked, ready-to-use product. The best solution is to have separate coolers for raw product and cooked product.

FEDERAL POULTRY INSPECTION AND GRADING

The USDA inspects all poultry since the passage of the Poultry Products Inspection Act of 1957, which covers all products that are shipped across state lines or to other countries. This law was expanded in 1968 to include the supervision of state **inspections** for birds that are consumed within a state.

Poultry is inspected before and after the kill by an agent of the USDA. This inspection is done by a trained veterinarian who ensures that the birds are healthy and free from any visible signs of disease. After the slaughter, the inspector checks that the carcass was not contaminated. This inspection is not a quality inspection; rather, it is a gauge of the wholesomeness of the bird and whether humans can consume it. The inspectors look for carcasses with excess pinfeathers, damaged limbs, and incomplete removal of the internal organs. All poultry must be slaughtered in a licensed, registered facility with USDA oversight. After the slaughter, the carcass must be packaged and labeled according to the regulations in the act. Unlike the beef inspection, the government pays for the inspection except when a plant is running on overtime or holidays. State plants, those that process poultry for sale within a state, must have the same level of inspection as the federal plants. The inspection mark (Figure 14.1) is required on consumer containers and shipping containers of poultry inspected under the Poultry Products Inspection Act.

The retail grading of poultry has much to do with the appearance and fat content of the bird. The procurement grading has more to do with useable yields. There are three retail grades and two procurement grades. The use of grading is voluntary, and anyone using it must pay for it. Those who do apply for the service must also provide the space, equipment, lighting, and any other facilities that the grader needs or that the regulations require. In addition, when grading is performed in a plant, the USDA must approve the plant and its facilities. (See Figure 14.2, Figure 14.3, and Figure 14.4 for sample grade marks).

14.1 **Inspection mark on consumer containers**

Courtesy USDA

Inspection Mark

14.2 **Grade mark on consumer containers**

Courtesy USDA

Federal–State Graded

Grade Mark

14.3 **Grade mark on shipping containers**

Courtesy USDA

FROZEN BROILER/FRYER CHICKEN BREAST QUARTERS AND LEG QUARTERS

Processor's
Name, Address, and Phone

Nutrition Facts Label
May Be Placed Here

Safe Handling Instructions
May Be Placed Here

KEEP FROZEN

Net Weight 40 LBS. (18.14 KG)

CONTRACT NO. _____
DATE PACKED <u>Month, Day, and Year</u>

UPC Symbol and Code

14.4 **Sample grading stamp on shipping containers**

Courtesy USDA

Quality Factors for Carcasses and Parts

The following factors must be considered in determining the quality of an individual ready-to-cook carcass or part.

- **Conformation.** This is the appearance or the shape of the bird. The inspectors will look for birds that meet the current shape guidelines.
- **Fleshing.** This is a measurement of how much flesh is on the drumstick, thighs, and breasts of the bird. The inspectors look for full, round pieces.

- **Fat covering.** The inspectors will look for fat covering the bird to see if the bird was not fattened correctly or if it is an older bird with fat accumulations in the abdominal areas.
- **Pinfeathers.** Pinfeathers are very small, fine hairs under the feathers. Most poultry farmers try to slaughter the birds right after a new layer of feathers has grown. If there are pinfeathers on the carcass, then the protruding ones (those poking out of the flesh) will need to be removed, and a lower grade will be assigned.
- **Exposed cuts, tears, and brokena bones.** Carcasses that are free from these defects always grade higher than a bird with cuts and broken bones.
- **Skin discoloration, blemishes, and bruises.** Most poultry must be packaged so that it is not exposed to air to prevent the skin from drying out and changing color. Bruises are only allowed at higher grades if there are no blood clots under the skin. Any dark or deep bruises are graded at a lower level, and the bruises are removed before the meat is sold.

STANDARDS FOR "A" QUALITY POULTRY

- **Ready-to-cook carcasses and parts.** All primal cuts should be long and deep enough to give a well-rounded appearance. The muscle meat should be plump, and the flesh should extend down the length of the cut. There should be no visible blemishes or bruises.
- **Ready-to-cook roasts.** The poultry used should be from a young bird, and all pinfeathers, blemishes, and excess fat should be removed. The majority of the finished product should be covered with skin, but the skin should not overlap. The product should be manufactured so that the shape is maintained throughout the preparation and cooking process so that the final product can be sliced with minimal separation. Any additives or flavorings should be evenly spread over the bird, and the packaging should be attractive and neat.
- **Ready-to-cook boneless poultry breasts or thighs.** All cuts should be as specified with the bones removed without damaging the surrounding meat. Skinless meat should be free of tendons, cartilage, blood clots, or any other blemishes. Some trimming around the inner muscle is permitted for cosmetic purposes.

Types of Poultry Eligible for Grading

The kinds of poultry that may be graded include, but are not limited to, chickens, turkeys, ducks, geese, pigeons, and guineas. They may be in the form of a ready-to-cook carcass or part, or a further-processed product. The following sections describe the different types of poultry. Also see Table 14.1.

Chicken

Chicken is the most common and most universal of all domesticated animals (Figure 14.5). This is for good reason. Chickens produce two major protein sources (eggs and meat), and chickens can be raised on a relatively small footprint. Chicken meat can be prepared any number of ways and can be adapted for almost any cooking style. Chicken is a cost-effective, lean protein source, especially compared with beef and pork. Chicken is available commercially in several different forms and packaging styles (see Table 14.2):

- **Poussin.** Poussin chickens are young immature birds. They are very small and are available as whole birds with giblets or as boneless specialty items.

- **Rock Cornish game hen, or Cornish game hen.** A Rock Cornish game hen, or Cornish game hen, is a young, immature chicken. Cornish game hens are usually sold in half or whole hens and are prepared as roasted hens.

- **Broiler, or fryer.** A broiler, or fryer, is a young chicken (usually 9 to 12 weeks of age). Broilers can be sold whole or in parts. Most cut-up chicken available to the food service industry is from broilers.

- **Roaster.** A roaster is a slightly older chicken (usually 3 to 5 months of age). Roasters are sold whole or in halves and roasted.

- **Capon.** A capon is a castrated male chicken (usually under 8 months of age). Capons are similar, in description and use, to broilers.

- **Stag.** A stag is an older male chicken (usually under 10 months of age) that has not been castrated. Stags have coarse skin, tough and dark flesh, and a hard breastbone cartilage.

- **Hen, stewing chicken, or fowl.** A hen, or stewing chicken or fowl, is a mature female chicken usually older than 10 months of age. These birds are by-products from egg production. They are used in slow-moist-heat recipes but are also often used in further-processed products.

14.5 **The anatomy of a bird**

© 2007 NAMP, reprinted with permission of John Wiley & Sons

ANATOMY OF A BIRD

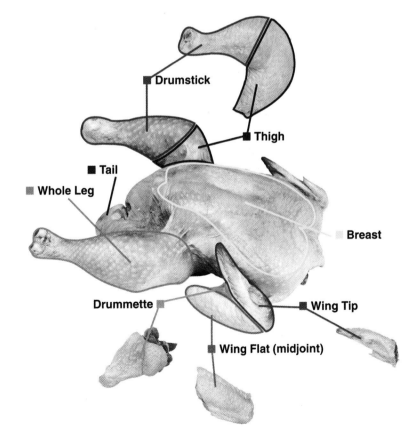

■ Drumstick

■ Thigh

■ Tail

■ Whole Leg

■ Breast

Drummette ■

■ Wing Tip

■ Wing Flat (midjoint)

TABLE 14.1 **Poultry Classification Chart**

© 2007 NAMP, reprinted with permission of John Wiley & Sons

Kind/Class	Description	Age	Weight Range	Market Form
CHICKEN				
Rock Cornish Game Hen	Special breed of young chicken, very tender and delicate.	5–6 weeks	0.75–2 pounds	Whole, Drawn, Fresh, Frozen
Broiler or Fryer	Young chicken of either sex. Tender flesh and flexible cartilage. Smooth skin.	9–12 weeks	Broiler: 1.5–2.5 pounds Fryer: 2.5–3.5 pounds	Whole, Drawn, Split, Quartered, Parts, Disjointed, Fresh, Frozen
Roaster	Young chicken of either sex. Tender flesh, smooth skin. Less flexible cartilage.	3–5 months	3.5–5 pounds	Whole, Disjointed, Fresh, Frozen, Canned
Capon	Castrated male chicken. Flesh very tender, well flavored, large breast, expensive.	Under 8 months	5–8 pounds	Whole, Fresh, Frozen
Hen or Fowl	Mature male, coarse skin, tough dark meat.	Over 10 months	3.5–6 pounds	Disjointed
Cock Rooster	Mature male, coarse skin, tough dark meat.	Over 10 months	4–6 pounds	Disjointed
TURKEY				
Fryer/Roaster	Young bird of either sex. Tender flesh, smooth skin, flexible cartilage.	Under 16 weeks	4–9 pounds	Whole
Young Turkey (Hen or Tom)	Bird with tender flesh, firmer cartilage.	5–7 months	8–22 pounds	Whole, Breast, Half Turkey, Fresh, Frozen, Canned
Yearling Turkey	Fully matured bird, still reasonably tender	Under 15 months	10–30 pounds	Whole, Breast, Half Turkey, Fresh, Frozen, Canned
Mature Turkey or Old Turkey (Hen or Tom)	Old bird, tough flesh, coarse skin.	Over 15 months	10–30 pounds	Whole, Breast, Half Turkey, Fresh, Frozen, Canned Processed
DUCK				
Broiler or Fryer Ducking	Young tender bird, soft bill and windpipe.	Under 8 weeks	2–4 pounds	Whole, Fresh, Frozen
Roaster Ducking	Young tender bird with bill and windpipe just starting to harden.	16 weeks	4–6 pounds	Whole, Fresh, Frozen
Mature Duck	Old bird, tough flesh, hard bill and windpipe.	Over 16 weeks	4–10 pounds	Whole, Fresh, Frozen

TABLE 14.2 **The Meat Buyer's Guide Index of Chicken Products**
© 2007 NAMP, reprinted with permission of John Wiley & Sons

Name Number	Product Name	Ustd Style Number	PG*
P1001	Whole Broiler with Giblets	70101	225
P1002	Whole Broiler without Giblets (WOG)	70102	225
P1003	Broiler, Front Half	70301	225
P1004	Broiler, Lower Portion	70401	225
P1005	Eight (8) Piece Cut Broiler — WOG	70204	225
P1006	Nine (9) Piece Cut Broiler — WOG	70206	226
P1007	Ten (10) Piece Cut Broiler — WOG	70208	226
P1008	2 Broiler Halves (Half Carcass)	70201	226
P1009	Broiler Quarters	70202	227
P1010	Broiler Breast Quarter	70501	227
P1011	Broiler Breast Quarter without Wing	70502	227
P1012	Broiler Breast with Ribs	70601	227
P1014	Broiler Breast Half with Ribs	70701	228
P1016	Broiler Airline Breast	70705	228
P1030	Broiler Leg Quarter	70901	228
P1031	Broiler Leg	71001	229
P1033	Broiler Thigh	71101	229
P1034	Broiler Thigh with Back Portion	71102	229
P1035	Broiler Drumstick	71201	229
P1036	Broiler Wing	71301	230
P1037	Broiler Wing Drummette	71304	230
P1038	Broiler Wing Flat (Mid Joint)	71305	230
P1039	Broiler Wingtip (Tip or Flipper)	71306	230
P1040	Broiler Wing Portion	71303	230
P1041	Broiler Back	71403	231
P1042	Broiler Neck	71601	231
P1043	Broiler Giblets	74002	231
P1044	Broiler Gizzard	71901	231
P1045	Broiler Liver	72001	231
P1047	Broiler Feet	71801	231
P1048	Broiler Paws	71803	231
P1052	Broiler Heart	72101	231

* Denotes page number in NAMP *Meat Buyer's Guide.*

Turkey

Turkey is a popular meat in the food service arena. Turkey is most commonly used in the form of deli breasts or lower fat versions of ham and bacon. Turkey is almost as versatile as chicken in form and function. The most popular form of turkey is the roast turkey often served during the holidays. Many food service operators know that turkey can be a cost-effective alternative in many applications. Turkey also is leaner then beef or pork and is perceived as a healthy alternative. (See Table 14.3.)

- **Fryer-roaster turkey.** A fryer-roaster turkey is a young, immature turkey (usually under 16 weeks of age). It is not normally used in food service applications.

- **Young hen turkey.** A young hen turkey is a young female turkey (usually 5 to 7 months of age). Hens can be used whole or cut up. Whole hens are usually sold in 2-pound increments.

- **Young tom turkey.** A young tom turkey is a young male turkey (usually 5 to 7 months of age). Toms can be used whole or cut up, but hens are used more often in cut processing. Toms are also sold in 2-pound increments.

- **Mature turkey or old turkey (hen or tom).** This is an old turkey of either sex (usually older than 15 months of age). Mature turkeys are usually used in further processing.

TABLE 14.3 **The Meat Buyer's Guide Index of Turkey Products**
© 2007 NAMP, reprinted with permission of John Wiley & Sons

Name Number	Product Name	Ustd Style Number	PG*
P2001	Whole Young Turkey with Giblets	710101	237
P2003	Young Turkey Front Half	710601	237
P2011	Young Turkey Breast Quarter without Wing	710704	238
P2012	Young Turkey Whole Breast with Ribs	710604	238
P2013	Young Turkey Whole Breast without Ribs	710614	238
P2014	Young Turkey Breast Half with Ribs	710701	238
P2015	Young Turkey Breast Half with Ribs	710705	238
P2030	Young Turkey Leg Quarter	710901	240
P2031	Young Turkey Leg	711001	240
P2033	Young Turkey Thigh	711103	240
P2035	Young Turkey Drumstick	711201	240
P2036	Young Turkey Whole Wing	711301	241
P2042	Turkey Neck	711601	241
P2051	Turkey Testicles (Fries)	712201	241

* Denotes page number in NAMP *Meat Buyer's Guide.*

Feathered Game

Feathered game birds comprise the remaining birds used in food service applications, such as wild turkey, goose, pheasant, duck, partridge, quail, and woodcock. Wild (hunt-harvested) birds cannot be sold in the United States. Any of these birds served in the food service application are farmed raised (including free range). For detailed information on the various game birds, see Table 14.4.

BUYING AND STORING

In general, game birds are available whole or precut into pieces, fresh or frozen; some of the smaller birds are canned. Game birds tend to have less fat than other poultry and require cooking techniques other than dry heat with little preparation. Great care must be taken in cooking game birds to eliminate any possible foodborne illness vectors while at the same time not overcooking the bird.

Factors affecting quality include the age of the bird and the manner of slaughter and packaging. Birds should

TABLE 14.4 **Game Bird Classification Chart**

Name and Servings	Approximate Age	Dressed Weight in Lbs	Market form
Goose (1 lb. (Raw) per serving)	9–10 Months	4–14	Whole
Pigeon, regular (1 serves 1)	28 Days	8–15 oz 12 oz	Whole
Pigeon, jumbo (1 jumbo serves 1–2)		14–16 oz	
Pheasant, baby (1 serves 1)	8–10 Weeks	1–1.25	Whole
Broiler (1 serves 2)	10 Weeks	3–3.5	Whole
Mature cock (1 serves 4)	20–22 Weeks	3–3.5	Whole
Mature hen (1 serves 3–4)	20–22 Weeks	1.75–2	Whole
Partridge, chukar (1 serves 1)	18 Weeks	1	Whole
Wild duck, mallard (1 serves 2)	6 Months	2	Whole (serve breast only)
Canvasback (1 serves 2)	6 Months	2–2.5	Whole (serve breast only)
Teal (1 serves 1)	6 Months	1.5–2	Whole (serve breast only)
Wild turkey, mature hen (1 serves 6)	6 Months	6	Whole
Mature gobbler (1 serves 12)	12 Months	12	Whole
Quail (1–2 per serving)	12–14 Weeks	4–5 oz	Whole

have no off odor; the skin should be springy, not dull or dry. Young birds are best and can be identified by their pliable breastbone, feet, and legs; their claws will be sharp (when still attached). Because of a lack of natural fat, particularly in younger birds, they must be basted or larded before roasting. Older birds are best cooked with slow, moist heat such as braising or used in soups or stews.

DUCK

Duck is a very popular bird in France and the rest of Europe. Most European ducks are raised for *foie gras*, or fattened duck liver. Asia also features several types of duck in its cuisine. Domesticated duck species include the Barbary duck, with a firm flesh, and the Nantes duck, which is fattier. For wild duck, the most popular species is the Mallard for its breast and thigh meat. There are roughly eighty species of duck that are available for food service. Each species has its own tastes and uses. A duckling is any duck that is younger than 2 months; ducks are older birds. Most of the time, the sex of the duck is not relevant when purchasing or cooking.

Duck is available in the following forms:

- **Broiler duckling or fryer duckling.** This is a young duck, less than 8 weeks old. It has tender meat and soft bills and windpipes.

- **Roaster duckling.** This is a duck that is between 8 and 16 weeks old. The meat is tender and the bill and windpipe are harder than the broiler ducklings.

- **Mature duck.** This is a duck that is older than 6 months. The flesh is tougher than the ducklings, and the bill and windpipes are hard.

GOOSE

Goose is another poultry bird that is more popular in Europe. In the United States, it is a Christmas and New Year's dish. Goose meat is darker than other poultry and even the breast is dark. The taste is gamier and has more fat than duck. In France, goose is also a source of *foie gras d'oie*, which is fattened goose liver. Goose meat from either sex can be sold.

Goose is available in the following forms:

- **Young goose.** Young goose weighs between 10 and 14 pounds (4 ½ and 5 ½ kilograms). These geese have tender meat and soft windpipes. Smaller geese are more popular with the customers for the flavor of the meat.

- **Mature goose.** Mature goose weighs between 18 and 19 pounds (8 and 9 kilograms). The flesh is tougher, and the windpipe is hard.

GUINEA

Guinea fowl are smaller birds with a gamey taste that originated in Africa. The meat is lean with many essential fatty acids. These birds are normally sold as whole birds, and the sex is not noted on the packaging. Guinea is available in the following forms:

- **Young guinea.** This is a young bird of either sex. It has very tender meat.

- **Mature guinea.** This is an older bird. The flesh is tougher than the younger variety.

PARTRIDGE

Partridge is a game bird that is available in several regions of the world. The gray and red-legged partridge is not native to the United States but is available in a frozen form. Partridges are very plump and have white gamy flesh and white meat. Commercial partridge is available frozen, weighing 12 to 14 ounces. Partridge is prepared by roasting or broiling.

PHEASANT

Pheasant is a mild-flavored bird, which can be roasted, stewed, or braised. It is raised on farms and is available fresh in some locales or frozen throughout the United States. Most birds weigh between 1 ½ and 2 ¼ pounds (680 grams and 1 kilogram). Pheasant is sold as a dish for two people.

PIGEON

Pigeon, or dove, is a small bird with large breasts. Pigeon is available from farms or as a wild game bird. Pigeon is sold without identifying the sex and is available in the following forms:

- **Squab.** This is a young bird with extra-tender meat and a light skin.

- **Pigeon.** This is an older bird with tougher flesh and a course, heavy skin.

QUAIL

Quail, related to the pheasant, is a small bird weighing about 3 to 7 ounces in total. Quail is tender enough to be grilled or cooked with dry heat. Most recipes indicate that the interior should be filled with stuffing. Quail is normally sold whole or in boneless quarters.

Furred Game

Furred game is wild animals that are rarely available from commercial wholesalers. Game meat has a dark color and a strong taste. Young animals are tender, while older ones have tough meat. The age of the animal and the cut of the meat are the determining factors when cooking. Younger animals and cuts from the loin areas can be cooked with dry heat. Older animals and other cuts should be cooked with moist heat, as they will be tough. Game meat can also be made into sausages and pates.

BUYING AND STORING

Fresh furred game is available from specialty wholesalers especially during hunting season. Other game is available from farms. Before purchasing, a chef should find out the age of the animal, how it was treated, and how long it was hung before processing. Game is available in cuts similar to beef such as tenderloin, ground meat, and roasts. Under no circumstances should game be purchased from unlicensed individuals. All game should be purchased from licensed, inspected purveyors with experience in the industry.

The taste of the meat will depend on the age of the animal and whether it was a wild or farm animal. Usually farm and younger wild animals have the mildest taste, while older wild animals will be the most gamey.

Game might be available fresh in certain areas. If it is fresh, the receiving clerk should check the texture of the meat. The meat should be firm and moist. If it is sticky or mushy, it should be rejected. Frozen game should be inspected to make sure the package is intact and there is no sign of thawing or excess liquid. Fresh game should be used within 1 to 2 days. Check with the supplier for the shelf life of the frozen game.

ANTELOPE

Antelope is an animal the size of a large deer and is raised on farms. Antelope is similar to deer meat and is normally cooked using those recipes and techniques.

WILD BOAR

Boar is the wild cousin of the domesticated pigs. Wild boar is only available in the autumn, and farm boar is available year-round. Boar has a stronger flavor than pork and can be used in any recipe that calls for pork or venison. Boar is sold as a young or mature animal.

BUFFALO (BISON/AMERICAN BUFFALO)

Buffalo is a large animal native to the United States. Larger than cows or other domesticated animals, its meat is very lean and nutritious with less cholesterol, fat, and calories than beef or chicken. Today, most buffalo is farm raised. Buffalo meat tastes like beef, but it is richer and sweeter.

BEEFALO

Beefalo is a cross between buffalo and domesticated cattle. A beefalo looks and tastes more like beef than the buffalo. The meat is very lean and dark with a slightly stronger flavor than beef. Beefalo can be cooked using any beef recipe. It is not readily available in most markets but can be special ordered through Internet specialty sites.

DEER (VENISON)

Venison is any meat from moose, elk, red-tailed deer, or white-tailed deer. Venison is available from wild sources and from farm-raised animals. Venison meat is dark red. It is leaner than beef, and it has almost no marbling. Venison is available in loin, leg, and rack cuts. It is also available in cuts similar to beef or as ground beef or sausages. Venison can be cooked using beef recipes. Match the venison cut to a beef chart, and then use the applicable cooking method.

HARE AND RABBITS

Rabbits are available from wild or farm-raised sources. **Hare** is the larger relative, which can weigh up to 14 pounds. Rabbits weigh between 3 and 5 pounds. Hare has a darker meat than rabbit, and wild versions must be marinated before cooking. Most hares are cooked with moist-heat methods. Rabbit meat is all white meat with a sweeter flavor than hares. Rabbit is also cooked with moist-heat methods but only needs marinating for flavor.

Rabbit is available whole or in cuts such as quarter rabbit or rabbit legs. The animals are also sold by age, with younger rabbits having a sweeter taste and older ones having a gamier taste. Rabbit is also available fresh or frozen from specialty meat vendors. Rabbit meat can be substituted for chicken meat in most recipes.

CONVENIENCE CORNER PRODUCT EXAMPLES

Poultry and Game

Company	Website	Products
Brakebush	http://www.brakebush.com	10# Chicken Tender
Grecian Delight	http://www.greciandelight.com	10# Meat Gyro Chicken
Hormel	http://www.hormelfoods.com	2/8-9# Turkey Breast, skin-on
Jennie-O	http://www.jennieofood service.com	12/1# Lunch Meat, Turkey 4/4-5# Turkey Great Raw
Lanova	http://www.lanova.com	2/4# Chicken Wings, boneless
Tyson	http://www.tyson.com	3/5 Chicken Strip Fries 2/7.5# Chicken Wings
Premium Elks	http://www.premiumelk.com	200/.5 oz Elk Jerky Sticks
Broad Leaf	http://www.broadleafgame.com	10/16 oz Buffalo T-Bone Steaks 20/8-9 oz Pheasant Breast
North American Provisioner Inc	http://www.nabison.com	8/1.5# Boar Tenderloin
New West	http://www.nabison.com	10# Antelope Leg, Denver 15# Rabbit Bone in Leg
Hudson Valley	http://www.hudsonvalleyfoiegras.com	8/1.25# Foie Gras Duck
Cavendish Game Birds	http://www.vermontquail.com	30/5 oz Quail Semi Boneless
Pierce	http://www.piercefoods.com	3/5# Chicken Wings, Brd
McCarty Farms	http://www.tyson.com	2/6# Chicken Ground Taco Meat
Advance Food Company	http://www.advf.com	36/4.5 oz Chicken Breast Brd
Koch Foods	http://www.kochfoods.com	10# Chicken Fajita Strip White

Johannes "Jan" Verdonkschot,

CEC, AAC, HOF

Place of Birth: Heemstede, The Netherlands

Educational Background and Work Experience

Chef Verdonkschot began his culinary career during World War II at the age of 14, when he worked for the Royal Canadian Army Service Corps in Holland, Germany, and Belgium. At the time, he didn't know that his work as an interpreter and cook's helper would lead to such an illustrious career in food service. After the war, "Jan" attended Pastry School and apprenticed as a pastry cook, cook, and aide de cuisine in the Netherlands. His desire for world travel led to a cook's position aboard the Royal Dutch Mail ocean liners for 7 years, eventually leading him to become the chef of his own cruise liner. He then worked at the Stadshottelt in Vasteras, Sweden, and later at the Chase Park Plaza Hotel. After working as the corporate executive chef for the Missouri Pacific Railroad for 2 years, he worked as the executive chef for the Missouri Athletic Club, as director of Hotel and Food service Operations for Grove Manufacturing, and for 13 years as executive chef/food service director for the May Company department stores. Although he was retired from the May Company, the indefatigable Chef Verdonkschot owned and operated his own business for 12 years, the Renée Café Corporation, while he also worked for 13 years as a corporate chef-consultant for the Hatco Corporation. Today, he still works part time as chef-consultant for the Piper Corporation.

Memberships and Career Highlights

As a longtime associate of the St. Louis Chefs de Cuisine Association, Chef Verdonkschot was an active member of the local American Culinary Federation chapter, being named its 1967 Chef of the Year. As a member of the American Academy of Chefs, Chef Verdonkschot was also very involved nationally, working to establish and lead the national certification program as the ACF National Secretary in 1968. This led to his being named ACF National Chef of the Year in 1970, being admitted into the Culinary Hall of Fame, and being inducted into the International Honorable Order of the Golden Toques.

Passions with the Food Service Industry

"One of my greatest pleasures was while I worked at the Missouri Athletic Club as the Executive Chef. I had 6 apprentice cooks in my kitchen brigade of over 60 culinarians and was able to share my knowledge with many interested young cooks and chefs. As a consultant, I've always enjoyed the opportunity to meet many great chefs around the world who have become my lifelong friends."

Advice to a Chef or Buyer

"Chefs or buyers should 'manage by objectives.' Set the objectives for each level; whether corporate, divisional, or individual. Be systematic: make decisions without prejudice, set plans that include both short- and long-range objectives, communicate well to the staff, analyze the results, and decide on future goals. Chefs should stay abreast of trends by reading, studying, and making contact with people who can teach you something useful. Chefs must also understand the tools of business and the needs of staff. People can be taught, and even good ones can be made better."

Courtesy Johannes "Jan" Verdonkschot.

It Happened to Me...

"While employed at the Missouri Pacific Railroad, my office was located near the commissary, where I noticed constant shortages. For example, I saw the potato person leave with a case of whole chickens! Whole pork loins would go out in the dirty linen carts. They had no platform scale with which to weigh the delivered food supplies. They received whole chickens packed in ice, which more than equaled the weight of the chickens. We needed chickens, not bloody ice! I immediately instituted wholesale changes to our storeroom operations. I introduced can cuttings for items like, fruit cocktail, peach halves, white asparagus, beans, tomatoes, and other vegetables. We measured the liquids in each can; we compared the firmness of the peaches, tomatoes, and asparagus. We started tracking the perpetual inventory and noted a minimum stock level needed by our operation. We used stock cards to note each time we received any food products and each time we issued an ingredient. We also noted each time the prices changed, either up or down. These systems of control dramatically reduced the costs of that food service operation."

Key Words and Concepts

---

beefalo	feathered game	hare	poultry
chicken	furred game	inspection	venison

Chapter in Review

The following exercises are provided to help the reader understand and apply the contents of this chapter. They may be completed individually or in a classroom environment.

REVIEW QUESTIONS

a. Define the term *game*.

b. How does game differ from domesticated animals?

c. Define the term *poultry*.

d. Describe the quality factors for carcasses and parts.

e. Describe the difference between a hare and a rabbit.

INDIVIDUAL ACTIVITIES

a. **Web based:** Research poultry websites to learn about uses for poultry and game birds.

b. **Experiential:** Visit a butcher shop or poultry processing facility to learn about poultry fabrication.

c. **Critical thinking:** Evaluate how game may be substituted in traditional or classically prepared dishes.

GROUP ACTIVITIES

a. **Lab experience:** Prepare various poultry and game birds in the same manner, and compare and contrast them for taste, texture, and moisture.

b. **Classroom action:** Discuss the storage and handling of poultry and game.

CHAPTER

15

© Randy Van Dam 2008

Fish and Shellfish

"Shellfish are the prime cause of the decline of morals and the adaptation of an extravagant lifestyle. Indeed of the whole realm of Nature, the sea is in many ways the most harmful to the stomach, with its great variety of dishes and tasty fish."

PLINY THE ELDER

After reading this chapter, you will be able to:

◎ List methods for harvesting seafood.

◎ Explain the purpose of the green sheet.

◎ Summarize the many quality points that should be inspected when receiving seafood.

◎ Differentiate between shellfish and bonefish.

◎ Define the term *mollusks*, and provide examples.

◎ Compare the differences between *univalves* and *bivalves*, and give examples of each.

◎ Define the terms *crustaceans* and *cephalopods*, and provide examples of each.

◎ Distinguish among *roundfish, flatfish, winged fish,* and *eels,* and provide examples of each.

◎ Identify the various market forms for shrimp and crab.

◎ List the various market forms for fish.

◎ Describe the proper method for icing fish for storage.

Introduction

Seafood is a protein source with an almost infinite variety of species—plenty to meet the needs of any food service establishment. Given the many varieties of fish, a wide range of cuts and forms can be found from most wholesalers. Each fish and shellfish has certain intrinsic characteristics that distinguish it from other seafood and from other foods.

Harvesting Seafood

Whole books have been written about the various methods for obtaining seafood, either by foraging for them in their natural habitat or by raising them in pens, ponds, or tanks. This section is meant to briefly distinguish among the various methods of harvesting fish and shellfish for the benefit of the consumer, while considering their effects on the fish habitat.

Some of these methods are more labor intensive and designed to selectively capture certain species of fish, while other methods are nonselective and efficient for volume harvesting. Each means of gathering seafood can have a direct effect on both the habitat and the product itself.

FISH HARVESTING

- **Gillnetting**. This technique uses a monofilament mesh suspended by a system of floats and weights to entangle (using tangle nets) or sandwich (using trammel nets) fish as they swim through, as illustrated in Figure 15.1a and Figure 15.1b. This indiscriminate method is meant to target salmon and shark, but it can also inadvertently trap and kill other nontargeted species, known as the **bycatch**. The flesh of the fish can sometimes be scarred using this method.

- **Handline**. Along with handcasting nets, similar to the *purse seine* method below, this method is the most ancient form of fishery. Using a single line and hook to cast and capture the fish, this method brings the catch onboard alive, allowing for greater selectivity and the least harm to the fish. Although it is not highly productive, because of the time it takes to cast and pull in the catch, this method is still used in tropical waters to capture grouper and snapper and in cold waters for cod, mackerel, and tuna.

- **Harpooning**. Although almost exclusively used in the past for whaling, this method now primarily exists for spearing mature bluefin tuna and swordfish and other fish that swim near the water's surface. This mode of harvesting is selectively effective without causing damage to the habitat.

- **Purse seine**. The purse seine method uses a large circular net to capture schools of herring, mackerel, or tuna by encircling them and then pulling the net together with a cable, as shown in Figure 15.2a and Figure 15.2b. The whole net is brought on board, or smaller amounts are hoisted or pumped aboard. This method does not harm the habitat bottom.

- **Hook and line**. This common method individually hooks fish either by trolling single lines and hooks or by using a series of branch lines connected to a single long main line. One of the major means used to catch fish, longlining allows nontargeted fish to be released alive and does not harm the habitat. (See Figure 15.3.)

- **Trawling**. This major form of commercial harvesting drags a funnel-shaped net through the water to gather fish and shellfish before bringing it onboard through gates in the ship's stern end. Bottom trawls are used for scallops, shrimp, cod, haddock, monkfish, rockfish, sole, and other bottom-feeding species, while midwater trawls capture whiting, pollock, herring, hake, and squid.

15.1a A gillnet hangs in the water

15.1b Fish gills are entangled in the net

15.2a A purse seine loosely surrounds a school of fish

15.2b The seine net is "pursed" to capture the fish

15.3 The hook-and-line, or trolling, method

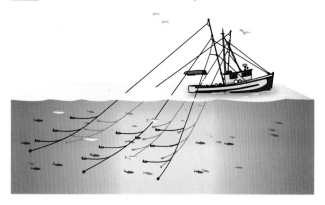

- **Trapping**. Constructed of wire cages and mesh netting held in place with floats and anchors, floating fish traps capture fish in perfect condition. The net size of the traps determines the selection intended for capture. The catch is then evaluated and either harvested or released live.

Fish Aquaculture

- **Open-ocean cages or net pens**. Used to hold large stocks of fish in submerged holding systems, these open-water pens provide flexibility to fish farmers. Salmon and trout are commonly farmed, but other fish such as tuna, cod, and halibut are also raised in this manner. This method can pollute the surrounding waters and ocean bottom and potentially threaten wild stock with parasites and disease.

- **Tanks, ponds, and raceways**. Catfish, tilapia, sturgeon, and trout are commonly raised in freshwater ponds, tanks, and raceways, while shrimp are now harvested from coastal saltwater ponds. Free-flowing water from rivers and streams are diverted into raceways while pumps aerate water in ponds and tanks.

SHELLFISH HARVESTING

- **Diving**. Hand harvesting is used to gather species such as scallops and red abalone. It has been used with mixed results, both successfully protecting the habitat while sometimes allowing for unregulated harvesting.

- **Dredging**. This method uses a sturdy rectangular frame with a net of metal rings attached at its bottom to rake the ocean floor. Dredging both reef and plant areas is generally destructive to the habitat and is nondiscriminatory in its harvesting. (See Figure 15.4.)

- **Trapping and pots**. Made of wood or wire mesh with funnel-shaped openings, traps and pots (or creels) are linked together by a system of longlines and buoys used for retrieval. Designed to rest on the ocean floor, they are positioned to capture shrimp, lobster, and crab. The habitat is generally left unaffected when placed on sandy bottoms. (See Figure 15.5.)

- **Tongs and rakes**. Similar to a broom and dustpan concept, basket rakes are used to manually scrape clams and oysters into wire-mesh baskets. The process is very selective and results in little environmental damage and no bycatch.

15.4 Dredging the ocean floor

15.5 Trapping fish in pots

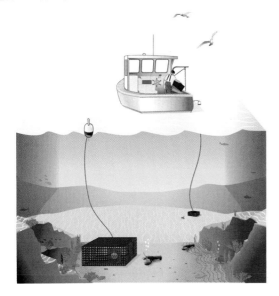

Shellfish Aquaculture

- **Beach culture.** This process uses sand-filled pens, often in beach locations, to farm filter-feeding shellfish such as oysters, clams, and mussels. Their impact on the surrounding beach area and water is generally negligible.

- **Suspended cable or bags.** Using dangling ropes or mesh bags on racks, this method suspends surface areas on which filter-feeding shellfish grow. This method has no impact on the surrounding habitat or other species.

Global Sourcing

The U.S. seafood market of the 21st century is vastly different from that of several decades ago. Chefs have far greater varieties from which to select, as middlemen from around the world work together to process, pack, and ship their products to the U.S. market. As Johnson writes, "It is not unusual to find Vietnamese tuna in New York City, Alaska king salmon in Boston, or New Zealand snapper in St. Louis" (2007, p. 1).

Buying and Storing

The **green sheet** is the name by which most people refer to the Market News Reports issued by the National Marine Fisheries Service (NMFS). The weekly summary lists first-receiver selling prices for most fresh and frozen seafood commodities in New York. It also gives fresh seafood receipts at Fulton Fish Market in New York and prices from New England. Some larger independent seafood suppliers maintain their own fishing fleets and processing plants, and provide weekly quote sheets to their customers, often independent from the NMFS.

A fuller service is published three times weekly, giving more data on fresh prices and movements than the weekly summary. The sheet is used all over the world as a source for seafood prices in the United States, and because packers in every country devoutly follow it, it has a substantial influence on the market.

NMFS publishes four other similar reports, each in a different color to identify it and each including particular regional items. The Boston Blue Sheet covers fish blocks and fillets, the Seattle sheet covers salmon, the New Orleans sheet covers shrimp, and the Los Angeles sheet covers tuna.

The grading and inspection of fresh fish are entirely voluntary, although local health departments are required to inspect all processing and packing plants for proper sanitation and handling procedures. The federal government has two different marks: one that indicates the fish was inspected and one that shows the quality level.

The designation "processed under federal inspection" (PUFI), as illustrated in Figure 15.6, is a product guarantee that:

- The seafood has been properly labeled.

- The seafood is pure, wholesome, and safe.

- The seafood has been processed and packaged under sanitary conditions.

- The product has not been graded as to a specific quality level.

Seafood so designated is of an acceptable quality as determined by federal inspectors. This standard applies to whole or dressed fish, fresh or frozen, of any species fit for human consumption and processed and maintained using good manufacturing practices. The Food and Drug Administration (FDA) regulates seafood labeling as to the product, net weight, and country of origin.

U.S. grade designations are as follows:

- **Grade A.** Top or best quality (can change season to season). Uniform in size and free from defects. Good condition and good flavor for the species.

- **Grade B.** Good quality but has less uniformity of size; some blemishes or defects.

- **Grade C.** Fairly good quality; little uniformity and many defects.

15.6 **Processed under federal inspection (PUFI) seal**

Courtesy U.S. Department of Commerce

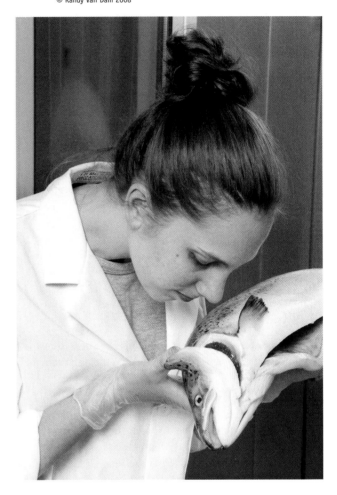

Grade B and Grade C are usually marketed without any grade designations on their labels.

The U.S. Department of Commerce provides grading and inspection services to processors for a fee. The grade or inspection shield (Figure 15.7) indicates the processors that choose to have their plants under continuous federal inspection. These packers display both the PUFI seal and a grading stamp. At the present time, the grades (A, B, and C) signify that:

- The product is clean, safe, and wholesome.
- The product is of a specified quality, indicated by the appropriate grade designation.
- The product was produced in an acceptable establishment, with proper equipment, and in an appropriate processing environment as required by food-control authorities.
- The product was processed under supervision by federal food inspectors and packed by sanitary food handlers.
- The product is truthfully and accurately labeled as to the common or usual name, optional ingredients, or quantity.

Food service establishments must inspect fresh fish deliveries upon arrival. If the fish is not fresh, it should be immediately rejected with a credit memo issued. A reputable wholesaler will also arrange for a quick replacement of the rejected product.

What to look for when the truck arrives depends on the product, of course, but there are a number of factors common to almost all fish and shellfish (see also Table 15.1):

- **Smell**. This is positively the best way to determine the quality of fresh seafood. Odors tell if the product is aging or stale or if it has been packed poorly. The wrong odor signals a problem. (See Figure 15.8.)

TABLE 15.1 **Freshness Chart for Fish**

1–2 Days	3–4 Days	6–7 Days	9–10 Days	12 and Older
Bright red, no bacterial slime	Darker red slime starting to appear	Thick slime, bloody briny odor	Bleached dark maroon slime, celery smell	Foul odor, very thick slime
Bulging black pupil, clear cornea	Graying and flattening pupils	Cloudy and sunken pupils	Flat, cloudy, and bloodshot	Flat, cloudy, swollen, and bloodshot
Fresh sea slime present, nice sheen	Slime thickens, loss of sheen	Very little sheen, fishy smell, lines on skin not so distinct	Very dull and lifeless looking	Starting to yellow in color and becoming slimy
Firm resilient and translucent	Beginning to appear less translucent	Soft to touch, no longer resilient to touch	Lost all clarity, waxy in appearance	Soft, darkening, and mushy
Flat to the body, plentiful, and very moist	Drying and reducing in number	Almost disappeared	Gone altogether	Nonexistent
Fresh sea smell	Still quite pleasant sea smell	Briny, yeasty, or malty	Distinctively fish and unpleasant	Bad fish smell, celery like

- **Whole and dressed fish.** It is far easier to determine the quality of fish that still has skin and a head than it is to determine the quality of fillets. If it is a whole fish, inspect the following:

  - **Eyes.** If the eyes are still around to look at, they should be convex with translucent corneas, and they should shine a little. Flat eyes, becoming opaque, indicate marginal quality. Sunken and discolored eyes call for rejection of the fish. (See Figure 15.9a.)

  - **Gills.** Normally, gills should be removed before the fish is shipped very far, because spoilage starts and spreads rapidly from the gills due to the amount of oxygen present. If the fish still have gills, they should be bright red and clean looking. Pink gills are acceptable. Gills may also be paler if the fish has been bled. Later, gills begin to turn gray and then brown. Brown is definitely not acceptable. Grey is marginal, and you should evaluate other factors before deciding whether the fish is of adequate quality. (See Figure 15.9b.)

- **Gut cavity.** Look for clean and rather glossy surfaces inside the gut cavity. If the belly bones are torn from the flesh or can be torn away easily, the fish may be "belly-burned," which is an enzymatic action on the flesh causing a burned or discolored appearance. Fish in good condition will have the belly wall bones adhering tightly to the flesh. The workmanship of your processor is also revealed by the gut cavity. All the guts should have been removed. Heads should be cut off cleanly without wasting edible flesh. The cavity should be washed and clean. There should be no cuts in the flesh of the fish. (See Figure 15.9c.)

- **Slime.** Fish naturally have a coating of slime that protects them in the water and helps to "oil" their movements, and makes fish slippery. Generally, the slime will have been washed off long before a fish reaches a distributor. If slime is still on the skin, it should be transparent or slightly milky. Yellow or brown slime is not acceptable.

15.9a Comparing fish eyes: clear and round (left) versus sunken and gray
© Randy Van Dam 2008

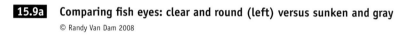

15.9b Comparing fish gills (freshest fish is to the right)
© Randy Van Dam 2008

15.9c A good gut cavity (right) versus a bad gut cavity
© Randy Van Dam 2008

15.10 Pressing the skin of fish to test its freshness

© Randy Van Dam 2008

15.11a Inspecting clams for freshness and looking for "yawners"

© Randy Van Dam 2008

- **Skin.** Skin should be shiny and bright, not dull or bleached. The flesh should spring back when pressed and should not fall away easily from the bones. The shiny, intact scales should adhere firmly to the skin. There should not be any visible breaks in the skin or scales. (See Figure 15.10.)

- **Temperature.** Correct temperature and plenty of ice are vital to maintaining quality of fish. Check the temperature of the product when it arrives. Use a probe thermometer on the thickest part of the fish or fillet. The temperature should be 32°F (0°C). Once the fish is received, the delivery ice should be discarded and fresh ice packed into the case.

- **Shellfish.** When inspecting shellfish, make sure the shells are closed. If the shell is open, tap it. If it closes, then the shellfish is still alive and can be cooked. If it does not, then it should be discarded. If the bag has more "yawners" than closed ones, then the bag should be rejected. (See Figure 15.11a and Figure 15.11b.)

15.11b Tapping open clam with another clam to see if it is still alive

© Randy Van Dam 2008

People, Places, Things

Foley School of Fish

Foley Fish House is a family business that has operated for four generations in Boston. It sells seafood to restaurants and specialty retail stores across the country, much like other fish processors, but is unique in several ways. One service it offers is a "School of Fish." Opened in 1981, the Foley School of Fish provides extensive hands-on training to culinary professionals in areas of best practices for handling seafood.

Packaging

Fish can be packaged in many different forms, such as in blocks, in layer or shatter packs, cello wrapped, or IQF. When purchasing fish, look for units that are compatible with the needs of the establishment. The following are the most common seafood packaging methods:

- **Block frozen**. Product is placed in a form or carton, topped up with water, and then frozen in a plate freezer. Block freezing is a popular method for seafood packaging. This technique is probably the most commonly applied to seafood. It gives good product protection and, because cartons are solidly filled, makes transportation and storage easier with less chance for damage. The product is protected because a relatively small surface area is exposed, and this is easy to cover with glaze. However, block-frozen product is the least convenient because you have to thaw the entire block, which is usually 5 pounds, so the end user must be able to use the full amount each time. Typical block-frozen products include all shell-on shrimp, most peeled shrimp, most scallops, all king crab, and snow crab meat. (See Figure 15.12a and Figure 15.12b.)

- **Cello wraps**. In this method, the fish fillets are wrapped together in cellophane film, and then packaged together in a smaller box, which is then placed within a larger, or master, cartoon. The standard master case is usually 50 pounds, either ten cartons with 5 pounds or five cartons with 10 pounds. This is a popular package as the smaller boxes can be frozen for later use. (See Figure 15.13.)

- **Individually quick frozen (IQF).** Product is individually frozen, then bagged and boxed. **IQF** product is preferred for retail sale because it can easily be repackaged. It is also good for institutional use because chefs can use only the amount needed, and most IQF seafood can be cooked without defrosting. (See Figure 15.14a, Figure 15.14b, Figure 15.14c, and Figure 15.14d.)

- **Layer packs.** This method puts product, usually fillets, into a carton in layers with a sheet of polythene between each layer. This enables the fish to be separated easily while still frozen, avoiding having to thaw entire blocks when less than the full block is required. Layer packs provide better product protection than IQF because less of the product is exposed to the air, thereby reducing the risk of dehydration. Layer packs are also easier to stack, which makes them easier than IQF packs to store and transport.

- **Shatterpack**. Shatterpack is similar to a layer pack except the fillets are stuck together. The only way to separate the fillets is to hurl the whole box at a concrete floor to break it apart. While there is almost no difference between the shatterpack and layer pack, shatterpacks are a bit harder to work with.

15.12a **Block-frozen shrimp, 5 pounds**© Randy Van Dam 2008; Courtesy SYSCO Food Services of Grand Rapids

15.12b **Block-frozen chopped clams and crawfish tail meat**
© Randy Van Dam 2008

15.13 **Cello-wrapped fillets**
© Randy Van Dam 2008

15.14a IQF bags of raw and cooked shrimp

Figures 15.14 a - d: © Randy Van Dam 2008

15.14b IQF lobster meat

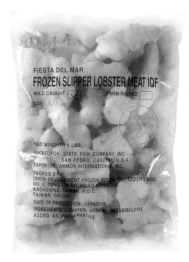

15.14c IQF hardshell clams

15.14d IQF mussels

Caviar

There are three kinds of sturgeon and variations within each of those. These major types of caviar are beluga, osetra, and sevruga. Some twenty-five species of sturgeon exist in the Northern Hemisphere. Additionally, in an effort to provide less expensive alternatives, other fish **roe** are sold as **caviar**. There are several sources for fish roe, chiefly from North America and the region surrounding the Caspian Sea.

The beluga is the largest source of fish roe followed by the osetra and then the sevruga. Regardless of the size of the fish, the roe is extracted in the same manner: The roe sac must be harvested from the fish while the fish is still alive. Then it is mixed with just enough salt to keep the eggs from clumping together.

Eggs prepared in this manner are referred to as *malossol*, or "little salt." The term is printed on the tin or jar lid and will only be used in reference to sturgeon roe. Lesser quality eggs will use more salt, but should not exceed 8% and are not considered lightly salted (malossol). The salt is used to preserve the quality and enhance the flavor of the fish eggs. It also prevents the eggs from freezing when they are stored at their usual holding temperature of 28°F to 32°F (−2.2°C to 0.0°C). Once salted, the eggs are packed in tins and allowed to cure for a minimum of 2 weeks before being sold. In addition to the malossol processing method, which ranges between 3.5 to 5% salt content, there are three other common processing methods. The next process increases the salt content up to 8%, and thereby increases the products' keeping quality. A third method involves pressing soft or damaged caviar into a delicate paste, which can intensify the flavor. The last method is designed to extend caviar's shelf life by heat-pasteurizing it, and then vacuum packing the caviar in glass containers.

AMERICAN CAVIAR

The United States was once one of the biggest worldwide sources of caviar, but later it was fished out. Recently, the United States has made a strong comeback in caviar production. U.S. laws allow only the roe of sturgeon to be called simply "caviar," while the roe of other fish must include the name of the fish before "caviar." The following is a list of caviars made from U.S. freshwater fish.

- **American sturgeon.** These fish can be as long as 10 feet and weigh more than 300 pounds. Many fish weighing 800 to 1,000 pounds or more were caught around the turn of the twentieth century, but by the 1920s the biggest sturgeon were gone.

- **Lake sturgeon.** Lake sturgeon run upwards of l00 pounds, spawn once every 5 to 7 years, and yield about 25 percent of their body weight in roe. The caviar is comparable in size, color, and flavor to Russian beluga. These fish are native to the northern waters of the Great Lakes.

- **Hackleback sturgeon.** This variety is native to the Mississippi–Missouri River system and is faster growing and smaller than most sturgeon. The eggs are small, almost always black or near black, and can have a sweet buttery flavor reminiscent of beluga caviar.

- **White sturgeon.** This variety is native to the waters and rivers of North America's Pacific Coast. It is the largest freshwater fish in North America.

- **Paddlefish roe.** These fish are a cousin to sturgeons and yield roe ranging in color from pale to dark steel-gray and golden "osetra brown." These fish are native to the South and are processed in the same manner as caviar from the Caspian Sea.

- **Salmon roe.** This is sometimes referred to as red caviar. It is prized for its large roe, which can be the size of a pearl and come in a glistening, orange-red color.

- **Whitefish roe.** Known as American golden caviar, this is a small freshwater fish found in the North. Like sevruga caviar, the tiny eggs pop in your mouth. It has an uncommon subtle flavor and fine crispy texture.

- **Trout roe.** These large, golden orange eggs come from the sac of the rainbow trout.

- **Bowfin roe.** This bony fish yields a black roe with a distinctive, lively flavor and makes a good, less expensive substitute for sturgeon caviar. Bowfin caviar is firm and shiny with natural black eggs resembling sturgeon caviar.

- **Lobster roe.** In contrast to all of the other caviar and roe, this product is cooked prior to service, creating a different texture.

IMPORTED CAVIAR

The Caspian Sea provides over 90 percent of the caviar available on the world market. Although there are 24 species of sturgeon still alive, the primary caviar sturgeons from the Caspian Sea are beluga, sevruga, and osetra.

- **Beluga sturgeon.** The largest and most rare, beluga caviar has the largest-sized grains and is the most sought after caviar in the world.

- **Sevruga sturgeon.** Sevruga is the smallest and most abundant of all sturgeon caviars. The eggs are predominantly steel-gray.

- **Osetra sturgeon.** The eggs are medium-sized and golden brown.

Other notable imported caviars are tobico, wasabi, and kaluga:

- **Tobico sushi caviar.** This caviar is used on many sushi dishes.

- **Wasabi caviar.** Capelia caviar is mixed with Japanese horseradish (wasabi) to create a bright green, and very spicy, caviar that goes well with smoked fish.

- **Kaluga caviar.** The color of this roe, from the Amur River system in Manchuria, China, varies from black to golden brown. It has a slightly spicy flavor and an intense salty nature similar to caviar from the Caspian Sea.

Fish

Seafood is a vital food source for people around the world. There are 20,000 known species of fish, and they can be identified in many ways: freshwater or saltwater, large or small, oily or flaky, thin or meaty. For ease of identification, fish are commonly categorized in this chapter as *roundfish, flatfish, winged fish,* or *eels.*

ROUNDFISH

Roundfish are the most common type of fish and populate both fresh and salt waters. (See Figure 15.15a and Figure 15.15b for a comparison of roundfish and flatfish.) The large number of species can make the selection and preparation of roundfish both exciting and confusing. A chef must know the fish's taste, texture, oil content, and bone structure when selecting fish for the menu. The following are the most common roundfish.

- **Smallmouth bass.** This usually measures between 8 and 15 inches and rarely weighs more than 3 pounds. This is a freshwater fish found in colder water.

- **Largemouth bass.** Also known as the speckled perch, it has a somewhat sturdier body than the smallmouth bass. It is a freshwater fish found in warmer waters.

- **Carp.** Carp is a large fish, between 14 and 18 inches long and often weighing more than 15 pounds, but can measure up to 30 inches and weigh as much as 55 pounds. It has heavy scales and a triangle-shaped head. Carp is a freshwater fish.

- **European pike perch.** This fish is between 24 and 40 inches and can weigh up to 22 pounds. It is bred intensively in Europe. Pike perch is very similar to perch, but it has an extra dorsal fin. This is a freshwater fish, popular in Europe.

- **Sauger.** It is usually between 10 and 16 inches long and weighs about 1 pound. Sauger is very similar to walleye and is sometimes substituted for it. It is another freshwater fish.

- **Walleye.** This is the largest member of the perch family. It is usually 13 to 20 inches long and weighs between 2 and 4 pounds. It is a cold freshwater fish.

- **Perch.** Perch is a smaller white, cold freshwater fish. Perch are between 10 and 20 inches long, and they average 1 pound but can be bigger.

- **Trout.** Trout is found in the cold waters of lakes, rivers, and seas. Trout that live in the sea return to freshwater to spawn. There are several species of trout, including:

  - **Brown trout** is usually about 16 inches long, but some sea-living versions can grow to almost 5 feet. They weigh from 2 to 12 pounds and up.

  - **Rainbow trout** is one of the most popular species in North America. It is frequently farmed and is the same size as the brown trout.

15.15a **Comparison photo of roundfish (salmon) to flatfish (flounder)**

© Randy Van Dam 2008

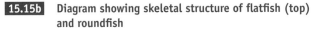

15.15b **Diagram showing skeletal structure of flatfish (top) and roundfish**

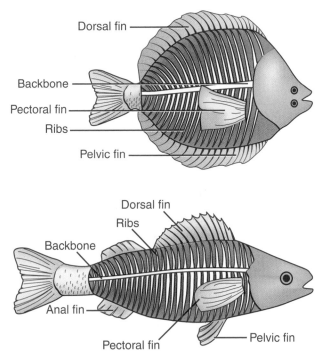

- **Lake trout** has a forked tail and is found in deeper lakes. It can grow up to 15 inches and weigh 4 pounds.

- **Brook trout** is a smaller fish that weights less than 3 pounds and is shorter than 12 inches. It is a very small cold-water fish.

- **Arctic char** is between 2 and 11 pounds and up. It is normally found in far north cold lakes.

- **Mullet.** This fish is usually between 12 and 16 inches but can grow to a maximum length of 40 inches. It is a sea fish, found in temperate zones.

- **Monkfish.** This sea fish ranges in size from 20 inches to 7 feet and can weigh as much as 90 pounds. Monkfish is sold fresh, frozen, or smoked. The skin and the head are usually removed before the fish is sold.

- **Sea bass.** This fish is found in the North Atlantic and Mediterranean Sea. It is also found in saltwater bays. Sea bass can grow to more than 3 feet, and the flesh will remain firm when the skin and scales are left on during cooking.

 Chilean sea bass is a different species that has been fished extensively and is close to extinction. Chefs who order this fish should make sure that it comes from legitimate sources and was not illegally obtained.

- **Sardine.** This is a small fish with thin skins. Sardines are sold smoked, salted, or packed in oil, wine, or tomato sauce as fresh sardines are very perishable.

- **Anchovy.** This is another small fish—5 to 8 inches long. There are roughly ten fish per pound. This is a saltwater fish, with warm- and cold-water varieties. Fresh anchovies are very perishable, so they are canned in brine, oil, or salt. They are also sometimes creamed or turned into pastes before sale.

- **Herring.** This is small saltwater fish, ranging from 6 to 12 inches and weighing 9 to 27 ounces, though bigger ones have been found. Herring is another highly perishable fish that is sold smoked or canned.

- **Mackerel.** Mackerel can weigh up to 4 pounds and can be as long as 2 feet. Mackerel is a saltwater fish and is usually sold salted, smoked, or canned in water, sauce, or oil. Fresh mackerel is available near the sea, but it must be consumed soon after harvesting.

- **Swordfish.** The swordfish is a large fish that can range from 6 to 10 feet and weigh 200 to 500 pounds. But, due to overfishing, swordfish is usually smaller. Swordfish is available whole but is normally sold in steaks for fillets.

- **Salmon.** Salmon is a fish with many different species. It is sold fresh, smoked, and as steaks and fillets. The most popular varieties include:

  - **Chinook salmon (king salmon)** measures 24 inches and up, and weighs up to 35 pounds. Its skin is olive green with silver sides. Its back, the top of its head, and its sides have black spots. Sold fresh, frozen, or smoked, it is rarely canned.

  - **Sockeye salmon (red salmon)** is similar in size to the Chinook. Its skin is bluish green with silver sides. Its firm flesh is red and remains quite red even when canned.

Sockeye salmon is almost always canned, but it is also available smoked or salted.

  - **Coho salmon (silver salmon)** measures between 18 and 24 inches and weighs between 4.5 and 10 pounds. Its skin has small black spots, and its sides are silvery. The coho salmon is the third most commercially important species. Its meat is not as prized as Chinook or sockeye, but it too breaks into large pieces. Often canned, coho salmon is also sold in other common ways.

  - **Pink salmon** is the smallest of the Pacific salmon. It measures up to 19 inches and 4 pounds. It has bluish-green skin with silver sides. It is usually canned.

- **Cod.** The cod has a large head and a deeply slit mouth. It usually weighs between 4 and 9 pounds and measures between 16 and 32 inches. The French make a clear distinction between salted or dried cod (morue) and fresh or frozen (cabillaud).

- **Haddock.** The haddock resembles a small cod. It measures between 15 and 25 inches and weighs between 2 and 5 pounds. It has a slightly prominent upper jaw and a small mouth. The haddock is found on both sides of the Atlantic. In France, the English word *haddock* refers specifically to smoked haddock. Milder than cod, the flesh of the haddock is lean and flavorful.

- **Smelt.** A small thin fish with an elongated silvery body, the smelt inhabits the temperate or cold waters of seas and lakes. It is available fresh or frozen.

- **Tuna.** Tuna are grouped into several species whose names highlight their distinguishing characteristics. The most common species include:

  - **Bluefin tuna (tunny)** is the largest member of the tuna family. It measures up to 7 feet and 400 pounds.

  - **Albacore (white tuna)** usually measures up to 40 inches and 130 pounds.

  - **Bonito** measures up to 20 inches and 5 pounds. The bonito has dark blue stripes on its sides. This fish is the most caught and canned species.

  - **Yellowfin tuna** measures up to 5 feet. Its skin is a dark blue with yellow tails. It is normally canned, with the exception of the loin, which is sold as steaks for fillets.

About ten different species of tuna are canned, but labels usually distinguish only between "white tuna" and "light tuna." Bluefin and yellowfin tuna should thus be marked "light tuna," while albacore should be labeled "white tuna." The bonito is usually marketed as "skipjack," the common name for the striped bonito. Solid tuna is always more expensive, but cheaper products such as crumbled tuna contain more fragments of bone and skin. When buying tuna, it may be helpful to consider how it is going to be used. If the appearance of the fish is important, buy solid tuna, but the other formats are fine for sauces or tuna salad (with mayonnaise).

FLATFISH

Flatfish are so named because their eyes are on the same side of the head, and their body is flattened, which allows them to live and feed on the bottom of the ocean.

- **Plaice.** Abundant in the Atlantic and the Pacific, this fish is less than 2 feet long and weighs between 1 and 4 pounds. Plaice is a very bony fish and is usually sold as fillets.

  - **American plaice** is abundant in New England and Canada, and is very common on both sides of the Atlantic. It can grow up to 2 feet.

  - **Common plaice.** This plaice rarely measures more than 16 inches but can grow to be 3 feet long.

  - **Winter flounder.** Usually about 18 inches long, the winter flounder can grow to a maximum length of almost 2 feet. It is particularly abundant in New England and the Gulf of St. Lawrence, but its natural habitat extends all the way from Labrador, in Canada, to Georgia. The winter flounder is fleshier than any other member of the plaice family.

  - **Witch flounder.** The witch flounder usually measures between 12 and 18 inches but can be longer than 30 inches. Found on both sides of the Atlantic, it is similar to the winter flounder but is brownish gray and has more rays on its dorsal and anal fins.

- **Common dab (plaice).** This dab is usually between 8 and 10 inches long but can grow up to 18 inches. It is found off the Atlantic coasts of Europe.

- **Yellowtail flounder.** The yellowtail usually measures between 10 and 16 inches but can be longer than 2 feet. Named for its yellow tail, it is commonly found in the Atlantic from Labrador to southern New England.

- **Lemon sole.** Despite its name, this fish is actually a plaice. It can grow to be longer than 2 feet, but its head and mouth are relatively small. Found in Atlantic coastal waters from France to Iceland, it is particularly abundant off the coast of France. Its flesh is bland and stringy.

- **Flounder.** This smaller fish, which is 12 to 20 inches, is abundant in the Baltic Sea. Its flesh is slightly less flavorful than that of the common plaice.

- **Summer flounder.** It can grow to be 3 feet long, the largest of all of the plaice species. The summer flounder is abundant in American coastal waters from Maine to South Carolina.

- **Turbot.** The turbot measures up to 20 inches and 55 pounds. The turbot has flavorful white flesh.

- **Halibut.** As one of the largest saltwater fish, the halibut thrives in the cold waters of northern seas and is very

People, Places, Things

Market Forms of Herring

Herring can be substituted for mackerel in most recipes. Frequently marinated, smoked, or canned, herring is usually sold as one following products:

- **Marinated herring** is completely deboned and fried. Marinated in oil, wine, tomato sauce, or vinegar, the canned sardines sold in North America are actually marinated herring.

- **Smoked herring** is either hot smoked (slightly cooked over direct heat) or cold smoked (smoked for a longer period of time away from the heat).

- **Saur herring** is named for the reddish-brown color the fish takes on when it is cold smoked for a long period of time. It is salted for 2 to 6 days before it is smoked and may or may not be gutted. Whole saur herring are stored in barrels or wooden crates and are sold individually; saur herring fillets are sold either in packages or in cans. It is also possible to buy marinated saur herring and canned saur herring eggs. This kind of herring will keep for 12 to 15 days.

- **Bloaters** are ungutted, usually whole herring that have been lightly salted (for 1 day at most) and then moderately hot or cold smoked. They will keep for about 5 days.

- **Bucklings** are herring that have been pickled in brine for a few hours and then smoked. Particularly popular in Holland and Germany, they are partially cooked during the smoking process and can be eaten without being cooked any further. This kind of herring will keep for about 4 days.

- **Kippers** are large herring that have been beheaded, slit open, deboned, flattened, and lightly cold smoked. Sold fresh, frozen, canned, or in ready-to-cook bags, they can be eaten as is or cooked for a few minutes. They will keep for 4 days.

common off the Atlantic coasts of Newfoundland and Greenland, as well as in the Pacific. It measures up to 55 inches and 155 pounds. Commercial overfishing has made large halibut quite rare. Halibut has very few bones and has lean, fine, firm, and flaky flesh.

- **Sole.** The sole thrives at the sandy bottom of several seas and oceans, though it is not found off the coasts of the United States or Canada. The sole measures up to 28 inches. The most sought-after species are the sole that are often identified with their place of origin, because they are frequently unique only to that area, and thus more rare. Dover sole, for example, is fished off the coasts of Dover, England.

TABLE 15.2		Yield chart of processed fish	
Courtesy of Plitt Seafood			
Turbot	30%	Jumbo fluke	39%
John Dory	35%	Catfish	50%
Red grouper	42%	Chilean sea bass	53%
Black grouper	43%	Lake trout	55%
Walleye pike	44%	Mackerel	56%
Mahi-Mahi	48%	Halibut	57%
Rainbow trout	60%	Monkfish	60%
Tuna	69%	Salmon	71%

WINGED FISH

Skate is a thin fish with a long tail and fins that look like large wings. The largest skates can weigh 1 ton and measure 20 feet. Smaller skates are sold whole and gutted, while larger ones are sold in pieces. The edible portions of the skate are the wings, the "cheeks," and the liver. Its boneless flesh can be pinkish or off-white and, depending on the species, may resemble that of scallops. When purchasing scallops, make sure they are not actually skate that were cut up into smaller circles. Skate needs to have the thick skin and spines removed before cooking.

EEL

The eel has a cylindrical body covered with small oval scales that are embedded in its skin. Eels, which are very popular in Europe and Japan, can be as long as 5 feet and can weigh more than 9 pounds, with males smaller than females. There are approximately 15 species of eels.

Eel is cut into fillets, slices, or pieces and sold fresh, smoked, marinated, or in cans. Eels can be kept alive in water tanks until they are sold. The firm flesh is fine and fatty. Eels are easy to debone, and much of the fat can easily be removed from larger eels because it is stored between the flesh and the skin. Fresh eel is extremely perishable and lasts only 1 or 2 days in the refrigerator.

MARKET FORMS OF FISH

Fresh fish is available in several market forms, ranging from the natural state to a processed end product. The price varies according to availability, amount of labor involved in processing, and market needs. See Table 15.2 for a yield chart of various fish. The market forms of fish include the following (see Figure 15.16):

- **Whole fish.** Some fish are sold whole, including shark, tuna, swordfish, salmon, tilapia, trout, mackerel, ocean perch, and black sea bass. A whole fish is the only way to completely confirm the quality of fresh fish. However, using whole fish can be expensive, as the fish must be processed before cooking.

- **Drawn.** This is a whole fish with all cavity organs removed. Drawn fish can be stored longer than whole fish.

- **Dressed.** These are the same as drawn fish but completely cleaned. They're usually served as a single serving.

- **H&G.** These are fish with heads and entrails (guts), or H&G, removed. H&G fish are available to food service operations and to processors that make steaks and fillets.

- **Loin.** Loins are taken from large fish like tuna, swordfish, or shark, cut from the backbone lengthwise into quarters. Flatfish are not typically loined. These are the thickest, best quality cuts and can be sold whole, cut into large pieces, or sliced. They often require further cutting and trimming into steaks before sale, which can result in unanticipated waste.

- **Fillet.** These are the sides of a fish that have been cut away from the backbone and removed in one piece. Fillets can vary in length and thickness, and are usually 100 percent edible:

  - **Thin fillets.** These cook quickly and benefit from moist cooking.

  - **Medium fillets.** These also cook fairly quickly and lend themselves to steaming, baking, braising, and frying.

  - **Thick fillets.** Meaty, they are used in a wide variety of ways. Whether they are thin, medium, or thick, fillets can be cut into different shapes and forms (see Figure 15.17). They include:

    - **Whole fillet.** This is the whole fillet cut from the fish. This cut is not common in the United States. Normally, it is sold to establishments that want to further trim it to meet their specific needs.

    - **V-cut.** This removes the pinbone along with a strip of flesh along the back. V-cut filets are boneless.

15.16   **Various market forms of fish**

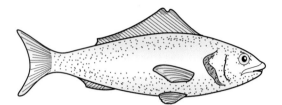

(a) Whole or round: completely intact, as caught.

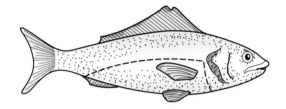

(b) Drawn: viscera removed.

(c) Dressed: viscera, scales, head, tail, and fins removed.

(f) Sticks: cross-section slices of fillets.

(d) Steaks: cross-section slices, each containing a section of backbone.

(e) Fillets: boneless sides of fish, with skin on or off.

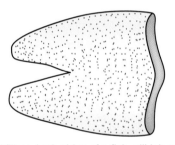

(g) Butterflied fillets: both sides of a fish still joined, but with bones removed.

People, Places, Things

Scaling Fish

Fish are easier to scale before they are gutted, when the ventral walls are still rounded. They are usually scaled with a scaler, a fork, the blunt edge of a knife, or a knife that has been dulled (to reduce the risk of cutting yourself). With one hand, hold the fish firmly by the tail, and use the other hand to scale the fish by placing the scaler at a 45-degree angle and scraping toward the head. You can do this under running water to prevent the scales from scattering. If the fish is going to be cooked with the skin on, be careful not to damage the skin. Fish can be skinned without removing the scales. Flatfish do

15.17 Various market forms of fish fillets and steaks

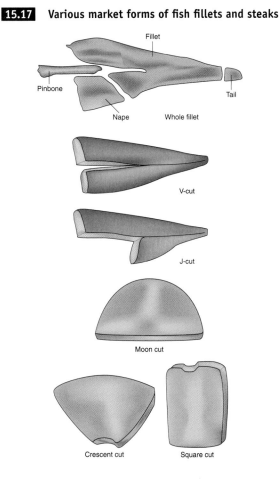

- Fillet
- Pinbone
- Tail
- Nape
- Whole fillet
- V-cut
- J-cut
- Moon cut
- Crescent cut
- Square cut

- **J-cut.** Premium, J-cut fillets are often the most expensive and usually offer slightly less yield than V-cut fillets. They are cut the same way but in a J shape.

- **Skin-on/skin-off.** Fish with soft flesh are rarely skinned because the fillets tend to fall apart. If the fish is firm-fleshed, the chef may ask that the skin be removed.

- **Deep-skinned.** Deep-skinned fillets have had their fatty layer removed to reduce the oily taste.

- **Tail-on/Tail-off.** Tail-on fillets cost less and provide a high degree of available flesh, but due to their gradually thinning shape close to the tail, they are prone to uneven cooking.

- **Steak.** Steaks often contain a thin band of skin, along with a piece of backbone. In smaller fish, bone-in steaks are uniform. In larger fish, they may have a variety of shapes. The edible portion is about 85 percent for each steak.

- **Fish sticks and patties.** These products are pieces of fish meat of uniform size, usually 3 inches by 1 inch. Some lesser-quality sticks are mechanically formed from fish meat and binders to appear like fillets, patties, or sticks. The edible portion is 100 percent.

BUYER'S NOTE *Shellfish should also be separated from ice using plastic or paper.*

People, Places, Things

Icing Fish for Storage

Fresh fish and shellfish must be handled carefully to ensure food safety. Refrigeration does not improve the quality of seafood; it only slows spoilage. Upon receipt of delivery, refrigerate fresh fish in the original leak-proof container immediately after inspection, until it can be stored properly. To store fresh fish:

1. Place a 6-inch perforated hotel pan inside a deeper hotel pan, leaving at least a 2-inch gap between the bottoms of the pans.

2. Fill the perforated hotel pan with a layer of crushed or cubed ice.

3. Place the whole fish (skin-on) directly on the ice. For fillets or sides, completely wrap the flesh in plastic wrap before placing on the ice (if the ice touches the flesh, it will cause the flesh to "burn.")

4. Cover the fish with a second layer of ice.

5. Place the filled hotel pans in the walk-in or reach-in cooler for storage.

6. As ice will melt and fill the bottom pan, repeat the process every 12 hours. (Seafood should not be allowed to remain in standing water for any length of time, as it leaches flavor from the fish and softens the flesh.)

7. Refrigerate (fresh fish) for only 1 or 2 days, or freeze

Crustaceans

Crustaceans are shellfish with external skeletons and jointed legs. Although there are thousands of species, there are only a couple of species that are commercially viable **crustaceans**: crab, shrimp, lobster, and crayfish are the most common.

CRAB

Crab are any of the numerous broadly built decapod crustaceans, each with a short, broad, and usually flattened, shell. They have a small abdomen that curls forward beneath the body, short antennae, and an anterior pair of limbs that are modified as grasping pincers. They are primarily marine animals that are prized for their fatty, moist, and flavorful meat.

Market Forms of Crab

- **Blue crabs**. An abundant small crab caught along the entire Atlantic coast, from Massachusetts southward into the Gulf of Mexico. The newly molted blue crab is the soft-shell crab widely used in food service operations. Blue crabs are sold alive in bushel baskets or cooked fresh. In some areas, blue crab meat is also canned. (See Figure 5.18.)

  - **Picked meat** is packed in containers, pasteurized, and refrigerated. This technique retains the flavor and texture much better than freezing does and still allows a shelf life of at least 6 weeks. There are a number of packs:

    - **Jumbo lump** are large pieces of body meat.

    - **Flake or body** are small pieces of meat from the body.

    - **Claw meat** is meat from the claws, which is brownish compared with the white meat from the body of the crab.

    - **Cocktail claws** are table-ready claws with part of the shell left attached.

- **Soft-shell crab.** These are in the "just-molted" stage of the blue crab, when it has shed its old shell and is just beginning to grow a new one. They are cleaned of gills and viscera, often breaded before being frozen, and then frozen. The trade in soft-shell crabs is substantial. Soft-shell crabs are graded by width of the shell from side to side, as illustrated in Table 15.3.

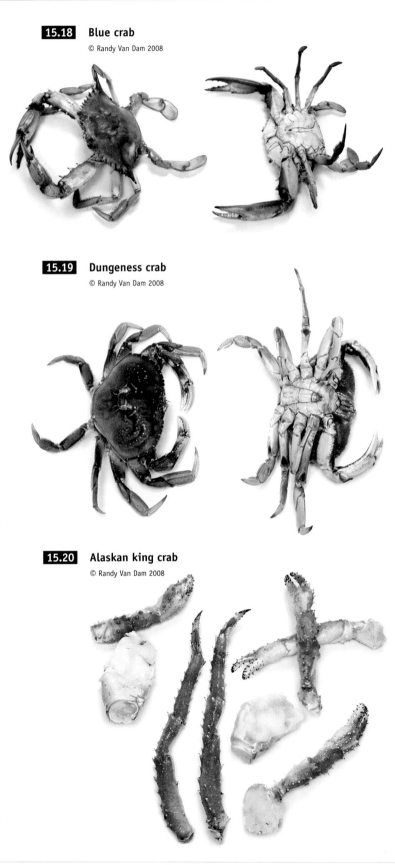

15.18   **Blue crab**
© Randy Van Dam 2008

15.19   **Dungeness crab**
© Randy Van Dam 2008

15.20   **Alaskan king crab**
© Randy Van Dam 2008

TABLE 15.3   Market Sizes of Soft Shell Crab

Market Name	Measurements
Whales or slabs	over 5 ½ inches
Jumbos	5 to 5 ½ inches
Primes	4 ½ to 5 inches
Hotels	4 to 4 ½ inches
Mediums	3 ½ to 4 inches

- **Dungeness crab.** Dungeness crabs come from the Northwest and are one of the best crabs to eat. They normally reach up to 3 ½ pounds, though most of the inshore (bay) crabs weigh 1 to 2 pounds. On the West Coast, frozen, cooked crabs are popular when fresh crab is out of season. Dungeness crab season is from September to February. Whole, cooked crabs are usually packed in a dozen, sometimes two dozen, per carton. Grading is 1½ to 2½ and 2½ to 3½ pounds per crab. Dungeness crab meat is packed in 5-pound cold-pack cans and frozen. Cases contain six 5-pound blocks. Meat from the legs is similarly packed, separately, and called fryer legs. (See Figure 15.19.)

- **Alaskan king crab.** This is a large spider crab found in the northernmost waters of the Pacific, from Alaska to northern Japan (see Figure 15.20). King crabs average 6 to 8 pounds, and those from Alaska sometimes grow as large as 20 pounds. King crab is harvested whole and then immediately cooked. The crab is then split and cleaned by removing the gills and viscera, the top shell is discarded, and the tail shell is separated. The remaining two pieces, which are made up of the legs and claw on one side connected by the shoulders, are called sections. These sections are the basic raw material from which all other king crab products are made. All products, therefore, are cooked before being processed and frozen. The various king crab products include:

  - **Whole merus meat (all-leg meat).** The merus is the largest segment of each of the six walking legs of the crab, and it is the segment closest to the shoulder. Whole pieces of meat from merus sections are roughly cylindrical in shape, red, and between 4 and 8 inches long. Five-pound blocks of merus meat are packed six per master carton. Often, the 5-pound block is split into two pieces each of nibs. Merus meat is the most expensive of the king crab products and indeed is one of the most expensive seafood products of any type.

  - **Fancy meat (60/40 meat or regular meat).** The most widely used king crab meat pack is also packed in six 5-pound blocks with each block divided in two, or 6 / 2 / 2 1/2 pounds, in the same way as the merus meat. Fancy meat should consist of three layers within each block: The bottom layer is 25 percent of the weight and consists of merus meat. Up to 70 percent of this layer may be broken merus meat. The top layer is 20 percent by weight and is

red meat. The remaining 55 percent is the middle layer and consists of large pieces of white meat. This layer should not include tail meat or meat from the walking tips of the legs.

The 60/40 designation, which is universally used as shorthand to specify king crab meat, means that there should be roughly 40 percent leg meat (the top and bottom layers) and 60 percent body meat (the middle layer). Most consumers prefer the leg meat, so chefs will normally ask for an even amount of leg and body meat.

- **Salad meat.** This is a cheaper pack and consists of smaller chunks of white and red meat mixed together. Salad meat chunks should be about 3/8-inch square for use in salads and other cold productions.

- **Shred meat.** This consists of the smallest pieces of meat from the body of the crab together with any small fragments broken from the leg pieces.

- **Minced meat (rice meat).** This is mixed meat put through a ricer to give it a uniform texture, for use in stuffing and similar applications. This is the cheapest king crab meat product. It is important that the mincing is not too fine; otherwise, the meat loses all texture and thaws to a mushy consistency that is not acceptable.

- **Tail meat.** The king crab has a triangular "purse" on the underside of the shell, and the meat in this tail is extracted and sold separately, as tail meat. Whole tail meat is extremely tough but has good flavor, and when chopped it is an excellent inexpensive product for sandwiches or salad mixtures.

- **Fancy legs.** These are the same as legs and claws but without the claws. They are sold when claws are not needed.

- **Large claws with arm (killer claws).** These are packed with the arm attached and should contain about 40 percent meat. The same boxes are used as for legs and claws, but sometimes 25 pounds (instead of 20 pounds) will be packed into one carton. The same quality considerations apply as for legs and claws.

- **Small claws with arm (feeder claws).** Like the previous item, these are cooked claws with the arm attached, but the feeder claw is the smaller of the two. These will contain only about 30 percent meat, so they are cheaper than large claws, or legs and claws. Small claws are generally packed in 25-pound boxes.

- **Split legs, or split legs and claws.** These are legs, or legs and claws, cut in half lengthwise, through the diameter of the leg section, so that the meat is exposed. Split legs are expensive, because they come ready for use and also require the processor to carefully handle and glaze the meat so it stays in place in the shells. Split legs alone are a more desirable pack than split legs and claws, but most packs include the split claws. In the past, it was possible to buy split legs graded according to length so that all the pieces were approximately the same size, but it was costly, so it lost its appeal. Quality considerations are similar to those for legs and claws, but, in addition, these must be cut accurately so that the two halves of the split legs are equal in thickness. Packs are either single 25-pound polylined cartons, known as bulk pack, or twelve 12-ounce retail polybags, when the price is quoted for 12-ounce units rather than pounds.

- **Rock crab (Jonah crab).** There are a number of different crabs with this name. Most are caught and consumed near where they are caught, and most contain good meat. Although this product may also be frozen, packers generally only freeze it as a last resort if they cannot sell it while fresh.

- **Snow crab (tanner crab, queen crab, bairdii, opilio).** Snow, or tanner, crabs come from the North Pacific and from Canadian waters in the North Atlantic (see Figure 15.21). The largest snow crab is the Alaskan crab, Latin name *Chionoecetes bairdii*, known as bairdii (pronounced "bird-eye") to distinguish it from the much smaller *C. opilio*. Alaskan snow crab is the most expensive. It is also far superior in taste to the Canadian crab; in fact, many users prefer the taste and texture of Alaskan snow crabmeat to that of king crab meat. However, king crab has a reputation with the consumer, and snow crab, whatever its intrinsic quality, sells for much less than king crab.

  - **Clusters.** Snow crab clusters are the equivalent of king crab sections, that is, three legs and one claw from one side of the crab joined at the shoulder with the gills, viscera, and top shell removed. Alaskan clusters are usually packed with the claw but may be sold without. Canadian snow crab is invariably claw on.

- **Snow crab claws (cocktail claws).** Cooked claws are scored around the top so that the shell cap may be removed easily. These are packed in 2-pound or 3-pound bags or boxes, usually six per master carton. Sometimes the cap is removed, and the exposed tip of meat is heavily glazed for protection.

- **Single legs.** The clusters may be cut at the shoulder and the legs sold separately. This has never been a particularly popular pack, probably because the small size of the snow crab makes a cluster a better portion for customers.

- **Snow crabmeat.** Alaskan snow crabmeat is packed in similar manner to king crabmeat (see above). Merus (all-leg meat) packs are also produced. Specification and packing are much the same as for Alaskan king crab, and the snow crabmeat is similarly offered in 60/40 ratios.

- **Stone crabs.** These are found almost exclusively along the Gulf Coast of Florida, and only the claws are used. One claw is removed, and the crab is thrown back into the water (in the belief or hope that it will regenerate the lost limbs). The claws are cooked and packed in 3-pound or 5-pound bags, eight or twelve per master carton. Gradings vary, but the largest claws may be 2/4 per pound (between 2 and 4 claws per pound), and the smallest about 16/20 (between 16–20 claws per pound). A small quantity of product is also imported from Chile. The stone crab there is very similar in taste and texture, but its shell is not as shiny as the Florida crab. Stone crabs from all sources have very hard shells, hence their name. When frozen, or directly iced, the claw meat tends to stick to the shell. They may be stored at 32°F (0°C) for 2 to 3 days. (See Figure 15.22.)

15.21 **Snow crab legs and claws**
© Randy Van Dam 2008

15.22 **Stone crab claws**
© Randy Van Dam 2008

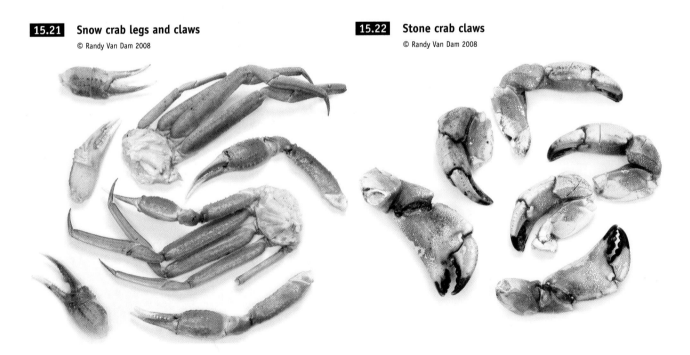

Claws regenerate usually within 12 months and can do so three to four times. (Regenerated claws are nicknamed "retreads.") It is illegal to harvest whole stone crabs, claws less than 2 ¾ inches from first joint to tip, or claws from egg-bearing females.

SHRIMP

Shrimp are small, mainly ocean-dwelling crustacean with ten legs, belonging to a suborder that includes several edible species. A shrimp has a long, thin semitransparent body, five pairs of jointed legs, a tail resembling a fan, and a pair of pincers. Like other crustacea, shrimp are prized for their tender, moist, and sweet-tasting meat.

Market Forms of Shrimp

Primary product forms for frozen shrimp (see Figure 15.23) are as follows:

- **Green head-on.** Includes the six tail segments with vein, shell, and tail fin and with head still intact.
- **Green headless.** Same as head-on but without the head. This is the common market form.
- **Peeled.** Green headless shrimp without the shell.
- **PUD.** Peeled, undeveined, tail fin on or off; raw or cooked.
- **P&D.** Peeled, deveined, tail fin on or off; raw or cooked.
- **Shell-on cooked.** Cooked tail with vein, shell, and tail fin.

- **Split, butterfly, fantail.** Tail-on shrimp that are cut deeply when being deveined.

Because shrimp are so small, they are sold by their number of shrimp per pound (known as the **count**). The count is expressed as a range, where the smaller the count, the larger the shrimp. For example, a U-15 count of green headless means that there are less than 15 shrimp per pound, weighing more than 1 ounce apiece. A count of 31/40 green headless shrimp consists of 31 to 40 shrimp in a pound, each weighing under 0.5 ounce (see Table 15.4).

TABLE 15.4 Shrimp Purchase Description and Count Chart

Purchase Description Name	Green Headless (Unpeeled) Count per pound
Extra Colossal	U-10
Colossal	U-15
Extra Jumbo	16-20
Jumbo	21-25
Extra Large	26-30
Large	31-35
Medium Large	36-42
Medium	43-50
Small	51-60
Extra Small	61-70
Tiny	Over 70

15.23 **Various market forms of shrimp**
© Randy Van Dam 2008

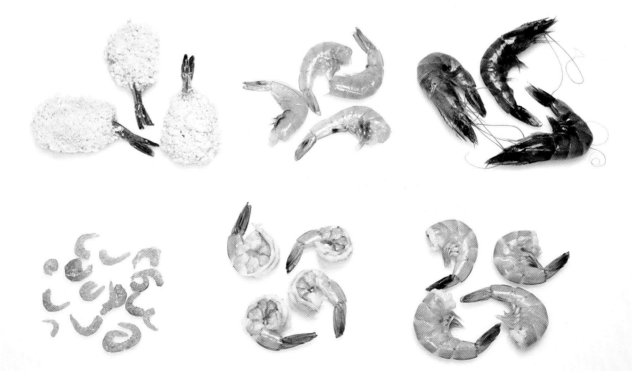

LOBSTER

Lobster is one of the most popular types of seafood. This, combined with increasing scarcity, makes lobster one of the most expensive seafood products. A lobster takes about 7 years to grow to 1 pound. From that point, it takes a lobster 4 years to gain each additional pound.

Market Forms of Lobsters

Fresh lobsters are available year-round and are most economical during spring and summer. There are two varieties common to the United States.

- **Maine lobster (American lobster, true lobster).** This is what most people think of when they hear "lobster." Maine lobsters are found off the Atlantic coast of the northern United States and Canada. Almost all of the meat is found in the claws and tail. (See Figure 15.24.)

- **Spiny lobsters (rock lobsters, Florida lobsters).** Spiny lobsters are found off the coasts of Florida and Southern California. Almost all of the meat is in the tail because the spiny lobster has no claws. Outside California and Florida, most of the spiny lobster meat sold in the United States is in the form of frozen tails, usually labeled "rock lobster tails." (See Figure 15.25.)

Fresh lobster has to be kept alive until needed for cooking. If a lobster dies before it is cooked, it should be discarded. When a lobster dies, the enzymes that normally digest food begin to digest the lobster. The by-product secretions are toxic to humans. Frozen lobster products, such as tails, are normally killed, cooked, and frozen within the fish plant, making them safe for consumption.

The easiest way to check if a lobster is alive is to pick it up. If the tail curls under the body or it begins waiving its claws, then it is alive. If the lobster is on ice, it might take awhile to "wake up." Lobsters that are kept in warmer boxes are usually livelier than the iced ones.

Lobster is one of the few seafood that do not freeze well. The flavor deteriorates, and the flesh toughens and shrinks in the freezing process. Freezing lobster in the shell also makes the animal brittle so that claws and legs often fall off. However, a live lobster, cooked and immediately brine frozen, and then packed in a sealed plastic "bubble" with water to keep it moist, can be an acceptable product. Alternative packing, using parchment or polywraps, or polystyrene tubes, does not protect the lobster as well, so breakage is high and shelf life short. "Bubble" packs are so far the best way of freezing lobsters. They, and other frozen whole cooked lobsters, are usually graded the same way as live lobsters.

Quarters to deuces are known as selects. Jumbos are seldom frozen, except for special order for buffet display or similar use. Although rare, lobsters that weighed up to 10 pounds used to be available, but due to overfishing, the numbers of giant lobsters available has virtually disappeared. Nowadays, 3-pound lobster is considered extraordinary.

Lobsters with one claw are called *culls*, and they are usually graded as chicken, select, and large culls. Lobsters without claws are called *bullets* are often available at a significant discount. Buyers should seriously evaluate the financial benefits of using bullets if they only need tail meat, and shells for stock or flavored butters. The edible portion (EP) cost may be more favorable than buying tails. Minimum sizes for lobsters are based on the length of the carapace of the body and not on weight. A few lobster tails, usually cooked, are frozen and may be available from time to time.

15.24 **Maine lobster**

© Randy Van Dam 2008

15.25 **Spiny lobster**

© Randy Van Dam 2008

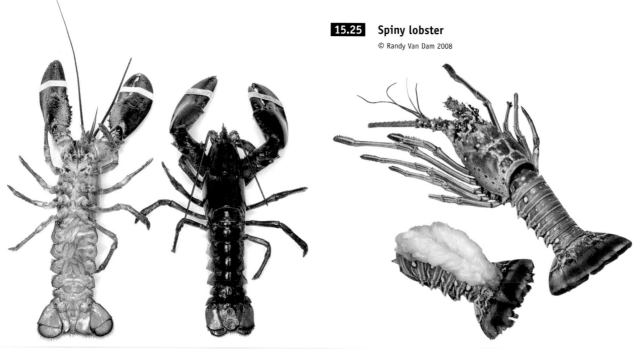

Frozen whole cooked Florida lobsters and other spiny lobsters are usually graded in 2-ounce or quarter-pound steps, and the spiny lobster produces a better frozen version than the northern lobster. Packs are 25 pounds each and individually wrapped.

There are two distinct types of lobster tail.

- **Cold-water tails** are the more expensive of the two. Most come from South Africa, which is the largest supplier of lobster tails (of any type) to the United States, and the rest come from Australia and New Zealand. Cold-water tails are a good, firm, tasty product, and they pack carefully and well. There are minor differences in appearance and taste among the different cold-water tails, but all offer a superior product and consistency. Sizes of South African tails are designated by letter codes illustrated in Table 15.5.

- **Warm-water tails** are cheaper and generally less tasty and less reliable. They come from a wider range of sources. Brazil and domestic packers in Florida are the major suppliers. Many warm-water tails come from the Bahamas, where the resource is shared with Florida fishermen, and from many parts of the Caribbean. Most Central American countries supply some lobster tails, and quantities also come from Asia, especially from India, Sri Lanka, the Philippines, and Japan. In general, the Atlantic tails are reddish brown, and the Pacific and Asian tails are slightly green, but the distinction between tails is slight. In practice, warm-water tails have become one of the most blatantly cheated products in seafood. Indian tails, which are comparatively cheap, are repacked as Florida tails, and many tails are reglazed to cheat the customer on both size and net weight. Florida tails usually come in four 10-pound packs and are graded in 2-ounce steps from 4/6 through

TABLE 15.5 **South African Lobster Tail Sizes**

Code	Ounces
K	2
KZ	2 ½
M	31
	4–4 ½
H	42–51
G	52–
F	61–
E	7 ½–8
D	8–9
C	9 1/2–11
B	11 ½–12
A	12–16
AA	16–20
AAA	20–40

TABLE 15.6 **Warm-Water Lobster Tail Sizes**

Size (in ounces)	Count per 10-lb box
3	over 50
3X	50
3XX	38–45
4	40
5	32
6	27
7	23
8	20
9	18
10	16
11	15
12	13
13	12
14	11

10/12; larger sizes are graded in 4-ounce steps. Brazil grading is in straight sizes from 3 ounces to 14 ounces, and this portion-control grading has given the Brazilian packers an important edge in the market: because the buyer knows how many tails she will get in every box, she can plan and control more effectively. Brazil tails always come in sets of four 10-pound packs, and size definitions are based on counts per 10-pound box, as illustrated in Table 15.6.

To clarify, 3-ounce Brazil tails are under 3 ounces, 3X tails are about 3¼ ounces, and 3XX tails are about 3½ ounces. All sizes are graded by eye to look similar. These grade scales do not imply that every tail in the box is identical in weight.

All lobster tails should show clean white meat at the end, which is broken out of the body, and this meat should be well glazed for protection. The shell should be lightly glazed overall. Each tail should be well wrapped or poly-bagged for protection.

CRAYFISH

Crayfish are known locally as freshwater lobsters, crawdads, and mudbugs. Crayfish are most popular in Louisiana. Almost all of the crayfish harvested in the United States come from Louisiana.

Crayfish are available live or frozen whole, or you can buy frozen shelled crayfish tail. Live crayfish should be very active. Put live crayfish in a bowl, cover with wet paper towels, and keep in the refrigerator for no more than 24 hours. To freeze, wrap crayfish meat carefully in freezer paper or plastic, and over-wrap with a plastic bag. Store for up to 2 months. (See Figure 15.26.)

15.26 Crayfish

© Randy Van Dam 2008

Mollusks (Molluscs)

Another category of shellfish is **mollusks**. The shells are the equivalent of the skeleton in higher animals, so this shellfish has no bones in the meat. There are three types of mollusks:

- **Bivalves**. These mollusks have two shells that enclose all or most of the animal when closed. Clams, oysters, mussels, and scallops are **bivalves**.

- **Univalves**. These mollusks have a single shell. The animal lives inside the shell and often has a shell-like plate that can be closed over the opening. Conch and abalone are **univalves**.

- **Cephalopods**. These mollusks do not usually have an external shell. The name indicates feet growing out of the head. Squid, octopus, and cuttlefish are the **cephalopods** most commonly used in food service. These varieties have a piece of cartilage inside the body that serves as the skeleton. It is called the "pen" or "quill" in squid, and the "bone" in the cuttlefish and "spine" in octopus.

CLAMS

Clams can be found in sand or mud close to shore and in bays just below the surface of the bottom. They are harvested with hand tools, such as rakes, shovels, or tongs. The two main varieties are hard shell and soft shell. The hard shell protects the meat. The most commercially important species of hard-shell clams harvested include:

- **Southern quahog and northern quahog.** These oval-shaped clams come in three sizes.

  - **Littleneck clams** are the smallest and most tender.

  - **Cherrystone clam** is medium sized, about 2½ inches across.

  - **Chowder clam** is the largest and has a shell diameter of at least 3 inches.

- **Steamer clam.** The most common East Coast soft shell is the steamer clam, which has an off-white thin, brittle shell that does not close entirely. They usually are 3 inches in diameter.

Clams are sold live in the shell, fresh or frozen shucked, and canned. Live hard-shell clams should be closed. If open, touch the shell to see if it closes. To test a soft-shell clam, lightly touch its neck; if it moves, it is alive. The guideline for buying shucked clams is plumpness and clear liquid.

All raw shellfish must be stored in refrigeration to slow or minimize bacterial growth. Direct storage in ice is not recommended as it may kill the shellfish. Store live clams up to 2 weeks in a 40°F refrigerator in containers with the lid slightly open. Refrigerate shucked clams up to 7 days in a sealed container. Clams can be frozen in the shell and kept up to 3 months. Place the live clams in moisture-vapor-resistant bags. Press out excess air and freeze. To freeze the clam meat, shuck the clams, and then clean and wash the meat thoroughly. Drain and pack in freezer containers, leaving 1/2-inch headspace. Frozen shellfish should be thawed in the refrigerator. (See Figure 15.27.)

15.27 Cherry stone, topneck, and littleneck clams, as shown from left to right

© Randy Van Dam 2008

OYSTERS

Oysters grow mainly in tidal mudflats, which are most vulnerable to pollution and to draining and silting of estuaries caused by commercial development. They are two-shelled (bivalve) mollusks with one shell fairly flat and the other deeper. Oysters are irregularly shaped: no two are exactly alike (see Figure 15.28a). When the baby oysters are established, the oyster-grower moves the material with its attached oysters to growing areas, or, in some cases, removes the baby oysters and lays them out in trays in suitable tidal areas to grow and fatten for market.

State authorities strictly monitor oysters under the **Shellfish Sanitation Program** (SSP) for contamination from viruses, bacteria, and "red tide" toxins. Imported raw fresh and frozen oysters are also subject to the SSP and must come only from approved growing beds. Recently, a process for sanitizing oysters in land-based holding tanks has been developed to avoid the problems of red tide and bacteria. The water is purified by ultraviolet light, and the "Ameripure oysters" eventually are purged of contaminants and then brought to the market. Popular standard oysters include:

- **Eastern oyster (Gulf, Atlantic, or American).** "Easterns" are very popular at seafood bars on both U.S. coasts. They thrive on reefs that are between 8 and 25 feet deep.

- **European flat oyster (Belon).** Introduced to the Northwest in the 1950s, the European flat has a rounder shell than other species and is possibly the most popular among half-shell enthusiasts.

- **Kumamoto.** Originally imported in the late 1940s to replace diminishing supplies of Pacifics, these oysters have a subtler flavor than Olympia oysters, and their shells hold considerably more meat.

- **Olympia.** Found all along the Pacific Coast, the Olympia oyster is the Northwest's only native oyster species. This species has become increasingly difficult to locate.

- **Pacific (Japanese).** The Pacific oyster is the largest of all commercial oysters. The meat of this oyster is sweet and rich.

There is an unlimited number of ways to enjoy oysters. Unlike most shellfish, oysters can have a fairly long shelf life: up to 2 weeks; however, they should be consumed when fresh. Dead oysters become dangerous to eat rather quickly because of the large bacteria colonies in the animal, which begin to multiply as soon as the oyster dies.

Oysters are easy to handle. Shelled stock should be kept in chilled storage. Remember that they are alive and are not adapted to living in freshwater, which can suffocate them, so they should not be near or in running or dripping water. Oyster bags should be handled carefully, never dropped or thrown around. Oysters may be shucked and eaten for as long as they are alive (see Figure 15.28b). Tightly closed shellfish, or ones that close their shells when tapped, are alive. Any gaping shells that do not close themselves when disturbed should be discarded.

15.28b Popping the hinge on an oyster (note the protective cloth being used)
© Randy Van Dam 2008

15.28a Eastern Delaware and Pacific Chef Creek oysters
© Randy Van Dam 2008

MUSSELS

Mussels are bivalve shellfish, like oysters and clams, and are subject to the controls of the Shellfish Sanitation Program. Unlike oysters and most clams, they are cheap and plentiful. They are considered by many chefs to be equally as good to eat, though mussels are seldom eaten raw. Fresh mussels, sold live in the shell, are one of the best opportunities for providing good quality seafood at modest prices.

Mussels grow in shallow water, attached to rocks, pilings, or other mussels, on both East and West coasts. Major harvests currently are from New England, but Washington is increasing supplies, and there are new flats for fishing. Aquaculture mussels are more likely to be evenly sized because they are planted and grown together.

Mussels are usually sold by the bushel bag. A bushel of mussels weighs about 45 pounds. Mussels, when properly handled and harvested, should be washed clean. Stones, seaweed, and empty shells should be removed before they are shipped. The shellfish should be fairly uniform in size, and the shells must be tightly closed. Open shells that do not close when touched or rinsed indicate the mussel is dead and unsafe for use. These should be discarded.

All bags and containers must display the license number of the shipper. Food service operators should keep the tags, even if the bag is repackaged, in case of a recall. Mussels are rather fragile out of water. The shells are thin and break easily, so gentle handling is important. Like all similar shellfish, they should be kept cool and not be mixed with ice. (See Figure 15.29a and Figure 15.29b.)

SCALLOPS

Scallops are the muscles holding the two halves of the scallop shell together. Only the muscle is harvested for consumption; the shell and insides are discarded. Scallops are only available as chucked—whole scallops cannot be opened without commercial equipment. Sea scallops are harvested from open waters and tend to be larger, while bay scallops are from sheltered coves and are much smaller.

It is necessary to mention that large quantities of frozen scallops are thawed and sold as fresh. Because frozen scallops tend to be quite tough when broiled, and fresh scallops are greatly preferred for broiling, this may present a problem. Canadian and domestic frozen sea scallops, available widely in 5-pound blocks, are often offered as fresh scallops. Institutional buyers that use larger quantities are rather more likely to buy a complete 30-pound bag of genuinely fresh scallops.

A more deceptive practice is offering thawed imported scallops, particularly queen scallops from the UK, as fresh bay scallops. Some packers of queen scallops produce an excellent product that is almost comparable in taste and texture to the true bay. Nevertheless, it is a different species. The law requires packers to report both this fact and their

15.29b   **Bearding the mussel**
© Randy Van Dam 2008

15.29a   **Mussels**
© Randy Van Dam 2008

imported origin to buyers, but not all foreign packers are virtuous. Some South American scallops, which are less like bays, are also "upgraded" in this way.

Perhaps the greatest problem associated with scallops, fresh or frozen, is the common practice of soaking them in phosphate dips. Phosphate helps the meats to hold this water, and it whitens the scallop, generally regarded as a marketing improvement. The use of phosphate dips or other additives is supposed to be noted on the label. These products purge the retained liquid when cooked, resulting in a smaller finished product and wetter pan.

All scallops should look and smell fresh. The odor should be sweet and reminiscent of seaweed. Any traces of sourness, gas, or iodine indicate spoilage. Sea scallops should be packed rather loosely in their bags. All scallops should look clear and shiny. Sea scallops are slightly creamy; bay scallops are definitely creamy. Calicos are whiter and less shiny. Traces of pink or orange-brown usually indicate that a roe was cut and are not a problem, unless you think customers might reject the scallops when displayed.

Market Varieties of Scallops

There are relatively few varieties of scallops sold for culinary use (see Figure 15.30a and Figure 15.30b); they are:

 Bay and sea scallops, as shown left to right
© Randy Van Dam 2008

 Removing the scallop and roe
© Randy Van Dam 2008

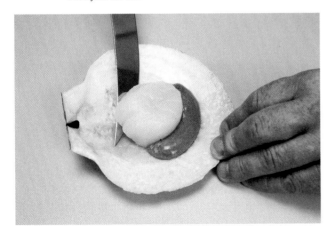

- **Bay scallops.** These are a smaller, inshore scallop found from Cape Cod to Long Island and nowhere else. This true bay scallop is also known as Cape Cod scallop or Cape scallop, Long Island scallop, Peconic scallop (Peconic Bay in Eastern Long Island being a major source area), and Rhode Island scallop. Fresh bays are excellent raw and require little cooking at any time. Because of their excellent quality, scarcity, and high price, many inferior scallops are passed off as bay scallops. Taste, however, is a simple and reliable test for the genuine article, once you have experienced the difference.

- **Calico scallops.** These are found from the Carolinas southward to Brazil and are landed fresh in large quantities from Florida and the Carolinas. Smaller quantities are landed from the Gulf Coast, also. Calicos are smaller than other domestic scallops, ranging from about 60 meats per pound down to 200 or more. Some packers are beginning to grade calicos, because there can be a substantial premium paid for the larger sizes (lower counts).

- **Sea scallops.** Generally, the term *sea scallops* describes, or should describe, the species of large, deepwater scallop caught by U.S. and Canadian vessels around the Georges Bank and other Northeastern fishing banks. This scallop is landed in Canada, Massachusetts, and Virginia. New Bedford, Massachusetts, is the major marketing center. The auction there plays a large part in determining the price of both fresh and frozen sea scallops.

- **Diver scallops.** Diver scallops refer to a method of harvesting, not a variety. Diver scallops are collected from the ocean by divers handpicking each one. The diver scallops are less gritty than the dragged ones. Diver scallops are also a much more ecologically friendly way of harvesting scallops.

- **Scallops on the half-shell.** These scallops are still attached to their original shell and then IQF frozen-processed and packaged for sale.

CONCH

Conch (scungilli, sea snail, snail, whelk, dog-whelk) are large sea snails of two different types: one from the Caribbean, especially the Bahamas, and the other from the Northern part of the Atlantic coastline (see Figure 15.31). The two types differ in appearance and in the way they are processed.

- The Bahamian or Caribbean conch is taken from the shell, eviscerated and washed, and then frozen in 5-pound boxes, ten to a master carton. It is sometimes offered uncleaned, similarly packed.

- The New England–type conch is generally smaller and darker in color; it is normally cooked before being shelled and cleaned. The meats are often packed in

15.31 **Conch shell and conch meat**
© Randy Van Dam 2008

BUYER'S NOTE *Conch is no longer available from American waters, as it is protected. Belize, Venezuela, and Puerto Rico have also closed conch fishing.*

ABALONE

Abalone is a large, single-shell mollusk and one of the most expensive varieties of seafood (see Figure 15.32.). Commercially fished quantities are limited to California and Alaska, and fishing is heavily controlled to protect the resources. Because the abalone eats kelp seaweed, it is immune to red tide, which affects the filter-feeding shellfish.

Abalone is cut from the shell, cleaned of viscera and frill, and sliced across the flesh into round steaks, which are then pounded lightly to soften the fibers. Abalone must be cooked only briefly, or it toughens. Additionally, prepared steaks, often already breaded, are commonly sold.

Because of the high price of abalone, it is a prime target for cheaper substitutions. Giant squid and cuttlefish are among the unlikely items that have been cut into similar shapes and passed off as abalone. If there is a thin membrane on part of the steak, it is actually cuttlefish or squid, not abalone. You can also test it by putting it through a meat tenderizer; the substitutes will leave telltale pin marks on the surface.

bags and frozen, and a few packers vacuum-pack the bags. There is no standard size bag or outer carton for this product.

Caribbean conch is whiter and larger than Rhode Island–type conch, and most users are not willing to substitute one for the other, either way, so the two conches are not particularly competitive with one another in the marketplace. Unclean and partially cleaned Caribbean conch can be a problem to handle, and it is best avoided unless you are sure that you have a use for it. It is cheaper than the fully cleaned pack, but it normally only sells when there is no cleaned conch available.

Conch is perhaps the only shellfish that becomes more tender with extended cooking. It needs several hours boiling, or alternatively plenty of beating with a mallet, to make it soft enough to eat. So the cooked conch originating in Rhode Island and other parts of the Northeast invariably requires further cooking before use. The processor in this case cooks the conch to facilitate its removal from the shell, not to prepare the meat for the user. Full cooking also reduces the yield substantially, so the saleable weight for the processor is less if the conch is fully cooked.

Be aware that every supplier will swear to you that the conch is not only fully cooked but that it is the only such genuinely described product on the market. Before you repeat such descriptions to your own customers, make sure you try to eat the conch yourself. The chances of the shellfish actually being fully cooked are remote. It may, however, be sufficiently cooked for certain uses, such as conch salad, where the ma rinade will soften the flesh.

15.32 **Removing abalone**
© Randy Van Dam 2008

SQUID (CALAMARI)

Commercially sold squid are usually between 12 and 16 inches long. It is available in a variety of market forms, including fresh, frozen, dried, and canned. Fresh squid should be moist, but firm with only a faint seawater odor.

15.33a **Cleaning squid (removing the head)**

© Randy Van Dam 2008

15.33b **Cleaned squid heads for sale in the marketplace**

Courtesy of Robert Garlough

When sold as fresh or thawed, it is often necessary to clean the squid prior to use, as shown in Figure 15.33a. The edible parts, representing approximately 80 percent of the squid, include the complete system of tenacles, and most of the cone-shaped body. However, cleaned and trimmed squid is also available as shown in Figure 15.33b. Squid has a very long shelf life if handled with reasonable care. Leaving the viscera in obviously reduces the shelf life. It becomes rather pungent with age. Squid is little affected by freezing; the texture is unchanged even if the flesh is frozen and thawed a number of times, so there is little reason to hold squid fresh for long periods when frozen product will be easier to keep.

OCTOPUS

The octopus is a shell-less cephalopod mollusk that is found in most of the world's seas. Related to the squid and the cut-

tlefish, it is the largest member of the family and can grow to almost 30 feet.

Octopus flesh is firm and flavorful, especially if it comes from a small animal. The tough flesh of large octopuses has to be pounded with a mallet before it is cooked, but flesh from octopuses smaller than 4 inches is more than tender enough to eat. The flesh of certain species, including one commonly found along the coast of Australia, is poisonous. The Japanese have established octopus farms. However, in many countries, including the United States and Australia, octopus is much less popular and is used as bait.

Look for octopuses with firm flesh that smells only slightly fishy. The skin is much easier to remove if the octopus has been pounded and then blanched for a couple of minutes. Octopus is usually cleaned and tenderized before it is sold. If it has not been prepared for cooking, start by removing the tentacles from the body and then turn the stomach cavity inside out to remove the intestines. After locating and removing the eyes and mouth at the center of the head, begin skinning the octopus. (See Figure 15.34.)

CUTTLEFISH

Very common in Europe and Asia, the cuttlefish is a cephalopod mollusk whose body is more oval and flatter than that of the squid. It contains an extremely light, chalky bone that

15.34 **Baby and larger octopus**

© Randy Van Dam 2008

is approximately 6 inches long. Rounded on one end and pointed on the other, the cuttlebone is used by birds as a beak sharpener.

The cuttlefish measures between 6 and 10 inches and is thus much larger than the little cuttle or lesser cuttlefish, a closely related species that is only 1 to 2 inches long. Look for fresh cuttlefish with moist, firm flesh that smells faintly of the sea. Cuttlefish is also sold frozen or canned. Fresh or cooked cuttlefish will keep in the refrigerator for 1 or 2 days and can be frozen for about 3 months. It should be washed before being refrigerated or frozen. The white flesh of the cuttlefish is very firm, and its slippery skin is difficult to remove. Prepared like octopus, cuttlefish also has to beaten before it is cooked. Unless cuttlefish is cooked rapidly, it tends to become tough. It can be poached or fried for 3 minutes per side, sautéed for 1 or 2 minutes per side, or steamed for 30 to 60 minutes.

SEA URCHIN

A sea urchin is a small invertebrate marine animal that lives in coastal waters (Figure 15.35a). The underside of the sea urchin is completely covered with spines and with the anus at its center. The edible portion of the sea urchin is located under the mouth and consists of the five sexual organs (the ovaries and testicles of the unisexual animal) known as the "coral," as well as the liquid that surrounds them. The coral is an orange color like that of the mussel and the scallop.

The sea urchin is found in most seas, but many of the almost 500 species are inedible. Sea urchins are sold whole or ready to serve and are extremely perishable. When buying them whole, look for urchins with firm spines and tightly closed mouth holes. Before storing whole sea urchins, remove the crunchy parts of the mouth.

When opening sea urchins, protect your hands with sturdy gloves or a thick cloth. Hold the sea urchin so that you can make an opening near the mouth with a small pair of scissors (see Figure 15.35b); then cut all the way around the soft spineless portion. Discard the black entrails. Remove the coral with a spoon and pour the liquid into a bowl; then remove any remaining pieces of the shell. Sea urchins can be refrigerated for 1 or 2 days in a tightly sealed container.

SEA CUCUMBERS

The sea cucumber is an echinoderm with an elongated body and leathery skin; it is found on the sea floor worldwide (Figure 15.36). Sea cucumber is considered a delicacy in Far East countries such as Malaysia, China, Japan, and Indonesia. It is often purchased dried and then rehydrated before use. The product is used in soups, stews, and braised dishes due to its gelatinous texture. Because of its texture, it is normally not eaten on its own.

15.35a **Sea urchins in the marketplace**
Courtesy of Robert Garlough

15.35b **Mouth of sea urchin**
© Randy Van Dam 2008

15.36 **Sea cucumber**
© Randy Van Dam 2008

Smoked Seafood

Smoking is a process by which salted seafood, fillets, steaks, loins, whole fish, and shellfish are flavored by being placed in a drying oven where dense smoke passes around and through the product. Finfish commonly smoked include salmon, herring, haddock, pollock, whiting, catfish, trout, and mackerel. Smoked shellfish include clams, oysters, shrimp, scallops, and mussels.

Good product can only be made from good fish. Stale fish does not smoke well; the staleness reappears within a day or two of smoking. There is a widespread belief that smoking is a useful way to salvage or disguise stale fish. This is not so. Herrings must have a high oil content, for example: herring that has recently spawned will give at best a dry and rather hard product. Bruises in fish flesh show up clearly after smoking, a particular problem with salmon, which leads many smokers to prefer line-caught (trolled) fish over netted fish, which is more likely to have been bruised in the nets. Similarly, inadequate bleeding can discolor the product.

The first step in the smoking process is to salt the fish. Salt preserves flesh by replacing some of the moisture in the tissue, making it less hospitable to spoilage bacteria. Of course, salt also brings out the flavor. Traditional salting processes used dry salt, but most modern products are brined in saturated salt solution. Sometimes dyes are added to the brine. Fish that tastes bitter may have been brined in the wrong type of salt: calcium and magnesium sulphates that are frequently found in salt have this effect. It is important that the brine is kept clean and at full strength. Blood, scales, and soluble proteins from the fish mix with the brine as it is used, so the solution must be regularly renewed.

After brining, the fish should hang in a gentle flow of cool air. This allows excess brine to drip from the flesh and gives time for a glossy surface to develop on the cut surfaces of the flesh. This gloss, which is called the pellicle, is both attractive to the consumer and protects the product a little.

Smoking is actually a combination of two separate processes: drying and smoking. Removal of some of the moisture from the fish is necessary to give the product the required texture of the smoked product; in smoking, chemicals are deposited on the flesh. These chemicals contribute to the flavor of the fish and help to preserve it, because some of them kill surface bacteria. Preservation depends partly on drying as well; in general, the more moisture remaining in the flesh, the shorter the shelf life. There are two basic methods of smoking: hot and cold.

- **Hot smoking.** This process essentially cooks the fish by heating it to a minimum internal temperature of 145°F for 30 minutes.
- **Cold smoking.** In this process, temperatures are kept below 95°F. Cold smoking produces a more delicate flavor and texture than hot smoking.

MARKET VARIETIES OF SMOKED SEAFOOD

- **Bloaters.** These are popular in Britain and Canada but are seldom seen in the United States. Bloaters are herrings that are dry-salted whole and then cold smoked for a short time. The product retains the silvery color of the raw herring and has a distinctive taste, probably from the fermentation of the contents of the gut. Smoked chub may sometimes be called a bloater, but there are very few similarities between the products.

- **Buckling.** This is hot-smoked herring, sometimes whole but more usually gutted. Buckling originated in Germany. The fish have an attractive golden brown color and are fully cooked. The flavor is rather strong.

- **Cod and haddock fillets.** These are largely interchangeable in practice, though because most of the product is described as "smoked haddock" it can be assumed that haddock is more desirable. The two can be distinguished by the haddock's "thumb mark" on the skin near the nape, which the cod lacks. Fish without the skin will probably need scientific analysis to determine the species. Smoked fillets without skin have a tendency to fall apart. Fillets are dyed and brined, and then cold smoked. It is possible to produce an acceptable product by using a smoke dip, which has the advantage that no weight is lost in the production process.

- **Eels.** Smoked eels are insufficiently appreciated in the United States but are a great delicacy in Germany, Holland, and other parts of Europe. Eels are exported from the United States alive for smoking in Europe. Few are processed and sold here. Eels are hot smoked and ready to eat. Small eels of about 1 pound, as well as large eels weighing up to 10 pounds, are used for smoking. Larger eels are sliced for serving. Smaller eels are usually served as fillets.

- **Finnan haddock (finnan haddie or smoked haddock).** Properly, a finnan is a small haddock that has been split along the backbone, leaving the backbone attached to the flesh of one side. The fish is lightly brined and cold smoked. It should be an attractive golden color. The term *finnan haddie* is widely (mis)used to describe any smoked haddock or cod, including the fillets, which are preferred by American consumers. See above for comments on smoked cod and haddock fillets.

- **Herrings.** This is the raw material for many smoked products, including bloaters, buckling, kippers, and blind robins.

- **Kippers.** Herrings are split along the back, brined, and cold smoked. Color develops slowly after smoking is completed: dyed kippers may turn very dark, even black. Canned kippers may turn black simply from an excess of smoke without any dye being used. Kipper fillets are more popular than regular kippers. It is important that the herring for kippering should have oil content of at least 10 percent and preferably far more. Herring with a low oil content makes a dry and unsatisfactory product.

- **Mackerel.** Smoked mackerel similarly requires an oily fish. The fish are generally nobbed, with the heads cut off and the guts drawn through the neck opening, or headed and gutted, then brined and hot smoked. They are ready to eat and make an excellent alternative to the more expensive smoked trout.

- **Oysters.** Oyster meats can be lightly brined, dipped in oil, and hot smoked. Generally, the product is then preserved in cans or jars. Similar use can be made of mussel meats.

- **Pollock.** An imitation smoked salmon product was produced in Germany during World War I. Known as "seelachs" (sea salmon), it is made by heavily salting large fillets of Atlantic pollock, slicing the fish, and soaking the slices in a mixture of brine, acetic acid, and dye. The slices are then processed in a very dense smoke, packed in vegetable oil, and either used fresh, with a shelf life under refrigeration of about 1 month, or canned.

- **Sablefish.** Filleted, hot-smoked sablefish is an excellent product, well known on the West Coast and in major cities, but by no means universally available. Like fresh sable, it deserves to be better known and appreciated.

- **Salmon.** Smoked salmon is probably the best known and most popular smoked fish product, and some forms are among the most expensive. The original product from Northern Europe is made from a fillet of Atlantic salmon heavily brined and then cold smoked for lengthy periods, with the exact time depending on the size and fat content of the fish. Scottish, English, Irish, Norwegian, Icelandic, French, and Danish smoked salmon are all made in similar fashion.

  Although cold smoked, the salmon is ready to eat without further processing. The hardened pellicle must be discarded and the rib bones removed one by one with long-nosed pliers. The side is then sliced very thinly and served. Removing the bones is important because, although they are soft and can be cut and eaten, the bones can tear the salmon when being cut, which spoils the appearance of the product and is wasteful.

  The most important factor in producing good smoked salmon is choosing good fresh salmon to start with. Fish that has soft flesh or is bruised will not make a good product. Many smokers prefer not to use frozen salmon, partly because the flesh is very slightly softer, but mainly because the yield from frozen fish is a little lower. Smokers expect approximately 20 percent loss in weight from headless dressed fish to smoked salmon sides. With an expensive product, a difference of 2 percent in yield makes a substantial difference to the profitability of the smokehouse. Following are some varieties of smoked salmon:

 The following list gives the usual meanings in the United States; however, there are other meanings, especially regionally. Be sure to describe what you mean if there is any chance of confusion between buyer and seller

- **Nova salmon** is a term used on the East Coast to describe a product very similar to the European smoked salmon defined above. The name may have originated from Nova Scotia, but most production now comes from New York City. Nova salmon tends to be slightly less salty than European and varies in quality from very fine to rather poor.

- **Lox,** strictly speaking, is cured, not smoked, salmon. Although originally salted sides, the cure is now lighter and includes sugar, making a mild product. Lox is soaked in freshwater to remove most of the salt before it is eaten. It is sliced and used much as smoked salmon. However, most of what is described and sold as lox is actually lightly smoked salmon, as the popular meaning of the term seems to have embraced the smoked product.

- **Kippered salmon** is fillets or pieces lightly brined and then hot smoked.

- **Indian-cure or hard-cure salmon** is a West Coast product originally used by coastal Indians to preserve the fish for long periods. It is cold smoked for a long time, around 2 weeks, yielding a product like fishy pemmican. It is similar in concept and execution to red herrings and equally unpalatable to most modern tastes.

- **Trout.** Smoked trout is an excellent gourmet item. It is hot smoked, ready to eat, and makes an impressive appetizer. Trout are smoked with the heads on because they are hung in the kiln and spearing the edible parts of the fish would tear the flesh and spoil the product. Most consumers prefer the heads removed before serving. Trout should not be dried too much while being smoked as it has comparatively low oil content, and over-drying results in a hard-textured product.

- **Whitefish (chub, cisco).** These freshwater fish are all excellent hot smoked. Main markets are in the Midwest and Northeast, especially New York. Chub are sometimes called bloaters.

SEAFOOD ANALOGS

In addition to traditional seafood, the flesh of fish and shellfish can be used to create **analogs**, substitutes for meat-based proteins. Common seafood analogs include (see Figure 15.37):

- **Burgers.** These are similar to patties, made from minced fish mixed with various seasonings. Soy protein is sometimes added to reduce cost and increase moisture. Available breaded and unbreaded, cooked or uncooked, burgers are often made from salmon, cod, tuna, or halibut.

- **Hams and loaves.** Spiced, seasoned, molded, ready-to-eat products shaped like hams or loaves, these can be sliced for sandwiches or entrées. Usually made of salmon and tuna, these are often high-quality products shaped from whole fillets, though minced fish meat is also used. Flavorings include smoked, garlic, and black pepper.

15.37 **Imitation crabmeat**

© Randy Van Dam 2008

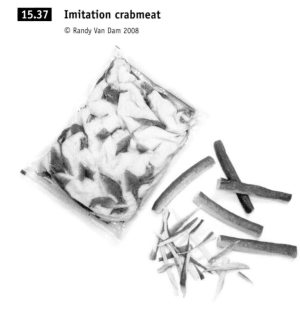

- **Hot dogs.** Typically made from salmon or minced groundfish like pollock, the meat for "sea dogs" is blended with herbs and spices, shaped to fit a hot dog bun, then steam cooked and/or smoked. Vacuum-packed, ready-to-eat franks are boneless. A typical serving is 1.5 ounces. Some seafood hot dogs are spiked with jalapeno peppers or stuffed with cheese.

- **Sausages.** Low-fat, high-protein sausages (or "breakfast links") are typically made of salmon, though tuna and several other species are used. The sausages are processed by binding together fish meat (with the help of 2 to 3 percent salt) and then adding spices and (optional) smoke or smoke flavoring. Some seafood sausages are briefly precooked, so they are ready to recook and serve. Others are fully cooked and ready to eat. Spicy, gourmet versions are available.

CONVENIENCE CORNER PRODUCT EXAMPLES

Fish and Shellfish

Company	Website	Products
Blount	http://www.blountseafood.com	4/4 # Soup Lobster Bisque
Fishery	www.fisheryproducts.com	10# Cod Scrod Soy Fillet 10# Pangasuis Breaded 4 oz 32/5 oz Tilapia Garlic Fillet
Hillman Oysters	http://www.Hillmanoysters.com	144 ct Oysters Half Shelled
Icelandic	http://www.icelandic.com	10# Halibut Redhook 2-3 oz
Norpac	http://www.norpac.com	5/5# Marlin Blue Fillet 6/4-6 # Wahoo Fillet 8/3# Seafood Fillet
Reser's	http://www.resers.com	2/5# Salad Tuna
Stockpot	http://www.stockpot.com	4/6# Soup Lobster Bisque
Tampa Maid	http://www.tampamaid.com	6/2# Grouper Fingers 4/2# Shrimp Jammer 4/3# Shrimp Brd Mini Round
Fortune Fish Company	http://www.fortunefishco.net	5# Striped Farm
The Crab Broker	http://www.crabbroker.com	20# Fish Char Arctic Fresh
Copper River	http://www.copperriver.com	10/2# Salmon Keta Fresh
Perona Farms	http://www.finesalmon.com	2/2.5# Salmon Smoked Lemon Pepper
King & Prince Seafood Corporation	http://www.kpseafood.com	4/2.5 Shrimp Brd Coconut 16/20

Robert Monaldo, CEC, CCE

Place of Birth: White Plains, New York

Educational Background and Work Experience

Growing up in New York's Westchester County, Bob Monaldo was exposed to the Big Apple at an early age. That experience with big-city dining, coupled with summers at his family's vacation home on Cape Cod, led to an early interest in food service and tourism. Starting out as a young teenager, Chef Monaldo worked in several family-dining restaurants, washing dishes and cooking fresh seafood for the Cape's summer tourists. After years of working in various kitchen positions, he eventually attended The Culinary Institute of America, where he graduated on the Dean's List while working in the food service department of Vassar College. After graduation, Chef Monaldo moved to West Yarmouth, Massachusetts, and became the executive chef of the Sword and Shield restaurant and, later, The Captain's Chair restaurant. Subsequently, he became manager of food and beverage operations for Gina's restaurant, a popular seaside eatery frequented by locals and celebrities alike. Chef Monaldo was then hired by Grand Rapids Community College (Grand Rapids, Michigan) to teach Advanced Food Production in its new Culinary Arts program. He opened the program's The Heritage restaurant dinner operation, guiding his students through all traditional restaurant procedures, from purchasing to plate presentation, while gaining immediate regional praise for the restaurant and notoriety for himself. In addition to sharing his skills in haute cuisine, Chef Monaldo offered his students more than 30 years of practical experience in selection and procurement, while teaching courses in food purchasing for culinary arts and culinary management majors, all the while continuing his own education through seminars, workshops, and college coursework. After 27 years of teaching, Chef Monaldo retired from GRCC and returned to his beloved home on Cape Cod to work as a chef-consultant.

Memberships and Career Highlights

Chef Monaldo joined the local chapter of the American Culinary Federation, becoming an active member in the ACF Greater Grand Rapids Chapter and certified as an executive chef (CEC) and culinary educator (CCE). One of Chef Monaldo's greatest joys as a teacher was sharing his skills in food show competition. Monaldo's own vast experience in culinary salon competition included many gold and best of show awards in state and regional competitions, including two medals earned at the 1988 Internationale Kochkunst Austellung, in Frankfurt, Germany, considered the "Culinary Olympics" of international culinary competition. As captain of the Grand Rapids Junior (Community) College team, the six faculty and alumni won a total of eleven Culinary Olympic medals. That experience later helped Chef Monaldo's student teams to become perennial powerhouses in state culinary salon competition. In 1999, Chef Monaldo was tapped to co-coach a team of American culinary arts students to represent the United States at the Malta International Student Culinary Salon. With his guidance in cold food presentation, the student team won an unprecedented 17 international awards in both hot and cold food presentation.

Courtesy Robert Monaldo

It Happened to Me... "In the early 1970s, when I accepted my first chef's position at a relatively new restaurant, it was a real eye-opener for me. As I was just acclimating myself to the menu, learning all of its idiosyncrasies and the nuances of some seafood products with which I was unfamiliar, I was truly at the mercy of the restaurant's purveyors. It didn't take me more than a few weeks to realize I was paying a premium for these products of which I had no previous knowledge. I knew right then that I had to reassess the menu and the ingredients I was using. And it was also time to reassess with whom I wanted to do business. I learned about acceptable substitutions to many of the premium ingredients; I bought receiving scales and books with product specifications. I needed to take control of my situation or be at the mercy of others who had more knowledge than I about the products I was receiving. From that day on, I made it my business to be informed as much as possible about my purchases. The Internet, text and reference books like this one, and the use of computerized inventory systems have been a blessing to those chefs who take their purchasing responsibilities seriously."

Passions with the Food Service Industry

"Working in the food industry is a wonderful way to make a living. The industry is extremely diverse, with job options that range from A to Z. For myself, it is very rewarding and satisfying because I can be creative and innovative. I thoroughly enjoy the spectrum of ingredients and cooking styles that I can use to create my food. Also, the interesting people that I meet and with whom I work ensure that each day will never be boring."

Advice to a Chef or Buyer

"If there were one piece of advice that I could offer to a young chef or buyer, it is to really know your product. With today's world of information being readily available at your fingertips, it is essential that the chef be armed with sufficient product knowledge. This background is essential in being able to select and procure the most appropriate ingredients, which is necessary for increased efficiency and profitability."

Key Words and Concepts

---

analogs	clam	green sheet	Shellfish Sanitation
bivalve	count	IQF	Program
bycatch	crustacean	mollusk	univalve
caviar	fillet	roe	
cephalopod	flatfish	roundfish	

Chapter in Review

The following exercises are provided to help the reader understand and apply the contents of this chapter. They may be completed individually or in a classroom environment.

REVIEW QUESTIONS

a. Distinguish shellfish from bonefish.

b. Identify the different methods used for harvesting seafood.

c. List the categories of shellfish, and define each.

d. Explain what to examine when determining the freshness of fish.

e. Distinguish the difference between caviar and other roe.

INDIVIDUAL ACTIVITIES

a. **Web based:** Research locations for, and types of, fish farms on the Internet.

b. **Experiential:** Visit a local fishery, fish store, fish farm, or processing facility to learn more about purchasing seafood.

c. **Critical thinking:** Consider how to check seafood for freshness once it has been cleaned and dressed.

GROUP ACTIVITIES

a. **Lab experience:** Have the class practice opening shellfish, and cleaning and filleting flatfish and roundfish.

b. **Classroom action:** Create a game for students using categories of seafood. Have one team of students take turns naming individual seafood items, and have the other team name a dish in which they could be used, without repeating.

CHAPTER

16

© iStockphoto.com

Fruits

"A fruit is a vegetable with looks and money. Plus, if you let fruit rot, it turns into wine, something Brussels sprouts never do."

P. J. O'ROURKE

After reading this chapter, you will be able to:

◎ List the five factors that affect a fruit's flavor and texture.

◎ Explain the buying and storing of fruits.

◎ Discuss and identify berries, and provide examples of different varieties.

◎ Discuss and identify melons, and provide examples of different varieties.

◎ Discuss and identify grapes, and provide examples of different varieties.

◎ Discuss and identify citrus, and provide examples of different varieties.

◎ Discuss and identify stone fruits, and provide examples of different varieties.

◎ Discuss and identify pome fruits, and provide examples of different varieties.

◎ Discuss and identify tropical and exotic fruits, and provide examples of different varieties.

Introduction

According to the *Oxford Encyclopedia of Food and Drink in America*, "Of the thousands of species of edible fruits growing wild and cultivated throughout the world, more than seventy are grown commercially or in home gardens in the United States" (Smith, 2004, p. 528). However, in modern food science, chefs are blessed with an unlimited supply of ripe fruits from around the corner, or around the globe.

The study of **fruit** is broad and complex, as there are many varieties that can be classified by several means. And as there are too many different products to study in depth, this chapter seeks to provide a primer on only the most commonly used fruit in today's U.S. food service operations.

Global Sourcing

The fruits produced in the United States range from indigenous stock to imports from European settlers during the colonization of Mexico and the United States.

There are several ways to categorize fruit. One method is by their climatic growing region, which includes:

- **Temperate fruits.** Berries, melons, pome fruits, stone fruits, grapes, and rhubarb.

- **Subtropical fruits.** Citrus, pear cactus, date, fig, kiwi, persimmon, and pomegranate.

- **Tropical fruits.** Banana and pineapple.

Table 16.1 illustrates the availability of various fresh fruits according to their growing season in the United States. Table 16.2 illustrates the U.S. grades, packing seasons, and production areas for different processed fruits.

Buying and Storing

For both the consumer and food service operator, the most important considerations when evaluating fruit are their flavor and texture. The following five factors can affect taste and texture:

- **Genetics.** The genetic heritage of a fruit strongly influences its eating quality. Its variety and rootstock affect its taste, size, color, hardiness, yield, season, and resistance to disease, among other horticultural characteristics. Some fruits have very little genetic variation, such as bananas, while others, such as apples, have an almost infinite variety.

- **Environment.** The environmental influences include soil, water, climate, weather, and general growing area. The environment affects the crop's flavor, taste, and aroma. Within a single field, there can be differences in the crop, and each year will produce slightly different fruits than previous years.

- **Farming practices.** This factor includes irrigation, pruning, and fertilizing. Better irrigation yields larger quantities, proper pruning maximizes exposure to sunlight, and fertilizing helps maintain proper nutrient levels in the soil.

- **Harvest maturity.** Fruits vary in their respiratory and ripening patterns. Climacteric fruits, such as bananas, can ripen off the tree when they are mature. Nonclimacteric fruits, such as berries and citrus, do not ripen after harvest and must be picked when ripe.

- **Post-harvest handling.** Because many fruits must be shipped long distances to reach their distribution centers and marketplaces, and then stored for prolonged periods of time, methods have been developed over decades to greatly extend the growing seasons and shelf lives of fruit. Handling procedures also affect the final taste of the fruit.

When purchasing fruits, the buyer must consider several factors relative to each individual product. Table 16.3 lists U.S. grades for fresh fruits.

TABLE 16.1 Fresh Fruit Seasonal Availability Chart

Product	JAN	FEB	MAR	APR	MAY	JUN	JUL	AUG	SEP	OCT	NOV	DEC
	WINTER DEC 21–MAR 19		SPRING MAR 20–JUN 20			SUMMER JUN 21–SEP 21			AUTUMN SEP 22–DEC 20			
Apples								X	X	X	X	
Apricots						X	X					
Blueberries					X	X	X	X				
Cantaloupe						X	X	X	X			
Cherries					X	X	X	X				
Citrus	X	X	X	X	X	X			X	X	X	X
Cranberries									X	X	X	X
Dates										X	X	X
Figs						X	X	X	X	X		
Grapes						X	X	X	X	X	X	
Lychees						X	X					
Mangos					X	X	X	X				
Papayas			X	X	X	X						
Peaches					X	X	X	X				
Pears	X	X	X	X						X	X	X
Persimmons										X	X	X
Pineapples			X	X	X	X	X	X				
Plums						X	X	X	X			
Pomegranates									X	X	X	X
Prickly pears									X	X	X	X
Raspberries						X	X	X	X			
Rhubarb		X	X	X	X							
Strawberries		X	X	X	X	X						
Watermelons						X	X	X				

TABLE 16.2   U.S. Grades, Packing Seasons, and Producing Areas for Processed Fruits

Product	U.S. Grades	Primary Packing Season	Primary Producing Area
Apples–Canned	A or Fancy (85) C or Standard (70)	October to December	Michigan, Washington, Virginia
Apples–Frozen	A or Fancy (85) C or Standard (75)	October to December	Michigan, Washington, Virginia
Apple Juice–Canned	A (90) B (80)	October to December	Michigan, Washington, Virginia
Applesauce–Canned	A or Fancy (90) B or Choice (80)	October to December	Michigan, Washington, Virginia
Apricots–Canned	A or Fancy (90) B or Choice (80) C or Standard (70)	June and July	California
Berries–Frozen	A or Fancy (85) B or Choice (70)	June to August	Northwest, California
Cherries, Red–Frozen	A or Fancy (90) B or Choice (80) C or Standard (70)	June to July	New York, Pennsylvania, Michigan
Cranberry Sauce–Canned	A or Fancy (85) C or Standard (70)	October to January	Massachusetts, New Jersey
Fruit Cocktail	A or Fancy (85) B or Choice (70)	June to September	California
Fruit Jelly	A (90) or B (80)	Year-round	California, Virginia, Michigan, Ohio
Fruit Preserves–Jam	A (85) or B (70)	Year-round	California, Virginia, Michigan, Ohio
Peaches–Frozen	A (90) B (80) C (70)	July to September	California, Virginia, Pennsylvania, Georgia
Peaches, Clingstone–Canned	A, B, C	July to September	California
Peaches, Freestone–Canned	A, B, C	July to September	California
Pears–Canned	A or Fancy (90) B or Choice (80) C or Standard (70)	July to November	Northwest California
Pineapple–Canned	A or Fancy (90) B or Choice (80) C or Standard (70)	January to September	Puerto Rico, Hawaii, Philippines
Pineapple–Frozen	A or Fancy (90) B or Choice (80) C or Standard (70)	January to September	Puerto Rico, Hawaii, Philippines
Pineapple Juice–Canned	A or Fancy (85) C or Standard (70)	January to September	Puerto Rico, Hawaii, Philippines
Plums–Canned	A or Fancy (90) B or Choice (80) C or Standard (70)	July to September	California, Northwest
Strawberries–Frozen	A or Fancy (90) B or Choice (80) C or Standard (70)	May to July	California, Northwest, Mexico

TABLE 16.3 U.S. Grades for Fresh Fruits

Product	U.S. Grades
Apples	Extra fancy, Fancy, #1, and Utility
Apricots	#1 and #2
Bananas	No U.S. grades
Blackberries/Raspberries	#1 and #2
Blueberries	#1
Cantaloupes	Fancy, #1, Commercial, and #2
Cherries	#1 and Commercial
Coconuts	No U.S. grades
Cranberries	#1
Grapefruit	Fancy, #1, Combo, #2, and #3
Grapes	Fancy, #1 Table Grapes, and #1 Juice Grapes
Honeydews	#1, Commercial, and #2
Lemons	#1, #1 Export, Combo, and #2
Limes	#1 and Combo
Nectarines	Fancy, Extra #1, #1, and #2
Oranges	Fancy, #1, Combo, and #2
Peaches	Fancy, Extra #1, #1, and #2
Pears	Extra #1, #1, Combo, and #2
Pineapples	Fancy, #1, and #2
Plums	#1
Strawberries	#1, Combo, and #2
Watermelons	Fancy, #1, and #2

Berries

A berry is a small sweet-tart flesh packed into a thin skin. Some berries, such as blackberries and raspberries, are made up of clusters of tiny sacs. Others, such as strawberries, have a skin that is speckled with dry, diminutive yellow seeds. Others, such as blueberries, cranberries, and currants, have a smooth, slick skin.

In addition to appearance, tartness is a major distinguishing factor among berries. Many, such as blueberries and strawberries, are sweet enough to eat as is. Other berries have super-tart flavor profiles; these include gooseberries, cranberries, and currants. They can be eaten as is, but most palates prefer an added sweetener.

BUYING AND STORING

When buying fresh, select vividly colored berries that are uniform in size, without mold, soft spots, or discoloration. If boxed, check to see if berries move freely when container is tilted; if they stick together, they are probably moldy. Discard any moldy, shriveled, or discolored berries. Strawberries should have a fresh, green cap, or hull. Other berries should not have a hull; if they do, it means they were picked before ripening and could taste tart. Berries should not be washed until it is time to use them, as water hastens rot and loss of shape.

Frozen berries are widely available. When receiving the frozen berries, make sure that the berries are moving freely and not clumped up. When the package is opened, the berries should have a uniform color and size.

Delicate berries, such as raspberries, blackberries, and boysenberries, can be stored up to 2 to 3 days. Refrigerate sturdier berries, such as cranberries, up to 7 days. To freeze, spread unwashed berries on sheet pans in a single layer; freeze, and then store frozen berries in an airtight container in the freezer. Traditional slow freezing in a walk-in or reach-in freezer changes the texture of all berries except cranberries; the berries become mushy and are generally best used in cooked dishes. Using a blast chiller to freeze berries will preserve their shape upon thawing. Most do not require defrosting before use in cooking or baking. Freezing reduces the pectin levels in berries, requiring the use of more pectin for pie and jam production.

- **Blackberry.** Blackberries are found in the wild and are also cultivated throughout the United States. The largest of the wild berries, blackberries are purplish black, sweet, and juicy. They should be stored unwashed in the refrigerator for 2 to 3 days. They are delicious cooked, which intensifies their flavor, or as a snack. They are also good for jams, coulis, and ice creams. (See Figure 16.1.)

16.1 **Blackberries**
© Randy Van Dam 2008

- **Blueberry.** Blueberries should have smooth, silver-frosted blue-black skins. They are delicious eaten alone, mixed into smoothies or yogurt, as a topping for cereal or pancakes, or mixed into baked goods. The modern cultivated varieties are much larger, sweeter, and juicier than their "wild" relatives. Look for plump, uniformly sized berries, and store them in the refrigerator, unwashed, for up to 5 days. (See Figure 16.2.)

16.2 **Blueberries**
© Randy Van Dam 2008

- **Boysenberry.** The boysenberry is a cross between the blackberry, raspberry, and loganberry. It looks like a large, purple-red raspberry and has a tart-sweet flavor. Store boysenberries in the refrigerator, unwashed, for 2 to 3 days. Use them in pies, on top of yogurt or cereal, mixed into fresh fruit salad, or as an ice cream topping.

- **Cranberry.** Cranberries are red, tart, and firm. They are usually sold in 12-ounce plastic bags and, if tightly wrapped, can be stored in the refrigerator for up to 2 months or frozen for up to a year. Cranberries are traditionally served with a holiday turkey dinner, but they are also excellent in muffins, sauces, chutneys, and relishes. Cranberry sauce is made by cooking the cranberries with sugar and water until their skins burst. Grinding berries in a food processor with apples, oranges, or dried apricots makes cranberry chutney. Sweetened, dried cranberries are great for sprinkling on top of salads and may be substituted for raisins when baking. (See Figure 16.3.)

- **Currants.** Currants are tiny berries that are related to the gooseberry. The white and red varieties are delicious eaten out of hand, served with cream or milk and sugar, or made into jams, jellies, and sauces. Black currants are usually used in sorbets, ice creams, preserves, syrups, and liqueurs like crème de cassis. Black currants are rarely eaten raw because of their acidity. Fresh currants can be stored in the refrigerator for up to 4 days. They need to have their stalks removed by stripping before use.

 BUYER'S NOTE *Don't confuse these fresh berries with dried currants, which look like miniature raisins. Those "currants" are actually dried Zante grapes.*

- **Gooseberry.** The tart gooseberry can be as small as a blueberry or as big as a cherry tomato. Gooseberries come in a variety of colors and can have a smooth or fuzzy skin. Due to their naturally high pectin content, they are well suited for pies, jellies, and sauces. Store them in the refrigerator for up to a week.

- **Loganberry.** The ruby red, blackberry-shaped loganberry is delicious cooked or fresh. Use loganberries in jams or preserves; add them to fruit salads, or top yogurt or ice cream with them. Store them, unwashed, in the refrigerator and use within a few days.

- **Raspberry.** Raspberries come in three main varieties: black, golden, and red. These intensely flavored berries can be stored, unwashed, in the refrigerator for 2 to 3 days. They are fragile, so they are best served fresh with a touch of cream or on top of a salad or ice cream. They are also used for pies and tarts. (See Figure 16.4a and Figure 16.4b.)

- **Strawberry.** Strawberries vary in size, color, and shape, depending on the variety. The miniature varieties, known as Alpine strawberries, are usually the sweetest. The larger varieties can also be sweet, but often they are sold

 Cranberries
Courtesy of Robert Garlough

 Red Raspberries
© Randy Van Dam 2008

16.4b **Golden raspberries**
Courtesy of Robert Garlough

16.5 **Strawberries**

© Randy Van Dam 2008

under-ripe. Store strawberries, unwashed, in the refrigerator for 2 to 3 days. Be sure to wash strawberries before hulling them because, once they are hulled, they soak up a lot of moisture. Use a sharp knife to remove the hull. Strawberries are delicious on their own or added to salad, baked into pie, sliced on top of pancakes or cereal, blended into smoothies or yogurt, or made into soufflés, sauces, jams, or frozen confections. (See Figure 16.5.)

Melons

Melons are widely available and grown in many parts of the world. They are juicy and grow on long vines on the ground. Melons are related to cucumbers, pumpkin, squash, and gourds. Some have netted, thinner skin; others have smooth, thicker skin. And some are in between, with skin that is almost smooth with very shallow netting. Melons have seeds in middle with a wide band of flesh covering the seeds. The flesh is held together by a thin flesh. Normally, the fruit is skinned, and then the seeds are removed. The remaining flesh is served.

BUYING AND STORING

There are hundreds of melon varieties. Although many are now available year-round, peak production is May to September. When receiving melons, inspect the stalk end, especially for muskmelons and cantaloupes; if it is very hard or unevenly colored, or if part of the greenish stalk is still attached, the fruit may not be sufficiently mature. In ripe melons, this part softens although this is not always an indication of ripeness, as excessive handling can also cause softening. The end opposite the stalk should have a delicate aroma if the melon is ripe.

A ripe melon will have a hollow sound when tapped. Melons should be heavy for their size and free of bruises or soft spots. Avoid overly soft melons or any melon that has a strong "off" smell. If it smells good, it will usually taste good. The skin should feel springy, not mushy. Refrigerate most ripe melons for up to 5 days, but pepinos should only be refrigerated for 3.

- **Bitter melon.** The fruit has a distinct warty-looking exterior and an oblong shape. Seeds are very bitter and must be removed before cooking. The flesh is crunchy and watery, similar to cucumber, green bell pepper, or chayote. The skin is tender and edible. The fruit is most often eaten green, as the ripe melons are too bitter to eat. (See Figure 16.6.)

- **Cantaloupe.** Cantaloupe is round with netted skin. When ripe, there is a light gold color between webbing. A perfectly ripe cantaloupe has raised netting on a pale gold or gray-green background, and the flesh is bright orange, juicy, fragrant, and sweet. (See Figure 16.7.)

- **Casaba.** The cassaba is a large yellow melon with a smooth skin and a globe shape. The ripe fruit has a white or yellow flesh that is sweet and juicy, with a cucumber flavor. (See Figure 16.8.)

16.6 **Bitter melon**

© Randy Van Dam 2008

16.7 **Cantaloupe**

Figures 16.7–.10b © Randy Van Dam 2008

16.8 **Casaba**

16.9 **Crenshaw**

16.10a **Green Honeydew**

16.10b **Golden honeydew**

- **Crenshaw.** Crenshaw melons, also known as *cranshaw*, are considered one of the sweetest muskmelons. The rind is slightly ribbed, and it turns golden green at peak ripeness. The flesh is salmon-orange and has a sweet, yet spicy, flavor. (See Figure 16.9.)

- **Honeydew.** Honeydew melons have a smooth rind and pale green flesh. Common green and gold varieties have the same light green flesh; orange variety has orange flesh. Honeydew is considered one of the sweetest melons and is known for its soft, silky texture. (See Figure 16.10a and Figure 16.10b.)

- **Juan Canary.** Juan Canary melons are somewhat oval shaped and have a bright canary yellow, smooth, slightly ridged rind. The flesh is pale green to cream in color with a pinkish tinge around the seed cavity. The taste is delicate, but the texture is crisp and firm. Avoid melons that are too firm or too soft. (See Figure 16.11.)

- **Kiwano (horned melon).** The kiwano, also known as *horned melon* or *horned cucumber*, has short "horns" on its bright yellow or orange skin. Kiwanos are about the size of a large pear with a pale yellow-green, soft pulp, and edible seeds. Select kiwanos with intact horns and no soft spots or bruises. Store at room temperature. Ripe kiwanos are good for 3 to 4 days. The sweet-tart flavor, with hints of bananas and cucumbers, is a welcome addition to fruit salads and even roasted meats. (See Figure 16.12.)

- **Pepino.** This fruit is a relative newcomer to Western markets. The fruit resembles a small melon; it has a slightly elongated shape and measures between 4 and 6 inches. Pepino melons can be as small as a plum or as big as a papaya. The entire melon is edible, but some people peel the melon before eating out of hand. The skin turns from pale green to golden yellow as the fruit ripens and is always streaked with purple. The flesh is slightly sweeter than most other melons. (See Figure 16.13.)

- **Persian melon.** Persian melons are close cousins to the cantaloupe, but the netting on their pale gray-green rind is finer and the salmon-colored flesh is firmer. They are medium sized, round to oval, with delicate netting set against grayish-green skin. Their pink-orange flesh is sweet with a firm, buttery texture.

- **Santa Claus *(Piel de Sapo)*.** This melon is round to oval with dark-green or yellow-green skin and a light green flesh similar to honeydew. The Santa Claus melon is mildly sweet and crunchy. (See Figure 16.14.)

16.13   Pepino

16.11   Juan Canary melon

Figures 16.11–.14 © Randy Van Dam 2008

16.12   Kiwano

16.14   Santa Claus melon

- **Watermelon.** Watermelons come in a variety of shapes and sizes, up to 90 pounds. Most watermelon varieties are large and have an elongated, oval shape. The rind of the watermelon is thick but fragile; it ranges in color from pale to dark green and is often striped or spotted. Red or deep pink flesh is typical with some exceptions. Some are considered "seedless" because they have very few seeds or those that are present are tiny, soft, and edible. Compared with other melons, the flesh of the watermelon is more crumbly and crisper. Watermelons should also be heavy, firm, and symmetrical. Avoid those with bruises or cuts, but don't worry about the creamy yellow spot on the bottom; that's where it sat on the ground, ripening in the sun. Uncut watermelons can be stored at room temperature for 7 to 10 days. Refrigerate after cutting. (See Figure 16.15a, Figure 16.15b, and Figure 16.15c.)

 Round seedless watermelon

Figures 16.15a–c © Randy Van Dam 2008

 Oval seeded watermelon

 Yellow watermelon

Grapes

When it comes to grapes, every element has culinary potential. The seeds can be used to make oil, the twisted vines can be used as fuel to flavor grilled foods, the leaves can be used for wrapping savory filling, and of course their alluring fermented juices become wine. It's impossible to imagine a culinary world without grapes.

With thousands of varieties, grapes can be classified several ways. First, some have seeds while others are seedless (though trace seeds, known as *vestigial seeds*, are commonly present even in seedless varieties). Second, they can be classified according to their use, either as table grapes (such as Flame) or wine grapes (such as Cabernet). Third, they can be categorized by color: green (pale yellow-green to light green), red (light red to dark red), or black (light red to very dark purple).

BUYING AND STORING

Look for firm grapes that are plump and fragrant. They should be fairly firm but not rock hard. Grapes are picked ripe; they do not ripen once removed from the vine (Figure 16.16). If grapes are detached from their stems, look at the area that once surrounded the stem; it should be free of discoloration, mold, or soft spots. Avoid shriveled fruit, and store unwashed grapes in perforated plastic bags in plastic storage bins for up to 10 days. They should be washed just prior to service. The following is a list of the most common table grapes.

- **Champagne (corinth).** These are tiny, pea-sized seedless grapes, deep purple to reddish purple, densely clustered on the stem. They have a sweet, mild flavor with crisp texture. (See Figure 16.17.)

- **Common black seedless (autumn royale, beauty, kyoho, maroo, ribier).** These are generally plumper than green grapes; color ranges from purple to almost black. Occasionally, they have seeds. They are very juicy and sweet with moderate acidity. (See Figure 16.18.)

- **Common green seedless (Thompson seedless, perlette, sugraone, calmeria).** These grapes are pale yellow-green to light green, are firmly attached to stem, and have a tangy sweetness with low tannin and acidity. (See Figure 16.19.)

16.16 **Grapes on the vine**
Courtesy of Robert Garlough

16.17 **Champagne grapes**
© Randy Van Dam 2008

16.18 Common black seedless grapes

Figures 16.18–.20 © Randy Van Dam 2008

16.20 Common red seedless grapes

16.19 Common green seedless grapes

These grapes are juicy, crisp, and crunchy with low acidity; they have a sweet-tart flavor. (See Figure 16.20.)

- **Concord.** These are deep blue and purple to almost black grapes with a dusty bloom. They are round and are encased in rather thick skin that slips off in the mouth. They come in both seeded and seedless varieties and produce the grape taste associated with commercial grape juice and jelly. They have a medium sweetness with slightly tart finish. The pulp is distinctively musky.

- **Globe.** These are large, oval red or green grapes, usually with seeds. Red globe grapes are the most common variety of globe. They have a similar flavor and texture to common red and green grapes. (See Figure 16.21a and Figure 16.21b.)

- **Muscat (green and red).** These are medium oval grapes that are typically red but can be green. They are juicy with intense sweetness and fragrance and are popular for dessert wines.

- **Common red seedless (flame, ruby, Christmas rose, emperor, crimson, rouge).** These grapes are medium sized, often with exterior bloom, which is a dusty film produced by cells on or near the surface that form a natural waterproofing and prevent delicate skin from cracking.

- **Muscato (green and red).** The muscato is a cross between Thompson seedless and muscat. They are medium-sized oval seedless grapes with green and gold or red skin. They are much sweeter than common green grapes. (See Figure 16.22a and Figure 16.22b.)

16.21a Green globe grapes

Figures 16.21a–.22b © Randy Van Dam 2008

16.21b Red globe grapes

16.22a Green muscato grapes

16.22b Red muscato grapes

Citrus Fruits

Citrus fruits are notable for their fragrance and juice content, which is high in citric acid, giving them their characteristic flavor. Many **citrus fruits** are picked while partially green, and their color changes while in transit to markets.

GLOBAL SOURCING

Citrus trees need sunny, humid environments and sufficent moisture. Fruit begins to ripen in fall or early winter and develops increasing sweetness afterward. Major commercial citrus growing areas include southern China, the Mediterranean region, Australia, South Africa, parts of South America, Florida, Texas, and California.

BUYING AND STORING

Citrus does not continue to ripen after it has been picked. Look for fruit that are firm and heavy for their size. Avoid bruised, wrinkled, or discolored fruit. Look for citrus fruit that is firm to the touch and free of soft spots. Generally, citrus will be brightly colored; sometimes you will see citrus with slightly green skin. Normally, fruit from Florida or California will be orange, yellow, or green while those from tropical countries have a greenish cast.

Fruit must be properly stored under refrigeration or in a cool, dry place. If it is refrigerated too long, citrus peel can develop dark, sunken patches. Natural blemishes on the peel do not affect the fruit's taste. Citrus fruit can be maintained at optimum quality for 6 to 8 weeks. Do not bag or wrap in storage. Allow for proper air circulation.

Grapefruit

Grapefruit, so named because it grows in clusters like grapes, comes in white, pink, and red fleshed varieties. All three have a yellow skin, sometimes with a pinkish tan. Grapefruit will keep in the refrigerator for up to 2 weeks. (See Figure 16.23.)

Kumquat

The kumquat looks like a miniature orange with a round or slightly oval shape. Although they are not much bigger than a cherry tomato, kumquats pack a lot of flavor. Their rind is sweet and edible, and they are usually eaten unpeeled. The fruit inside is dry and tart with hints of tangerine and orange flavors. Store them in the refrigerator for up to a month. Slice raw kumquats and serve on salad, or cook them to make marmalade or as a sauce or relish for meat, fish, or poultry. (See Figure 16.24.)

 16.23   **White, pink, and red grapefruit**
© Randy Van Dam 2008

Lemon

Lemons fall into two categories: tart and semi-sweet. Eureka and Lisbon are the two most common varieties of tart lemons. Bright yellow and highly acidic lemons vary in size, depending on the variety. Look for fruit that has brightly colored skin with no tinge of green and that feel heavy for their size. Refrigerate in covered plastic bin for 2 to 3 weeks or at room temperature for up to 1 week.

- **Lisbon lemon.** The Lisbon lemon is one of the most widely grown lemons in California and is planted extensively throughout the citrus-growing regions of the world. The fruits are medium sized, and the rind is yellow at full maturity. The flesh is pale greenish yellow, low seeded, and very acidic. (See Figure 16.25a.)

- **Eureka lemon.** Eureka lemons are medium-small and oblong. The fruits usually have a slight neck and a short nipple at the end. The rind is yellow at maturity with sunken oil glands. The flesh is pale greenish yellow, low seeded, and very acidic. (See Figure 16.25b.)

Limes

Limes are green-skinned with pale green pulp and a shape like a lemon. Select heavy limes with a smooth skin and refrigerate for up to 10 days. Limes are often used in Asian and Central American cuisines and in marinades.

- **Persian limes.** The Persian lime is the most widely available variety in the United States; it tastes tart and sour, but is more aromatic than a lemon. (See Figure 16.26.)

- **Key limes.** Key limes are a diminutive variety of lime that originated in Florida. Key limes have a tangy, tart flavor and are round and yellowish. Their most famous use is Key lime pie, but Key limes can also be substituted for Persian limes. (See Figure 16.27.)

- **Limequat.** Limequats have thin, yellow-green skin and bittersweet flesh. Developed in 1909, the limequat is a cross between a Key lime and a kumquat. The entire fruit may be eaten; the skin has a slightly sweet edge, while the flesh inside has a Key lime flavor and is dotted with tiny edible seeds. (See Figure 16.28.)

16.24 Kumquat

Figures 16.24–.28 © Randy Van Dam 2008

16.25a Lisbon lemon

16.25b Eureka lemon

16.26 Persian lime

16.27 Key lime

16.28 Limequat

Oranges

Select fruit that are firm and heavy for their size, without soft spots. They should be evenly colored, but don't worry if a ripe orange has a bit of green on it. Along with flavor, color and shape vary greatly. Some are round, others oval. Some have orange flesh, while others are purplish red or coral pink.

Oranges turn orange as they ripen, but in warm weather, the skins of some varieties may reabsorb chlorophyll and become slightly green. Some other citrus fruit may have small brown patches, called **russeting**, that do not affect the flavor. Oranges can be stored at cool room temperature for about 1 week or refrigerated for up to 3 weeks. Juice and zest can be frozen.

- **Blood orange.** Blood oranges have bright red flesh or white flesh streaked with red. Their flavor is sweet-tart with less acidity than navel oranges. Blood oranges can be eaten fresh or tossed in salads or salsas. (See Figure 16.29.)

- **Cara cara.** The exterior of the cara cara orange resembles the navel variety. The flesh is deep salmon-pink, and the skin is sometimes difficult to peel. Size varies and is generally seedless. Juicy and sweeter than navel, the cara cara has a subtle hint of grapefruit and tangerine. (See Figure 16.30.)

- **Navel orange.** The navel orange is one of the most common varieties of oranges. It has a medium-thick peel with a distinctive bump on the blossom end. These oranges are usually seedless and are easy to peel and section. (See Figure 16.31.)

- **Temple orange.** Often considered Florida's finest eating orange, temple oranges have a pebbly peel and deep orange color. They are a cross between a tangerine and an orange, and they have a flavor all their own. Temple oranges are fragrant, sweet, juicy, and easy to peel.

- **Valencia orange.** Valencias vary in size and shape; they are typically yellow with the occasional green tinge. They are tasty when eaten fresh, but a thin skin also means they are great for juicing. The juice is commonly added to marinades for meat, poultry, or fish. (See Figure 16.32a and Figure 16.32b.)

Pomelo (Pummelo, Pammelo)

These citrus fruits are the size of volleyballs and are popular in many Asian cuisines. Their taste can vary from tangy-tart to spicy-sweet. Their soft rinds

 Blood orange
Courtesy of Robert Garlough

 Cara cara orange
© Randy Van Dam 2008

16.31 **Navel orange**
© Randy Van Dam 2008

16.32a Valencia orange

Figures 16.32a–.34 © Randy Van Dam 2008

16.32b Red Valencia orange

are 1 to 2 inches thick and vary in color: yellow, brownish yellow, lime green, or pink. The flesh inside also varies in color, from light yellow to deep pink. The pomelo is generally drier than grapefruit, so it can be peeled and sectioned by hand. Its dryness also helps sections hold their shape better in salads.

Avoid fruit that has blemishes or is soft. The skin should be shiny and should not appear dried out. When pressed, the fruit should feel springy. This fruit can be stored 2 to 4 days at room temperature or 5 to 7 days in a refrigerator. The juice can be frozen. (See Figure 16.33.)

Tangerine and Mandarin

Look for fruit that is heavy for its size, without soft spots. Store at room temperature up to 1 week, or refrigerate in cov-

ered cases for 10 to 12 days. The juice can be frozen. There are several tangerine forms, including:

- **Clementine.** Imported from Spain, Morocco, and other parts of North Africa, clementines are a cross between a sweet orange and a Chinese Mandarin. They are small, very sweet, and usually seedless. The clementine is an excellent eating orange. (See Figure 16.34.)

- **Sweet tangerine.** Tangerines are deep orange, loose skinned, and small to medium sized. The taste is often more sour than that of an orange. Good quality tangerines will be firm, heavy for their size, and pebbly skinned with no deep grooves. Tangerines are easily peeled and eaten out of hand. (See Figure 16.35.)

16.33 Pomelo

16.34 Clementine

16.35 Florida sweet tangerine

Figures 16.35–.38 © Randy Van Dam 2008

16.36 Californian pixie tangerine

- **Pixie tangerine.** Pixie tangerines, also known as Ojai Pixies or California Pixies from the Ojai Valley in California from where they originated, are pale orange, moderately juicy, and always seedless. Pixies are small (1 to 3 inches in diameter), have a pebbly skin, and are easy to peel with segments that separate easily from one another. Pixies are a late-season variety, ripening in March and April. (See Figure 16.36.)

16.37 Minneola tangelo

- **Minneola tangelo.** Tangelos range from the size of a standard sweet orange to the size of a grapefruit, and they are usually necked at the base. The tangelo's rind and flesh are bright orange, a deeper shade than that of an orange. The peel is fairly loose and easily removed. The fruit is extremely juicy and sweet with a slight tartness. (See Figure 16.37.)

Ugli Fruit (Uniq Fruit)

Unique in its appearance and appealing flavor, this citrus fruit looks very rumpled. It peels away easily to reveal juicy, sweet sections that are often seedless. This tropical fruit ripens without the rind being fully yellow. A cross between grapefruit and Mandarin, Ugli fruit has grapefruit's juiciness but without its hallmark acidity. Look for those with skin that is more yellow than green. Brown blemishes on the skin do not affect taste. Refrigerate loose in covered plastic bins up to 2 weeks. (See Figure 16.38.)

16.38 Ugli fruit

Stone Fruits

Stone fruits all have pits in the center. This category of fruits includes peaches, nectarines, cherries, plums, apricots, and newer hybrids such as pluots (plum-apricot) and peacotums (peach-apricot-plum). The nonhybrids are thought to be native to China. California is the largest grower of all **stone fruits** in the United States, although Washington, Oregon, and Michigan are the largest producers of cherries. South Carolina, Georgia, and New Jersey are right behind California in peach production.

BUYING AND STORING

Summer is stone fruit season. Stone fruits ripen best on the tree but are often picked and shipped before fully ripe to keep the fruit from bruising. When peaches and nectarines are picked early and shipped under cold storage, they can become mealy. Plums do ripen after picking, and refrigerating ripe ones won't sacrifice juiciness. In all cases, look for heavy, unblemished fruit with deep color and a bit of give when you press the surface gently.

- **Apricots.** Apricots' skin color ranges from pale yellow to deep orange, and their flesh can be anywhere from a golden cream to bright orange. Select plump, firm (but not hard) fruit that are uniformly colored. Underripe apricots will keep 1 to 2 days at room temperature but must be refrigerated once fully ripened. Refrigerate ripe apricots in a plastic bag for 3 to 5 days. (See Figure 16.39.)

- **Cherries.** There are two main types of cherries: sweet and tart. They store for 4 to 6 days unwashed under refrigeration. Wash before service.
  - **Amarello.** A yellow-fleshed cherry.
  - **Bing.** Bing cherries are large, sweet, and juicy. Their color ranges from deep garnet to almost black. Look for plump, bright fruit with the stems attached. Bing cherries are excellent for cooking or snacking. (See Figure 16.40.)
  - **Lapin.** A dark, sweet cherry, becoming popular.
  - **Lambert.** A reddish, dark, sweet cherry. Great for eating.
  - **Montmorency.** A red-fleshed cherry ideal for jams, canning, and baking.
  - **Morello.** A dark, juicy cherry. It is inedible raw and is well suited when preserved in brandy or syrup.
  - **Rainier.** Rainier cherries are highly perishable, so store them unwashed in the refrigerator and consume soon after purchase. This cherry is so sweet that you can reduce the amount of sugar in recipes when cooking with it.
  - **Royal Annes.** A light-colored, semi-sweet cherry, good for cooking.
  - **Skeena.** A larger variety, dark and sweet, this cherry variety is popular with Canadian growers.
  - **Van.** A dark, sweet cherry, full of flavor.

- **Nectarines.** Nectarines have a smooth, golden-yellow skin that is blushed with red tinge. Nectarines taste similar to peaches; they are fragrant and will yield slightly to pressure. Store underripe nectarines at room temperature. Once ripe, they will keep in the refrigerator for a week or more. Eat nectarines alone, or use them to make fruit salads. (See Figure 16.41.)

16.39 **Apricots**

Figures 16.39–.40 © Randy Van Dam 2008

16.40 **Bing cherries**

16.41 Nectarines

- **Pluots (dinosaur eggs).** Pluots are a plum-apricot hybrid. They have a plum-like shape and a smooth skin that ranges from yellowish green to speckled red to deep purple, depending on the variety. Pluots contain more sugar than plums and have a firmer texture and longer shelf life than apricots. With their intensely sweet blend of flavors, pluots make a wonderful snack and work well in any recipe calling for plums. (See Figure 16.44a and Figure 16.44b.)

16.43 Black and red plums

- **Peaches.** Peaches have a fuzzy skin that can be pinkish white to red-tinged gold, with white to golden-yellow flesh. Peaches fall into two categories: clingstone and freestone. Clingstone peaches have a pit that "clings" to the flesh, while freestone peach pits pull away easily. Use freestone peaches when uniform slices are desired for a tart or composed salad. Under-ripe peaches will soften and become juicier and more flavorful when stored at room temperature for 1 or 2 days. They won't get any sweeter, however, so avoid fruit that is hard or tinged with green. Refrigerate ripe peaches for up to 5 days. (See Figure 16.42.)

- **Plums.** There are hundreds of varieties of plums that range from sweet to tart and come in yellows, greens, reds, purples, blues, and everything in between. There are two main varieties: Japanese and European. Japanese plums are larger and juicier than European plums, and they have a softer flesh. Both are great for eating fresh, but European plums are better for cooking and drying. Ripe plums are firm but yield to gentle pressure. Look for plums with a smooth skin that is free of blemishes or cracks. Store ripe plums in the refrigerator for up to 4 days. Dried plums are prunes. (See Figure 16.43.)

16.44a Assorted pluots

16.42 Peaches

16.44b Plumcot

Pome Fruits

Pome fruits are tree fruits that include apples, pears, and quince. Their name is derived from the *pome* shape they exhibit.

APPLES

Apples are an important food in all cooler climates. Apples store for months while still retaining much of their nutritive value. Some desirable qualities in apples are a colorful skin, lengthy storage ability, typical apple shape, and flavor. Most apples are bred for eating fresh, but some are bred for cooking or cider. Cider apples are too tart to eat fresh, but they give the beverage a rich flavor. Table 16.4 depicts culinary applications for the various varieties of apples. Because there are so many varieties of apples, most customers have preferences for which varieties they like to eat or use to cook with.

- **Braeburn.** This crisp and juicy apple varies from orange to red. Its spicy-sweet, rich flavor makes it a good multipurpose eating apple that is delicious by itself or served with cheese. (See Figure 16.45.)

- **Cortland.** The Cortland is a McIntosh cross, though it is a little sweeter than a McIntosh with only a hint of tartness. Cortland has white flesh that resists browning, making it a good choice for salads, fruit kabobs, and garnishes.

- **Crispin (Mutsu).** The Crispin apple originated in Japan, where it is called Mutsu. Similar in appearance to a golden delicious, the Crispin is sweet and juicy. It has a super crisp texture that is appealing for snacking, baking, and making applesauce.

- **Empire.** The empire, a cross between the McIntosh and red delicious, is a good all-purpose apple. It is crisp and juicy with a sweet-tart flavor and white flesh. Empires are great eaten out of hand or in salads. (See Figure 16.46.)

- **Fuji.** Fuji apples originated in Japan in the 1930s and are now one of the top-selling apples in the United States. This crisp and juicy apple is bicolored, usually striped with red and green to yellow. It makes a great snack and a fine addition to salads. (See Figure 16.47.)

- **Royal gala.** The extra-sweet royal gala is crisp and juicy and is good for snacking, sauces, and salads. Galas have a mottled skin and vary in color from cream to red and yellow striped. (See Figure 16.48.)

- **Golden delicious.** This sweet and mellow all-purpose apple is good for baking, sauces, or eating fresh. It has a pale yellow skin, sometimes with a red blush, and crisp, pale yellow flesh that resists browning, so it is a good choice for salads. (See Figure 16.49.)

- **Granny Smith.** The Granny Smith apple has a bright green skin and a distinctive greenish flesh, which is sometimes blushed with red. Its tart, full-bodied flavor and crisp texture make it a great choice for pies, as well as snacks and sauces. Many apple pie recipes call for Granny Smith apples because the flesh holds its shape when cooked. (See Figure 16.50.)

- **Honeycrisp.** The Honeycrisp apple is aptly named for its mild, honey flavor. Honeycrisps, a relatively new apple, have distinctive mottled red skin over a yellow background. Their flesh is coarse and very crisp. Honeycrisps are excellent for snacking, salads, and sauces.

- **Ida Red.** The Ida Red is a large Jonathan cross, and, like the Jonathan, it has a tangy flavor and bright red skin. The firm-textured flesh holds its shape well when cooked, making it a good choice for baking and pies. It is also used for making applesauce. (See Figure 16.51.)

- **Jonathan.** The Jonathan apple has a crimson color with occasional touches of green and is often used in pies and other baking. Its juicy, sweet-tart flavor also blends well with other apples when making apple cider or applesauce. (See Figure 16.52.)

- **McIntosh.** McIntosh apples are deep red and sometimes tinged with green. The tangy and tart flavor works well for snacks or applesauce. The McIntosh's tender white flesh cooks down quite a bit, so cut bigger slices or add a thickener when using this apple in pie recipes. (See Figure 16.53.)

- **Northern Spy.** The Northern Spy has a red skin that is streaked with yellow. It is a hard apple that ripens late and stores well. Its tart acidity makes it excellent for cooking and baking.

- **Pink Lady.** The aptly named Pink Lady has a pink skin and very white flesh. This apple has a sweet-tart flavor and crunchy texture that makes it great for all uses. (See Figure 16.54.)

TABLE 16.4 Culinary Applications for Apples

Snacking	Salad	Pie	Sauce	Baking
Braebum, Cameo, Cortland, Crispin Empire, Fuji, Gala, Golden Delicious, Granny Smith. Honeycrisp, Jonagold, McIntosh, Northern Spy, Pink Lady, Red Delicious, Winesap	Cameo, Cortland, Empire, Fuji, Gala, Golden Delicious, Granny Smith, Honeycrisp, Jonagold, Pink Lady, Red Delicious, Winesap	Cameo, Cortland, Golden Delicious, Granny Smith, Ida Red, Jonathan, McIntosh, Pink Lady, Rome Beauty, Winesap	Cameo, Cortland, Crispin/Mutsu, Gala, Golden Delicious, Granny Smith, Honeycrisp, Ida Red, Jonagold, McIntosh, Pink Lady, Rome Beauty, Winesap	Cameo, Cortland, Crispin/Mutsu, Golden Delicious, Granny Smith, Ida Red, Jonagold, Jonathan, Northern Spy, Rome Beauty, Winesap

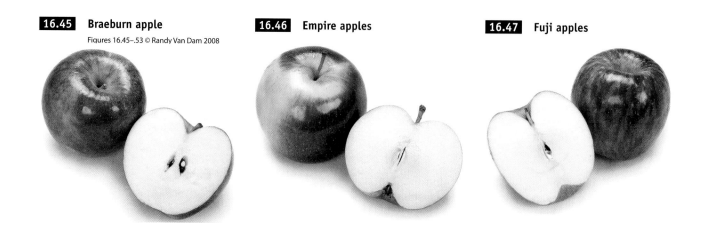

16.45 Braeburn apple

Figures 16.45–.53 © Randy Van Dam 2008

16.46 Empire apples

16.47 Fuji apples

16.48 Royal gala apples

16.49 Golden delicious apples

16.50 Granny Smith apples

16.51 Ida Red apples

16.52 Jonathan apples

16.53 McIntosh apples

16.54 **Pink Lady apples**

Figures 16.54–.56 © Randy Van Dam 2008

- **Red delicious.** The red delicious is probably the best-known apple in the United States. Its color varies from a striped red to a solid, deep red. Red delicious apples grown in the western United States have an elongated shape with pronounced "feet" (the five knobs at the bottom of the apple). Those grown in the east are rounder. Both are sweet and juicy and make tasty snacks and salads. (See Figure 16.55.)

- **Rome Beauty.** The Rome Beauty has a deep red skin, streaked with yellow. This apple is mildly tart and works so well for cooking that it is sometimes called the "baker's buddy." It is especially good baked whole or sautéed. (See Figure 16.56.)

- **Winesap.** The Winesap has a thick, deep red skin and a crisp, yellowish flesh. Its sweet-tart flavor has an appropriately winey aftertaste. This all-purpose apple keeps well and is good for snacking, salads, sauces, and pies.

BUYER'S NOTE *In addition to the varieties listed here, check with a local apple orchard for other local varieties.*

16.55 **Red delicious apples**

16.56 **Rome Beauty apples**

PEARS

Pears are picked when they are mature but not yet fully ripe. That is because, when left on the tree to ripen, pears become grainy mush. To allow time to ripen, it is best to buy pears several days before serving. They will continue to ripen at room temperature. Be sure to check them daily, and then refrigerate them when ripe. Don't go by color, as most varieties will not change as the pears ripen. Instead, you can tell they are ripe when they give to gentle pressure at the neck.

Look for unblemished fruit without bruises. There are hundreds of varieties with long arched necks, gentle teardrop curves, or charmingly rounded bodies. Handle gently, as even hard fruit can bruise.

- **D'Anjou.** There are both green and red D'Anjou pears, and both varieties are very sweet and juicy. These pears are served as hand fruit or sliced for salads. Under-ripe D'Anjous can be used for pies and chutneys. (See Figure 16.57.)

- **Asian (Chinese pear).** This was introduced into the United States only at the end of the nineteenth century. There are more than 100 varieties of the Asian pear, most of which are round and about the size of an apple. The thin, smooth edible skin may be yellow, green, or golden brown. The flesh is slightly sweet and mildly flavored and has the crispness of an apple. Unlike the pear, the Asian pear is picked when ripe and ready for consumption. Its crunchiness gives it a variety of uses. (See Figure 16.58.)

- **Bartlett.** Yellow Bartletts, which change from green to bright yellow as they ripen, possess the quintessential pear aroma and flavor. They make a succulent, fresh snack and are good for canning and cooking. Red Bartletts are bright red but otherwise have the same characteristics and uses as the yellow variety. (See Figure 16.59.)

- **Bosc.** This is a rather large pear, and its color ranges from deep yellow to dark tan. The Bosc has a sweet taste but is not particularly juicy. Its dense, tender flesh makes it a good utility pear. (See Figure 16.60.)

- **Comice.** Comice pears are bursting with sweet juice. They are often very large with a red blush on their green skin. Comice pears are refreshing on their own, or you can serve them with blue cheese as a simple dessert. They are too juicy for cooking. (See Figure 16.61.)

- **Forelle.** The Forelle is a small pear that turns from green to bright yellow with crimson freckles as it ripens. Forelles are slightly crisp, very sweet, and juicy.

- **Packham.** The Packham is a Bartlett cross with a bumpy, pale green skin and white flesh. Packhams are sweet and fragrant. Eat them fresh, add them to a salad, or poach them in red wine. (See Figure 16.62.)

- **Seckel.** Seckels are very sweet with a somewhat grainy texture. Their maroon and olive skin does not change color while ripening. Seckels can be used on their own or in some cooking applications.

- **Starkrimson (red pear).** The Starkrimson pear is a brilliant and solid red. This variety shares similar taste and texture with the Bartlett pears. (See Figure 16.63.)

- **Taylor's gold.** Offering a sweet taste, cinnamon-colored Taylor's gold pears have a smooth netlike uniform russet skin. Creamy, juicy, and very tender, its flesh has a rich, sweet flavor similar to a comice. (See Figure 16.64.)

16.57 D'Anjou pears

Figures 16.57–.58 © Randy Van Dam 2008

16.58 Asian pears

16.59   **Bartlett pears**

Figures 16.59–.64 © Randy Van Dam 2008

16.60   **Bosc pears**

16.61   **Comice pears**

16.62   **Packham pears**

16.63   **Starkrimson (red) pears**

16.64   **Taylor's gold pears**

BUYER'S NOTE   *Keep those fruits that produce ethylene gas stored away from those that would be harmed, or over-ripened, by the unwanted gas.*

16.65   **Quince**

© Randy Van Dam 2008

QUINCE

Quinces have yellow skin and yellowish-white flesh. This aromatic fruit looks and tastes like an apple-pear cross, but it is drier and more tart than either. Look for large, firm, brightly colored quinces with little greening. Wrap in plastic and store in the refrigerator for up to 2 months. Quinces are high in pectin and are excellent for making preserves, jams, and jellies. They can also be stewed, combined with apples in pies or other desserts, or added to meat stews. (See Figure 16.65.)

Tropical and Exotic Fruits

Tropicals are fruits that are native to tropical and subtropical climates. All can be eaten fresh without cooking or processing. They are often also referred to as *exotics,* as in earlier times, they were not readily available. However, improved systems for cultivating, harvesting, and transporting these unusual fruits have made them more commonplace in the American fruit market.

BUYING AND STORING

Many tropical fruits continue to soften or ripen after harvest, so they can be purchased in bulk while still firm, under-ripe, and slightly green. Most should be kept at room temperature as they ripen and then later refrigerated, unless otherwise noted.

Banana

Bananas are one of the few fruits that develop a better flavor when they ripen. They are often harvested green to protect them from bruising during shipping and handling, and they develop better flavor when ripened off the plant. About a dozen bananas grow in each bunch. Avoid bananas that has broken skin or moldy stems. Ripen at room temperature. Storing bananas in the refrigerator will slow the ripening process and will cause the skin to darken, but the flesh will be fine. Ripe bananas can be stored in the refrigerator for 3 to 4 days. Cut bananas will turn brown when exposed to air. To slow this process, toss them with a little lemon, lime, or orange juice before using.

- **Baby.** As their name suggests, these bananas are only 3 to 4 inches long. Their color is deep yellow with black-brown mottling. A typical bunch is eight to ten bananas. They are ripe when they give way to gentle pressure and are speckled with black. The baby banana is also called *finger banana* or *niño banana*. (See Figure 16.67.)

- **Blue java.** A small plump variety of banana that is commonly used as a dessert or snacking banana. This banana is also known as the blue java ice cream banana.

- **Burro.** The burro banana is thicker and shorter than a Cavendish banana and is sometimes called a chunky banana. It has creamy white flesh that yellows as it ripens. Burro bananas ripen more quickly than the common variety and develop black spots along the ribs when ripe. They are excellent to eat out of hand or added to fruit salads, and they can also be dried for banana chips.

- **Cavendish (common banana).** The Cavendish is the most widely available banana and most familiar to North American consumers, and they are available year-round. They are great as a snack, sliced on top cereal, added to fruit smoothies, or even peeled and frozen for a cool ice cream–like summer dessert. (See Figure 16.68.)

- **Manzano.** Manzano bananas are smaller than regular bananas. Their yellow skin turns completely black when ripe. The Manzano banana is delicious eaten out of hand and also cooks well.

- **Plantain.** The plantain is a cooking banana with a firm texture and mild flavor that is sometimes compared to squash. It has thick skin that varies from green to yellow to brownish black. Unlike most bananas, plantains have to be cooked before they are ripe and can be fried, braised, mashed, sautéed, or stewed. Plantains have more starch

16.66 Apple with enzymatic browning on left, versus freshly cut apple with no browning
© Randy Van Dam 2008

People, Places, Things

Enzymatic Browning

Bananas and apples are representative of the fruits very susceptible to enzymatic browning. The dining public is often concerned with different quality factors regarding their food, including its nutritional value, taste, texture, and appearance. And as the adage, "people eat with their eyes first" is a truism in food service, chefs need to be concerned about preventing the   of fruit to preserve its attractive appearance.

Enzymatic browning occurs when fruit is exposed to oxygen after it is peeled or cut. The melanins created by the fruit's natural enzymes cause the browning to occur. However, browning can be arrested by destroying the enzymes through exposure to intense heat or citric acid, such as lemon or pineapple juice

16.67 **Baby, or niño, banana**
© Randy Van Dam 2008

People, Places, Things

Ripening Fruit

is a chemical process that alters an inedible fruit, that is often tart and hard, into one more sweet, soft, and digestible. Oftentimes growers and packers will purposefully transport selected unripened fruit that can travel better when green, and be ripened later.

Ripening is caused by the action of ethylene gas on enzymes found in the cells of the fruit. All fruit gives off the same ethylene gas to some degree, causing a slow physiological change to the fruit. To stimulate this enzymatic process faster, and as needed, produce distributors will commonly subject differ-

16.68 Cavendish banana

© Randy Van Dam 2008

than sugar. They are often used as a savory side dish in Latin cuisine. As plantains ripen, they become sweeter and can be used in desserts; however, do not substitute plantains for other sweeter bananas. Ripen at room temperature. Plantains ripen more slowly than other bananas. They can take up to 2 weeks to ripen. Look for fruit that is unblemished and without signs of bruising. Ripe plantains can be stored in the refrigerator 5 to 7 days or frozen with skins on for 3 months. (See Figure 16.69.)

- **Red.** Red bananas are smaller than a common banana, and the peel is a deep red or purple. It is firmer and sweeter than the Cavendish banana, as well as plumper and shorter. This banana is better for baking. (See Figure 16.70.)

Carambola (Star Fruit)

Carambolas are typically 3 to 5 inches long with five distinct ribs running lengthwise. They are also called star fruit because cutting the fruit crosswise produces crisp, star-shaped slices. The flavor may be very sweet to slightly tart. Select firm, shiny carambolas that are mostly yellow. Store ripe carambolas in the refrigerator, tightly wrapped in a plastic bag for up to a week. They may be sliced for snacks or salads or juiced to add to fruit drinks. They do not need to be peeled before eating. Their distinctive shape makes them a beautiful garnish, especially in fruit salads and molded salads. (See Figure 16.71.)

Cherimoya

The cherimoya, sometimes called a *custard apple*, tastes like pineapple, papaya, and banana combined. It has a thin, green, and often scaly skin and can be round, oval, or heart shaped. Select fruit that is firm and heavy for its size and free of brown blotches. Wrap and refrigerate ripe cherimoyas for up to 4 days. Cut in half and serve fresh (remove the seeds first), or freeze for 30 minutes and eat like sorbet. (See Figure 16.72.)

Coconut

Select heavy coconuts that sound full of liquid, and avoid those with weeping "eyes." For brown coconuts or white coconuts, look for firm "eyes" free of mold. Some brown coconuts are sold with a "quick crack" feature for easier opening and are encased in plastic wrap. They are scored around the fruit's equator, deep enough to make them easier to open but not deep enough to penetrate the shell. Whole, unopened coconuts can be stored at room temperature for up to 6 months. Fresh, grated coconut meat should be tightly covered and stored in the refrigerator for up to 7 days or frozen in plastic wrap for up to 3 months. Coconuts are high in saturated fat, but small amounts add a nutty, candy-like natural sweetness to fruit salads, whole-grain cereals, and desserts. (See Figure 16.73.)

16.69 Plantain banana

Figures 16.69–.73 © Randy Van Dam 2008

16.70 Red banana

16.71 Star fruit

16.72 Cherimoya

16.73 Coconut

Date

Dates are typically 1 to 2 inches long with an oval shape, papery skin, and single, narrow seed. They might be yellow, golden brown, or black. Fresh dates should be plump, soft, and shiny. Avoid those that are shriveled, moldy, or encrusted with sugar crystals. Wrap them in plastic and refrigerate for up to 2 weeks. They are also delicious in salads, compotes, and baked goods.

Feijoa

The feijoa is 2 to 3 inches long and measures roughly 1 inch in diameter. It is an egg-shaped fruit with a thin, bitter, lime- to olive-green skin, which should be removed before use. Its cream-colored flesh is sweet and fragrant with a slightly granular texture resembling that of a pear. The flesh is strong tasting, with hints of quince, pineapple, and mint. The jel-lylike center has edible seeds. Ripe feijoas are fragrant and yield slightly to the touch; refrigerate them for 3 to 5 days. Feijoas are used in fruit compotes and as sauces for roasted meat. Depending on its stage of maturity, this fruit can have a sour taste. The feijoa is sometimes called a pineapple guava, but it is not related to the guava. (See Figure 16.74.)

Fig

There are more than 150 varieties of figs; colors vary from white to green, brown, red, or purple, and sometimes almost black. (See Figure 16.75a.) It is important to handle figs care-fully because they are extremely fragile and can bruise easily.

16.74 **Feijoa**
© Randy Van Dam 2008

Select plump, fragrant figs that have a little give when touched. Avoid those that are hard, mushy, or show signs of mold or splits. The most common commercial varieties include:

- **Calimyrna.** These fresh, green-skinned figs are thin skinned and juicy. They are popular for eating out of hand.

- **Kadota.** This variety is white-skinned and is considered and all-purpose fig. (See Figure 16.75b.)

- **Mission.** These dark-skinned figs are sweet and rather dry and are not as perishable as the others. (See Figure 16.75c.)

- **White Adriatic.** These white-skinned figs are grown commercially and are principally used for baking and drying.

Because they are highly perishable, fresh figs are most fre-quently dried or preserved. They can be dried artificially or through exposure to the sun. Figs are sometimes coated with sugar or soaked in water to increase their weight and moisture content. It takes more than 6 pounds of fresh figs to produce 2 pounds of dried figs. Fresh figs are highly perishable and should be refrigerated for just 2 or 3 days. Cut into quarters and serve with cheese and cured meat trays.

 BUYER'S NOTE *Figs contain enzymes that prevent gelatins from setting. They should not be used in gelatin desserts.*

Guava

There are many guava varieties. Some are as small as an egg, others as large as an apple. Their skin might be red, yellow, or purplish black, while their flesh ranges from pale yellow to vivid red. Look for firm guavas that yield to gentle pressure. Avoid bruised guavas or unripe ones (they are extremely

16.75a **Fresh figs in the marketplace**
Courtesy of Robert Garlough

16.75b **Kadota figs**

Figures 16.75b–.77 © Randy Van Dam 2008

16.75c **Black mission figs**

16.76 **Guava**

a jackfruit's weight is pulp, and 11 percent is seeds. While fertilized jackfruit flowers can be eaten, the fruit's skin and core, as well as the skin of the seeds, are inedible. These parts are commonly used for livestock feed. Like the banana, jackfruit continues to ripen after picking. Its flavor is not altered significantly, even when it is picked slightly under-ripe. (See Figure 16.77.)

16.77 **Jackfruit**

tart). Ripe guavas smell fragrant and fruity and can be stored in the refrigerator for up to 4 days. Puréed guavas can make a beverage base while the flesh can be made into jam, jelly, sauces, or preserves. (See Figure 16.76.)

Jackfruit

The many varieties of jackfruit are divided into two main categories: soft-flesh varieties, which have a sweet, juicy pulp, and crisp-flesh varieties, whose pulp is less sweet and juicy. The jackfruit's whitish or yellowish pulp becomes golden yellow when it is perfectly ripe. It contains numerous large seeds (depending on the variety, between 50 and 500 seeds) of a whitish color. Approximately 30 percent of

Kiwi (Gold and Green)

The kiwi fruit is an egg-shaped berry some 3 inches long and weighing between 2 and 4 ounces. There are two common varieties available in the U.S. market: golden and green. The emerald-green flesh is sweet and juicy. Small edible black seeds form a circle around the yellowish core of the fruit. Although the thin skin is edible, most people prefer to peel it. Today, about ten varieties of kiwi fruit are cultivated worldwide. In North America, the Hayward variety is the most common. (See Figure 16.78a and Figure 16.78b.)

 Green kiwi

Figures 16.78a–.80 © Randy Van Dam 2008

16.78b **Gold kiwi**

Lychee (Litchi)

Lychees are small fruits, 1 to 2 inches long. They have a thin, hard shell, which is removed before eating. Lychees are pink and then turn brown as they ripen. They have a sweet, crisp flesh with a large non-clinging stone. The stone should be removed before it is eaten. Lychees taste like a combination of strawberries and grapes. Lychees should be eaten when they are ripe. This fruit does not travel well, so it is frequently sold with the skin removed in cans. (See Figure 16.79.)

Longan

Longans grow in clusters and are covered with a smooth, thin orange shell that changes to brown and hardens when ripe. Inside, the transparent white flesh is juicy and sweet, although slightly less flavorful than that of the lychee. The flesh encloses a large, smooth brown seed that is inedible. The Chinese call this fruit "eye of the dragon" because of the white eye-shaped spot on the seed. (See Figure 16.80.)

 Lychee

 Longan

Mango

Mangos can be round, oblong, or kidney shaped and have a single, large seed. Their thin, tough skin is green at first and then turns a greenish yellow to bright yellow with red mottling as they ripen. Unripe mangoes will have a tough flesh that is harsh. Store mangoes at room temperature until they are ripe, and then use them within a few days. There are two commercial versions. The Kent mango has an oval shape with a yellow-green color (Figure 16.81a). The flesh is sweet and does not cling to the stone. The Ataufo mango (Figure 16.81b) has a creamy smooth flesh that is eaten as is. (See Figure 16.81c.)

16.81a Kent mango
© Randy Van Dam 2008

16.81b Ataufo mango
© Randy Van Dam 2008

16.81c Mangoes growing on trees
Courtesy of Robert Garlough

Mangosteen

The mangosteen is a round and peculiar-looking fruit that measures about 3 inches in diameter. Its thick, hard rind is inedible and contains tannins, which are used for dyeing leather. As the fruit ages, the rind takes on a deep purple color. Under this shell is a thick reddish membrane that encloses the flesh and is also inedible. The exquisite pearly white flesh inside is sweet and juicy; it is divided into five or six segments, some of which contain an edible pinkish stone. The fleshy part represents only a quarter of the fruit's total weight. The mangosteen is prized as one of the most succulent fruits of Asia.

Papaya

The papaya's thin, smooth skin is inedible; it ranges from orange to reddish yellow or yellowish green. Its texture is similar to that of the cantaloupe, yet softer. Its seeds resemble large peppercorns and have a peppery taste. The papaya's flavor resembles that of the melon. When buying papayas, choose fruits with an almost completely reddish-orange skin that yields slightly to the touch. Avoid hard, completely green papayas; they will never ripen. Also avoid very soft or bruised fruit. (See Figure 16.82a and Figure 16.82b.)

16.82a **Brazilian papaya**

Figures 16.82a–.83 © Randy Van Dam 2008

Passion Fruit

The most common varieties of passion fruit found on the market are the size of an egg, but passion fruit can grow to be the size of a small melon. It has a thick, smooth skin that is inedible. In commercially sold varieties, the skin is yellow, orange, or purple. As the fruit ripens, the skin becomes thinner and wrinkles. The pulp of passion fruit has a gelatinous texture and ranges from pinkish green to shades of orange or yellow; it may also be white or colorless. The pulp is sweet and juicy, slightly tart, and fragrant. The intense, sweetly tart flavor is described variously as lemon-jasmine-honey or jasmine-banana-lime. Unripe passion fruits are very tart. The pulp contains small blackish seeds that are crisp and edible. Choose deeply colored fruit that is heavy for its size, and store refrigerated for up to 5 days. Passion fruit puree adds a tropical flavor to drinks, vinaigrettes, sauces, syrups, and sorbets. (See Figure 16.83.)

Persimmon

Persimmons are yellow-orange to pumpkin in color. Fuyu persimmons are tomato shaped and have a spicy and sweet flavor that is reminiscent of mango and papaya. Fuyus remain firm when ripe, so they can be used in fruit salads. The Hachiya persimmon (also called Japanese persimmon) is large and round with a slightly elongated base. Ripe Hachiyas are almost mushy and very sweet, but unripe ones are unpleasantly high in tannins, much like red wine. Ripening greatly reduces their tannic acids.

16.82b **Caribbean red papaya**

16.83 **Passion fruit**

Pineapple

Fresh pineapples weigh from 1 to 6 pounds. Ripe pineapples are juicy and sweetly tangy with rough, diamond-patterned skins. The ripe fruit should not have a sour smell and is slightly soft to the touch. Fresh pineapple can be stored in the refrigerator up to 5 days. Under-ripe pineapples are firmer; they will soften and become less acidic after picking but will not get any sweeter.

- **Smooth cayenne.** These are large, firm, and quite sweet. They are also used for canning, having sufficient fiber for firm slices and cubes. (See Figure 16.84a.)

- **Red Spanish.** This pineapple is flavorful and has purple-hued skin, pale yellow flesh, and a large core.

- **Queen.** These weigh 1 to 2.5 pounds and are less fibrous than smooth cayenne. They are juicy with a small, tender core; they are sold fresh and keep well. (See Figure 16.84b.)

- **Abacaxi.** Rich, sweet, and juicy with a narrow core, these pineapples are not common in the food service industry.

Pomegranate

Pomegranates are small with a thick red skin that must be peeled. Inside, there are six sections with small edible seeds. The seeds look like tiny red balls and are used for garnishes, while the flesh is used for salads.

Select fruit that are heavy for their size with bright, unblemished skin. Store in a dark, cool place for a month or in the refrigerator for up to 2 months. To serve, cut pomegranates in half and scoop the juice sacs away from the tough, white membranes that separate them. Eat them fresh, use a sprinkling to garnish salads or dips, or add them to fish, poultry, or feathered game dishes.

Prickly Pear

Prickly pears are about the size and shape of regular pears, but they grow on a cactus. Prickly pears come in many different colors and have a soft texture with black seeds scattered through the flesh. Prickly pears taste like watermelon. Ripe prickly pears are evenly colored and yield slightly to pressure. Store in the refrigerator for up to a week. (See Figure 16.85.)

Rambutans

Originally from Malaysia, the rambutan grows in clusters on a small evergreen tree. Related to the lychee and the longan, it is widely grown in Southeast Asia, particularly in Indonesia. There are more than 50 varieties of this fruit. Covered on the outside with soft spikes, it looks rather like a small hedgehog. Its appearance accounts for its Malayan name, *rambout,* which means "hair;" it is also known as the "hairy lychee."

Rambutans have a diameter of about 2 inches and are covered with a fragile shell that is easily split open and varies from red to yellowish brown. The whitish pulp is juicy

16.84a Golden cayenne pineapple

Figures 16.84a–b © Randy Van Dam 2008

16.84b Queen pineapple

16.85 **Prickly pear**

and translucent and is similar in texture to the lychee. Like the lychee, the flesh surrounds a single inedible seed that is flat and almond-shaped. The flavor of the rambutan varies from sweet, mild, and fragrant to slightly sour or acidic, depending on the variety. Less fragrant than lychees, rambutans have a sweet-tart tropical flavor, a pineapple-cherry taste with a subtle tart edge, and a grapelike texture. Its scent is less pronounced than that of the lychee.

Red Tamarillo

There are three varieties of the tamarillo: red, amber, and yellow. Red tamarillos have a red skin and dark red pigmentation around the seeds. The remaining flesh is an amber color. The fruit is eaten by scooping the flesh from a halved fruit. Peel the tough skin before using. Sweeten with sugar, and then add raw to fruit compotes or cook and use in sauces, chutneys, relishes, or curries. Red tamarillos are also tasty and decorative in fresh salads. (See Figure 16.86.)

Rhubarb

Rhubarb is a long stalk with large leafy leaves. The leaves are inedible, and they must be discarded before use. Rhubarb is

16.86 **Red tamarillo**

a very sour plant, and, while it is sometimes eaten raw, it is more often used in pies and preserves. When buying rhubarb, look for crisp stalks that snap like celery. Rhubarb can be stored in the refrigerator if it is tightly wrapped. It can also be chopped and blanched and then frozen. (See Figure 16.87.)

Sapote (Sapota)

There are many varieties of sapote; the white sapote is the most common. It is about the size of an orange with a creamy, custard-like flesh surrounding three to five seeds. The skin ranges from chartreuse to yellow. Its sweet flavor has notes of peach, avocado, and vanilla. Store ripe sapotes in the refrigerator for up to 3 days. They are not used in cooking but are delicious eaten out of hand. They can also be puréed and added to fruit drinks or sauces. (See Figure 16.88.)

16.87 **Rhubarb**

16.88 **Sapote**

CONVENIENCE CORNER PRODUCT EXAMPLES

Fruit: Canned, Fresh, and Frozen

Company	Website	Products
Dole	http://www.dole.com	24/#2 Can pineapple slices
Smuckers	http://www.smuckers.com	200/0.5 oz Jam Strawberry
Knorr	http://www.knorr.com	4/ ½ gal Mango Sauce
Kellogg's	http://www.kelloggs.com	48/2.5 oz Kellog Snack Fruit Mix
Ms. Desserts	http://www.msdesserts.com	4/4.5# Crisp Apple
OceanSpray	http://www.oceanspray.com	24/16 oz Sauce Cranberry 24/1 lb Cranberry Whole
Reser's	http://www.Resers.com	215# Salsa Mango
Perfect Puree	http://www.perfectpuree.com	6/30 mg Puree Pineapple
Ferris Coffee & Nut	http://www.ferriscoffee.com	28# Apricot Dried
Musselman's	http://www.knouse.com	72/4 oz Applesauce Cinnamon
Mott's	http://www.motts.com	72/4 oz Applesauce Strawberry
Mr. Dell's Foods	http://www.mrdells.com	4/1 gal Cherries Maraschino w/ stem
Woodland Foods	http://www.woodlandfoods.com	5# Banana Chip Dried 5# Blueberries Dried 5# Blueberries Dried 24# Melon Halves
Sun Rich	http://www.sun-rich.com	36/2 oz Red Grapes Mini Bag
Saranac Brand Foods, Inc.	616-642-9463	5# Cranberry Relish

James M. Spilka

Place of Birth: Muskegon, Michigan

Educational Background and Work Experience

James Spilka is not a chef—not unless you want to count that 1-hour period when he cooked at a Produce Marketing Association (PMA) convention, or when he fusses over wild game in the family kitchen. But he did make 50 cents an hour working the grill for an A&W Root Beer stand when he was 11 years old, which eventually led to a grill job at the local McDonald's while in high school. But after graduation, he switched gears and studied law enforcement and criminal justice, receiving his B.S. degree from Ferris State University in 1975. However, he's not a police officer, either. Rather, Spilka is now vice president of produce for the tenth-largest privately held company in the United States: Meijer's Grocery. Spilka began his career with the Midwest-based chain in 1969 as a bagger and steadily worked his way up to his prominent position within the supermarket giant.

Meijer's Grocery was founded in 1934, when Hendrik Meijer purchased $338.76 of merchandise on credit to establish his first store in Greenville, Michigan. During the 1960s, the number of Meijer stores reached 26 with more than 4,000 team members. In 1962, it opened the first Meijer Thrifty Acres, a food and general merchandise store. It was the birth of one-stop shopping and the first "hyperstore" in the United States. Since then, Meijer stores have grown into "supercenters," each featuring more than 40 departments with more than 175 store locations across the Midwest. Jim's produce staff alone purchases from 34 countries around the world. Now employing more than 65,000 team members, Meijer reported revenue of $13.2 billion in 2005, making it the tenth-largest privately held company, according to *Forbes* magazine.

Memberships and Career Highlights

Spilka is a very active team member within his company, having been responsible for initiatives that have resulted in better

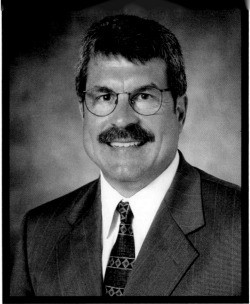

Courtesy James Spilka

It Happened to Me...

"As a Senior Buyer, I became responsible for all Product Promotions and Daily Retails with produce that would drive our sales and profit. During my training, there were no reports that measured the weekly retails, or profit, for advertised and non-advertised goods. My first assistant explained to me that he had a 'good feel' for the sales and margins each week, and I would learn to develop that same feel. Rather, it did not take long for me to begin working with our Information Technology department to develop a weekly report that gave me the ability to have a grip on the business and not just a good feel.

In a very short period of time, we doubled sales and profit and have been consistently outpacing our sales and margin goals... In our 'retail sales world,' quality of product is our success—I would think in a 'chef world,' consistent quality is your key to success and all the remaining management skills that go with the title."

service to customers, higher quality fresh foods, and improved sales. He has been instrumental in upgrading specifications for many fruit and vegetable items, including their packaging. And he is most proud of his efforts to create deli and bakery programs chainwide. This kind of creativity was recognized in 2004 when the United Fruit and Vegetable Association named him the Merchandiser of the Year. Jim is a member of the United Fruit and Vegetable Association and serves on the board of the Produce Marketing Association.

Meijer is known for developing relationships with growers and working with them to bring better products to market. That kind of communication is also stressed within Spilka's own staff, during their regular series of programmed meetings to evaluate customer and employee feedback. Jim values teamwork and enjoys an open relationship with all senior management, based on mutual respect.

Passions with the Food Service Industry

"In all of foods, the people are the difference maker. As a leader, it is vital to remain critical of yourself to ensure your team grows with the same passion for the business that you possess. Your team will be a reflection of your own actions... which control the success or failure of the business. When I have a team member make a misjudgment, I first review myself before passing on comments."

Advice to a Chef or Buyer

"Consistency in all you do in your personal or business life will ultimately dictate your success or failure. When people who serve the public become inconsistent in communication or training, quality or cost control, succession or personal life, their various deliverables will begin to falter. Attitude will affect your life and others around you, so again consistency will become essential."

Key Words and Concepts

---

citrus fruits	fruit	russeting	tropicals
enzymatic browning	ripening	stone fruits	

Chapter in Review

The following exercises are provided to help the reader understand and apply the contents of this chapter. They may be completed individually or in a classroom environment.

REVIEW QUESTIONS

a. Define the term *fruit*, and distinguish it from vegetables.

b. Describe the care in buying and storing berries.

c. What is enzymatic browning, which fruits does it affect, and how can it be prevented?

d. List four guidelines for the selection of fruit.

e. Identify the different uses for apples, and give examples of appropriate varieties for each.

INDIVIDUAL ACTIVITIES

a. **Web based:** Research fruit orchards in the area, and visit them to learn how the fruit is grown, harvested, packed, and shipped.

b. **Experiential:** Visit a canning and fruit packing plant to observe the process, and evaluate the quality of fruits used.

c. **Critical thinking:** Consider how one type of fruit may be substituted for another. For example, could melons be used to make a version of banana cream pie?

GROUP ACTIVITIES

a. **Lab experience:** Prepare pies, applesauce, and baked stuffed apples using different apples, and compare the results.

b. **Classroom action:** Divide the class into teams, and ask the groups to list as many varieties of oranges, apples, and melons as they can remember.

© Randy Van Dam 2008

Vegetables

"An old-fashioned vegetable soup, without any enhancement, is a more powerful anti-carcinogen than any known medicine."

JAMES DUKE, MD

After reading this chapter, you will be able to:

- ◎ Outline the growth stages of marketable greens, including micro-greens and baby greens.
- ◎ Explain the function of bulb vegetables.
- ◎ Compare the differences among leafy vegetables, including cabbage, chicory greens, and lettuces.
- ◎ List various root vegetables, including different varieties of potatoes.
- ◎ Explain the differences between heirloom and hybrid vegetables.
- ◎ Summarize the differences between fresh sweet and fresh chili peppers, and list several examples of each.
- ◎ Define the Scoville system for rating peppers.
- ◎ Explain how fresh peppers become dried peppers.
- ◎ Identify and discuss the differences between wild and cultivated mushrooms, and list several examples of each.

Introduction

According to *The Oxford Encyclopedia of Food and Drink in America*, "A vegetable is defined as any herbaceous crop grown for parts that can be eaten fresh or processed" (Smith, 2004, p. 570). It should be noted that **vegetable** is a culinary term. Parts of plants used as food are generally considered vegetables. Mushrooms, a fungus, which are covered in Chapter 19, are also commonly considered vegetables. Given this definition, vegetables can include any part of a plant. Some vegetables including squashes, tomatoes, avocados, and cucumbers are technically fruits but are treated as vegetables in the kitchen. This chapter will highlight some of the most common vegetables.

Global Sourcing

The world is a global marketplace, and vegetables are no longer only sourced from neighboring farms. Rising incomes, advancements in transportation, and international agreements have led to a rapid expansion of the global trade in produce. In an effort to make produce available when customers have a need, many national broadline distributors are using these international resources to supplement local growers. Still, many food service operators elect to use what is fresh and local. Locally grown, in-season produce appeals to both chefs and customers alike. Table 17.1 reflects the seasonal availability of fresh vegetables grown in the United States. Also see Table 17.2 for U.S. grades, packing seasons, and producing areas for common vegetables.

BUYING AND STORING

There are several methods of preserving vegetables, including refrigeration, cold storage, freezing, canning, drying, and marinating. While vegetables such as winter squash, garlic, potato, and taro tend to keep well even when stored at room temperature, most vegetables need to be refrigerated upon purchase. Table 17.3 lists U.S. Grades for common vegetables. When vegetables are stored in a general-use walk-in cooler, they should be kept in plastic storage bins with perforated lids to allow for less chill and more humidity.

Vegetables are stored differently depending on their specific characteristics. In general, it is preferable not to store or soak vegetables in cold water, as it changes their nutritional content. Instead, wilted vegetables can be refreshed and their crispness restored by adding a bit of moisture to the container using a wet paper towel, for example, or by misting them with water or immersing them in ice water for a few minutes. Avoid sealing the container completely, however, as this could cause the vegetables to rot.

When purchasing vegetables, the buyer must consider several factors relative to each individual product.

TABLE 17.1 Fresh Vegetable Seasonal Availability Chart

Product	Jan	Feb	Mar	Apr	May	Jun	Jul	Aug	Sep	Oct	Nov	Dec
	Winter Dec 21–Mar 19		Spring Mar 20–Jun 20			Summer Jun 21–Sep 21			Autumn Sep 22–Dec 20			
Artichokes			X	X	X							
Asparagus				X	X	X						
Avocados, Hass				X	X	X	X	X	X	X		
Beans, green					X	X	X	X	X			
Beets									X	X	X	
Broccoli	X	X	X						X	X	X	X
Brussels sprouts	X	X							X	X	X	X
Cabbage	X	X	X	X	X				X	X	X	X
Cauliflower	X	X	X	X	X				X	X	X	X
Celery root	X	X	X	X						X	X	X
Chestnuts									X	X	X	X
Collards	X										X	X
Corn						X	X	X				
Cucumbers					X	X	X	X				
Eggplants						X	X	X	X			
Greens			X	X	X	X						
Kohlrabi						X	X					
Leeks	X	X	X							X	X	X
Lettuce			X	X	X	X	X	X	X			
Mushrooms, morels			X	X	X							
Mushrooms, truffles	X	X									X	X
Okra					X	X	X	X	X			
Onions						X	X	X	X			
Onions, sweet				X	X	X						
Peas, English				X	X							
Peas, field							X	X				
Peppers, bell						X	X	X	X			
Peppers, chile									X	X	X	X
Potatoes								X	X	X		
Pumpkins									X	X	X	
Spinach	X	X	X	X	X					X	X	X
Squash, summer				X	X	X	X	X	X			
Squash, winter	X	X	X							X	X	X
Tomatoes						X	X	X	X			
Turnips				X	X					X	X	

TABLE 17.2 U.S. Grades, Packing Seasons, and Producing Areas for Processed Vegetables

Product	U.S. Grades	Primary Packing Season	Primary Producing Area
Asparagus—Canned	A or Fancy (85) C or Standard (70)	April to July	California, New Jersey, Michigan
Asparagus—Frozen	A or Fancy B or X-Standard	April to July	California, New Jersey, Michigan
Beans, Green and Waxed—Canned	A or Fancy (90) B or X-Standard (80)	June to October	Northwest, Wisconsin
Beans, Green and Waxed—Frozen	A or Fancy (90) B or X-Standard (80) C or Standard (70)	June to October	Northwest, California
Beans, Lima—Canned	A or Fancy (90) B or X-Standard (80) C or Standard (70)	August to October	California, East Coast
Beans, Lima—Frozen	A or Fancy (90) B or X-Standard (80) C or Standard (70)	August to October	California, East Coast
Beets—Canned	A or Fancy (85) C or Standard (70)	August ot December	California, Northwest, Michigan, New York
Broccoli—Frozen	A, B	June to August	California
Brussels Sprouts—Frozen	A, B, C	June to August	California
Carrots—Canned	A or Fancy (85) C or Standard (70)	August to May	California, Texas
Carrots—Frozen	A or Fancy (90) B or X-Standard (80)	July to October	California, Northwest, Texas
Cauliflower—Frozen	A or Fancy (85) B or X-Standard (70)	June to September	California
Corn on Cob—Frozen	A or Fancy (90) B or X-Standard (80)	June to August	Northwest
Corn, Whole Kernel—Canned	A or Fancy (90) B or X-Standard (80) C or Standard (70)	August to October	Northwest, Wisconsin, Minnesota
Corn, Whole Kernel—Frozen	A or Fancy (90) B or X-Standard (80) C or Standard (70)	June to August	Northwest, Wisconsin, Minnesota
Mushrooms—Canned	A or Fancy (90) B or X-Standard (80)	Year-round	Pennsylvania, North Carolina
Olives, Green—Canned	A or Fancy (90) B or X-Standard (80) C or Standard (70)	Year-round	California, Spain
Olives, Ripe—Canned	A or Fancy (90) B or X-Standard (80) C or Standard (70)	October to February	California
Onion Rings—Breaded Frozen	A or Fancy (85) B or X-Standard (70)	April to December	Various states
Onions—Canned	A or Fancy (85) C or Standard (70)	April to December	Various states
Peas—Canned	A or Fancy (90) B or X-Standard (80) C or Standard (70)	July to August	Wisconsin, Minnesota
Peas—Frozen	A or Fancy (90) B or X-standard (80) C or Standard (70)	June to July	Northwest, Wisconsin, Minnesota
Peas and Carrots—Canned	A or Fancy (90) B or X-standard (80) C or Standard (70)	June to August	Northwest, Wisconsin, Minnesota
Peas and Carrots—Frozen	A or Fancy (90) B or X-Standard (80) C or Standard (70)	June to July	Northwest, California
Pickles—Canned	A or Fancy (90) B or X-Standard (80)	Year-round	Michigan

TABLE 17.2   *(Continued)*

Product	U.S. Grades	Primary Packing Season	Primary Producing Area
Potatoes, French Fry—Frozen	A or Fancy (90) B or X-Standard (80)	September to May	Idaho, Washington, North Central, Maine
Potatoes, White—Canned	A (90) B (80)	September to March	Various states
Potatoes, Hash Brown—Frozen	A (90) B (80)	September to May	Northwest, North Central, Northeast
Sauerkraut—Canned	A or Fancy (90) B or X-Standard (80) C or Standard (70)	Year-round	New York, Pennsylvania
Spinach—Canned	A or Fancy B or X-Standard	June to October	California, Texas
Spinach—Frozen	A or Fancy (90) B or X-Standard (80)	June to October	California
Sweet Potatos—Canned	A or Fancy (90) B or X-Standard (80)	July to March	Southeast

TABLE 17.3   **U.S. Grades for Fresh Vegetables**

Product	U.S. Grades
Artichokes	#1 and #2
Asparagus	#1 and #2
Beans	Fancy, #1, Combo, and #2
Broccoli	Fancy, #1, and #2
Brussels Sprouts	#1 and #2
Cabbage	#1 and Commercial
Carrots	A, B, #1, and Commercial
Celery	Extra, #1, and #2
Corn	Fancy, #1, and #2
Cucumbers	Fancy, Extra #1, #1, #1 Small, #1 Large, and #2
Iceberg Lettuce	Fancy, #1, Commercial, and #2
Leaf Lettuce	Fancy
Boston Lettuce	#1
Onion	#1, Combo, #2, and Commercial
Romaine	#1
Sweet Peppers	Fancy, #1, and #2
Potatoes	Extra #1, #1, and #2
Sweet Potatoes	Extra #1, #1, Commercial, and #2
Tomatoes	#1, Combo, #2, and #3 (field grading standards; grade identification is lost in repacking)
Tomatoes—Canned	A or Fancy (90) B or X-Standard (80) C or Standard (70)
Tomato Catsup—Canned	A or Fancy (85) B or X-Standard (85) C or Standard (70)
Tomato Juice—Canned	A or Fancy (93) C or Standard (80)
Tomato Juice, Concentrate—Canned	A or Fancy (85) C or Standard (70)
Tomato Paste—Canned	A or Fancy (90) C or Standard (80)
Tomato Puree—Canned	A or Fancy (90) C or Standard (80)
Tomato Sauce—Canned	A or Fancy (85) C or Standard (70)
Vegetables, Mixed—Frozen	A or Fancy (90) B or X-Standard (80) C or Standard (70)

Leaf Vegetables

Leaf vegetables are plant leaves eaten as a vegetable. Leaf vegetables most often come from short-lived herbaceous plants such as lettuce and spinach. The most common leaf vegetables are discussed in this section.

CABBAGE

Cabbage is a heavy, compact leafy vegetable. All of the leaves encircle a core, and the leaves are removed from the core before serving. Choose firm crisp, heavy cabbages with no sign of browning. Ensure proper air circulation during storage. Discard the outer leaves and core before using.

- **Bok choy.** Bok choy resembles a bunch of wide-stalked celery with long, full green leaves. The smaller plants are tender and preferred. Bok choy cooks quickly and is often used in Oriental stir-fry dishes. (See Figure 17.1.)

- **Brussels sprouts.** Brussels spouts are tiny buds that look like mini cabbages. The edible portion is the small cabbage-like head. Brussels sprouts are a cool season crop, and they grow on long, thick stalks. Occasionally, the tops are used as greens. (See Figure 17.2.)

- **Celery cabbage.** Celery cabbage, also known as Chinese cabbage, is an elongated head of crisp celery-like stalks and light green leaves. It is used in Chinese cooking. (See Figure 17.3.)

- **Napa.** Napa cabbage is cylindrical with pale green leaves and white ribs. Napa cabbage is commonly used in Asian cooking. (See Figure 17.4.)

- **Green cabbage.** This familiar, round, compact cabbage is traditionally used in coleslaw or cooked with corned beef, but it also has many other applications. (See Figure 17.5a.)

- **Red cabbage.** Red cabbage is firm and round with shiny, dark red or purple leaves. It has a peppery taste and is a colorful addition to salads. (See Figure 17.5b.)

- **Savoy cabbage.** Savoy cabbage forms a loose head of crinkly, crisply succulent leaves. It has a mild, mellow flavor that makes it a favorite for Italian and other cuisines. (See Figure 17.6.)

17.1 **Bok choy**
Figures 17.1–.4 © Randy Van Dam 2008

17.2 **Brussels sprouts**

17.3 **Celery cabbage**

17.4 **Napa cabbage**

ENDIVE AND CHICORY

- **Belgian endive.** Belgian endive should be crisp with tightly furled heads tipped in a pale greenish yellow. Belgian endive is grown in the dark to keep it from turning green. (See Figure 17.7.)

- **Curly endive.** Curly endive is similar in appearance to chicory, a close cousin, and is often mistaken for it. Curly endive's lacy green leaves are a bit prickly and taste slightly bitter. It is used in small amounts in salads. (See Figure 17.8.)

- **Chicory.** Chicory is related to endive and radicchio. It has curly, green leaves with pale centers and is sometimes mistakenly called curly endive. Unwashed chicory can be kept in the refrigerator for up to 3 days. (See Figure 17.9.)

- **Escarole.** Escarole is another endive variety, but its broad leaves are milder in flavor than either curly or Belgian endive. Escarole looks like lettuce but is firmer and crunchier. Tightly wrap and refrigerate for up to 3 days. (See Figure 17.10.)

- **Frisee.** Frisee belongs to the chicory family. Its delicate, feathery leaves are curly and yellow-white to yellow-green. Store it unwashed in the refrigerator for up to 5 days. (See Figure 17.11.)

- **Radicchio.** Radicchio is a slightly bitter Italian chicory, with either a loose or tight head, pink to dark red leaves, and white ribs. The leaves should be crisp and full colored without any browning. Refrigerate in plastic for up to a week. (See Figure 17.12.)

17.5a **Green cabbage**

Figures 17.5a–.7

© Randy Van Dam 2008

17.5b **Red cabbage**

17.6 **Savoy cabbage**

17.7 **Belgian endive**

17.8 Curly endive

Figures 17.8–.12 © Randy Van Dam 2008

17.9 Chicory

17.10 Escarole

17.11 Frisee

17.12 Whole radicchio

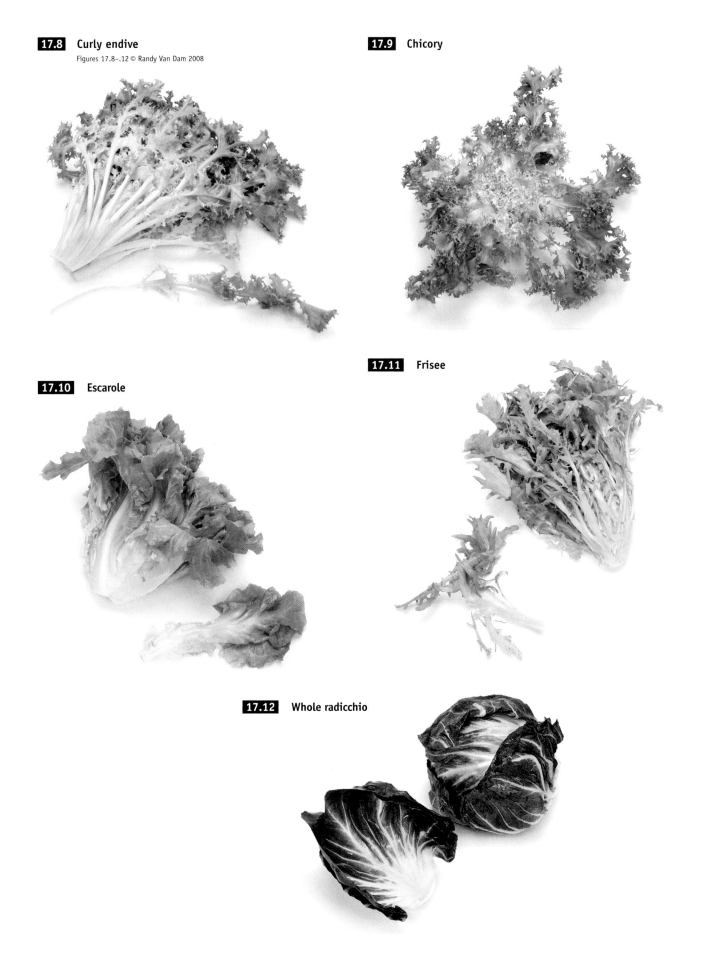

GREENS

Greens are different from lettuces in that they are cooked by braising, steaming, or sautéing to tenderize them. Only very young leaves are eaten raw.

- **Collard greens.** Collard greens have long stalks topped with a loose rosette of dark green leaves. Put them in a plastic bag and refrigerate for up to 5 days. In Southern kitchens, collard greens are traditionally slow cooked with salt pork or bacon. (See Figure 17.13.)

- **Dandelion greens.** Look for crisp, bright leaves, avoiding those with yellowing, browning, or wilted tips. Store them in a plastic bag in the refrigerator for up to 3 days. Dandelion greens have a taste similar to chicory and escarole. (See Figure 17.14.)

- **Kale.** Young, tender kale greens can provide an intense addition to salads, particularly when combined with

strongly flavored ingredients. Normally kale is sauteed or braised with onions or garlic. (See Figure 17.15a and Figure 17.15b.)

- **Mustard greens.** Mustard greens are dark green with oval leaves and scalloped edges. Wrap in plastic and refrigerate for up to a week. The peppery, pungent mustard flavor mellows with slow cooking. (See Figure 17.16.)

- **Rapini (broccoli raab).** Rapini, also called broccoli raab, grows on stalks with small, broccoli-like clusters at the end. This bitter green is favored in Italian cooking. (See Figure 17.17.)

- **Spinach.** Spinach is delicious raw or cooked. Look for crisp, dark green leaves and wash carefully to remove any grit. Store in a plastic bag in the refrigerator for up to 3 days. (See Figure 17.18.)

- **Swiss chard.** Swiss chard's broad green leaves grow on celery-like stalks that vary in color, depending on the type.

17.13 Collard greens

Figures 17.13–.15b © Randy Van Dam 2008

17.15a Green Italian kale

17.14 Dandelion greens

17.15b Red Russian kale

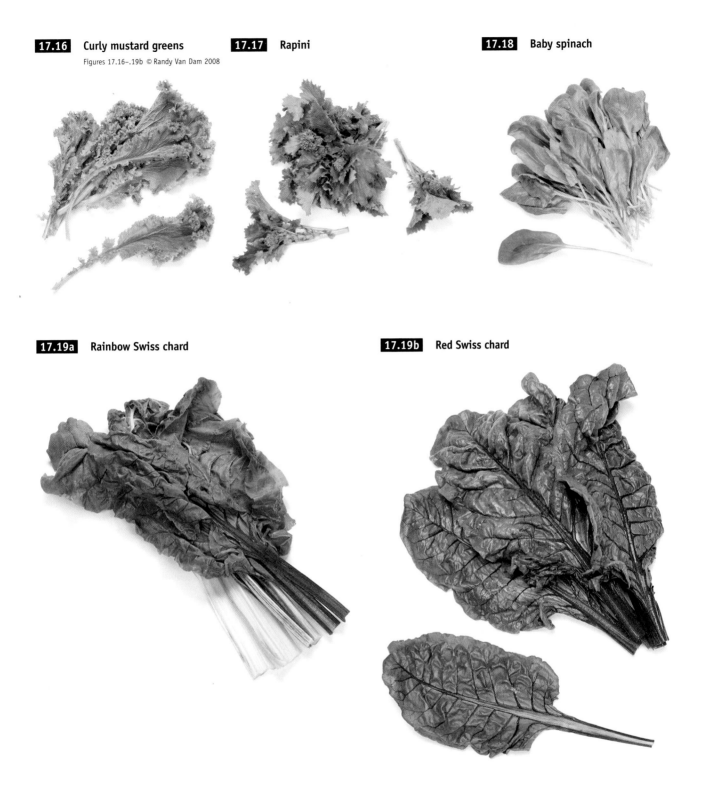

17.16 Curly mustard greens   **17.17** Rapini   **17.18** Baby spinach

Figures 17.16–.19b © Randy Van Dam 2008

17.19a Rainbow Swiss chard   **17.19b** Red Swiss chard

Green Swiss chard has a pale stalk; red has a red stalk, darker leaves, and a stronger flavor. Rainbow Swiss chard is the mildest of the three, and its stalks are a collection of reds, pinks, oranges, and yellows. (See Figure 17.19a and Figure 17.19b.)

- **Turnip greens.** Turnip greens have flat, fuzzy leaves on long stems. Tender and sweet when young, they grow tough and strong tasting with age. Refrigerate in a plastic bag for up to 3 days. To prepare, trim leaves from the thick rib, and then boil, sauté, steam, or stir-fry. (See Figure 17.20.)

- **Watercress.** Watercress belongs to the mustard family and shares its relatives' pungent, mustardy, peppery bite. The dark green, heart-shaped leaves make a pretty garnish, but watercress also adds a bold flavor to salads, sandwiches, soups, and other dishes. (See Figure 17.21.)

17.20 Turnip greens
© Randy Van Dam 2008

17.21 Watercress
© Randy Van Dam 2008

LETTUCE

Lettuce is another leafy vegetable, and there are many varieties available for commercial kitchens. Look for crisp lettuce with no blemishes or browning. Wash lettuce thoroughly by floating and soaking it in cold water. Lift the leaves from the water, rather than draining the sink with the lettuce. If washing a large quantity, bounce them in a colander or use a commercial-sized salad spinner to remove excess moisture. Store washed lettuce in plastic bins in the refrigerator for 3 to 5 days. See Table 17.4 for a list of salad green yields.

- **Arugula.** Arugula, also known as *roquette, garden rocket,* or *rocket lettuce,* has deeply notched bright green leaves and

a nutty, mustard-like flavor. Serve it raw in salad blends or cook it lightly in butter before serving. (See Figure 17.22.)

- **Bibb.** Bibb lettuce is one of the best-known butterhead varieties. The tender, dark green leaves form a loosely folded head, and they have a flavorful, almost buttery taste. (See Figure 17.23.)

- **Boston.** Boston lettuce is another butterhead variety and is similar to bibb lettuce. Its meaty, medium-sized leaves are smooth and slightly sweet. (See Figure 17.24a and Figure 17.24b.)

- **Green leaf.** Green leaf lettuce has ruffled leaves that are medium to dark green with a mild flavor and delicate

TABLE 17.4 **Comparison of Salad Green Yields**

Ingredient Name	As Purchased Weight (U.S.)	As Purchased Weight (Metric)	Edible Portion By Weight (U.S.)	Edible Portion By Weight (Metric)	Edible Portion By Volume (U.S.)	Edible Portion By Volume (Metric)
Arugula	6 ounces	168 g	3.5 ounces	98 g	2.5 cup	591 mL
Boston	5.25 ounces	147 g	4 ounces	112 g	2.5 cup	591 mL
Green Cabbage	2 lb	896 g	1 lb, 14 ounces	840 g	8 cup	1.89 L
Napa Cabbage	2 lb	896 g	1 lb, 12 ounces	784 g	7 cup	1.66 L
Dandelion Greens	6.5 ounces	182 g	3.25 ounces	91 g	3 cup	709 mL
Escarole	12.5 ounces	350 g	9 ounces	252 g	6 cup	1.42 L
Frisée	12 ounces	336 g	7.5 ounces	210 g	6 cup	1.42 L
Green Leaf Lettuce	11 ounces	308 g	7 ounces	196 g	4 cup	946 mL
Radicchio	9.5 ounces	266 g	4.5 ounces	126 g	2 cup	473 mL
Romaine	14 ounces	392 g	9.25 ounces	259 g	4.5 cup	1.06 L
Spinach, flat leaf	11 ounces	308 g	7.5 ounces	210 g	7 cup	
Watercress	5 ounces	140 g	3 ounces	84 g	2.5 cup	

17.22 **Arugula lettuce**

Figures 17.22–.24b © Randy Van Dam 2008

17.23 **Bibb lettuce**

17.24a **Green Boston lettuce**

17.24b **Red Boston lettuce**

crunch. The leaves form a loose bunch, rather than a tight head, and are more perishable than head lettuces such as iceberg. (See Figure 17.25a.)

- **Red leaf.** Red leaf lettuce has large, loose heads and thick leaves with a red tinge at the ends. This is a colorful addition to salad blends or sandwiches. (See Figure 17.25b.)

- **Iceberg.** Iceberg lettuce is a type of "crisphead" lettuce that has pale green leaves tightly packed into a round head. To prepare, loosen the core by smacking the head

on a hard surface. Twist the core and pull it out, and then rinse the remaining cavity with cold water. Iceberg's rather plain flavor and crunchy texture are well matched by most salad dressings; it is also often added to tacos or used for Asian-style lettuce wraps. (See Figure 17.26.)

- **Romaine lettuce.** Romaine lettuce grows in a long head of sturdy leaves with a firm rib down the center. Romaine is the standard lettuce used in Caesar salad. There are both green and red varieties of Romaine. (See Figure 17.27a and Figure 17.27b.)

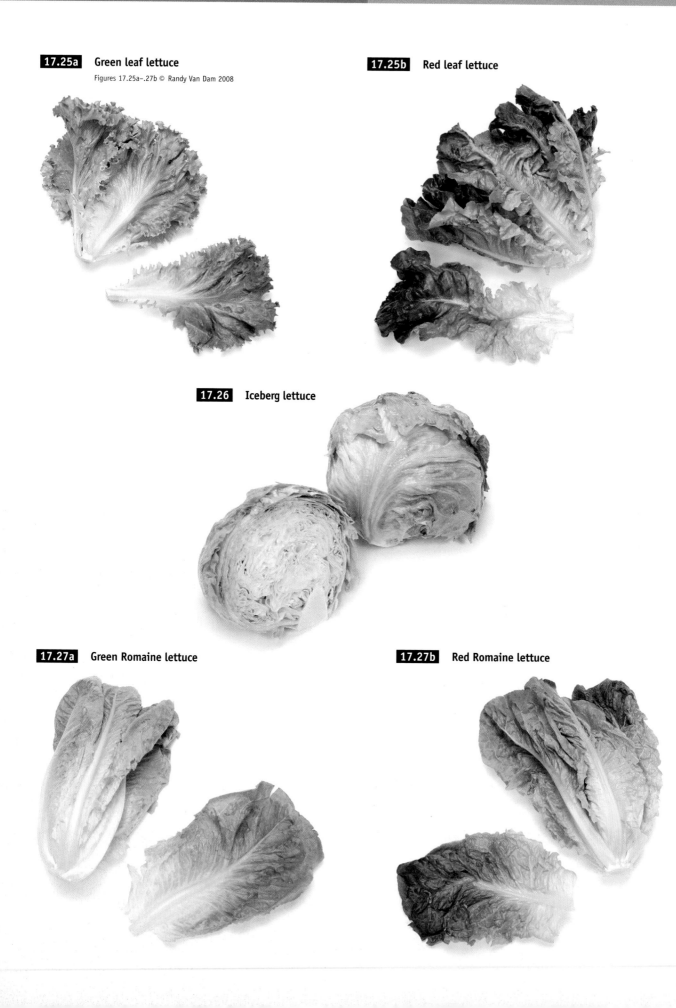

17.25a Green leaf lettuce

Figures 17.25a–.27b © Randy Van Dam 2008

17.25b Red leaf lettuce

17.26 Iceberg lettuce

17.27a Green Romaine lettuce

17.27b Red Romaine lettuce

Micro-Greens

Micro-greens are the plant's first true leaves. They are usually harvested with stalk or stem attached, making the unit of thin stem and just a few micro-leaves look like a sprout. They have a very intense flavor. They are also very expensive, as harvesting micro-greens means that less of a mature crop will be available. (See Figure 17.28a, Figure 17.28b, and Figure 17.28c.)

17.28b Onion (left) and broccoli sprouts (right)

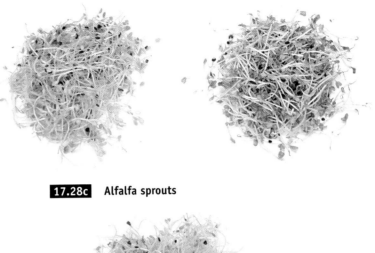

17.28a Bean sprouts

Figures 17.28a–c © Randy Van Dam 2008

17.28c Alfalfa sprouts

People, Places, Things

The Seven Stages of Growth for Marketable Greens

- **Stage #1: The Cotyledon Stage**
  These sprouts are considered very immature, and appear prior to the actual leaves. They are rarely used at this stage

- **Stage #2: The Micro Stage**
  These micro-leaves are the first actual growths that are considered edible greens. They have become increasingly popular in modern food service.

- **Stage #3: The Petite Stage**
  As the leaves begin to bunch, they are referred to as petite, just slightly larger than micro.

- **Stage #4: The Ultra Stage**
  These greens only range in size from 2 to 3 inches, and are carefully cultivated not to exceed these dimensions.

> **BUYER'S NOTE** *All harvests from the various plants are principally leaves.*

- **Stage #5: The Baby Stage**
  At this stage, the plant has developed a distinct root or head. The vegetable is often served whole as it is still tender.

- **Stage #6: The Young Stage**
  At this stage, the greens are nearly fully mature, making them larger and less delicate.

- **Stage #7: The Commercial Stage**
  These lettuces have achieved full maturity, and as full heads of greens, provide the greatest return on invest-

Bulb Vegetables

A bulb consists of an underground bud with overlapping leaves arising from a short stem. Bulbs can be used raw but most often are used in conjunction with other items to flavor dishes.

- **Fennel.** Bulb fennel, also known as *anise*, resembles onions in appearance, but the flavor is completely different, as bulb fennel is a delicate green. (See Figure 17.29.)

- **Garlic.** Some garlic head varieties are about the size of a marble, while others are as large as an orange. Select firm, plump heads with tight cloves and dry skin. Avoid shriveled, sprouting, or moldy bulbs. Store whole heads in a cool, dry, and dark place, not the refrigerator, for up to 2 months. Individual cloves can be stored for 3 to 10 days. Garlic is pungent, aromatic, and versatile. (See Figure 17.30.)

- **Onions.** Onions are one of the world's most popular ingredients. Dry onions are mature and have a thin, papery skin that can be yellow, red, or white. Their flesh is juicy, and the flavor is intense. Select dry onions that are firm and heavy for their size and that have dry, unblemished skins. Store in a cool, dry, well-ventilated place for up to 2 months. Wrap cut onions in plastic and refrigerate for up to 4 days. Refrigerating an onion for at least 30 minutes before chopping will help prevent the irritating juices from making your eyes water, as will using a freshly sharpened knife.

  - **Boiling onion.** Boiling onions measure about an inch across and can be white, yellow, or red. They are typically

17.30 Garlic head and loose cloves

boiled (as the name implies) and are easy to peel after cooking. They are best served whole. (See Figure 17.31.)

- **Globe onion.** Globe onions are between 1 and 4 inches across and have yellow, red, or white skins. Their flavor varies. (See Figure 17.32.)

- **Green/scallion.** Green onions have a small, white base that has not yet developed into a bulb; scallions have a flatter base and milder flavor. Both have long, straight, green leaves, and they can be used interchangeably in recipes. (See Figure 17.33.)

- **Knob onion.** Knob onions have thick green tops (similar to a leek) and a white, bulbous base. Sauté them in butter, add to a white sauce, or use in stir-fries. (See Figure 17.34.)

- **Leek.** Leeks look something like giant scallions with flat, green leaves and a thick, white base. Cut them in half and wash carefully to remove any sand or dirt between the layers. The leaves are usually discarded or used to make stock. (See Figure 17.35.)

- **Pearl onion.** Pearl onions are marble-size, mild-tasting, white boiling onions. They can be creamed, pickled,

17.29 Fennel

Figures 17.29–.31 © Randy Van Dam 2008

17.31 Boiling onions

marinated, or substituted for boiling onions in any recipe. (See Figure 17.36.)

- **Red onion (Italian).** Red onions are mildly sweet with a reddish-purple skin and white flesh with a red tinge that adds color to salads, pizza, and pasta dishes. (See Figure 17.37a.)

- **White onion.** White onions should be firm and free of blemishes. Store onions in a dry, dark, well-ventilated place—not in the cooler. (See Figure 17.37b.)

- **Yellow onion.** The yellow onion has a srong onion flavor and layers of papery skin. It is one of the most common onions used in the kitchen. (See Figure 17.37c.)

- **Shallot.** Shallots form in cloves, much like a head of garlic. Dry shallots will keep for a month in a cool, dry location. Fresh shallots can be refrigerated for up to a week. Avoid those that are wrinkled, soft, or sprouting. Shallots have a sweet, delicate flavor and can be used like other onions. (See Figure 17.38.)

- **Spanish onion.** These are the largest, most popular onion for slicing and eating raw because of its mild, sweet taste. They can also be baked, sautéed, or fried, and they store well. (See Figure 17.39.)

- **Sweet onion.** Sweet onions are succulent and mild, due to lower levels of the sulfuric compounds that make your eyes water. Varieties known for their high sugar content include Vidalia Sweets®, Maui Sweets, OSO Sweet, Walla Walla Sweets, and Texas 1015 SuperSweet®. (See Figure 17.40.)

17.32 **Globe onions**

Figures 17.32–.36 © Randy Van Dam 2008

17.33 **Scallions bunch**

17.34 **Knob onions**

17.35 **Leeks**

17.36 **Pearl onions**

17.37a Red onions

Figures 17.37–.40 © Randy Van Dam 2008

17.37b White onions

17.37c Yellow onions

17.38 Shallots

17.39 Spanish onions

17.40 Vidalia onions

17.42a Red beets with shoots and greens attached

Root and Tuberous Vegetables

Root and tuber vegetables are the underground portion of a plant that is used in cooking. (See, for example, arrowroot in Figure 17.41.) Most roots and tubers have long shelf lives. As these vegetables have been underground most of their growing cycle, you must wash them thoroughly or peel them before use.

- **Beet.** Beets may be garnet to white with firm, smooth skins. Small beets are tenderer than large ones. If the greens are attached, they should be crisp and bright. Remove greens, leaving about an inch of the stem; cook; and then peel. Refrigerate beets in a plastic bin for up to 3 weeks. (See Figure 17.42a and Figure 17.42b.)

- **Carrot.** Look for firm, smooth carrots; avoid withered or cracked ones. Wrap in plastic and refrigerate (store separately from apples, which emit ethylene gas and make carrots taste bitter). Very young or baby carrots do not need to be peeled before use. (See Figure 17.43a, Figure 17.43b, and Figure 17.43c.)

- **Celeriac.** Celeriac, also known as *celery root, celery knob,* or *knob celery*, is a knobby variation of celery. Look for small and firm roots without soft spots that are heavy for their size. Refrigerate in a plastic bin for up to 10 days. Celeriac has a celery-parsley flavor and can be eaten raw or cooked (peel first). (See Figure 17.44.)

17.42b Golden beets with shoots and greens attached

17.41 Arrowroot

Figures 17.41–.42b © Randy Van Dam 2008

17.43a Assorted carrots (horse, cello, baby)

Figures 17.43a–.44 © Randy Van Dam 2008

17.43b Organic cello carrot

17.43c Maroon carrot

17.44 Celeriac

- **Jicama.** Jicama is a large, heavy, crunchy bulb with a nutty taste. Look for firm, smooth roots. After the skin has been peeled, wrap in plastic and refrigerate for up to 2 weeks. (See Figure 17.45.)

- **Kohlrabi.** Kohlrabi is a stem vegetable that is also cooked like a root vegetable. Select those that are heavy for their size and firm. The edible leaves should be deep green with no yellowing. Tightly wrap and refrigerate for up to 4 days. The bulb tastes like a mild, sweet turnip, and it can be cooked like a turnip. The greens can be prepared like spinach. (See Figure 17.46.)

- **Lotus root.** The skin of the lotus root is smooth and green; the inside has several large air pockets for buoyancy in water. When a root is sliced in half, it resembles a wagon wheel because of these large air pockets. (See Figure 17.47.)

- **Parsnip.** Parsnips look like white carrots and have a sweet, nutty flavor. Look for small to medium, evenly tapered, and firm parsnips. Refrigerate in a plastic bin for up to 2 weeks. (See Figure 17.48.)

- **Potatoes.** Potato varieties are classified, named, and promoted according to their geographic location of production and intended use, such as Idaho baking potatoes. Potatoes fall into three general categories: *starchy or baking, waxy,* and *new*. Starchy potatoes are low in moisture and high in starch, which makes them the best choice for baking and mashing. Waxy potatoes contain more moisture and have a firmer texture that is ideal for boiling and roasting. New potatoes are immature potatoes of any variety; they are creamy, thin skinned, and small enough to serve whole.

17.45   **Jicama**

17.47   **Lotus root**

17.46   **Kohlrabi with shoots and greens attached**

17.48   **Parsnip**

Potatoes should be stored at room temperature. They should be stored in a well-ventilated, dark room. If they are packaged in a paper bag or box, they can be left in that container, but if they are delivered in plastic, they should be moved to a paper container. Potatoes should not be kept in the refrigerator, as the cold and moisture will convert the starch into sugars, which will affect the flavor when cooked.

Do not buy potatoes with a greenish tinge to their skins. This indicates that they have been badly stored. When they are exposed to light, they turn green, producing a toxic alkaloid called *solanin*. Cooking destroys it, but the potato flavor can turn bitter.

Common potato varieties include:

- **Red.** Red potatoes, sometimes called boilers, are a waxy potato with a rosy skin, white flesh, and smooth, firm texture. They hold their shape when steamed, roasted, or boiled. (See Figure 17.49.)

- **Russet (Idaho).** Russet potatoes are long and oval with a rough, brown skin and white flesh. This floury potato makes fluffy, light mashed potatoes. It also bakes well. (See Figure 17.50.)

- **White.** White potatoes can be short and round or long and oval. Both varieties are the waxy type with smooth and thin tan skins and white, creamy flesh. These all-purpose potatoes hold their shape well and can be used in most recipes. Tiny "baby whites" are called "fingerling potatoes." (See Figure 17.51a and Figure 17.51b.)

- **Yukon gold.** Yukon gold is one of the most popular waxy, yellow-fleshed potato varieties in the United States. They are buttery yellow to gold, inside and out, with a creamy texture that yields excellent mashed potatoes. (See Figure 17.52.)

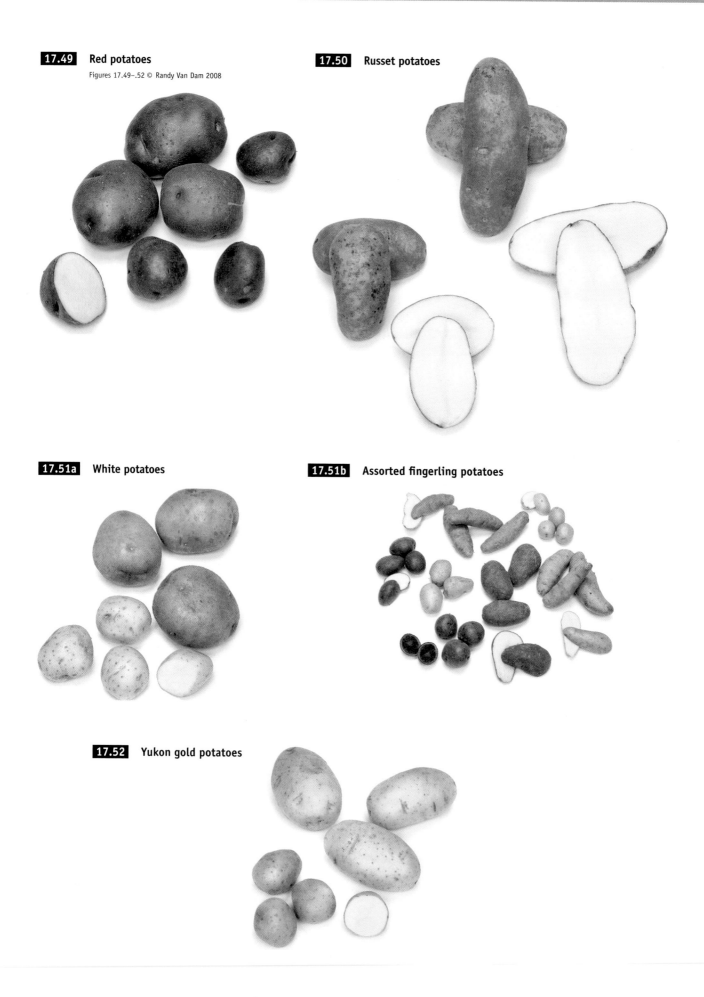

17.49 Red potatoes

Figures 17.49–.52 © Randy Van Dam 2008

17.50 Russet potatoes

17.51a White potatoes

17.51b Assorted fingerling potatoes

17.52 Yukon gold potatoes

- **Rutabaga.** Rutabagas, also known as *Swedes*, look like large, yellowish turnips. The yellow flesh is firm and slightly sweet. Look for hard, smooth, and heavy rutabagas, and refrigerate for up to 2 weeks. (See Figure 17.53.)

- **Sweet potatoes and yams.** These are root vegetables that resemble, but are not related to, regular potatoes. They should have smooth, unblemished skins. Use sweet potatoes within a week of purchase and yams within 2 weeks.

  - **Sweet potatoes.** Their skins and flesh may be light yellow to bright orange to dusty red. Lighter-skinned varieties tend to be drier and less sweet than dark ones, and they can be substituted for potatoes in many recipes. (See Figure 17.54a and Figure 17.54b.)

  - **Yams.** Yams are a tropical tuber similar to and often confused with the sweet potato. They are higher in moisture and sugar than sweet potatoes but can still be substituted for them in many recipes. (See Figure 17.55a and Figure 17.55b.)

- **Taro root.** Taro is a potato-like tropical tuber that can be up to a foot long. Taro root has a rough brown skin and gray-white flesh that tastes slightly nutty when cooked. Taro leaves are also edible and can be cooked like turnip or mustard greens. Select firm, smooth roots, and refrigerate for up to 4 days. Taro can be used like potatoes in soups or stews or baked, boiled, or fried. (See Figure 17.56.)

17.54a   Sweet potatoes

17.54b   Red sweet potatoes

17.53   Rutabaga

Figures 17.53–.54b © Randy Van Dam 2008

- **Turnip.** Turnips are white with a tinge of purple at the top and white flesh. Look for small turnips that are heavy for their size. They will be sweeter than large turnips, which may have a woody texture and peppery bite. Store in a cool, well-ventilated area or refrigerate for up to 2 weeks. (See Figure 17.57.)

17.55a   **Yams**

Figures 17.55a–.57 © Randy Van Dam 2008

17.55b   **Purple yams**

17.57   **Turnips**

17.56   **Large and small taro root**

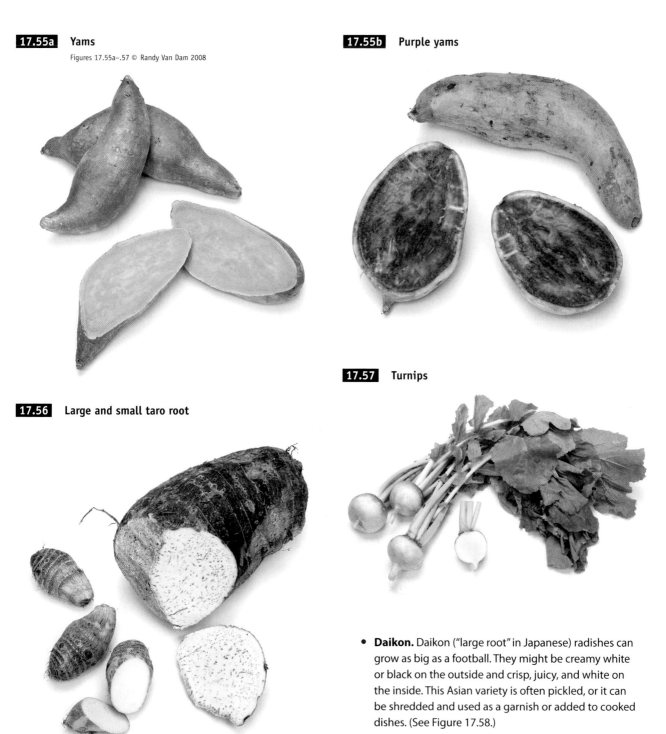

- **Radishes.** Radishes have a peppery flavor and come in a variety of colors, sizes, and shapes. Radishes should feel firm. Refrigerate radishes in a plastic bag for up to 5 days, depending on the variety.

  - **Black.** Black radishes are round with a rough, black skin and crunchy, white flesh. Although they can be horseradish hot, they do add a pleasing tang to salads and stir-fries and make an interesting side dish when braised or sautéed.

- **Daikon.** Daikon ("large root" in Japanese) radishes can grow as big as a football. They might be creamy white or black on the outside and crisp, juicy, and white on the inside. This Asian variety is often pickled, or it can be shredded and used as a garnish or added to cooked dishes. (See Figure 17.58.)

- **Red.** Red radishes are the most common and may be as small as a cherry or as large as an orange. They have a bright red skin with crisp, white flesh that has a mild bite. (See Figure 17.59a.)

- **Easter egg.** These clusters of colored radishes are named for their pastel colors, akin to traditional Easter eggs. (See Figure 17.59b.)

- **White.** White radishes are also called icicle radishes because of their long (up to 6 inches), tapering, and snowy white appearance. They are milder tasting than red radishes and are tasty raw. (See Figure 17.60.)

17.58 Daikon radish

Figures 17.58–.61 © Randy Van Dam 2008

17.59a Red radish

17.59b Easter egg radish

• **Yuca.** Yuca, also known as *cassava* or *manioc*, is a root vegetable with brown, bark-like skin and white flesh. Yuca may be sweet or bitter; bitter yuca is poisonous if undercooked or eaten raw. Sweet yuca is used to make tapioca. Look for firm, unblemished roots and refrigerate for up to 4 days. Sauté, boil, or stew yuca, or add to stir-fries, soups, or stews. (See Figure 17.61.)

17.60 White icicle radish

17.61 Yuca

Flowers

Flowers in the culinary sense are edible reproductive blossoms. There are some "true" flowers that are edible and used as garnishes, but this section deals with blossoms that are cooked as vegetables. The most frequent flowering vegetables include:

- **Broccoli.** Look for heads with tightly closed, vivid green buds; avoid those that are yellowing or brown. Refrigerate unwashed for up to 4 days. Trim and peel stalks before using. (See Figure 17.62.)

- **Cauliflower.** Cauliflower is usually white although green, purple, and yellow varieties are sometimes available. Look for firm heads with compact florets and green, crisp leaves. Wrap tightly and refrigerate for up to 5 days. (See Figure 17.63.)

 Broccoli

Figures 17.62–.64b © Randy Van Dam 2008

 Purple, white, and yellow cauliflower heads

Stem Vegetables

A stem vegetable is the stem section of certain plants used for culinary applications. Some vegetables have multiple parts that can be used (beets, for example), but this section focuses solely on the stem parts.

- **Asparagus, green.** Look for bright green stalks with compact and firm tips. Refrigerate for up to 4 days in a plastic bin or standing upright in water (like flowers in a vase). Before using, snap stalks off at their natural bend. Peel more mature or larger stalks. Boil, steam, or stir-fry until crisp-tender. (See Figure 17.64a.)

- **Asparagus, white.** White asparagus is grown underground, which keeps it from turning green (sunlight stimulates chlorophyll production in plants). Look for thick, smooth, pale ivory stalks with closed heads. Peel before cooking. Use like green asparagus. (See Figure 17.64b.)

17.64a **Green asparagus**

17.64b **White asparagus**

- **Fiddlehead ferns.** Fiddleheads, also nown as *ostrich fern* and *pohole*, are fern fronds that resemble the spiral end of a fiddle. Fiddlehead ferns are deep green and about the size of a silver dollar. They have a unique asparagus-like flavor and a chewy texture. Choose small, firm, brightly colored ferns. Refrigerate, tightly wrapped, for no more than 2 days. Fiddleheads should be washed and the ends trimmed before being briefly cooked by steaming, simmering, or sautéing.

- **Nopales (nopals).** Nopales are made from the young stem of prickly pear, carefully peeled to remove the spines.

Nopals are generally sold fresh or canned. They have a light, slightly tart flavor and crisp texture. (See Figure 17.65a and Figure 17.65b.)

- **Pascal celery.** The stems of this plant are eaten both raw and cooked. Choose firm bunches that are tightly formed. Store celery in plastic bins in the cooler for up to 2 weeks. Leave the ribs attached to the stalk until ready to use. Celery should be well washed and trimmed of leaves. (See Figure 17.66.)

17.65a **Woman selling fresh nopales in Guadalajara marketplace**
Courtesy of Robert Garlough

17.65b **Nopales**
© Randy Van Dam 2008

17.66 **Pascal celery and celery hearts**
© Randy Van Dam 2008

Podded and Seed Vegetables

Seed pods and the seeds they contain are an important and universal food item. Cost effective and nutritionally dense, these vegetables can stand alone or be used in stews, soups, salsas, dips, spreads, or vegetable blends.

- **Black beans.** Black beans, or turtle beans, are black with cream-colored flesh. They are popular in Latin and Caribbean dishes such as Cuban black bean soup. (See Figure 17.67.)

- **Chinese long bean.** These pencil-thin green beans are also called yard-long beans because they can grow up to 3 feet. They are usually shorter than that in the market. Chinese long beans are related to black-eyed peas, but they taste more like green beans. (See Figure 17.68.)

- **Fava beans.** Fava beans are pale green when fresh, and tan and flat like a lima bean when dried. They are popular in Mediterranean and Middle Eastern cooking and also make a tasty addition to soups. (See Figure 17.69.)

- **French green beans.** French green beans, also known as *haricot vert,* which is French for "green bean," are tiny, slender, young green beans with a delicate flavor. They are not the same as French-cut or "frenched" green beans, terms referring to any green bean cut lengthwise into thin strips. (See Figure 17.70.)

- **Garbanzo beans.** Garbanzo beans, or chickpeas, are round, buff colored, and firm textured. They are often used in Mediterranean, Indian, and Middle Eastern cooking and are the main ingredient in hummus and falafel. (See Figure 17.71.)

- **Green peas.** Fresh green peas are sweet and work well in a variety of recipes. "English pea" is the proper name for what is often called a green or garden pea. (See Figure 17.72.)

- **Lima beans.** Lima beans are green and kidney shaped, and the two most

17.67 Black beans

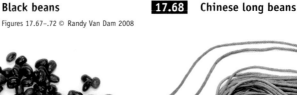

Figures 17.67–.72 © Randy Van Dam 2008

17.68 Chinese long beans

17.69 Fava beans

17.70 French green beans

17.71 Garbanzo beans

17.72 Green peas

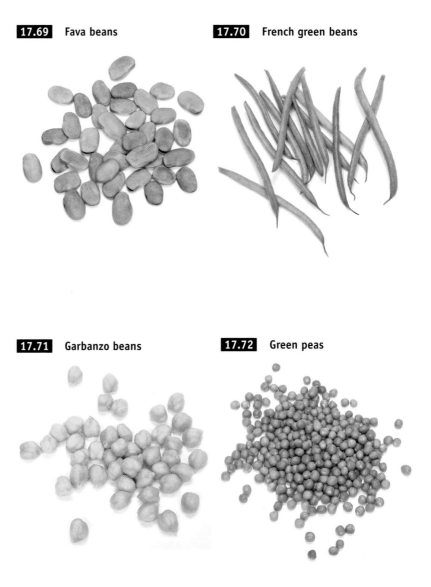

popular varieties are Fordhook and baby lima. Fordhooks are plumper and more flavorful. Baby limas are fully mature but naturally petite. With their creamy, sweet taste, lima beans can stand on their own as a side dish. (See Figure 17.73.)

- **Okra.** Okra is full of round, white seeds, which, when picked young, are eaten as a vegetable. Okra is also used to thicken stews. (See Figure 17.74.)

- **Pinto beans.** Pinto beans are oval and beige with streaks of red; they turn brown when cooked. These beans are a staple in Latin American and Southwestern cooking and are often used to make refried beans, burritos, and tacos. (See Figure 17.75.)

- **Pole bean.** Many chefs prefer pole beans for their distinctive "beany" flavor. The dark green pods are tender and rich, filled with white seeds and an incomparable flavor. (See Figure 17.76.)

- **Red bean.** *Red bean* is a broad category that includes kidney beans of different colors and sizes. They range from light brownish red to crimson and are cream colored inside. Red beans hold their shape and texture when cooked, so they are perfect for *chili con carne* and Louisiana-style dishes such as red beans and rice. (See Figure 17.77.)

- **Snap/string beans.** Green beans have tender pods with immature seeds, and the entire bean is eaten. Although they are often called string beans, modern varieties no longer have the stringy fiber along the side that earned the name. (See Figure 17.78.)

- **Snow peas.** Snow peas are thin and crisp with an edible green pod that encases tiny, tender peas. They are a common addition to Chinese-style stir-fries and salads. (See Figure 17.79.)

- **Soybeans.** Soybeans can be grown on a variety of soils and a wide range of climates. Green soybeans (edamame) should be refrigerated and used within 2 days. Dried soybeans can be kept in an airtight container for a long period of time. As soybeans mature in the pod, they ripen into a hard, dry bean. (See Figure 17.80.)

17.73 Lima beans

Figures 17.73–.78 © Randy Van Dam 2008

17.74 Okra

17.75 Pinto beans

17.76 Pole beans

17.77 Red beans

17.78 Snap/string beans

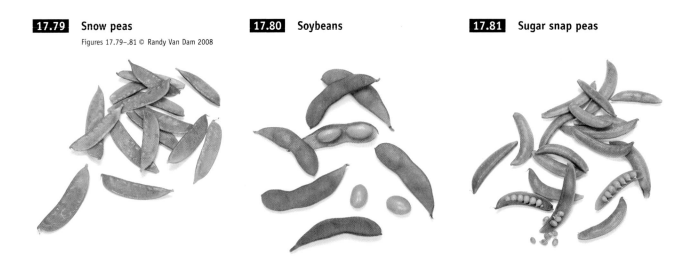

17.79 Snow peas   **17.80** Soybeans   **17.81** Sugar snap peas

Figures 17.79–.81 © Randy Van Dam 2008

- **Sugar snap peas.** Sugar snap peas are a cross betwen English and snow peas. The plump, bright green pods are entirely edible and have a pleasing sweetness and crunch.

Serve them raw in salads or dress sautéed sugar snap peas with soy sauce, rice vinegar, and toasted sesame seeds. (See Figure 17.81.)

CONVENIENCE CORNER PRODUCT EXAMPLES

Vegetables: Canned, Fresh, and Frozen

Company	Website	Products
Carla	http://www.carlaspasta.com	2/5# Eggplant cutlet
Del Monte	http://www.delmonte.com	12/14.75 oz Carrot Puree
Frito Lay	http://www.fritolay.com	8/16 oz Potato Chip Kettle
Garden Burger	http://www.gardenburger.com	48/3.2 oz Vegetable Mal
Heinz	http://www.heinz.com	2/4# Chicken Wings, boneless
Lamb Weston	http://www.lambweston.com	6/2.5# Potato Wedge Red
McCain	http://www.mccainusa.com	200/.5 oz Elk Jerky Sticks 54/5 oz Potato Stuffed with Cheese
Mission	http://www.missionfoods.com	30# Corn Tortilla
Morning Star	http://www.morningstarfarms.com	48 ct Patty Vegetable 48/4.25 oz Patty Black Bean
Reser's	http://www.resers.com	2/8# Dip Spinach
Tantalizers	http://www.tantalizers.com	8/2# Onion Rings Steakhouse
Omstead	http://www.omsteadfoods.com	6/2 kg Onions Diced
General Mills	http://www.generalmills.com	6/2.25# Potato Scallop Dry
Bombay	http://www.bombaybrand.com	6/10 oz Bombay Egg Plant Pickled
Traina Foods	http://www.trainafoods.com	12/32 oz Tomato Sundried Halves

- **Sweet corn.** Purchase corn as fresh as you can find it, and cook it on the day you purchase it. Choose corn that is tightly wrapped in bright light green husks. The kernels, when pierced, should give out a milky juice. Tough skin indicates over-maturity. (See Figure 17.82a and Figure 17.82b.)

- **Yellow wax bean.** Wax beans can be light to deep yellow, and they have a subtle flavor. (See Figure 17.83.)

17.82a **Woman making fresh corn masa tamales in a Oaxacan food market**

Courtesy of Robert Garlough

17.83 **Yellow wax beans**

© Randy Van Dam 2008

17.82b **Sweet corn**

© Randy Van Dam 2008

Botanical Fruits Used as Vegetables

There are many vegetables that meet the definition of a fruit. An informal definition for a fruit is any seed-bearing pod from a flowering plant. There are several fruits that are treated like vegetables within the kitchen.

- **Artichokes.** Artichokes are the head of an edible thistle, and they come in many sizes. Look for deep green artichokes that are heavy for their size and that have tightly formed leaves that "squeak" when pressed. Avoid those with dry, brown, or split leaves. Refrigerate unwashed in a plastic bag for up to 4 days, and then boil, steam, or microwave. (See Figure 17.84.)

- **Cucumbers.** Cucumbers are long and round with green skin and pale greenish-white flesh. The seeds are edible, but those of more mature cucumbers can taste bitter and should be removed. Look for firm cucumbers with unblemished, brightly colored skins. Some cucumbers are coated with wax to prevent moisture loss; these should be washed thoroughly before using. Wrap unwashed cucumbers in plastic, or store in covered plastic bins, and refrigerate for up to 10 days.

  - **Armenian.** Armenian cucumbers, also called Turkish or Syrian cucumbers, have corduroy-like ribs and thin skin (no peeling required) and grow into long, twisted shapes.

  - **Common.** Common cucumbers are available year-round. Serve them sliced with a sprinkle of salt and fresh-cracked pepper. (See Figure 17.85.)

  - **English/burpless.** English cucumbers, also called hothouse or burpless cucumbers, are virtually seedless. They can grow up to 2 feet long and are usually sold shrink-wrapped in plastic. They add extra crunch to salads and sandwiches and can be used in any recipe that calls for cucumbers.

  - **Japanese.** Japanese cucumbers have tiny white bumps on their thin, green skin. They are crisp, mild, and sweet with fewer seeds than the common cucumber. Add them to salads, or make quick pickles by brining them overnight.

  - **Kirby.** Kirby cucumbers are small and perfect for pickling. They are firm and crunchy with a waxy green skin and tart flavor. Use Kirby cucumbers in homemade pickles or other recipes.

- **Eggplant.** Eggplants come in a range of whites, mauves, and purples although there are also orange, yellow, and green varieties. Choose firm, unblemished eggplants that are heavy for their size. They are highly perishable and grow bitter with age. Store them in a cool, dry place, and use within a few clays of purchase. Eggplants can be baked, broiled, or grilled. Eggplants are also tasty when fried, but they absorb more fat during cooking than most other vegetables. (See Figure 17.86a and Figure 17.86b.)

17.84 Artichokes

Figures 17.84–.85 © Randy Van Dam 2008

17.85 English, Kirby and Common cucumbers

17.86a Purple eggplant

Figures 17.86a–b © Randy Van Dam 2008

17.86b Italian and Chinese eggplant

- **Chinese eggplant.** Chinese eggplants are long and slim, and they may be white to lavender in color. They are delicately flavored with a meaty flesh and tender skin. Chinese eggplant is a good choice for stir-fries and sautéed dishes.

- **Japanese eggplant.** Japanese eggplants are long and thin with a light purple skin that darkens as it matures. They resemble Chinese eggplants in texture and flavor and can be used interchangeably with them.

- **Italian eggplant.** Italian eggplants, sometimes called baby eggplants, look like smaller versions of common purple, mauve, and white varieties. They are also slightly sweeter. Try substituting Italian eggplant for pasta in lasagna or grilling over charcoal.

- **Purple (American) eggplant.** Purple eggplant is the most common variety. Its dark purple skin is smooth and glossy, and it is typically large and pear shaped. Try adding slices to pizza.

- **White eggplant.** White eggplant is egg shaped, and the white skin is thick and tough. The flesh is firm with a delicate taste. It can be prepared in the same way as other varieties but may require less cooking time.

People, Places, Things

Where's the Heat?

Dr. Paul Bosland of the Chile Pepper Institute explains that there is no heat in chili seeds or pod walls. According to Shirley Corriher, author of Cookwise, all of the five capasainoid compounds are produced by, and located in, small bubble-like glands that lie between the placenta and pod wall. When the chili is cut, the knife pierces many of the pods and splatters the hot capasainoids throughout the inside of the pod. Each time the chili is cut, more of the heat is released.

- **Peppers.** There are two types of peppers in common culinary use: sweet peppers and chili peppers. Sweet peppers are generally larger and have a much milder, "sweet" taste. Chili peppers are smaller and have a more pointed shape than sweet peppers. Chili peppers are much hotter than sweet peppers and are not interchangeable with sweet peppers. Chili peppers add flavor and "heat" to many recipes.

  - **Fresh chili peppers.** Chili peppers may be large or small (general rule: the smaller, the hotter); plump or skinny; and yellow, green, red, or black. The fire in each comes from the capsaicin found in its veins and seeds. Remove those parts, and you automatically get a milder pepper. (To do that, slice off the stem, cut the pepper in half lengthwise, and use a spoon to scrape out the veins and seeds.)

BUYER'S NOTE *For the hottest peppers, it is recommended to wear latex gloves when handling deliveries and issues.*

  - **Anaheim.** Anaheim chilies are green or red and a slender 6 to 8 inches long. Their sweet flavor and small bite makes Anaheims a zesty addition to salsas and stuffed dishes such as chiles rellenos. (See Figure 17.87.)

  - **Arbol.** Arbol, also known as *bird's beak* or *rat's tail*, are narrow, curved chilies that start out green and mature to bright red. The arbol chili is very hot and is related to cayenne pepper. Be careful during preparation. (See Figure 17.88.)

  - **Cherry.** Cherry peppers, also called Hungarian cherry peppers, are small, round, and deep orange to bright red. They are mild to medium-hot and slightly sweet. Pickled cherry peppers often appear on antipasto platters, while fresh ones are useful in meat and poultry dishes. (See Figure 17.89.)

  - **Chilaca.** Fresh chilaca peppers are long and thin. They ripen from green to a deep chocolate brown, but they are rarely used fresh. (See Figure 17.90.)

  - **Cubanelle.** Cubanelle peppers, also known as *banana peppers*, are long and tapered. They can be substituted in recipes calling for Anaheim peppers. The cubanelle should be firm, smooth, and glossy. (See Figure 17.91.)

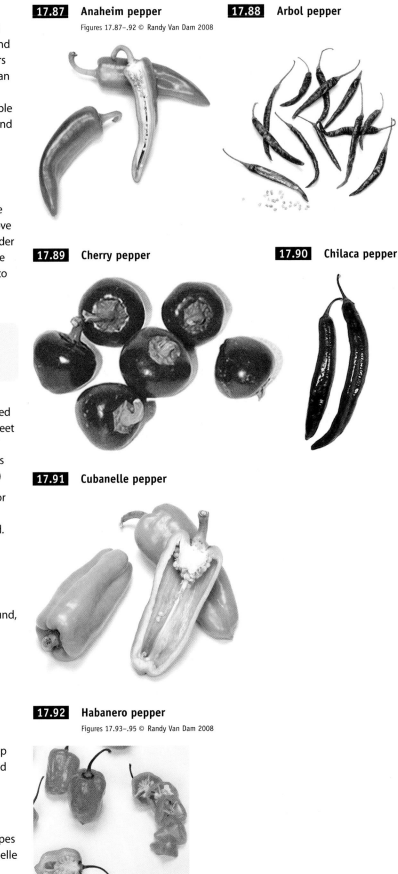

17.87 Anaheim pepper

Figures 17.87–.92 © Randy Van Dam 2008

17.88 Arbol pepper

17.89 Cherry pepper

17.90 Chilaca pepper

17.91 Cubanelle pepper

17.92 Habanero pepper

Figures 17.93–.95 © Randy Van Dam 2008

- **Fresno.** Fresno chilies start out a light green and mature to bright red. They are short and cone shaped with a jalapeno-like kick. Use them sparingly to season casseroles and savory dishes.

- **Habanero.** Habanero peppers top the Scoville Heat Unit scale, which measures pepper pungency, and should be handled cautiously. They are lantern shaped and come in shades of green, red, orange, and yellow. Their intensity is accompanied by a fruity, tropical flavor and apricot aroma, which makes them perfect for Jamaican jerk chicken and other Caribbean-style recipes. (See Figure 17.92.)

- **Hungarian wax.** Hungarian wax peppers are 3 to 5 inches long and not quite 2 inches across. This yellow chili may seem tame early in the season, but it will be fiery hot when fully mature. They are sometimes confused with banana peppers, which look much the same but are sweet and mild. Be sure you know which you are buying. (See Figure 17.93.)

- **Jalapeño.** Jalapeño chilies may be green or red, hot or very hot. They are about 2 inches long, rounded at the tip, and smooth skinned. They are a mainstay in U.S. kitchens, mostly because they're flavorful, widely available, and easy to prepare. Use fresh jalapeños in salsas, nachos, sauces, or vegetable dishes. (See Figure 17.94.)

- **Poblano.** Poblano chilies are a dark (almost black) green. They warm to a reddish-brown and sweeten when ripe. They grow up to 5 inches and are triangular in shape. Their rich flavor is spiked with varying amounts of heat. (See Figure 17.95.)

- **Serrano.** Serrano chilies are at first green, then scarlet, and finally yellow and very spicy when fully ripe. They are about an inch and a half long with a slightly pointed tip. (See Figure 17.96a and Figure 17.96b.)

- **Thai.** Thai "bird" chilies may be tiny (a little more than an inch long and quarter-inch around), but they are startlingly potent. (See Figure 17.97.)

- **Dried chili peppers.** Many times farmers would have an excess of fresh chili peppers that they were unable to sell. They would take their extra peppers to a drying shed, similar to a tobacco drying shed of the U.S.

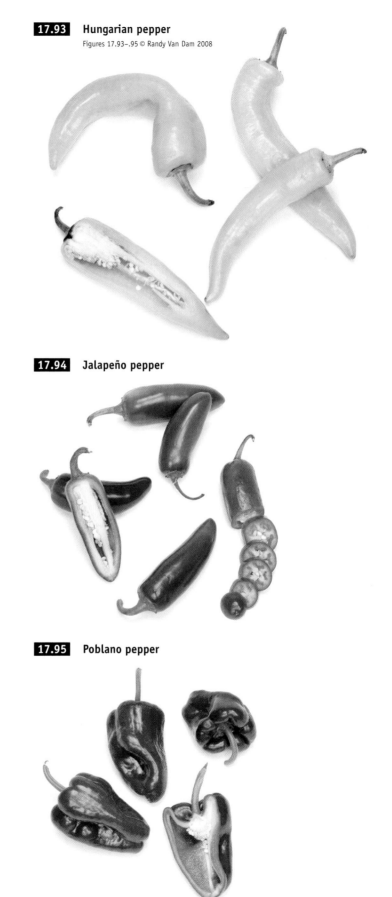

17.93 **Hungarian pepper**
Figures 17.93–.95 © Randy Van Dam 2008

17.94 **Jalapeño pepper**

17.95 **Poblano pepper**

17.96a **New serrano pepper growing on the bush**

Courtesy of Robert Garlough

17.96b **Serrano pepper**

© Randy Van Dam 2008

17.97 **Thai pepper**

Figures 17.97–.99 © Randy Van Dam 2008

17.98 **Ancho pepper**

17.99 **Chipotle pepper**

southeast, and allow their peppers to dry. Oftentimes, they would also smoke the peppers (for example, the *mulato* is a smoked *poblano* chili) in a drying shed to hurry the process and to impart a smoke flavor to the dried pepper.

- **Ancho.** When poblano chilies are dried, they are called ancho chilies and are the sweetest of the dried varieties. They are triangular shaped, very dark brownish red, and wrinkled. Ancho chilies are the most commonly used chilies in Mexican cuisine. They have a wonderful earthy flavor. They range from mild to medium in heat. They are the most popular chili used for commercial chili powder. (See Figure 17.98.)

- **Chipotle.** Dried jalapeños, called chipotles, are a standard ingredient in Southwestern and Mexican recipes. (See Figure 17.99.)

- **Guajillo.** The color is a brick red with deep burgundy tones, and the skin is smooth. The guajillo is the most common chili in Mexico after the ancho. (See Figure 17.100.)

- **Mulato.** Mulato chilies are a smoked, dried poblano. They are large, flat, and wrinkled. The mulato is one of the several chilies essential to Mexican cookery.

- **Pasilla.** Dried chilacas, called pasilla peppers, are the more common use of the chilaca. They may be medium to very hot and add a rich and fruity complexity to sauces. (See Figure 17.101.)

- **Fresh sweet peppers.** Sweet peppers elong to the same capsicum family as chili peppers, but their flesh is mild and sweet, rather than spicy hot. They add crunch, flavor, and a rainbow of colors to salads, crudités platters, stir-fries, sandwiches, soups, and casseroles. They can be grilled, roasted, steamed, sautéed, braised, or stuffed with savory fillings.

  - **Bell (green, red, yellow, orange).** Bell peppers may be green, red, yellow, orange, or even purple. Immature red peppers are green and then turn color as they ripen. Bell peppers are shaped like bells with a thick, crunchy flesh. (See Figure 17.102.)

  - **Sweet banana.** Sweet banana peppers are aptly named as they look like a long, yellow banana. Be careful: they also resemble the hotter Hungarian wax chilies that are sometimes sold as banana chilies or banana peppers.

17.100 Guajillo pepper

Figures 17.100–.101 © Randy Van Dam 2008

17.101 Pasilla pepper

People, Place, Things

Scoville Heat Units

In 1912, pharmacist William Scoville invented the Scoville Heat Unit (SHU) scale to assess the heat level of chili peppers. In this somewhat subjective test, chili "tasters" sampled a chile and recorded its heat level. The chili was then diluted in the laboratory until the taster couldn't taste any more *capsaicin*, the compound that gives chilies their heat. The Scoville unit is a measure based on the amount of dilution; the higher the Scoville unit, the hotter the chili. Today, more sophisticated chemical tests are often used to test heat, but the results are still called Scoville units. The Chile Pepper Institute at the University of New Mexico rates orange habanero chilies a fiery 210,000 Scoville units and a bell pepper 0 Scoville units. Other chilies generally fall somewhere between those

Red, yellow, green, and orange bell peppers
© Randy Van Dam 2008

TABLE 17.5 Scoville Chile Pepper Heat Ratings

Heat Rating in Scoville Units	Pepper Varieties
350,000–1,000,000	Red Savina Habanero, Indian Tezpur
100,000–350,000	Habanero, Scotch Bonnet
50,000–100,000	Chiltecpin, Red Amazon, Santaka, Thai
30,000–50,000	Aji, Cayenne, Chilipiquin, Tabasco
15,000–30,000	Chile Arbol
5,000–15,000	Chipolte, Serrano, Yellow Wax
2,500–5,000	Chipolte, Mirasol
1,500–2,500	Cascabel, Poblano
1,000–1,500	Anaheim, Ancho, Pasilla
100–1,000	Cherry, New Mexico, Pepperoncini
0–100	Pimento, Sweet Banana, Sweet Bell

- **Squash.** In addition to the fruit, other parts of the plant are edible. Squash seeds can be eaten directly, ground into paste, or (particularly for pumpkins) pressed for vegetable oil. The blossoms are an important part of Native American cooking and are also used in many other parts of the world.

  - **Summer squash.** They are consumed almost immediately and require little or no cooking.

    - **Chayote.** Chayote looks something like a furrowed, pale green pear. The white flesh surrounds a single seed and has a zucchini-cucumber-apple flavor. They can be split and baked like acorn squash, sautéed in butter, or used raw in salads. (See Figure 17.103a and Figure 17.103b.)

    - **Pattypan.** Pattypan squash is a summer squash notable for its small size and its round and shallow shape. Pattypan comes in yellow, green, and white varieties. The squash is most tender when relatively immature; it is generally served when it is no more than 2 to 3 inches in diameter. (See Figure 17.104.)

    - **Yellow crookneck.** Yellow crookneck squash is a variety of summer squash with bumpy, yellow skin and sweet flesh. (See Figure 17.105.)

    - **Zucchini (courgette).** It can be either yellow or green and generally has a similar shape to a ridged cucumber. Zucchini are traditionally picked when very immature. Mature zucchini can be as long as 3 feet, but then they are often fibrous and not useable. (See Figure 17.106.)

  - **Winter squash.** Winter squashes are harvested at maturity and stored in a cool place for eating later. They generally require longer cooking time than summer squashes.

    - **Acorn.** Acorn is a winter squash with ridges and sweet, yellow-orange flesh. The most common variety is usually dark green. As the name suggests, its shape resembles that of an acorn. (See Figure 17.107.)

    - **Buttercup.** Buttercup squash are a type of turban squash. They grow to about the size of a salad plate and have a sweet, orange flesh that tastes a bit like a sweet potato. Their dark green shells are flecked with gray; there is also an orange variety. (See Figure 17.108.)

    - **Butternut.** Butternut has a sweet, nutty taste that is similar to pumpkin or sweet potato. It has yellow skin and orange flesh. When ripe, it turns increasingly deep orange and becomes sweeter and richer. (See Figure 17.109.)

    - **Calabaza.** Calabaza, also known as a *West Indian Pumpkin*, is often sold already cut into chunks, and the bright orange flesh is sweet. Look for unblemished squash that are heavy for their size

 Chayote squash

© Randy Van Dam 2008

17.103b **Chayote hanging from a tree**

Courtesy of Robert Garlough

17.104   Pattypan squash

Figures 17.104–.107 © Randy Van Dam 2008

17.105   Yellow crookneck squash

17.106   Zucchini squash

17.107   Acorn squash

and store in a cool, dark place for up to 6 weeks. Wrap cut squash in plastic and refrigerate for a week. Calabaza can be substituted for butternut or other winter squash. (See Figure 17.110.)

- **Hubbard.** Hubbard squash is typically found in a tear-drop shape. It is often used as a cheaper replacement for pumpkins.

- **Pumpkin.** Store pumpkins at room temperature for up to a month or in the refrigerator for 3 months. The pumpkin varies greatly in form: sometimes nearly globular but more generally oblong or ovoid. The rind is smooth and variable in color.

- **Spaghetti.** When raw, the flesh is solid and similar to other raw squash; when cooked, the flesh falls away from the fruit in ribbons or strands like spaghetti. It tastes nothing like spaghetti, however; it has a slight sweetness and, if not overcooked, is crunchy and watery like cucumber. Spaghetti squash can be baked, boiled, or steamed, and served with sauce as for pasta. (See Figure 17.111.)

- **Turban.** Turban squash has a hard, bumpy shell that is bright orange with touches of green. There is a turban-shaped cap on the blossom end, hence the name. The finely textured orange flesh may taste mild to sweet. (See Figure 17.112.)

17.108 Buttercup squash

Figures 17.108–.112 © Randy Van Dam 2008

17.109 Butternut squash

17.110 Calabaza squash

17.111 Spaghetti squash

17.112 Turban squash

- **Tomatillo.** Tomatillos look like green cherry tomatoes wrapped in papery husks. They are also called Mexican green tomatoes. Select firm tomatillos with tight-fitting husks; refrigerate in a paper bag for up to a month. Tomatillos have a lemon-apple-herb flavor that works well in a variety of Mexican and Southwestern dishes. (See Figure 17.113.)

- **Tomatoes.** Choose firm, smooth tomatoes with good color and no wrinkles or cracks. Avoid soft or bruised fruits, as they are likely to be watery, flavorless, and will spoil rapidly. Fresh tomatoes are best bought at the end of summer, when local vine-ripened tomatoes are abundant. Overripe tomatoes should be stored in the refrigerator, where they will keep for 2 or 3 days. For the fullest flavor, take them out of the refrigerator about 30 minutes before serving. Tomatoes should be washed just before use. Green tomatoes can be ripened slowly at room temperature and will keep for several weeks away from direct sunlight.

  An *heirloom* is a vintage that perseveres because it has qualities such as size, coloring, and taste that are not common among modern varieties. Most heirloom tomatoes have not been cross-bred, so they don't usually have much disease resistance.

  A *hybrid* is a variety created by cross-breeding different varieties. The advantage of hybrids is their ability to resist diseases.

  - **Beefsteak tomatoes.** Beefsteaks are the very biggest tomatoes. Beefsteaks hold together well when sliced, which, together with their large size, makes them ideal for sandwiches. They also cook down well for sauces. (See Figure 17.114a and Figure 17.114b.)

17.114a **Vine-ripened tomatoes**

17.114b **Hydroponic tomatoes**

17.113 **Tomatillo**

Figures 17.113–.114b © Randy Van Dam 2008

- **Cherry tomatoes.** Known to most as the small round tomatoes that accompany a garden salad, the cherry tomato plant produces a cherry-sized (or slightly larger) fruit. (See Figure 17.115.)

- **Grape tomatoes.** Grape tomatoes are smaller than cherry tomatoes and are an excellent size for salads. They usually have sweet intense flavor. (See Figure 17.116.)

- **Heirloom.** Heirloom tomato varieties can be found in a wide variety of colors, shapes, flavors, and sizes. (See Figure 17.117.)

- **Plum tomatoes.** Plum tomatoes have thick flesh and reduced amounts of pulp. They are commonly used for making ragu, marinara, pizza, and spaghetti sauces. (See Figure 17.118.)

- **Avocado.** A ripe avocado will yied to gentle pressure when held in the palm of the hand and squeezed. The flesh turns brown quickly after exposure to air. To prevent this, lime or lemon juice can be added to avocados after they are peeled. The avocado is very popular in vegetarian cuisine and is also known as *avocado pear* or *alligator pear.* (See Figure 17.119.)

17.117   Heirloom tomatoes

17.115   Vine-ripened ripened cherry tomatoes

Figures 17.115–.119 © Randy Van Dam 2008

17.118   Plum tomatoes

17.116   Grape tomatoes

17.119   Haas avocado

Michael Whitman, CEC

Place of Birth: San Bernardino, California

Courtesy Michael Whitman

Educational Background and Work Experience

After starting in the dishroom, as most talented chefs have, Mike Whitman finally earned his chance to work in a local fine dining restaurant under a British chef. After gaining a solid foundation in the kitchen, he then headed off to the Caribbean to work a 6-month season on a charter sailboat, working both as a private chef and all-around deck hand. Whitman returned to West Michigan to apprentice under his mentor, Executive Chef Robert Schafer, while working at the Thornapple Village Inn, in Ada, Michigan. All the while, he worked on his AAAS degree from Grand Rapids Junior College. That position led to a job as sous chef at the celebrated 1913 Room, at the new Amway Grand Plaza Hotel in Grand Rapids, Michigan. From there, he worked at the haute cuisine restaurant Gibsons as its sous chef. Whitman later returned to the Thornapple Village Inn, this time as its new executive chef. Years later, Chef Whitman's vast experience and interest in seafood landed him a sales representative position for Triar Seafood, out of Hollywood, Florida. After 5 years with Triar, Whitman returned to the kitchen as the executive chef of the prestigious Kent Country Club and began taking classes for his bachelor's degree in post-secondary technical education from Ferris State University. After many years at Kent Country Club, he moved to the Wuskowhan Players Club in West Olive, Michigan, and he also began teaching culinary arts classes part time for the Hospitality Education Department at Grand Rapids Community College (GRCC). Chef Whitman, who is both respected and appreciated by his students, finally completed his bachelor's degree from FSU after 7 years of dogged determination to become a full-time chef-instructor. Chef Whitman now proudly teaches food purchasing and other hospitality courses for Grand Rapids Community College.

Memberships and Career Highlights

Whitman has had many special moments in his career, such as winning medals in

It Happened to Me...

"As Executive Chef of a private club, I had a dish on the menu that included sautéed morels as a component. My source could provide fresh morels into August, from the slopes of mountains on the West Coast. The dish was hugely popular and brought a great contribution to sales, so I was hesitant to take it off the menu in the fall. My supplier recommended using dried morels and quoted me some prices on grades A, B, C, from both domestic and foreign sources. I went with a foreign "A" grade and eagerly awaited my first shipment. Upon arrival, I visually inspected them and noticed some 'rattled' a bit when handled. I discovered a pebble inside one of the caps and upon further inspection found several more in the pound of dried morels. I mentioned this to my supplier, who said he had heard that from several chefs and had since eliminated that source. It seems the pickers would place a pebble in a few mushrooms per pound, and when dried, the pebbles would remain and be weighed along with the mushrooms. At my cost of $80 per pound, a few pebbles can add up soon to real money. I also discovered the mushrooms were dried over a dung fire imparting a very 'special' bouquet when rehydrated and cooked. I requested and was given full credit and have only used domestic ever since. The experience reinforced the fact that most often, price follows quality."

culinary salon competition and having his restaurant, the Thornapple Village Inn, being named Restaurant of the Year. An active member of his local American Culinary Federation (ACF) chapter, including serving in the capacity of committee chair and chapter president, he was named ACF Greater Grand Rapids Chef of the Year in 2000 and Chef Professional of the Year in 2002. For his many contributions to the West Michigan hospitality industry, Chef Whitman was inducted into the Hospitality Hall of Fame of GRCC, an honor only presented twenty times in the 85-year history of the college. Even after all of these proud events, his special moment was being a part of the inaugural planning committee that started "Chefs for Kids," a very successful event that annually raises tens of thousands of dollars to feed hungry children in his community.

Passions with the Food Service Industry

"This industry is unique in that, on a daily basis, we get to engage all of our senses, as well as use our hands and minds to create wonderful food from the earth's bounty. Then we get to serve it, bringing pleasure to different guests every day! Where else can you find that kind of satisfaction?"

Advice to a Chef or Buyer

"After negotiating the best prices, cost all recipes with care to detail, and make portion control a priority. Train, train, train your staff to be mindful of waste. Every dollar lost to spoilage or poor handling costs you approximately $3, or more, in lost sales. Develop strong relationships with your purveyors, learn their strengths and weaknesses, and play to their strengths. Always support local suppliers and agriculture, as much as possible!"

Key Words and Concepts

---

greens   micro-greens   Scoville Heat Units   vegetable

Chapter in Review

The following exercises are provided to help the reader understand and apply the contents of this chapter. They may be completed individually or in a classroom environment.

REVIEW QUESTIONS

a. Define the term *vegetable*.

b. Explain how some vegetables are considered fruits and some fruits are treated as vegetables.

c. Define the differences between heirloom and hybrid vegetables.

d. Discuss the creation and application of Scoville Units as they apply to chili peppers.

INDIVIDUAL ACTIVITIES

a. **Web based:** Research local farmers, co-ops, or farmer's markets that will sell fresh vegetables to food service operators.

b. **Experiential:** Conduct a blind tasting of different vegetable groups, such as leaf vegetables, to distinguish their flavor characteristics.

c. **Critical thinking:** Identify vegetables that are used like fruits and fruits that are used like vegetables.

GROUP ACTIVITIES

a. **Lab experience:** Conduct a product identification quiz with different vegetable groups, such as leafy vegetables, pod and seed vegetables, root and tuberous vegetables, chilies, and fungi.

b. **Classroom action:** Divide the class into teams and have them develop five appetizers, five side dishes, five salads, five entrees, and five desserts or sorbets where vegetables are the only, or primary, ingredient. Create a point system for the use of highly unusual vegetables, creative use of vegetables, and artistic use of vegetables. Apply bonus points for items that only use vegetables and seasonings.

CHAPTER

18

Eggs, Dairy, and Cheese

"A meal without cheese is like a beautiful woman who lacks an eye."

JEAN ANTHELME BRILLAT-SAVARIN

After reading this chapter, you will be able to:

◎ Define the terms *eggs* and *dairy*.

◎ Identify the parts to an egg.

◎ List egg sizes and the weight of the average egg.

◎ Identify the most commonly used dairy products.

◎ Summarize the butterfat content of dairy products.

◎ Explain the process for making butter.

◎ List the main varieties of cheese, and provide examples of each.

◎ Review the proper procedures for purchasing and storing different egg and dairy products.

Introduction

Eggs and dairy products have sustained humankind long before history was recorded. According to the *Encyclopedia of Food and Culture*, "Eggs have been known to, and enjoyed by, humans for many centuries. Jungle fowl were domesticated in India by 3200 B.C. Records from China and Egypt show that fowl were domesticated and laying eggs for human consumption around 1400 B.C., and there is archaeological evidence for egg consumption dating back to the Neolithic age. The Romans found egg-laying hens in England, Gaul, and among the Germans. The first domesticated fowl reached North America with the second voyage of Columbus in 1493." (Katz, 2003, p. 558)

Dairy products have been used and enjoyed as long as humans have had access to milk. Most common dairy products are made from cow's milk although some products are made from other animals' milk. Milk and cheese are the most popular dairy products. Milk also serves as the primary ingredient for cheese.

Eggs

Eggs are packed with protein; in fact, eggs are the standard on which other protein sources are measured. Eggs are a culinary staple with many uses in the kitchen. They combine with many other staples or stand alone equally well.

PARTS OF THE EGG

The egg is composed of four main parts: *the shell, the membranes, the albumen,* and *the yolk.* (See Figure 18.1 and Table 18.1.)

- **Shell.** The eggshell is the porous covering that protects the egg, and its multiple tiny pores allow air and water into the egg. The shell is a barrier against germs and controls the humidity of the egg. Eggshells are often coated with an odorless mineral oil that partially clogs the pores, thus prolonging freshness.

- **Membranes.** The shell membranes are made up of two or three thin layers of protein fibers that cling to the shell and provide additional protection against undesirable elements such as mold and bacteria.

- **Albumen.** The albumen, or "white," consists of 87 percent water and 12.5 percent albumin, a protein substance; it represents two-thirds of the total weight of the egg.

- **Yolk.** The yolk is centered in the albumen. The yolk is where the embryo would be attached. The yolk contains most of the egg's protein and nutrients.

BUYING AND STORING

After they have been laid, eggs are examined to determine their quality. Following inspection, the eggs are washed, graded, and packaged. When buying eggs, make sure that the shells are not cracked, and choose refrigerated eggs, as they will stay fresh much longer. Always check the side of the carton for the expiration date, which indicates when the quality will deteriorate. The "best before" date is reliable only if the eggs are stored at an adequate temperature (below 40°F/4°C) and degree of humidity (70 to 80 percent). Eggs that are left out above this temperature spoil many times faster than eggs stored in proper conditions. Expiration dates are generally 4 to 5 weeks after packaging.

The criteria for grading eggs differ from one country to another. In the United States, eggs are graded AA, A, B, and C, with grade AA being the best quality. Eggs graded C are used in the food processing industry only. (See Figure 18.2.)

Eggs are also classified according to their weight per dozen: a dozen "small" eggs weigh at least 18 ounces (540 grams), "medium" eggs weigh at least 21 ounces (600 grams), "large" eggs at least 24 ounces (720 grams), and "extra-large" eggs 27 ounces (810 grams). The smallest eggs ("peewee") weigh a minimum of 15 ounces (450 grams), and the largest ("jumbo") weigh a minimum of 30 ounces (900 grams) per dozen. (See Table 18.2 and Figure 18.3a.)

Eggs left out at room temperature will lose as much freshness in 1 day as eggs that are properly stored (at 40°F/4°C and 70 to 80 percent humidity) will lose in a week. The best place to keep eggs is in the refrigerator, where they will stay fresh for over a month; store them in their carton or in a covered container to prevent the loss of humidity and the absorption of odors. Place eggs with the pointed end downward to prevent compression of the air chamber and displacement of the yolk.

Avoid washing eggs, as this removes their protective layer and allows germs to penetrate; if they are dirty, wipe them with a dry cloth. Place unused raw whites or yolks in a covered container in the refrigerator, where they will keep for 4 days (cover the yolks with cold water to prevent them from drying out, and simply drain them before using them). Slightly beaten whole eggs or egg whites can be frozen for 4 months; yolks can be frozen on their own or beaten with whites. Never freeze eggs in their shell, as the cold causes them to crack. Hard-boiled eggs will keep in the refrigerator for a week. (See Figure 18.3b.)

18.1 The composition of an egg

Shell
- Outer covering of egg, composed largely of calcium carbonate
- May be white or brown depending on breed of chicken
- Color does not effect egg quality, cooking characteristics, nutritive value or shell thickness

Vitelline (Yolk) Membrane
- Holds egg yolk contents

Chalazae
- Twisted, cordlike strands of egg white
- Anchor yolk in center of egg
- Prominent chalazae indicate freshness

Thin Albumen (White)
- Nearest to the shell
- Spreads around thick white of high-quality egg

Thick Albumen (White)
- Major source of egg riboflavin and protein
- Stands higher and spreads less in higher-grade eggs
- Thins and becomes indistinguishable from thin white in lower-grade eggs

Yolk
- Yellow portion of egg
- Color varies with feed of the hen, but doesn't indicate nutritive content
- Major source of egg vitamins, minerals, and fat
- Germinal Disc

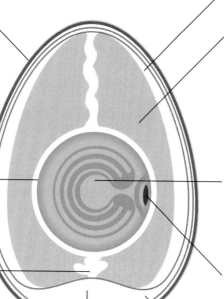

Air Cell
- Pocket of air formed at large end of egg
- Caused by contraction of the contents during cooling after laying
- Increases in size as egg ages

Shell Membranes
- Two membranes—inner and outer shell membranes—surround the albumen
- Provide protective barrier against bacterial penetration
- Air cell forms between these two membranes

TABLE 18.1 USDA Standards for Quality of Individual Shell Eggs

Courtesy USDA

Quality Factor	AA Quality	A Quality	B Quality
Shell	Clean. Unbroken. Practically normal.	Clean. Unbroken. Practically normal.	Clean to slightly stained. Unbroken. Abnormal.
Air cell	1/8 inch or less in depth. Unlimited movement and free or bubbly.	3/16 inch or less in depth. Unlimited movement and free or bubbly.	Over 3/16 inch in depth. Unlimited movement and free or bubbly.
White	Clear. Firm.	Clear. Reasonably firm.	Weak and watery. Small blood and meat spots present.
Yolk	Outline slightly defined. Practically free from defects.	Outline fairly well defined. Practically free from defects.	Outline plainly visible. Enlarged and flattened. Clearly visible germ development but not blood. Other serious defects.

18.2 Quality levels of eggs

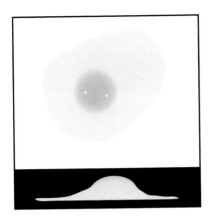
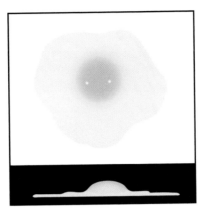
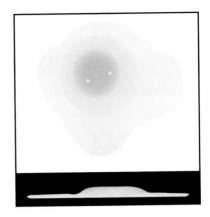

TABLE 18.2 Egg Size Chart

U.S. Weight Classes, Consumer Grades	Minimum net Weight per		Minimum Quantity of Product Approximately the Amount in One Dozen Eggs						
	Case (30 doz.)	Dozen	Liquid or Frozen			Dried			
	Pounds	Ounces	Whole Pounds	Yolk Pounds	Albumen Pounds	Whole Pounds	Yolk Pounds	Albumen Pounds	Pounds
Shell eggs:									
Jumbo	56.0	30	1.88	1.64	0.71	0.93	0.42	0.32	0.12
Extra large	50.5	27	1.69	1.48	0.64	0.84	0.38	0.29	0.11
Large	45.0	24	1.50	1.32	0.57	0.75	0.34	0.26	0.10
Medium	39.5	21	1.31	1.16	0.50	0.66	0.30	0.23	0.09
Small	34.0	18	1.12	1.00	0.43	0.57	0.26	0.20	0.08
Peewee	28.0	15	0.94	0.80	0.35	0.47	0.21	0.16	0.06
Avg. weight									
Sold at retail	47.0	25	1.57	1.38	0.60	0.78	0.35	0.27	0.10

People, Places, Things

Checking the Freshness of Eggs

To check the freshness of an egg, place the egg in a bowl or pan with enough cold water to cover the egg:

- If the egg lies on its side on the bottom, the air cell within is small and it is very fresh.

- If the egg stands up and bobs on the bottom, the air cell is larger and it isn't quite as fresh.

- If the egg floats on the surface, it should be discarded.

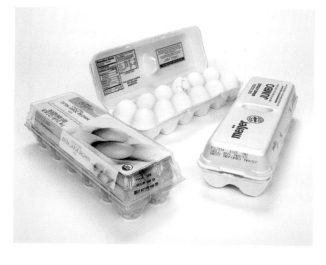

Dairy

There are more than thirty main products made from milk (see Figure 18.4a, Figure 18.4b, Figure 18.4c, and Figure 18.4d). The mostly commonly used dairy products include:

- **Milk.** Milk is primarily water, but it does contain significant amounts of saturated fat, protein, and calcium.

- **Butter.** Butter is made by churning milk or cream. Butter is used in cooking, as a spread, and as a condiment. Butter consists of butterfat surrounding tiny droplets of water and milk proteins. The most common form of butter is cow's milk, but it can also be made from the milk of other mammals.

- **Casein.** Casein is the primary protein found in fresh milk and cheese. As it exists in milk, it is a source of calcium.

- **Yogurt.** Yoghurt, or **yogurt**, is a dairy product produced by bacterial fermentation. It can be made from any milk, but cow's milk is primarily used. The fermentation of lactose produces lactic acid, which gels to give yoghurt its texture and characteristic tang.

- **Gelato.** Gelato contains 4 to 8 percent butterfat. Gelato is usually made with whole milk, which is 3 to 4 percent

18.4a **Assorted milk with varying milkfat percentages (note the different packaging sizes)**
© Randy Van Dam 2008. Courtesy Meijer, Inc.

Instant and condensed milk
© Randy Van Dam 2008

 Evaporated milk
© Randy Van Dam 2008

 Reddi-wip
© Randy Van Dam 2008

butterfat, and often cream is added to increase creaminess. Unlike ice cream, gelato ingredients are not mixed together, so it melts faster than ice cream.

- **Ice cream.** Modern industrially produced ice cream is made from a mixture of ingredients and air incorporated during the stirring process. Generally, less expensive ice creams contain lower quality ingredients and more air is incorporated, sometimes as much as 50 percent of the final volume. Premium ice creams have between 3 percent and 15 percent air. Because ice cream is sold by volume, it is economically advantageous for producers to reduce the density of the product.

- **Other.** There are other lesser known ethnic forms of dairy products made around the world, such as *airag*, *kajmak*, and *kephir*.

BUYING AND STORING

In the United States, there are federal standards for butterfat content of dairy products.

Nondairy and Non-Bovine Milk

In addition to the milk that is available from cows, there are a number of other products offered in the market, such as:

- **Nondairy.** This includes milk made from soya, rice, oat, and coconut products (Figure 18.5a).

- **Non-bovine mammals.** This includes milk from goats, buffalo, and sheep (Figure 18.5b).

CULTURED DAIRY PRODUCTS

Milk or cream that has been thickened by heat or sharpened by bacterial cultures, or both, becomes buttermilk, sour cream, or yogurt. These dairy products have a unique role in the kitchen. All three can be used as the basis for dips and dressings, can be used in cake batters or bread dough, and can greatly enhance many soups. Cuisines the world over use cultured dairy products in a number of ways. Sour cream is used extensively in the cuisines of Central and Eastern Europe. Yogurt is used in both sweet and savory dishes throughout India and the Middle East. And in North America, buttermilk flavors many baked goods or serves as the foundation for fruit-flavored drinks.

USING CULTURED DAIRY PRODUCTS IN COOKING

Cultured dairy products are difficult to use in cooking because they curdle when overheated, and, for this reason, they must never be boiled. For best results, always add them at the end of cooking time, and stir in by spoonfuls. Alternatively, a teaspoon or so of cornstarch can be stirred in before heating. This will help to stabilize these delicate ingredients and reduce the risk of curdling.

18.5a **Soy milk**
© Randy Van Dam 2008

18.5b **Rice milk and goat milk**
© Randy Van Dam 2008

Buttermilk

A by-product of butter making, this is the liquid that is drained from the churned milk after the fat has coagulated to form butter. Old-fashioned **buttermilk** was simply pasteurized before packaging, and it had a rich, full flavor.

Nowadays, a culture is added, and it is left to ferment for about 12 to 14 hours at a very low temperature, giving modern-day buttermilk a more acidic tang. Buttermilk marries well with the sweetness of fruits such as pears and cherries. In some recipes, where sharpness is welcome, buttermilk can be substituted for ordinary milk; try making fruit custards or flans with buttermilk. In baking, it is best to use recipes that are specially adapted for buttermilk because the quantities of yeast or baking powder are calculated to accommodate the acidity of buttermilk. (See Figure 18.6.)

Clotted Cream

Clotted cream is one of the gems of Britain's culinary heritage, made from the rich milk of Devon and Cornwall. It is so thick that you can literally stand your spoon up in it. Traditionally, it is made by slowly heating great bowls of creamy milk to a temperature of 176–185°F (80–85°C), holding it at that temperature 30 minutes or so, and then cooling it. The heating gives the cream its "cooked" flavor and prolongs shelf life. Clotted cream has a butterfat content of 55 percent or more.

Kaymak (Kaimaki, Eishta)

The British are not the only makers of clotted cream. Middle Eastern kaymak is another "cooked" cream, made not from cow's milk but from sheep or water buffalo's milk, both of which have very high fat contents, perfect for cream making. Though the method is similar to clotted cream, the end result has a distinctive flavor and can be even thicker than Cornish clotted cream.

18.6 **Buttermilk**
© Randy Van Dam 2008

18.7 **Crème fraiche**
© Randy Van Dam 2008

skim milk and light cream, a richer version of buttermilk. It has a relatively low butterfat content, around 10 percent, similar to half-and-half. When used in cooking, it should be treated like yogurt and never overheated.

Crème Fraiche

Crème fraiche ("fresh cream" in French) is the standard French cream, thick and voluptuous (Figure 18.7). It is a cultured cream, similar to sour cream, but richer with a minimum 30 percent butterfat content. The high fat content means that it can be added to sauces with little fear of curdling.

Mixing heavy or whipping cream with half its volume of sour cream in a small pan produces the closest substitute for crème fraiche. Heat very gently, stirring constantly, to a temperature of 85°F (29°C) or until it is warm but not hot. Do not let it boil. As you heat it, you can see it thickening. Remove from the heat and scrape it into a bowl. Cover loosely, and keep in a warm place for about 8 hours. Store in the refrigerator once it has thickened. Buttermilk or yogurt can be used instead of sour cream.

Almost as good, and slightly cheaper too, is whipping cream "ripened" with lemon juice; to every quart of whipping cream, add 2 tablespoons (scant) lemon juice. Stir well, and let stand, loosely covered, in a warm place for 4 to 6 hours until thickened. Keep in the refrigerator.

Smatana

Russian smatana is sour cream mixed with sweet cream to give thick, lightly sour cream used in sauces and soups. In the United States, the smatana we buy is cultured but made with

Sour Cream

While sour cream is, in effect, sour, it is not ordinary cream that becomes sharp over time. Commercial sour cream is made from a homogenized cream that has about the same fat content as light cream, plus a bacterial culture. As with buttermilk, it is the culture that imparts the tang. Especially popular in the cuisines of Central and Eastern Europe, sour cream is essential in the classic Russian dish beef stroganoff and beet soup, or borscht, which is common to many cuisines of the area.

Sour cream can be used like ordinary heavy cream to enrich meat or game casseroles, sauces, and soups; sour cream with chopped fresh chives is the classic baked potato topping. Sour cream also provides the ideal base for dipping sauces and salad dressings. A popular addition to chocolate cakes, cheesecakes, and coffee cakes, sour cream adds a pleasant tang and texture. (See Figure 18.8.)

French-Style Yogurt

French-style yogurt is generally set, and it is made from low-fat homogenized milk. As a rule, set yogurts can be used for cooking, although they are best appreciated when eaten in their natural state, with vanilla sugar or enhanced with honey or fruit compotes. To avoid the crunchy texture of superfine sugar, use confectioners' sugar because it dissolves more easily.

18.8 **Assorted sour creams (left to right: whole milk, light, fat free)**
© Randy Van Dam 2008

Greek Sheep's Yogurt

Greek yogurt is made with sheep's milk, which has a higher fat content than cow's milk and a sweetish flavor. The bacterial culture used to make yogurt in Greece is not the same as those used for commercial yogurt making in the United States. Thick Greek yogurt is good enough to serve as a dessert, with honey or homemade jam and perhaps a sprinkling of toasted nuts or coconut flakes. Use it in savory dishes as well. Like all yogurts, it will curdle if overheated, so, to incorporate it into a hot sauce, it must be added when the sauce has cooled enough to avoid danger, or it must be stabilized. Yogurt drinks, like the Indian lassi, and iced soups are better if made with sheep's milk yogurt.

Strained Yogurt

This is concentrated yogurt with some of the watery whey removed to make it thicker and richer. The more whey is drained off, the thicker the texture and the more concentrated the flavor. Any yogurt can be strained, but better yogurt produces a better end result. Strain a yogurt that is fairly acidic in the first place, and you will get an even sharper taste. Greek strained yogurts are particularly good because the original yogurt has only the mildest acidity, which concentrates down to a welcome hint of sharpness to balance the richness.

The Greek strained yogurt sold commercially, made from sheep's milk or cow's milk, still has a spoonable consistency, so it should be treated as a more luxurious version of yogurt. (See Figure 18.9.)

People, Places, Things

How to Strain Yogurt

To strain yogurt, place in a sieve lined with a double layer of cheesecloth and leave to drip over a bowl, or gather up the ends of the cheesecloth, knot, and suspend over the sink, until the yogurt is as thick as you want it. Exact timing will depend on the thickness of the yogurt, but allow at least 3 to 4 hours for a thick but spoonable consistency or a minimum of 6 hours, preferably 8 or overnight, for a strained yogurt with the consistency of soft cream cheese.

18.9 **Assorted yogurts (left to right: whole milk, low fat, nonfat)**
© Randy Van Dam 2008

Ricotta

"Ricotta" means recooked. The first "cooking" is part of the process of making other cheeses, when the curds are separated from the whey by heating. The curds are trundled off to make whatever cheese it happens to be, while the whey is reheated (the second "cooking") to a temperature of around 176°F (80°C). Granules of white ricotta rise to the surface and are skimmed out into a basket or, more likely these days, a perforated plastic bowl. The basket or bowl gives the cheese its characteristic pudding-basin shape. Ricotta is a neutral cheese that can be served alone but normally is used as a filling for many dishes.

Fresh ricotta, if not used in a few days, develops an aftertaste and should be discarded. Always purchase fresh ricotta from a reputable source and only on the day you intend to use it. The packaged ricotta sold in little tubs is less desirable than fresh.

Ricotta *affumicata* is lightly salted, smoked, and firmer but still soft. Ricotta *salata* is salted—a matured ricotta that is hard and suitable for grating. (See Figure 18.10.)

Mascarpone

Mascarpone is a very rich Italian cream cheese; the fat content is extremely high (around 90 percent). It is made from

18.10 **Assorted ricotta (left to right: whole milk, part skim, low fat)**
© Randy Van Dam 2008

fresh cream, heated, and whipped to give it a velvety smooth texture. The flavor is sweetish but basically neutral. It is usually used to make desserts, often beaten with egg yolks and a drop of something alcoholic, although it occasionally finds its way into savory dishes, often as a sauce for pasta. In Italy, it may come in blocks wrapped in cheesecloth, but in North America, it is packaged in plastic tubs, as sold through food service distributors and many specialty stores and supermarkets. (See Figure 18.11.)

 Mascarpone
© Randy Van Dam 2008

Cottage Cheese

Cottage cheese is a cheese curd product with a mild flavor. Different styles of cottage cheese are made from milks with different fat levels and in small curd or large curd preparations (see Figure 18.12). It is made from fresh milk and is not aged.

Fromage Frais

Fromage frais is *fromage blanc*, unripened cheese, beaten until it is smooth and creamy, with the consistency of thick yogurt. Commercially made, fromage frais is absolutely velvety smooth and rarely salted. The fat content ranges from virtually nothing to 8 percent or more, when it has been enriched with cream. Farmhouse fromage frais whipped with less aggressive machinery has a very pleasing graininess and a fuller flavor, though by no means so strong as to be positively cheesy.

Like yogurt, fromage frais can be strained to make it thicker. French *cremets* or *coeurs a la creme* are often made with fromage frais, enriched perhaps with creme fraiche, lightly sweetened and lightened with stiffly beaten egg white, then drained in cheesecloth-lined perforated molds, traditionally heart shaped, to serve alongside fresh fruit.

Fromage frais is used like yogurt in mousses, fools, ice creams, or in cold sauces. It can be used to enrich hot sauces but only if you take great care. When overheated, it coagulates to rubbery blobs, which not only look unsightly but are quite inedible. When fromage frais is mixed with eggs or

18.12 **Assorted cottage cheeses (left to right: large curd 4%, small curd 4%, low fat 1%)**
© Randy Van Dam 2008

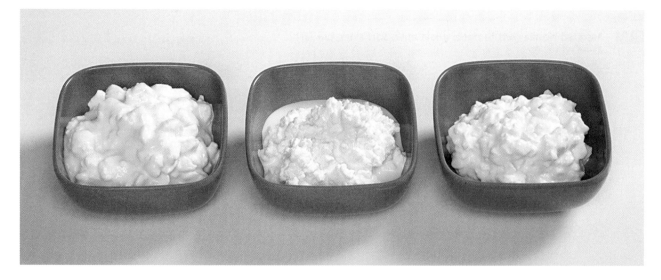

flour, as with a quiche filling or for a gratin, it is less likely to turn rubbery. Even so, remove the dish from the oven as soon as the mixture is set to prevent overcooking.

Butter

Butter is the fat of the milk. It is made by beating cream until it thickens and separates. Butter is used for many recipes. Butter made from cow's milk is the norm in most countries, although other animals' milk is used in some locations. In the kitchen, heat alters the form and flavor of butter.

BUTTER PRODUCTION

Pasteurized cream is placed in large vats and churned repeatedly. This causes the fat particles to pull together and solidify, leaving buttermilk. This is drawn off, leaving small lumps of solid butter that are washed and drained. The butter is then churned until it forms a solid mass that is ready for packaging. The flavor varies according to several factors, such as diet of the animal and time of year.

BUYING AND STORING

There are two basic types of butter: sweet cream butter and lactic butter. Both of these may be salted or unsalted. Butter that is labeled "salted" contains at least 3 percent salt; "slightly salted" butter contains 1 to 2.5 percent salt. Sweet cream butter is made from pasteurized cream that is placed in a tank at a low temperature for about 12 hours before churning. This butter has a sweet creamy taste and a golden yellow color, and it is ideal for baked goods.

Pasteurized cream combined with a lactic acid culture produces lactic butter. The resulting butter has a much lower moisture content, only about 10 percent, while sweet cream butter can contain as much as 18 percent moisture.

Butter is best kept in the refrigerator, but it easily absorbs other flavors, so it should be well wrapped and kept away from strong-smelling foods, especially melon and cauliflower. Whipped butter is often used in food service, mainly for its increased spreadability at lower temperatures. Whipping is achieved by injecting an inert gas (nitrogen) into the butter after churning.

 Butter is also discussed in detail in Chapter 12, "Bakery Supplies."

Cheese

In general, it takes 11 pounds of milk to make 1 pound of cheese. It is thought that the discovery of cheese was an accident. Having observed that milk curdled when left out at room temperature, the first cheese makers found that the curd could be drained to separate it from the whey (a process accelerated by heat) and thus obtained cheese.

Cheeses made from goat's and ewe's milk were common fare in ancient Roman times, an era that saw cheese making attain an unprecedented level of sophistication. Knowledge of cheese making spread throughout the empire, and a number of firm cheeses were developed by the Romans, including Parmesan and Pecorino. After the fall of the Roman Empire and the barbarian invasions, Benedictine and Cistercian monasteries became the major centers of cheese making during the Middle Ages. A number of cheeses still bear the name of their monastic origin (Saint-Paulin, Pont-l'Eveque, Livarot, Limburger, Munster).

There are more than 1,500 varieties of cheese in the world, with France alone producing more than 500 of these varieties. The quality, nutritive value, and characteristics of cheese are dependent on many factors, such as the type of milk, method of production, and local preferences. To the connoisseur, cheeses are too often robbed of their full flavor to conform with strict rules of food hygiene whose purpose is to protect the public against the spread of bacteria. This has led to standardized production methods, which include the pasteurization of milk. This process destroys the bacteria present in milk, but these organisms cannot survive more than 60 days in cheese if the milk was not previously pasteurized. In a number of countries, including Canada, cheeses that are sold without having been aged for at least 2 months must be made from pasteurized milk.

CHEESE PRODUCTION

Although it is understood that each variety of cheese has its own unique procedure that differentiates it from the other cheeses on the market, certain steps are common to most cheeses: pasteurizing the milk (Figure 18.13a, Figure 18.13b, and Figure 18.13c), adding starter cultures, separating curds and whey (Figure 18.13d), salting and flavoring the curds, pressing the cuds into molds (Figure 18.13e), and curing (if necessary) the final product (Figure 18.13f).

 Some commercially made cheeses are brined, or coated with Penicillium candidum, *before ripening or drying (see Figure 18.13g).*

18.13a Heating milk in a vat

Figures 18.13a–f Courtesy of Robert Garlough

18.13b Stirring milk with a harp

18.13c Taking the temperature

18.13d Splitting cheese curds in two while hanging in cheesecloth over whey, before being placed in their mold

18.13e Placing cheese in mold and labeling with vegetable dye

18.13f Cheese floating in brine tanks

18.13g **Cheese in drying room**
Courtesy of Robert Garlough

 Some important cheeses are branded with a trademark that is similar to the concept of "appellation d'origine controlée" used with wine. Figure 18.14a and Figure 18.14b illustrate the markings on Italy's famous Parmigiano Reggiano cheese.

 18.14a **Pointing to the branded registry trademark**
Courtesy of Robert Garlough

 18.14b **Close-up of the Parmigiano Reggiano cheese trademark**
Courtesy of Robert Garlough

 18.15 **Assorted firm, or hard, cheeses**
© 2005 Wisconsin Milk Marketing Board

CATEGORIES OF CHEESE

- **Firm (or hard) cheeses** are cheeses that have been cooked and pressed. The curd is heated for at least 1 hour to make it more concentrated, which, upon pressing, produces a more compact cheese. Firm cheeses, which include Gruyere, Emmenthal, Jarlsberg, Comte, Raclette, Beaufort, Parmesan, and Romano, may or may not have a hard rind; the rind is sometimes rubbed with oil to reduce moisture loss, or washed and scraped, which helps to ripen the cheese. The fermentation process usually lasts for 4 to 12 months. In certain cases, carbon dioxide forms and is trapped in the cheese, producing holes (eyes) that vary in size and quantity from one cheese to another. The texture of the cheese is usually firm, although some hard cheeses, such as Parmesan and Romano, may have a rather granular texture. These cheeses are sometimes produced in wheels that can weigh as much as 85 to 300 pounds. (See Figure 18.15.)

- **Soft cheeses** are ripened for a relatively short period of time before being drained and turned into molds without being pressed or cooked. They have a moisture content of 50 to 60 percent, and their fat content represents 20 to 26 percent of the cheese's weight. Cheeses in this category develop a soft rind that can be somewhat satiny. Fermentation starts on the surface of the cheese and moves toward the interior. Soft cheeses are rarely used in cooking because they tend to lose a lot of flavor when heated. Soft cheeses are divided into two categories, according to the characteristics of the rind:

  - **Surface-ripened soft cheeses** are covered with a thin layer of a white down or mold that is satiny in appearance (Camembert, Brie, Brillat-Savarin, Coulommiers); this rind is edible but should be removed if its flavor is too pronounced. (See Figure 18.16.)

  - **Interior-ripened soft cheeses** are washed in light brine to maintain the moisture level and softness of the cheese and the rind and to eliminate certain ferments. These delicately flavored and strong-smelling cheeses include Munster, Pont-l'Eveque, Livarot, Bel Paese, and Epoisses. To ensure an appropriate interior degree of humidity and adequate fermentation, these cheeses are stored in a humid atmosphere (close to 90 percent humidity) at a mild temperature varying between 53°F and 59°F (12°C and 15°C). Some of the cheeses in this category are soaked in alcohol such as wine or beer as part of the ripening process. (See Figure 18.17.)

- **Semi-firm cheeses** are uncooked, pressed cheeses that are ripened for a relatively long period in a cool (45–50°F, or 7–10°C) and very humid (90 percent) atmosphere. The curd is cut into small grains, pressed, and turned out of the molds to be soaked in brine. Semi-firm cheeses are dense and are usually pale yellow. This family of cheeses includes Cheddar, Cantal, Reblochon, Gouda, Edam, Fontina, Saint-Nectaire, Morbier, Tommes, Tilsit, and Monterey Jack. (See Figure 18.18.)

- **Pasta filata cheeses (unripened stretched-curd cheeses)** are produced by kneading and stretching the curd (known as "stringing"), which is then stored in water until the desired consistency is obtained. This process gives it a slightly rubbery texture. Cheeses in this category include mozzarella, Scarmoza, Provolone, Bocconcini, and Caciotta. Mozzarella is widely used as a topping on pizzas and pasta dishes baked au gratin. (See Figure 18.19.)

> **BUYER'S NOTE** Curds can be purchased, and fresh mozzarella can be warmed and stretched "a la minute" for appetizers or salads.

- **Blue-veined (or blue) cheeses** are neither cooked nor pressed; the curd is first cut into pieces, then molded, drained, salted, and inoculated with a species of blue-green mold such as *Penicillium roqueforti* or *P gorgonzola*, which is injected into the cheese by means of long needles. Fermentation occurs from the inside out; the action of the bacterial culture causes a network of blue-green veins to form, which becomes denser over time. These cheeses (Roquefort, Gorgonzola, Bleu de Bresse, Danish Blue, Stilton) have a strong and sharp, peppery flavor and are often crumbly. (See Figure 18.20.)

- **Process cheeses** are made from one or a blend of pressed cheeses (cooked or uncooked) that are melted and to which milk, cream, or butter is added. They have the advantage of keeping longer than natural cheeses. These cheeses may contain stabilizing agents, emulsifiers, salt, food coloring, sweeteners (sugar, corn syrup), or flavorings (herbs, spices, fruits, nuts, Kirsch). They are somewhat soft and rubbery with a flavor that is usually quite mild. In North America, most process cheeses are made using Cheddar, while Emmenthal and Gruyere are more commonly used in Europe. Process cheeses are labeled differently depending on the amount of cheese they contain (processed cheese, process cheese food, and cheese spread are all available on grocery shelves). (See Figure 18.21.)

- **Cheese substitutes** are imitation cheeses that are often made using only the casein element in milk, to which emulsifiers (disodium phosphate, sodium citrate) and artificial flavoring and food coloring are added. Natural ingredients like soybean or corn are also sometimes added after being processed.

- **Goat's milk cheeses** are available in several different styles and degrees of firmness. Whiter than cheeses made from cow's milk, goat cheeses also tend to have a more pronounced flavor. These cheeses are often very salty, which prolongs their storage life. Most goat cheeses today are made from a blend of goat's and cow's milk. Cheeses in this family include Crottin de Chavignol, Valencay, Chevrotin, and feta.

18.16 Assorted surface-ripened soft cheeses

Figures 18.16–.21 © 2005 Wisconsin Milk Marketing Board

18.17 Assorted interior-ripened soft cheeses

18.18 Assorted semi-firm cheeses

18.19 Assorted pasta filata cheeses

18.20 Assorted blue-veined cheeses

18.21 Assorted process cheeses

BUYING AND STORING

When purchasing cheese, check the expiration date on the package and avoid cheeses that have been stored at room temperature. Each category of cheese has specific characteristics that are important to look for when purchasing. Certain problems are easy to spot, and any cheese showing signs of these defects should be avoided.

For example, soft cheeses should be soft both inside and out; they are fully ripe when the cheese is creamy, smooth, and uniformly colored, and when it fills out the crust. The crust itself should be soft, not too dry, and uncracked. Avoid cheeses that are overly firm or chalky white in the center, a sign of underripeness. Overripe soft cheeses have a sticky rind that is often darker or that smells like ammonia. Soft cheeses that have been improperly stored will have a hard crust and will be dry on the inside. They should be sliced using a cheese wire rather than a cheese knife, as soft cheeses adhere to the blade and result in both lost product and uneven slices (see Figure 18.22a).

Semi-firm cheeses should be neither too dry nor too crumbly; if the cheese near the crust is darker than at the center, the cheese has likely been improperly stored. These cheeses should be neither rancid nor sharp tasting.

Firm cheeses should be uniform in color and texture, with a firm rind. Avoid dried-out, bulging, pasty, or overly granular cheeses with a cracked rind, all of which point to improper storage conditions. Firm cheeses should be neither too salty nor too bitter. Firm cheeses can be sliced using either a cheese knife or cheese wire; a cheese knife is best for larger slices (Figure 18.22b) while a cheese wire is best for thin slices (Figure 18.22c).

Blue cheeses should be generously veined, depending on the variety, and the veining should be evenly distributed throughout the cheese. The cheese, which is usually white, should be neither too crumbly, too dry, nor too salty.

Only firm cheeses are suitable for grating, and they are easier to grate when cold than when at room temperature. Once grated, hard cheeses will stay fresh for about a week in the refrigerator.

The shelf life of cheeses is determined mainly by moisture content. For example, because soft cheeses have higher moisture content than firm cheeses, they do not keep as long.

- Fresh cheeses and blue-veined cheeses will keep for only a week to 10 days and must be refrigerated in airtight wrapping.

 18.22a **Cutting soft cheese with cheese wire**

Figures 18.22a–b © Randy Van Dam 2008

18.22b **Cutting hard cheese with cheese knife**

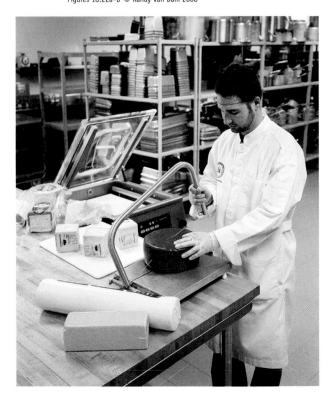

18.22d   **Wrapping cheese in waxed paper while wearing sanitary gloves**

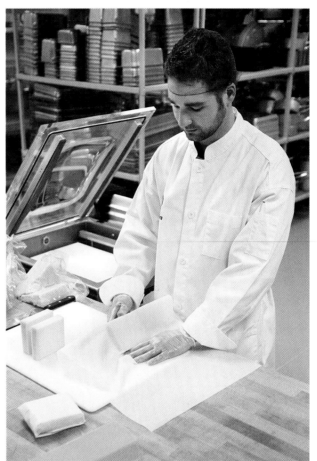

- Soft cheeses do not keep for very long once they are fully ripened.

- Semi-firm cheeses can be stored for several weeks in the refrigerator, provided they are well wrapped.

- Firm cheeses will keep for 2 weeks in the refrigerator or in a cool place if they are well wrapped in wax paper or aluminum foil.

All cheeses can be stored in the refrigerator, although it is not an ideal location. They should be well wrapped in waxed paper or aluminum foil and placed in the warmest section of the refrigerator (some cheeses, including soft cheeses, lose flavor when stored at inappropriate temperatures). It is important to wear protective latex or plastic gloves when handling cheese to prevent contaminating the cheese with bacteria (see Figure 18.22d). Surface-ripened cheeses should not be stored in vacuum-sealed or airtight packages.

Cheese is best enjoyed at room temperature. To minimize the potential for damaging the cheese with constant trips in and out of the cooler, only take out what you expect to use in 1 hour.

If mold has developed on the surface of a firm cheese, cut out 1/2 to 1 inch of the cheese around the mold just to be safe, and cover the cheese with a fresh piece of wrapping. It is preferable to discard fresh and soft cheeses that contain mold, as they could cause food poisoning. While it is possible to freeze cheese, this method of preservation is not recommended, as it tends to detract from the flavor and to make it more crumbly. Should freezing prove necessary, it is best to cut the cheese into wedges about 1-inch thick and weighing no more than 1 pound. Dry cheeses stand up better to freezing than those with high moisture content; fresh cheeses cannot be frozen. When well wrapped, cheese will keep for 2.5 to 3 months in the freezer. Frozen cheeses are best thawed in the refrigerator to minimize alteration of their texture; it is better to reserve frozen cheeses for cooking.

According to Max McCalman, maître fromager at New York's Picholine and Artisanal restaurants, cheeses are happiest when stored at cool temperatures ranging from 45 to 60°F (7 to 16°C) with relative humidity of 80 percent or higher. However, many local health departments require cheese to be stored below 40°F. And most walk-in coolers operate at around 30 percent relative humidity. See Table 18.3 for ideal storage conditions for cheese. Check with the local health department regarding its regulations.

TABLE 18.3 Ideal Storage Conditions for Cheese

Cheese	Temperature (°F)	Relative Humidity (%)
Blue	42–46	85–95
Soft-ripened	50–52	80–90
Wash-rind	50–55	90 +
Hard, aged	55–60	80 +

CONVENIENCE CORNER PRODUCT EXAMPLES

Dairy: Eggs and Cheese

Company	Website	Products
Butterball Farms	http://www.butterball.com	6/3# Butterballs
Dannon	http://www.dannon.com	6/32 oz Dannon yogurt plain
Smucker's	http://www.smucker.com	200/0.5 oz Apple Butter
Kraft	http://www.kraftfoods.com	4/5# Kraft American Cheddar 160 ct 5/5# Grated Parmesan Cheese
Land O' Lakes	http://www.landolakes.com	450/10 gr. Butter with honey 6/5# Cheese Golden Velvet 360/ 3/8 oz Half & Half Creamer 60/3.8 oz Sauce Cheese Nacho Cup
Reser's	http://www.resers.com	2/5# Salad Egg
Rich's	http://www.richs.com	12/32 oz Rich's Quiche Mix 12/32 oz Richs Topping Whip
Roth Kase	http://www.rothkase.com	2/5# Cheese Fontina & Gryere 14# Cheese Montanella
Sunny Fresh	http://www.sunnyfresh.com	288/1oz Egg Patty
Crystal Lake	http://www.conceptfoodbrokers.com/product.cfm	415# Egg Diced
Papetti	http://www.michaelfoods.com/papettis.htm	15/2# Egg Yolk Liquid
Dean	http://www.deanfoods.com	24/8 oz Milk Chocolate
Reddi-Wip	http://www.reddi-wip.com/products.html	12/15 oz Cream Whipped Aerosol

Art Davis

Place of Birth: Plymouth, Indiana

Educational Background and Work Experience

Sales and marketing manager Art Davis has enjoyed a career in sales for more than 28 years. But he didn't start out at the top of his game. After spending 3 years taking business courses at Western Michigan University, Davis decided his best education would come by way of employment. So Davis left college to labor in a warehouse, where his diligent efforts and responsible behavior were eventually rewarded when he became warehouse supervisor. But this promotion didn't come quickly. He had to first demonstrate a commitment to his job and the ability to get along with both staff and customers. His affable personality helped him to get along with all of the delivery drivers who came to the warehouse. Eventually, ready for a change, Davis became a truck driver himself. Although he was successful, Davis missed the interaction of working with many people. So he left truck driving to take his first sales position in street sales. Twenty-eight years later, Davis is still in sales, working with the prestige accounts of SYSCO Food Service of Grand Rapids.

Memberships and Career Highlights

Davis is an active member in his community and takes pride in his support of local charities, particularly those associated with the area chef's association. Because of his staunch support of culinary education, he was named to the Grand Rapids Community College Hospitality Hall of Fame in 2003. His long success in food sales and marketing over the years was recognized in 2000, when he received the Torch Bearer Award from SYSCO.

Passions with the Food Service Industry

"The greatest pleasure of my occupation is the satisfaction of helping others accom-

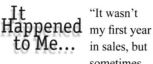

Courtesy Art Davis

It Happened to Me...

"It wasn't my first year in sales, but sometimes we get in a pattern and just routinely perform our daily duties. I took a hard look at a particular account that SYSCO had 40 percent of the business. We had a good relationship with the account, but our sales were always the same. The owner wanted to lessen his role in the business, and he was looking for someone to trust and support his purchasing plan. SYSCO was his choice on which to rely. We began by studying the non-food products he was using. Often the non-food items cost you significant money, so our intention was to change items that would lower his costs. We changed the napkins, toilet paper, and foam containers. Next, we looked at the food items, switching to Angus burgers, fresh orange juice, and new breads. We upgraded the quality of several important ingredients, with little or no overall increase in costs. Our relationship of trust was intact with our available products. We took over 80 percent of the business, and a year later we had 100 percent. The lesson to learn is (1) to look at what is not selling and to ask yourself why, and (2) establishing a trusted relationship with the vendors will result in a positive experience and increased success."

plish their objectives. I enjoy being there for the chefs and making things happen for them. I look for the opportunities that arise and try to come up with a solution; many times you can work out a solution that meets their needs when you try. I want to be the biggest reason that they trust their sales representatives."

Advice to a Chef or Buyer

"Everyone is in the (food service) business to make money. It's how you get there that makes you successful. Buying a quality product and serving tasteful food will bring clientele to your restaurant. If you control your waste in the kitchen and your menu is priced correctly, then you will reach your 'success goals.' A lot of salespeople will call on you, but very few will invest themselves in your business. You need to align yourself with the marketing manager (sales representative) who will be committed and invested in your projects and passions. Be open to the suggestions from professionals who are invested in your success."

Key Words and Concepts

buttermilk	dairy	pasta filata cheeses	surface-ripened soft cheeses
crème fraiche	eggs	process cheeses	
cultured dairy products	interior-ripened soft cheeses	soft cheeses	yogurt

Chapter in Review

The following exercises are provided to help the reader understand and apply the contents of this chapter. They may be completed individually or in a classroom environment.

REVIEW QUESTIONS

a. Define the terms *egg* and *dairy*.

b. List the parts to the egg.

c. Define *cultured dairy products*, and list several examples.

d. Explain the process for making cheese.

e. Explain the process for making butter.

INDIVIDUAL ACTIVITIES

a. **Web based:** Research artisan cheese makers in your area.

b. **Experiential:** Visit an artisan cheese maker, and learn how the cheese is made.

c. **Critical thinking:** Consider the effect of substituting cheeses with different fat and moisture contents in recipes.

GROUP ACTIVITIES

a. **Lab experience:** Bring in a large variety of cheeses to class and present them to the students without identifying their names. Have the class separate the cheeses into different categories as discussed in this chapter and identify them based on appearance, taste, and texture.

b. **Classroom action:** Divide the students into teams, and have them list as many cheeses as they can remember by category.

CHAPTER

19

Image copyright ultimathule, 2009. Used under license from Shutterstock.com

Vegetarian and Special Dietary Products

"A small garden, figs, a little cheese, and, along with this, three or four good friends—such was luxury to Epicurus."

FRIEDRICH NIETZSCHE

After reading this chapter, you will be able to:

◎ Define the term *vegetarian*, and identify other forms of vegetarianism.

◎ List the six food groups of the vegetarian diet, and provide examples from each.

◎ Outline the various cereals and grains and the role of whole grains in diets.

◎ Identify the different categories of pasta, and give examples of each.

◎ Distinguish the different forms of oats and how they are used.

◎ Distinguish the different forms of barley and how they are used.

◎ List the different types of rice and their features.

◎ Identify the different pulses and their uses.

◎ Explain the process for making seitan.

◎ Explain the uses of tempeh and tofu.

◎ Identify the more popular varieties of edible nuts.

◎ Identify dried fruits and the methods used to dry them.

◎ List examples of fresh and dried mushrooms.

◎ Identify the more popular varieties of olives produced globally.

Introduction

Simply stated, a **vegetarian** is someone who avoids meat. But there are so many types and levels of vegetarians that one definition cannot encapsulate them all. Whether an occasional vegetarian or a true vegan, being a vegetarian can be more of a lifestyle choice than dietary habit. Veganism may be defined as a way of living that seeks to exclude all forms of animal exploitation for food, clothing, or any other purpose. Today, there are several forms of vegetarianism:

- **Vegetarian.** A vegetarian eats most culinary items except meat, poultry, game, fish, shellfish, or crustaceans. Vegetarians might, however, consume dairy or dairy by-products.

- **Vegan.** A **vegan** excludes all animal flesh and animal by-products from his or her diet, including milk, cheese, and possibly honey.

- **Strict vegetarian.** This term, also called pure vegetarian, originally meant vegan, but now it can mean vegan or vegetarian.

- **Ovo-lacto vegetarian.** This is the same as a vegan, but the person eats eggs and milk products.

- **Semi-vegetarian.** Also known as *selectarian* or *pseudo vegetarian*, this person eats less meat than the average person, generally for health reasons.

- **Pescetarian.** This is a vegetarian who consumes fish.

- **Fruitarian.** This is the same as a vegan, but the person only eats fruits that do not kill the plant.

- **Veggie.** This is a nickname for a vegetarian.

This chapter highlights foods that are of growing interest to consumers and have not yet been covered in other chapters. It is estimated that 15 percent of the dining public is either vegetarian or will select vegetarian dishes when offered on menus. Modern managers, chefs, and food buyers cannot ignore this demographic; they must be versed in this important cuisine and its ingredients.

Vegetarian Foods

Vegetarians must be mindful of their protein intake. Proteins are made from 20 amino acids, 10 of which are said to be essential. Animal protein contains all of the essential amino acids that fulfill human needs. But plant proteins are deficient in certain essential amino acids and are only partially digested by humans. When a plant protein is short of a particular amino acid, this amino acid is referred to as the limiting factor, because its limited quantity reduces the overall efficiency of the protein by 30 percent.

Proteins of animal origin have been referred to as "complete," while proteins of plant origin are said to be "incomplete." When certain food groups are combined, they complement each other (see Figure 19.1). These examples show that the perfect combination of different plant proteins provide the complete protein that is required by the human body. Cereals complement legumes (like bread complements peanut butter), as do nuts and seeds; in the same way, dairy products complement cereals (like cheese and crackers). All foods belonging to the same family can be interchanged in such combinations.

Although it is difficult to classify vegetarian foods into strict and all-inclusive categories, the Vegetarian Society of the United Kingdom has identified the following food groups:

- **Cereals and grains:** wheat (bread and pasta), oats, maize, barley, rye, rice

- **Pulses:** kidney beans, baked beans, chickpeas, lentils

- **Nuts and seeds:** almonds, walnuts, hazelnuts, sesame seeds, sunflower seeds

- **Fruit and vegetables:** all varieties of fruits, vegetables, and fungi

- **Dairy products or soya products:** tofu, milk, and cheese

- **Vegetable oils and fats:** margarine and butter

19.1 Diagram of complementary foods

Some foods which may be combined to provide a good balance of amino acids are:

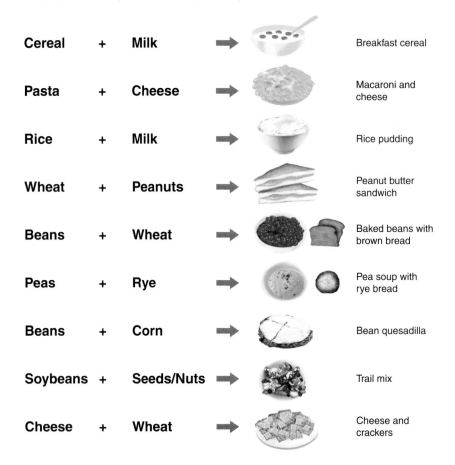

Cereal	+	**Milk**	⟹	Breakfast cereal
Pasta	+	**Cheese**	⟹	Macaroni and cheese
Rice	+	**Milk**	⟹	Rice pudding
Wheat	+	**Peanuts**	⟹	Peanut butter sandwich
Beans	+	**Wheat**	⟹	Baked beans with brown bread
Peas	+	**Rye**	⟹	Pea soup with rye bread
Beans	+	**Corn**	⟹	Bean quesadilla
Soybeans	+	**Seeds/Nuts**	⟹	Trail mix
Cheese	+	**Wheat**	⟹	Cheese and crackers

CEREALS AND GRAINS

Made from the edible seeds of various plants belonging to the grass family, cereals have been an essential part of the human diet since the beginning of agriculture. Inhabitants of Syria, Palestine, and the eastern shores of the Mediterranean were already cultivating primitive varieties of barley and wheat more than 8,000 years ago. By 3,000 B.C., the Egyptians had mastered the techniques of irrigation, allowing for further development of cereal cultivation.

While cereal consumption has declined in industrial countries in the past century, cereals remain the most important crop in the developing countries, where they represent the major source of food energy and up to 90 percent of protein intake, compared with a mere 25 percent in industrialized countries.

All cereals belong to the family of grasses. The seed is enclosed in an outer shell, or hull, that humans cannot digest. For this reason, the grains must be hulled to make them edible. As first discussed in Chapter 12, "Bakery Supplies," the cereal grain (caryopsis) consists of three main parts: an outer layer (the bran), the endosperm (or kernel), and the germ:

- The *endosperm* (kernel) is the largest part of the grain and is composed of starch, a complex carbohydrate that is absorbed slowly by the body.

- The kernel is enclosed in the *bran* (pericarp). High in vitamins and minerals, it also plays an important role in digestion.

- The *germ* (embryo) contains the seed of a new plant. The germ has the highest concentration of nutritional elements.

Cereal grains play a central role in the human diet and are used in a variety of ways. While the word *cereal* is most commonly associated with the ready-to-eat breakfast food, cereal grains are available in many forms; for example, they can be ground or crushed to make pasta, flour, semolina, and starch, as well as being sold in puffs or flakes. Wheat, triticale, barley, and rye grains can be added to soups and legume dishes, to which they lend an original note while at the same time improving their nutritional quality. (See Figure 19.2.)

Buying and Storing

Cereals are best kept in an airtight container away from heat and moisture. Storing them in the refrigerator or at a temperature of about 40°F (4°C) delays rancidity and mold while also preventing insect infestation. See Table 19.1 for cooking times.

19.2 From left to right, wheat berry, cracked wheat, and flour

© Randy Van Dam 2008

TABLE 19.1 Cooking Times for Grains

1 Cup	Liquid (in Cups)	Cooking Time
Oats (Grains)	2–3	1 hr
Cracked Wheat	2–3	30–40 min
Wheat (Grains)	2	60–90 min
Bulgur	2	Cover and simmer 25–35 min
Cous Cous	1	Add boiling water, let stand 5 min
Rolled Oats	1	5 min
Wheat Flakes	2	1 hr
Rye Flakes	2	1 hr
Soya Flakes	2	1 hr
Millet	2	30–40 min
Barley (Grains)	2	45 min
Hulled Barley	3–4	1 hr
Brown Rice	2	45–60 min
Wild Rice	3	45–60 min
Buckwheat (Kasha)	2	10–15 min
Cornmeal	4	25–30 min

Buckwheat

Buckwheat is the fruit of a plant, technically not a grain. Buckwheat grains must be hulled in order to be edible. They are then sold, either roasted or plain, and graded according to size. Roasted buckwheat is called **kasha**, a dish that is popular in Eastern Europe. Flour made from buckwheat is dark and high in nutritional value. (See Figure 19.3.)

Oats

The several hundred varieties of oats are divided into two classes: winter oats and summer oats. The hulled seed, or *groat*, can be sold as is, rolled, or ground. Oats retain their bran and germ during processing. The different stages and methods of processing produce steel-cut oats, old-fashioned rolled oats, quick-cooking oats, instant oats, oat bran, and oat flour. (See Figure 19.4.)

19.3   **Light and dark buckwheat grains**
© Randy Van Dam 2008

19.4   **Oats (Top row: rolled oats (left), instant rolled oats; bottom row: steel-cut (left), quick-cooking steel-cut)**
© Randy Van Dam 2008

- **Steel-cut oats.** Oats are passed between steel blades that cut them into slices of varying thickness.

- **Old-fashioned rolled oats.** The hulled grains are steamed and rolled to produce flat flakes.

- **Quick-cooking oats.** These are old-fashioned rolled oats that have been cut finely to shorten their cooking time.

- **Instant oats.** The grain is partially cooked and then dried and rolled very thin. The different types of oatmeal on the market almost always contain sugar and salt and often contain food additives.

- **Oat bran.** Located in the outer layers of the grain under the inedible hull, oat bran is longer and narrower than wheat bran. It is available as a separate product but may also be present in rolled oats and steel-cut oats. It can be cooked on its own, like oatmeal, or used in combination with other foods, in the same way as wheat germ.

- **Oat flour.** Oat flour does not contain gluten and therefore does not rise during baking. It must be combined with wheat flour to make breads and other leavened foods, and it tends to produce denser products.

People, Places, Things

Making Seitan

Because the process of making seitan is rather long, it is a good idea to prepare a large quantity and then freeze a portion of it. It is recommended that durum wheat flour be used.

Kneading

1. Pour 4 cups of water into a large bowl, and add enough flour to obtain the consistency of a thick soup.

2. Stir vigorously with a wooden spoon and add the rest of the flour for a total of 8 cups of durum whole-wheat flour.

3. Form the dough into a ball (at this point, there should be roughly 2 1/2 cups of raw seitan, which expands during cooking).

4. Knead the dough for 10 to 20 minutes, adding flour or water as needed to work the dough (this operation is important because the kneading binds the gluten mol-

5. Let the dough stand, covered with cold water, for 30 minutes to 8 hours; although this step is not essential, it shortens the rinsing time, thus facilitating the separation of the starch and the gluten.

Rinsing

1. Fill a large bowl with cold water; place the dough in a strainer in the water.

2. Gently knead the dough in the water until it thickens and takes on a whitish color.

3. The rinsing process is finished when the dough becomes rubbery and has been rid of its starch; change the water as many times as necessary until it is clear. Do not worry about over-kneading the dough; it regains its elasticity quickly.

The rinse water containing the starch and bran can be used to thicken soups, sauces, braised dishes, and desserts. Another alternative is to slowly pour out the water and to keep the starch that has settled at the bottom of the bowl, which can be dried and used like cornstarch.

Cooking

1. Prepare a stock with 8 cups of water, 1/2 cup or more of tamari sauce, a 3-inch piece of kombu, and a pinch of salt.

2. If desired, flavor the stock by adding vegetables, spices, and fines herbes (garlic, onion, ginger, thyme, bay leaf, etc.).

3. Cut the gluten into pieces the size of a potato; because it expands during cooking, it is better to separate it this way, especially when making a large quantity.

4. Bring the stock to a boil; add the gluten to the stock, cover the casserole, lower the heat, and let simmer. Stir occasionally, adding water if necessary.

Cooking time varies depending on the size of the pieces and their intended use; allow about 30 minutes if planning to recook the seitan in another dish, and 1 hour if planning to eat the seitan in strips.

Barley

Barley grains are oval and white. For the grains to be edible, the hull must be removed. The various stages of processing produce hulled barley, pot (or scotch) barley, and pearled (or pearl) barley. Whole grain barley flour must be combined with gluten flours for it to leaven. Barley malt is used in the production of alcohol and as a sweetener. (See Figure 19.5.)

- **Hulled barley.** The outer husk has been removed, but the bran is maintained. This is the most nutritious form of barley.

- **Pot, or scotch, barley.** At this stage, the barley has been subjected to a triple polishing process, which causes the grain to lose almost all of its bran.

- **Pearled barley.** The barley has undergone multiple polishing operations to create consistent grains. The grain is stripped of its germ.

- **Barley flakes.** The barley has been processed and is used like rolled oats. Whole grain barley flour has a nutty flavor and is darker than whole grain wheat flour.

Millet

Millet can be used in place of most other cereals, although it does have a strong flavor. It can be added to soups, omelets, croquettes, meat pies, puddings, and muesli. Because millet flour does not contain gluten, it is unsuitable for making leavened breads, although it is commonly made into flat breads, which are widely consumed in Africa and Asia. Millet is also cooked to make porridge, fermented to make alcohol or beer (particularly in Africa), or sprouted like alfalfa sprouts and used to enrich other foods. Millet meal or ground millet can be incorporated into breads, cakes, pies, and biscuits. (See Figure 19.6.)

Teff is eaten whole or ground into slightly granular flour; although this flour does not rise, it is baked into delicious flat breads and sweet breads, such as *injera*, the national bread of Ethiopia. *Faffa* is a dietary supplement that is prepared from a finely ground mixture of teff flour, chickpeas, skim milk, sugar, and salt.

19.6 **Millet**
© Randy Van Dam 2008

19.5 **Hulled barley, pearled barley, and barley flakes**
© Randy Van Dam 2008

Rice

Rice can be divided into two basic groups: long grain and specialty. All-purpose long grain rice can be used for all styles of cooking. Long grain rice is a slim grain that is four to five times as long as it is wide. It undergoes different milling techniques to produce the different types of rice. (See Figure 19.7.)

- **Long grain white rice** (roughly 6 millimeters, or 1/4 inch) is light, and the grains remain separate when cooked; however, this rice can become sticky if it is overcooked or stirred too frequently during cooking. There are many different hulling methods, from the traditional practices of hand threshing and pounding to the more modern industrial methods using mechanical brushes. The market offers several kinds of rice that vary according to the degree of milling. In some countries, including the United States, white rice is commonly enriched with iron, niacin, and thiamine to restore some of its nutritional value.

- **Instant rice** is white rice that is precooked and then dried to shorten its cooking time. It is fairly bland tasting and even less nutritious than white rice, although it is more expensive than the latter because it requires more processing. It is often referred to as Minute Rice, a familiar brand name that is available for both retail and commercial use.

- **Brown rice** (or whole rice) is the whole grain with the fibrous inedible outer hull removed. Brown rice almost always contains some green grains that were not fully ripe at the

19.7 Structure of the rice grain

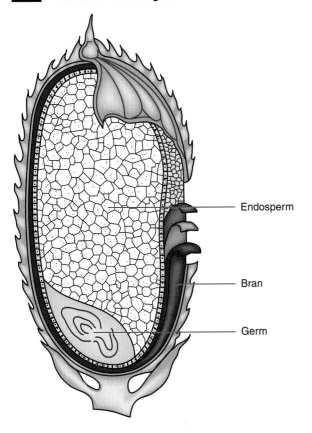

Endosperm

Bran

Germ

19.8 Long-grain brown rice

© Randy Van Dam 2008

time of harvesting. While these immature grains are also found in white rice, they are less noticeable because white rice is milled to a greater degree. Brown rice is the most nutritious form of rice and has a nutty flavor. (See Figure 19.8.)

- **Instant brown rice** has been treated in the same way as instant white, which reduces the cooking time to 5 minutes, with a 5-minute rest period, as opposed to the normal cooking time of 45 minutes for brown rice.

- **Parboiled white rice,** or **converted white rice,** is soaked and then steamed before being milled. The parboiling process transfers the water-soluble vitamins and minerals contained in the germ and outer layers to the interior so that they are not eliminated during polishing. It does not usually stick and is lighter than brown rice. Next to brown rice, this is the most nourishing rice. (See Figure 19.9a.)

- **Parboiled brown rice** (ready in 25 minutes) is processed in the same way as parboiled white rice to shorten its cooking time. Parboiling has the added advantage of improving the keeping qualities of brown rice by neutralizing the substances that cause the oils in the germ to turn rancid. Unlike parboiled white rice, parboiled brown rice always retains the bran and germ. (See Figure 19.9b.)

Specialty rice is often used for a particular dish, style, or type of cuisine. There are many different varieties. (See Figure 19.9c.)

- **Arborio rice.** This is the classic round white rice that is essential to Italian risotto. It can absorb large quantities of liquid without becoming too mushy. (See Figure 19.10.)

- **Basmati rice.** This is the best known of the perfumed varieties. It has a light, dry texture. (See Figure 19.11.)

- **Jasmine rice.** This white rice can be interchanged with white Basmati rice. It is just slightly sticky when compared with Basmati. (See Figure 19.12.)

19.9a White rice. Top row: medium grain (left), extra long grain; bottom row: parboiled (left), instant

Figures 19.9a–.10 © Randy Van Dam 2008

19.9b Brown rice. Top row: short grain (left), extra long grain; bottom row: parboiled (left), instant

19.9c Specialty rice examples: Purple sticky rice (top), Himalayan red (bottom right), Chinese black (bottom right)

19.10 Arborio rice

19.11 White and brown basmati rice

Figures 19.11–.13 © Randy Van Dam 2008

19.12 Brown and white Jasmine rice

19.13 Sushi rice

- **Sushi rice.** All sushi rice is a white, short-grain variety. Short-grained rice has higher levels of starch, which is why the grains are so sticky. (See Figure 19.13.)

- **Sweet rice.** Sweet rice, also known as *sticky rice, waxy rice, botan rice, mochi rice,* and *pearl rice,* is a type of short-grained Asian rice that is especially sticky when cooked. (See Figure 19.14.)

- **Wild rice.** Wild rice is not rice; it is a grain (specifically, it is the seed of a water grass). Wild rice taken from lakes is far superior to cultivated wild rice and is your best option. (See Figure 19.15.)

- **Seasoned rice.** This is almost always made from precooked or parboiled rice to which salt and various seasonings have been added. They also often contain food additives. (See Figure 19.16.)

19.14 **Japanese sweet rice**

19.15 **Wild rice**

19.16 **Seasoned rice**

Quinoa

Quinoa seeds are covered with a layer of saponin, a bitter, soapy resin that forms a lather on contact with water and that must be washed off before the seeds can be eaten. During commercial processing, the seeds are washed or agitated to remove the resin. One of the world's true super foods, quinoa is the only vegetable complete protein, containing all essential amino acids. Quinoa is also a great source of fiber, iron, and magnesium. Quinoa is an especially valuable food for vegetarians and vegans who are concerned about getting enough protein in their diets. It is commonly used in pilafs, risottos, salads, and mixed with cooked vegetables. (See Figure 19.17.)

19.17 **Quinoa**

Corn

Upon arriving in the New World, the first explorers found corn growing all the way from Canada to Chile. Native Americans from Mexico northward to lower Canada consumed a type of cornmeal sweetened with honey or spiced with peppers and accompanied by vegetables, meat, or fish. Early colonists were attracted by this cereal grain, which the natives had adapted to various climatic and soil conditions. Christopher Columbus provided the first reports of corn's existence back to the Old World. Spanish explorer Hernán Cortés introduced corn to Europe in the early sixteenth century, and the Portuguese brought it to Africa at the same time. Today, there are two main types of corn. *Dent corn* is grown for livestock feed, and it is the predominant corn crop. *Sweet corn* is the second most common form of corn grown, and it is used for human consumption and to make corn-based products. Sweet corn should be eaten as close to harvesting as possible or refrigerated to prevent the sugars from converting to starches.

Pasta and Noodles

Pasta is made from the flour of certain grains mixed with water and/or eggs. The most common forms of pasta are associated with Italian cooking, but they are used in many different cuisines.

COMMON PASTA SHAPES

- **Shaped.** This pasta is molded to resemble objects such as stars, bowties, and other novelty shapes. (See Figure 19.18.)

- **Tubular.** Tubular pastas have a hole in the middle. They are used for stuffing (manicotti) or for dishes with chunky sauces. The tubes catch and hold the sauce. (See Figure 19.19.)

- **Strand.** Strand pastas look like long strings, which vary in width and length. Stand pastas are used with delicate sauces. (See Figure 19.20.)

- **Ribbon pasta.** Ribbon pastas are similar to strand pastas, except they have a ruffled or scalloped edge. They are a heavier pasta used for stuffing and heavy sauces. (See Figure 19.21.)

- **Micro pasta.** These are very small pastas such as stars. They can be substituted for grains. (See Figure 19.22.)

- **Stuffed pasta.** These are pastas made to be stuffed (e.g., manicotti and stuffed shells). (See Figure 19.23.)

- **Irregular shape.** These do not have a similar or regular shape. (See Figure 19.24.)

Noodle is a generic term for a variety of unleavened dough that is sliced, boiled, and dried. Noodles can be made from many grains. The majority of Asian noodles are made from rice, wheat, mung bean, and buckwheat, although some regions also produce noodles from corn or seaweed. Most other noodles are similar to pasta as they are usually made of flour, eggs, and water.

Although there are many exceptions, most noodles fall approximately into one of the following descriptions.

- **Rice noodles.** These are made with just rice flour and water. Rice noodles should be soaked in hot water for 15 to 20 minutes before using. (See Figure 19.25.)

- **Cellophane noodles.** Cellophane noodles are made from mung bean starch. Cellophane noodles work well in soups and stir-fries, absorbing the flavor of the foods they are cooked with. When deep-fried, they puff up and become crispy. (See Figure 19.26.)

- **Egg noodles.** Made with eggs, wheat flour, and water, they come in a number of widths and shapes, from the thinner vermicelli to flat, thicker noodles. (See Figure 19.27.)

- **Wheat noodles.** These are made from wheat flour and water. (See Figure 19.28.)

- **Buckwheat noodles.** These are noodles made from buckwheat flour. (See Figure 19.29.)

19.18 **Assorted shaped pastas**

© Randy Van Dam 2008

19.19 Assorted tubular pastas

Figures 19.19–.20 © Randy Van Dam 2008

19.20 Assorted strand pastas

19.21 **Assorted ribbon pasta**

Figures 19.21–.22 © Randy Van Dam 2008

19.22 **Assorted micro pasta**

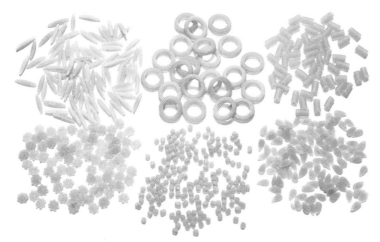

19.23 Assorted stuffed pasta

Figures 19.23–.25 © Randy Van Dam 2008

19.24 Assorted irregularly shaped pasta

19.25 Assorted rice noodles

19.26 Assorted cellophane noodles

Figures 19.26–.27 © Randy Van Dam 2008

19.27 Assorted egg noodles

19.28 **Assorted wheat noodles**

Figures 19.28–.29 © Randy Van Dam 2008

19.29 **Assorted buckwheat noodles**

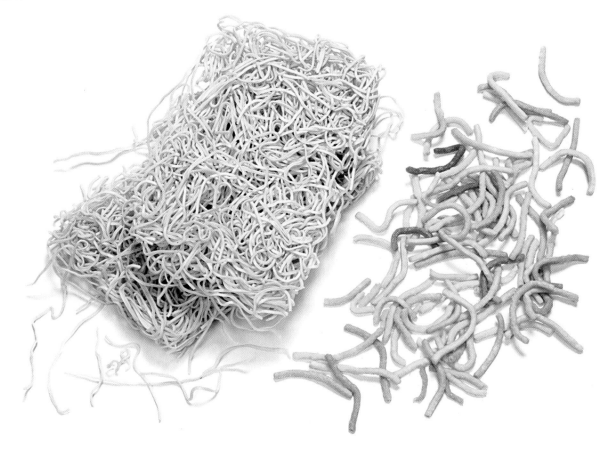

PULSES

The United Nations Food and Agricultural Organization (FAO) defines **pulses** as annual leguminous crops yielding from one to twelve grains or seeds of variable size, shape, and color within a pod. In regards to their essential amino acid and high protein content, pulses are considered an important agricultural product. They can be eaten fresh or dried and come in a great number of varieties. In spite of its common name, the peanut or groundnut is considered a legume rather than a nut.

Global Sourcing

Pulses and legumes are in the class of vegetables that includes beans, peas, lentils, and garbanzo beans. Peas, chickpeas, and lentils are produced and consumed mainly in Africa, India, Pakistan, Bangladesh, Turkey, and the Middle East.

Buying and Storing

One advantage of dried pulses is that they store very well for long periods if kept in a dry, airtight container away from the light. Pulses toughen during storage, and older ones will take longer to cook, though this won't affect the eating quality. Avoid beans, peas, and lentils with cracked seed coats, foreign materials, and pinholes caused by insect damage.

The FAO recognizes eleven categories of pulses, including the following.

- **Dry beans.** Dry edible beans, or field beans, come in a wide variety of market classes, including kidney bean, navy bean, pinto bean, and black bean. (See Figure 19.30.)

- **Dry broad beans.** The broad bean is also known as the horse bean, Windsor bean, English bean, tick bean, fava bean, field bean, and pigeon bean. Pods are large and thick but vary from 2 to 12 inches. (See Figure 19.31.)

- **Dry peas.** Dry peas are most commonly split, which speeds up cooking time. Americans are most familiar with green peas, but yellow peas are also grown. (See Figure 19.32.)

- **Chickpeas (garbanzo beans).** The greatest production of the plant takes place in India, where it is used to make "dhal," and in the Mediterranean area the cooked seeds (plus sesame oil and other flavoring) form the well-known dish hummus. (See Figure 19.33.)

- **Dry cow peas.** Also known as *black-eyed peas*, these have a pea-like flavor with a firm, resilient texture (if not overcooked). A popular legume in the South, black-eyed peas are essential in the traditional dish Hoppin' John. They do not need soaking and cook fairly quickly. (See Figure 19.34.)

- **Pigeon peas (Congo bean).** These are usually sold dried, but other forms are available. They have a strong flavor, and they are popular in the South and in the Caribbean. (See Figure 19.35.)

- **Lentils.** These have an earthier flavor than green peas. It is best to buy them split, because split peas don't need to be soaked and cook fairly quickly. They are sold in many forms, with or without the pods, whole or split. (See Figure 19.36.)

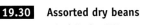
19.30 **Assorted dry beans**
© Randy Van Dam 2008

19.31 **Dry split broad beans**
© Randy Van Dam 2008

Yellow and green dry split peas

Figures 19.32–.35 © Randy Van Dam 2008

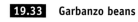 **Garbanzo beans**

19.34 **Black-eyed peas**

 **Pigeon peas**

19.36 Assorted whole and split lentils
© Randy Van Dam 2008

NUTS AND SEEDS

The term **nut** is applied to various fruits having a hard outer shell enclosing a kernel (also called a nut). *Seeds* are found in the fruits of plants and are capable of producing a new plant when released from the fleshy part of the fruit. Humans have consumed nuts and seeds for thousands of years; they were an essential part of the diet for primitive hunter-gatherers and are also sources of nourishment for many animal species.

Nuts and seeds have a wide array of culinary and decorative uses. They go just as well with savory dishes as with sweet dishes, and they make an ideal snack or appetizer. They are also a good complement to or replacement for meat. Oils are extracted from nuts and seeds, which are also processed to make butter and flour.

Buying and Storing

When buying shelled nuts, it is best to buy those in vacuum-sealed glass jars, in cans, or in sealed bags, all of which ensure maximum freshness. It is also a good idea to buy nuts in stores with a rapid turnover.

Nuts sold in the shell tend to keep better than shelled, cut, chopped, or ground nuts. Broken pieces are more perishable than halves or whole kernels. A rancid nut will have a flat metallic taste and a lingering aftertaste. Nuts should be stored in an airtight container away from direct light, heat, and moisture. Depending on the variety, nuts will keep for 2 to 9 months in the refrigerator. Unshelled nuts freeze well and will keep for about a year in the freezer.

Popular Varieties of Edible Nuts

Although there are hundreds of nut varieties consumed around the world, the following nuts are the most common to industrialized societies.

- **Almond.** Almond trees originated in the Mediterranean region, though California is currently the largest producer of almonds. Almonds are used in many desserts but are also used as a garnish for salads, fish, or meat. (See Figure 19.37.)

- **Brazil nuts.** The Brazil nut tree produces large fruits, each containing up to two dozen nuts. Brazil nuts are used in pastries and as snacks. (See Figure 19.38.)

- **Cashews.** Cashews are among the most widely cultivated nut. Cashews are used in snacks, confectionery, and cooking. (See Figure 19.39.)

- **Hazelnuts.** Hazelnuts, also known as *filberts*, are used in snacks, baking, and confectionery. They are also essential to the Spanish dish *picadas*. (See Figure 19.40.)

- **Macadamia nuts.** Hawaii is the leading producer. Macadamia nuts are used as snacks, in baked goods, and in exotic dishes. (See Figure 19.41.)

- **Peanuts.** Although a nut in the culinary sense, in the botanical sense, the fruit of the peanut is *not* a nut. Peanuts are sold dry roasted in the shell, green, boiled, and roasted in the skin or skinless. (See Figure 19.42.)

 19.37 **Different market forms of almonds**
© Randy Van Dam 2008

19.38 Brazil nuts

Figures 19.38–.41 © Randy Van Dam 2008

19.39 Cashews

19.40 Hazelnuts

19.41 Macadamia nuts

Figures 19.42–.45 © Randy Van Dam 2008

19.42 Assorted peanuts

19.43 Pecans

- **Pecans.** These are native to North America, where they are cultivated today. Pecans are used in ice cream, baking, and as a topping or filling for some entree recipes. (See Figure 19.43.)

- **Pine nuts.** Harvesting pine nuts is difficult and expensive. Pine nuts are a staple in Asian, Mediterranean, and Middle Eastern cuisines. (See Figure 19.44.)

- **Pistachios.** Pistachios are not only a popular snack nut but are also used as an ingredient in many desserts. Pistachios are also used as a source for green food coloring. (See Figure 19.45.)

- **Soy nuts.** Soy nuts are not actually nuts. Soy nuts are soybeans that have been soaked in water, drained, and then baked or roasted. Soy nuts are available in a variety of flavors. (See Figure 19.46.)

- **Walnuts.** Walnuts have many uses, including being a popular source for oil. Cheaper than pecans, they are frequently substituted in baking. (See Figure 19.47.)

19.44 Pine nuts

Popular Varieties of Edible Seeds

All pumpkin, melon, and squash seeds are edible and sources of protein. Seeds are very diverse in size. (See Figure 19.48.)

- **Melon seeds.** Many varieties are enjoyed worldwide, and they can also be pressed for oils.

- **Pumpkin seeds.** Green hulled pumpkin seeds are called *pepitas* and are often used in southwestern and Mexican cooking. Pumpkin seeds can turn rancid quickly and should be kept in an airtight container in the refrigerator or freezer.

- **Squash seeds.** These are used much the same way as pumpkin seeds.

- **Sunflower seeds.** Sunflower seeds/kernels are a popular snack and also serve as a source for cooking oil.

19.45 Pistachio nuts

19.46 Soybeans with roasted and salted soy nuts

Figures 19.46–.48 © Randy Van Dam 2008

19.47 Walnuts

19.48 Melon, pumpkin, squash, and sunflower seeds

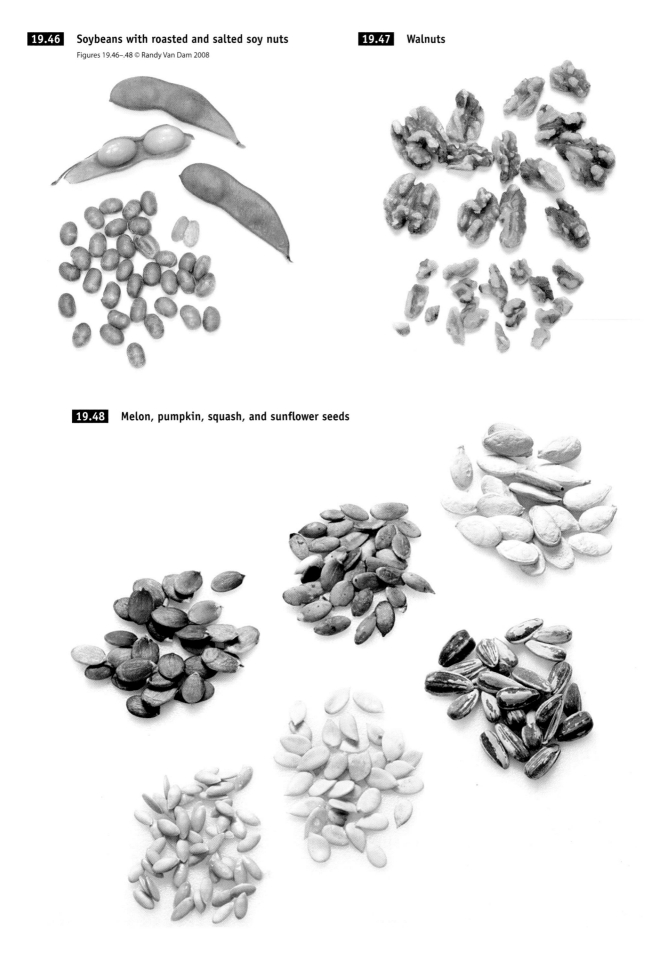

FRUITS AND VEGETABLES

Fresh fruits and vegetables are covered in detail in Chapter 16, "Fruits," and Chapter 17, "Vegetables." In this chapter, dried fruits, fungus, seaweed, and olives are discussed.

Dried Fruits

As long as there have been fruit trees and bushes, there have been dried fruits available for consumption. In North America, the first of these that come to mind are probably tree-hard or top fruits. They consist of two main groups: the *pome fruits*, including the apple and pear-like members, and the *stone fruits*, which include plums, peaches, cherries, and apricots. The pomes have small seeds in a core around which the stalk forms and the flesh encases. The stone fruits have a single seed in a hard shell around which the flesh forms.

BUYING AND STORING

Some dried fruits (such as raisins, figs, prunes, dates, and persimmons) are subject to *sugaring* on the surface. Incidence and severity of sugaring increase with storage temperature and time. The lower the moisture content, the longer the post-harvest life. Many dehydrated fruits have sulfur in them to prevent the natural browning. (See Figure 19.49.)

SULFURING AND DRYING FRUITS

Many commercially dried fruits are **sulfured** with sulfur dioxide (SO_2). This process preserves their original color. Typically all white, yellow, and orange fruits have been sulfured. The process of drying is intended to reduce the moisture content to below 25 percent of its normal levels, thereby delaying the time for the fruit to spoil. There are many ways to dry fruits; some of the most common include the following. (Also see Figure 19.50.)

- **Sun-dried.** Fruits are laid out to dry in the sunshine. Larger fruits are usually cut in half. The fruits typically dried this way include apricots, currants, figs, peaches, pears, and raisins.

19.49 **Example of sugaring on dried fruit**

© Randy Van Dam 2008

 BUYER'S NOTE *Chefs also place sliced fruits on perforated sheet pans in 160°F (71°C) ovens for 45 minutes to simulate sun-drying.*

- **Air or tunnel dried.** The fruit has warm air blown over it to dry. The fruits commonly dried in this fashion include apples, coconut, raisins, and tomatoes.

 BUYER'S NOTE *Chefs often use kitchen dehydrators to air-dry fruits, vegetables, and meats such as jerky.*

- **Naturally dried.** Fruits naturally dry on the trees before they are harvested.

- **Infused with sugar.** The fruit is cut and peeled, and then placed in a large container. Water is heated with a high concentration of sugar. The sugar water exchanges with the lower viscosity water in the fruit. Once the fruits are partially dried this way, they are air dried to complete the drying process.

- **Dried by frying.** The fruits are fried in oil to raise the temperature of the water in the fruit to rapidly boil away. Bananas and plantains are dried this way before the fruits have ripened and their starches are turned into sugar.

Fungus

Mushrooms are commonly listed as a vegetable, but they are actually a fungus. There are approximately 38,000 different mushroom varieties, and not all are edible. In fact, some are poisonous, and you must be sure to purchase mushrooms from reliable sources. Many of these mushroom varieties grow in the wild, but most of the mushrooms found in the market are now grown in controlled environments. Like most things, increased availability has resulted in more affordable prices.

BUYING AND STORING

Mushrooms are sold fresh, dried, frozen, canned, blanched, whole, chopped, sliced, and in stems and pieces. Loose mushrooms are always the best choice; plastic packaging suffocates the mushrooms, making them soggy. Make sure they exhibit appropriate white, tan, or cream color, depending on the variety you are buying. Mushrooms typically darken as they age. When selecting specialty mushrooms, like portabella and shiitake, try to select the firmest and meatiest ones you can find. Most specialty mushrooms will be dry to the touch, but they should not be too fragile. With wild mushrooms, check for any holes that indicate insect damage. Shiitake mushrooms caps should curl under slightly. Only cultivated mushrooms will keep, and even then only for a short period, about 3 days in good condition. Wild mushrooms are best used on the same day they are purchased.

TYPES OF MUSHROOMS

- **Cultivated mushrooms.** Mushrooms that are grown commercially are called **cultivated mushrooms**. Cultivated varieties are the most readily available and the most versatile.

19.50 **Assorted dried fruits**
© Randy Van Dam 2008

- **Button, or white, mushrooms.** The most immature variety, these milky white mushrooms are harvested at a very early stage of development. Cultivated white mushrooms are creamy white to light brown. They are called button mushrooms when small, but they can grow to a jumbo size suitable for stuffing. The flavor has not had much time to mature, but these mushrooms are good in salads, alone, or in combination with other mushrooms or foods. (See Figure 19.51.)

- **Cremini (crimini) mushrooms.** A dark brown variety of the *agaricus bisporus*, this type has a pleasant flavor that can be appreciated in dishes both cooked and raw. (See Figure 19.52.)

- **Cup mushrooms.** These mushrooms are available with the cups either closed or open. The closed types are barely distinguishable from button mushrooms in appearance, although the taste is slightly stronger. Open-cup mushrooms have a speckled cap and exposed brownish gills on the underside. These are mature mushrooms with a fully developed flavor. They are delicious when filled with a savory, herb-specked stuffing and baked.

- **Flat mushrooms.** The most mature of all the common mushrooms, these also have the most intense flavor. Their fanned-out cap and exposed brown gills make them unattractive to many, but it would be a mistake to let their appearance interfere with their great flavoring potential.

19.51 **Button mushrooms**
© Randy Van Dam 2008

19.52 Cremini mushrooms

© Randy Van Dam 2008

19.53 Portabella mushrooms

© Randy Van Dam 2008

- **Portabella (portobello) mushrooms.** Portabellas are mature crimini. Freshly harvested portabella caps are light tan, rounded, and slightly textured with somewhat uneven edges and visible gills on the underside. Their flavor will be richer and more intensely mushroom as they grow larger. Portabellas may be marinated and grilled. (See Figure 19.53.)

- **Wild mushrooms.** In many countries, mushroom gathering is a popular pastime and an extremely rewarding one because **wild mushrooms** are one of the most delicious woodland offerings. Many mushrooms, however, are poisonous, and the inexperienced gatherer should be wary. Never eat any mushroom garnered in the wild if it cannot be positively identified as safe for consumption. There are a number of books that can help you identify nonpoisonous edible mushrooms, although appearance varies from one area to another. For this reason, an expert should authenticate any suspicious type of mushrooms, and wild mushrooms should only be purchased from known suppliers.

  - **Boletus (cepes, porcini).** Boletus have a long, fleshy stalk up to 10 inches high. Thick and firm, it is topped by a fleshy cap. Anywhere from 2.5 to 12 inches across, it can be a number of different colors: yellow, red, brown, pink, whitish, or grayish. The underside of the cap is covered with vertical tube-like pores; this aids identification, as most other mushrooms have gills. Young boletuses are more tender and flavorful. Their taste improves with cooking. (See Figure 19.54.)

  - **Chanterelles.** Chanterelles are horn-shaped mushrooms and have a cup-shaped cap ranging from ¾ to 4 inches across. The cap's wrinkled underside distinguishes chanterelles from most other mushrooms, which are gilled. All types of chanterelles are edible. They can be gently sautéed and served on their own. Gray chanterelles are known as *Girolles*. (See Figure 19.55.)

  - **Chicken-of-the-woods mushroom.** This fungus got its name because it has the texture of cooked chicken. You

can sauté it or, if you want to make mock chicken (as a vegetarian dish), simmer it in salty vegetable stock.

- **Horns of plenty.** These are dark brown, almost black, mushrooms with a deep, rich flavor. They are less common but easily recognizable in markets by their funnel-shaped stem. They offer a pleasing contrast when combined with other mushrooms.

- **Huitlacoche.** This is a fungus that forms black kernels on ears of corn in damp weather. It is a prized delicacy in Mexico and tastes a bit like wild mushrooms. You can get it fresh or frozen by mail order, or canned in some Hispanic markets. It is also known as *maize mushroom*.

- **Morels.** The conical cap looks rather like a sponge with many small crevices. The morel's globular or conical cap is honeycombed, which makes it look porous. Yellowish, brown, or whitish, the cap is from 1 to 5 inches high. It grows atop a fairly thick stalk of the same color and height. (See Figure 19.56.)

- **Shiitake.** Shiitake, also known as *Chinese black* or *forest mushrooms*, can be eaten raw, but their meaty flavor is best appreciated when cooked. (See Figure 19.57.)

- **Oyster mushrooms.** Oyster mushrooms range from soft brown to gray, and their fanned shape resembles that of an oyster shell. They are velvety with a robust flavor that turns subtly sweet when cooked; however, they lose their flavor when overcooked. (See Figure 19.58.)

- **Truffles.** The king of wild mushrooms, truffles have an incomparable flavor. The most sought after is the *black truffle* (see Figure 19.59), a globular fungus covered with small blackish warts, which grows abundantly but not exclusively in the French region of Perigord. The *white truffle* is also highly esteemed, particularly specimens gathered around Alba, Italy. Somewhat rough textured, it is whitish, yellowish, or greenish yellow and resembles an irregularly shaped tuber. Its white or ochre flesh, streaked with white veins, has a garlic-like or cheese-like taste.

The odor of truffles and the aroma that they add to foods is their appeal, compared with their bland taste and chewy texture.

19.54 Cepes, or porcini, mushrooms

Figures 19.54–.58 © Randy Van Dam 2008

19.56 Morels

19.55 Chanterelle mushrooms

19.57 Shiitake mushrooms

- **Cultivated wild mushrooms.** Some popular varieties are now grown commercially and are more widely available.

  - **Enoki mushrooms (velvet shank).** The delicate-tasting enoki mushroom has a long stem (up to 4 inches) topped with a tiny white cap. It grows in clusters on live or dead tree trunks, as well as on tree roots and branches covered with soil. The mushrooms are cultivated on stumps or in a sawdust medium and are picked about 2 months after inoculation. Cultivated enoki mushrooms are paler than those that grow wild. (See Figure 19.60.)

  - **Oyster mushrooms.** With a firm texture and neutral flavor, oyster mushrooms are ideal for a mixed mushroom sauté. High heat will draw out all of the liquid and, with it, all the texture and flavor.

  - **Shiitake mushrooms.** With a meat-like flavor, these mushrooms lend themselves well to long cooking. Their fleshy brownish caps are generally from 2 to 4 inches across, and their stems are woodier than those of most other mushrooms.

19.58 Oyster mushrooms

19.59 **Perigord black truffle**

Figures 19.59–.61 © Randy Van Dam 2008

19.60 **Enoki mushrooms**

- **Dried mushrooms.** The taste of certain mushrooms, such as morels and boletus, is even more intense when dried. The general rule is to allow one part dried mushrooms for every eight parts fresh. (See Figure 19.61.)

  - **Morels.** These are the most expensive of the dried mushrooms, but only a few add a lot of flavor (1 pound equals 2 to 3 ounces dried).

  - **Shiitake.** When dried, these have a smoky flavor. For best results, chop shiitake finely before use.

  - **Wood ears (cloud ears, tree ears).** While they add little in flavor, they are valued for their gelatinous, seaweed-like texture. Reconstitute them by soaking or simmering them in lots of water for a few hours.

Seaweed

Seaweed is an important food source in many Asian cultures. Japanese cuisine employs multiple varieties for different uses. Laver, also known as purple laver, is one of the most commonly consumed seaweeds. Sheets of dried laver look somewhat like purple cellophane. (See Figure 19.62.)

19.61 **Assorted dried mushrooms (morels, shiitake, wood ears)**

People, Places, Things

Reconstituting Dried Mushrooms

Reconstituted dried mushrooms can be used in place of fresh in most recipes. Be sure to adjust the cooking time because they can be a bit tough and require additional simmering.

To reconstitute, soak the mushrooms for 15 to 30 minutes in enough warm water to cover; then, strain through a lined sieve. (The liquid can also be added to the dish.) If needed, dry the wet mushrooms on side towels and pat with another side towel. They should be dry before use, or they may dilute the

19.62 **Seaweed and nori**

© Randy Van Dam 2008

Cooking with Mushrooms

Mushrooms are quite porous, which makes cleaning them a delicate task. Cultivated mushrooms can be gently rinsed, but for salads it is best to trim the stems and wipe the caps with a paper towel to keep them crisp and dry. While it is common practice to peel mushrooms, this is not necessary unless the color or texture of the cap is uninviting; be sure to reserve the trimmings for the stockpot. Wild mushrooms should never be rinsed or peeled. Simply trim off the thick, rough part of the stems and gently brush off any dirt with a soft brush.

Olives

The following olives are representative of the many table varieties available, and they include many of the most popular olives on the world market.

BUYING AND STORING

In contrast to the popular misconception, green and black olives do not come from two different trees. Although there are many varieties of olives, their color indicates the degree of ripeness at which they were picked. Olive packers select their olives based on desired characteristics, and degree of ripeness contributes greatly to an olive's texture and flavor. As a general rule, the darker the color, the riper the olive when it was picked. (See Table 19.2 for typical olive sizes and counts.)

The overall quality of an olive depends very much on the method of harvesting. In these modern times, commercial growers often use tree shakers to vibrate the fruit from their branches onto tarps lying on the ground below. Less mechanical methods, sometimes used in smaller groves or poorer countries, include beating the branches with sticks to hasten the olive's fall onto the tarps. Either method will generally result in bruised olives that have been picked at varying degrees of ripeness.

Olives that are handpicked can be carefully plucked (see Figure 19.63) or raked at the proper stage of ripeness and with little bruising to the fruit. This results in a consistent texture and even flavor, which is crucial to a quality product.

There are several important considerations to make when selecting table olives. It is generally best to use olives that are:

- Handpicked (not roughly harvested in batches)
- Naturally cured (never in lye)
- Fresh (not pasteurized)

TABLE 19.2 **Olive Sizes and Counts**

Green		Ripe Counts**	
Type	Count*	Whole	Pitted
Small	737	557	578
Medium	644	466	486
Large	539	404	402
X-Large	457	338	334
Mammoth	385	288	278
Giant	312	228	245
Jumbo	253	192	199
Colossal	199	152	163
Super-Colossal	172	128	---

*Approximate count per gallon container.
**Approximate count per #10 size can.

19.63 **Picking olives by hand**

© Randy Van Dam 2008

- **Argentina**
  - The Alfonso olive is large, meaty, and purple or green, with a uniquely fruity flavor. They are common to the north and west coasts of South America. (See Figure 19.64.)

- **France**
  - Niçoise olives are some of the most coveted of all. Real Niçoise olives are tiny and black, and they possess a uniquely delicate flavor. They are essential to the preparation of many authentic regional Mediterranean dishes, such as *salade Niçoise with tuna*. (See Figure 19.65.)
  - Picholines are the crisp, uncracked green olives from southern France with a nutty flavor and anise undertones. Besides their use as table olives, they are pleasant additions to stews and fennel dishes.
  - Nyons olives are often expensive and imitated. They are first dry-cured and then aged in brine to plump them. Authentic Nyons are slightly wrinkled and a bit duller than the North African imitations that lack the rich flavor.

- **Greece.** Greece grows more than 1.5 million acres of olives. Marketplaces will generally offer more than twenty varieties from which to choose.
  - Greek olives include Amfissa, Elitses (tiny), Hondroelia (gigantic), Konservolia (or natural black olives), Nafplion, and Kalamata, which are allowed to ripen on the tree until their skin turns purple black. (See Figure 19.66.)

19.64	Alfonso (alphonso) olives

Figures 19.64–.67b © Randy Van Dam 2008

19.66	Kalamata olives

19.65	Niçoise olives

19.67a	Barese olives

19.67b	Sicilian Castelvetrano olives

- **Italy**
  - Mildly fruity and slightly bitter in taste, the Barese olive is meaty and provides a good amount of oil when used in the production of olive oil. (See Figure 19.67a.)
  - Sicilian-style Castelvetrano is a large green variety that is highly seasoned in a marinade of herbs and has a somewhat salty or sour flavor. (See Figure 19.67b.)
  - Naturally cured Cerignola olives, from the Province of Puglia, are medium-ripe and light brown.
  - Purple-brown Gaeta olives are frequently used in pasta dishes or on pizzas.

- **Morocco.** The olive is the most predominant fruit tree in Morocco. Moroccan olives are commonly sun dried.
  - Morocco grows Picholine, Marocaine, and Zitoun olives, and they are used in both table olives and olive oil. (See Figure 19.68.)
- **Spain**
  - Spain is the world's largest exporter of table olives. The majority of its exports are the Spanish-style pimento-stuffed green olives.
  - The varieties grown in Spain are Gordal, Arbequina, Manzanillas, and Hojiblanca. The large, green Gordals have a firm, meaty texture. Manzanillas are smaller, crisper, and nuttier than Gordals. Hojiblancas are used primarily for olive oil production and make marginal quality table olives. (See Figure 19.69a, Figure 19.69b, and Figure 19.69c.)

19.69b **Arbequina olives**

19.68 **Moroccan sun-dried olives**

Figures 19.68–.69c © Randy Van Dam 2008

19.69c **Manzanilla olives**

19.69a **Gordal olives with pits and stuffed**

- **United States.** California produces nearly all the olives in the United States—more than 34,000 acres. (See Figure 19.70, Figure 19.71a, and Figure 19.71b.)
  - Manzanilla olives represent more than 70 percent of the olives grown in the United States. Other varieties are produced in lesser quantities. Although most olives become the California black ripe olives, the Sevillano are large, brine-cured, green, and meaty, similar to the Spanish-style Gordal.

19.70 **Assorted sizes of California black-ripened olives**

Figures 19.70–.72 © Randy Van Dam 2008

19.71a **Assorted loose olives being sold in marketplace**

Courtesy of Robert Garlough

19.71b **Market forms of packaged olives**

SOYA PRODUCTS

Proteins that are extracted (isolated) from certain vegetable plants by a chemical process are known as textured vegetable proteins, which are added to a wide array of food products primarily as a meat substitute. The nutritional quality of the soya bean is superior to that of other pulses. It contains more protein and is also a good source of iron and calcium. A large number of soya-based foods including tofu, tempeh, and textured vegetable protein (TVP) are available.

Tofu

Tofu is made by grinding soybeans in water, extracting the liquid, adding a coagulant to create curds, and then straining to create a solid block. Attention needs to be paid to the expiration date. Shelf life is only a few weeks, and it is best to open the container and change the water daily until it is used. Tofu is also sold in a foil-lined pouch that has an extended shelf life. (See Figure 19.72.)

Tofu can have a variety of textures, depending on the type of coagulant used and how it is compressed in the straining process. Silken varieties are never pressed; when pureed, it can replace eggs in baking and mayonnaise in salad dressings. Pressed tofu needs to be marinated, as the moisture has been pressed out. It can be flavored, and also freezes well. Generally, tofu is found in four textures:

- **Soft.** Best for use in dressings and sauces (Figure 19.73a).

- **Medium.** Best if marinated, like all pressed tofus, to absorb flavor.

- **Firm.** Works well in salads and soups (Figure 19.73b).

- **Extra-firm.** Best for stir-frying and broiling (Figure 19.73c).

Although it has a mild taste of its own, tofu easily picks up flavors with whatever it is cooked (Figure 19.74). The soybean, from which it is made, contains all eight essential amino acids, is high in calcium, low in sodium, and is low in fat compared with other proteins.

19.72 **Fried tofu**

19.73a Soft tofu

Figures 19.73a–.75 © Randy Van Dam 2008

19.74 Flavored tofu examples

19.73b Firm tofu

Tempeh

Tempeh is a cake of soybeans made by removing the hulls of cooked soya beans, mixing with tempeh starter, and then ageing and fermenting for a day or two. The starter culture helps hold the soybeans together in a cake form. Because of its nutritional value, tempeh is used worldwide in vegetarian cuisine. Tempeh has a high protein, dietary fiber, and vitamin content. (See Figure 19.75.)

19.75 Tempeh

19.73c Extra-firm tofu

Textured Vegetable Proteins

The composition of textured soybean proteins is extremely variable because it depends on the manufacturing process as well as on the ingredients used. In cooked commercial preparations, there is so much variety that it is often very difficult to know the nutritional value of the product unless it is indicated on the label. The advantage of **textured vegetable proteins (TVPs)** from a nutritional standpoint is that they are extremely low in fat and rich in proteins. (See Figure 19.76.)

19.76 Assorted TVP products

© Randy Van Dam 2008

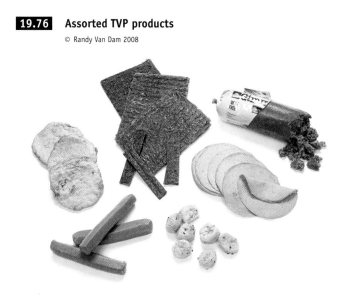

[ASK THE EXPERT]

Christopher Koetke
Soyfoods Council Spokesperson

Name: Christopher Koetke

Title: Dean of the School of Culinary Arts

Employer: Kendall College School of Culinary Arts

Education/Training:

Chef Koetke began cooking professionally in 1982, starting at local restaurants in his hometown of Valparaiso, Indiana. He soon moved to Chicago and procured a position at L'Escargot on Halsted. Eager to expand his knowledge of fine cuisine, Koetke traveled to France, where he worked in some of the country's finest kitchens: Pavillon Elysees, Pierre Gagnaire, Taillevent, and Pierre Orsi. Upon his return to the United States, Koetke began a 5-year tenure at the world famous Le Français in Wheeling, Illinois. During this time, Koetke finished third in the U.S. finals of the Bocuse d'Or culinary competition. In 1992, Koetke became the executive chef of Chicago's Les Nomades restaurant. Chef Koetke has earned a BA from Valparaiso University and an MBA from Dominican University.

Awards/Honors:

CEC and CCE certifications from the American Culinary Federation
International Green Award by FCSI International
FCCLA honorary member
Chef of the Year, Chicago Chapter of the International Food and Wine Society

General Responsibilities:

Over the past 5 years, Chef Koetke has had the pleasure of working closely with the Soyfoods Council, the Idaho Potato Commission, the National Pork Board, and the Wisconsin Milk Marketing Board. These professional relationships have generally consisted of presentations and video projects.

Ask the Expert Questions:

1) What was the reason behind your interest in soy products?
For a number of years, I have worked closely with the ever-changing world of soy. Over this time, I have witnessed the United States warming up to soy, and the soy producers have made products that increasingly appeal to the American's taste profile and lifestyle. The reason behind my initial interest in soy was a reaction to an elevated cholesterol level that was certainly linked to years of teaching charcuterie. Like many Americans, I first saw soy as a nutritional remedy to a medical issue.

2) Beyond the nutritional benefit, was there any other appeal to the use of soy products?
As a chef, I started focusing on the myriad of tastes and textures of the many different soy foods. This started a personal journey to create dishes with soy that married nutrition and taste. While I was intrigued, others wrinkled up their noses and muttered something about not liking soy and believing it to be too healthy to be likeable. First, I worked with soy in an Asian context. Then I started slipping it into other cuisines like Italian and regional American and was amazed at its ability to adapt to other flavors. One day I prepared a spicy mushroom tofu tomato sauce to go over pasta. The combination was simply delicious and broke many of soy's stereotypes. My wife, too, then became a soy convert.

3) What are you doing to promote healthful cooking and dietary practices?
At Kendall College, we believe that all food service professionals entering the world of food today need to have a strong understanding of nutrition. Without this, they will be at a competitive disadvantage. At the present time, we are exploring ways to make nutrition an increasingly important focus across the curriculum. This will not only improve the student's nutritional prowess but also communicate to them the value that we place on nutrition.

CONVENIENCE CORNER PRODUCT EXAMPLES

Vegetarian and Special Dietary Products

Company	Website	Products
Carla's Pasta	http://www.carlaspasta.com	2/2.5 # Ravioli Shrimp 36 ct/2.57 oz Manicotti Seafood
Kraft	http://www.kraftfoods.com	36/7 oz Macaroni and Cheese
Kellogg's	http://www.kelloggs.com	48/1.3 oz Breakfast for Nutri-grain 10/18.3 oz Cereal All Bran 10/18 oz Cereal Granola
Reser's	http://www.resers.com	2/5# Salad Pasta Greek Feta
Simplot	http://www.simplotfoods.com	6/2.5# Bean Soy Edamame
Woodland Foods	http://www.woodlandfoods.com	10# Bean White Sweet Runner 6/5# Noodle Lo Mein
Uncle Ben's	http://www.unclebens.com	2/5# Rice Arborio 6/24 oz Rice Mexican Fiesta
Indian Harvest	http://www.indianharvest.com	12/2# Rice Basmati Brown 12/1 # Grain Muesli Whole
Near East	http://www.neareast.com	6/2.25 # Rice Spinach
Mama Mucci Pasta	http://www.mamamuccispasta.com	20# Pasta Cavatappi
Barilla	http://www.barilla.com	2/10# Pasta Gemelli
Ferris Coffee & Nut	http://www.ferriscoffee.com	5# Nut Almonds Sliced
Planters	http://www.planters.com	12/6.5oz Nuts Mixed Salt
Mo-Na Foods	http://www.monafood.ca	5/1# Mushroom Forest Blend

Margaret "Mokie" Steiskal, PhD

Place of Birth: Lansing, Michigan

Educational Background and Work Experience

Mokie (as she's called by her friends) Steiskal was fortunate to grow up near one of the country's leading hotel, restaurant, and institutional management programs. After graduating from Michigan State University with a bachelor of arts degree, she went to work for the local YWCA as its food service manager. That position lead to a job with the Bill Knapp's Restaurants chain as the Michigan Director of Service Training based in Battlecreek, Michigan. Steiskal worked with new and pre-existing service staff while helping to open new restaurant units. After a few years in the restaurant setting, Dr. Steiskal moved to Columbus, Ohio, and the Mount Carmel Medical Center in 1974, working as an administrative dietitian, supervising the cafeteria and catering operations in an institutional food service setting. It was during this period when Dr. Steiskal began her celebrated career as an educator, serving as an adjunct instructor for Columbus State Community College (CSCC) in 1981. In 1982, she moved to the Riverside Methodist Hospital, also in Columbus, to work as its Food Production and Cafeteria manager, managing 50 employees and producing and serving 3,000 meals a day to patients, employees, and visitors. In 1984, CSCC came knocking on her door with a full-time position as a hospitality management instructor for its growing program. After Steiskal earned her MBA in 1992 from the University of Dayton, she was made a professor of hospitality management. In 2002, Steiskal graduated from Ohio University with a Ph.D. in higher education administration, and in 2006 she was named chairperson of the Hospitality, Massage Therapy, Sport and Exercise Studies Department at Columbus State Community College. Steiskal still finds time to instruct and advise her students, teaching courses in food purchasing, menu development, introduction to hospitality and tourism management, and hospitality supervision and quality management.

It Happened to Me...

Courtesy Margaret Steiskal

"In my first position after graduating from Michigan State, I was food service manager of the YWCA. Included in my responsibilities was purchasing for the operation. The YWCA served breakfast and lunch cafeteria style to the public, Monday through Friday. There was also occasional on-site catering involved for United Way agencies. It was a relatively low-volume operation with a limited budget.

My major faux pas was to purchase 25 cases of six #10 cans of sliced peaches. Why is this a faux pas you ask? The sales representative that I was working with at the time represented a large distributor, and I was new and young. He told me that if I bought the peaches on sale I would get two free blankets . . . and my apartment needed stuff. I fell for his 'bargain,' bought the peaches, and enjoyed the blankets. Sounds great—right? The YWCA probably took 3 years to use up the peaches. So what did I learn? What looks like a 'bargain' often isn't; not all sales representatives have your best interest at heart, and I have felt guilty ever since!"

Memberships and Career Highlights

People who know Dr. Steiskal see her as a dynamic force—capable of multitasking and making improvements wherever she serves. She is an active member of the American, Ohio, and Columbus Dietetic Associations; a registered dietitian by the Commission on Dietetic Registration, American Dietetic Association; and a licensed dietitian by the Ohio Board of Dietetics, State of Ohio. A Certified Culinary Educator by the American Culinary Federation and a member of the ACF Columbus Chapter, she served as program chair for 5 years, co-chaired the program committee for 2005 Northeast Regional, and served as Hospitality Chair for 2006 and as Secretary for 2007–2008. With the Council on Hotel Restaurant and Institutional Educators, Steiskal served as the 2-year representative to the board, on the Strategic Planning Committee, and was elected as the organization's vice president in 2007. Programmatic accreditation for 2- and 4-year schools has always been important to Steiskal, as she has served in a variety of capacities, including as chairperson, commissioner and site-team visitor for the American Culinary Federation Foundation (ACFF), Commission on Accreditation of Hospitality Management Programs (CAHM), and the Accrediting Commission for Programs in Hospitality Administration (ACPHA).

Her studies and work have always received praise, as demonstrated by her induction into Beta Gamma Sigma, an honor society for collegiate schools of business, University of Dayton chapter, in 1993. That same year, Steiskal received the Reverend Raymond A. Roesch, S.M., Award of Excellence for outstanding academic achievement in the MBA program from the University of Dayton. She is also a member of the honor society of Phi Kappa Phi, Ohio University chapter. In 2002, the International Council on Hotel, Restaurant, and Institutional Education awarded Dr. Steiskal the prestigious Chef Herman Breithaupt Award, which recognizes achievement and contributions to food service education by a chef or educator.

Passions with the Food Service Industry

"This business is about serving the very best food every time, providing the

(continued)

very best service every time, and pleasing your customer every time. And it is an industry that gets in your blood and heart and mind. The pleasure is from the positive responses one gets from the customer, the smiles of satisfaction, and the joy of having served another customer who appreciates what you do. It takes hard work and energy, but it is so worth it!"

Advice to a Chef or Buyer

"'Organize this mess!' This is a phrase I often use in purchasing class to express the attention to detail that purchasing requires. How often did you take produce inventory on an old napkin and then complain to the produce delivery driver that you got the wrong order? Understand your customers' expectations and budget. The temptation to buy the most expensive item might be there, but will it truly provide a return on your investment? And pay attention to how the product is prepped, handled, cooked, and served in your operation. Make sure the product you have purchased works best in your kitchen, and it should ideally provide the best product at the best cost for your customers. Do not limit your freedom of action by buying into the company that provides you with the 'free' software for ordering and never comparing prices and services that another company might provide. And remember, the purchasing function isn't over when the food comes in the back door."

Key Words and Concepts

cultivated mushrooms	seitan	textured vegetable proteins (TVPs)	vegetarian
kasha	sulfured		wild mushrooms
nut	tempeh	tofu	
pulses		vegan	

Chapter in Review

The following exercises are provided to help the reader understand and apply the contents of this chapter. They may be completed individually or in a classroom environment.

REVIEW QUESTIONS

a. Define the term *vegetarian* and its other dietary forms.

b. List the six major food groups of the vegetarian diet, and provide examples from each.

c. List the different types of rice and their features.

d. Discuss dried fruits and the methods used to dry them.

e. Define the term *pulses*, and list several different types.

INDIVIDUAL ACTIVITIES

a. **Web based:** Research sources for TVPs and other vegetarian products on the Internet. Try to find sources for all six vegetarian food groups.

b. **Experiential:** Make *seitan*, and try substituting it for other ingredients in recipes.

c. **Critical thinking:** Consider what meat products you use in your own lifestyle and how you could eliminate their use if you chose to do so.

GROUP ACTIVITIES

a. **Lab experience:** Prepare a variety of TVPs and have students compare their tastes to meat-based products during a blind tasting.

b. **Classroom action:** Divide the class into two groups, and debate the merits of a vegetarian lifestyle.

CHAPTER

20

Image copyright Katarzyna Malecka, 2009. Used under license from Shutterstock.com

Beverages

"When I sell liquor, it's called bootlegging: when my patrons serve it on Lake Shore Drive, it's called hospitality."

AL CAPONE

After reading this chapter, you will be able to:

◎ Describe the production of coffee beans, and list the different varieties available.

◎ List the types of roasts and grinds used for coffee beans.

◎ Explain the production of tea, and list the different varieties available.

◎ Identify the different fruit and vegetable juices.

◎ Discuss bottled water, and list the types of water available based on their standard of identity.

◎ Explain the concepts of Alcohol Beverage Control and control states, as they relate to alcoholic beverage sales.

◎ Define wine and its proper storage.

◎ Summarize the international wine production laws and regulations.

◎ Define fortified wines and aperitifs, and provide examples.

◎ Identify the most common types of port and Madeira available.

◎ Define craft beers and their different terms for production and sales capacity.

◎ Explain *vital statistics* as they relate to beer production.

◎ Summarize the types of beers and their characteristics.

◎ Describe the distillation process for spirits, including the use of pot stills and column stills.

◎ List the different products from which spirits are distilled.

Introduction

Beverages are the most universal form of purchase to any food service operation. Nearly every item in a food service operation can be served with a beverage. Water is one of the most popular beverages, followed by tea, coffee, and then other nonalcoholic drinks. Alcoholic beverages are also very popular with patrons, especially when they match the food served. Although almost impossible to catalogue in their entirety, this chapter discusses the most common beverages sold in modern food service operations.

Coffee

Coffee dates back to the sixth century. It originated in Africa and spread rapidly across Europe and other continents. Today, coffee is drunk around the world, and each nation has its own ways of preparing and serving it.

COFFEE PRODUCTION

Coffee is now grown in more than fifty countries, although production is not at all straightforward. Because it is vulnerable to frost, coffee can be grown only in the tropics. Crop maintenance is labor intensive. The plants require careful tending, pruning, hoeing, and weeding, and in most areas picking is done by hand. (See Figure 20.1.)

The harvested berrylike fruits are called *cherries*. These ripen over a period of 6 to 8 months and turn a deep red when ripe, hence their name. Inside, there are two beans that have to be separated from the pulp and skin, and then dried. This process is known as *curing*, and it can be done by one of two methods:

- For the traditional **dry method of curing**, the cherries are laid out in the sun until completely dry, and then a hulling machine removes the dried skins and pulp.

- The **wet method of curing** is a more recent development and is employed for high-quality, hand-picked beans. The outer, fleshy layer is removed, and then the cherries are

20.1 **Coffee cherries ripe for harvest**
Photo Courtesy Robert Garlough

soaked and fermented, followed by washing and drying. Finally, a hulling machine removes the skins.

In both cases, the hulled or "polished" green coffee beans are sorted, graded, and packed for export. Roasting is usually done in the country of import. It is possible to buy green beans, but most coffee is sold after it has been roasted. The roasting process is necessary to reduce the acidity of the beans and to develop the aromatic oils that give the coffee its aroma and flavor. Finally, grinding exposes a larger surface area to the water, ensuring optimum contact between the grounds and water, which results in a richer cup of coffee. (See Figure 20.2.)

GLOBAL SOURCING

The following are some of the most common types of coffee available (also see Figure 20.3):

- **Brazilian Santos.** Brazil is the world's largest coffee grower, producing every grade of bean, but the majority is used to make instant coffee. Brazilian Santos gets its name from the port through which it is shipped, and it is held to be the best of the Brazilian coffees. Usually medium roasted, this has a flavor that is soft and mellow but full bodied.

20.2 **Coffee roaster used at Mexican organic coffee finca**

Photo Courtesy Robert Garlough

- **Colombian.** This is a fine coffee that can be enjoyed either medium or dark roasted. *Medellin excelso,* with its slightly nutty flavor, is probably the most well-known Colombian coffee, but *Libana supreme* is reputed to have more flavor than other varieties of bean from this country.

- **Costa Rican.** Prized for the elegant richness of its flavor, as well as its delicate acidity, this is popular as a breakfast coffee. *Tarrazu* is one of the best from this area.

- **Guatemalan.** All the beans from this country have a characteristic rich spiciness and a smoky character. Medium roasting is recommended to bring out the full body and pleasant, flavorful acidity.

- **Indonesian.** The most well known are *Java* and *Sumatra,* and both have a heavy-bodied, smooth flavor with little acidity. Java beans have a unique, slightly smoky taste, whereas Sumatra beans have a flavor that is vaguely reminiscent of chocolate.

- **Jamaican Blue Mountain.** With a smooth, subtle delicacy and gentle acidity, plus a rather distinctive nutty flavor, this coffee is in great demand. Not surprisingly, this is one of the more expensive coffees.

- **Kenyan.** Aromatic with a clean, sharp, bright taste and good acidity, this is one of the classic coffees. *Kenyan Peaberry* is an especially prized type of coffee; this should be medium roasted and preferably drunk black.

- **Kona Kai.** Grown in Hawaii, this is another of the world's fine, rare coffees. Rich, earthy and full flavored with a pleasant acidity, this is best when medium roasted.

- **Mexican Maragogipe.** Originally from Brazil, this Mexican strain produces a fine coffee. *Mexican coatapec* is another good quality coffee, exported mainly to the United States.

- **Mocha.** Strictly speaking, this is the name given to coffee from Arabia, but in practice, the trade applies the name to coffee from Ethiopia. *Ethiopian mocha* has a rich, complex flavor that is often described as "gamy" or "veiny." With an excellent aroma and good balance, it is the choice of many connoisseurs; the best example is *Harrar longberiy.* This is also the type used for traditional Turkish coffee.

- **Mysore.** The best-known Indian coffee, this has a delicate aroma and smooth, soft flavor with no acidity. It is often blended with mocha to give *Mysore mocha.*

- **Nicaraguan.** A mild non-acidic coffee, this is well suited for breakfast-time drinking.

- **Tanzanian Kilimanjaro.** Stronger than Central American coffees but less acidic than East African coffees, this has a distinctive well-balanced flavor. It can be satisfactorily medium or dark roasted.

BUYING AND STORING

Coffee sold on the world market is still "green," that is, unroasted, as green beans can be stored for several years with no loss in flavor. Indeed, aging in warehouses enhances the characteristics of certain coffees. Before roasting, the beans undergo a final grading to eliminate any remaining impurities and to discard unripe or fermented beans, and then they are blended with other varieties to improve the quality of individual batches and to ensure a consistent taste.

Coffee beans start to lose their flavor as soon as they are roasted, and this flavor loss accelerates after grinding. Store coffee away from air and light, ideally in an airtight container made of opaque glass kept in the refrigerator or freezer. Ground coffee keeps well at room temperature for 7 to 10 days and up to a month in the freezer. Whole coffee beans can be stored for several months in the refrigerator.

Types of Coffee

The flavor, character, and quality of coffee vary tremendously, not only among countries, but also among estates within the same country. The soil, altitude, and climate all affect the character of the bean and, therefore, the final taste.

Coffea arabica grows on steep mountain slopes at high altitudes and accounts for 70 percent of world production. Coffee experts agree that the arabica bean has a far superior flavor than other types.

Coffea canepbora produces the coffee known as *robusta.* Robusta beans have a higher caffeine content than arabica

Assorted coffee beans (top: Java; middle row from left: Kenya, Sumatra, Ethiopia; bottom: Columbia)
© Randy Van Dam 2008

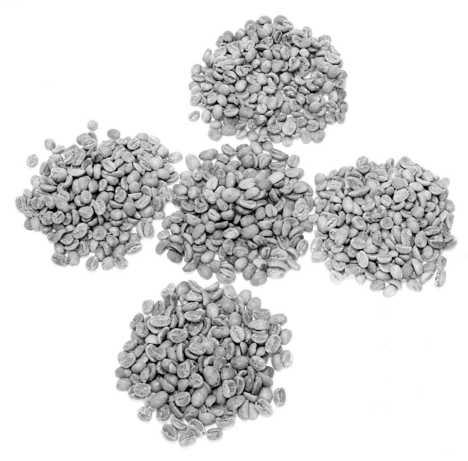

People, Places, Things

Fair Trade Certification of Coffee

In 1988, world coffee prices began a sharp descent, triggering the birth of the first Fair Trade certification initiative. It was branded "Max Havelaar," after a fictional Dutch character who opposed the exploitation of coffee pickers in Dutch colonies. The *Netherland's Max Havelaar* label offered mainstream coffee industry players the opportunity to adopt a standardized system of Fair Trade criteria. In 1997, FLO, the international umbrella organization for Fair Trade labeling, brought "Max Havelaar" together with its counterparts in other countries. Today, TransFair USA is a member of FLO, which now has representation in nineteen countries across Europe, North America, and Japan. Fair Trade–certified coffee is now the fastest-growing segment of the U.S. specialty coffee market. Building on the success of Max Havelaar and ATOs, TransFair USA opened its doors in late 1998, and began certifying Fair Trade coffee in 1999. In addition to coffee, TransFair has introduced Fair Trade–certified tea and cocoa to the U.S. market.

beans and a rougher flavor. It costs about half the price of arabica. Both arabica and robusta coffee are served in commercial food service operations, and blends of the two beans are also available.

Types of Roasts

When coffee beans are roasted, they expand to nearly double their original size. **Roasting** transforms the chemical and physical properties of green coffee beans into roasted coffee products. As the bean absorbs heat, the color shifts to yellow, then to a light "cinnamon" brown, and then to a dark and oily color. During roasting, oils appear on the surface of the bean. The roast will continue to darken until it is removed from the heat source. The degree of roasting determines the delicacy or richness of a coffee; strength is determined by the amount of coffee used. The following are the common levels of roasting:

- **Light.** This roast is used for beans with subtle flavors. (See Figure 20.4.)

- **Medium.** With a more pronounced flavor and smell, this roast results in a stronger and more balanced coffee. (See Figure 20.5.)

- **Dark.** This coffee provides a strong flavor and aroma. (See Figure 20.6.)

- **Continental.** A very dark roast, this is the preferred roast of those who like strong coffee. (See Figure 20.7.)

Types of Grinds

The coarseness or the fineness of the grind determines the surface area of the coffee that will come into contact with the water. Because some brewing methods have a very long or very short contact period between grounds and water, they must always be matched with a suitable grind. For example, in espresso machines, the water spends little time in contact with the grounds, so the grounds must be very fine to ensure that the flavor is passed to the water.

20.4 **Light-roasted coffee beans (Kent Club)**

Figures 20.4–20.5 © Randy Van Dam 2008

20.5 **Medium-roasted coffee beans (New Guinea)**

People, Places, Things

Instant Coffee

There are three types of instant coffee. The cheapest is made from robusta beans that have been brewed into a concentrate. This is sprayed into a stream of hot air that instantly evaporates all moisture, leaving a fine powder. Some of these spray-dried powders undergo further heating to produce granular coffees; the better ones include some arabica beans. The best instant coffees are freeze-dried. For these, an arabica coffee concentrate is frozen and processed in a vacuum to produce crisp, dry particles of coffee.

20.6 Dark-roasted coffee beans (Nicaragua)

Figures 20.6–20.7 © Randy Van Dam 2008

20.7 Continental-roasted coffee beans (Colombia Supremo)

With a coffee grinder on hand, you can grind the beans to order. If not, buy ground coffee in small quantities and store in an airtight container in the refrigerator. The flavor of coffee depends on its highly volatile oils, so it is best to buy freshly roasted beans in small quantities. The following are the common levels for grinding coffee:

- **Coarse grind.** It is possible to obtain this grind only at home. It may be used for the jug method and for percolators and will produce a lighter brew than medium grind. (See Figure 20.8.)

- **Medium grind.** The most versatile grind, this is suitable for use in jugs, percolators, cafeterias, and Neapolitan flip pots. Use a fine strainer with jugs and percolators. (See Figure 20.9.)

- **Fine grind.** For coffee made by the filter or drip method, this is the grind to choose. It produces a large surface area of coffee that allows the water filtering through to take

the maximum flavor. The coffee will be strong because the fineness of the grind prevents the water from filtering through too fast, thereby lengthening the contact time between coffee and water. (See Figure 20.10.)

- **Espresso grind.** An especially fine grind, this is designed specifically for use in espresso machines and moka espresso pots. (See Figure 20.11.)

- **Pulverized.** Also known as *powdered coffee* or *Turkish*, this is the finest grind available. The heat generated during the grinding process contributes to its distinctive flavor. (See Figure 20.12.)

 BUYER'S NOTE — *Most fresh coffee suppliers will provide commercial coffee grinders, and often coffee makers, "free of charge" if you use their product in a food service operation.*

People, Places, Things

Decaffeinated Coffee

Caffeine is a stimulant that is present in coffee. It has the effect of making the nervous system more active, which is usually the desired effect, although some people react badly to it and prefer to buy coffee without caffeine. Decaffeinated coffee is available in all the regular coffee forms: whole beans, ground, and instant. Caffeine is removed by soaking the beans in water or by using solvents or carbon dioxide. The last is thought to be the best method as it does not affect the flavor and there is no residue. To qualify as decaffeinated, coffee must contain less than 0.9 percent dry weight of caffeine. A 5 fl oz (150 ml)

20.8 Coarsely ground coffee beans (Brazilian Santos)

Figures 20.8–20.12 © Randy Van Dam 2008

20.9 Medium-ground coffee beans (Brazilian Santos)

20.10 Finely ground coffee beans (Brazilian Santos)

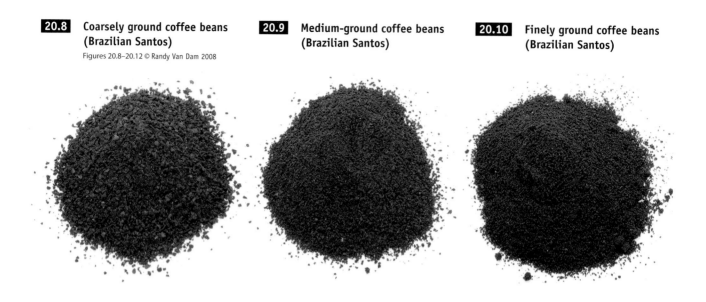

20.11 Espresso-ground coffee beans (Brazilian Santos)

20.12 Pulverized coffee beans (Brazilian Santos)

People, Places, Things

Coffee Substitutes and Flavorings

Roasted chicory root is a popular coffee extender in Europe. During the Civil War, when food was scarce, chicory was first added to coffee in the United States. The roots impart a characteristic bitter taste that is unpleasant to some. Dandelion root is toasted for a drink similar to coffee that is sold in health-food stores as dandelion coffee. Toasted barley is used to produce a drink called *malted coffee*. Spices and floral waters are often added in the Middle East, while in Austria, ground, dried figs are added for a thick, sweet flavor. Some coffees are

Tea

Tea is made from the dried leaves of the tea plant. The leaves have been used since ancient times to produce a drink even more popular than coffee. Indeed, next to water, tea is the world's leading beverage. Although where the Chinese originally grew the tea plants is uncertain, it is believed a Chinese emperor initiated the practice more than 4,500 years ago.

TEA PRODUCTION

All true teas come from the leaves of the tea bush or tea tree (*Camellia sinensis*), which is native to Asia. Depending on the process, the leaves are used to produce black tea (fermented), oolong tea (semi-fermented), green tea (unfermented), or white tea.

GLOBAL SOURCING

The tea plant's elliptical, persistent leaves are bright green, slightly hairy, partially serrated, and scattered with glands containing an essential oil. The best teas are cultivated at high altitudes where the plants grow slowly in relatively cool climates. Once a year, they bear tiny white flowers similar in appearance to camellias; these lightly scented blossoms fetch a high price. Tea plants continue to produce leaves for close to a century.

There are three broad categories of tea plants, originating from China, Southeast Asia, and India. These varieties are divided into a huge range of subcategories. In tea plantations, the leaves are picked up to twenty or thirty times a year. Increasingly, traditional hand picking is being replaced by mechanized means. Only the young leaves at the tips of the branches are harvested. The end bud is known as "pekoe," a term derived from the Chinese *pako,* meaning "white down," in reference to the delicate down that covers the lower surface of the emerging leaf.

Tea Terroir

Terroir is a term usually associated with regional wines but is also appropriate for tea. It refers to the growing area and climate. It is the sum of sun, soil, precipitation, temperature, and elevation in a specific area that conspires to produce particular qualities in tea leaves (or grapes) particular to that area or region. Here are the categories of tea from the five major tea-producing nations:

- **India** is known for its black teas. India is the largest producer with close to 2 billion pounds of annual production, much of which is consumed domestically.

- **China**, the second largest producer, is home to all tea types. It produces the largest variety of leaf styles and more specialty types than any other country.

- **Sri Lanka** produces the classic black teas associated with this island nation, known as "Ceylon teas."

- **Taiwan** produces the world's finest oolong teas.

- **Japan** exports fine green teas.

BUYING AND STORING

When buying herbal teas, ensure that the mixtures contain only nontoxic plants. To be absolutely safe, buy products whose ingredients are listed on the package. Responding to the recent surge in popularity of herbal teas, the U.S. Food and Drug Administration (FDA) has published a list of plants that cannot be used in foods, drinks, and medicines. Canada's health department requires that manufacturers document any health claims made about their products. It is thus important to read the label when buying herbal teas and other herbal products. Most of the herbal teas on the market are composed of well-known, harmless products, but some ingredients in herbal teas could interact with medications and certain conditions.

Keep tea in an airtight container in a dark, cool place (under 85°F). Ideally, it should be stored in a sealed metallic container, which will protect it from dampness and odors. Less fragile than coffee, it can be kept for up to 18 months; for optimum flavor, however, you should use it within 6 months. Chinese teas keep for up to 3 years.

Types of Teas

- **White.** A minimally processed form of green tea, white tea is the least processed of all teas. The leaves and buds are merely dried (withered), sorted, and packaged. White tea is generally more expensive than other types. (See Figure 20.13a.)

- **Green.** Green tea is unfermented. It is available in an innumerable array of infusions and styles that can be traced to two general regions: China and Japan. Green tea is particularly popular in China, Japan, and Muslim countries. (See Figure 20.13b.)

- **Oolong.** Oolong tea, which comes from Taiwan, is partially fermented. Its characteristics are halfway between those of black tea and green tea. Its antioxidant levels are high, and the caffeine content is somewhat higher than green tea. (See Figure 20.13c.)

- **Black.** The most widely consumed tea in the world, black tea is so called because the relatively lengthy oxidation period (several hours) darkens the leaves.

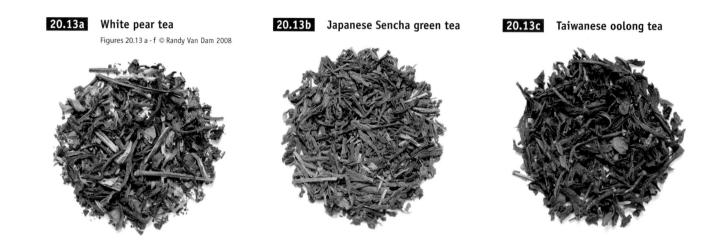

20.13a White pear tea

Figures 20.13 a - f © Randy Van Dam 2008

20.13b Japanese Sencha green tea

20.13c Taiwanese oolong tea

Black tea flavors can be differentiated by region more so than other teas.

- **India.** Darjeeling: teas with light, complex muscatel flavors and flowery aromas (Figure 20.13d). Assam: strong and malty (Figure 20.13e and Figure 20.13f).
- **Sri Lanka (Ceylon).** This has a straightforward flavor, good straight up.
- **China.** This has a wine-like flavor with a sweet finish.

- **Other teas.** The following are some additional terms used in tea classifications.

  - **Flavored and scented teas.** Flavored and scented teas are true teas mixed with various spices and additives. The best teas of this sort use natural flavors or essential oils derived from natural or organic sources. Avoid teas with artificial flavors or those that do not declare whether their flavorings are natural or artificial. (See Figure 20.14a,

Figure 20.14b, Figure 20.14c, and Figure 20.14d for various flavored varieties.)

- **Instant tea.** Instant teas are made from tea that has been steeped and evaporated. The resulting powder, which has been very popular in the United States since the 1950s, has existed for much longer in countries such as Japan.
- **Decaffeinated tea.** In decaffeinated tea, part of the caffeine (an alkaloid also known as "theine") has been removed; this reduces the stimulating effect of the resulting beverage. As the caffeine content of tea varies widely, however, some decaffeinated teas can contain almost as much of the alkaloid as regular teas.
- **Specialty teas.** Specialty teas are unadulterated teas of exceptional quality and flavor.
- **Estate teas.** These teas are named after specific tea gardens.

20.13d Darjeeling tea

20.13e Assam ebony flowers

20.13f Assam Choice Estate

20.14a California blend (China black and green teas scented with California sunflowers, cactus flowers, and rhubarb)

Figures 20.14 a - d © Randy Van Dam 2008

20.14b Florence (black tea, chocolate, hazelnut)

20.14c Exotic wedding tea (white buds and green leaves of Mutan, blended with vanilla, lemon, and rosebuds)

20.14d Tangerine white tea (white leaves, green tea, sweet tangerine peel)

- **Blended teas.** Blended teas are various combinations of tea leaves from more than one region or crop to obtain a desired outcome.
- **Chai tea.** Chai means "tea with spices"; it is usually made with ginger or cinnamon for a strong spicy taste. (See Figure 20.15.)
- **Russian tea.** Russian tea can refer to tea produced in Russia or drunk in the Russian style, in a glass with lemon.

TEA SUBSTITUTES

Tea substitutes are dried herbs and spices that are steeped to form an infusion. Chamomile tea, for example, is used as a relaxant, while peppermint is considered a digestive aid (Figure 20.16a). It is always a good idea to ask a qualified medical professional before taking any unfamiliar herbs. For other tea substitutes, see Figure 20.16b, Figure 20.16c, Figure 20.16d, Figure 20.16e, and Figure 20.16f.

20.15   **Voodoo chai (red rooibos, ginger, cinnamon, coriander, allspice, safflowers, mulberry leaf, clove, star anise, black peppercorn)**

© Randy Van Dam 2008

20.16a   **Chamomile flowers**

Figures 20.16 a - f © Randy Van Dam 2008

20.16b   **Red tea (organic red tea, honey bush, lemongrass, kaffir leaves)**

20.16c   **Rose petals and flowers**

20.16d   **Hibiscus flowers**

20.16e   **Dried lavender**

20.16f   **Orange passion fruit**

Nonalcoholic Beverages

Nonalcoholic beverages account for the vast majority of the beverage market. These drinks are generally chosen for their refreshment purposes, to quench people's thirst. With the increased market focus on health and wellness, it is likely the nonalcoholic beverage market will continue to be the segment leader in beverages.

JUICE

Juice is the liquid extracted from fruits and vegetables. Juice may be supplied in concentrate form, requiring the user to add water to reconstitute the liquid back to (an approximation of) the original state. Vegetable juice is an alternative to fruit juice. If making vege juice commercially in a food service operation, you will need a juicer that can process vegetables. Vegetable juice cannot be made from every vegetable, unlike fruit juices, which can be made from almost any edible fruit. Vegetable juices are usually made from carrots, beets, pumpkins, and tomatoes.

Global Sourcing

Fruit juices are available worldwide. Fresh-squeezed juice has become more available but is somewhat limited to the original fruit source, unless the establishment purchases the whole fruit and juices it at the establishment.

Buying and Storing

A number of new companies have had considerable success supplying prepackaged fruit juice combinations as a result of increasing popularity. Popular juices include:

- **Apple.** Apples cultivated specifically for cider and juice are typically too tart and astringent to eat fresh, but they give the beverage a rich flavor that dessert apples cannot. (See Figure 20.17a.)

- **Berry (mixed).** Although processors can choose to use different ingredient blends, the following are most common: apple, grape, raspberry, strawberry, and blueberry. (See Figure 20.17b.)

- **Carrot.** A pound of carrots will yield about a cup of juice, which is not a bad yield compared with fruits like apples and oranges. (See Figure 20.17c.)

- **Cherry.** Cherry juice can be frozen or refrigerated in storage. (See Figure 20.17d.)

- **Cranberry.** Cranberry juice is usually sweetened to reduce its natural tartness. It is also blended with other fruit juices. Unsweetened cranberry juice is available from specialty vendors. (See Figure 20.17e.)

- **Grape.** Grape juice is a fruit juice obtained from crushing grapes. Preserving grape juice requires pasteurization because the unprocessed juice will naturally ferment from yeast on the grapes.

- **Grapefruit.** The most popular varieties of grapefruit juice cultivated today are red, white, and pink hues. The family of flavors range from highly acidic to sweet-tart, offering something for everyone. (See Figure 20.17f.)

- **Orange.** The largest exporter of orange juice is Brazil, followed by the United States (predominantly from Florida). Juice that is shipped in liquid form is traded as *direct juice* between producers. It is sold to consumers (in the United States and Canada) with the label "Not from concentrate." (See Figure 20.17g.)

- **Pineapple.** Pineapple mill juice is extracted from the waste trimmings from the cutting and canning of the valued pineapple core cuts. (See Figure 20.17h.)

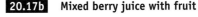
20.17a Apple juice with fruit

Figures 20.17 a - b © Randy Van Dam 2008

20.17b Mixed berry juice with fruit

20.17c Carrot juice with fruit

Figures 20.17 c - h © Randy Van Dam 2008

20.17d Cherry juice with fruit

20.17e Cranberry juice with fruit

20.17f Grapefruit juice with fruit

20.17h Pineapple-orange juice with fruit

20.17g Orange juice with fruit

- **Pomegranate.** Pomegranate juice is extracted from the seeds of the fruit. Pomegranate juice contains antioxidants at much higher levels than other fruit juices. (See Figure 20.17i.)

- **Tomato.** Tomato juice is made from squeezed tomatoes. It can be used either plain or in cocktails such as a Bloody Mary. (See Figure 20.17j.)

- **Organic juice.** This juice is made from all natural and organic juices and other products. Certified organic means the product is from fresh fruit grown naturally, without synthetic chemicals such as pesticides, fertilizers, herbicides, or fungicides. (See Figure 20.17k.)

CARBONATED SOFT DRINKS

The term **soft drink** originally applied to carbonated drinks and noncarbonated drinks made from concentrates, although it now commonly refers to almost any cold drink that does not contain alcohol. In the broader sense, beverages like colas, sparkling waters, lemonade, and fruit punch may be considered soft drinks; however, sales of water and juices have exploded in recent years, giving rise to their own categories of beverages.

There are a wide variety of soft drinks, including "clear," cola, fruit flavors, and other flavors such as root beer and cream sodas. Today the soft drink industry is highly

20.17i **Pomegranate juice with fruit**

Figures 20.17 i - k © Randy Van Dam 2008

20.17j **Tomato juice with fruit**

20.17k **Organic juice with fruit**

competitive with both carbonated and noncarbonated drinks going head to head in the marketplace (see Figure 20.18a). A broad array of bottled waters and juice drinks (see Figure 20.18b) are also available. However, for some, the carbonated, thirst-quenching pleasure of soda pop cannot be surpassed. In fact, estimates show that, in 2002, Americans consumed almost 53 gallons of carbonated soft drinks per person per year. (See Figure 20.18c.)

BOTTLED WATER

Water is classified as "bottled water" or "drinking water" when it meets all applicable federal and state standards, is sealed in a sanitary container, and is sold for human consumption. By law, FDA standards for bottled water must be at least as stringent and protective of public health as standards set by the U.S. Environmental Protection Agency (EPA) for public water systems. Some beverages containing certain ingredients or additives may cause that product to be classified as a soft drink, dietary supplement, or some other categorization.

Global Sourcing

Any imported bottled water brand sold in the United States must meet all of the same federal and state regulations that apply to domestically produce bottled water brands.

20.18a **Soft drinks for sale in a supermarket**

Photo Courtesy Robert Garlough

20.18b **Iced herbal teas**

Figures 20.18 b - c © Randy Van Dam 2008

20.18c **Assorted soft drinks with real juice**

BUYING AND STORING

Bottled water products meeting the Standard of Identity may be labeled as bottled water or drinking water, or one or more of the following terms:

- **Spring water.** This bottled water derived from an underground formation from which water flows naturally to the surface of the earth. (See Figure 20.19a and Figure 20.19b.)

- **Purified water.** This water has been distilled or filtered in some way.

- **Mineral water.** Bottled water containing no less than 250 parts per million total dissolved solids may be labeled as mineral water. No minerals can be added to this product.

- **Sparkling bottled water.** Water that, after treatment, contains the same amount of carbon dioxide that it had when it emerged from the source. (See Figure 20.20a and Figure 20.20b.)

- **Artesian water, or artesian well water.** This is bottled water from a spring well, where the source is above the ambient water table level.

- **Well water.** Bottled water from a well.

The FDA has not established a shelf life for bottled water. The International Bottled Water Association advises consumers to store bottled water at room temperature (or cooler), out of direct sunlight, and away from solvents and chemicals such as gasoline, paint thinners, and dry cleaning chemicals. Bottled water can be used indefinitely if stored properly.

20.19a Assorted bottled still water (plain)   **20.19b** Assorted bottled still water (flavored)

Figures 20.19a–20.20b © Randy Van Dam 2008

20.20a Plain sparkling water   **20.20b** Flavored sparkling water

Alcoholic Beverages

According to a survey conducted in 2006 by Technomic, Inc., a Chicago-based market research firm specializing in the food service industry, "Within the Top 500 chains, 48 percent offer alcohol of some type to the guest. These include not only casual dining chains, but a significant number of limited service players such as Chipotle Mexican Grill and Fuddruckers. There were also some midscale restaurants serving alcohol." *Casual dining* is the chain category in which the majority offer beverage alcohol, so Technomic whittled the top 500 down to the top 50 casual dining chains. On average, alcohol sales comprise 17 percent of total sales among these operators (Technomic, 2006).

THE CONTROL STATES

Alcoholic beverage **control states** are those that have state monopoly over the wholesaling and/or retailing of some or all categories of alcoholic beverages, such as beer, wine, and distilled spirits. Following the federal repeal of prohibition in the United States in 1933, some states decided to continue their own prohibition against the production, distribution, and sale of alcoholic beverages within their borders. Other states decided to leave the issue to local jurisdictions, including counties and cities, a practice called local option. Among those states that did not choose to maintain complete prohibi-

tion, some chose to establish government monopolies over the sale of alcoholic beverages within their borders. Most of these states have an **Alcoholic Beverage Control (ABC)** board and run package stores, called ABC stores. Most food service establishments are prohibited from purchasing alcohol from stores that sell to the public.

Table 20.2 identifies those states that exercise more distribution control than simply issuing and enforcing licenses to private establishments that sell and distribute alcoholic beverages. State control of alcoholic beverages varies by kind of beverage, level of distribution, and exclusivity. (See Figure 20.21.)

> **BUYER'S NOTE**
> A distilled spirits plant (DSP) may be established to produce, bottle, rectify, process, or store beverage spirits. Examples of beverage-distilled spirits include neutral spirits or alcohol (i.e., vodka or grain spirits), whiskey, gin, brandy, blended applejack, rum, tequila, cordials, and liqueurs. Alcohol by volume (ABV) simply represents what portion of the total volume of liquid is alcohol.

20.22   **Three tiered wine distribution system**

3-Tiered System of Distribution

20.21   **Martha's Vineyard wine shop exterior**

© Randy Van Dam 2008

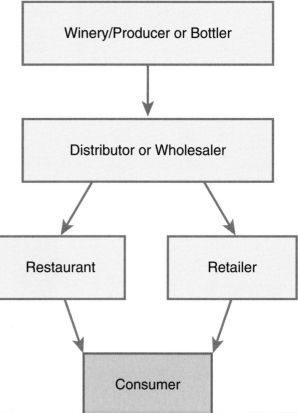

WINE

Wine is an alcoholic beverage produced by fermenting the juice of fruits, usually grapes. Although a number of other fruits, such as plum, elderberry, and blackcurrant may also be fermented, grapes are naturally chemically balanced to normally ferment completely without requiring extra sugars, acids, enzymes, or other nutrients. Non-grape wines are called fruit wine or country wine. Other products made from starch-based materials, such as barley wine or rice wine, are more similar to beer. The English word *wine*, and its equivalents in other languages, is protected by law in many jurisdictions. (See Figure 20.22.)

Buying and Storing

Not all wines are bottled with the intention of being aged. Most of the wines of the world are meant to be drunk young while they still possess their youth and freshness. Most of the wines that are destined for the cellar are red. Very few white wines need time to mature. For this reason, most white wines are purchased on an as-needed basis.

Wine is alive. As such, it reacts either positively or negatively to its environment. How it is treated will determine how fast or slow it will age. Essentially, wine needs to be kept in a clean, dark, damp place with good ventilation, where it can be stored vibration-free at a constant temperature.

Temperature is the most important factor in storing wine. The optimum temperature is 50 to 55°F (10 to 12°C). However, any constant temperature within 40 to 65°F (5 to 18°C) will do. Quick temperature fluctuations should be avoided. Moderate humidity is important so as to keep the corks in good resilient condition and thereby preventing them from shrinking. A relative humidity of 50 to 80 percent is the acceptable range. (See Figure 20.23a and Figure 20.23b.)

Light will prematurely age a bottle of wine. Ultraviolet light may give wine unpleasant aromas and ruin it, even in a dark bottle. The space should be free from smells and debris. Extraneous smells can enter through the cork and contaminate the wine. Proper ventilation will help with this problem. Table wine is stored horizontally so that the wine stays in contact with the cork (Figure 20.24a). This keeps the cork moist, thereby preventing air from entering the wine. Fortified wines other than port are stored standing (Figure 20.24b). See Table 20.1 for standard bottle sizes.

People, Places, Things

Alcohol Purchase Guidelines for a 150-Person Event

Based on a 150-person event of average consumers, the following guidelines for alcohol beverages are suggested to purchase:

Beer: 12 total cases

- 4 domestic cases
- 5 premium cases
- 3 light cases

Wine: 9 total cases

- 5 sauvignon blanc cases
- 1–2 white zinfandel cases
- 1–2 cabernet sauvignon cases
- 2 merlot cases

Hard liquor: 19 bottles

- 6 liters vodka
- 4 liters gin
- 2 liters light rum
- 2 liters dark rum
- 2 liters scotch
- 1 liter bourbon
- 2 liters Bailey's Irish Cream
- Kahlua
- Grand Marnier

20.23a Wine cellar with humidity and temperature control system

Figures 20.23a–20.24b © Randy Van Dam 2008

20.23b Wine storage bins labeled for ease of identification

20.24a Still wines lying horizontally in storage

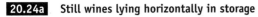

20.24b Fortified wines being stored upright

TABLE 20.1 Standard Bottle Sizes

Number of Standard Sized Bottles	Volume	Name for Bordeaux Shaped Bottle	Name for Sparkling Wine Bottle
½	375 ml	Half bottle or "tenth"	Same
1	750 ml	Bottle or "fifth"	Same
2	1.5 liters	Magnum	Same
4	3 liters	Double magnum	Jéroboam
6	4.5 liters	Jéroboam	Rehoboam
8	6 liters	Impériale	Methuselah
12	9 liters	Usually used for sparkling wine	Salmanazar
16	12 liters	Usually used for sparkling wine	Balthazar
20	15 liters	Usually used for sparkling wine	Nebuchadnezzar

People, Places, Things

Required Information on Wine Labels

In the United States, ten specific pieces of information are required on wine labels:

- Name of the wine
- Name of the producer
- Name and address of the bottler
- Name of the importer
- Name of the shipper
- Alcohol content (expressed as a percentage of the volume)
- Volume of the bottle's content
- Country of origin
- Sulfite advisory (According to U.S. laws, wine producers must warn if the wine contains sulfites because some people are allergic to them. These sulfites might be added to wine as sulfur dioxide to act as an antibacterial agent for the wine.)
- Government warning

Sometimes the information might be duplicated. For example, the producer and the bottler might be one and the same. When this is the case, this information only has to be listed on the label once. In addition to the required information, there are five optional pieces of information that the wine label also can include:

- Quality of the wine
- Vintage of the wine
- Type of wine
- Growing region, or *appellation*
- Descriptive information about the wine

Still Wines

Still wines include the broad categories of white, red, and rosé wines that contain no carbon dioxide, which would make them sparkling or effervescent. See Figure 20.25 and Figure 20.26 for more on how red and white wines, respectively, are made.

INTERNATIONAL WINE PRODUCTION LAWS AND REGULATIONS

Different countries have different laws regarding the production of wine. Most countries have an agency or several agencies that regulate how the grapes are grown and how the bottle is labeled. In the United States, wine production is regulated by the Department of the Treasury and enforced by the Bureau of Alcohol, Tobacco, and Firearms. Companies or individuals from other countries that import wine into the United States must follow all of the U.S. laws regarding labeling. (See Figure 20.27.)

Many of the areas that grow grapes in the United States are broken into what are referred to as American Viticulture Areas (AVA). The areas are similar to the regions in other countries and are specific geographical locations that have been given appellation status by the Bureau of Alcohol, Tobacco, and Firearms. Appellations are specific regions in which wine grapes can be grown and are determined by a country's regulatory agency.

20.25 Flowchart of operations in making red wine

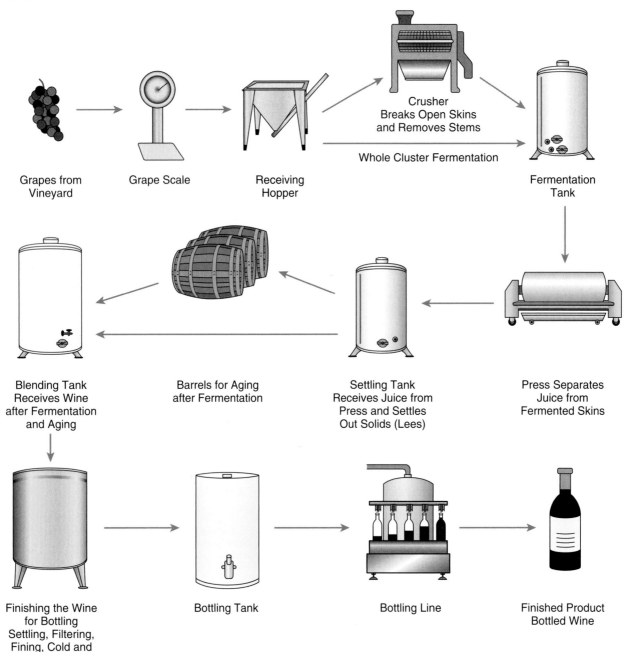

Grapes from Vineyard

Grape Scale

Receiving Hopper

Crusher Breaks Open Skins and Removes Stems

Whole Cluster Fermentation

Fermentation Tank

Blending Tank Receives Wine after Fermentation and Aging

Barrels for Aging after Fermentation

Settling Tank Receives Juice from Press and Settles Out Solids (Lees)

Press Separates Juice from Fermented Skins

Finishing the Wine for Bottling Settling, Filtering, Fining, Cold and Heat Stabilizing

Bottling Tank

Bottling Line

Finished Product Bottled Wine

20.26 Flowchart of operations in making white wine

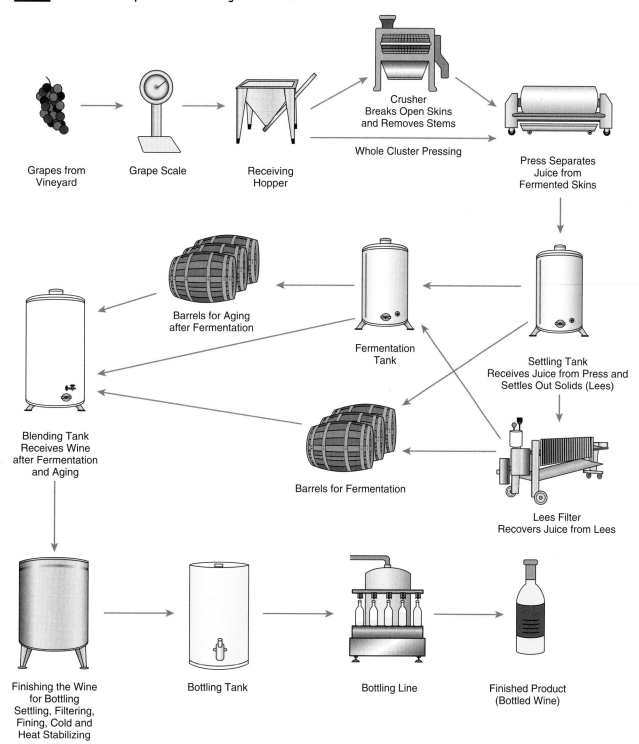

Grapes from Vineyard

Grape Scale

Receiving Hopper

Crusher
Breaks Open Skins
and Removes Stems

Whole Cluster Pressing

Press Separates
Juice from
Fermented Skins

Barrels for Aging
after Fermentation

Fermentation
Tank

Settling Tank
Receives Juice from Press and
Settles Out Solids (Lees)

Blending Tank
Receives Wine
after Fermentation
and Aging

Barrels for Fermentation

Lees Filter
Recovers Juice from Lees

Finishing the Wine
for Bottling
Settling, Filtering,
Fining, Cold and
Heat Stabilizing

Bottling Tank

Bottling Line

Finished Product
(Bottled Wine)

20.27 Reading U.S. wine labels

Reading a United States Wine Label

As the wine industry has advanced in recent decades, wine labels have become much more elaborate. While in the 1960s wine was usually bottled with relatively plain labels with a minimum of information, today they are designed to be more eye-catching with multiple colors, embossing, gold leaf, and distinctive shapes. This is to try to get potential customers to notice the wine on the shelf; also, expensive labels are used to try to convey an impression of quality for the wine in the bottle. The importance of packaging to wineries is evidenced by the industry saying, "you sell your first bottle of wine to a customer with the outside of the bottle, and the second bottle of wine to the customer with what is inside." In addition to their importance in selling wine, labels must also provide information to the consumer. Some of the information on wine labels is provided by the winery to describe what the wine tastes like and how it was made. The federal government also mandates what information must be placed on a bottle of wine to accurately describe what the wine is, including standards of composition that must be met before certain claims can be made on the label. In recent years the amount of information required by law has expanded to include warnings about health and whether there are sulfites present in the wine.

The next three pages outline the basic requirements for wine labels in the United Sates. Different countries have different standards and terms that they use to describe their wines. Information on the labels of imported wines is outlined in their respective chapters of this book.

Front Label

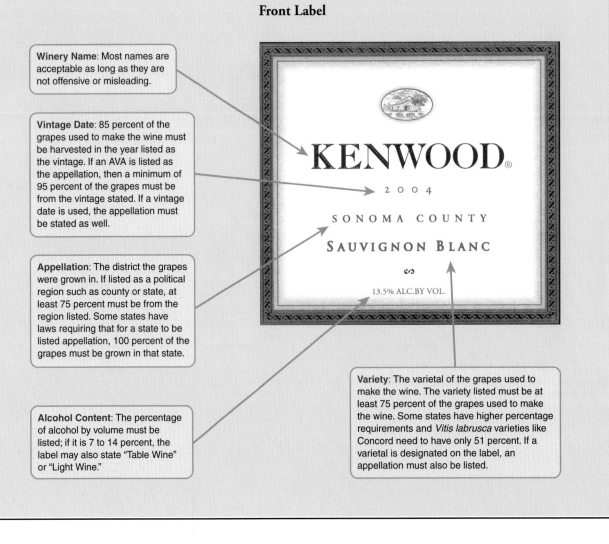

Winery Name: Most names are acceptable as long as they are not offensive or misleading.

Vintage Date: 85 percent of the grapes used to make the wine must be harvested in the year listed as the vintage. If an AVA is listed as the appellation, then a minimum of 95 percent of the grapes must be from the vintage stated. If a vintage date is used, the appellation must be stated as well.

Appellation: The district the grapes were grown in. If listed as a political region such as county or state, at least 75 percent must be from the region listed. Some states have laws requiring that for a state to be listed appellation, 100 percent of the grapes must be grown in that state.

Alcohol Content: The percentage of alcohol by volume must be listed; if it is 7 to 14 percent, the label may also state "Table Wine" or "Light Wine."

Variety: The varietal of the grapes used to make the wine. The variety listed must be at least 75 percent of the grapes used to make the wine. Some states have higher percentage requirements and *Vitis labrusca* varieties like Concord need to have only 51 percent. If a varietal is designated on the label, an appellation must also be listed.

20.27 (continued)

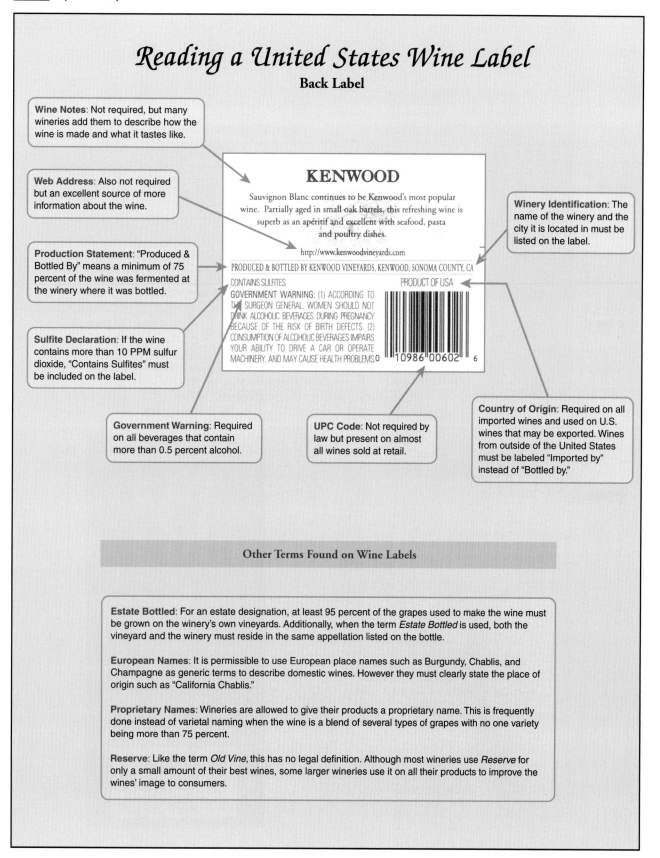

Reading a United States Wine Label
Back Label

Wine Notes: Not required, but many wineries add them to describe how the wine is made and what it tastes like.

Web Address: Also not required but an excellent source of more information about the wine.

Production Statement: "Produced & Bottled By" means a minimum of 75 percent of the wine was fermented at the winery where it was bottled.

Sulfite Declaration: If the wine contains more than 10 PPM sulfur dioxide, "Contains Sulfites" must be included on the label.

Government Warning: Required on all beverages that contain more than 0.5 percent alcohol.

UPC Code: Not required by law but present on almost all wines sold at retail.

Winery Identification: The name of the winery and the city it is located in must be listed on the label.

Country of Origin: Required on all imported wines and used on U.S. wines that may be exported. Wines from outside of the United States must be labeled "Imported by" instead of "Bottled by."

Label content:

KENWOOD

Sauvignon Blanc continues to be Kenwood's most popular wine. Partially aged in small oak barrels, this refreshing wine is superb as an apéritif and excellent with seafood, pasta and poultry dishes.

http://www.kenwoodvineyards.com

PRODUCED & BOTTLED BY KENWOOD VINEYARDS, KENWOOD, SONOMA COUNTY, CA

CONTAINS SULFITES   PRODUCT OF USA

GOVERNMENT WARNING: (1) ACCORDING TO THE SURGEON GENERAL, WOMEN SHOULD NOT DRINK ALCOHOLIC BEVERAGES DURING PREGNANCY BECAUSE OF THE RISK OF BIRTH DEFECTS. (2) CONSUMPTION OF ALCOHOLIC BEVERAGES IMPAIRS YOUR ABILITY TO DRIVE A CAR OR OPERATE MACHINERY, AND MAY CAUSE HEALTH PROBLEMS.

0 10986 00602 6

Other Terms Found on Wine Labels

Estate Bottled: For an estate designation, at least 95 percent of the grapes used to make the wine must be grown on the winery's own vineyards. Additionally, when the term *Estate Bottled* is used, both the vineyard and the winery must reside in the same appellation listed on the bottle.

European Names: It is permissible to use European place names such as Burgundy, Chablis, and Champagne as generic terms to describe domestic wines. However they must clearly state the place of origin such as "California Chablis."

Proprietary Names: Wineries are allowed to give their products a proprietary name. This is frequently done instead of varietal naming when the wine is a blend of several types of grapes with no one variety being more than 75 percent.

Reserve: Like the term *Old Vine*, this has no legal definition. Although most wineries use *Reserve* for only a small amount of their best wines, some larger wineries use it on all their products to improve the wines' image to consumers.

20.27 (continued)

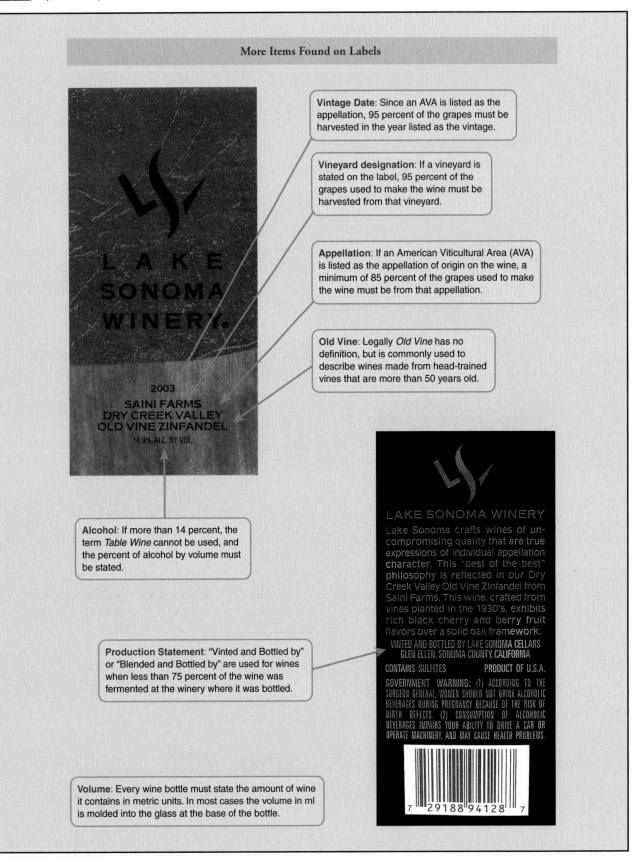

More Items Found on Labels

Vintage Date: Since an AVA is listed as the appellation, 95 percent of the grapes must be harvested in the year listed as the vintage.

Vineyard designation: If a vineyard is stated on the label, 95 percent of the grapes used to make the wine must be harvested from that vineyard.

Appellation: If an American Viticultural Area (AVA) is listed as the appellation of origin on the wine, a minimum of 85 percent of the grapes used to make the wine must be from that appellation.

Old Vine: Legally *Old Vine* has no definition, but is commonly used to describe wines made from head-trained vines that are more than 50 years old.

2003
SAINI FARMS
DRY CREEK VALLEY
OLD VINE ZINFANDEL
14.9% ALC. BY VOL.

Alcohol: If more than 14 percent, the term *Table Wine* cannot be used, and the percent of alcohol by volume must be stated.

Production Statement: "Vinted and Bottled by" or "Blended and Bottled by" are used for wines when less than 75 percent of the wine was fermented at the winery where it was bottled.

Volume: Every wine bottle must state the amount of wine it contains in metric units. In most cases the volume in ml is molded into the glass at the base of the bottle.

LAKE SONOMA WINERY
Lake Sonoma crafts wines of uncompromising quality that are true expressions of individual appellation character. This "best of the best" philosophy is reflected in our Dry Creek Valley Old Vine Zinfandel from Saini Farms. This wine, crafted from vines planted in the 1930's, exhibits rich black cherry and berry fruit flavors over a solid oak framework.

VINTED AND BOTTLED BY LAKE SONOMA CELLARS
GLEN ELLEN, SONOMA COUNTY, CALIFORNIA

CONTAINS SULFITES   PRODUCT OF U.S.A.

GOVERNMENT WARNING: (1) ACCORDING TO THE SURGEON GENERAL, WOMEN SHOULD NOT DRINK ALCOHOLIC BEVERAGES DURING PREGNANCY BECAUSE OF THE RISK OF BIRTH DEFECTS. (2) CONSUMPTION OF ALCOHOLIC BEVERAGES IMPAIRS YOUR ABILITY TO DRIVE A CAR OR OPERATE MACHINERY, AND MAY CAUSE HEALTH PROBLEMS.

7 29188 94128 7

France has a similar system, known as *Appellation d'Origine Controlee* (AOC), which was founded in the 1930s. The AOC system establishes regulations for winemaking and provides quality control for French wine. A winemaker in France must follow rules concerning where grapes can be grown, which grapes can be grown in different areas, the minimum alcohol content, and how many grapes can be grown per acre. AOC also is the highest quality rank for wine in France. (See Figure 20.28.)

There are three additional levels denoting quality in French wine:

- *Vin Delimite de Qualite Superieure* (VDQS)
- *Vin de Pays* (Country Wine)
- *Vin de Table* (Table Wine)

In Italy, the *Denominazione di Origine Controllata* (DOC) and DOCG (the "G" stands for *Garantita* and means *guaranteed*) are very similar to the AOC in France and AVA in the United States. The DOC, however, is a much newer system, begun in 1963. The DOC regulates the size of the regions, the grapes that can be used, how many grapes can be grown per acre, and the minimum alcohol content of the finished wine. Its control also extends to the percentage of each variety of grapes used in a wine and the length of aging. The DOCG is the highest quality rating for wine in Italy. To protect the quality of wine within this category, the National DOC committee has adopted standards for wines admitted into the DOCG category. These standards include limits on the number of grapes grown per acre and a higher minimum alcohol level. (See Figure 20.29.)

Spain's classification system is broken down into five quality levels. The first two levels represent the top wines of Spain. The last three are comparable to the Vins de Pays wines of France. (See Figure 20.30.) The DOC level, added in 1991, includes only the very best wine of Spain:

- *Denominación de Origen Calificada* (DOC)
- *Denominación de Origen* (DO)
- *Vino de la Tierra* (VdlT)
- *Vino Comarcal* (VC)
- *Vino de Mesa* (VdM)

Australia has a more limited labeling program known as the Label Integrity Program (LIP). In general, the LIP regulates vintage, varietal, and geographic claims on labels. (See Figure 20.31.)

The German system of regulation started in 1971. The system is fairly simple but extensive. German wine is first graded into one of two categories:

- *Qualitatswein* (quality wine)
- *Tafelwein* (table wine)

The Qualitatswein category is then divided into two types:

- *Qualitatswein mit Pradikat* (QmP)
- *Qualitatswein bestimmter Anbaugebiete* (QbA)

The difference between the two types is that QbA wines are region-specific (from one of the thirteen regions in Germany) quality wines that meet certain alcohol content and grape variety requirements and are examined by authorities. QmP is quality wine with distinction from the thirteen regions or the top wine of Germany. Every requirement for QbA must be met, but also the wine must not be chaptalized. *Chaptalization* is the process of adding sugar to the unfermented grape juice, which raises the potential alcohol content after fermentation. This means that the grapes that constitute these wines must ripen longer on the vine, thus gaining natural sugar and hence a higher alcohol content when fermented. (See Figure 20.32.)

There are six levels within this higher wine category. The six levels of QmP are listed in descending order of quality:

- ***Eiswein*** (German for *ice wine*). This is a rare wine produced from grapes that are left on the vine until they freeze. Then, the grapes are picked and crushed while they are still frozen. The grapes must be at least ripe enough to make beerenauslese.

- ***Trockenbeerenauslese*** (German for *dry-berries-out-picked*) These grapes literally dry on the vine, resembling raisins when picked. The sugar and the juice are very concentrated and produce a very sweet wine. Many times the grapes also are infected with Noble Rot *(Botrytis cinerea)*. This wine was first made in 1921 and tends to be the most expensive German wine. (A bottle simply marked *trocken* is a dry wine.)

- ***Beerenauslese*** (German for *berries-out-picked*). These grapes are individually picked out of the grape bunches. The grapes are sometimes infected with Noble Rot.

- ***Auslese*** (German for *out picked* or *selectively picked*). This wine is made from grapes that are very ripe when picked; the other clusters of grapes are left on the vine to ripen more.

- ***Spatlese*** (German for *late picking*). The grapes for this wine are picked at least a week after the normal harvest. The extra time allows the grapes more sunlight, which in turn increases the sugar level in the fruit. The wine tends to be more intense and sweet than Kabinett.

- ***Kabinett*** (German for *cabinet*). This wine is the least expensive and driest of the German wines in the QmP category.

For more information on reading Chilean wine labels, see Figure 20.33; South African labels, Figure 20.34; and Canadian labels, Figure 20.35.

20.28 **Reading French wine labels**

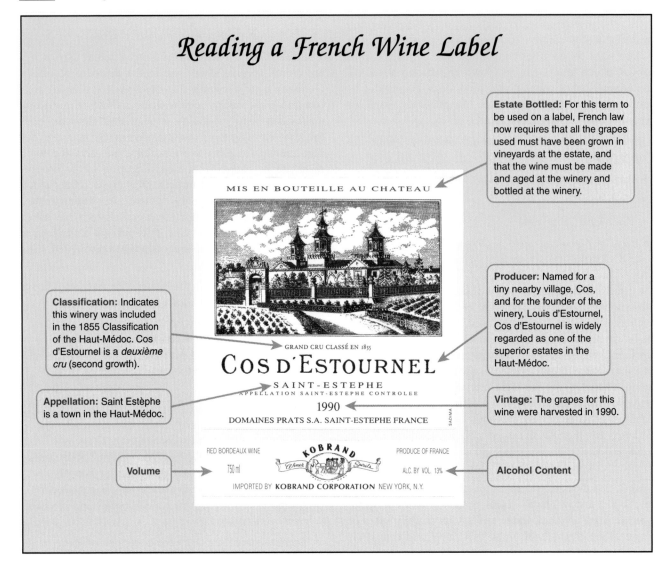

Reading a French Wine Label

Estate Bottled: For this term to be used on a label, French law now requires that all the grapes used must have been grown in vineyards at the estate, and that the wine must be made and aged at the winery and bottled at the winery.

Producer: Named for a tiny nearby village, Cos, and for the founder of the winery, Louis d'Estournel, Cos d'Estournel is widely regarded as one of the superior estates in the Haut-Médoc.

Classification: Indicates this winery was included in the 1855 Classification of the Haut-Médoc. Cos d'Estournel is a *deuxième cru* (second growth).

Appellation: Saint Estèphe is a town in the Haut-Médoc.

Vintage: The grapes for this wine were harvested in 1990.

Volume

Alcohol Content

20.29 Reading Italian wine labels

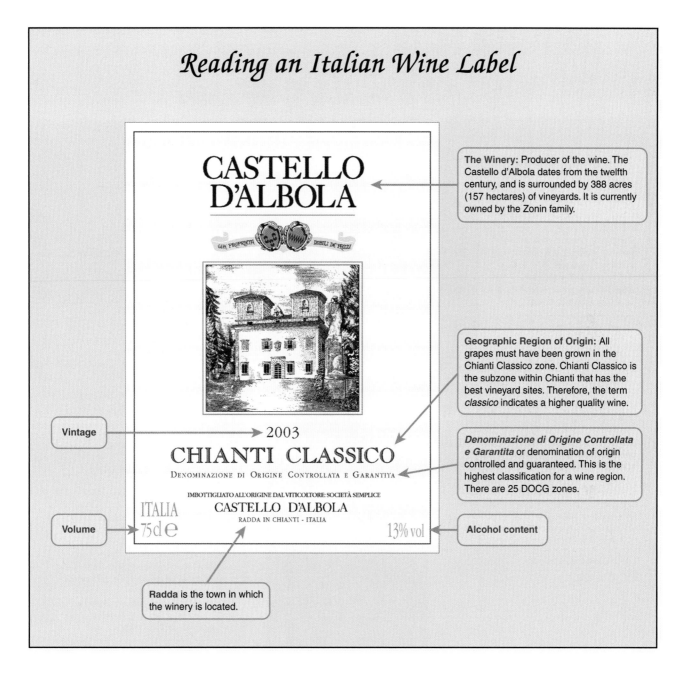

Reading an Italian Wine Label

The Winery: Producer of the wine. The Castello d'Albola dates from the twelfth century, and is surrounded by 388 acres (157 hectares) of vineyards. It is currently owned by the Zonin family.

Geographic Region of Origin: All grapes must have been grown in the Chianti Classico zone. Chianti Classico is the subzone within Chianti that has the best vineyard sites. Therefore, the term *classico* indicates a higher quality wine.

Denominazione di Origine Controllata e Garantita or denomination of origin controlled and guaranteed. This is the highest classification for a wine region. There are 25 DOCG zones.

Vintage

Volume

Alcohol content

Radda is the town in which the winery is located.

20.30 **Reading Spanish wine labels**

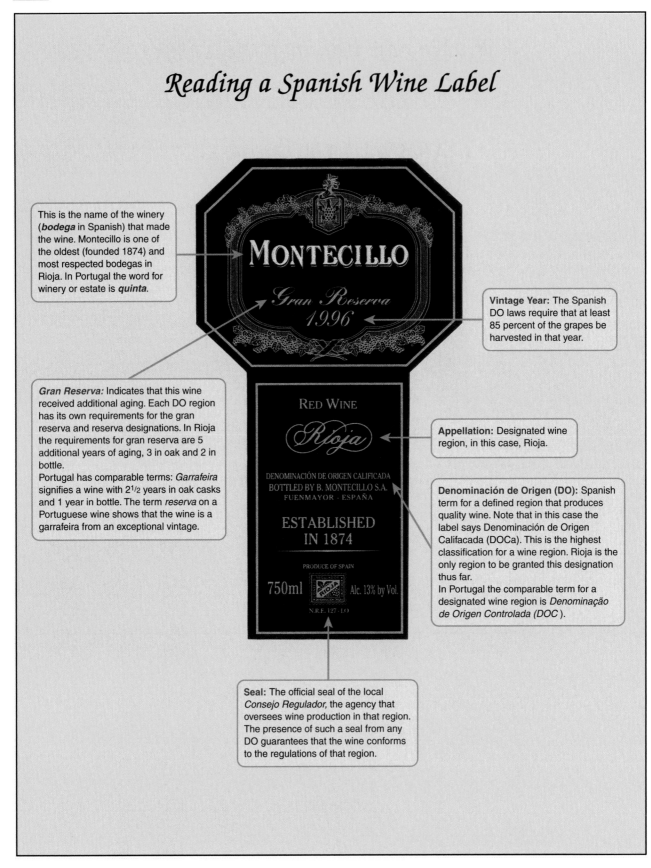

Reading a Spanish Wine Label

This is the name of the winery (***bodega*** in Spanish) that made the wine. Montecillo is one of the oldest (founded 1874) and most respected bodegas in Rioja. In Portugal the word for winery or estate is *quinta*.

Gran Reserva: Indicates that this wine received additional aging. Each DO region has its own requirements for the gran reserva and reserva designations. In Rioja the requirements for gran reserva are 5 additional years of aging, 3 in oak and 2 in bottle.

Portugal has comparable terms: *Garrafeira* signifies a wine with 2½ years in oak casks and 1 year in bottle. The term *reserva* on a Portuguese wine shows that the wine is a garrafeira from an exceptional vintage.

Vintage Year: The Spanish DO laws require that at least 85 percent of the grapes be harvested in that year.

Appellation: Designated wine region, in this case, Rioja.

Denominación de Origen (DO): Spanish term for a defined region that produces quality wine. Note that in this case the label says Denominación de Origen Califacada (DOCa). This is the highest classification for a wine region. Rioja is the only region to be granted this designation thus far.

In Portugal the comparable term for a designated wine region is *Denominação de Origen Controlada (DOC)*.

Seal: The official seal of the local *Consejo Regulador*, the agency that oversees wine production in that region. The presence of such a seal from any DO guarantees that the wine conforms to the regulations of that region.

20.31 Reading Australian and New Zealand wine labels

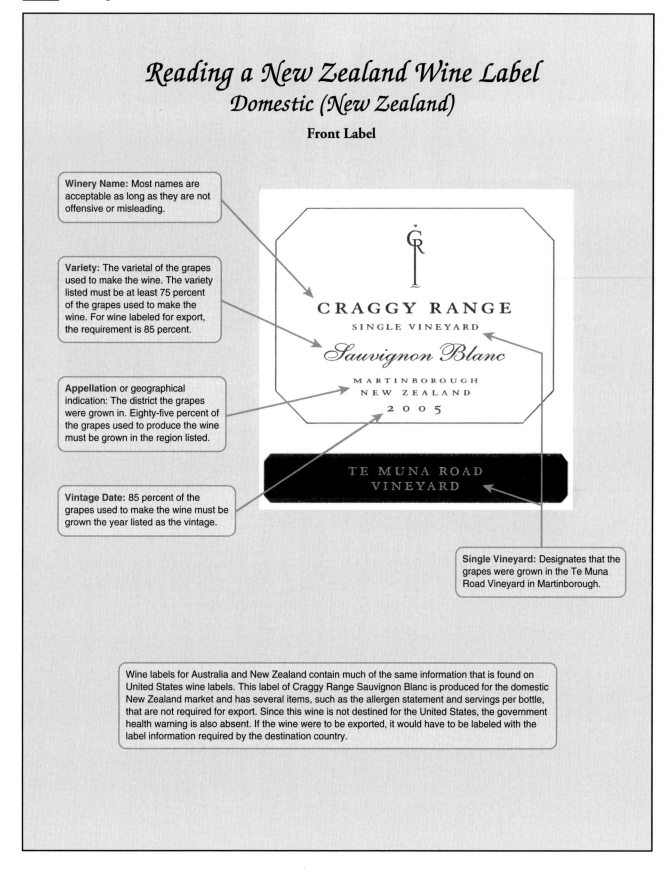

Reading a New Zealand Wine Label
Domestic (New Zealand)
Front Label

Winery Name: Most names are acceptable as long as they are not offensive or misleading.

Variety: The varietal of the grapes used to make the wine. The variety listed must be at least 75 percent of the grapes used to make the wine. For wine labeled for export, the requirement is 85 percent.

Appellation or geographical indication: The district the grapes were grown in. Eighty-five percent of the grapes used to produce the wine must be grown in the region listed.

Vintage Date: 85 percent of the grapes used to make the wine must be grown the year listed as the vintage.

CR

CRAGGY RANGE
SINGLE VINEYARD
Sauvignon Blanc
MARTINBOROUGH
NEW ZEALAND
2 0 0 5

TE MUNA ROAD
VINEYARD

Single Vineyard: Designates that the grapes were grown in the Te Muna Road Vineyard in Martinborough.

Wine labels for Australia and New Zealand contain much of the same information that is found on United States wine labels. This label of Craggy Range Sauvignon Blanc is produced for the domestic New Zealand market and has several items, such as the allergen statement and servings per bottle, that are not required for export. Since this wine is not destined for the United States, the government health warning is also absent. If the wine were to be exported, it would have to be labeled with the label information required by the destination country.

20.31   (continued)

Reading a New Zealand Wine Label
Domestic (New Zealand)
Back Label

Wine Notes: Not required but many wineries add them to describe how the wine is made and what it tastes like. They must not be misleading.

Alcohol Content and Container Volume: The percentage of alcohol by volume must be listed. If it is under 15 percent the label may also state "Table Wine." The volume of wine must also be listed in metric units.

Allergen Statement: Since 2002 both Australia and New Zealand have required that potential allergens, such as egg or milk products, be listed when they have been used (typically for fining) in the production of a wine.

Sulfite Declaration: If the wine contains any added sulfur dioxide it must be listed on the label. Here sulfur dioxide is referred to as "preservative 220."

Servings per Bottle: The number of "standard drinks" or servings must be listed. A standard drink is equal to the amount of the wine that contains 10 grams of alcohol.

TE MUNA ROAD VINEYARD

Craggy Range is a family owned winery specialising in the production of expressive Single Vineyard wines. Our Te Muna Road Vineyard is in the famous Martinborough Appellation. This wine is sourced exclusively from several parcels of vines growing on a stony, limestone influenced soil adjacent to the Huangarua River. The wine has rich ripe flavours of limes, peaches and apples alongside the characteristic herbaceous components and a unique dry grainy texture on the palate. As with all our Sauvignon Blanc wines intervention in the cellar is minimal out of care and respect for characters of the vineyard. Enjoy within three years of vintage, lightly chilled, wherever there is sun, surf or seafood.

SAUVIGNON BLANC
MARTINBOROUGH   2005

Alc 13% by vol 750ml

This wine was fined with traditional fining agents based on milk and fish products.
Contains preservative 220
Contains approx. 7.7 standard drinks

PRODUCED AND BOTTLED BY CRAGGY RANGE VINEYARDS LIMITED,
WAIMARAMA RD, HAVELOCK NORTH, N.Z. WWW.CRAGGYRANGE.COM
WINE OF NEW ZEALAND

Production Statement: The name and address of the winery that produced the wine.

Country of Origin: Required on all New Zealand wines.

20.32 **Reading German wine labels**

Reading a German Wine Label

Designation, or Prädikat: the designation indicates level of ripeness of the grapes at harvest, and therefore, the style of the wine. There are six Prädikat categories in chronological order of picking and in descending order of ripeness.
Kabinett: The lowest level of ripeness. Wines at this level are slightly off-dry.
Spätlese: Grapes for this category are picked later (*spät* means "late"). The wines are off-dry with more body.
Auslese: "Selected" grapes are picked later, and have higher sugar levels. The wines are definitely off-dry and quite rich.
Beerenauslese: Individual bunches are picked after being partially infected with *Botrytis cinerea,* the "noble rot." These wines are rich, sweet dessert wines.
Eiswein: Eiswein, like Beerenauslese, are partially botrytized bunches of grapes picked after the first hard frost in which the grapes are frozen.
Trockenbeerenauslese: Literally translates as "selected dried berries." These grapes are picked once they are fully botrytized, that is, shriveled up by the fungus. Sugars are very concentrated, and the resulting wine is very sweet and rich in texture.

Region: Mosel-Saar-Ruwer is one of the 13 official wine regions.

Gutsabfüllung: Estate-bottled. This means the Weis family owns the portion of the Goldtröpfchen vineyard from which these grapes were harvested.

Quality Level: Qualitatswein mit Prädikat indicates this wine belongs to the highest level of quality.

Government Approval Number: All Prädikat wines and QbA wines must display an official approval number on their label, indicating the wine has met all standards for its level of quality.

Alcohol Content: The percentage of alcohol by volume.

Village: All grapes were grown within the borders of the town of Piesport.

VDP Logo: The initials stand for "Verbands Deutscher Prädikats-und-Qualitäts-weingüter," Germany's most prestigious growers' association for Riesling.

Varietal: 85 percent must be the grape indicated.

MOSEL SAAR RUWER
GUTSABFÜLLUNG
Estate bottled
Qualitätswein mit Prädikat
White Wine/Product of Germany
A. P. Nr. 3 529 290 012 02
9% alc./vol.
750 ml
AUSLESE
2001
PIESPORTER GOLDTRÖPFCHEN
Riesling AUSLESE
WEINGUT
St. URBANS-HOF
OEKONOMIERAT NIC. WEIS
D-54340 LEIWEN / MOSEL

Winery Name: St. Urbans-hof, named for the German saint of wine, is owned by the Weis family.

Vineyard: Goldtröpfchen is a famous single vineyard in the town of Piesport. 85 percent of the grapes must come from this vineyard. In Germany, there are over 2,500 individual vineyards that can be indicated on labels.

Vintage Date: By German law, 85 percent of the grapes must have been harvested in this year.

20.33 Reading Chilean wine labels

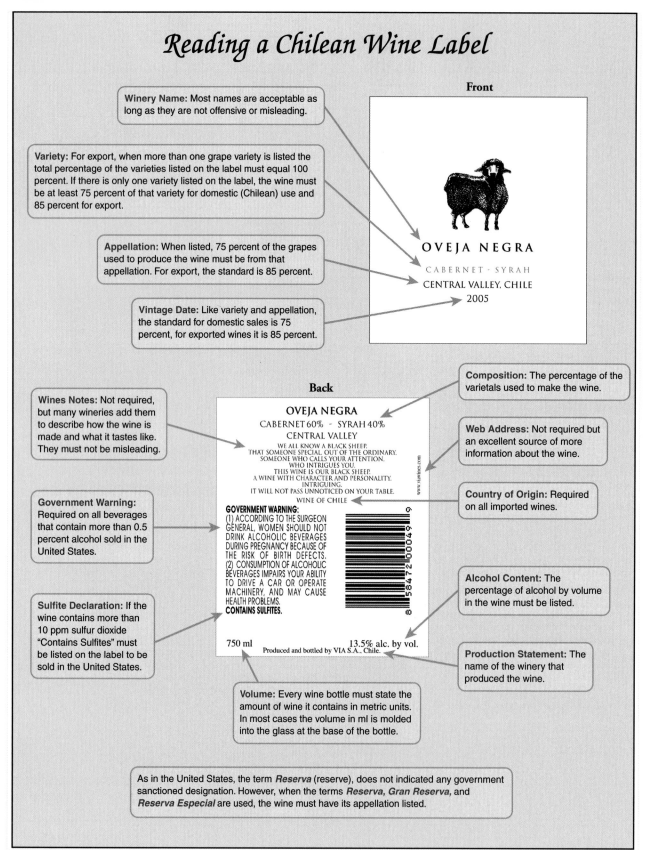

Reading a Chilean Wine Label

Winery Name: Most names are acceptable as long as they are not offensive or misleading.

Variety: For export, when more than one grape variety is listed the total percentage of the varieties listed on the label must equal 100 percent. If there is only one variety listed on the label, the wine must be at least 75 percent of that variety for domestic (Chilean) use and 85 percent for export.

Appellation: When listed, 75 percent of the grapes used to produce the wine must be from that appellation. For export, the standard is 85 percent.

Vintage Date: Like variety and appellation, the standard for domestic sales is 75 percent, for exported wines it is 85 percent.

Front

OVEJA NEGRA
CABERNET - SYRAH
CENTRAL VALLEY, CHILE
2005

Back

OVEJA NEGRA
CABERNET 60% - SYRAH 40%
CENTRAL VALLEY
WE ALL KNOW A BLACK SHEEP.
THAT SOMEONE SPECIAL. OUT OF THE ORDINARY.
SOMEONE WHO CALLS YOUR ATTENTION.
WHO INTRIGUES YOU.
THIS WINE IS OUR BLACK SHEEP.
A WINE WITH CHARACTER AND PERSONALITY.
INTRIGUING.
IT WILL NOT PASS UNNOTICED ON YOUR TABLE.
WINE OF CHILE

www.vianics.com

GOVERNMENT WARNING:
(1) ACCORDING TO THE SURGEON GENERAL, WOMEN SHOULD NOT DRINK ALCOHOLIC BEVERAGES DURING PREGNANCY BECAUSE OF THE RISK OF BIRTH DEFECTS. (2) CONSUMPTION OF ALCOHOLIC BEVERAGES IMPAIRS YOUR ABILITY TO DRIVE A CAR OR OPERATE MACHINERY, AND MAY CAUSE HEALTH PROBLEMS.
CONTAINS SULFITES.

750 ml   13.5% alc. by vol.
Produced and bottled by VIA S.A., Chile.

Composition: The percentage of the varietals used to make the wine.

Web Address: Not required but an excellent source of more information about the wine.

Country of Origin: Required on all imported wines.

Alcohol Content: The percentage of alcohol by volume in the wine must be listed.

Production Statement: The name of the winery that produced the wine.

Wines Notes: Not required, but many wineries add them to describe how the wine is made and what it tastes like. They must not be misleading.

Government Warning: Required on all beverages that contain more than 0.5 percent alcohol sold in the United States.

Sulfite Declaration: If the wine contains more than 10 ppm sulfur dioxide "Contains Sulfites" must be listed on the label to be sold in the United States.

Volume: Every wine bottle must state the amount of wine it contains in metric units. In most cases the volume in ml is molded into the glass at the base of the bottle.

As in the United States, the term *Reserva* (reserve), does not indicated any government sanctioned designation. However, when the terms *Reserva, Gran Reserva,* and *Reserva Especial* are used, the wine must have its appellation listed.

20.34 **Reading South African wine labels**

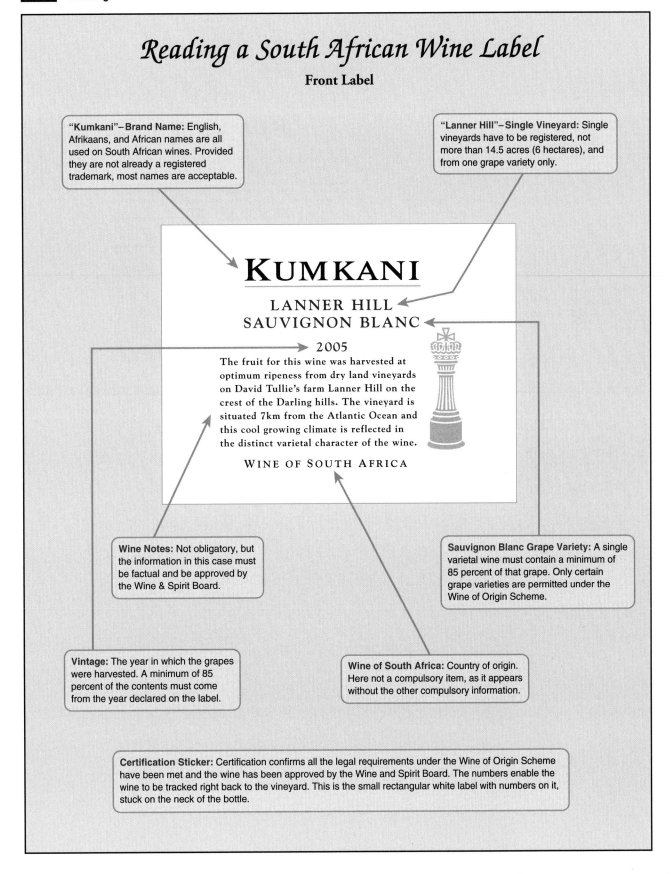

Reading a South African Wine Label

Front Label

"Kumkani"–Brand Name: English, Afrikaans, and African names are all used on South African wines. Provided they are not already a registered trademark, most names are acceptable.

"Lanner Hill"–Single Vineyard: Single vineyards have to be registered, not more than 14.5 acres (6 hectares), and from one grape variety only.

KUMKANI

LANNER HILL
SAUVIGNON BLANC

2005

The fruit for this wine was harvested at optimum ripeness from dry land vineyards on David Tullie's farm Lanner Hill on the crest of the Darling hills. The vineyard is situated 7km from the Atlantic Ocean and this cool growing climate is reflected in the distinct varietal character of the wine.

WINE OF SOUTH AFRICA

Wine Notes: Not obligatory, but the information in this case must be factual and be approved by the Wine & Spirit Board.

Sauvignon Blanc Grape Variety: A single varietal wine must contain a minimum of 85 percent of that grape. Only certain grape varieties are permitted under the Wine of Origin Scheme.

Vintage: The year in which the grapes were harvested. A minimum of 85 percent of the contents must come from the year declared on the label.

Wine of South Africa: Country of origin. Here not a compulsory item, as it appears without the other compulsory information.

Certification Sticker: Certification confirms all the legal requirements under the Wine of Origin Scheme have been met and the wine has been approved by the Wine and Spirit Board. The numbers enable the wine to be tracked right back to the vineyard. This is the small rectangular white label with numbers on it, stuck on the neck of the bottle.

20.34 (continued)

Reading a South African Wine Label

United States Export Back Label

KUMKANI
SINGLE VINEYARD

2005 LANNER HILL SAUVIGNON BLANC
WINE OF ORIGIN GROENEKLOOF

Derived from of the Xhosa word meaning King – Kumkani is a leader amongst South African wines. A wine with stature & pedigree, it epitomises the quality inherent in the rich diversity of the ancient soils, unique climates and winemaking heritage of South Africa.

The grapes for the Single Vineyard range of wines are grown in partnership with private, family owned farms – each wine reflecting a specific terroir.

This expressive, classic Sauvignon blanc reflects its cool climate origins. Ripe gooseberry flavours, flinty and full-bodied with a crisp lingering finish.

PRODUCT OF SOUTH AFRICA
CONTAINS SULFITES
ALC 14.5% BY VOL A581 750ML

Produced and bottled by Omnia Wines, Stellenbosch, South Africa.

GOVERNMENT WARNING: (1) ACCORDING TO THE SURGEON GENERAL, WOMEN SHOULD NOT DRINK ALCOHOLIC BEVERAGES DURING PREGNANCY BECAUSE OF THE RISK OF BIRTH DEFECTS. (2) CONSUMPTION OF ALCOHOLIC BEVERAGES IMPAIRS YOUR ABILITY TO DRIVE A CAR OR OPERATE MACHINERY, AND MAY CAUSE HEALTH PROBLEMS. IMPORTED BY: SOUTHERN STARZ, INC., HUNTINGTON BEACH, CA www.southernstarz.com

BARCODE NO: 00000000000000

Government Warning: A requirement for wines exported to the U.S. market.

20.35 Reading Canadian wine labels

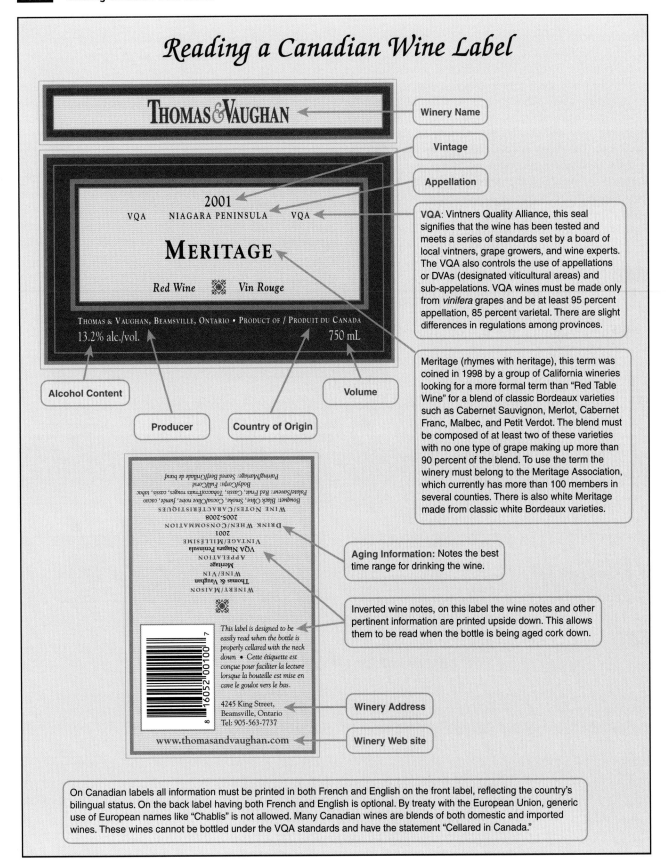

Reading a Canadian Wine Label

THOMAS & VAUGHAN ← Winery Name

← Vintage

← Appellation

2001
VQA   NIAGARA PENINSULA   VQA

MERITAGE

Red Wine ❈ *Vin Rouge*

THOMAS & VAUGHAN, BEAMSVILLE, ONTARIO • PRODUCT OF / PRODUIT DU CANADA

13.2% alc./vol.   750 mL

Alcohol Content

Producer   **Country of Origin**

Volume

VQA: Vintners Quality Alliance, this seal signifies that the wine has been tested and meets a series of standards set by a board of local vintners, grape growers, and wine experts. The VQA also controls the use of appellations or DVAs (designated viticultural areas) and sub-appelations. VQA wines must be made only from *vinifera* grapes and be at least 95 percent appellation, 85 percent varietal. There are slight differences in regulations among provinces.

Meritage (rhymes with heritage), this term was coined in 1998 by a group of California wineries looking for a more formal term than "Red Table Wine" for a blend of classic Bordeaux varieties such as Cabernet Sauvignon, Merlot, Cabernet Franc, Malbec, and Petit Verdot. The blend must be composed of at least two of these varieties with no one type of grape making up more than 90 percent of the blend. To use the term the winery must belong to the Meritage Association, which currently has more than 100 members in several counties. There is also white Meritage made from classic white Bordeaux varieties.

Pairing/Mariage: Seared Beef/Grillade de boeuf
Body/Corps: Full/Corsé
Palate/Saveur: Red Fruit, Cassis, Tobacco/Fruits rouges, cassis, tabac
Bouquet: Black Olive, Smoke, Cocoa/Olive noire, fumée, cacao
WINE NOTES/CARACTÉRISTIQUES
2005-2008
DRINK WHEN/CONSOMMATION
2001
VINTAGE/MILLÉSIME
VQA Niagara Peninsula
APPELLATION
Meritage
WINE/VIN
Thomas & Vaughan
WINERY/MAISON

❈

This label is designed to be easily read when the bottle is properly cellared with the neck down • Cette étiquette est conçue pour faciliter la lecture lorsque la bouteille est mise en cave le goulot vers le bas.

4245 King Street,
Beamsville, Ontario
Tel: 905-563-7737

www.thomasandvaughan.com

8 16052 00100 7

Aging Information: Notes the best time range for drinking the wine.

Inverted wine notes, on this label the wine notes and other pertinent information are printed upside down. This allows them to be read when the bottle is being aged cork down.

Winery Address

Winery Web site

On Canadian labels all information must be printed in both French and English on the front label, reflecting the country's bilingual status. On the back label having both French and English is optional. By treaty with the European Union, generic use of European names like "Chablis" is not allowed. Many Canadian wines are blends of both domestic and imported wines. These wines cannot be bottled under the VQA standards and have the statement "Cellared in Canada."

Sparkling Wines and Champagne

Sparkling wine has significant levels of carbonated dioxide in it, thereby making it fizzy. This can occur naturally in the bottle or as a part of a production process. In some parts of the world, the word *champagne* is used as a synonym for sparkling wine, although only sparking wine from the Champagne region of France can truly be called champagne. Sparkling wine and champagne are rated by their relative sweetness. The driest is brut, followed by extra dry, sec, and the sweetest of all, demi-sec. See Figure 20.36 and Figure 20.37 regarding the process of making champagne. See Figure 20.38 regarding classification of champagne styles. Also see Figure 20.39, Figure 20.40, and Figure 20.41 for examples of various champagnes.

Fortified Wines and Aperitifs

Fortified wines are those that are manipulated primarily after fermentation by adding other types of alcohol to achieve a bolder taste, higher alcohol content, and a longer shelf life. An aperitif can be made in the same way as sweet fortified wines, but an aperitif is consumed before the meal to stimulate the appetite. Some of the wines in this chapter are appropriate served as **aperitifs** as well as after meals.

PORT

Port is named for the city of Oporto, Portugal, a port city at the end of the Douro River. Port grapes are grown in the Douro River area. More than forty different varieties of grapes can be used when making Port. The producer's aim is to make this wine a strong (about 18 to 22 percent alcohol), sweet

20.36 **Methode Champenoise flowchart**

MÉTHODE CHAMPENOISE FLOWCHART

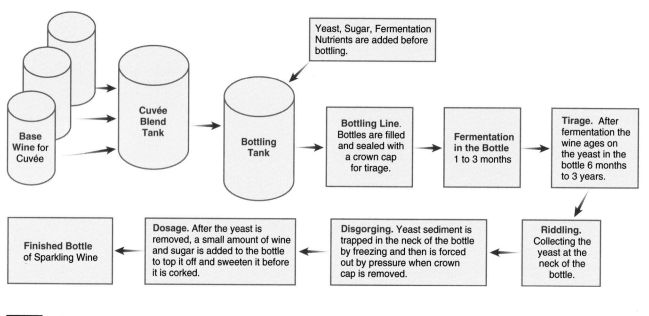

20.37 **Charmat process flowchart**

CHARMAT (BULK) PROCESS FLOWCHART

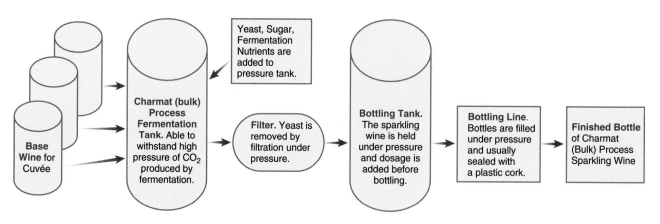

20.38 Classification of champagne styles

Classification of Champagne Styles

Extra Brut: Bone dry. Residual sugar is less than 0.6 percent per liter. At this level there is usually no dosage.

Brut: This is the most common classification, and forms the backbone of any house's line. Residual sugar is 0.5–1.5 percent per liter.

Extra Dry: These Champagnes are off-dry, with residual sugar 1.0-2 percent.

Sec: Although *sec* means "dry," these Champagnes have noticeable sugar—between 2 and 3.5 percent. They are rarely seen in the United States.

Demi-Sec: The literal translation is "off-dry" but these Champagnes are quite sweet. The dosage causes residual sugar to be between 3.5 and 5 percent. These Champagnes are meant to be served with dessert.

Doux: The sweetest form of Champagne has a minimum of 5.5 percent sugar, and in some cases contains as much as 8 percent.

Label for nonvintage Brut from the house of Taittinger.

20.39 Veuve Cliquot champagnes

Figures 20.39–20.41 © Randy Van Dam 2008

20.40 Dom Perignon champagnes

20.41 Inexpensive sparkling wines (Asti and Cook's)

drink. The alcohol level was originally increased with brandy to help preserve the wine during long voyages from Portugal to England. The following are the various types of port:

- **Ruby port.** Lower-quality wine is made into ruby port and aged in wood for approximately 3 years before being released for sale. These ports are, as the name suggests, very red. The flavor displays the fruity characters of a young wine, and it is meant to be drunk young. Ruby port is usually consumed in the winter months, and it is the least expensive of the ports.

- **Late bottled vintage (LBV) port.** This is a very high-quality ruby port. It must be aged in wood for at least 4, but no more than 6, years. If the port produced from a single year's grape production is of high quality, the shipper can declare it to be "late bottled vintage." (See Figure 20.42.)

- **Crusted ports.** Crusted ports have been, for the most part, replaced by LBV port.

- **Tawny port.** Tawny port takes its name from its color. This port is a blend of several vintages that have been aged in wood. The aging can last for almost 40 years; however, most are aged closer to the 6-year minimum.

- **Colheita port.** This port is also called dated port. It is similar to LBV, but it is a tawny port. This port is aged for a minimum of 7 years before it is bottled.

- **Vintage port.** This is considered by most to be the best port available. Only the best grapes from the best growing site make this wine, but it is made only during the best years. A vintage is not declared every year.

- **Second label vintage port.** When a firm feels that its port is very good but not vintage, it will call it a second label vintage port. It is made the same way as vintage port.

- **Single quinta port.** This port is similar to high-quality estate, chateau, or single-vineyard reserve wine. All of the wine is from a single estate, usually labeled as such, in nonvintage years to establish the vineyard's claim of a superior port.

- **White port.** This port is made from white grapes. The producers make white port using the same methods as for ruby or tawny port, but they allow the white wine to ferment a little longer. This makes for a dryer finished product. White ports range from medium sweet to almost dry, and they are mainly served as an aperitif. (See Figure 20.43.)

MADEIRA

Madeira comes from the Island of Madeira, which is located in the Atlantic Ocean off the coast of northwest Africa, about 350 miles from Morocco. Brandy is added to wine to make Madeira just as it is added to wine to make port. Unlike port, however, Madeira is then exposed to air and heat, two things that would ruin any other wine. In the nineteenth century, Madeira shippers found that the wine was better when it arrived at the destination than when it left the Island of Madeira. This difference was caused by the wines' exposure

20.42   **Bottle of LBV port**

Figures 20.42–20.43 © Randy Van Dam 2008

20.43   **Bottles of ruby, tawny, and white ports**

to heat and air aboard the ship. Unlike port, Madeira is not always sweet. There are five levels of Madeira.

- **Malmsey.** Malmsey has a honey flavor with overtones of chocolate and figs. It is the sweetest of the five levels.

- **Bual.** This wine is medium-sweet to sweet and is distinctive because of the fruit and butter flavor.

- **Rainwater.** This was first made by accident when a shipper's Madeira became "waterlogged" in heavy rain from the island to the Americas.

- **Verdelho.** The wine has a gentle, smooth, smoky flavor and is great for use in cooking.

- **Sercial.** This is the driest style of Madeira, which has been compared to Fino Sherry.

MARSALA

The name of this wine is taken from the port city of Marsala, located on the western end of Sicily. Marsalas are classified according to three characteristics. Each of these characteristics has three manifestations; therefore, these characteristics become a "Triple Trinity." The first characteristic concerns the level of sweetness, the second concerns color, and the third concerns class, or ranking.

Marsala has three levels of sweetness: *secco, semisecco,* and *dolce* (Figure 20.44).

- **Secco.** This designation indicates that the Marsala is dry.

20.44 Dry and sweet Marsala

© Randy Van Dam 2008

- **Semisecco.** This category indicates that the Marsala is semi-dry.

- **Dolce.** This indicates that the Marsala is sweet.

Marsala's three color classifications are *oro, ambra,* and *rubino.*

- **Oro.** Oro means *gold.*

- **Ambra.** Ambra means *amber.* The wine is reduced to one-third of its original volume, which gives the Marsala its cooked taste. A *sifone* (a mixture of semi-dried grapes and alcohol) is also added to the wine; the *sifone* is responsible for the wine's sweetness.

- **Rubino.** Rubino means *ruby.* Red grapes are used to make this wine and provide its color.

The third part of the trinity refers to Marsala's quality ranking. The three classifications are *Marsala Fine, Marsala Superiore,* and *Marsala Vergine* (also known as Vergine Soleras).

- **Marsala Fine.** This Marsala can have any of the sweetness or color rankings.

- **Marsala Superiore.** This Marsala can come in any color and level of sweetness. The wine must be aged for at least 2 years in wood and have at least 18 percent alcohol.

- **Marsala Vergine (Vergine Soleras).** This Marsala can come in any color, but it is limited to *secco* in its level of sweetness. This is the best Marsala made. It is aged in wood for 5 years and has at least 18 percent alcohol. It should always be served as an aperitif.

SHERRY

Sherry is Spain's addition to the ranks of fortified wine. Like other fortified wines, sherry has several levels that are categorized in various ways. There are only two grape varieties used to produce sherry: Palomino Fino and Pedro Ximenez. The Palomino grapes comprise about 90 percent of the grape production for sherry. Sherry has between 17 and 22 percent alcohol by volume. (See Figure 20.45.)

Oxidation is an important part of sherry's production process. There are several ways the producers ensure that oxidation happens. One way is to store the wine in an above-ground cellar called a *bodega.* The second is to make sure the barrels are not filled to the top, leaving an air gap so that the wine is exposed to the air. Barrels are only filled two-thirds full, and the bung (cork) is not completely shut; this allows air to circulate. (See Figure 20.46.)

- **Fino.** These are the lightest of the sherries. They are pale and dry but fragrant, refreshing, and tangy. They should not be aged because they will decline with age rather than improve.

- **Manzanilla.** This sherry has a hint of saltiness, which may have something to do with where it is produced. It is made in the Sanlucar de Barrameda region, which is close to the sea.

- **Amontillado.** This sherry also is classified as a Fino. Amontillado has a little more age to it and tends to be dry unless it is blended. It should be served at room temperature or with ice.

20.45 The Solera system for making sherry

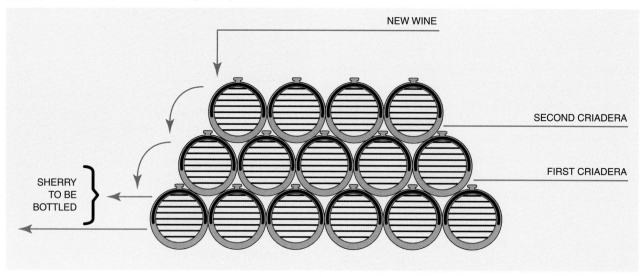

NEW WINE

SECOND CRIADERA

FIRST CRIADERA

SHERRY
TO BE
BOTTLED

- **Oloroso.** Some Oloroso sherries can be aged for many years; in some cases, they can be aged a full century. The flavors of this type of sherry vary greatly. Some need to be blended to enjoy, while others are good to drink as they are.

- **Palo Cortado.** These sherries tend to develop like an Oloroso, but they are lighter in flavor. This style varies from producer to producer.

- **Cream sherries.** This class of sherry has given the other styles a bad name, even though some cream sherries can be quite good. A cream sherry is a sweet oloroso.

- **PX.** This group of sherries is small and hard to find. These are very sweet sherries and can be used to top ice cream or to blend with other sherries such as Fino or Oloroso. (See Figure 20.47.)

BEER

The family of beverages generally referred to as **beer** has been brewed for centuries. Beers are obtained by the yeast fermentation of malted cereal grains, to which hops and

20.46 Bottles of Cream, Fino, and Amontillado sherries

© Randy Van Dam 2008

20.47 Bottle of PX sherry

© Randy Van Dam 2008

water have been added. Germans consume the most beer per person per year.

Global Sourcing

Commercially available beers are produced in more than 30 countries and exceed 1,500 different choices of international and micro-brewed beverages. According to the 2004 Brewers Association Craft Beer Industry statistics, there were 1,396 craft breweries, 988 brewpubs, 351 microbreweries, and 57 regional specialty breweries in the United States (www. nysaes.cornell.edu).

Buying and Storing

The color of beer is measured at two steps of the brewing process: the color of the malt is graded after kilning, and the color of the finished beer is assessed when ready for packaging and consumption. Brewers tend to describe their finished beers in Standard Reference Method (SRM) numbers. Although the beer community uses these numbers as color scales, they really are measurements of light. The color of beer is affected by the ambient lighting and by the width of the glass in which it is served. For example, a darker beer will be perceived lighter if served in a thin glass.

AMERICAN CRAFT BEER PRODUCTION

An **American craft brewer** is *small, independent,* and *traditional.* Craft beer comes only from a craft brewer. The best-known craft beers are national brands like Samuel Adams or Sierra Nevada, but there are hundreds of small breweries nationwide that distribute their own brews locally and regionally. Craft beer accounts for just 3.5 percent of U.S. beer sales, and imports make up 12.5 percent, according to Eric Shepard, executive editor of *Beer Marketer's Insights.* But those numbers are going up, while the market share of mainstream beers is declining.

Craft breweries can be defined in the following ways:

- **Small.** Annual production of beer is less than 2 million barrels.

20.48a **Brewpub**
© Randy Van Dam 2008

- **Independent.** Less than 25 percent of the craft brewery is owned or controlled (or equivalent economic interest) by alcoholic beverage industry members who are not themselves craft brewers.

- **Traditional.** A brewer who has either an all-malt flagship (the beer that represents the greatest volume among that brewer's brands) or has at least 50 percent of its volume in either all malt beers or in beers that use adjuncts to enhance rather than lighten flavor.

The different craft brewers are defined as follows:

- **Microbrewery.** A brewery that produces less than 15,000 barrels (17,600 hectoliters) of beer per year.

- **Brewpub.** A restaurant-brewery that sells 25 percent or more of its beer on site (see Figure 20.48a). The beer is brewed primarily for sale in the restaurant and bar. (See Figure 20.48b.)

- **Contract brewing company.** This is a business that hires another brewery to produce its beer or to produce additional beer.

- **Regional brewery.** A brewery with an annual beer production of between 15,000 and 2 million barrels.

- **Regional craft brewery.** An independent regional brewery that has either an all-malt flagship or has at least 50 percent of its volume in either all malt beers or in beers that use adjuncts to enhance rather than lighten flavor.

20.48b **Customer enjoying beer at a brewpub**
© Randy Van Dam 2008

Types of Beer

Beers are produced in a variety of recipes or styles, many with a long history. A beer's style is a label that describes the overall flavor and often the origin of a beer, according to a system that has evolved by trial and error over many centuries. A style of beer is defined by the ingredients used in its production, the method of production, and other factors. There are several quantifiable characteristics of a beer, often referred to as "vital statistics." These include:

- **Bitterness (IBU).** The amount of bitterness imparted to a beer from the hops, as calculated by a moderately complex formula, that is measured in International Bitterness Units (IBUs)
- **Color.** As measured by the Standard Reference Method (SRM)
- **Original specific gravity (OG).** A measure of the amount of sugars in a beer before fermentation
- **Final specific gravity (FG).** A measure of the amount of unfermented sugars remaining in a beer after fermentation
- **Alcohol content by volume (ABV).** May be calculated from the OG and FG, or measured directly

Beer might be strictly categorized simply as ales, lagers, or hybrid beers, but that would eliminate some products and confuse others. For purposes of using this text as a reference manual, beer is broadly divided into the following categories, as they all use the same yeast-based biochemical reaction to ferment:

- **Ales.** An ale is a fermented malt beverage, full-bodied, and somewhat bitter with a strong flavor of hops. Modern ale is made with top-fermenting yeast and processed at higher temperatures than lager beer. Pale ale has up to 5 percent alcohol content; the darker, strong ale contains up to 6.5 percent. (See Figure 20.49 and Figure 20.50.)
- **Ciders.** Cider is a natural, liquid beverage that is obtained by pressing finely ground fruit such as apples. Under the proper conditions, it undergoes a natural fermentation process, which yields an alcoholic juice. However, most products on the market today that are labeled cider are not fermented. (See Figure 20.51.)
- **Lagers.** This is a general style of beer that was brewed in cool conditions using a slow-acting brewers yeast, known as bottom-fermenting yeast, and originally stored and aged (lagered) in its cask or vat for 1 to 3 months. The most popular examples of beer brewed using the lager method are pale lagers, also known as pilsners. Lager is a light, bubbly, golden brew that ranks as the United States' most popular beer. (See Figure 20.52.)

20.50 **Assorted bottles of Bocks. Originally brewed with malt in the northern German town of Einbeck since the 1300s, modern flavored bock beer can be dark, amber, or pale in color.**

© Randy Van Dam 2008

20.49 **Assorted bottles of ale**

© Randy Van Dam 2008

20.51 **Assorted bottles of cider**

Figures 20.51–.54 © Randy Van Dam 2008

20.52 **Assorted bottles of lager**

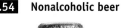

- **Meads.** Dating back to Biblical times, mead is a beverage made by fermenting honey, water, and yeast with flavorings such as herbs, spices, or flowers. Mead was popular in early England and, though not widely distributed today, is still bottled. (See Figure 20.53.)

- **Low alcohol.** Low-alcohol (or nonalcoholic, N/A, or NAB) beer is beer with very low or no alcohol content. The vast majority of NABs are lagers, but there are also some ales. Legally, in the United States, beers containing up to 0.5 percent alcohol by volume can be called nonalcoholic. In Europe, it must be lower than 1 percent. Although they are called nonalcoholic, they still contain some alcohol, and all states have laws that prohibit their sale to minors. (See Figure 20.54.)

- **Sake.** Made from rice, *sake* is an alcoholic beverage particular to Japan. (See Figure 20.55.)

- **Specialty beers.** These are beers made from fruits or other nontraditional food products. (See Figure 20.56.)

- **Stouts and porters.** Stouts and porters are dark beers made using roasted malts or roasted barley. Guinness is the most famous of the dry stouts. Sweet stout, an English version, is less bitter and often lower in alcohol content. (See Figure 20.57a, Figure 20.57b, and Figure 20.57c.)

- **Wheat beers.** This beer is brewed with a significant proportion of malted wheat. The addition of wheat lends wheat beers a light flavor and pale color. Wheat beers are usually top-fermented (in Germany, they have to be by law). (See Figure 20.58 and Figure 20.59.)

20.53 **Bottle of mead**

20.54 **Nonalcoholic beer**

20.55 Bottle of sake

Figures 20.55–.59 © Randy Van Dam 2008

20.56 Pumpkin ale (specialty beer)

20.57a Various bottles of porters

20.57b Various bottles of stouts

20.57c Bottle of extra stout

20.58 Bottles of wheat beer

20.59 Organic beer

DISTILLED SPIRITS

Distilled spirits are a liquid preparation meant for consumption and contain ethyl (ethanol) purified by distillation from a fermented substance such as fruit, vegetables, or grain. The word *spirits* generally refers to distilled beverages low in sugars and containing at least 35 percent alcohol by volume. Gin, vodka, rum, whiskey, brandy, and tequila are types of spirits. Beverages high in alcohol and with added flavorings such as Grand Marnier, Frangelico, and schnapps are generally referred to as liquers. Aside from specific product categories, another method for classifying distilled spirits is as aged or unaged. Whiskies, cognacs, and other products must be aged for specific periods (the minimums are usually mandated by law) in wooden barrels in order to develop specific characteristics of taste, color, and aroma.

The Distillation Process

Alcohol is not created by distillation; it is just concentrated. A weak alcoholic beverage such as wine or beer is heated to boiling in a still (see Figure 20.60a and Figure 20.60b). Because the various constituents of the resulting vapor (like water, ethyl, methyl, and isopropyl alcohols) will vaporize and condense at different temperatures, they may be selectively extracted to create a new mixture that may then be further aged or flavored by the distiller.

The container at the center of the pot still receives both the distillate from the first pot, which must be further purified, and the undesirable portions (the foreshots and feints) of the second distillation, more of whose alcohol can thereby be extracted.

The plates in each column of the column still (see Figure 20.61) are hottest at the bottom and coolest at the top. Liquids with low boiling points are concentrated in the vapor that leaves the first column and rises in the second. As is the case with the pot still, the impurities are recycled to extract their fraction of desirable ingredients.

Types of Distilled Beverages

In recent history, worldwide distribution has made it possible for us to taste beverages from around the world. The following common spirits are categorized by their foundation ingredients.

People, Places, Things

The Brewing Process

The steps a brewer may follow are similar, whether they are a small craft brewer or large national brand brewery. The steps generally include the following, although craft brewers may purchase ground grist rather than grind it themselves.

1. Malt is fed into the mill.
2. The mill grinds the malt into grist.
3. The grist is fed into the mash tun, where it is mixed with warm or hot water. If the infusion method is used, only the mash tun is utilized.
4. If infusion is not used, it is during the decoction phase of the brewing process that the mash is sent through the lauter tun, where the mash is clarified and becomes the refined wort.
5. Hops are added to the wort in the brew kettle, where the actual brewing of the mixture occurs.
6. The hops are removed from the mixture, and the wort passes through the hop back and is flavored by the hops.
7. The whirlpool removes the undesirable proteins by centrifugal force.
8. The wort moves through a cooling area, the heat exchanger, where it is brought down to a temperature suitable for fermentation.
9. The yeast is added to the wort in the fermentation tank.
10. Following fermentation, the wort moves along to the conditioning tanks, where it sits undisturbed until it reaches its finished, aged state (depending on the style).
11. The finished beer is filtered, although some styles are not filtered at all.
12. The beer passes to a holding tank, where it remains until it is bottled or kegged for transport, sale, or consumption.

20.60a   **Diagram of the pot still**

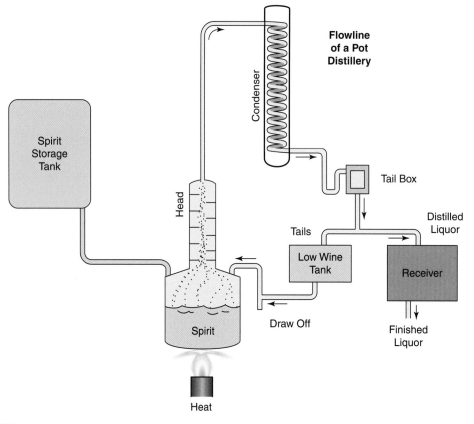

Flowline of a Pot Distillery

Condenser

Head

Spirit Storage Tank

Tail Box

Tails

Low Wine Tank

Draw Off

Distilled Liquor

Receiver

Finished Liquor

Spirit

Heat

20.60b   **Pot still**

Photo Courtesy Robert Garlough

20.61   **Diagram of the column still**

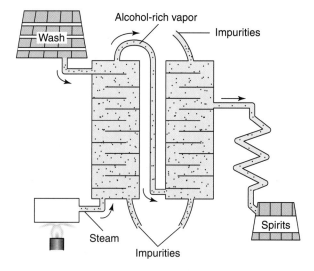

Alcohol-rich vapor

Impurities

Wash

Steam

Impurities

Spirits

WHEAT, CORN, AND RYE

Whiskey or whiskey-like products are produced in most grain-growing areas. They differ in base product, alcohol content, and quality.

- **Scotch whisky** is divided into four distinct categories: single malt (Figure 20.62a), vatted malt (also called "pure malt"), blended (Figure 20.62b), and single grain.

- **Irish whiskey** is a grain whiskey made in Ireland. There are several types of whiskey common to Ireland: single malt, pure pot still, and blended whiskey. (See Figure 20.62c.)

- **American straight whiskey** must be made using a mash bill that consists of at least 51 percent and no more than 79 percent of a single grain. Bourbon is made from at least 51 percent corn; straight mash is made from at least 51 percent rye, and so on. (See Figure 20.62d and Figure 20.62e.)

- **Grain whiskey** differs from malt in that it is usually made from corn, maize, or other grains rather than malted barley.

- **Blended whiskey** is a mix of different types of whiskies, usually some combination of single-malt and grain whiskies. (See Figure 20.62f.)

- **Vatted malt.** When single-malt whiskeys from different distilleries are mixed together, the term *vatted* or *blended malt* is used. They do not contain any grain whiskey.

- **Corn whiskey.** Corn whiskey is a U.S. whisky made from a mash (a mixture of hot water and crushed grain) made up of at least 80 percent corn. The whiskey is distilled to no more than 80 percent alcohol by volume.

- **Rye whiskey.** Rye whiskey describes two types of whiskeys, theoretically distilled from rye.

"Whiskey" is spelled "whisky" in Scotland, Japan, New Zealand, and Canada.

GRAINS

- **Vodka.** Vodka is typically a colorless spirit, distilled from fermented rye or wheat grains. Except for various types of flavorings, vodka consists of water and ethanol alcohol. It usually has an alcohol content ranging from 35 to 50 percent by volume (70 to 100 proof). The classic Russian vodka is 40 percent (80 proof). (See Figure 20.63.)

RICE

- **Shōchū.** In English, this is often dubbed "Japanese vodka." Most shochu is around 25 percent alcohol, although some varieties can go as high as 43 percent. Shochu can be made from rice, although it is more commonly made from barley, sweet potato, or sugarcane.

- **Baijiu.** The name *baijiu* literally means "white liquor," "white alcohol," or "white spirits." *Baijiu* is a clear drink, usually distilled from sorghum, although sometimes other grains, such as rice, may be used.

20.62a **Various bottles of single-malt scotch whiskeys**

Figures 20.62a–c © Randy Van Dam 2008

20.62b **Various bottles of blended scotch whiskeys**

20.62c **Various bottles of Irish whiskeys**

20.62d American bourbon whiskey

Figures 20.62d–.63 © Randy Van Dam 2008

20.62e American sour mash whiskey

20.62f Various bottles of Canadian blended whiskeys

20.63 Various bottles of vodka

FRUITS

- **Brandy.** Brandy is a general term for distilled wine, usually 40 to 60 percent ethyl alcohol by volume. In addition to wine, this spirit can also be made from grape pumace or fermented fruit juice. (See Figure 20.64.)

- **Cognac.** Cognac, named after the town of Cognac in France, is a brandy that is produced in the region surrounding the town. It must be made from at least 90 percent Ugni Blanc, Folle Blanche, or Colombard grapes. It must be distilled twice in copper pot stills and aged at least 2.5 years in French oak barrels in order to be called cognac. (See Figure 20.65.)

- **Gin.** Gin is a spirit made from the distillation of white grain spirit and juniper berries, which provide its distinctive flavor. The taste of ordinary gin is very dry, and, as such, it is frequently mixed with other beverages. (See Figure 20.66.)

APPLES

- **Applejack.** Applejack is produced from apples, originating from the U.S. colonial period. It is made by concentrating hard cider (fermented alcoholic apple juice) either by the traditional method of freeze distillation or by true evaporative distillation. The term *applejack* comes from "jacking," a nickname for the freeze distillation procedure originally used.

- **Calvados.** Calvados is an apple brandy from the French region of Lower Normandy. The fruit is picked and pressed into a juice that is then fermented into a dry cider. It is then distilled into *eau de vie*, a French term for a colorless brandy distilled from fermented fruit juice. (See Figure 20.67.)

SUGARCANE/MOLASSES

- **Rum.** Made from sugarcane or sugarcane by-products, the clear liquid distillate is then usually aged in oak and other casks. Rum is produced in a variety of styles. Light rums are commonly used in mixed drinks, while golden and dark rums are appropriate for use in cooking as well as cocktails. (See Figure 20.68a, Figure 20.68b, and Figure 20.68c.)

- **Cachaça.** Cachaça, made from sugarcane juice (also called garapa), is the most popular distilled alcoholic beverage in Brazil. The legal definition for cachaça is the product of the distillation of the fermented sugarcane juice, with alcohol strength between 38 and 51 percent by volume. Cachaça is often said to differ from rum in that it is made from sugarcane juice, while rum is made from molasses. (See Figure 20.69.)

AGAVE

- **Tequila.** Tequila is a spirit made primarily in the area surrounding Tequila, a town in the western Mexican state of Jalisco, 65 km northwest of Guadalajara. Most common tequilas are 35 to 65 percent alcohol (70 to 110 proof). By Mexican law, all 100 percent agave or aged tequila is bottled in Mexico. All 100 percent agave tequila is labeled

People, Places, Things

My Meeting with the Little Peasant Girl

Many years ago, I lead a group of culinary students on a cuisine and culture study tour of Brazil. My colleague at Grand Rapids Community College, Chef Angus Campbell, and I would lead tours every year to foreign destinations. Our goal was to learn about the local culture, indigenous ingredients and topography, and their impact on the cuisine. We accomplished this by visiting food markets, plantations, and restaurants, and taking cooking classes from local chefs. Upon landing in Manaus, an important trading spot midway along the 1,000-mile long Amazon River, we gave our student group the afternoon off to acclimate to their jungle resort surroundings. Chef Campbell and I wandered down a dirt road until we came across a quaint outdoor *barra*, located along one of the mighty river's many tributaries. Seated at a table was a lone guest, who was amusing himself with drink. After a few minutes, he directed the server (who was also the busser, bartender, cook, and dishwasher) in slurred German to bring us two drinks. Not wishing to be rude, and in the spirit of adventure, we gratefully accepted his cold beverages called a *Caipirinha* (nicknamed "little peasant girl"). This powerful cocktail is Brazil's favorite drink, and after only a few of them, we could see why. We happily spent the afternoon with our new German comrade and the "little peasant girl."

To make a Caipirinha: In a rock's glass, muddle half a lime with 1 tablespoon of sugar. Add ½ cup of cachaça and ½ cup of ice. Stir.

20.64 Bottle of brandy

Figures 60.64–.68c © Randy Van Dam 2008

20.65 Various bottles of Cognac

© Randy Van Dam 2008

20.66 Various bottles of gin

20.67 Various bottles of apple brandy

20.68a Various bottles of Puerto Rican rum

20.68b Various bottles of Jamaican rum

20.68c Various bottles of spiced and dark rum

20.69 Various bottles of Cachaça

Figures 60.69–.71c © Randy Van Dam 2008

20.70 Various bottles of tequila

as such; otherwise, it is a "mixto," which is made from fermented agave juice and other sugars. (See Figure 20.70.) Tequila is labeled in the following manner:

- **Silver or blanco.** This is aged 60 days or less, or not at all.
- **Gold.** Gold is usually a "mixto" and is made from unaged silver tequila plus caramel for color.
- **Reposado.** Aged in wooden tanks or casks for at least 2 months; the better quality reposado tequilas are aged from 3 to 9 months.
- **Añejo.** These are aged in wood at least 1 year. High-quality "mixtos" are aged from 1.5 to 3 years, and high-quality agaves are aged up to 4 years.
- **Mezcal.** Mezcal is a Mexican distilled spirit made from the agave plant. There are many different types of agaves, and each produces a slightly different mezcal. While Tequila is a mezcal made only from the blue agave plant in the region around Tequila, Jalisco, spirits labeled "Mezcal" are often made using other agave plants. Mezcal is primarily made in the Mexican state of Oaxaca. (See Figure 20.71a and Figure 20.72.)

20.71a Bottle of mezcal

20.71b Person standing next to mature agave plant

Photo Courtesy Robert Garlough

20.71c Pile of agave piñas

Photo Courtesy Robert Garlough

20.71d Pile of roasted and cut agave piñas, ready for crushing

Figures 20.71d–.71i © Photos Courtesy Robert Garlough

20.71e Roasted agave being crushed under stone wheel drawn by donkey

20.71f Shredded agave being turned

20.71g Agave being fermented in vat

20.71h Agave juice being distilled

20.71i Variety of mezcal available for sale in Mexican shop

20.72 Blue agave growing on a hillside near the town of Tequila (in the state of Jalisco, Mexico)

Photos Courtesy Robert Garlough

POMACE

Grappa is a fragrant grape-based pomace brandy of between 40 and 60 percent alcohol by volume (80 to 120 proof), of Italian origin.

ANISE

- **Absinthe.** This is a distilled, highly alcoholic, anise-flavored spirit derived from herbs, including the flowers and leaves of the medicinal plant *Artemisia absinthium*, also called grand wormwood. Although it is sometimes incorrectly called a liqueur, absinthe is not bottled with added sugar and is therefore classified as a liquor or spirit.

 Buyer's Note: Liquors that contain extracts from the Artemisia absinthium cannot be imported to the United States.

- **Ouzo.** Ouzo is a Greek anise-flavored spirit that is widely consumed in Greece. The name dates back to the late nineteenth century but is of uncertain origin. It is similar to absinthe but without the wormwood. (See Figure 20.73.)

POTATO

- **Aquavit.** This is a Scandinavian distilled beverage of about 40 percent alcohol by volume. Like vodka, it is distilled from potato or grain. It is flavored with herbs such as caraway seeds, anise, dill, fennel, and coriander, among others. (See Figure 20.74.)

People, Places, Things

Making Mezcal

Mezcal is made from the agave plant and is harvested when it is 7 or 8 years old (see Figure 20.71b). After the agave is harvested, the spines of the plant are cut off. The remaining heart, called the piña (which is Spanish for pineapple), can weigh up to 220 pounds. (See Figure 20.71c). The piñas are split or cut into quarters and roasted inside a rock-lined pit called a palenque. Agave leaves and matting are used to cover the pit allowing the piñas to roast for up to a week (see Figure 20.71d). The roasted agave is crushed using a special stone grinding wheel pulled by a horse or mule (see Figure 20.71e and Figure 20.71f). Once the agave has been crushed, it is fermented in wooden barrels with water for several days (see Figure 20.71g). After the fermentation process is complete, the mash is distilled. The first distillation yields low-grade alcohol. The fibers are then removed from the still and the alcohol from the first distillation is distilled a second time (see Figure 20.71h). After the second distillation, the mezcal is blended to obtain a consistent grade of alcohol. Then, the mezcal is either bottled or left to age in oak barrels (see Figure 20.71i), which takes less time than most other spirits.

20.73 **Ouzo**
© Randy Van Dam 2008

20.74 **Aquavit**
© Randy Van Dam 2008

CONVENIENCE CORNER PRODUCT EXAMPLES

Beverage: Juices, Coffee, Tea, and Water

Company	Website	Products
Campbell's	http://www.campbellsoupcompany.com	12/46 oz Juice Tomato
Lipton	http://www.lipton.com	4/24 ct Tea bag Ice 6/40 ct Tea bag Green
Nestle	http://www.nestle.com	12/1.75# Cocoa Mix
Ocean Spray	http://www.oceanspray.com	8/60 oz Orange Juice 8/60 oz Cranberry Juice
White Lion	http://www.whiteliontea.com	12 ct Tea Hot Ginger
Sunny Delight	http://www.sunnyd.com	24/6.75 oz Drink Citrus Punch
Tropicana	http://www.tropicana.com	48/10 oz Juice Orange
Seattle's Best	http://www.seattlesbest.com	42/2 oz Coffee Cinnamon
Maxwell House	http://www.maximuscoffeegroup.com	6/4# Coffee Regular Grind
Folgers	http://www.folgers.com	30/5.4 oz Coffee Regular Ultra
Liquid Planet	http://www.liquidplanet.com	2/5# Coffee Bean Blend
Vitality Food service, Inc.	http://www.vitalityfoodservice.com	3/59 oz Coffee Decaf Concentrate
Sunkist	http://www.sunkist.com	4/3 liter Juice Grape 3.5 +1
Tazo	http://www.tazo.com	6/24 ct Tea African Red Bush
Bigelow	http://www.bigelowtea.com	6/28 Tea Hat Asst.
Minute Maid	http://www.minutemaid.com	12/16 oz Lemonade Mix 7x1
Old Orchard	http://www.oldorchardjuice.com	2.5 gal Juice Cranberry 4x1
Very Fine	http://www.veryfine.com	12/16 oz Juice Grape 100%

Kathy Talis, RD,
Registered Dietitian

Place of Birth: Jackson, Michigan

Educational Background and Work Experience

Kathy Talis can't think of a time when she didn't have an interest, curiosity, or passion for food. At about 5 years of age, rather than make mud pies as her sisters did, Talis made a simulated full mud turkey dinner with all the trimmings. She took a large foundation stone, wrapped it in burlap to be the turkey skin, and basted it with mud water while baking it in the sun. She fed her dolls and teddy bears mud mashed potatoes, dirt pies, and dandelion greens. However, by the age of 13, Talis had learned of an occupation that incorporated food, nutrition, and education. Registered dietitian became her career goal from that point on. Now as director of Nutrition Services for Spectrum Health Services in Grand Rapids, Michigan, Talis manages 30 supervisors and 450 staff covering three shifts of services at three health care facilities across West Michigan. As an important part of her daily routine, she oversees the production of 6,000 meals and the medical nutrition therapy for 1,000 patients each day. She earned her associate of arts degree from Jackson Community College, and later pursued a bachelor of science degree in dietetics from Michigan State University. Talis later earned her dietetic registration after serving an internship in the Flint area. While working in health care

management, Kathy returned to school to earn a master's in business administration from Grand Valley State University. In addition to her daily work in health care, Kathy regularly consults on food service and has taught at the community college and university level.

What have you done to teach your staff about nutrition?

"As I progressed with my educational pursuits, my interest in teaching expanded to managing people. I thrived on teaching any nutrition topic to people one-on-one, in seminars, or in the classroom. To incorporate quality food services, nutrition education, and promoting a positive work environment, whether teaching church groups, "TOPS," weight management clubs, Head Start children, or provide in-service to our staff at work. Any one of these activities is enjoyable for me."

What activity at work are you doing to promote healthful cooking?

"Working in a health care setting, it is natural to promote healthy lifestyles. The skill is to create appealing, appetizing food when preparing a multitude of therapeutic diets served to our patients. To improve the quality of food we serve, we have employed many culinary graduates. To have our chefs modify recipes developed for special diets in a creative way that meet the specific diet restrictions but enhance the taste. I challenge our chefs to create appetizing, flavorful healthy foods.

Courtesy Marvis Hinson

We teach our chefs an accurate definition as to what "healthy" means as publicized through the American Dietetic Association. There is a misnomer in the media what is considered nutritious, and it can be confusing or deceiving for chefs.

Health care in the 1960s served more patients than retail customers, a 30/70 percent ratio. Today this has changed where health care institutions are feeding more retail customers than patients (60 percent staff or visitors and 40 percent patients). To educate retail customers, our department created the Smart Choice program for all of our retail operations, for example, meals that meet certain criteria as healthy (low calorie, low fat, moderate sodium). We use simple definitions so as to not confuse the customer. In addition, we are expanding this program to label numerous other food items, snacks, desserts, and salad bar in our retail operations to assist the customer in choosing healthier food choices."

Key Words and Concepts

Alcoholic Beverage Control (ABC)

American craft brewer

aperitif

beer

control states

distilled spirits

roasting (coffee beans)

soft drink

wine

Chapter in Review

The following exercises are provided to help the reader understand and apply the contents of this chapter. They may be completed individually or in a classroom environment.

REVIEW QUESTIONS

a. List the types of roasts used for coffee beans.

b. List the types of bottled water available, based on their standard of identity.

c. Define *Alcohol Beverage Control*, and give examples of its practice.

d. Define the *vital statistics* as they relate to beer production.

e. Define the term *spirits*, and list examples of beverages made from the distillation of different foundation ingredients.

INDIVIDUAL ACTIVITIES

a. **Web based:** Research the Alcohol Beverage Control laws for your own state, using the Internet.

b. **Experiential:** Go to a large liquor or wine shop, and evaluate the varieties and sources for each category of beverage. Talk to a sales representative at the store to learn about how the store purchases its stock.

c. **Critical thinking:** Evaluate the distillation process to determine how the process works.

GROUP ACTIVITIES

a. **Lab experience:** Purchase supplies to brew "home beer," and practice making several varieties for educational purposes.

b. **Classroom action:** Discuss the merits of alcohol laws and controls, as they relate to purchasing and distribution.Pomace

PART IV

Postscript: Looking Ahead

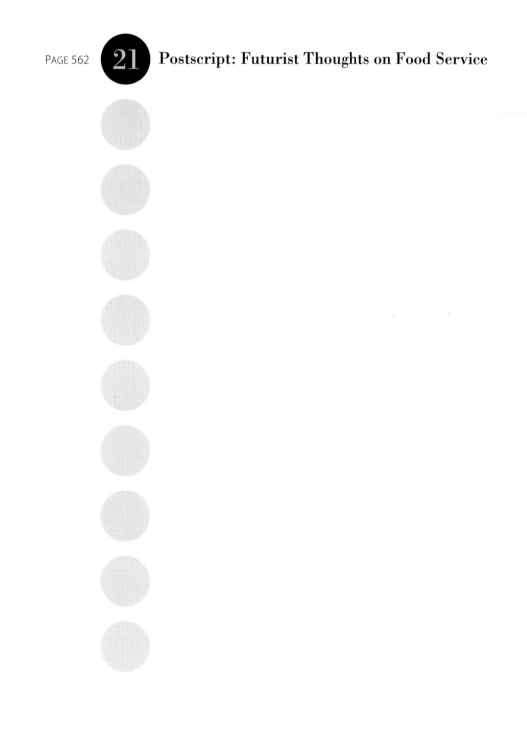

© iStockphoto.com

21

Postscript: Futurist Thoughts on Food Service

"The future is called 'perhaps,' which is the only possible thing to call the future. And the important thing is not to allow that to scare you."

TENNESSEE WILLIAMS

Introduction

Although the basics in food service have remained relatively constant over centuries, history has proven that changes periodically occur throughout the food distribution channel. Innovative products are cultivated or manufactured on a regular basis, new intermediaries enter the marketplace, and numerous factors affect the purchasing, receiving, storing, issuing, and preparing of food and supplies.

This postscript is included as a mechanism for thoughtful discussion on future initiatives and innovations that may affect the selection and procurement in the food service industry. The contents that follow are not meant to guarantee any particular direction but to identify some likely areas of change that will occur in the foreseeable future. Market research can't predict the future with absolute certainty in this rapidly changing world; it can only reflect the thoughts that exist with consumers in the moment. However, it is prudent for modern food service managers, chefs, and purchasing agents to keep one eye to the future to stay fully informed and prepared for the changes to come.

Food Philanthropy

In 1996, President Bill Clinton signed into law the Bill Emerson Good Samaritan Food Donation Act to promote food donations and gleaning. The law provides liability protection for organizations and businesses donating food in good faith to nonprofit organizations.

No matter the state of the economy, food and drink remain essential. **Food philanthropy** will become part of corporate mission statements. With the amount of hunger in the world, more and more companies will recognize the need to contribute to food pantries and to raise donations for their communities.

The Greening of Food Service

Although once an innocuous color, **green** has become a major focus of both the environmentally concerned and the savvy business operator. Efforts to *reduce, reuse, and recycle* energy and consumable materials will undoubtedly continue to accelerate in the food industry. Great strides have already been made in this area, but continued efforts are certain to come about. New equipment designed to lessen energy consumption, coupled with new practices by operational staff, will continue to reduce the amount of water, electricity, and gas used in food service. Chefs and managers will also evaluate the use

of their disposables in an effort to reduce landfills. Ad ally, with linen costs already hurting the bottom-line, op tors may look to reduce or eliminate them altogether. The fa that "green" can mean efficiency and cost savings makes it a really strong trend for years to come.

CERTIFIED GREEN RESTAURANT

The Green Restaurant Association (GRA) is a national non-profit organization that promotes environmental responsibility among food manufacturers, distributors, restaurants, and consumers. According to its website, with 20 years of experience, the GRA is the expert in helping restaurants become more environmentally sustainable, and it has the world's largest database of environmental solutions for the restaurant industry.

The GRA provides consultation and environmental assessment as part of its environmentally sustainable certification program. Increasing numbers of restaurants will likely choose to pursue this certification in an effort to be ecologically proactive and business minded.

UTILITIES

Utilities are a necessity in virtually all food service operations. On average, energy bills represent 30 percent of a building's annual budget. From the simple pizza parlor to the complex Las Vegas hotel, a certain amount of utilities are used to power the food preparation equipment, heat and cool the rooms, and light the overall facility. All of these energy-consuming activities can be improved upon with the deliberate use of controls and energy-efficient devices. Methods of reducing utilities include:

- Installing air dryers in bathrooms
- Installing automatic switches or motion sensors in rooms
- Installing timers on signage
- Eliminating the practice of quick-thawing frozen foods under running water (instead, stage thaw under refrigeration)
- Replacing hand sink faucets with infrared auto faucets
- Activating auto shutdown programs on all office and point-of-service (POS) computers
- Not keeping gas flames running constantly without use
- Replacing incandescent bulbs that do not need to be dimmed with compact fluorescents (CFLs)
- Replacing 10 to 20 percent of bulbs with LED
- Replacing paraffin candles with rechargeable LED lights at the dinner tables to reduce ambient heat

To quote Sheryl Crow, "the cheapest energy is the energy you don't use in the first place."

rs will be seeking to gain "Cer-
tract eco-conscious customers.
g for restaurants that care about
it publicly with recycling con-
back the use of Styrofoam. Sustainable
packaging is one of an increasing number of consumer issues
motivated by environmentalism and moral values; therefore,
more brands will consider adopting sustainable packaging.

Consumers will expect food outlets to use renewable
eco-friendly packaging like biodegradable Bagasse food
and soup containers made from sugar cane and compostable
food containers made from corn. Other methods of reducing
landfill waste include:

- Convert all bleached paper products to unbleached
- Change plastic disposable products, such as straws, to
  biodegradable products
- Use foil or reusable lids instead of plastic wrap
- Eliminate or reduce bottled water and replace with filtered
  tap water
- Purchase only Energy Star
- Use reusable hemp or organic take-out bags
- Purchase office paper with a minimum 30 percent post
  consumer waste (PCW) recycled product

COMPOSTING

Many food service operations are already composting their
food waste, and technology is making it easier to do so. The
timing is important, as more and more community landfills
are beginning to restrict organic food waste.

Future Food

In a world of supply and demand, it is likely that "future
food" will cater to personal health. It is thought by nutrition-
ists that once the medical community has a better understanding of human metabolism, people will personalize their diets
to meet their own health needs.

CLONED FOOD

On January 15, 2008, the federal Food and Drug Administration concluded that milk and meat from clones of cattle,
swine, and goats, and the offspring of clones from any genus
customarily eaten as food, are as harmless to consume as
food from conventionally bred animals.

After a failed attempt to pass a law that requires cloned
foods to be labeled as such (H.R. 992 Cloned Food Labeling

ACT), the offspring of cloned animals have already entered
the food supply. Cloned animals are used for breeding, as
they are presently far too expensive for general consumption.

Cultured Meat

In-vitro meat, also known as **cultured meat**, is considered the manufacturing of meat products by using "tissue-
engineering" technology. The process produces animal meat
without actually using an animal. *Starter cells* are painlessly
taken from live animals by biopsy, without hurting the animals, and placed in a culture media to grow independently
from the animal. Proponents suggest this method would create enough cultured meat to feed the planet.

HYDROPONICS

Although they have existed for more than 1,500 years, hydroponics have been used to a greater extent in the past 60 to
70 years. Their benefits are many: their production requires
80 percent less growing space, 90 percent less water, and
75 percent less fertilizer than traditional farming methods. As
the world's arable land continues to shrink every year (nearly
25 million acres are lost per year), consumers and growers
concern themselves with environmental conservancy, and
sanitation fears swirl around agricultural products. The production of hydroponics is certain to expand.

AQUACULTURE

Many suggest that the only way our planet's oceans, lakes,
and rivers will be able to meet a growing demand for seafood
is through fish farming. According to Johnson, in an article
from *Aquavision* magazine in which he is quoted suggests,
"the ocean and its resources are clearly in crisis. Codfish,
bluefin tuna, Chilean sea bass, and red snapper are just a few
of the fish species that have fallen victim to overfishing and
mismanagement" (2007, p. 2).

Opinions differ on the future of aquaculture. Those who
believe there is a future in aquaculture argue the following:

- The supply of wild-caught fish will greatly diminish as their
  stock diminishes.
- Hatcheries can be a conservation tool.
- Aquaculture products are far less prone to harmful toxins
  and disease.

Those who don't believe aquaculture will greatly expand
point to the following issues:

- The regulatory process of gaining approval is difficult.
- There are legitimate concerns over the environmental
  impact of fish farms producing a concentration of waste
  material, thereby polluting the host rivers and oceans.
- The public may prefer the taste and texture of
  wild-caught seafood.

ORGANIC FOOD

Analysts report that the number of people using organic foods on a regular basis will double by 2010. Reasons for this broadened appeal include greater availability, greater variety, lower costs, and expanded educational information. According to the Biodelice website, which is dedicated to green living and organic gardening:

> The future of organic food and the future of organic agriculture appears to be rather bright on many levels. Perhaps the most important reason as to why proponents of organic agriculture are optimistic rests in the reality that an ever growing segment of the general public is beginning to use at least some organic food and other types of organic products in their everyday lives.

Food Sanitation and Inspection

The jurisdiction for monitoring the United States' food supply is confusing, at best. Marion Nestle reports in her book *Safe Food* that presently there are thirty-five separate laws, administered by twelve agencies, located in six cabinet-level departments. Laws are always in flux, and reforms are often vigorously debated. On July 29, 2009, the U.S. House narrowly defeated proposed reforms that would have resulted in sweeping changes to the federal food safety system. The bill would have allowed the U.S. Food and Drug Administration (FDA) power to order food recalls, increase the frequency of inspections for food processing plants, increase FDA access to company records, and require Hazard Analysis and Critical Control Points (HACCP) and food safety plans for all food operations.

The FDA maintains a website listing recalls, market withdrawals, and safety alerts. The website includes the most noteworthy product events over the past 5 years, based on their widespread nature and the extent of the health risk.

In October 2007, the Topps Meat Company went out of business after it was forced to recall 21.7 million pounds of ground beef due to E. coli contamination. It was the second-largest beef recall in U.S. history. The contaminated meat was believed to have sickened more than twelve people in eight states. In November and December 2006, a multistate outbreak of E. coli contamination was traced to onions from Taco Bell restaurants. A total of fifty-three people from five states were hospitalized, while eight developed kidney failure. In September and October 2006, nearly 200 people from 26 states were infected; 102 were hospitalized, 31 developed kidney failure, and 3 died. The illness was traced to fresh spinach grown in California. All of these incidences are examples of the need for increased vigilance in the food chain. (FDA, 2009)

The general public needs reassurance from the food industry that their health is both important to, and protected by, the individual food service operator. Otherwise, customers may elect to redirect their purchasing dollars. For example, a 2008 Guelph research study showed that, due to a listeria outbreak in Canada, 27 percent now eat less often at restaurants and fast food outlets, 52 percent pay more attention to food labels, 32 percent cook at home more, and 30 percent take more time over their own food preparation (University of Guelph, 2008).

Equipment

Equipment and food products are the primary capital assets of a food business, and, along with facilities and available funds, they make up the variables with which staffing has to work. And, as working capital is generally limited, operators must always be judicious with their purchases. Affordability, practicality, dependability, and flexibility are the equipment requirements that businesses desire when making their selection decisions.

REFRIGERATION

Due to ever-increasing concerns over food safety, health departments will likely stress the need for proper quick-cooling methods of heated foods. The United States could follow in the footsteps of France, which enacted laws requiring foods to be sufficiently chilled *before* being stored in refrigerators or walk-in coolers. Food service personnel habitually place large containers of hot liquids or hot foods in refrigeration, which, in extreme cases, causes the cooler to overheat and endangers the safety of the other foods being stored. This concern by health officials may cause a marked increase in the demand for flash freezers in the United States.

Flash Freezers and Chillers

Flash freezing, also known as *blast freezing*, is used in the food industry to rapidly freeze food items that are prone to spoilage. In addition to their ability to quickly cool hot foods to protect them against harmful bacterial growth, flash freezers also provide multiple benefits in the area of improved food quality, extended shelf life, increased moisture retention, and reduced shrinkage due to less evaporation while cooling. The process freezes food products fast enough that large ice crystals cannot form and damage the cell structure of the food, particularly with high moisture items such as fruits and vegetables. When the items are thawed, their shape is not distorted from the freezing, and they don't "bleed" moisture loss.

Irinox, a company that specializes in blast chilling, has recently developed a combination Bread Blast Chiller and Shock Freezer. Among several examples, reported benefits include less shrinkage, minimal damage to products, shorter oven-to-packaging time, shortened relaxation time, and ease of work for laminate doughs.

BEVERAGE EQUIPMENT

As operators seek to meet customer demands while reducing their disposable material costs, the increased use of in-house beverage equipment is likely. As customers enjoy quality beverages and are usually willing to pay a premium for fresh and healthful products, the use of juicers and espresso coffee makers will continue to rise.

Coffee Makers

The design and application of coffee makers will continue to evolve, both for small units that can be used tableside or larger units designed for multiple brews. One example includes the *Mypressi Twist*, a nonelectric handheld espresso maker that uses gas cartridges to extract espresso, making it ideal for tableside service.

Juicers

There are several designs of **juicers** available on the market today. Their design makes some better matched for juicing certain kinds of produce than other styles. Unfortunately, there is no single juicer that will perform each juicing operation with comparable quality. The centrifugal ejection juicers are fast, easiest to use, and easy to clean. They are good for juicing most fruits and vegetables and, therefore, are the recommended style for most establishments.

Blixers, Blenders, and Mixers

A **blixer** is a hybrid of a blender and mixer, with a design similar to a food processor. Traditional blenders and food processors only function up to 1,725 revolutions per minute (RPM), while blixers are capable of reaching twice that RPM at operating level. Chefs can blend both solid foods and beverages using this machine, making it highly versatile.

COOKING EQUIPMENT

The design and application of cooking equipment will undoubtedly seek to reduce operating costs relative to utilities while also reducing cooking time and improving food quality. The following examples of cooking equipment typify the nature of improvements already in existence but not yet commonly used.

Induction cooking surfaces, TurboChef ovens, Hot Logic Technology rethermalization systems, and immersion circulators are entering kitchen operations across the country because they provide dependable cooking abilities not available with traditional kitchen equipment.

Induction Cooking Surfaces

With **induction cooking**, each induction coil generates a magnetic field that induces heat in the steel pots and pans placed on its top. The pot becomes the actual element that cooks the food, becoming the fastest of all cooktops to heat and cook food. The induction cooktop surface doesn't heat up like traditional gas or electric burners, staying cool throughout the cooking process, although they have the same instant control as gas. Induction cooking uses 90 percent of the energy produced compared with only 65 percent for traditional electric ranges and 55 percent for a gas burner. Although initially more expensive than traditional cooking surfaces, their user-safety and energy-efficiency will undoubtedly add to their widespread appeal.

TurboChef Ovens

The redesigned convection oven uses patented Airspeed Technology™ to evenly circulate the heated air from the top and bottom of the oven cavity to superheat and brown the food, accelerating the cooking time up to fifteen times faster than a conventional oven. Some TurboChef ovens also incorporate nearly 500 preset cooking profiles to accurately heat the food based on food type and portion count. Many of the units are ventless, thereby saving the expense of both exhaust hoods and make-up air.

Rethermalization Units

Rethermalization units have been used for decades to warm precooked meals. In the past, trays of cooked foods were placed in a cabinet that was outfitted with a steam generator. The generator provided steam to the entire cabinet interior, where it is continuously mixed with air. Thermocouples controlled the temperature of both the air and steam for rethermalizing and holding the food products.

Institutional food service, including health care, military, and school lunch programs, were the primary users of these systems. However, the food quality was drastically compromised as the holding time lengthened. In time, the use of rethermalizing units diminished because of their poor performance.

Recently, however, a new rethermalization concept named Hot Logic Technology was developed. Hot Logic units are designed to heat and hold individual units of canned, pouched, or trayed food. The food can be frozen, refrigerated, tepid, or hot when placed on the shelves. Each individual shelf uses micro sensors to detect the temperature of the food item placed on that shelf and then quickly heats the container accordingly. Then, it maintains a safe holding temperature. This design allows greater flexibility and holding times for the operator, up to 4 to 8 hours without appreciable food degradation. It will likely find uses in establishments where there is no ability to prepare food on-site, for low-density feeding, or with institutional meal programs.

Immersion Circulator Cooking

Sous vide is a method of cooking food at a specific temperature while under vacuum pressure. The raw foods are usually seared, placed in heat-stable vacuumized pouches, and submerged in an **immersion circulator** that precisely controls the temperature of the water bath. Foods are cooked at such exact temperatures the results generally exceed the ability of traditional cooking methods.

Although sous vide cookery has been used in Europe for decades, the cooking method has not been widespread in the United States until recently—mainly because of state health department restrictions and the lack of dependable cooking appliances. One major benefit of the process is its ability to tenderize tougher cuts of meat by allowing the collagen to gelatinize while the meat slowly cooks in the bag. Other benefits include increased moisture retention, flavor and texture enhancement, time savings, productivity, and temperature control.

With the recent introduction of the immersion circulators, sous vide cookery will become more commonplace in the industry. Harold McGee, a food science writer, describes the sous vide technique as "one of the most important culinary innovations of modern times"in his introduction to chef Thomas Keller's celebrated book, *Under Pressure: Cooking Sous Vide*.

COMPUTERIZATION AND DIGITAL CONNECTIVITY

As a digital society, we are increasingly using speech recognition, scanning, networking, e-commerce, and virtual reality in business applications. The impact of these technological advances will also continue to change customer behavior. Consumers want a community built around food, and they are building it virtually. Food websites with greater interactivity and direct-to-Internet TV, Twitter exchanges, amateur restaurant reviewers on Yelp, and iPhone apps related to food are all growing in popularity.

Miniaturization and portability will also be the goal of manufacturers as they seek to create devices that are smaller, more powerful, and interactive. The increased use of digital cameras, barcode scanners, netbook computers, and PDAs for storeroom operations is certain.

Word-of-Mouth Marketing

More companies will use their own customers to help promote the unique qualities of their business products and services through digital social media sites. They are engaged in **word-of-mouth marketing** strategies through vehicles such as Twitter, Facebook, and Flickr. According to Andy Sernovitz, leading word-of-mouth marketing expert and author of *Word of Mouth Marketing: How Smart Companies Get People Talking* (2009), "happy customers are your best ad." Operators will use the Internet and social media sources to communicate their food business and reduce their advertising expenditures with traditional static media such as newspapers, Yellow Pages, and magazines.

Legislation

In Mississippi, House Bill 282 was introduced in 2008 to prohibit certain food establishments from serving food to any person who is obese. The criteria would be set by the State Department of Health, and it would apply to restaurants that sat five or more people. Their license to operate could be suspended if they chose to ignore the decree.

In the U.S. Congress, House Bill 875, known as the Food Safety Modernization Act of 2009, was introduced in an attempt to strengthen the food safety system. The bill would "establish the Food Safety Administration within the Department of Health and Human Services to protect the public health by preventing food-borne illness, ensuring the safety of food, improving research on contaminants leading to food-borne illness, and improving security of food from intentional contamination, and for other purposes."

These bills are examples of continued legislation aimed at protecting the dining public. Although they have virtuous intentions, some of the laws can also have potentially negative consequences for food service operators. It behooves the food service professional to stay abreast of the political climate.

Global Ethics

As the world continues to shrink and grow interconnected, many people around the world have recognized the need to promote ethical behavior in individuals, institutions, businesses, and nations. To accomplish this goal, society needs to conduct research, convey public discourse, and engage in practical action.

On the local level, we as operators must regularly commit ourselves to ethical and responsible practices. As owners, chefs, managers, and purchasing agents, we are obliged to keep the best interests of the business, staff, suppliers, and buying public in the forefront of our decisions. Protecting the economy of our nations and the public health of its citizens is certain to be an escalating focus of many in the coming years.

[ASK THE EXPERT]

Bruce Kraig, PhD

Courtesy Bruce Kraig

Name: Bruce Kraig, PhD

Educational Background and Work Experience

Bruce Kraig is emeritus professor of history at Roosevelt University in Chicago, an adjunct instructor for Kendall College, and the president of the Culinary Historians of Chicago. He has given many lectures worldwide, including the keynote address to Pillsbury Bakeoff, 1998; keynote address, Australian Symposium on Gastronomy 1996; many lectures at the Oxford Symposium on Food and Cookery (UK), Smithsonian Institution, 2005; Fullbright Association, Les Dames d'Escoffier; many at ASFS conferences; and several hundred—most on food history and food culture—at schools, historical societies, museums, and clubs throughout the United States. His many appearances include as an authority on food history and culture, having been on television programs such as *ABC Nightline*, *ABC National News*, *Good Morning America*, Fox News, NBC News, *Good Morning Australia*, BBC News, Public Television in Los Angeles, Telemundo (Mexico), and various cable shows. Radio appearances have been frequent, including multiple appearances on National Public Radio, WGN-Chicago, and many other Chicago stations. Dr. Kraig has also appeared on stations in Canada; Detroit; San Jose, California; San Francisco; Los Angeles; New York; and Boston and on national networks such as The History Channel, among others. He has been the main speaker on national programs such as *Talk of the Nation*, National Public Radio's *History of the Hot Dog*, the Travel Channel in 2004, radio programs in Minneapolis and throughout the Midwest, podcasts, and a recent BBC Radio documentary on American popular culture. In 1962, he earned his BA in history from the University of California, Berkeley; an MA in history with archaeology from the University of Pennsylvania in 1963; and a PhD from the University of Pennsylvania in 1969, majoring in history with archaeology.

Memberships and Career Highlights

Among his many distinctions, Dr. Kraig has been honored with Two Lente de Plata Awards (Mexico), Silver Apple Award (National Education Media Competition), Gold Apple Award, CHRIS (top award, Columbus International Documentary Comp), two Bronze Medals (Columbus International Documentary Competition), and four Emmys for PBS programming. He was the Scholar-in-Residence, International Association of Culinary Professionals, 2007; an Illinois Scholar, Key Ingredients Project, Smithsonian Institution, from 2004 to 2007; and is the Illinois Road Scholar, Illinois Humanities Council, from 2004 to the present.

How did you first become interested in food history?

"It began with working as an apprentice with European-trained chefs when I was a teenager; I learned to appreciate the art and craft of cooking. The food history part came from my early archaeological work on medieval villages in Europe when I began to wonder just how ordinary people ate, since most were farmers raising their own food. That led to work with medieval recipes, then to basic nutritional questions about medieval diets."

When was your *wow* moment in food and culture?

"Teaching courses in the Politics of Food has made me much more aware of the importance of scientific nutrition combined with traditional, sustainable, food production. The real WOW moment came when I was doing research on early civilizations in Mexico. Going to rural villages, seeing and eating "real" Mexican food, brought home not just one of the world's great cuisines, but the whole history of modern food and just how nutritious traditional country food can be."

How important is it for culinary students and working chefs to understand food sustainability?

"I regard teaching courses in this field—the critical need to build sustainable and organic food systems—to culinary students and students in a liberal arts university to be about the most important work that I've ever done. In this regard, I organized and chaired a series of panels for a large public audience on food history, local sourcing of food, and chefs' work in the field, at the Chicago History Museum in April 2008."

Financial and Cost Control Formulas

Appendix A

The Percent Triangle

The following triangle is a tool used to find part, whole, or percent.

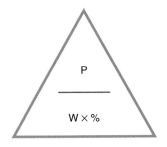

APQ, EPQ, and Yield Percent Triangle

The following triangle is a tool used to find the as-purchased quantity, edible portion quantity, and yield percent.

Part = Edible portion quantity (EPQ)

Whole = As-purchased quantity (APQ)

Percent = Yield percent (Y%)

The Cost Per Portion, Selling Price, and Food Cost Percent Triangle

The following triangle is a tool used to find the cost per portion, selling price, and food cost percent.

Part = Cost per portion

Whole = Selling price

Percent = Food cost percent

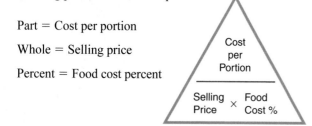

The Cost Per Beverage, Selling Price, and Beverage Cost Percent Triangle

The following triangle is a tool used to find the cost per beverage, selling price, and beverage cost percent.

Part = Cost per beverage

Whole = Selling price

Percent = Beverage cost percent

Calculating the As-Purchased Quantity

$$\text{As-purchased quantity (APQ)} = \frac{\text{Edible portion quantity (EPQ)}}{\text{Yield percent (in decimal form)}}$$

Calculating the Edible Portion Quantity

$$\text{Edible portion quantity (EPQ)} = \text{As-purchased quantity (APQ)} \times \text{Yield percent (in decimal form)}$$

Determining Cost Per Unit

$$\text{Cost per unit} = \frac{\text{As-purchased cost}}{\text{Number of units}}$$

Calculating Total Cost

Total cost may be calculated using the following formula:

Total cost = Number of units × Cost per unit

Note: units must be the same

Formula for Edible Portion Cost

$$\text{Edible portion cost (EP)} = \frac{\text{As-purchased cost (AP)}}{\text{Yield percent (in decimal form)}}$$

Determining Food Cost Percent

The food cost percent is the percent of the selling price that pays for the ingredients. The formula for the food cost percent is

$$\text{Food cost percent} = \frac{\text{Food Cost}}{\text{Food sales}} \quad \text{or} \quad \frac{\text{Cost per portion}}{\text{Selling price}}$$

Determining Cost Per Portion

The cost per portion can be calculated with the following formula:

$$\text{Cost per portion} = \frac{\text{Total recipe cost}}{\text{Number of portions}}$$

Determining Selling Price

The cost per portion is used to calculate the selling price based on a desired food cost percent:

$$\text{Selling price} = \frac{\text{Cost per portion}}{\text{Food cost percent (in decimal form)}}$$

Beverage Costing

$$\text{Beverage cost percent} = \frac{\text{Beverage cost}}{\text{Beverage sales}}$$

Calculating the Recipe Conversion Factor (RCF)

A recipe conversion factor (RCF) is a number that represents the relationship between the new and old recipe yields.

$$\frac{\text{New recipe yield}}{\text{Old recipe yield}} = \frac{N}{O} = \text{Recipe conversion factor (RCF)}$$

Calculating for Break-even

There are several methods available to determine the break-even

A) $$\text{Breakeven (BE)} = \frac{\text{Fixed Cost Dollars (FC\$)}}{\text{Fixed Cost Percent (FC\%)}}$$

or

B) $$\text{Breakeven (BE)} = \frac{\text{Fixed Cost Dollars FC\$}}{\text{Gross Margin Percent (GM\%)}}$$

or

C) Breakeven (BE) =

$$\frac{\text{Fixed Cost Dollars (FC\$)}}{\text{Selling Price Per Unit (SP\$)} - \text{Variable Cost Per Unit (VC\$)}}$$

Calculating Turnover Rates

$$\text{Turnover} = \frac{\text{Cost of Goods Sold}}{\text{Average Inventory Value}}$$

Calculating the Cost of Goods Sold (COGS)

Opening Inventory
+ Purchases
− Closing Inventory
= Cost of Goods Sold

Measurement Conversions

Appendix B

A: To convert this Item	B: Into this item	Multiply "A" by:	Or, to convert to	Multiply "A" By:
LIQUID VOLUME				
U.S. Fluid Ounce	Milliliters	29.57353	Liters	0.02957353
U.S. Cup, Liquid	Milliliters	236.588	Liters	0.236588
U.S. Pint	Milliliters	473.1765	Liters	0.473176
U.S. Quart	Milliliters	946.3529	Liters	0.94635
U.S. Gallon	Milliliters	3785.41	Liters	3.785412
Imperial Fluid Ounce	Milliliters	28.413	Liters	0.028413
Imperial Cup, Liquid	Milliliters	227.304	Liters	0.227304
Imperial Pint	Milliliters	568.26	Liters	0.56826
Imperial Quart	Milliliters	1136.52	Liters	1.13652
Imperial Gallon	Milliliters	4546.08	Liters	4.54608
Milliliters	U.S. Fl. Oz.	0.033814	Imperial Fluid Oz.	0.0351951
Milliliters	Cup of US Fl. Oz.	0.0042265	Cup of Imp. Fl. Oz.	0.00439938
Milliliters	U.S. Pint	0.002113376	Imperial Pint	0.0017952
Milliliters	U.S. Quart	0.001056688	Imperial Quart	0.0008796
Milliliters	U.S. Gallon	0.0002641721	Imperial Gallon	0.000219961248
Milliliters	Liters	0.001		

Book of Yields - Wiley

A: To convert this Item	B: Into this item	Multiply "A" by:	Or, to convert to	Multiply "A" By:
Liters	U.S. Fl. Oz.	33.814	Imperial Fluid Oz.	35.195
Liters	U.S. Cup	4.22675	Imperial Cup	4.33938
Liters	U.S. Pint	2.113	Imperial Pint	1.75975
Liters	U.S. Quart	1.05669	Imperial Quart	0.879877
Liters	U.S. Gallon	0.26417	Imperial Gallon	0.219969
Liters	Milliliters	1000		
U.S. Fluid Ounce	Imperial Fl. Oz.	1.04084	Imperial Cup Lq.	0.130105
U.S. Cup, Liquid	Imperial Cup Lq	1.04084	Imperial Pint	0.416337
U.S. Pint	Imperial Pint	0.832674	Imperial Quart	0.416337
U.S. Quart	Imperial Quart	0.83267	Imperial Gallon	0.208169
U.S. Gallon	Imperial Gallon	0.832674		
Imperial Fluid Ounce	U.S. Fluid Oz.	0.96076	U.S. Cup, Liquid	0.120095
Imp. Cup, Liquid	U.S. Cup, Lq.	0.96076	U.S. Pint	0.48038
Imp. Pint	U.S. Pint	1.20095	U.S. Quart	0.600475
Imp. Quart	U.S. Quart	1.20095	U.S. Gallon	0.300327
Imp. Gallon	U.S. Gallon	1.20095		

U.S. SYSTEM

U.S. Fluid Ounce	U.S. Cup	0.125	U.S. Pint	0.0625
U.S. Fluid Ounce	U.S. Quart	0.03125	U.S. Gallon	0.0078125
U.S. Cup	U.S. Fluid Ounce	8	U.S. Pint	0.5
U.S. Cup	U.S. Quart	0.25	U.S. Gallon	0.0625
U.S. Pint	U.S. Fl. Oz	16	U.S. Cup	2
U.S. Pint	U.S. Quart	0.5	U.S. Gallon	0.125
U.S. Quart	U.S. Fluid Ounce	32	U.S. Cup	4
U.S. Quart	U.S. Pint	2	U.S. Gallon	0.25
U.S. Gallon	U.S. Fl. Oz.	128	U.S. Cup	16
U.S. Gallon	U.S. Pint	8	U.S. Quart	4

IMPERIAL SYSTEM

Imp. Fluid Ounce	Imp. Cup	0.125	Imp. Pint	0.05
Imp. Fluid Ounce	Imp Quart	0.025	Imp. Gallon	0.00625
Imp. Cup	Imp. Fluid Ounce	8	Imp. Pint	0.4
Imp. Cup	Imp. Quart	0.2	Imp. Gallon	0.05
Imp. Pint	Imp. Fluid Ounce	20	Imp. Cup	2.5
Imp. Pint	Imp. Quart	0.5	Imp. Gallon	0.125
Imp. Quart	Imp. Fluid Ounce	40	Imp. Cup	5
Imp. Quart	Imp. Pint	2	Imp. Gallon	0.25
Imp. Gallon	Imp. Fluid Ounce	160	Imp. Cup	20
Imp. Gallon	Imp. Pint	8	Imp. Quart	4

A: To convert this Item	B: Into this item	Multiply "A" by:	Or, to convert to	Multiply "A" By:
CUPS & SPOONS				
Fluid Ounce	Tablespoons	2	Teaspoons	6
Cups	Tablespoons	16	Teaspoons	48
Teaspoons	Tablespoons	0.33333		
Tablespoons	Teaspoons	3		
Tablespoons	Cup	0.0625		
U.S. Tablespoon	Milliliters	14.78677	U.S. Fluid Ounces	0.5
U.S. Teaspoon	Milliliters	4.92892	U.S. Fluid Ounces	0.16666666
U.S. Tablespoon	Imp. Tablespoon	1.04084	Imp. Fluid Ounces	0.5204
U.S. Teaspoon	Imp. Teaspoon	1.04084	Imp. Fluid Ounces	0.173474
Imperial Tablespoon	Milliliters	14.20655	Imp. Fluid Ounces	0.5
Imperial Teaspoon	Milliliters	4.735516	Imp. Fluid Ounces	0.1666666
Imperial Tablespoon	U.S. Tablespoon	0.96076	U.S. Fluid Ounces	0.4803806
Imperial Teaspoon	U.S. Teaspoon	0.96076	U.S. Fluid Ounces	0.1601268
U.S. Cup (Liquid) 237 mL	Imperial Cup. Lq.	1.04084	Imp. Tablespoon	16.65346195
Imperial Cup (Lq.) 227 mL	U.S. Cup Liquid	0.96076	U.S. Tablespoon	15.372179107
Milliliters	U.S. Tablespoons	0.067628	U.S. Teaspoons	0.20288
Milliliters	Imp. Tablespoons	0.07039	Imp. Teaspoons	0.21117
WEIGHT (MASS)				
Ounce (avoirdupois)	Pound (avdp)	0.0625		
Ounce (avoirdupois)	Gram	28.349523125		
Ounce (avoirdupois)	Kilogram	0.028349523125		
Pound (avdp)	Ounce (avdp)	16		
Pound (avdp)	Gram	453.592		
Pound (avdp)	Kilogram	0.45359237		
Kilogram	Gram	1000		
Kilogram	Ounce (avdp)	35.27396		
Kilogram	Pound (avdp)	2.204623		
Gram	Kilogram	0.001		
Gram	Ounce (avdp)	0.035274		
Gram	Pound (avdp)	0.002204623		

Weight Measures		
oz	lb.	Decimal Unit Conversion
½		.031
1		.063
1½		.093
2	$\frac{1}{8}$	.125
2½		.156
3		.188
3½		.218
4	¼	.250
4½		.281
5		.313
5½		.343
6	$\frac{3}{8}$	.375
6½		.406
7		.438
7½		.469
8	½	.500
8½		.531
9		.563
9½		.594
10	$\frac{5}{8}$	.625
10½		.656
11		.688
11½		.719
12	$\frac{3}{4}$	.750
12½		.781
13		.813
13½		.844
14	$\frac{7}{8}$	.875
14½		.906
15		.938
15½		.969
16	1	1.000

Volume Measures		
cup	qt	gallons
½		
1	¼	
1½		
2	½	
2½		
3	¾	
3½		
4	1	¼
4½		
5	1¼	
5½		
6	1½	
6½		
7	1¾	
7½		
8	2	½
8½		
9	2¼	
9½		
10	2½	
10½		
11	2¾	
11½		
12	3	¾
12½		
13	3¼	
13½		
14	3½	
14½		
15	3¾	
15½		
16	4	1

Temperature Equivalents (Fahrenheit/Celsius Scales)		
	Fahrenheit	**Celsius**
Water Freezes	32°	0°
	40°	4.4°
	50°	10°
	60°	15.6°
	70°	21.1°
	80°	26.7°
Water Tepid	90°	32.2°
	100°	37.8°
	110°	43.3°
	120°	48.9°
	130°	54.4°
	140°	60°
	150°	65.6°
	160°	71.1°
	170°	76.7°
	180°	82.2°
	190°	87.8°
	200°	93.3°
Water Boils	212°	100°
	250°	121°
	300°	149°
	350°	177°
	400°	205°
	450°	235°
	500°	260°

$1.8 \times C + 32 = F$

$(F - 32) \times .5556 = C$

Appendix C

Approximate Volume to Weight Chart

Item	Volume T = Tablespoon C = Cup	Weight (oz)
Allspice, ground	T	1/4
Almonds, blanched	C	5 1/3
Apples, peeled, 1/2" cubes	C	3 1/3
Apples, pie, canned	C	6
Applesauce, canned	C	8
Apricots, cooked	C	3 1/3
Apricots, drained	C	5 1/3
Apricots, halves	C	8
Apricots, pie, packed	C	9
Asparagus, cut, canned	C	6 1/2
Baking powder	T	1/2
Baking powder	C	8
Bananas, diced	C	6 1/2
Barley	C	8
Beans, baked	C	8
Beans, cut, canned, drained	C	4 1/2
Beans, kidney	C	6
Beans, kidney, cooked	C	6 3/4
Beans, lima, cooked	C	8
Beans, lima, dried	C	6 1/2

(Continued)

Item	Volume T = Tablespoon C = Cup	Weight (oz)
Beans, navy, dried	C	6 3/4
Bean sprouts	C	4
Beets, cooked, diced	C	6 1/2
Beets, cooked, sliced	C	6 1/2
Blueberries, canned	C	6 1/2
Blueberries, fresh	C	7
Bread crumbs, dried	C	4
Bread crumbs, soft	C	2
Brussel sprouts*	C	4
Butter	C	8
Cabbage, shredded†	C	4
Cake crumbs, soft	C	2 3/4
Carrots, raw or cooked, diced	C	5 1/3
Celery, diced†	C	4
Celery seed	T	1/4
Cheese, cottage or cream	C	8
Cheese, grated	C	4
Cherries, glacéed	C	6 1/2
Chicken, cooked, cubed	C	5 1/3
Chili powder	T	1/4
Chili sauce	C	11 1/4
Chocolate, grated	C	4 1/2
Chocolate, melted	C	8
Cinnamon, ground	T	1/4
Citron, dried, chopped	C	6 1/2
Cloves, ground	T	1/4
Cloves, whole	C	3
Cocoa	C	4
Coconut, shredded	C	2 1/2
Corn, canned	C	8
Corn flakes	C	1
Cornmeal*	C	5 1/3
Corn syrup	C	12
Cornstarch	C	4 1/2
Cracker crumbs	C	3
Cranberries, raw	C	4
Cranberry sauce	C	8
Cream, whipped	C	4
Cream, whipping	C	8
Cream of tartar	T	1/3

* As-purchased quantity.
† Edible portion quantity.

(Continued)

Item	Volume T = Tablespoon C = Cup	Weight (oz)
Cream of wheat	C	6
Cucumbers, diced	C	5 1/3
Currants, dried	C	5 1/3
Curry powder	T	1/4
Dates, pitted	C	6 1/5
Eggs, dried, whites	C	3 1/4
Eggs, dried, yolks	C	2 3/4
Eggs, fresh, whites (9)	C	8
Eggs, fresh, yolks (10)	C	8
Eggs, raw, shelled (5 eggs)	C	8
Farina, raw	C	5 1/3
Figs, dried, chopped	C	6 1/2
Flour, all-purpose	C	4
Flour, bread, sifted	C	4
Flour, bread, unsifted	C	4 1/2
Flour, cake/pastry, sifted	C	3 1/3
Flour, rye	C	2 3/4
Flour, soy	C	3 1/4
Flour, whole wheat	C	4 1/4
Gelatin, granulated	T	1/4
Gelatin, granulated	C	5 1/3
Ginger, ground	T	1/5
Ginger, ground	C	3 1/4
Grapes, cut, seeded	C	5 3/4
Grapes, whole	C	4
Ham, cooked, diced	C	5 1/3
Honey	C	12
Horseradish	T	1/2
Jam	C	12
Jelly	C	10 2/3
Lard	C	8
Lettuce, shredded	C	2 1/4
Margarine	C	8
Marshmallows, large	80 ea	16
Mayonnaise	C	8
Meat, cooked, chopped	C	8
Milk, condensed	C	10 2/3
Milk, evaporated	C	9
Milk, liquid	C	8 1/2
Milk, nonfat dry	T	1/4
Milk, nonfat dry	C	4
Mincemeat	C	8
Molasses	C	12
Mustard, dry, ground	C	3 1/2

(Continued)

Item	Volume T = Tablespoon C = Cup	Weight (oz)
Mustard, prepared	T	1/2
Mustard seed	T	2/5
Noodles, cooked	C	5 1/3
Nutmeats	C	4 1/2
Nutmeg, ground	T	1/4
Oil, vegetable	C	8
Onions, chopped	C	6 1/2
Oysters, shucked	C	8
Paprika	T	1/4
Parsley, coarsely chopped	C	1
Peanut butter	C	9
Peanuts[†]	C	5
Peaches, chopped	C	8
Pears, canned, drained/diced	C	6 1/2
Peas, canned, drained	C	8
Peas, dried, split	C	6 3/4
Pecans[†]	C	4 1/2
Pepper, ground	T	1/4
Pepper, ground	C	4
Peppers, green, chopped	C	5 1/3
Pimiento, chopped	C	6 1/2
Pineapple, crushed	C	8
Poppy seed	C	5
Potato chips	C	1
Potatoes, cooked, diced/mashed	C	8
Prunes, cooked, pitted	C	5
Prunes, dried	C	6 1/2
Pumpkin, cooked	C	6 1/2
Raisins	C	5 1/3
Raisins, after cooking	C	7
Raspberries[*]	C	4 3/4
Rhubarb, cooked	C	6 1/2
Rhubarb, raw, 1" dice	C	4
Rice, cooked	C	8 1/2
Rice, puffed	C	3/5
Rice, uncooked	C	8
Rutabaga, cubed	C	4 3/4
Sage, ground	C	2
Salad dressing	C	8
Salmon, canned	C	8
Salt	T	2/3

[*] As-purchased quantity.

[†] Edible portion quantity.

(Continued)

Item	Volume T = Tablespoon C = Cup	Weight (oz)
Sauerkraut	C	5 1/3
Sesame seed	T	1/3
Sesame seed	C	5 3/8
Shallots, diced	T	2/5
Shortening	C	7
Soda, baking	T	2/5
Soybeans	C	7
Spinach, cooked	C	8
Spinach, raw	qt	3 1/4
Squash, Hubbard, cooked	C	8
Strawberries	C	7
Suet, ground	C	4 1/2
Sugar, brown, lightly packed	C	5 1/3
Sugar, brown, solidly packed	C	8
Sugar, granulated	C	8
Sugar, powdered, sifted	C	5 1/3
Tapioca, pearl	C	5 3/4
Tapioca, quick-cooking	C	5 1/3
Tea, instant	C	2
Tea, loose-leaf	C	2 2/3
Tomatoes, canned	C	8
Tomatoes, fresh, diced	C	7
Tuna	C	8
Vanilla	T	1/2
Vinegar	C	8
Walnuts, shelled	C	4
Water	C	8
Yeast, compressed cake	ea	3/5
Yeast, envelope	ea	1/4

Food Service Industry Resources

Appendix D

The following is a partial list of the important resources involved in the food service industry.

FOOD SERVICE DISTRIBUTOR RESOURCES

The following businesses are among the leaders in food manufacturing, distribution, and sales. They include both regional and national service companies.

Allen Foods

Food service distribution and equipment servicing within 300 miles of St. Louis, MO.

www.allenfoods.com

AlliantLink.com

E-commerce food service company providing a catalog, order fulfillment, and distribution

www.alliantlink.com

Arrow-Sysco Food Service Distributors, Inc.

A subsidiary of Sysco, serving South Louisiana and the Mississippi Gulf Coast markets

www.syscono.com

Benchmark Sales & Marketing, Inc.

Food broker and distributor for New England and Upstate New York

www.benchmarksales.com

Bidvest

Broadline food service wholesale distributor in Australasia

www.bidvest.com.au

Canteen Vending Services

National vending company operating 150 branches and 18,500 client sites

www.canteen-usa.com

Catanzaro Foods

Family-owned full service food distributorship

www.catanzarofoods.com

CSV Sales, Inc.

National distributor of frozen food/food broker/consulting

www.csvsales.com

Custom Food Service

Food service distributor

www.customfoodservice.com

Diamond Crystal Specialty Foods

Specializes in nutritional products used by the health care industry, drink and dessert mixes, and packets and shakers for salt, pepper, non dairy creamer, and more

www.diamondcrystal.com

Diversified Foods Inc.

Provides import and export, custom manufacturing, ingredients for manufacturing, and food service/retail distribution

www.diversifiedfoods.com

Dole & Bailey, Inc.

Distributor of fresh meats, poultry, seafood, and specialty groceries

www.doleandbailey.com

Dot Foods, Inc.

Provides sales and redistribution for food processors and food service distributors

www.dotfoods.com

Dulin Food Service

Food broker for major manufacturers, distributors, and operators serving south Florida, specifically the food service industry

www.dulinfoodservice.com

Dutch Creek Foods

Distributors of a full food service line of fresh and frozen meats, fruit, vegetables, salad dressings and mixes, noodles, oils, and more

www.dutchcreekfoods.com

Fair Market Inc.

Specializes in the distribution of frozen meat, prepared foods, fruits and vegetables, dry goods, and seafood

www.fairmarketinc.com

Food Marketing Specialists, Inc.

Food service broker serving the state of Oklahoma

www.fmsokc.com

Food Services of America

Nationwide privately held food distributor

www.fsafood.com

Good Source

Food distributor to schools, universities, correctional facilities, and nonprofit organizations

www.goodsource.com

Gordon Food Service

Broadline food service distributor in the United States and Canada

www.gfs.com

Groupex Canada

Offers discount volume food buying services to member restaurants and hotels

www.groupex.com

H & M Wagner & Sons, Inc.

Full line food service and equipment distributor

www.hmwagner.com

Harker's Distribution, Inc.

Distribution services for schools, health care, restaurants and more

www.harkers.com

HAVI Food Services Philippines

Provides warehousing and distribution services; also offers wholesale of baking goods and lease of temperature-controlled delivery equipment

www.haviphils.com.ph

International Multifoods Corporation

Manufacturer and marketer of consumer brands and food service products and distributor to vending operators and food service customers

www.multifoods.com

Joseph Campagna & Sons, Inc.

Wholesale distributors of food products and supplies for restaurants and pizza shops in the metro New York City area

www.campagnafoods.com

JW Holding Group & Associates, Inc.

International full service, full line food distributor specializing in government contract work

www.jwholding.com

Mamma Roma Ltd

Carries food, drink, ingredients, and ancillary products for the catering, restaurant, and manufacturing industries; specialists in Italian and French items

www.mamma-roma.com

Martin Brothers Distributing Co., Inc.

Full line food service distributor

www.martinsnet.com

Menu Magic New Zealand Ltd.

Marketer of mainly portion control foods, both frozen and fresh chilled; also a distribution agent in the Bay of Plenty and Waikato regions for Tegal Foods Ltd.

www.menumagic.co.nz

Micucci Wholesale Foods

Distributor of food products and supplies for pizza shops and restaurants in New England

www.micucci.com

MIDEX

Supplier of dairy products, fruit desserts, organic food, soups, and baby food

www.midex.com

Nestlé FoodServices

Manufacturer of food service products; includes a catalog, recipes, branded systems, and meal planning tools

www.nestlefoodservices.com

NuCo2

Provides food service establishments with the carbonation in fountain beverages

www.nuco2.com

Ocean Spray Foodservice

Developing product and packaging solutions that help grow food service businesses

www.oceansprayfoodservice.com

Palmex Alimentos

Manufactures and distributes potatoes, wheat, corn, bacon, and multi-grain pellets as well as other snack seasoning products

www.palmex.com

Pocahontas Foods USA

National food distribution company with local branches

www.pocahontasfoods.com

Premier Foodservice Distributors of America

Member owned cooperative

www.pfda.com

Ravensbergen Bakery Supplies

Bakery and ice cream supplies including ingredients and equipment

www.ravensbergen.com

RC Fine Foods

Manufacturers of over 250 specialty food products

www.rcfinefoods.com

Reinhart FoodService

Midwest food distributor

www.ReinhartFoodService.com

Roma Food Enterprises Inc.

Distributor of Italian food products

www.romafood.com

Shamrock Foods Company

Provides customers and associates with the latest information about the food service industry

www.shamrockfoods.com

Sharin' Foodservice Sales, Inc.

Coverage in the Carolinas

www.sharinfoods.com

Southern Foods

Supplier of food to restaurants and homes

www.southernfoods.com

Sysco Corporation

Marketer and distributor of food service products in North America

www.sysco.com

Tannis Food Distributors

Supplier of major brands to the food industry in Eastern Ontario and Western Quebec.

www.tannisfood.com

Thomas & Howard

Food service distributor providing a broad range of food services and supplies to restaurants, convenience stores, schools, and institutions

www.tohoco.com

Trujillo and Sons

Distributes vegetable oil, rice, beans, fresh vegetables, and sugar all over the world

www.trujilloandsons.com

U.S. Foodservice

Broadline food service distributor of national, private label, and signature brand items

www.usfoodservice.com

UniPro Foodservice, Inc.

Broadline food service procurement and marketing distribution group

www.uniprofoodservice.com

FARM-TO-TABLE RESOURCES

The following organizations provide information on sustainable agriculture and seafood, community supported agriculture, local purchasing practices, and food philanthropy.

Blue Ocean Insitute

www.blueocean.org

Chef's Collaborative

www.chefscollaborative.org

Community Supported Agriculture

www.localharvest.org/csa

Earth Pledge

www.farmtotable.org

Eat Well Guide

www.eatwellguide.org

Eatwild

www.eatwild.com

Edible Communities

www.ediblecommunities.com

Foodbuy-Atlanta

www.foodbuy.com

Food Routes

www.foodroutes.org

Heritage Foods USA

www.heritagefoodsusa.com

Local Harvest

www.localharvest.org

Oldways Preservation Trust

www.oldwayspt.org

Share Our Strength

www.strength.org

Slow Food USA

www.slowfoodusa.org

The Sustainable Table

www.sustainabletable.org

TECHNOLOGY SOFTWARE AND HARDWARE RESOURCES

The following companies provide computer software and hardware products used in food service operations.

Aceeca
www.aceeca.com

Aloha-Radiant Systems, Inc.
www.alohapos.com

Ameranth
www.ameranth.com/home

Barrington Software, Inc.
www.cooken.com

Central Point Technologies
www.centralpointtech.com

Cheftec
www.culinarysoftware.com

Chef2Chef
Forums.chef2chef.net

CNET
www.cnet.com

Compaq
www.compaq.com

CookenPro
www.cooken.com

Dell
www.dell.com

Digital Dining
www.menusoft.com

DinersChoice
www.13solutions.com

Foodservice
www.foodservicei.com

HanDBase
www.ddhsoftware.com

Handhelds for Chefs
www.handheldsforchefs.com

Hewlett-Packard
www.hp.com

Hotelware Corporation
www.hotelwarecorp.com

Infogenesis,
www.infogenesis.com

Javelin Systems
www.jvln.com

J. Kings Food Service Professionals, Inc.
www.jkings.com

la Madeleine
www.lamadeleine.com

MAI Systems
www.maisystems.com

MasterCook Deluxe
www.valusoft.com

MICROS
www.micros.com

Multi-Systems, Inc.
www.msisolutions.com

My Technology Partners, Inc.
www.MTPonline.net

NextStep Edge Technologies
www.inextstep.com

OBI Software
www.obisoft.com

Otter Box
www.otterbox.com

Palm
www.palm.com

PalmBrew and PDABrew
http://choiceway.com/palmbrew

Pocket PC platform
www.pocketpc.com

PocketSolutions
www.thepocketsolution.com

Pokky Manufacturing
www.pokky.com

Red-M
www.red-m.com

Sales Partner Systems, Inc.
www.spsi.com

Sony
www.sony.com

Spice-o-pedia
www.13solutions.com

Symbol Technologies
www.symbol.com

The Book of Yields
www.wiley.com/college/lynch

The CBORD Group Incorporated
www.cbord.com

USDA National Nutrient Database
www.nal.usda.gov/fnic/foodcomp/srch/search.htm

Vindigo
www.vindigo.com

Webfoodpros
www.webfoodpros.com

Wine Enthusiast Guide
www.landware.com

Zagat
www.zagat.com

State Alcohol Control Boards

The following is a list of state and territorial offices that administer and enforce laws regarding the manufacture, distribution, and dispensing of alcoholic beverages. It is recommended to review the laws in your state before trying to buy wine by mail-order.

Alabama

Alcoholic Beverage Control Board

2715 Gunter Park Drive

West Montgomery, AL 36109-1021

Fax: (334) 277-2150

Alaska

Alcoholic Beverage Control Board

550 W. Seventh Ave., Suite 350

Anchorage, AK 99501-3510

Arizona

Liquor Licenses and Control Department

800 W. Washington St., Fifth Floor

Phoenix, AZ 85007

Phone: (602) 542-5141; fax: (602) 542-5707

E-mail: liqr@ll.state.az.us; Internet: http://www.azll.com

Arkansas

Alcoholic Beverage Control

Administration Technology Center

100 Main, Suite 503

Little Rock, AR 72201

Fax: (501) 682-2221

California

Alcoholic Beverage Control Department

3801 Rosin Court, Suite 150

Sacramento, CA 95834-1633

Phone: (916) 263-6900; fax: (916) 263-6912

Colorado

Liquor Enforcement Division

Department of Revenue

1881 Pierce Drive, Room 108A

Lakewood, CO 80214

Phone: (303) 205-2300; fax: (303) 205-2341

Connecticut

Liquor Control Commission

165 Capitol Ave.

Hartford, CT 06106

Phone: (860) 566-4687

Delaware

Alcoholic Beverage Control Division

Carvel State Office Building

820 N. French St.

Wilmington, DE 19801

Fax: (302) 577-3204

Florida

Department of Business and Professional Regulation

Alcoholic Beverages & Tobacco

1940 N. Monroe St.

Tallahassee, FL 32399-1020

Phone: (904) 488-3227; fax: (904)922-5175

Georgia

Department of Revenue

Alcohol & Tobacco Tax

Unit 270, Washington St. SW

Atlanta, GA 30334

Hawaii

Department of Liquor Control County of Hawaii

101 Aupuni Street, Room 230

Hilo, Hawaii 96766

Idaho

State Liquor Dispensary

7185 Bethel St.

P.O. Box 59

Boise, ID 83704

Alcoholic Beverage Control Division

Department of Law Enforcement

P.O. Box 700

Meridian, ID 83680-0700

Phone: (208) 884-7003

Illinois

Liquor Control Commission

100 W. Randolph St., Suite 5-300

Chicago, IL 60601

Phone: (312) 814-2206; fax: (312) 814-2241

Internet: http://www.state.il.us/lcc

Indiana

Alcohol Beverage Commission

302 W. Washington St., Room E114

Indianapolis, IN 46204

Phone: (317) 232-2430; fax: (317) 233-6114

Iowa

Alcoholic Beverages Division

1918 SE Hulsizer

Ankeny, IA 50021

Phone: (515) 281-7407; fax: (515) 281-7385

Kansas

Department of Revenue

Alcoholic Beverage Control Division

4 Townsite Plaza, Room 210

200 SE Sixth St.

Topeka, KS 66603-3512

Phone: (913) 296-3946; fax: (913) 296-0922

Kentucky

Alcoholic Beverage Control Department

1003 Twilight Trail

Suburban Park Building A2

Frankfort, KY 40601

Phone: (502) 564-4850; fax: (502) 564-1442

Louisiana

Alcohol & Beverage Control

P.O. Box 201

Baton Rouge, LA 70806

Phone: (504) 925-4041; fax: (504) 925-3975

Maine

Alcoholic Beverages and Lottery Operations Bureau

8 State House Station

Augusta, ME 04333-0008

Phone: (207) 287-3721; fax: (207) 287-6769

Maryland

Alcohol & Tobacco Tax Division

State Treasury Building, Room 310

Annapolis, MD 21401-3311

Phone: (410) 974-3311; fax: (410) 974-3201

Massachusetts

Alcoholic Beverages Control Commission

100 Cambridge St., Room 2204

Boston, MA 02202

Phone: (617) 727-3040; fax: (617) 727-1258

Michigan

Liquor Control Commission

7150 Harris Drive

P.O. Box 30005

Lansing, MI 48909

Phone: (517) 322-1345; fax: (517) 322-5188

Minnesota

Department of Public Safety

Liquor Control Division

444 Cedar St., Suite 100L

St. Paul, MN 55101-2149

Phone: (612) 296-6212; fax: (612) 297-5259

Mississippi

Alcoholic Beverage Control Bureau

P.O. Box 540

Madison, MS 39130-0540

Phone: (601) 856-1301; fax: (601) 856-1390

Missouri

Liquor Control Division

Department of Public Safety

P.O. Box 837

Jefferson City, MO 65102

Montana

Revenue Department

Liquor Division

Sam W. Mitchell Building, Room 455

Helena, MT 59620

Fax: (406) 444-3696; TTY: (406) 444-2830

Nebraska

Liquor Control Commission

301 Centennial Mall South

P.O. Box 95046

Lincoln, NE 68509-5046

Phone: (603) 471-2571; fax: (402) 471-2814

Nevada

Nevada Department of Taxation–Liquor Division Capitol Complex

1340 South Curry St.

Carson City, NV 89710

Phone: (702) 687-4820

New Hampshire

Liquor Commission

Storrs St.

P.O. Box 503

Concord, NH 03302-0503

Phone: (603) 271-3134; fax: (603) 271-1107

New Jersey

Department of Law & Public Safety

Alcoholic Beverage Control Division

140 E. Front Street, CNO87

Trenton, NJ 08625-0087

Phone: (609) 984-2830; fax: (609) 633-6078

New Mexico

Department of Regulation & Licensing

Alcohol & Gaming Division

P.O. Box 25101

Santa Fe, NM 87503

Phone: (505) 827-7003; fax: (505) 827-7168

New York

Alcoholic Beverage Control Division State Liquor Authority

84 Holland Ave.

Albany, NY 12208

Phone: (518) 474-3114; fax: (518) 402-4015

TTY: (518) 474-9888

North Carolina

Alcoholic Beverage Control Commission

3322 Garner Road

Raleigh, NC 27610

Phone: (919) 779-0700; fax: (919) 662-1946

North Dakota

Licensing Administration
Office of the Attorney General
State Capitol, 17th Floor
600 East Boulevard Ave.
Bismarck, ND 58505
Phone: (701) 328-2210; fax: (701) 328-3535

Ohio

Department of Liquor Control
2323 W. Fifth Ave.
Columbus, OH 43266-0701
Phone: (614) 644-2472; fax: (614) 644-2480

Oklahoma

Alcoholic Beverage Control Board
4545 N. Lincoln Blvd., Suite 270
Oklahoma City, OK 73105
Phone: (405) 521-3484

Oregon

Liquor Control Commission
9079 SE McLoughlin Blvd.
Portland, OR 97222-7355
Phone: (503) 872-5000; fax: (503) 872-5266
TTY: (503) 872-5013

Pennsylvania

Liquor Control Board
Northwest Office Building
Harrisburg, PA 17124-0001
Phone: (717) 783-7637; fax: (717) 783-6614
TTY: (717) 772-3725

Rhode Island

Department of Business Regulation
Liquor Control
233 Richmond St.
Providence, RI 02903
Phone: (401) 277-2562

South Carolina

Department of Revenue & Taxation
Division of Alcohol Beverage Control
301 Gervais Ave.
Columbia, SC 29201
Phone: (803) 734-0477

South Dakota

Division of Special Taxes
Department of Revenue
Kneip Building, 3rd Floor
700 Governor Drive
Pierre, SD 57501
Phone: (605) 773-3311

Tennessee

Alcoholic Beverage Commission
226 Capitol Blvd., Suite 300
Nashville, TN 37243-0755
Phone: (615) 741-1602; fax: (615) 741-0847

Texas

Alcoholic Beverage Commission
P.O. Box 13127
Austin, TX 78711
Phone: (512) 206-3333; fax: (512) 206-3350
TTY: (512) 206-3270;
E-mail: questions@tabc.state.tx.us

Utah

Alcoholic Beverage Control
Department 1625 South
900West
P.O. Box 30408
Salt Lake City, UT 84130-0408
Phone: (801) 977-6800; fax: (801)977-6888
E-mail: kwynn@state.ut.us

Vermont

Liquor Control Department
Green Mountain Drive, Drawer 20
Montpelier, VT 05620-4501
Phone: (802) 828-2345; fax: (802)828-2803
E-mail: norrie@dlc.state.vt.us

Virginia

Alcoholic Beverage Control Board
2901 Hermitage Road
P.O. Box 27491
Richmond VA 23261
Phone: (804) 213-4405; fax: (804) 213-4411

Professional Organizations

Appendix F

The following is a partial list of the important professional trade organizations involved in purchasing and/or the food service industry.

American Cheese Society

304 West Liberty Street

Suite 201

Louisville, KY 40202

(502) 583-3783

www.cheesesociety.org

American Culinary Federation

180 Center Place Way

St. Augustine, FL 32095

(800) 624-9458

www.acfchefs.org

American Dietetic Association

120 South Riverside Plaza

Suite 2000

Chicago, IL 60606-6995

(800) 877-1600

www.eatright.org

American Institute of Baking

P.O. Box 3999

Manhattan, KS 66505-399

(785) 537-4750

www.aibonline.org

American Institute of Wine & Food

1303 Jefferson Street

Suite 100B

Napa, CA 94559

(800) 274-2493

www.aiwf.org

American Personal & Private Chef Association

4572 Delaware Street

San Diego, CA 92116

(800) 644-8389

www.personalchef.com

American Purchasing Society

P.O. Box 256

Aurora, IL 60506

(630) 859-0250

www.american-purchasing.com

American Spice Trade Association

2025 M Street, NW

Suite 800

Washington, DC 20036

(202) 367-1127

www.astaspice.org

Black Culinary Alliance

55 West 116th Street

Suite 234

New York, NY 10026

(646) 548-2949

www.blackculinarians.com

Chef's Collaborative

262 Beacon Street

Boston, MA 02116

(617) 236-5200

www.chefscollaborative.org

Club Managers Association of America

1733 King Street

Alexandria, VA 22314

(703) 739-9500

www.cmaa.org

Community Supported Agriculture

LocalHarvest

220 21st Avenue

Santa Cruz, CA 95062

(831) 475-8150

www.localharvest.org/csa

International Association of Culinary Professionals

304 West Liberty Street

Suite 201

Louisville, KY 40202

(502) 581-9786

www.iacp.com

International Food Service Executives Association

836 San Bruno Avenue

Henderson, NV 89015

(888) 234-3732

www.ifsea.org

The James Beard Foundation

167 West 12th Street

New York, NY 10011

(800) 36-BEARD

www.jamesbeard.org

Les Dames d'Escoffier International

P.O. Box 4961

Louisville, KY 40204

(502) 456-1851

www.ldei.org

Multicultural Foodservice and Hospitality Alliance

P.O. Box 25661

Providence, RI 02905

(401) 461-6342

www.mfha.net

National Ice Carving Association

P.O. Box 3593

Oak Brook, IL 60522-3593

(630) 871-8431

www.nica.org

National Restaurant Association

1200 17th Street, NW

Washington, DC 20036

(202) 331-5900

www.restaurant.org

North American Meat Processors Association

1910 Association Drive

Reston, VA 20191

(703) 758-1900

www.namp.com

Oldways Preservation Trust

266 Beacon Street

Boston, MA 02116

(617) 421-5500

www.oldwayspt.org

Produce Marketing Association

1500 Casho Mill Road

P.O. Box 6036

Newark, DE 19714-6036

(302) 738-7100

www.pma.com

Research Chefs Association

5775 Peachtree-Dunwoody Road

Building G, Suite 500

Atlanta, GA 30342

(404) 252-3663

www.culinology.com

Seafood Choices Alliance

8401 Colesville Road, Suite 500

Silver Spring, MD 20910

(301) 495-9570

www.seafoodchoices.com

Share Our Strength

1730 M Street, NW

Suite 700

Washington, DC 20036

(800) 969-4767

www.strength.org

Slow Food USA

20 Jay Street

Suite 313

Brooklyn, NY 11202

(718) 260-8000

www.slowfoodusa.org

Women Chefs and Restaurateurs

304 West Liberty Street

Suite 201

Louisville, KY 40202

(502) 581-0300

www.womenchefs.org

Commodity Organizations

Appendix G

MEAT:	
www.mla.com.au	Australia—beef and lamb
www.nzbeeflamb.co.nz	New Zealand—beef and lamb information and recipes
www.veal.org	veal
www.beeftips.org	beef and veal—Wisconsin Beef Council
www.beef.org	beef
www.angusbeef.com	beef
www.beeffoodservice.com	beef
www.otherwhitemeat.com	pork
www.lambchef.com	lamb
POULTRY:	
www.mapleleaffarms.com	duck
www.turkeyfed.org	turkey
www.eatchicken.com	chicken
www.tyson.com	chicken
SEAFOOD:	
www.seafoodno/worldwide	Norwegian Seafood Export Council
www.ca.seafood.com	California seafood
www.floseafood.com	Florida seafood
www.nf.org	National Fisheries Institute
www.seafood.is	seafood
www.horizonfoods.com	seafood
www.alaskaseafood.org	Alaska seafood
www.seafood.com	seafood
CHEESE:	
www.polliofs.com	cheese company
www.cheesefromspain.com	Spanish cheeses
www.cheese.com	cheeses from many countries
www.cheese-online.com	French cheeses
www.aco-igp.com	Designation of Origin (DO) cheeses

(Continued)

BEANS:	
www.americanbeans.org	American Dry Bean Board
www.pea-lentil.com	USA Dry Pea and Lentil Council
FRUITS AND VEGETABLES:	
www.avocado.org	avocado
www.idahopotato.com	potatoes
www.mainepotatoes.com	potatoes
www.aboutproduce.com	produce
www.caltreefruit.com	peaches, plums, nectarines
OLIVE OIL:	
www.bertolli.com	
www.colavita.com	
www.asoliva.com	Spanish olive oil
SEASONINGS:	
www.astaspice.org	information on spices
www.monafederzoni.com	balsamic vinegar
www.kikkoman.com	Kikkoman soy sauce and other products
MISCELLANEOUS:	
www.abika.com	various countries and food products (click on "How To" Guides on side menu bar, then click on Food and Recipes)
www.foodgalaxy.com	check industry links
www.vino.eunet.es	Spanish products—olive oil, Serrano ham, wine
www.riceusa.com	rice
www.riceweb.org	rice history, production, and recipes
www.macsoc.com.au	macadamia nuts
www.almondsarein.com	almonds
www.dececco.it	pasta
www.pasta.com	pasta
www.pastalabella.com	pasta
www.ilovepasta.org	pasta
www.professionalpasta.it	pasta
www.landolakes.com	butter
www.cuisinenet.com	various ingredients
www.unlv.edu/tourism	links to many food-related sites
www.aeb.org	American Egg Board
www.goya.com	Goya Foods—Latin American and Caribbean recipes

Glossary

Every industry has their unique vernacular that separates their business from others. To excel in the food service industry, one must speak the language. The following terms are basic to *kitchenspeak* … the dialect of the food and beverage manager, chef, kitchen manager, food buyer, and storeroom manager. Although this glossary reflects some innovations by the author, many of the terms listed in this glossary are not the original definitions of the author, but are a compilation derived from sources formally published.

A

ABC analysis A technique used to measure and compare the cost of each item held in stock and to rate their cost contribution to overall purchases for purposes of controlling investments and inventory control.

accounting period The period of time, whether days, weeks, or months, in which an operator chooses to measure specific revenue and expense activity.

accounts payable The term used to represent debts owed by a business, but not yet paid.

accounts receivable The term used to represent bills issued to customers, but not yet collected.

actual cost A method for determining total inventory value by using the actual price paid for each item held in inventory.

Alcoholic Beverage Control (ABC) Charged with enforcing the alcoholic beverage control laws and regulations in the states with ABC boards; they run package stores called ABC stores.

American craft brewer An American craft brewer is a small, independent, and traditional brewery. Craft beer comes only from a craft brewer.

analogs A meat substitute made from vegetable protein (usually soy). Most analog products provide more protein than meat with fewer calories and no cholesterol.

aperitif An alcoholic drink taken as an appetizer before a meal.

as-purchased cost (AP cost) The cost of a product on its initial purchase, before being trimmed, cooked, or portioned.

as-purchased weight (AP weight) The weight of a product on its initial purchase, before being trimmed, cooked, or portioned.

assets Any item of economic value owned by an individual or corporation, especially that which could be converted to cash, such as CDs, inventory, equipment, property, and accounts receivables.

aquaculture The science, art, and business of cultivating marine or freshwater food, fish, or shellfish, such as oysters, clams, salmon, and trout, under controlled conditions.

B

backdoor selling Bypassing the buyer and going directly to an individual who will use the product.

balance sheet A statement of the book value of a business at a certain date in time, often at the end of the fiscal (business) year.

balsamic vinegar Traditional sweet-sour flavored vinegar commonly used in Italian cuisine. The finest and most traditional balsamic vinegar is very labor-intensive to produce; while it ages and gradually evaporates over a minimum of 12 years, the liquid is transferred to successively smaller casks made of different woods, absorbing the flavor characteristics of each wood and becoming more concentrated with each transfer. Oak, mulberry, chestnut, cherry, juniper, ash, and acacia are the most commonly used woods.

bank lines of credit A limited amount of money made available for borrowing from a bank, as needed in the future, usually by securing the bank loan using assets owned by the client.

barter The direct exchange of goods and services.

beefalo A fertile hybrid offspring of domestic cattle (*Bos taurus*) and the American Bison (generally called buffalo).

beer A fermented alcoholic beverage brewed from malt and flavored with hops. The fermented beverage, brewed by traditional methods, is de-alcoholized so that the finished product generally contains no more than 0.5 percent alcohol.

beverage A drink specifically prepared for human consumption.

beverage cost Those material costs related to the sale of alcoholic beverages, and often nonalcoholic beverages.

beverage cost percent Calculated by dividing the beverage costs by beverage sales during the same period of time.

bid request form A formal document, issued by the buyer to potential sellers requesting a quote for various products or services specified in the document over a specified period of time.

bin tag An identification tool assigned to individual bottles or racks of wine containing information about the wine.

biochemistry The study of the chemistry of life processes in plants and animals.

biodiversity The number and variety of organisms found within a specified geographic region.

biological hazard Refers to microorganisms (including bacteria, viruses, and parasites) that can cause the risk of foodborne illnesses if they reach a sufficient number of cells, or when they contaminate food.

biotechnology The use of microorganisms, such as bacteria or yeasts, or biological substances, such as enzymes, to perform specific industrial or manufacturing processes, including food development. Biotechnology refines and extends methods that produce new plants and animals.

Bioterrorism Act of 2002 The Public Health Security and Bioterrorism Preparedness and Response Act of 2002 (the Bioterrorism Act), an amendment of the Safe Water Drinking Act of 1974, requires domestic and foreign facilities that manufacture, process, pack, or hold food for human or animal consumption in the United States to register with the FDA.

bivalve These mollusks have two shells that enclose all or most of the animal when closed. Clams, oysters, mussels, and scallop are bivalves.

blackball The act of excluding someone by a negative vote or veto, or to refuse to do business with a person or entity.

blanched To plunge food (usually vegetables and fruits) into boiling water briefly, then into cold water to stop the cooking process. Blanching is used to firm the flesh, to loosen skins (as with peaches and tomatoes) and to heighten and set color and flavor (as with vegetables before freezing).

blanket purchase order A financial arrangement between buyer and seller that authorizes the buyer to spend up to a specified dollar amount during a specified period of time with the seller.

blind receiving A process requiring an extra level of responsibility from the receiving clerk: The delivery people bring only a list of the items in the shipment. The receiving clerk must count and weigh the order for them to be able to complete the receiving check sheet. In this practice, the full invoice—complete with the purveyor's counts and weights—is sent directly to the accounting office. The accounting office compares the completed check sheet from the receiving clerk to the invoice from the purveyor and verifies that all is as billed, and prices charged are as quoted.

blind tests Performed to evaluate similar items, often from competing suppliers; certain tests are applied on a selection of ingredients to draw comparisons between those like items available in the marketplace. Also known as a *can cutting*.

blixer A hybrid of a blender and mixer, with a design similar to a food processor.

boiling water bath method Jars of food are completely covered with boiling water and heated for a specific period of time.

bonefish A gamefish found off the coast of Florida. In the broader sense, bonefish include roundfish and flatfish that have their skeletal structure on the inside.

bottom-line bidding To select a vendor by comparing quotes from different purveyors and purchasing the lowest priced product. Also known as *bottom-line buying*.

bran The fibrous pericarp (hard, dry shell) that encloses the grain's kernel.

break-even analysis A management tool that can aid food service managers in examining the relationship between various revenues, costs, and sales volume. Also known as *cost-volume-profit (CVP) analysis.*

break-even point The volume of sales needed for a business to generate zero profit; the point at which the sum of all costs is equal to sales, with no profit or loss.

broadline vendor A large food service distributor that sells a broad variety of products, including food, supplies, and equipment.

brokers Independent sales and marketing representatives who contract with different growers, manufacturers, and fabricators to both sell and conduct local promotional programs with distributors, suppliers, and/or food service operators.

business-to-business (B2B) e-commerce The area that encompasses electronic buying and selling transactions between organizations and in which e-procurement is a central function.

butcher's yield test A test used by butchers, chefs, or buyers to evaluate the difference in the cost of cutting their own portions (including the resultant by-products of trim, bones, and fat) or buying them preportioned.

butter Used as a cooking ingredient, it is the fatty substance created by churning or agitating cream. It contains not more than 16 percent water and must contain a minimum of 80 percent milkfat.

buttermilk The liquid that is drained from the churned milk after the fat has coagulated to form butter. A culture is added to the liquid and it is left to ferment for about 12–14 hours at a very low temperature, giving it a more acidic tang.

buyer The person primarily responsible for the purchase of all food, beverages, and supplies that are issued to the different outlets of the food service operation.

buyer's order form Lists created by the buyer, and separated by the nature of their contents, to assist in purchasing different categories of goods.

buying To obtain goods or services by spending money.

bycatch The nontargeted or immature fish that are caught and later discarded.

C

can cuttings See *blind test.*

canning Packing and preserving of food in cans or jars subjected to sterilizing temperatures.

casein The major protein in milk. Many soy cheeses contain casein, which may be problematic to those with dairy sensitivities.

cash and carry A business, generally operated by food service distributors, that sells products at close to wholesale prices, but who don't deliver products.

cash flow The expression used to compare cash on-hand to pay bills, or accounts payable, coming due.

cash flow statement A financial report that shows incoming and outgoing money during a particular period (often monthly or quarterly).

caviar U.S. Government law allows only the roe of sturgeon to be called caviar, whereas the roe of other fish must only be called caviar if the name of the fish comes first.

central processing unit (CPU) Component of a computer hardware system that combines control unit, storage unit, and arithmetic unit; the part of a computer that interprets and executes instructions.

cephalopod These mollusks do not usually have an external shell. The name indicates feet growing out of the head. Squid, octopus, and cuttlefish are the cephalopods most commonly used in food service. These varieties have a piece of cartilage inside the body that serves as the skeleton called the "pen" or "quill" in squid and the "bone" in cuttlefish.

chemical hazard Chemical hazards in food processing can include chemicals that are intentionally added to foods, incidental or unintentionally added chemicals, as well as naturally-occurring toxins.

chicken A kind of poultry recognized by the USDA. The term includes any of several varieties of common domestic fowl used for food as well as egg production.

citrus fruits A common term and genus of flowering plants in the family *Rutaceae*, originating in tropical and subtropical southeast Asia. Citrus fruits are notable for their fragrance, partly due to flavonoids and limonoids contained in the rind, and most are juice-laden. The juice contains a high quantity of citric acid giving them their characteristic sharp flavor.

clam Generally applied to a wide variety of bivalve (two-shelled) mollusks.

clostridium botulinum Anaerobic bacterium producing botulin—the toxin that causes botulism. These rod-shaped organisms grow best in low-oxygen conditions forming spores that allow them to survive in a dormant state until exposed to conditions that can support their growth.

cocoa powder Made by pulverizing partially defatted chocolate liquor and removing nearly all of the cocoa butter.

code of ethics A set of principles established to govern an organization's employees.

cold-pressed oils Oils that are cold pressed are expeller pressed in a heat-controlled environment to keep temperatures below 120° F.

cold smoking Cold smoking is done without any heat being present; it merely imparts a smoke flavor and color without increasing the internal temperature of the food product, allowing it to remain raw if desired.

commerce A branch of production that deals with the exchange of goods and services from producer to final consumer.

commodity money Objects with intrinsic value, whether rare or common, used as currency.

common costs A cost that is common to a number of costing objects but cannot be easily traced to them individually. Also known as *joint costs*.

community-supported agriculture (CSA) CSA aims to restore a sense of place to the food that people eat. Members of CSA clubs support their local farmers by agreeing to pay a lump sum in advance for a "seasonal share" of the harvest.

compatible When the same computer program can run on two different computer brand products.

competitive buying The application whereby the buyer solicits quotes from various sellers, either orally or written, and compares them to discover the lowest price for the same product.

conceptual skill Involves the ability to see the enterprise as a whole; it includes recognizing how the various functions of the organization depend on one another, and how changes in any one part affect the others.

conching A final stage in chocolate production that involves slowly stirring melted chocolate in large vats to remove excess moisture and volatile acids while creating a very smooth texture.

consumer protection A government regulation to protect the interests of consumers. For example, the FTC requires businesses to disclose detailed information about their products, particularly in areas where safety or public health is an issue, such as food.

consistency A recipe to be reproduced to the same standard of appearance, taste, yield, and cost.

contamination Refers to the presence, generally unintended, of harmful organisms or substances. Contaminants, or hazards, can either be *biological, chemical,* or *physical*.

control process Steps taken to maintain standards of production and profitability.

control states Those states (in the United States) that have state monopoly over the wholesaling and/or retailing of some or all categories of alcoholic beverages, such as beer, wine, and distilled spirits.

convenience foods Any food items on which some prepreparation labor has already been performed, prior to purchase.

conversion costs The sum of direct labor and the business overhead.

cooking oils Vegetable oils used in cooking.

cooperative buying Where an association of persons voluntarily joins together to achieve a common economic end through the formation of a democratically controlled business organization.

cost of goods Food and beverage costs jointly calculated by subtracting the closing inventory value from the combined total of opening inventory value plus purchases.

cost plus fixed-fee A food service operator agreement to purchase most of the needed products from one broadline or full-line food service distributor for a fixed mark-up beyond the seller's actual costs.

cost-volume-profit (CVP) analysis An equation stating that sales is equal to the sum of variable costs, fixed costs, and profit (or loss).

count Refers to the specific quantity of product measured for purchase or production. May also refer to the number of guests served.

cracked wheat Milled wheat grains that are broken into pieces and particles.

credit memo A document completed and signed by the driver and given to the receiving clerk, for the value of rejected product. The memo instructs the seller to deduct the value of the rejected product from the invoice.

crème fraiche Literally translated from French to mean "fresh cream," it is the standard French cream, thick and voluptuous. It is a cultured cream, similar to sour cream, but richer with a minimum 30 percent butterfat content.

cross-contamination When safe foods come into contact with harmful organisms or substances, often by contact with human hands, dirty side towels, cutting boards, work surfaces, or chef's knives.

cross-utilization Both raw and prepared products are used in multiple fashions.

crustacean A large group of arthropods, that have a stiff exoskelton which must be shed to allow the animal to grow. They include various familiar aquatic animals, such as lobsters, crabs, shrimp, and crayfish.

Cryovac® Barrier Bag A form of flexible packaging for fresh foods; these bags are used for vacuum packaging perishables along with extending the distribution and merchandising life of meats, poultry, cheeses, and many other foods.

cultivated mushrooms Commercially grown mushrooms.

cultural heritage Encompasses the qualities and attributes of places that have aesthetic, historic, scientific, or social value for past, present, or future generations. These values may be seen in a place's physical features, but can also be intangible qualities such as people's associations with, or feelings for, a place.

cultural relativity To understand a culture within the context of that culture, without the filters and biases of the observer affecting his observations.

cultured dairy products Milk or cream thickened by heat or sharpened by bacterial cultures, or both.

cultured meat (in-vitro meat) The manufacturing of meat products by using "tissue-engineering" technology. The process produces animal meat without actually using an animal.

curds The part of milk that coagulates when the milk sours or is treated with enzymes. Curd is used to make cheese.

current assets From an accounting aspect, cash and short-term items convertible into cash within one year.

customary units Standard units of measure that were widely adopted for use in commerce. In modern times, the use of U.S. Customary and Metric Measures are considered customary in most countries.

D

daily bid Daily pricing offered by a supplier for goods or services for a short period of time, usually no longer than a week. Also known as a *daily quotation*.

daily order Food that is ordered on a daily basis from a vendor.

daily quotation See *daily bid.*

dairy Generally speaking, dairy is "food that is produced by animals" rather than as milk specifically. Under this definition, eggs are grouped with milk products. Defining dairy as limited to milk products, however, is more common.

desired profit The sales necessary to cover the costs of construction or acquisition; otherwise defined as the profit an owner seeks to achieve on a predicted quantity of revenue.

deterioration All foods (agricultural and aquatic products) undergo varying degrees of loss in nutritional value, safety, or esthetic appeal (color, texture, flavor) as they are subjected to a variety of forces. Physical, chemical, or biological deterioration in food can be caused by heat, cold, light, moisture, dryness, food enzymes, and microorganisms.

dextrose A food additive used as a nutritional sweetener in processed foods. It is glucose produced from cornstarch that has been treated with acids or enzymes, and heated.

digital camera An electronic device used to capture and store photographs electronically in a digital format.

direct costs Costs are those that can be easily assigned to a product.

direct issues When products arrive to the receiving dock and are issued immediately into production without going through storage.

discounts Various methods used to save money by reducing costs.

distilled spirits A liquid preparation meant for consumption containing ethyl (ethanol) purified by distillation from a fermented substance such as fruit, vegetables, or grain.

distribution The means by which products are transferred in the marketplace, moving in turn through a series of intermediaries from the source (grower, manufacturer, or fabricator) to the hospitality operation. The circulation of goods in the marketplace.

drained weight test Used to determine the servable weight of ingredients generally co-packed in cans, pouches, or tubs with a protective packing medium.

drop shipment A type of retailing where the seller does not keep goods in stock, but instead passes the customer's order and shipment details to the wholesaler, who then dispatches the goods to the customer directly.

dry-age Dry-aging was the standard aging process up until the mid-1970s. In this process, carcasses are hung for up to five weeks in a cool, well-ventilated meat locker at 85 percent relative humidity. During aging, natural enzymes break down proteins in the muscle fibers, resulting in improved tenderness. The meat also acquires a unique flavor. Dry-aging is costly, as the meat loses something like 6 percent of its weight every week.

dunnage rack Low and sturdy shelving used for stacking cases of products, such as frozen cases of bread dough, frozen cases of snap-n-bake cookies, or frozen cases of chicken breasts that the operation uses in high volume.

Dutch-processed cocoa Cocoa powder ground from beans that have been treated with an alkali solution, such as potassium carbonate, to raise its pH level. The resultant powder is less acidic, milder tasting, and darker in color than untreated cocoa powder. Also known as *alkalized cocoa.*

E

ecology The branch of biology that deals with the relations between living organisms and their environment.

e-commerce The area that encompasses electronic buying and selling between companies and in which e-procurement has been the primary method of purchase.

economic order quantity (EOQ) The economic order quantity (EOQ) concept is derived from a sensible balance of ordering cost and inventory holding cost.

edible portion cost (EP cost) The cost of a product after it has been trimmed, cooked, and portioned.

edible portion weight (EP weight) The weight of a product after it has been trimmed, cooked, and portioned.

eggs An organic reproductive body lay by the female of bird and animal species; it contains the germ of an embryo and nutritional reserves. Eggs from various different birds are used for human consumption, with the chicken egg being the most common.

emic approach The emic approach to studying a culture is from the viewpoint of an insider, someone who lives among the people to gain a sense of understanding.

endangered species A population of organisms, usually a species (a basic unit of biodiversity) that is either few in number or threatened by changing environmental or predation parameters, which makes it at risk of becoming extinct.

endosperm The largest part of the grain and is composed mainly of starch (flour), a complex carbohydrate that is absorbed slowly by the body, producing a long-lasting feeling of satiety.

Environmental Protection Agency (EPA) An agency of the U.S. government created to protect human health and the environment.

enzymatic browning A chemical process involving enzymes that create melanins, resulting in a brown color. Lemon, orange, and pineapple juice, along with other acids, are used to preserve color in fruit, particularly apples and pears.

ethics The branch of axiology (one of the four major branches of philosophy) which attempts to understand the nature of morality; to define that which is right from that which is wrong. It is oftentimes described as moral philosophy.

etic approach The etic approach to studying culture is from the viewpoint of an outsider, which is the more common method.

exempt employees Those employees not covered by (exempt from) the provisions of the Fair Labor Standards Act (FLSA) requiring, among other things, premium pay for hours worked over forty hours in one week.

expenses The price paid to obtain the items required to operate the business. Also known as *cost.*

F

fabricators The fabricator is responsible for the many forms of food available to the buyer. They take raw food or other raw materials and process them further, such as processing whole poultry into portions, making cheese, or fabricating cans from sheets of tin.

Fair Labor Standards Act (FLSA) The Fair Labor Standards Act (FLSA) establishes minimum wage, overtime pay, recordkeeping, and child labor standards affecting full-time and part-time workers in the private sector and in Federal, State, and local governments. The Department of Labor enforces the Fair Labor Standards Act (FLSA).

Fair Packaging and Labeling Act (FPLA) A U.S. law that applies to labels on many consumer products.

fats Organic compounds that are made up of carbon, hydrogen, and oxygen. They are a source of energy in foods. Fats belong to a group of substances called lipids, and come in liquid or solid form. All fats are combinations of saturated and unsaturated fatty acids.

feathered game Wild birds hunted for sport or food, as well as the flesh of these animals. Common examples include duck, goose, pheasant, quail, and pigeon.

Federal Trade Commission (FTC) An independent agency of the U.S. government whose principal mission is the promotion of consumer protection and the elimination and prevention of anticompetitive business practices.

FIFO A storeroom storing and issuing policy meaning "first in, first out."

fillet A longitudinal slice or boned side of a fish. (*Filet* is the French spelling.)

financial statements Financial documents that food service operations use to manage and control their capital; they include: *income statements, balance sheets, cash flow statements,* and *operating budgets.*

fixed assets A long-term, tangible asset held for business use and not expected to be converted to cash in the current or upcoming fiscal year, such as manufacturing equipment, real estate, and furniture. Also known as *capital assets.*

fixed bids Established pricing offered by a supplier for goods or services for an extended period of time. Often used by larger organizations, such as universities, hospitals, or restaurant chains, which buy great quantities of perishable or nonperishable items over a long period of time.

fixed costs The costs that do not vary with the number of goods or meals produced or sold.

flatfish Flatfish are so named because their eyes are on the same side of the head, and their body is flattened, which allows them to live and feed on the bottom of the ocean.

flavoring agents Flavoring agents are focused on altering or enhancing the flavors of natural food product such as meats and vegetables, or creating flavor for food products that do not have the desired flavors, such as candies and other snacks.

flexible packaging This packaging includes the paper sacks that dog food comes in, the plastic bags that hold potato chips, and the paper or plastic sacks in which we carry home our purchases.

flour The finest grind of a grain used for food.

foie gras Duck or goose liver that has been hypertrophied (enlarged) by force-feeding the birds; prepared and cooked with great care, it is regarded as a delicacy by food connoisseurs.

Food Allergen Labeling and Consumer Protection Act (FALCPA) The act requires food labels to identify in plain English if the product contains any of the eight major food allergens responsible for over 90 percent of all allergic reactions—milk, eggs, fish, crustacean shellfish, peanuts, tree nuts, wheat, and soybeans.

Food and Drug Administration (FDA) An agency of the U.S. Department of Health and Human Services and is responsible for regulating food (human and animal), dietary supplements, drugs, cosmetics, and a variety of medical devices and blood products in the United States.

foodborne illnesses An illness caused by contaminants that are chemical, physical, or biological being mixed with food.

food composition The organic or inorganic chemical substances in most foods including water, fats, carbohydrates, and proteins (including enzymes). Additionally, acids, minerals, vitamins, flavoring agents, and pigments contribute to the makeup of the ingredient.

food cost The material costs associated with actually producing the food items offered on the menu.

food cost percentages Calculated by dividing the food costs by food sales during the same period of time.

Food, Drug, and Cosmetic Act (FDCA) A set of laws passed by Congress in 1938 giving authority to the FDA to oversee the safety of food, drugs, and cosmetics.

food drying Drying food takes the water from the product; to make or become no longer fresh or shapely because of loss of moisture.

food in service The value of inventory considered "in-use." That is to say, the raw product that is in the kitchen and available for production. Also known as *in-use inventory*.

food irradiation A food safety technology designed to reduce disease-causing germs from food. It is the process of exposing food to high levels of radiant energy. Irradiation penetrates deeply into food, killing microorganisms without significantly raising the temperature of the food.

food philanthropy Organizations and businesses donating food, and related financial support, to nonprofit organizations such as food pantrys and homeless shelters.

Food Safety and Inspection Services (FSIS) The public health agency in the U.S. Department of Agriculture responsible for ensuring that the nation's commercial supply of meat, poultry, and egg products is safe, wholesome, and correctly labeled and packaged.

food service distributor The supplier to the restaurant. The purchase from producer-packers and distribute to restaurants.

formal issuing The process of releasing products from the storeroom into production by use of requisitions. Also known as *controlled issuing*.

Form I-9 The Form I-9, employment eligibility verification, is used to establish the employment eligibility of persons being considered for employment, and therefore requiring employers to hire only those persons who are eligible to legally work in the United States. The law also obliges U.S. employers not to discriminate against individuals on the basis of national origin or citizenship, or require different documents from an individual.

fraudulent invoices Falsified invoices to customers, caused by a variety of reasons, including the supplier padding invoices by charging for products never shipped.

Frankenfood A derogatory nickname used to describe genetically engineered food.

freezing food Subjecting food to below 32°F to solidify the moisture within the food in order to extend its useable storage life and quality.

fruit Ripened ovary of a seed plant and its contents, including such adjacent tissues as may be inseparably connected with it. A culinary fruit is any sweet, edible part of a plant that resembles fruit, even if it does not develop from a floral ovary.

furred game Wild mammals hunted for sport or food, as well as the flesh of these animals. Common examples include rabbit, hare, deer, elk, bear, and boar.

G

game Any animal hunted for food or not normally domesticated (such as venison). Game animals are also hunted for sport. The type and range of animals hunted for food varies in different parts of the world. This will be influenced by climate, animal diversity, local taste, and locally accepted view about what can or cannot be legitimately hunted. Sometimes a distinction is also made between varieties and species of a particular animal, such as wild or domestic pigs.

game birds Birds that are hunted for sport or food. They are considered any wild bird suitable for food, including the larger species (such as wild turkey and goose), medium-size birds (including pheasant and wild duck), and smaller game birds (such as partridge, quail, and woodcock). Also known as *feathered game*.

gelatinization Starch granules swell as they absorb moisture when placed in liquid and heated. Gelatinization occurs gradually over a range of temperatures (150°F–212°F/ 66°C–100°C) as the granules continue to absorb moisture, the mixture thickens.

genetically engineered foods Also known as *genetically modified foods*. See *genetically modified organisms*.

genetically modified organisms (GMOs) A food product containing some quantity of any genetically modified organism (GMO) as an ingredient. Genetic recombination techniques consist of introducing into a crop or other organisms a gene extracted from another organism that gives useful characteristics to the crop or organism.

germ Located in the lower end of the grain, and contains the seed of a new plant.

Global Alliance for Improved Nutrition (GAIN) A worldwide consortium of corporations and charities providing grants and research to reduce global hunger and improve the nutritional habits of world populations.

green Proactive environmental effort to reduce, reuse, and recycle energy and consumable materials.

greens Any various leafy plants or their leaves and stems eaten as vegetables. They may be consumed in either a cooked or raw state.

green sheet The name by which most people refer to the Market News Reports issued by the National Marine Fisheries Service from New York.

H

hare The larger relative of the rabbit, and can weigh as much as 12 to 14 pounds, compared to a rabbit at about 5 pounds. Whether wild or domesticated, hares have a darker flesh and earthier flavor than rabbits.

Hazard Analysis and Critical Control Point (HACCP) HACCP focuses on preventing food safety problems before they occur. HACCP does this by assessing the risks associated with a food product or process, and then establishing necessary steps needed to control the risk.

hedging The practice of investing in the futures market, by the buyer, for products that are forecasted to increase in price. Also known as *forward contracting* or *forward buying*.

heirloom An *heirloom* is an old variety that has been maintained either because it has appealing attributes like extra large size, unusual coloring, special connoisseur qualities, or because of family sentimental reasons. Because heirloom tomatoes haven't been "worked on" by plant breeders, they don't usually have much disease resistance.

herbs Leaves of low-growing shrubs and herbaceous (non-woody) plants.

Hierarchy of Needs (Maslow's) A theory in psychology that Abraham Maslow proposed in his 1943 paper *A Theory of Human Motivation*, which he subsequently extended to include his observations of man's innate curiosity. His theory contended that as humans meet "basic needs," they seek to satisfy successively "higher needs" that occupy a set hierarchy (ranking order).

holding costs The total of all expenses in maintaining an inventory: the cost of capital tied up in inventory, obsolescence of products, storage, insurance, handling taxes, depreciation, deterioration, and breakage.

hot smoking Hot smoking raises the internal temperature of the product and helps to render the food cooked while imparting a mild smoke flavor.

hybrid A variety created by deliberately and painstakingly taking pollen from an existing open-pollinated tomato and putting it onto a different open-pollinated tomato. The advantage of hybrids is vigor, and the ability to use a parent known to be disease resistant.

hydroponics The growing of plants without soil.

I

I-9 form See *Form I-9*.

immersion circulator Cooking equipment where packaged foods are submerged and cooked in a temperature-controlled water bath.

IMPS (Institutional Meat Purchase Specifications) Specifications describing various meat cuts, meat products, and meat food products derived from all livestock species, commonly abbreviated "IMPS," and intended for use by any meat procuring activity.

income statement A detailed listing of the revenue and expenses for a given time. Also known as a *profit & loss statement (P&L)*.

induction cooking Uses magnetic fields where each induction coil generates a magnetic field that induces heat in the steel pots and pans placed on its top.

informal issuing Allowing staff to enter and exit the storeroom with product, without the requirement of submitting a formal requisition for the supplies. It is the opposite of *formal issuing*.

ingredient room An area where specified quantities of dry ingredients, fresh fruits and vegetables, and meat items required for food preparation are weighed, measured, packaged, and assembled according to standardized recipes.

inspection Refers to the wholesomeness of meat or poultry and its fitness for food. It is not concerned with quality or grade. The inspection mark means that the meat or poultry has passed examination by a qualified USDA veterinarian or inspector during slaughter and/or processing.

intermediaries The middlemen between the sources and the food service operators or buyers.

interior-ripened soft cheeses These cheeses are washed in light brine in order to maintain the moisture level and softness of the cheese and the rind, and to eliminate certain ferments.

inventory management The process of controlling the inventory volume until it is to be issued.

inventory shrinkage Loss of inventory due to any number of reasons, including theft, poor management, poor controls, and product deterioration.

inventory value padding Involves intentionally overstating the economic value of the products held in inventory.

IQF A food processing term meaning "Individually Quick Frozen" generally applied to separate portions of seafood.

irradiation A technique used by producers to improve the shelf life and overall quality of vegetables. They are exposed to radiation in the form of cobalt 60 or cesium 137, which act directly on the molecules without making the vegetables radioactive. Radiation reduces germination, destroys bacteria and insects, and reduces the need to treat fruits and vegetables with pesticides following harvesting.

issues/issuing Product given to the staff for use in production. The issuing process takes one of two methods, either informal or formal; or said another way, uncontrolled or controlled.

J

joint cost A cost that is common to a number of costing objects but cannot be easily traced to them individually. Also known as *common costs*.

juice A fluid naturally contained in animal or plant tissue.

K

kasha Made from roasted, cracked, or whole buckwheat.

keyboard A data input device for computers; arrangement of keys is modeled after the typewriter keyboard.

key stop A delivery driver is entrusted with an entrance key to an establishment, and often their coolers and freezers, in order to have access for making deliveries. Also known as *drop stop*.

kickbacks The form of cash payments or products of value being given to a food operation's employee, by a vendor, in exchange for special consideration.

L

labor cost Payroll costs, including salaries, wages, and employee benefits.

labor cost percentage Calculated by dividing the labor costs of preparing food by the food sales during the same period of time.

lard The white solid or semisolid rendered fat of a hog. Also means to cover or coat lean meat with lard or a similar fat.

latest purchase price Valuing inventory based on the most recent price paid for the group of like products held in inventory.

leavening agent A substance used in doughs and batters that causes them to rise. In the presence of moisture, heat, acidity, or other triggers, the leavening agent reacts to produce gas (often carbon dioxide) that becomes trapped as bubbles within the dough.

liabilities The value of what the company owes to creditors.

lifestyle The way of living based on identifiable patterns of behavior. It is based on an individual's choice, influenced by the individual's personal characteristics, their social interactions, and socioeconomic and environmental factors.

LIFO A storeroom storing and issuing policy meaning "last in, first out."

line-item bidding Selecting the vendor who quotes the lowest price for a single product. Also known as *bottom-line bidding*.

line positions Those employees directly involved in the food production or service.

live tanks Similar to freshwater or saltwater aquariums, these holding tanks vary in size, with the largest ones (upwards of 330 gallons) able to hold up to 200–250 pounds of lobster, 150 pounds of catfish, or 100 pounds of trout for approximately one week, and are often placed in the lobby for customers to see.

long-term contracts A contract that makes the supplier responsible for purchasing the needed product for the buyer, and then having it available as needed.

M

make-or-buy decision To decide whether to make a product from scratch, or to purchase it from an outside source.

manufacturers Manufacturers create new products by combining goods from several growers or fabricators.

manufacturer's agents They differ from representatives in that they virtually always work directly for only one manufacturer or fabricator.

manufacturer's representatives They differ from brokers in that they carry products in inventory, set the local price for those products, and usually deliver them directly to the buyer. Also known as *commission houses*.

margarine As a generic term, can indicate any of a wide range of butter substitutes.

market A social arrangement that allows buyers and sellers to discover information and carry out a voluntary exchange; the mechanism that allows for trade.

marketing channel (distribution channel) A system of buyers and sellers that allows for the exchange of goods.

market research The process of systematicly gathering, recording, and analyzing data about ingredients, the market, and potential suppliers.

Maslow's Hierarchy of Needs See *Hierarchy of Needs (Maslow's)*.

meal The texture of milled grain between cracked wheat and flour.

measuring The process of calculating and determining the specific amount of an ingredient required by using a standard measurement device, such as a measuring spoon, measuring cup, or measuring utensil.

meat The flesh of domesticated animals used as food. Most often it references the skeletal muscle and associated fat, but it may also refer to non-muscle organs such as liver, and meat mixtures such as sausages.

Meat Buyer's Guide See *The Meat Buyer's Guide*.

menu analysis The disciplined act of recording the sales history of all menu items sold, and evaluating both the item's contribution to profit and customer appeal.

menu engineering The science of menu analysis and modification used to create a menu that is both profitable to the operation, and acceptable to the customer.

merchant wholesalers Distributors who purchase products from various sources, provide storage, resell them at a profit, and deliver them to the buyer's business.

metrification Introduction of the SI (International System of Units) metric system as the international standard for physical measurements.

micro-greens The plant's first true leaves, replacing the cotyledon leaves, after a seed sprouts. They are usually harvested with stalk or stem attached, making the unit of thin stem and just a few micro-leaves look like a sprout.

minerals Nonliving crystal solids or natural compounds formed through geological processes.

modified atmosphere packaging (MAP) Similar to vacuum-processing, it involves the removing of oxygen from plastic packaging materials that contain perishable foodstuffs in order to extend the shelf life and improve the food quality. A gas is added to prevent oxygen degradation to the foodstuffs.

mollusk Members of the large and diverse phylum *Mollusca*, which includes a variety of familiar animals well-known as seafood, or for their decorative shells. They range from tiny snails, clams, and abalone to larger organisms such as squid, cuttlefish, and the octopus. Mollusks may be either "univalves" (single shell) or "bivalves" (two-shells).

monitor display The term "monitor" usually refers to the entire box, whereas display screen can mean just the screen. Also known as *display screen*.

monoculture The practice of growing the same crop each year on a given acreage.

mushrooms Mushrooms are the reproductive structure of the fungus, called "fruit-bodies," which function much like the flower of a green plant. Unlike green plants, fungi cannot manufacture their own food and instead create an extensive network of filaments (called *mycelium*), which convert organic materials (called *substrates*) into compounds absorbable by the fungi. Successful cultivation produces an abundant harvest of the fungal fruit-bodies we collectively call "mushrooms."

N

NAMP North American Meat Processor's Association.

National Shellfish Sanitation Program See *Shellfish Sanitation Program*.

natural casings Sausage casings consisting of a piece of animal (mainly pork or lamb) intestine or the lining of a pig's intestine (a thin, transparent membrane or caul that is veined with fat).

negotiate To discuss a matter of business with a view to reach agreement between all parties.

nonexempt employees Those employees that are covered by Fair Labor Standards Act (FLSA) protections, and must be paid at time-and-a-half their normal hourly rate for any hours worked above forty in one work week.

nut Various fruits having a hard outer shell enclosing a kernel (also called a nut), while "seeds" are contained in the fruits of plants and are capable of producing a new plant when released from the fleshy part of the fruit.

nutritional value The measured nourishment gained by consuming an ingredient or combination of ingredients.

Nutrition Labeling and Education Act Requires that food manufacturers include nutrition information on all packaged foods.

O

offal Consists of the edible nonmuscular parts of slaughter animals. Offal is generally broken down into organ meats; red offal (heart, tongue, lungs or "lights," liver, and kidneys) and white offal (brains, marrow, testicles or "mountain oysters," feet, thymus or "sweetbreads," head, and tripe). Also called *variety meats*.

operating budget Financial plan that forecasts the estimated expenses that will be incurred in achieving estimated sales revenues.

optimal purchasing The concept of matching the specific characteristics of the product to the specific needs of the business.

ordering cost The total operating expenses of the purchasing and receiving departments, expenses of purchase orders and invoice payment, and data processing costs for purchasing and inventory.

organic Organic food is produced according to certain production standards and without the use of synthetic chemicals. For crops, it means they were grown without the use of conventional pesticides, artificial fertilizers, human waste, or sewage sludge, and that they were processed without ionizing radiation or food additives.

Organic Foods Production Act Calls for national organic food guidelines, including: certification of growers and standards for organic food production, monitoring crops for chemical contamination and livestock for living conditions, and screening organic imports.

organizational charts A document showing the arrangement of staff according to traditional vertical and horizontal lines of authority and responsibility.

oven drying The simplest method of drying food, as it requires almost no special equipment, except what is already available in a commercial kitchen. It tends to be a lot faster than sun drying, and is generally more reliable.

P

P&D Peeled and de-veined; usually refers to processing shrimp.

packer's brand A packer's brand system is essentially that particular food processor's personal grading system, often used in lieu of the government's federal quality grade.

packing medium The packing medium can be salted water, natural juices, heavy syrup, or oil, and is used to protect the primary ingredient from damage while in the can.

palatable A food that is pleasant or acceptable to the taste or mind.

par stock A "partial stock" located near the main kitchen for access by the kitchen staff.

pasta filata cheeses These cheeses are produced by kneading and stretching the curd, known as "stringing," which is stored in water until the desired consistency is obtained. This process gives them a slightly rubbery texture.

pathogens An agent that causes disease, especially a living microorganism such as a bacterium or fungus.

pellicle A tacky film that forms on the surface of smoked foods, consisting of numerous tiny droplets of various natural chemicals, such as aldehydes, phenols, ketones, and carbolic acid that condense.

personal digital assistant (PDA) A portable computer that is small enough to be carried in the pocket, and then held in the palm for immediate use when needed. It is powerful enough to exchange data with a larger, desktop computer system via cable, modem, or wireless connectivity.

perpetual inventory An estimation of the stock that is supposed to be held in inventory, based on records. A perpetual inventory is constantly maintained, and adjusted each time product is added or deducted from the inventory. Also known as *virtual inventory.*

personal handheld device (PHD) A pocket-sized computing device, typically utilizing a small visual display screen for user output and a miniature keyboard for user input. Also commonly uses a line-of-sight infrared light to scan bar codes and communicate with other infrared storage devices.

pH levels pH is defined as a measure of free acidity. (The pH value is a direct function of the free hydrogen ions present in that food. Acids present in foods release these hydrogen ions, which give acid foods their distinct sour flavors.) The range of pH is commonly considered to extend from 0 to 14. A pH value of 7 is neutral because pure water has a pH value of exactly 7. Values less than 7 are considered acidic, while those greater than 7 are considered basic or alkaline.

physical hazard Physical hazards in food processing can include such objects as metal fragments, nuts and bolts, glass and plastic, wood splinters, nut shells and fruit pits, and bone fragments.

physical inventory The counting of stock done physically in the storeroom and coolers among the stored goods. It requires a complete accounting of all items still in inventory, Also known as *periodic* or *actual inventory.*

pick-slip Initiated by requisitions, and printed by the storeroom staff, it is used in collecting the requisitioned items from their storage locations.

plate costs The total of all ingredients appearing on the same plate, including the "center of the plate" item.

policies and procedures manual A living document used to provide guidance to the staff in matters such as purchasing, receiving, storing, and issuing.

poultry Refers to edible birds domestically raised for human consumption.

prepared meats The products intended for human food which are obtained by subjecting meat to drying, curing, smoking, cooking, grinding, seasoning, or flavoring, or to any combination of such procedures, and to which no considerable quantity of any substance other than meat or meat byproducts has been added.

preserving food The process of treating and handling food in such a way as to stop or greatly slow down spoilage to prevent foodborne illness while maintaining nutritional value, density, texture, and flavor.

pressure canner method Jars of food are heated under pressure to 240°F (116°C), a temperature above boiling.

prime costs The sum of direct materials and direct labor expended by a business to derive income.

prime vendor Sellers agreeing to sell their products at a set price, often based on cost plus fixed-fee, to the buyer; similar to a cost plus fixed-fee contract.

printer A device that accepts text and graphic output from a computer and transfers the information to paper, usually to standard size sheets of paper. Printers vary in size, speed, sophistication, and cost.

process cheeses These cheeses are made from one or a blend of pressed cheeses (cooked or uncooked) that are re-melted and to which milk, cream, or butter is added.

procurement The orderly and systematic exchange of payment, for goods or services, between the buyer and the seller.

product rejection The action by the receiving staff to purposely elect to refuse acceptance of a delivery. When a product fails to meet the quality standards of a food service establishment, the operator has the right to reject the delivered product before signing acceptance of the delivery. Also known as *rejecting.*

product specifications A statement of all the factors required in a product to satisfy a purchase need. It typically includes product information that can be validated upon delivery, and that can be communicated clearly between the buyers and the sellers.

production reports An instrument of control used to record the activity surrounding all prepared menu items.

profit and loss statement (P&L) A detailed listing of the revenue and expenses for a given time. Also known as an *income statement.*

property A societal convention that means "one's own thing."

pulses Annual leguminous crops yielding from one to twelve grains or seeds of variable size, shape, and color within a pod.

purchase order (P.O.) A business document issued by the buyer to the seller, indicating the products, quantities, and agreed prices for products or services that the seller will provide to the buyer.

purchase requisition An internal document, used by businesses that have formal purchasing departments or storeroom operations, which detail the specifications of desired equipment or materials not normally carried by the storeroom.

purveyor A supplier with goods or services for sale. Also known as a *vendor, seller,* or *supplier.*

Q

quality (food) A combination of the inherent properties of a product which determines its relative degree of excellence.

quality grade A composite evaluation of factors that affect palatability of meat (tenderness, juiciness, and flavor). These factors include carcass maturity, firmness, texture, and color of lean, and the amount and distribution of marbling within the lean.

quality standards A preset list of agreed-upon measurable values that companies use to measure goods and services.

R

radura The international symbol, located on the packaging, which indicates food has been "Treated with Radiation" or "Treated by Irradiation."

receiving Involves many duties by the clerk or chef, including verifying the delivered order by inspecting the product for quality, wholesomeness, and count; confirming the order matches established product specifications; obtaining any required credit memo; checking the math calculations; properly storing the products; and filing the paperwork immediately.

receiving clerk The person primarily responsible for the receipt and storage of all food items and equipment received by the food service operation. It is the receiving clerk's responsibility to inspect all products being delivered, and to determine if they match the product specifications required by the food service organization.

reciprocity When a company purchases from a source when it is otherwise advantageous for the company to do so.

recycling To extract useful materials from (garbage or waste). The three R's of recycling include reduce, reuse, and recycle.

rennet Product made from rennin, the enzyme secreted by the lining of a calf's stomach. Rennet is used in the cheese-making process.

revenues Income resulting from the exchange of products and services for value.

Right-To-Know regulations Rules instituted by the federal, state, and municipal governments to inform all hospitality employees and to protect them against any potentially harmful chemicals.

rigid packaging Forms of rigid packaging include crates, glass bottles, and metal cans.

ripening A process in fruit that causes them to become more edible. In general, a fruit becomes sweeter, less acidic, less green, and softer as it ripens.

roasting (coffee beans) Transforms the chemical and physical properties of green coffee beans into roasted coffee products. When roasted, the green coffee bean expands to nearly double its original size, changing in color and density. As the bean absorbs heat, the color shifts to yellow and then to a light "cinnamon" brown, then to a dark and oily color. During roasting, oils appear on the surface of the bean. The roast color will continue to darken until it is removed from the heat source.

roe The eggs or the egg-laden ovary of a fish, often having a grainy texture. Also means the egg mass or spawn of certain crustaceans, such as the lobster. Caviar is the salted roe of sturgeon.

roundfish Any ordinary market fish with a rounded body and eyes on both sides of its head. Roundfish are the most common type of fish, and populate both fresh waters and salt waters.

russeting A brown, corky netlike condition on the skin of apples. It may appear on only a small portion of each fruit, or may cover its surface. Severe russeting may be accompanied by fruit cracking which usually renders the fruit useless.

S

safety stock The minimum quantity of product that must be available in storeroom inventory at all times.

sanitation Refers to the creation and maintenance of conditions that will prevent food contamination or foodborne illness.

scale Mechanical or electronic equipment used to accurately measure the weight of an ingredient or product.

scanner A type of optical scanner that consists of a flat surface on which documents are layed to be scanned. Flatbed scanners are particularly effective for bound documents.

Scoville Heat Units The Scoville Heat Unit (SHU) scale is used to assess the heat level of chile peppers. The Scoville unit is a measure based on the amount of dilution; the higher the Scoville unit, the hotter the chile.

sealed bid Goods or services, offered at a specific price for a specific period of time, confidentially submitted to a company by an announced deadline, and then publicly opened by the buyer.

seasonality Food is grown or raised during a specific period of the calendar year. Generally speaking, climate and soil conditions have the greatest impact on plant life, while the birthing season dictates animal and seafood production.

seitan A protein-rich food made from wheat gluten. It has a firm, chewy texture and bland flavor suitable for mixing and cooking with other flavors and ingredients.

selection Choosing from among many alternatives.

selling To exchange goods or services for money.

semi-flexible packaging An example of semi-flexible packaging is the paperboard boxes in which cereal and many other food products are packaged. Semi-flexible plastics are also used as tray packs for cookies, crackers, and soft foods.

servable weight The weight or volume of the primary product, less the packing medium (which can be salted water, natural juices, heavy syrup, or oil), measured separately.

service contracts A business arrangement, between two or more parties, that details specific work for specific compensation.

shellfish Any of many species of aquatic invertebrates with shells or carapaces found in saltwater and freshwater regions worldwide. They are categorized as either crustaceans or mollusks.

Shellfish Sanitation Program All interstate shipments of fresh and frozen clams, mussels, and oysters are supervised by the Food and Drug Administration (FDA) to ensure that only uncontaminated product reaches the consumer, as part of their National Shellfish Sanitation Program.

shelf life The length of time product can exist in storage without perceived deterioration.

shrinkage The difference between the actual inventory at the end of the accounting period and the balance in the perpetual inventory identifies the amount of goods that are (a) not at hand and (b) were not sold.

Siamese twins of management A system of planning and controls used by management to ensure the business accomplishes its goals.

single-source buying The buyer orders what is needed from one source with the hope that the price and quality are favorable.

Slow Food Movement Founded in 1986 by Carlo Petrini, Slow Food's main tenet is to protect "the right to taste." Protecting taste means protecting artisan foods and food products, promoting sustainable agriculture, preserving food traditions, educating people about quality foods and enjoying the slow life—good friends, good food, and good wine.

smoke point The temperature at which the oil begins to decompose and visible fumes (smoke) are given off. The oil begins to breakdown creating *acreolein*, an obnoxious-smelling compound.

soft cheeses These cheeses are ripened for a relatively short period of time before being drained and turned into molds without being pressed or cooked. They have moisture content of 50 to 60 percent and their fat content represents 20 to 26 percent of the cheese's weight.

soft drink Originally applied to carbonated drinks and noncarbonated drinks made from concentrates, although it now commonly refers to almost any cold drink that does not contain alcohol.

sources Products originate from three major sources (where things are first created) that supply wares to the food service industry. These sources include the growers, manufacturers, and fabricators.

spices Spices come from the bark, roots, buds, seeds, berry, or the fruit of tropical plants and trees.

sous vide A method of cooking food at a specific temperature while under vacuum pressure.

staff position Employees in support of others who are directly involved in food production or sales.

standing order (S.O.) An established contract from a buyer for repetitive or specified services or items from a single supplier.

standardized recipes The measured use of tightly specified ingredients prepared and cooked in a consistent manner; written to ensure regularity in costs, preparation, appearance, taste, and yield.

statement of cash flows One of the main financial statements, it reports the cash generated and used during a specific time interval, often a month or three-month period.

stockouts The lack of available product in inventory needed to fill requisitions with specific product requests.

stone fruits Stone fruits all have pits in the center, and include peaches, nectarines, cherries, plums, apricots, and newer hybrids such as pluots (plum-apricot), and peacotums (peach-apricot-plum).

storeroom assistants Storeroom assistants perform a wide variety of tasks for the storeroom. They may help portion items purchased in bulk, such as cheese and nuts, pick items for issue, and assist during inventory. They are responsible for maintaining the sanitation of the storeroom facilities, including mopping the coolers and washing the sinks.

storeroom manager The individual who supervises and coordinates the activities of all workers concerned with storeroom operations, including the ordering, receiving, storing, inventorying, issuing, and delivering of the food, materials, supplies, tools and equipment. Also known as *stockroom manager*.

storeroom requisition The formal document completed by the production staff to request food and supplies from the storeroom. Also known as *product requisition*.

storing The act of placing food, beverages, supplies, and equipment in their proper location, as determined by their need for refrigeration, air, light, water, and security.

sugar spotting A crystallization of sugars under the skin and in the flesh of dried fruits.

sulphured Many commercially dried fruits are sulfured with sulfur dioxide (so2) or meta bisulfate to keep them from oxidizing during and after the drying process. To sulfur the fruits, they are put into a room in which the mineral rock sulfur is burned to produce sulfur dioxide gas that permeates the fruits. This process preserves their original color.

sun drying The ancient method used to dry food; it uses the warmth from the sun and the natural movement of the air to dehydrate the food.

supply and demand In economics, supply and demand describes the market relationship between prospective sellers and buyers of a product. It is based on the amount of product available in relationship to the interest in the product; a greater interest, or a limited supply, can both increase the selling price.

surface-ripened soft cheeses These cheeses are covered with a thin layer of a white down or mold that is satiny in appearance. Examples include Camembert, Brie, Brillat-Savarin, Coulommiers; this rind is edible but should be removed if its flavor is too pronounced.

sustainable agriculture Farming that provides a secure living for farm families; maintains the natural environment and resources; supports the rural community; and offers respect and fair treatment to all involved, from farm workers to consumers to the animals raised for food.

sweetbreads The name for the thymus gland of the calf and the lamb; a whitish gland found only in young animals, because it atrophies with age. Located at the entrance to the chest, below the windpipe, the thymus gland consists of two parts: a central lobe known as the "heart sweetbread" or "kernel," and two lateral lobes known as the "throat sweetbread."

synthetic casings Sausage casings made from collagen (edible) or cellulose (inedible); have almost completely replaced natural casings.

systems of measurement A specific means used to quantify volume or weight with vessels or scales and recording by use of established U.S. Customary or Metric numerical systems.

T

tempeh A cake of soybeans prepared by removing the hulls of cooked soya beans, mixing with a culture of *Rhizopus oligosporus* or *Rhizopus oryzae* (tempeh starter), and then aging and fermenting for a day or two.

temperature danger zone The Temperature Danger Zone refers to the broad range of temperatures between 41–135°F (5–57°C) when most bacteria that cause foodborne illnesses multiply rapidly.

tempered A process involving heating and cooling chocolate to stabilize the cocoa butter crystals into more uniform size. The resultant chocolate is hardened, shiny, smooth, and unblemished by bloom.

terroir A term usually associated with wine, but is also appropriate for tea. It is the sum of sun, soil, precipitation, temperature, and elevation in a specific area that conspires to produce particular qualities in tea leaves or grapes peculiar to that area or region.

textured vegetable proteins (TVPs) A meat substitute made from defatted soybeans that are often found in prepared vegetarian foods. TVP's texture is similar to ground beef, so it's a natural for tacos, casseroles, and stews.

The Meat Buyer's Guide A publication of the North American Meat Processor's Association that identifies specific food service cuts. These codes describe the exact trim dimensions and weight ranges for each cut of beef, lamb, veal, pork, chicken, turkey, duck/goose, and game birds.

tofu Tofu is made by grinding soybeans in water, extracting the liquid, adding a coagulant (such as nagari or calcium sulfate) to create curds, and then straining to separate the curds from the whey to create a solid block of tofu. Tofu is sold in block form (light, medium, firm, or extra firm press) or in smooth liquid form (silken).

trade The voluntary exchange of goods and services, or both. Also known as *commerce*.

tripe A food made from the stomachs of cud-chewing animals (beef, mutton, and veal prepared in various ways), but the word "tripe" also refers to the intestines of butchered animals.

tropicals Considered those fruits that are native to the world's tropical and subtropical climates.

U

Uniform Commercial Code (UCC) One of the uniform acts that has been promulgated in attempts to harmonize the law of sales and other commercial transactions in all 50 states within the United States. The overriding philosophy of the UCC is to allow people to make the contracts they want, but to fill in any missing provisions where the agreements they make are silent. The law also seeks to impose uniformity and streamlining of routine transactions like the processing of checks, notes, and other routine commercial paper.

Uniform System of Accounts for Restaurants Developed by the National Restaurant Association, it is designed to include all forms of revenues and expenses common to food service operations.

univalve These mollusks have a single shell. The animal lives inside the shell and often has a shell-like plate that can be closed over the opening. Conch and abalone are univalves.

U.S. Code The official record of all federal laws; its database is available from the Government Printing Office (GPO).

U.S. Department of Agriculture (USDA) Responsible for the safety of meat, poultry, and egg products.

USDA Quality Grades See *quality grades*.

V

vacuum packing (sealing) A vacuum sealer removes air from a bag or a container, creating a vacuum, and then seals it (for bags a heated strip actually melts the plastic sides together). The vacuum environment removes atmospheric oxygen and any free moisture making it very difficult for bacteria or fungus to grow, thus preventing the food from spoiling.

variable costs Costs that can often be adjusted through proper controls. They may be controlled, to some degree, by management. Also known as *controllable costs.*

variety meats Consists of the edible nonmuscular parts of slaughter animals. Variety meats are generally broken down into organ meats; red offal (heart, tongue, lungs or "lights," liver, and kidneys) and white offal (brains, marrow, testicles or "mountain oysters," feet, thymus or "sweetbreads," head, and tripe). Also known as *offal.*

veal The meat from a calf or young beef animal. A veal calf is raised until about 16 to 18 weeks of age, weighing up to 450 pounds.

vegan(ism) A way of living that seeks to exclude, as far as possible and practical, all forms of exploitation of, and cruelty to, animals for food, clothing, or any other purpose. In dietary terms, it refers to the practice of dispensing with all animal produce, including: meat, fish, poultry, eggs, animal milks, honey, and their derivatives.

vegetable Any herbaceous crop grown for parts that can be eaten fresh or processed. Vegetables can include leaves (spinach), stems (asparagus), roots (carrots), flowers (broccoli), bulbs (garlic), seeds (peas and beans), and the botanical fruits like avocados, cucumbers, pumpkins, and squash.

vegetable shortening Created by the complete hydrogenation of vegetable oil. (Hydrogenation is the process of forcing hydrogen atoms into the holes of unsaturated fatty acids.)

vegetarian A vegetarian is someone living on a diet of grains, pulses, nuts, seeds, vegetables, and fruits with or without the use of dairy products and eggs (preferably free-range). A vegetarian does not eat any meat, poultry, game, fish, shellfish or crustacea, or slaughter by-products such as gelatin or animal fats. The word was derived from the Latin *vegetus,* meaning whole, sound, fresh, and lively.

vendor dishonesty Purposely misleading the buyer, by a vendor, by delivering inferior products to those which were ordered, shorting the deliveries by weight or count, or billing for products neither sold nor ordered.

vendor error The unwitting sending of products or invoices, by a vendor, that are either flawed in price, quantity, or quality.

venison Meat from any of the deer family, including elk, moose, reindeer, red-tailed deer, whitetailed ricer, and mule deer.

vinegar Comes from the French *vin aigre,* or sour wine, and it is also used to describe other soured, alcohol-based liquids, such as those made from cider, malt, or rice wine.

volume buying and warehousing The ability to negotiate a contract for large quantities of singular products to be received over an extended period of time. Also known as *stockless purchasing.*

W

weight A term of measurement referring to either an object's mass or to the gravitational force acting on the object.

weighted average The average cost of the same items held currently in inventory. The inventory value is calculated based on the total quantity of like products purchased at different unit prices times the average cost of purchase. The average price is weighted according to the quantity of products available in inventory that are purchased at each price.

weight tag A small document attached to individual large portions of expensive products, such as beef tenderloin or whole salmon. Used to charge actual weight/costs to departments upon issue of product, and to track their usage for loss prevention. Also known as *fish tag* or *meat tag.*

wet-age The meat is sealed in Cryovac® and set aside for a period of time. Natural enzymes break down the proteins, but without any loss in weight. Wet-aged steaks are often just as tender as dry aged meat, and because they retain more water, they're juicer than dry-aged steaks.

whey The liquid by-product of the cheese-making process; an ingredient in crackers, cakes, and processed foods.

wild mushrooms There are several thousand varieties of wild mushrooms. Some are poisonous and some are edible and delicious when properly prepared. The edibility of the majority is either not known, or they are not considered for food because of their small size, poor flavor, or texture.

wine An alcoholic beverage produced by the fermentation of the juice of fruits, usually grapes.

word of mouth marketing Operators use the Internet and social media sources to communicate their food business, and often reduce their advertising expenditures.

Y

yeast A microscopic fungus that converts its food (carbohydrates) into carbon dioxide and alcohol through a metabolic process called fermentation. It comes in several forms, including active dry yeast, instant dry yeast, brewer's yeast, and compressed yeast.

yield The amount of fully prepared, ready to consume food product that should result if directions for a specific recipe or procedure are properly followed.

yield cost analysis The purpose of a yield cost analysis is to determine the edible portion cost (EP cost), which is also known as the serving portion cost (SP cost) or plate cost, of a recipe. The data required for this calculation are the purchase price of the ingredients and their edible yield.

yield grades Yield grades estimate the amount of boneless, closely trimmed retail cuts from the high-value parts of the carcass: the round, loin, rib, and chuck. However, they also show differences in the total yield of retail cuts. (The USDA Yield Grades of beef are rated numerically and are 1, 2, 3, 4, and 5. Yield Grade 1 denotes the highest yielding carcass and Yield Grade 5, the lowest.)

yogurt A dairy product produced by bacterial fermentation of milk. Fermentation of the milk sugar (lactose) produces lactic acid, which acts on milk protein to give yogurt its gel-like texture and its characteristic tang.

The following publications were used as resources for writing this textbook.

Chapter 1

Coltman, M.M. *Hospitality Industry Purchasing.* New York: Van Nostrand Reinhold, 1990.

Feinstein, A.H., and Stefanelli, J.M. *Purchasing: Selection and Procurement for the Hospitality Industry,* 6th Ed. Hoboken, NJ: John Wiley & Sons, 2005.

Gunn, M. (1992). Professionalism in Purchasing. *School Food Service Journal,* 46 (9), 32–34.

Harrison, J.S., and Enz, C.A. *Hospitality Strategic Management: Concepts and Cases.* Hoboken, NJ: John Wiley & Sons, 2005.

Kotschevar, L.H., and Donnelly, R. *Quantity Food Purchasing,* 5th Ed. Upper Saddle River, NJ: Prentice Hall, 1998.

Neef, D. *e-Procurement: From Strategy to Implementation.* Upper Saddle River, NJ: Prentice Hall, 2001.

Paquette, L. *The Sourcing Solution: A Step-By-Step Guide to Creating a Successful Purchasing Program.* New York: AMACOM, 2004.

Peddersen, R.B. *Food Service and Hotel Purchasing.* Boston: CBI Publishing, 1981.

Shapiro, R.M., Jankowski, M.A., Dale, J., and Ripkin, C. *The Power of Nice: How to Negotiate So Everyone Wins—Especially You.* New York: John Wiley & Sons, 2001.

Spears, M.C. *Purchasing for Profit.* Upper Saddle River, NJ: Prentice Hall, 1999.

Spears, M.C., and Gregoire, M.B. *Food service Organizations,* 5th Ed. Upper Saddle River, NJ: Prentice Hall, 2003.

Walker, J.R. *Introduction to Hospitality Management.* Upper Saddle River, NJ: Prentice Hall, 2004.

Warfel, M.C., and Cremer, M. *Purchasing for Food Service Managers,* 5th Ed. Berkeley, CA: McCutchan Publishing Corporation, 2005.

Virts, W.B. *Purchasing for Hospitality Operations.* East Lansing, MI: Educational Institute of the American Hotel & Motel Association, 1987.

http://www.sba.gov

http://en.wikipedia.org/wiki/Food

http://www.ams.usda.gov/nop/

Chapter 2

Coltman, M.M. *Hospitality Industry Purchasing.* New York: Van Nostrand Reinhold, 1990.

Feinstein, A.H., and Stefanelli, J.M. *Purchasing: Selection and Procurement for the Hospitality Industry,* 6th Ed. Hoboken, NJ: John Wiley & Sons, 2005.

Potter, N.N. *Food Science,* 4th Ed. Westport, CT: AVI Publishing Company, 1986.

Spears, M.C. *Purchasing for Profit.* Upper Saddle River, NJ: Prentice Hall, 1999.

Virts, W.B. *Purchasing for Hospitality Operations.* East Lansing, MI: Educational Institute of the American Hotel & Motel association, 1987.

Walker, L. (2006). Codex Alimentarius Demystified. *Natural Awakenings Healthy Living,* November, pp. 14–15.

World Health Organization. *More Than 30 New Food Safety Standards Adopted,* news release, July 6, 2009.

http://www.usda.gov/wps/portal/usdahome

http://vm.cfsan.fda.gov/list.html

www.cfsan.fda.gov/label.html

http://www.fsis.usda.gov/Food_Safety_Education/

http://www.fda.gov/oc/bioterrorism/bioact.html

http://www.ams.usda.gov/farmersmarkets/facts.htm

http://www.ams.usda.gov/nop/archive/OFPA.html

http://www.census.gov/mrts/www/efaq.html

http://www.organicconsumers.org/organic/newyork102703.cfm

http://www.csacenter.org

http://www.fda.gov/FoodGuidanceComplianceRegulatoryInformation/GuidanceDocuments

Chapter 3

The Culinary Institute of America (Ed.). The Professional Chef, 7th Ed. New York: John Wiley & Sons, 2002.

Devine, M.M., and Pimentel, M.H. *Dimensions of Food.* Westport, CT: AVI Publishing Company, 1985.

Eilperin, J. (2007). At the End of the Line. *WashingtonPost.com,* May 2.

French, S., Story, M., & Jeffery, R. (2001). Environmental Influences on Eating and Physical Activity. *Annual Review of Public Health,* 22, 309–335.

Grossman, D. (2007) Farming for Freshness and Health. *The National Culinary Review,* June, 14–18.

Kant, A., & Graubard, B. (2004). Eating Out in America, 1987–2000: Trends and Nutritional Correlates. *Preventive Medicine,* 38, 243–249.

Kittler, P., and Sucher, K. *Food and Culture in America.* New York: Van Nostrand Reinhold, 1989.

Spears, M.C. *Purchasing for Profit.* Upper Saddle River, NJ: Prentice Hall, 1999.

Terry, L. (2002). Building a Better Menu. *Hospitality Technology.* Retrieved from http://www.htmagazine.com/archive/june2002/june2002_7.html.

Wansink, B. (2004). Environmental Factors That Increase the Food Intake and Consumption Volume of Unknowing Customers. *Annual Review of Nutrition,* 24, 455–479.

Warfel, M.C., and Cremer, M. *Purchasing for Food Service Managers,* 3rd Ed. Berkeley, CA: McCutchan Publishing Corporation, 1996.

Williams, F. (2007). US Proposes Global Ban on Fishing Aid. *FT.com,* May 1.

http://www.cfsan.fda.gov/~lrd/haccp.html

http://www.slowfoodusa.org/raft/initiatives.html#a

http://ft.com/cm/s

http://www.seafoodwatch.org

http://www.oceansalive.org/eat.cfm

http://www.blueocean.org/welcome.html

http://www.msc.org

http://www.docstoc.com/docs/9099015/The-Restauran

Chapter 4

Allen, P. *Food for the Future.* New York: John Wiley & Sons, 1993.

Bennion, M., and Scheule, B. *Introductory Foods,* 12th Ed. Upper Saddle River, NJ: Prentice-Hall, 2004.

Berry, W. "The Pleasures of Eating." *What Are People For?: Essays.* Harper Collins Canada, Ltd., 1990, 145.

Briefly Noted. *Food Ingredient News,* August 2003.

Charles, D. *Lords of the Harvest.* Cambridge, MA: Perseus Publishing, 2001.

Clark, R. (Ed.) *Our Sustainable Table.* San Francisco: North Point Press, 1990.

Cloud, J. My Search for the Perfect Apple. *Time,* March 12, 2007, 42–50.

Devine, M.M., and Pimentel, M.H. *Dimensions of Food.* Westport, CT: AVI Publishing Company, 1985.

Eilperin, J. At the End of the Line. *WashingtonPost.com,* May 2, 2007.

Envirolink. Green Restaurant Association. December 2004. Available from: http://www.envirolink.org/resource.html?catid=5&itemid=860516214793.

Foley, Michael. 2013: FENI Futurists Mini-Conference held on February 15, 2003 in Chicago, Illinois.

Horovitz, B. Can Restaurants Go Green, Earn Green? *ABC News,* May 15, 2008.

Kittler, P., and Sucher, K. *Food and Culture in America.* New York: Van Nostrand Reinhold, 1989.

Lambrecht, B. *Dinner at the New Gene Café.* New York: St. Martin's Press, 2001.

McWilliams, M. *Foods: Experimental Perspectives.* Upper Saddle River, NJ: Prentice Hall, 2001.

Mepham, B. (Ed.). *Food Ethics.* London: Routledge, 1996.

Orr, D. (1991). What Is Education For? *The Learning Revolution,* 27, 52.

Pollack, A., and Martin, A. F.D.A. Tentatively Declares Food From Cloned Animals to Be Safe. *The New York Times,* December 29, 2006.

Robson, J.R.K. (Ed.). *Food, Ecology and Culture.* New York: Gordon and Breach Science Publishers, 1980.

Shee, J. Shape Your Culinary Footprint: Do Chefs Have a Debt to Consumers and the Planet? *Sizzle Magazine,* 4, Winter 2006, 14–16.

Singh, R.P., and Heldman, D.R. *Introduction to Food Engineering,* 3rd Ed. Chestnut Hill, MA: Academic Press, 2001.

Symons, M. *A History of Cooks and Cooking.* Champaign, IL: University of Illinois Press, 2000.

Tork USA. (2009). Green Dining: Catering for Environmental Health. Interview with Chris Moyer, NRA. *TorkUSA.com.*

Toussaint-Samat, M. *History of Food.* Cambridge, MA: Blackwell Publishers, 1992.

Trager, J. *The Food Chronology.* New York: Henry Holt and Company, 1995.

Waters, A. (1989). "The Farm-Restaurant Connection." *The Journal of Gastronomy,* 5 (2).

Welti-Chanes, J. et al. (Eds.). *Engineering and Food for the 21st Century.* Boca Raton, FL: CRC Press, 2002.

Zaccarelli, H. *Management Without Reservations: Leadership Principles for the Manager's Life Journey.* Lincoln, NE: iUniverse, 2007.

http://www.foodallergy.org/research.html
http://www.wfp.org,
http://www.timesonline.co.uk
http://www.gainhealth.org,
http://www.health.gov/dietaryguidelines
http://www.obviously.COM/recycle
http://www.washingtonpost.com
http://www.seafoodwatch.org
http://www.oceansalive.org/eat.cfm
http://www.msc.org
http://www.blueocean.org/welcome.html
http:// www.micro-climes.co.uk www.emcarthur.com
http://www.onlinepot.org/hyrdoponics
http://www.commercial-hydroponics.com
http://www.bbc.co.uk/schools/gcsebitesize/biology/livingthings.com
http://www.thecampaign.org/index.php
http://ccr.ucdavis.edu/biot/what/index.shtml
http://www.thecampaign.org/index.php
http://www.iht.com/articles/2006/12/29/business/food.php
http://www.bio.org/foodag/priorities/fact4.asp
http://www.ar.gov/ha/nutrition/
http://www.bio.org/foodag/priorities/fact4.asp
http://www.endocrinology.org
http://www.jifsr.org/topics/tpfdirrad.htm
http://www.env.qld.gov.au/cultural_heritage/
http://culturalheritage.utah.gov/index.html
http://darwin.bio.uci.edu/~sustain/bio65/lec01/b65lec01.htm
http://historymatters.gmu.edu
http://www.emcarthur.com/shrpduck/resource/book_003_HistoryOf Hydroponics/book_003_HistoryOfHydroponics.htm
http://www.oneota.net/~foodcoop/organic.html
http://www.ams.usda.gov
http://www.conserve.restaurant.org
http://www.enn.com/wildlife/article/36390
http://www.okspecialtyfruits.com/mb-industry-growth-statistics.php
http://www.unicef.org/mdg
http://one.wfp.org/country_brief/hunger_map/facts.html

Chapter 5

Ball/Alltrista Corporation. *Ball Blue Book* (Vol. 1). Muncie, IN: Ball/Alltrista Corporation, 1995.

Centers for Disease Control and Prevention. Foodborne Illness. October 25, 2005. Available from: http://www.cdc.gov/ncidod/dbmd/diseaseinfo/foodborneinfections_g.htm.

Garlough, R., and Campbell, A. *Modern Garde Manger.* Clifton Park, NY: Thomson Delmar Learning, 2006.

Greene, J., Hertzberg, R., and Vaughn, B. *Putting Food By,* 4th Ed.. Lexington, MA: The Stephen Greene Press, 1992.

Home Economics Library Program, *Preserving Food Safely* (V. 3). Cooperative Extension Service, Michigan State University.

Kuhn, G.D., and Resurricion, A.V.A. *How to Freeze the Right Way.* Cooperative Extension Service, The Pennsylvania State University.

Kurlansky, M. *Salt: A World History.* New York: Penguin Books, 2002.

Shephard, S. *Pickled, Potted, and Canned: How the Art and Science of Food Preserving Changed the World.* New York: Simon & Schuster, 2000.

Soroka, W. *Fundamentals of Packaging Technology,* 2nd Ed. Institute of Packaging Professionals, 2000.

So Easy to Preserve, 3rd Ed. Cooperative Extension Service, University of Georgia, 1993.

Strianese, A.J., and Strianese, P.P. *Math Principles for Food Service Occupations,* 5th Ed. Clifton Park, NY: Thomson Delmar Learning, 2007.

http://www.mealtime.org/default.aspx?id=316
http://www.foodreference.com/html/artcanninghistory.html
http://www.ext.vt.edu/pub/foods
http://web.aces.uiuc.edu
http://essence-of-life-com
http://www.fao.org
http://www.e-packaging.com
http://edis.at.ufl.edu
http://www.dupagehealth.org
http://www.cvpsystems.com
http://www.ianr.unl.edu
http://161.58.185.53/food/freezingfoods.html
http://www.preservefood.com
http://www.coe.uh.edu
http://www.cypsystems.com/packaging.html
http://www.wsu.ed
http://www.foodreference.com
http://www.nasm.edu
http://sarasota.extension.ufl.edu
http://foodhistorynews.com
http://dbs.extension.iastate.edu

Chapter 6

Bennion, M., and Scheule, B. *Introductory Foods,* 12th Ed. Upper Saddle River, NJ: Prentice-Hall, 2004.

Coltman, M.M. *Hospitality Industry Purchasing.* New York: Van Nostrand Reinhold, 1990.

Cost, B. *Bruce Cost's Asian Ingredients.* New York: William Morrow and Company, 1988.

Feinstein, A.H., and Stefanelli, J.M. *Purchasing: Selection and Procurement for the Hospitality Industry,* 6th Ed. Hoboken, NJ: John Wiley & Sons, 2005.

Garlough, R., and Campbell, A. *Modern Garde Manger.* Clifton Park, NY: Thomson Delmar Learning, 2006.

Kotschevar, L.H. and Donnelly, R. *Quantity Food Purchasing,* 5th Ed. Upper Saddle River, NJ: Prentice Hall, 1998.

Mooney, J. (2006) A Convenience Truth, *Sizzle,* 3, Fall, pp. 18–21.

Pavesic, D.V., and Magnant, P.F. *Fundamental Principles of Restaurant Cost Control,* 2nd Ed. Upper Saddle River, NJ: Prentice Hall, 2005.

Spears, M.C. *Purchasing for Profit.* Upper Saddle River, NJ: Prentice Hall, 1999.

Wade, M.A. (2005). Balancing Acts: Food service Manufacturers Are Trying to Juggle Quality, Cost, Convenience, and Health. *Prepared Foods,* Nov.

Warfel, M.C., and Cremer, M. *Purchasing for Food Service Managers,* 5th Ed. Berkeley, CA: McCutchan Publishing Corporation, 2005.

Virts, W.B. *Purchasing for Hospitality Operations.* East Lansing, MI: Educational Institute of the American Hotel & Motel Association, 1987.

http://www.fsis.usda.gov/Fact_Sheets/Inspection_&_Grading/index.asp
http://www.pma.com/template
http://capmic.org
http://business.gourt.com
http://www.tpub.com
http://www.fcsi.org
http://hireachef.com
http://www.digiprisma.de/usdameatgrades
http://www.preparedfoods.com/articles/newsletter-business/BNP

Chapter 7

Bensky, G. (2001) Irradiation Using Electricity May Ease Resistance to Food Safety Procedure. *Nation's Restaurant News,* November 12.

Chesser, J.W. *The Art and Science of Culinary Preparation.* St. Augustine, FL: The Educational Institute of the American Culinary Federation, 1992.

Coltman, M.M. *Hospitality Industry Purchasing.* New York: Van Nostrand Reinhold, 1990.

Feinstein, A.H., and Stefanelli, J.M. *Purchasing for Chefs: A Concise Guide.* Hoboken, NJ: John Wiley & Sons, 2007.

Feinstein, A.H., and Stefanelli, J. M. *Purchasing: Selection and Procurement for the Hospitality Industry,* 7th Ed. Hoboken, NJ: John Wiley & Sons, 2008.

Garlough, R., and Campbell, A. *Modern Garde Manger.* Clifton Park, NY: Thomson Delmar Learning, 2006.

Garlough, R., Finch, R., and Maxfield, D. *Ice Sculpting the Modern Way.* Clifton Park, NY: Thomson Delmar Learning, 2004.

Kotschevar, L.H., and Donnelly, R. *Quantity Food Purchasing,* 5th Ed. Upper Saddle River, NJ: Prentice Hall, 1998.

Labensky, S.R., and Hause, A.M. *On Cooking: A Textbook of Culinary Fundamentals,* 4th Ed. Upper Saddle River, NJ: Prentice Hall, 2007.

Lachney, A. *The HACCP Cookbook and Manual,* 4th Ed. Eatonville, WA: Nutrition Development Systems, 2002.

National Restaurant Association Educational Foundation (NRAEF). *Inventory and Purchasing Competency Guide.* Upper Saddle River, NJ: Pearson Prentice Hall, 2007.

Reed, L. *SPECS: The Food Service and Purchasing Specification Manual.* Student Edition. Hoboken, NJ: John Wiley & Sons, 2006.

Ryser, E.T., and Marth, E.H. (1989). New Foodborne Pathogens of Public Health Significance. *Journal of the American Dietetic Association,* 948.

Scriven, C., and Stevens, J. *Food Equipment Facts.* New York: Van Nostrand Reinhold, 1989.

Warfel, M.C., and Cremer, M.L. *Purchasing for Food Service Managers,* 5th Ed. Berkeley, CA: McCutchan Publishing Corporation, 2005.

http://www.dol.gov/dol/topic/wages/index.htm
http://www.dol.gov/compliance/laws/comp-flsa.htm
http://www.reliabilityweb.com
http://www.paytemps.net
http://restaurantbiz.com
http://www.howardresh.com
http://www.timecentre.com
http://www.tempwebpage.com
http://www.nonprofitexpert.com
http://www.inventory-mgt.com
http://www.ece.purdue.edu
http://desktop.dau.mil
http://mail.mcintosh.k12.ga.us
http://66.54.186.169/pdf_files
http://dsf.chesco.org
http://www.world-news-report.com
http://www.optics.arizona.edu
http://www.environmentalhealthguide.com
http://encyclopedia.infonautics.com
http://acquisition.jpl.nasa.gov
http://www.english.uga.edu

Chapter 8

Coltman, M.M. *Hospitality Industry Purchasing.* New York: Van Nostrand Reinhold, 1990.

Dittmer, P.R., and Keefe III, J.D. *Principles of Food, Beverage, and Labor Cost Controls,* 8th Ed. Hoboken, NJ: John Wiley & Sons, 2006.

Feinstein, A.H., and Stefanelli, J.M. *Purchasing: Selection and Procurement for the Hospitality Industry,* 6th Ed. Hoboken, NJ: John Wiley & Sons, 2005.

Garlough, R., and Campbell, A. *Modern Garde Manger: A Global Perspective.* Albany, NY: Thomson Delmar Learning, 2006.

Hendee, S.S., and Al-Ubaydli, M. *Handheld Computers for Chefs.* Hoboken, NJ: John Wiley & Sons, 2008.

Karimi, B., Fatemi Ghomi, S.M.T., and Wilson, J.M. (2003). The Capacitated Lot Sizing Problem: A Review of Models and Algorithms. *Omega,* October.

Kim, I.Y., Finley, D.H., Fanslow, A.M., and Hsu, C.H.C. *Inventory Control Systems in Food service Organizations: Programmed Study Guide.* Ames, IA: Iowa State University Press, 1992.

Levinson, C. *Food and Beverage Operation: Cost Control and Systems Management,* 2nd Ed. Englewood Cliffs, NJ: Prentice Hall, 1989.

Miller, J.E., Dopson, L.R., and Hayes, D. K. *Food and Beverage Cost Control,* 3rd Ed. Hoboken, NJ: John Wiley & Sons, 2005.

Pavesic, D.V., and Magnant, P.F. *Fundamental Principles of Restaurant Cost Control,* 2nd Ed. Upper Saddle River, NJ: Prentice Hall, 2005.

Schmidgall, R.S., Hayes, D.K., and Ninemeier, J.D. *Restaurant Financial Basics.* Hoboken, NJ: John Wiley & Sons, 2002.

Spears, M.C. *Purchasing for Profit.* Upper Saddle River, NJ: Prentice Hall, 1999.

Warfel, M.C., and Cremer, M. *Purchasing for Food Service Managers,* 5th Ed. Berkeley, CA: McCutchan Publishing Corporation, 2005.

www.culinarysoftware.com
www.foodservicei.com
www.handheldsforchefs.com
www.palm.com
www.webfoodpros.com
http://en.wikipedia.org
http://montanapk.com
http://bibleocean.com
http://www.computerhoe.com
http://aliciasrecipes.co.uk
http://www.csun.edu
http://money.howstuffworks.com
http://www.reliabilityweb.com
http://practicalorganization.com
http://neena.blogdrive.com
http://www.mgmgrand.com
http://newmediamedicine.com
http://wwwponcatech.com
http://hfpa.otsg.ameed.army.mil
http://www.telmedpak.com
http://ara.pdaorder.com
http://www.freehotelsearch.com

Chapter 9

Cookingham, V. (1989). Accounting: The Language of Business. *Security Management,* November.

Culinary Institute of America (Ed.) *The Professional Chef,* 7th Ed. New York: John Wiley & Sons, 2002.

Deloitte and Touche LLP (Ed.) *Uniform System of Accounts for Restaurants,* 7th Ed. Washington, DC: National Restaurant Association, 1998.

Dittmer, P.R., and Keefe III, J.D. *Principles of Food, Beverage, and Labor Cost Controls,* 8th Ed. Hoboken, NJ: John Wiley & Sons, 2006.

Feinstein, A.H., and Stefanelli, J.M. *Purchasing: Selection and Procurement for the Hospitality Industry,* 6th Ed. Hoboken, NJ: John Wiley & Sons, 2005.

Garlough, R., and Campbell, A. *Modern Garde Manger: A Global Perspective.* Albany, NY: Thomson Delmar Learning, 2006.

Miller, J.E., Dopson, L.R., and Hayes, D.K. *Food and Beverage Cost Control,* 3rd Ed. Hoboken, NJ: John Wiley & Sons, 2005.

Pavesic, D.V., and Magnant, P.F. *Fundamental Principles of Restaurant Cost Control,* 2nd Ed. Upper Saddle River, NJ: Prentice Hall, 2005.

Reed, L. *SPECS.* Hoboken, NJ: John Wiley & Sons, 2006.

Schmidgall, R.S., Hayes, D.K., and Ninemeier, J.D. *Restaurant Financial Basics.* Hoboken, NJ: John Wiley & Sons, 2002.

Spears, M.C. *Purchasing for Profit.* Upper Saddle River, NJ: Prentice Hall, 1999.

Warfel, M.C., and Cremer, M. *Purchasing for Food Service Managers,* 5th Ed. Berkeley, CA: McCutchan Publishing Corporation, 2005.

http://www.cafemeetingplace.com
http://www.bizbound.com
http://www.richdadthai.com
http://www.starchefs.com
http://www.wrnich.edu
http://www.taxopedia.com
http://www.allaccounts.com
http://www.stockformation.investopedia.com
http://www.cisaurora.org
http://sbinfocanada.about.com/accounting
http://facstaff.bloomu.edu
http://www.northonline.northseattle.edu
http://www.acs.utah.com
http://www.nunavuteda.com
http://cash-flow.vladzone.com
http://www.legamedia.net

Chapter 10

Aidan Murphy, CMC, the Executive Chef of Old Warson Country Club in St. Louis, MO, Has Become One of Only 61 Chefs in the United States to Earn the Coveted Certified Master Chef (CMC) Designation from the American Culinary Federation (ACF). *Club Management*, August 2006.

Coltman, M.M. *Hospitality Industry Purchasing*. New York: Van Nostrand Reinhold, 1990.

Feinstein, A.H., and Stefanelli, J.M. *Purchasing: Selection and Procurement for the Hospitality Industry*, 6th Ed. Hoboken, NJ: John Wiley & Sons, 2005.

Feinstein, A.H., and Stefanelli, J.M. *Purchasing for Chefs: A Concise Guide*. Hoboken, NJ: John Wiley & Sons, 2007.

Kotschevar, L.H., and Donnelly, R. *Quantity Food Purchasing*, 5th Ed. Upper Saddle River, NJ: Prentice Hall, 1998.

LaJeunesse, T.L. (1987). Is Your Company Safe from Embezzlement? *The Bottomline*, August–September, pp.7–11.

NRAEF ManageFirst. *Inventory and Purchasing Competency Guide*. Upper Saddle River, NJ: Pearson Prentice Hall, 2007.

Pavesic, D.V., and Magnant, P.F. *Fundamental Principles of Restaurant Cost Control*, 2nd Ed. Upper Saddle River, NJ: Prentice Hall, 2005.

Spears, M.C. *Purchasing for Profit*. Upper Saddle River, NJ: Prentice Hall, 1999.

Thorn, B. (2002). ACF Finalizes Culinary Olympics Team Lineup. *Nation's Restaurant News*, June 3.

Warfel, M.C., and Cremer, M. *Purchasing for Food Service Managers*, 5th Ed. Berkeley, CA: McCutchan Publishing Corporation, 2005.

Virts, W.B. *Purchasing for Hospitality Operations*. East Lansing, MI: Educational Institute of the American Hotel & Motel Association, 1987.

http://www.avendra.com
http://www.ncdmag.com

Chapter 11

American Spice Trade Association. *A History of Spices*. New York: Bernard L. Lewis, 1960.

Bennion, M., and Scheule, B. *Introductory Foods*, 12th Ed. Upper Saddle River, NJ: Prentice Hall, 2004.

Diggs, L. *Vinegar: The User-Friendly Standard Text Reference & Guide to Appreciating, Making, and Enjoying Vinegar*. San Jose, CA: Authors Choice Press, 2000.

Hill, T. *The Spice Lover's Guide to Herbs & Spices*. Hoboken, NJ: John Wiley & Sons, 2004.

Grigson, S. *Gourmet Ingredients*. New York: Van Nostrand Reinhold, 1991.

Kurlansky, M. *Salt: A World History*. New York: Penguin Books, 2002.

Miloradovich, M. *Cooking with Herbs and Spices*. Mineola, NY: Dover Publications, 1989.

Norman, J. *The Burns Philp Book of Spices*. London: Dorling Kindersley Limited, 1990.

Ortiz, E.L. *The Encyclopedia of Herbs, Spices & Flavorings*. New York: Dorling Kindersley, 1992.

Rosengarten, Jr., F. *The Book of Spices*. New York: Pyramid Books, 1973.

Swahn, J.O. *The Lore of Spices*. London: Grange Books, 1991.

Tannahill, R. *Food in History*. Briarcliff Manor, NY: Stein and Day, 1973.

Trager, J. *The Food Book*. New York: The Grossman Publishers, 1970.

www.foodreference.com/html/artbalsamicvinegar.html

Chapter 12

Connelly, P., and Pittam, M. *Practical Bakery*. London, England: Hodder & Stoughton, 1997.

Corriher, S. O. *Cookwise*. New York, NY: Harper Collins, 1997.

Figoni, P. *How Baking Works*, 2nd Ed. Hoboken, NJ: John Wiley & Sons, 2008.

Gisslen, W. *Professional Baking*, 5th Ed. Hoboken, NJ: John Wiley & Sons, 2009.

Labensky, S. R., VanDamme, E., Martel, P., and Tenbergen, K. *On Baking*. Upper Saddle River, NJ: Pearson Prentice Hall, 2005.

Labensky, S. R. and Hause, A. M. *On Cooking*, 4th Ed. Upper Saddle River, NJ: Pearson Prentice Hall, 2007.

McGee, H. *On Food and Cooking*. New York, NY: Fireside, 1984.

Chapter 13

North American Meat Processors Association (Eds.). *The Meat Buyer's Guide*. Hoboken, NJ: John Wiley & Sons, 2007.

TryFoods International (Eds.). *Meat & Seafood Guide*. Apopka, FL: TryFoods International, 2006.

http://www.fsis.usda.gov/Fact_Sheets/Inspection_&_Grading/index.asp
www.crabtreefoods.com
www.foodtrader.com
www.askthemeatman.com
www.usmef.org
www.meatnplace.net

Chapter 14

Johnson, B.A. (1994). What's Your Game? Game Meats Offer Nutritional Benefits and Profits While Luring Curiosity. *Restaurants and Institutions*, December 15.

Minton, M. U.S. Agriculture Officials Are Revising Chicken Classification Standards. *The News & Observer*, December 23, 2003.

Wishnow, S.J. (1997). Look to Food service for Innovation, Not in the Supermarket Freezer! *Quick Frozen Foods International*, July.

http://www.victoriapacking.com
http://www.namp.com
http://www.msstate.edu/dept/poultry
http://www.piercefoods.com
http://www.foodreference.com
http://www.chickeniworld.com
http://www.kraft.com
http://www.mda.state.mn.us
http://www.foodnetwork.com

Chapter 15

Anderson, C. (2004). Smoked Salmon: The Market Has Expanded Beyond Farmed Atlantics to Meet Greater Demand for Smoked Wild. *Seafood Business*, July.

The Basics of Buying Frozen Fish. *Food Management*, February 2000.

Bittman, M. *Fish: The Complete Guide to Buying and Cooking*. New York: Macmillan Publishing, 1994.

Garlough, R., and Campbell, A. *Modern Garde Manger: A Global Perspective*. Albany, NY: Thomson Delmar Learning, 2006.

Johnson, P. *Fish Forever*. Hoboken, NJ: John Wiley & Sons, Inc., 2007.

Nicolas, J.F. *The Complete Cookbook of American Fish & Shellfish*, 2nd Ed. New York: Van Nostrand Reinhold, 1990.

Seafood Business (Eds.). *Seafood Handbook*. Portland, ME: Diversified Business Communications, 2005.

Shellfish Sells. *Institutional Distribution*, August 1989.

Weise, E. Only a Sliver of Foods Eaten in USA is Made in China. *USA Today*, May 22, 2007, p. D10.

http://www.911caviar.com/
http://www.duwe-gt.de
http://www.foodtrader.com
http://whatscookingamerica.net
http://www.profish.com
http://sarasota.extension.ulf.edu

http://www.allrecipes.com
http://www.wsg.washington.edu
http://www.montereybayaquarium.com
http://www.truestarhealth.com
http://206.3.133/dir_aaa?top_amercav.html
http://www.beck-liner.com
http://seafoodhaccp.com
http://www.fishandaquaria.com
http://www.northwindhighlanders.net
http://www.ticketsofrussia.ru
http://web2.winespectator.com
http://www.theage.com
http://www.cheftalk.com
http://www.whatscookingamerica.net
http://www.seafood-norway.com
http://www.neptunetrading.com
http://www.gourmetfoodstore.com
http://www.iht.com
http://www.phantomgourmet.com
http://www.victoriapacking.com
http://www.whatscookingamerica.net
http://www.ed.org
http://www.worldwideseafoods.com
http://www.fasthealth.com
http://www.fanice.com
http://www.gormetdelish.com
http://www.plittcompany.com
http://www.kraft.allrecipes.com
http://www.wync.com
http://wwwsan.pablo.bay.en
http://www.agen.ufl.edu
http://www.library.uncc.edu
http://www.greatpartyrecipes.com/caviar-types.html
http://www.payvand.com/news/05/may/1162.html

Chapter 16

Bennion, M., and Scheule, B. *Introductory Foods,* 12th Ed. Upper Saddle River, NJ: Prentice Hall, 2004.
Citrus Rundown. *The Orange County Register,* February 12, 2002.
Cost, B. *Bruce Cost's Asian Ingredients.* New York: William Morrow and Company, 1988.
Fresh Finds: Rambutan. *Chicago Tribune,* January 15, 2007.
McClure, B.H. Prime Time for Winter Vegetables. *Supermarket Business,* December 1988.
Richter, H. *Dr. Richter's Fresh Produce Guide.* Apopka, FL: Try-Foods International, 2005.
Roehrig, E. Make Over My Grocery Shopping! Save Time, Money, and Your Sanity with Tips That'll Have You Breezing. *Redbook,* September 2003.
Smith, A.F. (Ed.) *The Oxford Encyclopedia of Food and Drink in America,* Volume 1. New York: Oxford University Press, 2004.
Thomas, C. *Melissa's Great Book of Produce.* Hoboken, NJ: John Wiley & Sons, 2006.
http://www.sunkist.com
http://citrusvariety.ucr.edu
http://www.victoriahansen.com
http://www.newcrop.hort.purdue.edu
http://en.wikipedia.org
http://www.merexfoodcorp.com
http://www.friedas.com
http://www.medaus.com
http://www.pixietangerine.com
http://www.itopack.com
http://www.manic-organic.com
http://www.tonytantillo.com
http://recipes.jennieoturkeystore.com
http://www.citrusfruitworld.com
http://www.hugusfruitfarm.com
http://www.lizzieandrewborden.com
http://www.nowfoods.com
http://essenes.crosswinds.net
http://www.melissas.com
http://www.pureprescriptions.com
http://producepete.com
http://www.agmrc.org

http://www.brazilianfruit.com
http://www.innvista.com
http://www.gladescropcare.com
http://www.midweek.com
http://www.porcelainartist.proboards25.com
http://www.fruit-center.com
http://www.produceoasis.com
http://www.colimport.com
http://www.hbrooks.com
http://www.usapear.org
http://www.chef2chef.net
http://www.countrymeadowsoaps.com
http://www.fruitcenterpieces1.com
http://www.aracaria.com
http://www.community.cookinglight.com
http://kategoria.zdobnictwo.pl.com
http://www.fruit-center.com
http://www.tampamaster.com
http://www.pshm.org
http://newbernsunjournal.com
http://www.south.africa.en
http://www.rickerhill.com
http://www.halloweeniworld.com
http://www.ogtr.gov
http://www.marsanta.co
http://www.melissas.com
http://www.pellcitrus.com
http://bilo.lifeware.com
http://newbernsunjournal.com
http://www.intesource.net
http://wwww.care2com.
http://www.growquest.com
http://agni.en.wikimiki.net
http://www.r.no.wikimiki.org
http://www.samcooks.com
http://www.sweetdbz.com
http://here.alfalaval.com
http://www.fas.usdagov/htp/hort_circular/2005/09-05/handling%20charts.pdf
http://www.britannica.com/ebchecked/topic/189243/enzymatic-browning

Chapter 17

Bennion, M., and Scheule, B. *Introductory Foods,* 12th Ed. Upper Saddle River, NJ: Prentice Hall, 2004.
Cost, B. *Bruce Cost's Asian Ingredients.* New York: William Morrow and Company, 1988.
D'Amico, S. (Ed.). *The Visual Food Encyclopedia.* New York: Macmillan, 1996.
DeWitt, D., and Gerlach, N. *The Whole Chile Pepper Book.* Boston: Little, Brown and Company, 1990.
Garlough, R., and Campbell, A. *Modern Garde Manger: A Global Perspective.* Albany, NY: Thomson Delmar Learning, 2006.
Lettuce…: Be. *High Point Enterprise,* August 1. 2007.
Richter, H. *Dr. Richter's Fresh Produce Guide.* Apopka, FL: Try-Foods International, 2005.
Rosengarten, D, *The Nine Stages of Growth in Greens,* September 3, 2002. Available from: http://www.davidrosengarten.com.
Smith, A.F. (Ed.) *The Oxford Encyclopedia of Food and Drink in America,* Volume 2. New York: Oxford University Press, 2004.
Thomas, C. *Melissa's Great Book of Produce.* Hoboken, NJ: John Wiley & Sons, 2006.
http://nctomatoman.topcities.com
http://www.cuesa.org/seasonality/charts/vegetable.php
http://www.acasatv.ro
http://www.naturalhub.com
http://commhum.mccneb.edu
http://en.wikipedia.org
http://www.soya.be
http://news.milesfarmersmarket.com
http://www.calliesorganics.com
http://yourproduceman.com
http://www.mdidea.com
http://www.gilroygarlicfestival.com
http://chefpedia.com
http://www.produceoasis.com

http://www.missvickie.com
http://www.currypantry.com
http://seedswestgardenseeds.com
http://aggie-horticulture.tamu.edu
http://www.vrichards.com
http://www.truestaraffiliate.com
http://encycl.opentopia.com
http://www.entrepreneurship.fiu.edu
http://www.homecooking.miningco.com
http://giantfood.com
http://www.merefoodcorp.com
http://www.fqqd.com
http://www.chinesefood-recipes.com
http://dog.en.ogarnij.info
http://bg.pl.wikimiki.org
http://www.gilroygarlicfestival.com
http://www.softwaretechnics.co.uk
http://envirodocs.com
http://www.tomato-cages.com
http://seedman.com
http://lyceum.lv0.net
http://www.thefreshspicemarket.com
http://www.gourmetstore.com
http://www.joson.com
http://www.honestweight.coop
http://www.lesliebeck.com
http://www.yutopian.com
http://www.supermarketsiworld.com
http://user.orac.net.au
http://www.spiceidea.com
http://www.allag.com
http://bellaonline.com
http://www.cookingvillage.com
http://www.thespicehouse.com
http://www.yahooligans.com
http://www9.siteamerica.com
http://www.users.bigpond.com
http://www.evergreenherbs.com
http://www.infoplease.com
http://www.allherb.com
http://www.parole-web.de
http://www.newmoonfarmorganic.com
http://alibi.com
http://www.answers.com
http://www.photography-cafe.com
http://www.heisse-teens-paradies.de
http://www.rso.wmich.edu
http://www.scottrobertsweb.com
http://www.ichef.com
http://koshursaal.com
http://www.netaffiliateprograms.com
http://homecooking.about.com/library/weekly/blhotchiles.htm

Chapter 18

Carroll, R. *Home Cheese Making.* North Adams, MA: Storey Publishing, 2002.
Comfort Food. *Publishers Weekly*, March 4, 2002.
Garlough, R., and Campbell, A. *Modern Garde Manger.* Clifton Park, NY: Thomson Delmar Learning, 2006.
Katz, S.H. (Ed.). *Encyclopedia of Food and Culture,* Volume 1. New York: Charles Scribner's Sons, 2003.
McCalman, M., and Gibbons, D. *The Cheese Plate.* New York: Clarkson Potter, 2002.
http://www.usda.gov/fcs/commodities/a12b.htm
http://www.ilovecheese.com/about/abfaq.html
http://www.saucecafe.com
http://www.policeiworld.com
http://en.wikipedia.org
http://www.isbog.org
http://www.egglandsbest.com
http://www.gti.net
http://cufan.clemson.edu
http://www.foodsci.uoguelph.ca
http://www.bestegg.com
http://www.chefs-food.tripod.com
http://www.supermarketsiworld.com

http://www.stocksiworld.com
http://eaa-smt.org
http://www.milk.en.ogarnij.info
http://anthing.oingo.com
http://www.cuisine-et-terroirs.com
http://www.eat-online.net
http://www.opparers.com
http://www.artistbooking.com
http://www.consisted.net
http://www.aps.uoguelph.ca
http://www.milk.drinkdigest.com
http://wilmette.nttc.org
http://www.answers.com
http://ams.usda.gov/AMSv1.0/getfile?dDocName=STELDEV3004376

Chapter 19

Beech, H. Truffle Kerfuffle. *Time*, February 14, 2005.
Fi Asia Singapore: Fi Asia 2003 Is to Be Held in the Suntec Centre in Singapore from December 9–11. *International Food Ingredients*, August–September 2003.
Garlough, R., and Campbell, A. *Modern Garde Manger: A Global Perspective.* Albany, NY: Thomson Delmar Learning, 2006.
Ingredients and Implements: Rice and Woks. *Gourmet Retailer*, July 1, 2007.
Miller, O.K. *Mushrooms of North America,* 7th Ed. New York: Chanticleer Press, 1985.
Nicholls State University. *Nation's Restaurant News*, October 4, 2004.
Through-Tubing Whipstock to Exit Two Casing Strings. *World Oil*, May 1997.
http://www.vegsoc.org/info/definitions.html
http://www.vegsoc.org/food.html
http://www.vaughns-1-pagers.com/food/amino-acids-summary.htm
http://en.wikipedia.org/wiki/Amino_acid
http://www.answers.com
http://www.ivu.org
http://fishernuts.com
http://www.bulkfoods.com
http://www.tonytantillo.com
http://216.166.134.3/vlong/veggiewrangler
http://www.3emarket.com
http://www.marsanta.co.nz
http://whatscookingamerica.net
http://www.olives.com
http://www.riceassocation.org.uk
http://beanslentils.com
http://www.enonline.sh.con
http://switcheroo.com
http://www.vegsoc.org
http://www.moondragon.org
http://www.grainfieldsaustralia.com
http://www.foodtrader.com
http://www.ricegourmet.com
http://www.websters-online-dictionary.org
http://www.midweek.com
http://www.foodsubs250x.com
http://www.weaverstreetmarket.org
http://www.producepete.com
http://www.chinesefood.miningco.com
http://osh3.datasync.com
http://www.i-asianwomen.com
http://www.nowfoods.com
http://www.khinfo.com
http://.www.coolforce.com
http://lve.scola.ac-paris.fr
http://www.farmbuilt.com
http://www.falconblanco.com
http://kraft.allrecipes.com
http://www.usaemergencysupply.com
http://www.tempeh.info
http://chichissalsa.com
http://www.pixelbomb.com
http://www.florilegium.org
http://www.cheffy.spike-jamie.com
http://pccnaturalmarkets.org
http://www.foodreference.com
http://www.leschefs.com
http://www.kosherconsumer.org
http://www.sunflowerseed.com

http://www.crapshop.com
http://www.seedman.com
http://www.ellenskitchen.com
http://www.indianvegan.com
http://www.awomansviews.com
http://www.nzgirl.com
http://pearlina.proboards36.com
http://www.oktoberfest.en.infox.org
http://www.caviarmore.com
http://www.vitaminexpress.com
http://www.goodfood.com
http://www.akron.com
http://www.palatkaforum.com
http://www.riceassociation.org
http://www.shizenworld.com
http://www.chinesefood-recipes.com
http://public2.bcm.tmc.edu
http://www.hrsynergy.com
http://www.chrie.org
http://the-wanderer-blogspot.com
http://www.sicountsportsnutrition.com
http://www.tempeh.com
http://www.balancedlivingmag.com
http://www.johnbudzinski.com
http://www.freecholesterol.com
http://www.tekki.fi.wikimiki.net
http://www.wikimirror.com
http://www.iranian.com
http://www.vegsoc.org/info.html
http://www.absoluteastronomy.com/topics/pulse

Chapter 20

Bell, D.A. *Wine and Beverage Standards.* New York: Van Nostrand Reinhold, 1989.

Brandes, R. Spirits Training Guide. *StateWays*, March 2001.

Brewer's Association, *Top 50 American Breweries Reflect the Diversity of American Beer,* March 2005.

Brewers Association Announces Craft Beer Segment Is the One to Watch. *Business Wire*, April 11, 2007.

Brewers Association of Boulder, CO. *unnamed beverage survey*, December 2005.

Crecca, D. Distilling a Dream: Bardenay, the Nation's First Distillery Restaurant, Serves up Distinctive Cocktail. *Cheers*, May 2006.

Crecca, D. By the Numbers: Just How Much Does Beverage Alcohol Contribute to Overall Sales? *Cheers*, October 2006.

Henderson, J.P., and Rex, D. *About Wine.* Clifton Park, NY: Thomson Delmar Learning, 2007.

Hilton, G. *Infuse: Discover the World of Tea.* Bristol, UK: Origin Publishing, 2003.

International Journal of Wine Marketing, 18(3) 2006.

Lipinski, B., and Lipinski, K. *Professional Beverage Management.* New York: Van Nostrand Reinhold, 1996.

Mariani, J.F. *The Dictionary of American Food & Drink.* New Haven, CT: Ticknor & Fields, 1983.

Rhodes, C. P. (Ed.). *Encyclopedia of Beer.* New York: Henry Holt and Company, 1995.

Shepard, E. unknown article, *Beer Marketer's Insights.*

Seville & Western Andalusia. *Fodor's Seville & Western Andalusia*, Annual 2007.

Technomic Inc, *unnamed beverage survey,* 2006.

http://www.tea.co.uk/index.
http://www.wholefoodsmarket.com/products/tea/index.html
http://www.clearwatersprings.net/FAQ.html
http://www.intowine.com/cellar.html
http://www.madehow.com/Volume-2/Beer.html
http://www.alexreisner.com/spirits
http://micro.magnet.fsu.edu/micro/gallery/softdrink/softdrink.html
http://www.winelaw.org/controlstates.htm
http://theteahousetimes.com/tea_facts.htm
http://www.notbeer.com/wiki/?title=Beer_style
http://www.bridgehead.ca/coffeetea/ourcoffees
http://en.wikipedia.org
http://www.liquormarts.com/
http://www.mountainbrookwater.com/
http://www.beertown.org
http://transfairusa.org
http://www.liquidpoets.com/
http://www.brew-wineforum.com

http://www.chinesefood-recipes.com
http://www.whatscookingamerica.net
http://www.foreverd.com/articles/Alcoholic_beverage_control_state
http://www.truewoman.org
http://www.champagne-and-flowers.com/x12800.html
http://www.usabride.com/wedplan/a_liquor.html
http://www.abcworld.net/Orange_juice.html
http://www.homebrew.org/craftbrewing
http://www.yemeniworld.com/wiki-Coffee_Roasting
http://www.ohiohealth.net/
http://www.halloweeniworld.com/
http://www.wine-storage.net/wine-storage-basic-storage-darkness.htm
http://angelfire.com/pa/herbs/HerbMixtures.html
http://www.yahooligans.com/
http://www.jasonzada.com/
http://web.sakra.ch/
http://southernfood.miningco.com/library/weekly/aa071397.htm
http://themythmagikshoppe.com/american-express-merchant-services/sitemap.php
http://gomexico.about.com/od/fooddrink/ss/mezcal_process.htm
http://www.boliviaiworld.com/wiki-Gin
http://www.a1b2c3.com
http://www.mauritiusiworld.com/wiki-Cranberry
http://www.madehow.com/Volume-4/Cider.html
http://www.winebuyer.co.uk/sparkling_wine.htm
http://www.wikimirror.com/Rum
http://www.alcbev.state.ut.us/Background/regulate.html
http://www.bottledwater.org/public/pdf/USAtoday_final.pdf
http://recreation.gourt.com/Food/Drink/Liquor.html
http://www.dow.com.au
http://witheid.nl.infoax.org/en/cider
http://omnipelagos.com/entry?n=soft_drink
http://www.weekendbrewer.com/brewingformulas.htm
http://kraft.allrecipes.com
http://midd-milltol.seesaa.net/
http://www.notbeer.com
http://www.mi-cherries.com/tips.htm
http://www.azstarnet.org/business/121964
http://mezcal.quickseek.com/
http://www.brainyquote.com
http://www.nationmaster.com/encyclopedia/Music-of-Norway
http://www.sportsmans4wine.com/glossaryofterms.html
http://www.thedemocraticrepublicofcongoiworld.com/wiki-Scotch_whisky
http://www.fitnessexposed.com/exercise/
http://www.cnpropertysales.com/encyclopedia/Whiskey/
http://www.die-weinkiste.com/Weingesetz/
http://www.black-and-white-der-film.de/
http://www.internationalrecipesonline.com
http://www.orangejuiceweb.co.uk
http://www.samdosha.net/info/Herbs-for-Asthma
http://www.bristolmanor.com
http://www.outofrange.net/blogarchive/archives/000398.html
http://admin.tobacco.org/articles/org/fda/
http://www.wichitamountains.org
http://www.fruittree.co.za/
http://oktoberfest.en.infoax.org
http://www.vinyl-rocker.de/cognac.php
http://transfairusa.org/content/about/history.php
http://www.nysaes.cornell.edu/fs430/lock/beerhistory.pdf
http://www.mezcal-de-oaxaca.com/mezcal-making.htm

Chapter 21

Biodelice. The Future of Organic Food and Agriculture: A Look at Emerging Trends. Available from: http://www.biodelice.com/future-organic-food.asp.

FDA. (2009). Recalls, Market Withdrawals, & Safety Alerts. Available from: www.fda.gov/safety/recalls.

Johnson, P. *Fish Forever.* Hoboken, NJ: John Wiley & Sons, Inc. 2007.

Keller, T. and McGee H. *Under Pressure: Cooking Sous Vide.* New York, NY: Artisan Publisher, 2008.

Nestle, M. *Safe Food.* Los Angeles: University of California Press, 2004.

Sernovitz, A. *Word of Mouth Marketing: How Smart Companies Get People Talking*, Rev. Ed. New York: Kaplan Publishing, 2009.

U.S. Congress. House. *Food Safety Modernization Act of 2009.* HR875. 11th Cong. Available from: http://thomas.loc.gov/cgi-bin/bdquery/z?d111:HR00875:@@@D&summ2=m&.

http://ag.arizona.edu/hydroponictomatoes/future.htm
http://www.plantcare.com/gardening-guides/hydroponic-gardening/benefits-of-hydroponic-gardening.aspx
http://www.sba.gov/OIT/info/links.html
http://en.wikipedia.org/wiki/Food
http://www.ams.usda.gov/nop/
http://www.globalchange.com/fishfarm.htm
http://hmsc.oregonstate.edu/projects/msap/future.html
http://www.culinate.com/articles/opinion/slow_food_nation_panel
http://www.slowfoodusa.org/index.php/slow_food/
http://www.csmonitor.com/2008/1124/p17s01-hfgn.html
http://www.biodelice.com/future-organic-food.asp
http://abeacon.wordpress.com/2009/03/02/the-future-of-cooking-is-sous-vide/
http://online.wsj.com/article/SB122004224561584255.html
http://www.eartheasy.com/blog/2009/01/induction-cooking/

www.turbochef.com/
http://www.fesmag.com/article/CA6592693.html
http://www.discountjuicers.com/bestjuicer.html
http://www.fda.gov/Safety/Recalls/default.htm
http://www.foodchannel.com/stories/1464-social-media-survival-stories
http://www.foodchannel.com/stories/1056-top-ten-trends-going-going-green
http://www.foodchannel.com/stories/1065-top-ten-trends-food-insecurity
http://www.dinegreen.com/restaurants/default.asp
http://www.cnn.com/2009/HEALTH/02/18/foods.future/
http://www.foodservicewarehouse.com/education/going-green/default.aspx
http://www.washingtonpost.com/wp-dyn/content/article/2009/07/29/AR2009072902753.html
http://www.globalchange.com
http://www.uoguelph.ca/news/2008/12/post_157.html

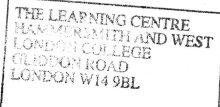